A Concise History of the American Republic

A CONCISE HISTORY

OF TH

Volume 1   To 1877

An Abbreviated and Revised Edition of

The Growth of the American Republic

NEW YORK   OXFORD 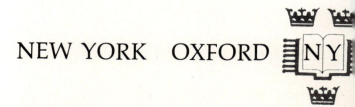

AMERICAN REPUBLIC

Second Edition

SAMUEL ELIOT MORISON

HENRY STEELE COMMAGER

WILLIAM E. LEUCHTENBURG

XFORD UNIVERSITY PRESS   1983

Picture Adviser
JUDITH MARA GUTMAN

Library of Congress Cataloging in Publication Data
Morison, Samuel Eliot, 1887–1976.
A concise history of the American Republic.
Bibliography: v. 1, p.   v.2, p.   Includes indexes.
Contents: v. 1. To 1877—v. 2. Since 1865.
1. United States—History.
I. Commager, Henry Steele, 1902–   . II.
Leuchtenburg, William Edward, 1922–   . III. Title.
E178.M83 1983   973   82-3622
ISBN 0-19-503181-4 (pbk. : v. 1) AACR2
ISBN 0-19-503182-2 (pbk. : v. 2)

Printing (last digit): 9 8 7 6 5 4 3 2

Printed in the United States of America

Samuel Eliot Morison

1887–1976

For the whole earth is the sepulchre of famous men, and their story lives on, woven into the stuff of other men's lives.

PERICLES, The Funeral Speech

Preface

A Concise History of the American Republic is a shortened and revised edition of *The Growth of the American Republic*, which first appeared in 1930. Over the next three decades, the two senior authors brought out four more editions. In the fifth edition, which appeared in 1962, Morison was responsible for the period up to the Civil War, and for the chapters on World War II; Commager for the period since 1860, except for the chapters on World War II. In the sixth edition, published in 1969, Leuchtenburg had the main responsibility for revision, and for writing new chapters on the recent period, but Morison and Commager also made revisions.

Leuchtenburg has written *A Concise History of the American Republic,* but the book draws largely upon the work of the two senior authors in *The Growth of the American Republic.* Furthermore, the senior authors made numerous editorial recommendations at different stages in the preparation of the manuscript for the first edition of this book, which was published in 1977. In particular, Leuchtenburg closely followed Morison's suggestions for abridgment for the period up to the American Revolution and Commager's on the most recent period. *A Concise History of the American Republic* aims to reach a wide audience that prefers a more compact historical account, but effort has been made to preserve the essence of *The Growth of the American Republic* and to maintain the stylistic integrity of those volumes. Leuchtenburg has again been responsible for writing this revised edition, which carries the narrative into the second year of the Reagan administration, but Commager has made a number of editorial emendations. In preparing this new edition, we have sorely missed the counsel of Admiral Morison, whose death on 15 May 1976 evoked widespread expressions of sorrow together with a sense of fulfillment for a life so rich in achievement.

Our sincere thanks are extended to authors and publishers who have allowed us to quote passages from prose and poetry, to Esta Sobey for bibliographical assistance and to Delight Ansley, who prepared the index. We are especially happy to have an opportunity to acknowledge our debt to Judith Mara Gutman, whose contribution to illustrating this volume was indispensable, and to Byron S. Hollinshead, Jr., and the proficient staff of the Oxford University Press, especially Nancy Lane, Leona Capeless, and Joyce Berry.

We write for young men and women of all ages. We believe that history embraces the whole of a people's activity: economic and social, literary and spiritual, as well as political and military. We have endeavored therefore to give such stress to these different aspects that our story will be that of a growing and changing civilization in an expanding United States of America.

HENRY STEELE COMMAGER
WILLIAM E. LEUCHTENBURG

March 1982

Contents

Maps

A Concise History of the American Republic

1

The New World

*

?–1615

Indian Culture

One summer day somewhat over 25,000 and less than 40,000 years ago, a Mongolian tribe stood on lofty Cape Dezhnev, the easternmost promontory of Siberia, about 30 miles south of the Arctic Circle. They or their parents had abandoned their old home in what is now the Gobi Desert, because that area was beginning to dry up. They had had a hard trek of at least 3000 miles, living off the country and fighting the natives along the way for several years. Perhaps only the magic of their medicine man, his promise of a new world toward the rising sun, had kept them going. Food was scarce, the latest enemy to resent their intrusion followed hard at their heels, and their skin garments were in tatters; in fact they were a tough-looking lot, even according to Siberian standards of that unrefined era. Looking southeastward over Bering Strait, our hard-pressed wayfarers saw clearly, only 23 miles away, a dome-shaped island over 1700 feet high rising above the sea. They had no experience in navigation, but something had to be done quickly. So, either by fastening together whatever logs and driftwood they could procure,

or (more likely) by stealing native kayaks, they ferried themselves over to Big Diomede Island and shook off their pursuers. Big Diomede and its companion Little Diomede, between which runs today the U.S.-U.S.S.R. boundary, are barren, affording little in the way of food. So our harassed pioneers, unconscious that they were men of destiny, resumed their voyage to a high rocky land 25 miles to the eastward on the Seward Peninsula of Alaska, now the westernmost point of continental United States. Our Mongolian pilgrim fathers were the forerunners of the mighty race which Christopher Columbus mistakenly named the Indians.

Indulge your historians this little flight of imagination before they settle down to hard fact! After all, the consensus of scientists is that the American continent was discovered by man in some such way as we have described. *Homo sapiens* is a relative newcomer on our planet, and he must have come from some other continent, because no near relatives, such as the bigger and brighter apes, have been found here. Great animals like the dinosaur had it all their own way in the pre-glacial age, 50,000 years ago and earlier.

1

This is not to say that all the many million Indians who inhabited North, Central, and South America in 1492 were descended from the passengers on our hypothetical fleet. Biologically it was possible, but other migratory bands from Siberia must have followed the same course to safety and a square meal.

All ancestors of the Indians came from Asia via Siberia, and America received no addition from any other source for at least 25,000 years. Africa was once joined to South America, and there was a bridge for plant and insect life between the Old World and the New; but that was long before humankind appeared on the earth. The 'lost continents' of Atlantis and Mu are myths. The Polynesians, although very skillful in canoe navigation, never reached America, because in the South Pacific the prevailing winds are easterly, and in the North Pacific there is a 2000-mile jump from the Hawaiian Islands to California. An occasional Chinese junk or Japanese fishing boat may have drifted across to the coast of Vancouver Island or Oregon; but the human survivors, if any, were undoubtedly killed and probably eaten.

During the next twenty-five to perhaps thirty-five millennia, these Asiatic immigrants drifted southward, perhaps through a corridor in the ice cap that then covered much of North America, until they had reached the southernmost part of Patagonia. Although they lived in the Western Hemisphere for a period some fifty to seventy times as long as the interval from Columbus's landfall to the present day, we know little of their history save what may be surmised from scattered artifacts and skeletons. In these silent eons, Niagara Falls was created, Crater Lake erupted into birth, and mastodons, enormous ground sloths, and camels roamed the continent. The Indians hunted mammoths with spears tipped with ivory; painted pictures and made beads; and showed their precocity by working copper and planting maize at a surprisingly early point in time.

Somewhere between 500 B.C. and A.D. 500, the pace of Indian life quickened, especially among the Maya of northern Central America, the Inca of Peru, and the Chibcha of Colombia. In Guatemala arose the Maya empire, a civilization so advanced that its calendar was more accurate than the Julian calendar. It abandoned the stone-built cities of Guatemala in favor of Yucatán, where its civilization reached its height around A.D. 1100. About a hundred years later the Toltec, a warrior tribe from the north traditionally led by a remarkable king named Quetzalcoatl, conquered most of the Maya and absorbed their culture, much as the Romans did that of the Greeks. The Toltec empire fell before the onslaught of a new warrior race from the north, the Aztec, a ruthless people who practiced human sacrifice to satisfy the blood lust of their unattractive deities. In South America, the Inca ruled over a great Andean empire; a totalitarian society, it excelled in stone architecture and imperial organization.

The only area north of Mexico where any long historical sequence can be given to Indian life is New Mexico and Arizona. Here a hunting group that had learned the rudiments of agriculture settled down somewhere about the beginning of the Christian era and erected adobe-walled towns with apartment-house dwellings, community courts, and buildings where religious dances and other ceremonies were practiced. These pueblos were so defensible that succeeding waves of Indian conquerors passed them by, and their inhabitants, of the Hopi, Zuñi, and other tribes, were such good farmers and weavers that they seldom lacked food or clothing. First conquered by the Spaniards in the sixteenth century, they managed to throw out their masters in 1680; and although reconquered, they, more than other North American Indians, have been unmolested by Spaniards and Americans, so today they afford the best example of a well-rooted Indian culture.

Using a 'tree-ring' method of dating,[1] one can establish a sequence of basket weaving and pottery for the Pueblos, in different styles, from the first centuries of the Christian era to the present. In the 1300 years that elapsed between A.D. 217 (year of the oldest pueblo roofbeam that can be dated) and

1. Rings of trees make definite patterns, owing to the amount of sunshine and moisture they receive in the growing season. Thus, in the Southwest, where wooden beams were used for the pueblos, the rings on them can be compared with those of a pueblo known to have been destroyed four centuries ago, and these with rings on deeper buried beams, giving us a dating sequence extending about 2100 years.

1540, when the Spaniards burst in on them, these Indians became fairly sophisticated. In the oldest culture, that of the basket-makers, the people lived in caves or built round adobe huts, wove baskets in which they stored nubbin-like ears of corn, which they cultivated with a digging-stick, hunted with flint-headed spears, and went completely naked, except for sandals on their feet and fur in the winter. In their second stage, the basket-makers learned to make pottery, as the inhabitants of Mexico had done somewhat earlier, and the women began to adorn themselves with bracelets of shell, seed, and turquoise beads. The bow and arrow, another independent invention of the Indians which had already been adopted in the Old World, replaced the spear. The third Pueblo period, from about A.D. 1050 to 1500, curiously corresponds to the 'glorious thirteenth century' in Europe. It was the golden age of cliff-dwellings, which discouraged enemies, of great masonry-walled communal dwellings built in the open, with terraced set-backs like modern skyscrapers; of big *kivas* like built-in drums where the priests danced. The close-weave basketry and decorated black-on-white pottery of this period are remarkable. After 1300 the area occupied by the Pueblo civilization was seriously reduced; the people were forced together into larger pueblos which had a good water supply, and their arts, ritual, and organization expanded. The Navajo and Apache moved in and absorbed the Pueblo culture, which the Navajo maintain to this day.

This drawing by Jacques Le Moyne, a member of an ill-fated Huguenot expedition to the Floridas in 1564, shows Indian women sowing seeds in coastal Florida. After the men broke and leveled the ground, women planted beans, millet, and maize. This sketch was first published by the gifted engraver Theodor de Bry (1528–98), who, with the aid of the distinguished geographer Richard Hakluyt, initiated the voluminous *Peregrinationum in Indiam Orientalem et Indiam Occidentalem* that gave many Europeans their main impression of the New World. From Theodor de Bry, *America*, part II, 1591. (*Rare Book Division, New York Public Library*)

Of Indian history east of the Rockies even less is known because the Indians there did not stay put, as did those of the pueblos. Whence came the 'mound-builders,' the older Indians of the Ohio and upper Mississippi valley, we do not know. The mound-builders tilled the earth with stone and shell hoes, carved out of stone elaborate tobacco pipes with realistic pictures of birds and fishes, and painted their bodies with red ochre. They were the best metal workers north of Central America before the European discovery, and even used a musical instrument, panpipes of bone and copper.

4

These disappeared when they disappeared, along with the tunes that a thousand years ago resounded through the oak groves of our Middle West. Above all, these people were famous for the massive earthen mounds, sometimes built in shapes of serpents and birds, in which they buried their dead.

At the time the first white men arrived in North America, the Indians of the Great Plains between the Rocky Mountains and the forested areas bordering on the Mississippi lived mostly by hunting the buffalo, on foot with bow and arrow. Although Europeans regarded all Indians except the Pueblos as nomads (a convenient excuse for denying them title to the land they occupied), only the Plains Indians really were nomadic; and even they did not become so until about A.D. 1550, when they began to break wild mustangs, offspring of European horses brought in by the Spaniards. The horse gave the men mobility in pursuit of the buffalo herds, while women followed with children and baggage on *travois*, shafts attached to big dogs or old horses; or, in winter, on toboggans, another Indian invention.

Semi-sedentary and agricultural, the Algonquin included the Abnaki of Maine and Nova Scotia, all the Indian tribes of southern New England, the Delaware and Powhatan of the Middle States and Virginia, the Sauk and Fox, Kickapoo and Pottawatomi in the Middle West, and Blackfoot in the Plains. The New England settler found the Indians not in the forest primeval but in the fields, tending crops. They cultivated beans, pumpkins, tobacco, and maize, which on many occasions saved English colonists from starvation. The Algonquin was an excellent fisherman with nets and a good hunter. He lived sociably and filthily in long bark-covered communal houses. He invented one of the lightest and most efficient of the world's small boats—the birch-bark canoe; and in regions where no white birch of sufficient girth was available he built dugouts, as did the other coastal Indians. He hunted deer and moose with bow and arrow for meat and skins, and trapped beaver, with which the women made smart jackets. The men went almost naked, even in winter, except for 'shorts' and moccasins of deerskin. They got about easily in winter on snowshoes, an Algonquian invention. These tribes produced some great and even noble characters: Powhatan, Massasoit, King Philip, Tammany, Pontiac, Tecumseh, and Keokuk. The Algonquin were susceptible to Christianity and assimilated European culture somewhat better than most Indians, although some of the chiefs tried to unite their people against the English and perished in the attempt.

The Five Nations (Mohawk, Cayuga, Oneida, Onondaga, and Seneca) of the Iroquois had the reputation of being the toughest fighters in North America; and they had to be, to hold their own against the Algonquin. In 1600, when first seen by Europeans, they occupied the territory from Lake Champlain to the Genesee river, and from the Adirondacks to central Pennsylvania. Hard pressed when the Europeans arrived, the Iroquois survived, and even extended their dominion, partly by Hiawatha's League which prevented war among themselves, and later through alliance with the Dutch and English. Their folkways were similar to those of the Algonquin. Among their famous leaders were Hendrick, Cornplanter, Red Jacket, Brant, and Logan. The Tuscarora, who in 1720 moved north and became the Sixth Nation, and the southern Cherokee were also of Iroquoian stock. The Cherokee produced one of the greatest of American Indians, Sequoya, who invented an alphabet for his people and led them in a great advance in civilization.

In the Southeast the Muskhogean stock, which included the Apalachee, Chickasaw, Choctaw, Creek, Natchez, and Seminole nations, was regarded by Europeans as the elite of North American Indians. They had an elaborate system of castes, from the 'Suns' down to the 'Stinkards,' which were not allowed to intermarry. All Muskhogean tribes were planters of maize, which they accented with the annual 'busk,' or green corn festival; and they were expert potters, weavers, and curers of deerskin for clothing. They learned very quickly from Europeans to plant orchards and keep cattle.

Even the most advanced Indian civilizations never discovered some simple things of immemorial use in Europe. Although they mined, smelted, and worked gold, silver and platinum, tin, lead, and copper, their use of iron was limited to chance finds of meteoric deposits. Indians invented the bark and the dugout canoes, yet only one or two primitive tribes in California learned to build a boat from plank and timber. They never discovered the potter's, or any other kind of wheel; the only beasts of burden in all the Americas (apart from the women) were the dog and the llama. But despite their deficiencies—notably in political organization—the American Indians were a great and noble race.

Indian and European

Since most Indians lived in a state of permanent hostility with their neighbors, and knew nothing of what went on elsewhere, it was possible for Europeans to impinge here and there on the New World without affecting tribes a few hundred miles away. One such impingement, the only one which is positively known to have occurred before Columbus, was that of the Norsemen in the eleventh century A.D. In the ninth century Scandinavians from Norway occupied Iceland, and in the late tenth century a tough Norseman from Iceland named Eric the Red discovered Greenland. On its west coast he founded a colony that flourished for several centuries by raising cattle and exporting walrus ivory and white falcons to Norway. After one Biarni Heriulfson had seen land to the west c. 986, Eric's son Leif in 1001 reached a coast where he saw long sand beaches; he spent a winter in northern Newfoundland and returned to Greenland.

Around 1010–15 another Icelander, Thorfinn Karlsefni, with a group of Eric the Red's kindred and neighbors, explored the coast of this 'Vinland the Good,' and attempted to found a colony where Leif had been. They spent two or three winters in northern Newfoundland, but the natives, whom they called 'Skrellings,' proved so hostile that the Norsemen gave up and returned to Greenland. These Norsemen were not Vikings, but ordinary farmers and traders; with weapons little better than those of the American natives, they were unable to cope. The significance of their discovery as the key to a New World never seems to have occurred to the Norsemen, or to anyone else.

Biarni Heriulfson may justly be called the European discoverer of America; but he only lifted a corner of the veil, and his people let it drop. Nothing that he or Thorfinn Karlsefni observed was of any interest to a Europe just emerging from the Dark Ages. And there is no trace of Norse influence in the legends or customs of the northern Indians, or in American fauna and flora.

Thus America enjoyed almost five centuries more of complete isolation. Nothing was done to prepare for the next European attack, because the existence of Europe and Asia was unsuspected. No Indian tribe or nation knew much about its own continent a few hundred miles away. Among them there was nothing even approaching a sentiment of racial or continental solidarity, not even a name for race or country. Almost every Indian tribe called itself something equivalent to 'We the People,' and used some insulting title for its near neighbors. Wherever Europeans appeared, for a century or more after 1492, the first thought of the Indians was 'Men from the Sky,' and the second, 'Heaven-sent allies against our enemies.' The white man did not have to divide and conquer; he only had to overcome the tribes piecemeal, and he found plenty of native assistance for the task. Lack of iron and gunpowder, ships and horses, handicapped the Indians, but the earliest Europeans who came had few of these, and the Indians in time learned to use them well enough. Certain tribes, like the Cuna Cuna of Panama and others in Colombia and Brazil, have retained their lands and their cultural integrity to this day because they combined the offensive power of poisoned arrows with lack of anything valuable to Europeans. Primarily, inability to unite was responsible for the European conquest. If, for instance, the Aztec 'emperors' had had a little more time to consolidate their empire, Mexico might have emerged as a native state like Japan. As it was, the three authoritarian Indian empires were the first to fall. For, as a conquistador put it, when you captured *the* Inca or *the* Montezuma, it was as if a keystone fell from an arch. In Mexico, Peru, and Colombia the Spaniards simply took the place of an Indian aristocracy or theocracy, and exploited the natives for their own profit.

There was no consistent pattern of conquest. Certain feeble peoples, such as the Arawak of the

West Indies, were exterminated by being forced to labor. Others, like the Plains Indians, were humbled in the nineteenth century because their food supply was destroyed. Some nations managed for many years to live peaceably side by side with a European colony. But if a tribe wished to keep its virtue, it had to raid or fight; and the lower sort of white men could always be counted on to provoke hostilities, which at best ended in land cession and removal. However, war was far less important in the extermination of the Indian than the ravages of new forms of disease, imported by the white man.

Since Indian societies were diverse, and since their experience with whites differed, the intrusion of the European had a variety of unexpected results. In New England, the Puritans, who regarded the redmen as potential Christians descended from the ten lost tribes of Israel, sought to convert and educate them and to deal with them fairly. In the South, the Indian, adapting himself to the white man's ways, acquired Negro slaves. In the Great Plains, the Spaniards' horses had the unanticipated consequence of the explosive development of the horse-and-bison culture. Yet even where the initial result of the advent of the white man was benign, the ultimate outcome of the pressure of a technologically advanced European civilization on the Indian was almost always extinction or dispersal. Still, the Indians are so far from being exterminated that in the United States and Canada today their numbers are approaching the estimated 1.5 million of 1492.

The Decadence of Europe

At the end of the year 1492 most thinking men in western Europe felt gloomy about the future. Christian civilization appeared to be shrinking in area and dividing into hostile units. For over a century there had been no important advance in natural science, and registration in the universities dwindled as instruction became increasingly lifeless. Many intelligent men were endeavoring to escape the present through studying the pagan past. Islam was expanding at the expense of Christendom. Every crusade to recover the Holy Sepulchre at Jerusalem had failed. The Ottoman Turks,

after snuffing out all that remained of the Byzantine Empire, had overrun most of Greece, Albania, and Serbia. In 1492 the papacy touched bottom when Rodrigo Borgia, a corrupt ecclesiastical politician, was elected to the throne of Saint Peter as Alexander VI. If one turned to the governments, the prospect was no brighter. The amiable but lazy Emperor Frederick III, driven from his Austrian lands by the king of Hungary, had retired to dabble in astrology and alchemy. In England the Wars of the Roses were over, but few expected the House of Tudor to last long. Only in the Iberian peninsula, in Portugal and Castile, were there signs of new life; but these kingdoms were too much on the periphery of Europe to alter the general picture of decay. Throughout western Europe the feeling was one of profound disillusion, cynical pessimism, and black despair.

The colophon of the *Nuremberg Chronicle*, dated 12 July 1493, declares that it contains 'the events most worthy of notice from the beginning of the world to the calamity of our time.' That time was painted in the most somber colors, suggesting the end of the world; a few blank pages were left to record events between 1493 and the Day of Judgment. Yet, even as the chroniclers of Nuremberg were correcting their proofs, a Spanish caravel named *Niña* scudded before a winter gale into Lisbon, with news of a discovery that was to give old Europe another chance.

In a few years we find the picture completely changed. Strong monarchs are stamping out privy conspiracy and rebellion; the Church, purged and chastened by the Protestant Reformation, puts her house in order; new ideas flare up throughout Italy, France, Germany, and the northern nations; faith in God revives and the human spirit is renewed. The change is complete and astounding. A new world view has begun, and people no longer sigh after an imaginary golden age in the distant past, but lay plans for a golden age in the near future.

Columbus Discovers America

Christopher Columbus discovered America by accident when looking for Japan and China. Few people cared anything about it, when found; and

Christopher Columbus (1451–1506). No portrait of 'the Admiral of the Ocean Sea' was painted during his lifetime, and various purported likenesses bear no resemblance to him. This sixteenth-century 'giovio' portrait (for a gallery of notable men at Bishop Paolo Giovio's villa at Lake Como) is regarded as the most authentic, although it was not painted until thirty years or more after his death. It depicts the explorer, wearing a sort of monastic robe, in a downcast and reflective mood after his third expedition, which ended with his return to Spain in chains. (*Museo Giovio, Como*)

the Atlantic coast from Hudson's Bay to the Strait of Magellan was explored by navigators seeking a passage to India through or around this unwanted continent. Yet Columbus was the effective discoverer of America for Europe, because he was the first to do anything with it. The 'Enterprise of the Indies,' as he called his plan of sailing west to the Orient, was his very own, suggested by no previous information, produced by no economic forces. He promoted this design for at least eight years before he could persuade any prince to grant him the modest equipment required; and a less persistent or stout-hearted captain would have turned back before reaching land. News of his discovery was immediately spread throughout Europe by the recent invention of printing. Columbus led the first colony to the New World in 1493; he discovered the South American continent in 1498; and he obtained the first definite news of the Pacific Ocean. The history of the Americas stems from his four voyages.

Born at Genoa in 1451, the son of a weaver of woolen cloth, this great mariner went to sea at about the age of twenty, and after making voyages in the Mediterranean, suffered shipwreck in Portugal, settled in Lisbon around the year 1477. Portugal was then the most progressive of the European kingdoms. Under Prince Henry the Navigator, the Portuguese sought a sea route to 'the Indies' (India, China, and the eastern islands), to obtain at their source the spices, drugs, and gems which reached Europe in small quantities over caravan routes, and the gold and silver about which Marco Polo had told tall tales. The most promising route lay to the southward; and by the time Columbus settled in Portugal, the mariners of that nation were opening up new stretches of the West African coast every year. As early as 1460 they had passed the site of Dakar, and had dispelled the Arabian legends of a 'sea of pitchy darkness.' Fifteen years later they had completed the exploration of the Gulf of Guinea, and opened up a trade in gold and ivory, slaves and pepper, that made Lisbon the envy of Europe. For this traffic, which required a round voyage of many thousand miles, the Portuguese developed the caravel, a sailing vessel, which was fast, seaworthy, and weatherly. Ships capable of making

the voyage to America and back had existed long before Columbus was born; but the caravel made the voyage far less difficult and dangerous.

Columbus proposed to open a much shorter sea route to 'the Indies' by sailing west, around the world. A poor mathematician, he had satisfied himself by a series of lucky miscalculations that Japan lay only 2400 to 2500 miles west of the Canaries. In 1484 he began his efforts to obtain backing. But the learned men to whom the plan was referred had more accurate notions of the globe than he had. Not that he needed to demonstrate the earth was round. It had been known to be spherical for centuries; a spherical earth was taught in all European universities. Everyone agreed that a westward route to 'the Indies' was theoretically possible, like flying in 1900; but nobody considered it practicable with such means as were then available.

After eight years of agitation, the intuition of Queen Isabella gave Columbus his chance. After all, the man might be right about the size of the earth: it was simply one theory against another. The equipment he asked for was cheap enough; the honors he demanded were not unreasonable, if he succeeded, and the glory and gain for Spain would be incalculable. If he failed, little would be lost. So Ferdinand and Isabella, the joint sovereigns of Spain, undertook to pay the bills and to make Columbus viceroy, governor, and admiral over any lands he might acquire. They gave him a Latin letter of introduction to the Emperor of China, and a passport stating that he was on a legitimate voyage 'to regions of India.'

Columbus sailed from Palos on 3 August 1492, as commander of a fleet of three vessels, *Niña*, *Pinta*, and *Santa Maria*, each about 70 to 80 feet long. They were manned by about 90 picked Spaniards. His plan was to sail due west from the Canary Islands, because according to the best available maps these lay on the same latitude as Japan; if these islands were missed, the fleet would be sure to hit China. Their course lay along the northern edge of the belt of northeast trade winds which blow steadily in late summer between the Canaries and America. This most important voyage in history was also one of the easiest; they generally enjoyed fair wind, soft air, a serene sky, and an ocean smooth as a river. The three vessels departed the westernmost Canaries on 9 September. Mutiny flared on 10 October but Columbus persuaded his men to go on for three days more. At 10 p.m. on 11 October, Columbus and a few others saw for a short time a dim light ahead. This may have been a brush fire kindled by natives on a high point of an island, whose sand cliffs showed up in the moonlight at 2 a.m. on the 12th. It was the Bahamian island that Columbus named, and we call, San Salvador.

Many other discoveries have been more spectacular than that of this small, low, sandy island that rides out ahead of the American continent, breasting the trade winds. But it was there that the Ocean for the first time 'loosed the chains of things' as Seneca had prophesied, gave up the secret that had baffled Europeans since they began to inquire what lay beyond the western horizon's rim. San Salvador, rising from the sea at the end of a 33-day westward sail, was a clean break with past experience. Every tree, every plant, that the Spaniards saw was strange to them, and the natives were completely unexpected, speaking an unknown tongue and resembling no race of which even the most educated of the explorers had read. Never again may mortal man hope to recapture the wonder, the delight of those October days in 1492 when the New World gracefully yielded her virginity to the conquering Castilians.

Several of the natives, whom Columbus hopefully called Indians, welcomed the 'Men from the Sky,' and several were impressed to act as guides to 'Cipangu' (Japan) and 'Cathay' (China). They piloted Columbus through the Bahamas to northwestern Cuba. There he dispatched his Arabic interpreter inland to meet a cacique whom he took, from the Indians' description, to be the Emperor of China. But the village of thatched huts that they found bore little resemblance to the Cambaluk where Marco Polo had hobnobbed with Kubla Khan. Columbus persisted in his quest, eagerly examining every new plant for evidence that Cuba was the southeastern promontory of China. On *La Isla Española*, 'The Spanish Island,' which we still call Hispaniola, he found golden grains in river sands, rumors of a gold mine up-country, and an abundance of gold ornaments on the Indians which they readily swapped for brass rings, glass beads, and bits of cloth. When the flagship ran on a coral reef, Columbus built a fort of her timbers, garrisoned it with her crew, and sailed for home on board *Niña*, accompanied by *Pinta*.

Columbus and his men were received as heroes, and everyone assumed that they had discovered islands 'in the Indian Sea,' if not the continent of Asia. The Pope conferred on Spain sovereignty of all lands beyond the meridian 100 leagues (318 nautical miles) west of the Cape Verde Islands. Portugal protested, and by mutual consent the next year the line was moved 270 leagues farther west; this new line of demarcation gave Portugal her title to Brazil. After six months in Spain Columbus sailed in command of a gallant fleet of seventeen vessels which discovered all the Caribbee Islands north and west of Martinique, and Puerto Rico. At Hispaniola, after ascertaining that his garrison had been wiped out, he began building a fortified trading station.

There his troubles began. The first European colony in America was nothing more than a glorified gold hunt. Columbus expected to obtain the precious metal by trade; but the Indians' demand for trading truck was soon exhausted, and the Spaniards began taking gold by force. As elsewhere in America where Europeans came, the newcomers were first welcomed by the Indians as visitors, then resented as intruders, and finally resisted with fruitless desperation. The Spaniards, who had come only for gold, resented their governor's orders to build houses, tend crops, and cut wood; the wine and food supplies from Spain gave out; and before long bands of men in armor were roving the fertile interior, living off the country, and torturing the natives to obtain gold. In the summer of 1494, which Columbus spent exploring the southern coasts of Cuba and Hispaniola and discovering Jamaica, the colonists got completely out of hand; and the Admiral's attempts to impose an iron discipline resulted in malcontents seizing vessels and returning to Spain to complain. So Columbus, leaving his brother Bartholomew in charge, sailed for home in 1496. After a year's lobbying at court, Columbus could only obtain grudging consent to send out convicts as colonists, and to let him make a new voyage in search of the Asiatic continent.

Meantime, a second nation had stumbled on America when searching for Asia, and through the efforts of another Genoese. John Cabot, a compatriot of Columbus but a naturalized citizen of Venice, believed that the Far East could best be reached by sailing westward in the short high latitudes. After making a contract with Henry VII of England similar to that of Columbus with the Spanish sovereigns, he sailed from Bristol in 1497 and reached the New World, probably northern Newfoundland, where he spent less than a month. All we know of Cabot's second voyage in 1498 is that he never returned. The English did practically nothing to follow up Cabot's voyages for three-quarters of a century, and their only influence was to give the English Crown a 'legal' title to North America against the claims of Spain and France.

When on his third voyage Columbus returned to Santo Domingo, the new capital of Hispaniola that had been established in his absence, he found the island in turmoil. Most of the Indians had been brought under subjection, but the chief justice, Francisco Roldán—first of a long line of American rebels—was heading a revolt of ex-criminals and robust individualists against the government of Columbus's brother, in the hope of obtaining a larger share of the women and the gold-diggings. Columbus was forced to appease Roldán. To each man was granted a tract of land with the Indians who lived on it, whose labors he was entitled to exploit as he saw fit. These *encomiendas*, as they were subsequently called, marked the beginning of a system the Spaniards applied throughout their conquests in order to induce settlement and supply the colonists with cheap servile labor.

Several Spaniards who had been officers under Columbus made voyages to South America, and on one of them sailed a Florentine merchant, Amerigo Vespucci. Amerigo's inflated and pre-dated account of a voyage in 1499 made his name familiar to northern Europe. Thus, when a German geographer in 1507 suggested that the new continent be called *America*, after him, the name caught on. A year earlier Columbus, after an unsuccessful fourth voyage to try to find a strait through his 'Other World,' as he called America, had died in obscurity.

No discoverer in the world's history had such marvelous success as Columbus, even though he never found what he first sought; no navigator save Magellan or da Gama may be compared with him for courage, persistence, and skill; no other great benefactor of the human race was so ill rewarded in his lifetime; none other is so justly revered today in the New and Other World of his Discovery.

The Spanish Empire

For about twenty years after the first voyage of Columbus, Hispaniola was the only European colony in America. It was based on cattle and cotton raising, gold mining, and the culture of the sugar cane introduced from the Canaries. In 1512 Hispaniola was exporting annually to Spain not far short of a million dollars in gold. The enslaved Indians died off under forced labor, and were replaced, first by Indians kidnapped from other islands, who suffered the same fate, and then—beginning in 1510—by black slaves, bought from the Portuguese, who procured them in Africa, largely from other blacks. Santo Domingo became the center from which much of the rest of America was explored and colonized.

Juan Ponce de León, the first of the *adelantados* (advancers), explored in 1506 the island of Puerto Rico, which, with Jamaica and Cuba, was conquered and colonized, and then extended his explorations to the mainland. Ponce de León had heard the story of a marvelous spring on an island named Bimini which restored youth and vigor to the old and impotent, and he decided to search for it. In April 1513, after threading his way through the Bahamas and ascertaining that there were neither springs nor streams in the islands, Ponce landed near Daytona Beach and named the land Florida after that fair Easter season (*Pascua Florida*). Hugging the coast to avoid the Gulf stream, he rounded the Florida Keys and sailed up into the Gulf of Mexico, and then discovered Yucatán. But he returned to Puerto Rico without an ounce of gold or a drink of invigorating water. Though St. Augustine was founded by Menéndez de Aviles in 1566 in order to protect the treasure fleets from French and English marauders, Florida during three centuries of Spanish rule remained little more than a military outpost of Mexico and Cuba.

Vespucci 'Discovering' America. In this late sixteenth-century work, Stradanus depicts the New World as an abundantly endowed woman burdening a hammock, while a tapir and a sloth prowl around the trees. In the background cannibals are cooking dinner. Vespucci, in a handsome garment, carries an astrolabe in his left hand; in his right, he holds the Southern Cross. (*The British Museum*)

The Pacific Ocean was discovered by Vasco Núñez de Balboa, a stowaway from Hispaniola who had made himself master of a relatively insignificant Spanish post on the Gulf of Darien. In 1513 Balboa had several hundred Indians hack the way across the difficult isthmus of Darien for him and his 189 hidalgos to the spot where 'silent, upon a peak in Darien,' he first gazed upon the Pacific. The discoverer was soon after put to death by his rival Pedrarias, whose energy was so vast that small sailing vessels and their gear were transported across the divide in sections, and set afloat on *El Mar del Sur*, the great South Sea.

Presently the city of Panama was founded, and Spain had a Pacific base.

Across that ocean—how far across nobody had yet guessed—lay the Spice Islands, whence the king of Portugal was deriving far greater wealth than did his Spanish cousins from the gold-washings of Hispaniola, for the epic voyage of Vasco da Gama around the Cape of Good Hope to India had given the Portuguese the long-sought sea route to the Orient. Ferdinand Magellan, a captain who had spent seven years with the Portuguese in the Far East, believed that the Spice Islands—modern Indonesia—could better be reached by sailing westward. Rebuffed by the king of Portugal, he turned to the king of Spain (Charles I, later Emperor Charles V), who gave him a fleet of five ships. They sailed from Seville in August 1519, reached the River Plate in January, and continued south along the coast of Patagonia. While the fleet was wintering, the captains of four ships mutinied; Magellan hanged some of the leaders, and marooned the others. At the Antarctic summer solstice the voyage was renewed, and on 21 October 1520, Magellan discovered the entrance to 'the Strait that shall forever bear his name,' as Camoëns wrote in the *Lusiads*. The fleet, reduced by shipwreck and desertion to three sail, required 38 days to thread the dangerous 334-mile passage that cuts through the tail end of the Andes.

Then came the most terrible part of the voyage. This South Sea was calm enough, once they were off shore—that is why Magellan renamed it the Pacific Ocean—but they were fourteen weeks without sight of land, excepting two small coral atolls where neither water nor food was found. The scurvy-ridden men were reduced to eating sawdust and biscuit which had become mere powder swarming with worms, even to broiling the leather chafing-gear of the yards. Relief was obtained on 6 March 1521, at Guam, and ten days later they reached Leyte Gulf in the Philippines. On the tiny island of Limasawa, off Leyte, there occurred the most dramatic event of the voyage. Magellan's Malay servant Henriquez, whom he had brought home from a previous voyage, was able to make himself understood. West had met East.

After Magellan was slain in a battle and two of the three vessels ran into grief, the *Vittoria*, laden with spices, set forth alone, on 21 December 1521, under Captain Juan Sebastian de Elcano. She crossed the Indian Ocean, rounded the Cape of Good Hope, and on 9 September 1522, this greatest voyage of all time ended at Seville, with only eighteen of the 239 men who set forth three years earlier. Captain de Elcano was ennobled, and Europe for the first time learned the width of the Pacific Ocean and the real relation of the New World to the Orient.

Magellan was already on his way and the entire east coast of South America had been explored before the two most splendid native civilizations in America, Mexico's and Peru's, yielded their secrets. In 1519 the governor of Cuba, wishing to establish a trading post on the Mexican coast, sent an expedition of eleven ships, carrying only 550 Spaniards, under 32-year-old Hernando Cortés. Arriving at a time when the caciques of Mexico were chafing under the cruel sovereignty of the Aztecs, Cortés was welcomed by many as their fabled hero, Quetzalcoatl, and he had the wit to take advantage of it. For all that, the conquest of Mexico was one of the most amazing military and diplomatic feats in the world's history. The march up from Vera Cruz to the great interior plateau, the audacious capture of Montezuma's lake-rimmed capital (1521), and the defeat of a vast army on the plains of Teotihuacan completed the ruin of Aztec power and firmly established Cortés as master of Mexico.

Spanish conquistadors explored the whole southern expanse from South Carolina across to California in search of more valuable treasure and of new empires. Pánfilo de Narváez, who sailed from Spain in 1527, landed somewhere on the Gulf coast of Florida, where he built a fleet from native wood fastened with spikes fashioned from spurs and stirrups, rigged with hair cordage and sails made from the hides of horses which his men had eaten. In these crazy craft Narváez made his way to Texas, where the fleet was wrecked. The survivors, Cabeza de Vaca, two other Spaniards, and a Negro, Esteban, spent six years among the Indians, eventually reaching Mexico with tales of wild 'hunchback cows' that covered the plains as far as the eye could see, and of cities with emerald-studded walls, of which they had heard. These 'Seven Cities of Cibola' were more readily believed in than were the buffalo. In 1539 the viceroy of Mexico sent Fray Marcos, accompanied by Esteban, up into the future New Mexico in search of the fabled 'Seven Cities.' There they discovered the disappointing foundation of this myth, the Zuñi pueblos, and the honest Fray Marcos so reported. Nevertheless the viceroy sent forth the most splendid expedition of all, that of Francisco Vásquez Coronado. One of Coronado's lieutenants discovered the Grand Canyon in 1540; Coronado himself marched eastward across the panhandle of Texas into eastern Kansas, only to return, disappointed, to Mexico. Yet another explorer led on by tales of splendid cities, Hernando de Soto, landed in Florida, marched about the interior of the future Gulf States, and in 1541 came upon the mighty Mississippi.

Owing to their failure to find treasure or a strait, these explorations had no immediate result. Only at the end of the sixteenth century did Juan de Oñate formally take possession 'of all the kingdoms and provinces of New Mexico.' The Pueblos submitted, colonization began, and the next governor founded Santa Fe in 1609. Thus New Mexico, the forty-seventh state to be admitted to the Union, was settled at the same time as the first permanent English colony in North America. Well before then Spain had conquered almost the whole of Latin America. Francisco Pizarro had overthrown the mighty Inca empire of Peru and founded Lima by 1535, and by mid-century the foundations had been laid for every one of the twenty republics of Central and South America, excepting the Argentine.

There has been no other conquest like this in the annals of the human race. In one generation the Spaniards acquired more new territory than Rome did in five centuries. Genghis Khan swept over a greater area, but left only destruction in his wake; the Spaniards organized all that they conquered, brought in the arts and letters of Europe, and converted millions to their faith. Our forebears in Virginia and New England, the pathfinders of the Great West, and the French-Canadian pioneers were stout fellows indeed; but their exploits scarcely compare with those of the conquistadors and friars who hacked their way in armor through solid jungle, across endless plains, and over snowy passes of the Andes to fulfill their dreams of gold and glory, and for whom reality was greater even than the dream.

Hispanic America is rich in paradox. The Spanish, who encountered an Indian population more numerous and more advanced than England and France found, incorporated the Indian into their society, unlike the English and the French, and the intermarriage of whites, Indians, and blacks created a heterogeneous culture less marked by racial prejudice. But it was also a highly stratified social order in which social distinction rested on pigmentation, with a white elite at the top. Guilty of revolting cruelty toward the Indian, Spain also sought persistently to preserve his personal liberty. A medieval society, it nonetheless welcomed modern advances. Mexico City and Lima, the 'City of Kings,' became seats of urban civilization within fifteen years of the conquest; in each a university was founded in 1551; the first printing press in the New World came to Mexico City in 1539. Even today an air of superb magnificence rests on the churches and palaces built by these 'children of the sun' in their provincial capitals hundreds of miles from the sea.

Thus the Spanish empire had more than a century's head start on the English and French; and the stupendous results of that conquest were the envy of every European power. Spanish prestige reached its height in 1580 when Philip II succeeded to the throne of Portugal as well as that of Spain, uniting under his person two vast empires that now stretched their arms around the world, the left arm to the west coast of Mexico, the right arm to Manila. At that moment not another nation had placed a single permanent settler on the shores of the New World.

Yet the end of that monopoly was near. The autumn gales of 1580 blew up the English Channel and into Plymouth harbor Francis Drake in the *Golden Hind*, worm-eaten and weed-clogged after her three years' voyage around the world, laden with the spoil of a Peruvian treasure ship. Only eight years more, and Spain suffered her first major defeat on the ocean that she had mastered; twenty years more, and Virginia was founded.

Enter France and England

Spanish conquest was too swift and successful for the health of Spain. American treasure ruined her manufactures, financed useless military adventures of her kings, and finally led to poverty and stagnation. Yet the immediate success, which alone was visible, stimulated three other nations, France, England, and the Netherlands, to acquire colonial possessions of their own. As early as 1521 French corsairs bagged part of the booty that Cortés was sending home; and this process of muscling into the Spanish empire continued until England and France were firmly established in North America, and the Dutch in the Far East.

Jacques Cartier is the Columbus of French Canada. This hardy seaman of St.-Malo made three voyages to the Gulf of St. Lawrence (1534–41) in search of a passage to the Orient. On the second he discovered the rock of Quebec, in a region which the natives called Canada, and then proceeded upstream, past Montreal (so named by him), to the lowest rapids of the St. Lawrence, the La Chine. From the Indians he collected a cycle of tall tales about an inland kingdom of the Saguenay, where gold and silver were as plentiful as in Peru. Cartier brought back nothing save a shipload of iron pyrites, or fool's gold, and quartz crystals that he believed to be diamonds, but he did discover one of the two leading axes of penetration of the continent. France then fell into a cycle of religious wars, and no progress was made toward an empire in America until the next century.

England approached America gingerly, for it was a small and poor country, hemmed in by enemies and anxious to placate Spain. Yet England was growing stronger year by year. No small share of the treasure from Mexico and Peru went to buy English woolens. Henry VIII's breach with the Church of Rome stimulated English nationalism and made a break with Spain inevitable sooner or later. Under Queen Elizabeth I (1558–1603) it became a religious as well as a patriotic duty to 'singe the king of Spain's beard.' On Francis Drake's memorable voyage to California and around the world (1577–80) he terrorized the coasts of Chile and Peru, and in 1587 Captain Thomas Cavendish bagged the grandest prize of all, a Manila galleon. His ships entered the Thames rigged with damask sails, and each sailor wore a silk suit and a chain of pure gold round his neck.

The great age of Elizabeth and of Shakespeare, in which English genius burned brightly in almost every aspect of life, was reaching its acme.

> This happy breed of men, this little world,
> This precious stone set in the silver sea,

awakened from long lethargy to a feeling of exuberant life, such as few people had known since ancient Greece. That was an age when the scholar, the divine, and the man of action were often one and the same person—for the Elizabethans knew, what many of us have forgotten, that life is empty without religion, that the tree of knowledge is barren unless rooted in love, and that learning purchased at the expense of living is a sorry bargain. Man in those days was not ashamed to own himself an animal, nor so base as to quench the divine spark that made him something better; but above all, he exulted in the fact that he was a man. Chapman spoke for his age when he cried out, 'Be free, all worthy spirits, and stretch yourselves!'

The age of discovery in England was closely integrated with literature and promoted by her governing class. Sir Humphrey Gilbert, Oxonian, educational reformer, and courtier, published a *Discourse of a Discovery for a New Passage to Cataia* (China), and attempted the first English colony. His half-brother Sir Walter Raleigh, courtier, soldier, and historian, founded Virginia and sought El Dorado up the Orinoco. And the Reverend Richard Hakluyt, student of Christ Church, Oxford, compiled his great collection of *Navigations, Voiages, Traffiques and Discoveries of the English Nation* in order to fire his countrymen to worthy deeds overseas. These men wanted an overseas empire that would make England self-sufficient and employ a great merchant marine. It should be in a climate where Englishmen might live, and where they and the natives would provide a new market for English goods. The colonies should produce tar and timber for shipbuilding, gold and silver, dyewoods, wine, spices and olives, and everything else that England was then buying from abroad. The Indians must be converted to Protestant Christianity, in order to stay the progress of the Counter-Reformation, and a passage through to the real Indies was sought.

Yet, with all this energy and gallantry, English colonization in the sixteenth century repeatedly failed. Gilbert took possession of Newfoundland for the Queen in 1583, but was lost on the voyage home. Raleigh then took over his patent to the whole of North America above Florida, named it Virginia, and planted two successive colonies on Roanoke Island. The first gave up after a year; the second, a well-chosen group of 117 men, women,

Sir Walter Raleigh (*c.* 1552–1618), organizer of the Roanoke Island expeditions, failed either to achieve a permanent settlement in Virginia or to find El Dorado up the Orinoco, but quickened interest in colonizing the New World. This portrait by Marcus Gheerhardts the Younger depicts Queen Elizabeth's favorite shortly after he was knighted. (*Colonial Williamsburg*)

and children, had completely disappeared by the time a relief expedition arrived in 1590. The experience of Gilbert and Raleigh proved that 'it is a difficult thing to carry over colonies into remote countries upon private men's purses.' The Crown was too impecunious to finance colonies; and individual enterprise preferred the gay adventure and certain profit of raiding the Spanish Main. So the sixteenth century closed like the fifteenth, without a single Englishman on American soil— unless survivors of Raleigh's lost colony were still wandering through the forests of Carolina.

This should have been discouraging, but the English were past discouragement. For, underlying all their efforts, the earlier failures as well as later successes, was a powerful drive. This *daimon* of the English was the burning desire to found a new England, a new society, in which all the best of the past would be conserved, but where life would have a better quality than anything conceivable in Europe, where men might even create a commonwealth that would be, in a word borrowed from Sir Thomas More's great work of 1516, Utopia.

2

First Foundations

*

1600–1660

Virginia

Two waves of colonizing activity were responsible for founding twelve of the thirteen English colonies which federated as the United States of America, and the French colonies which became the nucleus of the Canadian Commonwealth. The first wave, which began in 1606 and lasted until 1637, planted three groups of English colonies and three French colonies: Virginia and Maryland on the Chesapeake, the Puritan commonwealths of New England, and the British West Indies; French L'Acadie (Nova Scotia), Quebec, and the Antilles; and also the Dutch colony of New Netherland, which became New York.

The death of Elizabeth I and the accession of James I in 1603 brought peace with Spain and Scotland, and released capital and men for fruitful purposes. The lesson that 'private purses are cold comforts to adventurers' had been well learned. Excellent results had already been obtained in foreign trade by joint-stock corporations, which combined the capital of many under the management of a few. The Muscovy Company and the Levant Company had done well in trading with Russia and the Near East; spectacular profits were in store for the East India Company. Each firm received a monopoly of English trade with a specified portion of the world, and full control over whatever trading posts or colonies it might see fit to establish.

In such wise the English colonization of Virginia was effected. Two groups of capitalists were formed, one centering in Bristol and the other in London. Every stockholder could take part in the quarterly meetings (called general courts) and had a vote in choosing the board of directors, known as the treasurer and council. Between these two companies, the English claim to North America was divided. Northern Virginia, renamed New England in 1620, fell to the Bristol group; Southern Virginia, which also included the future Maryland and Carolina, to the Londoners. The Northern Company's one attempt to plant came to grief because of an 'extreme unseasonable and frosty' Maine winter. But the 'Old Dominion' of Virginia was established by the London Company. That corporation was no mere money-making scheme, although the expectation of profit certainly existed; rather was it a national

18

enterprise with hundreds of stockholders great and small.

Three ships under Captain Christopher Newport, *Susan Constant, Godspeed,* and *Discovery,* dropped down the Thames at Christmastide 1606, and 'Virginia's Tryalls' (as an early tract was entitled) began at once. The long voyage proved fatal to sixteen of the 120 men on board—no women were taken. The company expected to convert Indians, locate gold, discover the Northwest Passage, and produce 'all the commodities of Europe, Africa and Asia.' But no gold was found, neither the James nor the Chickahominy rivers led to the Pacific, and the only commodities sent home for several years were of the forest, such as oak clapboard. The company proposed to establish a new home for the unemployed who swarmed into English towns, but these 'sturdy beggars' did not care to emigrate as landless wage-slaves. So the first colony consisted largely of decayed gentlemen, released prisoners, and a few honest artisans. For Jamestown Captain Newport had selected a very malarial site which was eventually abandoned. As in Columbus's first colony, the men were upset by the strange food, drenched in flimsy housing, racked by disease, and pestered by mosquitoes and Indians. By the spring of 1608 only 53 Englishmen were left alive; and they were saved only through the bustling activity of Captain John Smith in placating the natives and planting corn.

The Virginia Company sent relief in 1608, and again in 1609—a fleet of nine ships under Sir Thomas Gates. The flagship was wrecked on the Bermudas, providing material for Shakespeare's *Tempest,* and securing for England the lovely islands that are now her oldest colony. When the survivors reached Jamestown, that colony was reduced to the last stage of wretchedness. 'Everie man allmost laments himself of being here,' wrote Governor Dale in 1611. He despaired of making a success with 'sutch disordered persons, so prophane, so riotous . . . besides of sutch diseased and crased bodies.' He hoped the king would send to Virginia, out of the common jails, all men condemned to die; they at least might be glad 'to make this their new Countrie.' One is not astonished at the 'treasonable Intendments' of these

workers when one reads of their regime. Twice a day they were marched into the fields by beat of drum or into the forests to cut wood, and twice a day marched back to Jamestown to eat and pray. The only thing that kept the colony alive was the deep faith and gallant spirit of men who believed that they had hold of something which must not be allowed to perish. 'Be not dismayed at all,' says the author of *Newes from Virginia* (1610):

> Let England knowe our willingnesse,
> For that our worke is good;
> *Wee hope to plant a nation,*
> *Where none before hath stood.*

Virginia needed more than faith and gallantry to ensure permanence. She needed a profitable product, a system of landholding that gave immigrants a stake; discipline to be sure, but also liberty. In ten years' time she obtained all these. Between 1615 and 1625 Virginia was transformed from an unsuccessful trading post, ruled by iron discipline and hated by most of the settlers, into a commonwealth that began to open a new and wonderful life to the common man of England.

Tobacco culture, which never entered into the founders' plans, saved Virginia. Smoking was brought to England by Sir John Hawkins in the 1560's. The English complained that the tobacco the Indians cultivated around Roanoke bit the tongue, and so continued to import West Indian leaf through Spain. John Rolfe, husband to Pocahontas, is said to have been responsible for procuring seed from the West Indies around 1613, and the leaves grown from this seed on Virginian soil smoked well. Some 2500 pounds were exported in 1616; 20,000 in 1617; 50,000 in 1618. Here at last was something to attract capital and labor, and make large numbers of Englishmen wish to emigrate.

Private property in land also stimulated growth. As the indentures of hired servants expired, they became tenant farmers on a sharecropping basis; by 1619 tenant farms extended twenty miles along the James. Groups of settlers organized by some man of substance were granted large tracts called 'hundreds,' which formed autonomous communities within the colony. And in 1618 the company devised 'head-rights,' which

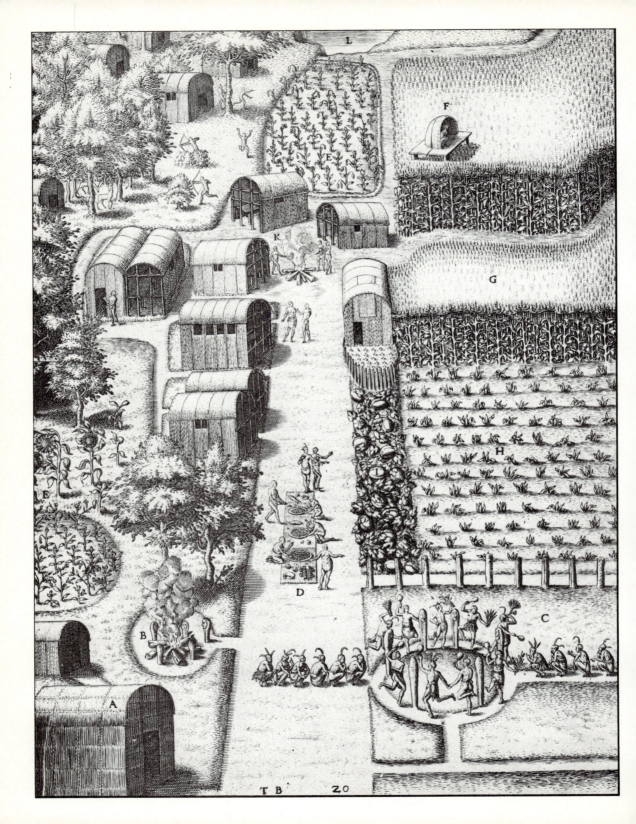

became the basis of land tenure in all the Southern English colonies. By this system persons who emigrated at their own expense were granted 50 acres free for each member of their party, or for any subsequent immigrant whose passage they paid. Thus private gain was enlisted to build the colony, and the labor supply kept pace with that of arable land.

English law and liberty came as well. In 1618 the company instructed the governor to introduce common law and summon a representative assembly with power to make by-laws, subject to the company's consent in England. Democracy made her American debut on 30 July 1619, when 22 'burgesses,' two from each settled district, elected by vote of all men seventeen and upward, met with the governor's council in the church at Jamestown. From that time forth, government of the people, however limited or thwarted, and the rule of law have been fundamental principles of the English colonies and the United States.

The parent company in England exerted far more power in Virginia than this popular assembly, but the company itself was democratic in spirit. Stockholders in 1619 unseated Sir Thomas Smyth, the London merchant adventurer who had headed it during the most difficult years, and elected Sir Edwin Sandys, an opposition leader in the House of Commons, tolerant in religion and liberal in outlook. Convinced that the colony's exclusive preoccupation with tobacco was unsound, Sandys induced the stockholders to adopt a five-year plan for Virginia. French vines, vintners, and olive trees, lumbermen from the Baltic, ironworkers from England were procured or hired to start new industries, and thousands of poor English men and women were assisted to emigrate. Unfortunately this required more expense than the company could bear, and the colony was ill-prepared to receive an influx of 4000 people in four years. Of those sent from England in the Sandys regime, more than three-fourths perished. Ships were overcrowded, housing facilities inadequate, and the loss of life from typhus, malaria, malnutrition, and overwork was appalling. Plantations were laid out too far apart, defense was neglected, and in 1622 a surprise attack by Indians destroyed the infant ironworks

This depiction of a Pamlico river Indian village in sixteenth-century Virginia derives from a watercolor by John White, a settler on Roanoke Island who subsequently became governor of the doomed colony. It is the earliest printed picture of tobacco fields, marked *E*. In the lower half, as Thomas Hariot explained, *A* indicates a building housing 'the tombes of their kings and princes,' *B* the site of their 'solemne prayers,' *C* where they met with their neighbors to 'make merrie together' after they had feasted with them in a broad plot, *D*. In the structure designated *F* in the upper right, an Indian keeps vigil, 'for there are such number of fowles, and beasts, that unles they keepe the better watche, they would devour all their corne. For which cause the watcheman maketh continual cryes and noyse.' From Theodor de Bry, *America*, part I, 1590. (*Rare Book Division, New York Public Library*)

at the falls of the James, erased almost every settlement outside Jamestown, massacred more than 300 men, women, and children, and in a night wiped out the gains of three years. This gave the enemies of Sandys a handle against him, convinced the king that the bankrupt, faction-torn colony had been grossly mismanaged, and produced, in 1624, a judicial dissolution of the Virginia Company of London.

Virginia now became a royal province or Crown colony; but she did not lose her large measure of self-government. Assembly and courts of justice were retained, though governor and council were now appointed by the king and subject to royal instructions. Charles I, not unaffected by the large revenue he was obtaining from the duties on tobacco, interfered with the colony less than the company had, and development continued along tobacco plantation lines.

When we think of seventeenth-century Virginia we should first banish from our minds the cavalier myth of gallants and fair ladies living a life of silken ease. We must picture a series of farms and plantations lining the James, the York, and the Rappahannock up to the fall line, and along the south bank of the Potomac. Few houses are more than a mile from tidewater. The average farm, not above 300 or 400 acres, is cultivated by the owner and his family and a few white indentured servants of both sexes. Around a story-and-a-half frame cottage are a vegetable garden and orchard; beyond, corn and tobacco fields, enclosed by zigzag fences of split rails; and beyond that, woodland, where cattle and hogs fend for themselves. In the course of a few years, when the original tobacco fields are exhausted, the woodland will be cleared and put under tillage, while the 'old fields,' after a few diminishing crops of corn, will revert to brush and woodland. Few horses and still fewer wheeled vehicles will be seen outside Jamestown until after 1650, but almost every farmer keeps a yoke of oxen for plowing and a boat on the nearest creek or river. If the owner prospers, he will procure more land from someone who has more head-rights than he cares to take up, or by importing his poor relations as servants.

The few great plantations, established by men who came out with considerable capital, have large houses and more outbuildings, keep a shop for selling English goods to their neighbors, and a wharf and warehouse for handling their tobacco. Every so often the big planter orders the London merchant who handles his tobacco crop to send him out another parcel of indented servants, for each of whom he will obtain 50 acres more land; if no ungranted land is available near the homestead he will 'seat' a second plantation elsewhere, and put his son, or a trusty servant whose time is up, in charge. Virginia was a colony with a sharply defined ruling class, although it took almost a century for a stable aristocracy to develop.

During the first half-century, the manners and customs of Virginia were Puritan. The code of laws adopted by the first Virginia Assembly 'Against Idleness, Gaming, drunkenes and excesse in apparell,' might well have been passed by a New England colony. Yet there were important differences, too, between Virginia and New England. The Church of England was early established in Virginia, and Puritan congregations were outlawed in 1643. And as time flowed on, and great fortunes were built from tobacco, the Puritan tinge faded from the Old Dominion.

Below the independent landowners in Virginia were the English and Irish indented servants, the main source of labor in the Chesapeake colonies throughout this pioneer period. Indented servants were mostly lads and lasses in their late 'teens or early twenties, members of large families in the English towns and countryside, who were looking for a better chance than the overcrowded trades of the old country. Men and women servants alike performed any sort of labor their master required for a period of five years, which might be extended for ill-conduct; at the end of that time they were dismissed with a few tools and clothes; in Maryland each servant was given 50 acres by the Lord Proprietor. The more energetic freedmen would then earn money by wage labor, and set up as farmers themselves. A hard system it was, according to modern lights; yet it enabled thousands of English men and women, and, in the eighteenth century, tens of thousands of Scots, Irish, Germans, and Swiss, to make a fresh start and take an active part in forming the American nation.

A Dutch ship brought the first Africans to

Jamestown as early as 1619. The first blacks appear to have been indented servants; slavery is not mentioned in any statute until after 1660, although it may have developed before that. Slavery did not become a characteristic feature of Virginia until nearly the end of the seventeenth century. It became so then for three reasons: England restricted the emigration of white bond servants; the Royal African Company became more efficient in the slave trade; and a catastrophic fall in the price of tobacco ruined the small farmers, permitting profits only to men who had the capital to purchase cheap and self-propagating labor.

Lord Baltimore's and Other Proprietary Colonies

Maryland, a colony with the same soil, climate, economic and social system as Virginia, owed her separate existence and her special character to the desire of one Englishman to create a feudal domain for his family, and a refuge for members of his faith. Sir George Calvert, first Lord Baltimore, aspired to found his own colony. Ordered out of Virginia because he was a Roman Catholic convert, he asked for and obtained from Charles I a liberal slice of the Old Dominion. Lord Baltimore died while the Maryland charter was going through, but it was confirmed to his son and heir Cecilius, the second Lord Baltimore, who dispatched the first group of colonists in 1634. Cecilius Calvert planned Maryland to be not only a source of profit, but a refuge for Catholics. Yet almost from the start the colony had a Protestant majority. Calvert coped with this situation in a statesmanlike manner by inducing the Maryland Assembly to pass a law of religious toleration in 1649. But civil war broke out in 1654, a class war of Protestant small farmers against the Catholic magnates and lords of manors. The majority won, and the Act of Toleration was repealed; but Lord Baltimore eventually recovered his rights.

In the West Indies, English, French, and Dutch used the proprietary method of colonization with success. The extension of sugar culture around 1650 and the importation of slaves made even the smallest of the islands immensely valuable. Far more money and men were spent on defending and capturing these islands than on the continental colonies that became Canada and the United States, because they were much more profitable.

These West Indian colonies were closely integrated with the English colonies in New England. Slave labor made it more profitable for the planters to concentrate on tropical crops of high profit, and procure elsewhere every other essential, such as salt meat and fish, breadstuffs and ground vegetables, lumber and livestock. These were exactly the commodities that New England produced, yet could find no vent for in England; and New England built the ships to carry these products of her farms, forests, and fisheries to the West Indies. The Chesapeake colonies, and later the Middle Colonies and the Carolinas, also shared this trade and, like New England, imported molasses and distilled it into rum. New England would have long remained a string of poor fishing stations and hardscrabble farms but for commerce with these superb tropical islands set in the sapphire Caribbean.

The Puritan Colonies

New England was founded without reference to the West Indies, and largely as a result of the religious movement known as Puritanism. The Puritans were that party in the Church of England who wished to carry through the Protestant Reformation to its logical conclusion, and establish both a religion and a way of living based on the Bible—as interpreted by themselves. The Church of England, a compromise between Rome and the reform, did not satisfy them. With official Anglican doctrine the Puritans had no quarrel; but they wished to do away with bishops and all clergy above the rank of parish priests, to abolish set prayers, and to reorganize the Church either by a hierarchy of councils (Presbyterianism), or on the basis of a free federation of independent parishes (Congregationalism). They were disgusted with the moral corruption that pervaded English society and wished to establish such patterns of living as would make it possible for people to lead something approaching the New Testament life. Eng-

Cecilius Calvert, second Baron Baltimore, sought to make Maryland a refuge for
Catholics, but the settlers turned out to be predominantly Protestant. In this
Gerard Soest portrait, he is shown with his young grandson Cecil. (*Enoch Pratt
Free Library*, *Baltimore*)

lish Puritan divines frowned on idleness as a sin, eschewed mysticism and monasticism, and taught that a good businessman served God well, provided he were honest; hence Puritanism appealed to the middle class of tradesmen and rising capitalists whose center was London. It made a wide appeal also in rural regions such as East Anglia and the West Country, where 'the hungry sheep look up and are not fed' (to use Milton's phrase) by the common run of English clergyman, incapable of delivering a proper sermon. And it enlisted the devoted support of many young intellectuals in the universities, especially in Cambridge; hence the stress of the Puritans on education. Puritanism was no class revolt, or economic movement in religious clothing, as sundry writers have claimed, but a dynamic religious revival with a burning desire to do the will of God. Their desires were thwarted by the first two Stuart kings. James I promised to harry the Puritans out of the land if they would not conform, and under Charles I, clergymen who refused to follow the Anglo-Catholic polity of Bishop Laud were persecuted.

The Pilgrim Fathers were a group of Separatists who, unlike the majority of Puritans, despaired of reforming the Church of England and broke away to create a new institution. This small band of humble folk of East Anglia, whose religious meetings were so interfered with that they removed to Leiden in 1609, formed an English Congregational Church in that Dutch city. After ten years' exile in a foreign land where the people were tolerant but the living was hard, and where war threatened, they decided to remove to America. Sir Edwin Sandys procured for them a grant from the Virginia Company, and a group of English merchants financed their migration. The *Mayflower*, after a rough passage, anchored on 11 November 1620 in the harbor of Cape Cod, outside the Virginia jurisdiction. Accordingly, the Pilgrims signed a compact to be governed by the will of the majority until permanent provision should be made for their colony. This Mayflower Compact of 1620 stands, with the Virginia Assembly of 1619, as one of the two foundation stones of American institutions. Nothing similar occurred anywhere else in the world for almost two centuries.

No group of settlers in America was so ill-fitted by experience and equipment to cope with the wilderness as this little band of peasants, town laborers, and shopkeepers; yet none came through their trials so magnificently. For, as Bradford put it, 'they knew they were pilgrims, and looked not much on those things, but lift up their eyes to the heavens, their dearest country.' Their only good luck was to find deserted fields ready for tillage at the harbor already named Plymouth by Captain John Smith, and to be joined by Squanto, a lonely Indian who taught them how to catch fish and plant corn. Half the company died the first winter; but when the *Mayflower* set sail in April not one of the survivors returned in her. Around mid-October 1621, after the gathering of a fair harvest and a big shoot of waterfowl and wild turkey, the Pilgrims held their first Thanksgiving feast, with Chief Massasoit of the Wampanoag and 90 of his subjects, 'whom for three days we entertained and feasted.' For several years thereafter the colony ran neck-and-neck with famine. But the Pilgrims never lost heart, and their stout-hearted idealism made Plymouth Rock a symbol. For, as Governor Bradford concluded his annals of the lean years,

Thus out of small beginnings greater things have been produced by his hand that made all things of nothing, and gives being to all things that are; and as one small candle may light a thousand; so the light here kindled hath shone unto many, yea, in some sort, to our whole nation.

Only 'small beginnings' were apparent for ten years; at the end of that time the Colony of New Plymouth numbered just 300. In the meantime a dozen straggling fishing and trading posts had been founded along the New England coast from southern Maine to Massachusetts Bay, with or without permission from the Council for New England.

One of these developed into the important Bay Colony. A company, which planted a small settlement at Salem in 1628, was taken over by a group of leading Puritans, including Sir Richard Saltonstall, Thomas Dudley, and John Winthrop, who wished to emigrate. Obtaining from Charles I a royal charter as the Massachusetts Bay Company in 1629, when Anglo-Catholic pressure began to be severely felt, they voted to transfer charter, government, and members to New England. A fleet of seventeen sail bearing 900 to 1000 men and women, the largest colonizing expedition yet sent out from England, crossed in the summer of 1630 to Massachusetts Bay and founded Boston and six or seven nearby towns.

This transfer of the Massachusetts Bay charter had an important bearing on colonial destiny and American institutions. With both charter and company in America, the colony became practically independent of England. The 'freemen,' as stockholders were then called, became voters; the governor, deputy-governor, and assistants whom the freemen annually elected, and who in England had been president and directors of a colonizing company, were now the executives, upper branch of the legislative assembly, and judicial officers of a Puritan commonwealth. A representative system was devised, as it was inconvenient for the freemen to attend the 'general court' or assembly in person, and by 1644 the deputies and assistants had separated into two houses. Neither king nor parliament had any say in the Massachusetts government. The franchise was restricted to church members, which prevented non-Puritan participation in the government; but this did not matter in the long run. What mattered was that this organization made for independence, and that the annual election on a definite date of all officers—governor and upper branch as well as deputies—became so popular in the colonies as to be imitated wherever the king could be induced to grant his consent. This feature survives in the Federal Government, and the corporate precedent has given the American system of government a very different complexion from the parliamentary system that was slowly developing in England.

The Puritan leaders had proposed to set up and maintain what they deemed to be true religion. That included an insistence on sobriety of manners, purity of morals, and an economy that would neither exalt the rich nor degrade the poor. Unlike the Pilgrims of Plymouth, they were not Separatists, but remained nominally within the Church of England. Unlike the Presbyterians, they were Congregationalists, who denied the need for a church superstructure and who stipulated that membership in the church would be restricted to those 'visible saints' who gave unmistakable evidence of their Christian belief. Each Congregational church was formed by a new covenant, and so was each new settlement. It soon appeared that Massachusetts Bay was the sort of colony that English Puritans wanted; for heavy Puritan migration to it continued until the outbreak of civil war in England. By that time New England had some 20,000 people. Most of this emigration, unlike that which was going on at the same time to Virginia, Maryland, and the West Indies, was against the will of the royal government; but nothing could stop it.

The community character of the New England migration dictated the method of land settlement. Neighborhood groups from the old country, often accompanied by an ousted parson, insisted on settling together, obtained a grant of land from the general court, established a village center, laid out lots, and so formed what was called in New England a town. Around each village green were situated the meeting-house (as the Puritans called a church edifice), the parsonage, and the houses of the principal settlers. Each person admitted as an inhabitant received a house lot, a planting lot for his corn, and a strip of river mead or salt meadow for winter forage. The cattle ranged the common woods, attended by the town herdsman. In town meeting, each settlement determined local affairs such as support of the school. Here democracy seeped into New England, unwanted by the founders.

The Puritan leaders were disturbed, too, by the rising spirit of egalitarianism. Men like John Winthrop, a superior statesman of noble character, had no doubt that God had ordained a hierarchy of classes, so that 'in all times some must be rich some poore, some highe and eminent in power and dignitie; others meane and in subieccion.' When a Puritan synod met in 1679, it expressed its concern not only about the rise of bastardy, the attempt to set up a brothel in Boston, and the displaying of naked necks and arms, 'or, which is more abominable, naked Breasts,' but, above all, about the spirit of insubordination of inferiors toward their betters. In particular, the church leaders noted: 'Day-Labourers and Mechanicks are unreasonable in their demands.'

The Puritan clergyman Richard Mather (1596–1669). His grandson Cotton
Mather observed: 'His voice was loud and big, and uttered with a deliberate
vehemency, it procured unto his ministry an awful and very taking majesty.' This
1670 depiction by John Foster, a recent graduate of Harvard who had been baptized
by Richard Mather, is the earliest portrait in a woodcut in America. (*American
Antiquarian Society*)

As the population of the towns grew, clashes frequently developed between the first generation, which insisted on respect for rank, and the second generation, determined on winning a share of meadow rights. If demands of the new generation were not met, they would threaten to secede from the town. 'If you persecute us in one city, wee must fly to another,' a Sudbury man warned. When such clashes were unresolved, a few hardy spirits would break away and repeat the process of town-building farther west.

Education was a particular concern of the Puritans. Their movement was directed by university-trained divines, and embraced by middle-class merchants and landowning farmers who had received the excellent education of Elizabethan England. Moreover, it was necessary for godliness that everyone learn to read the Bible. There had come to New England by 1640 about 130 university alumni, who insisted that their children have the same advantages as themselves, or better. Consequently, in the New England colonies, parents were required to teach their children and servants to read, or to send them to a village school. Above these primary schools, about two dozen of the larger New England towns had secondary public grammar schools on the English model, supported by taxation, which boys entered at the age of eight or nine, and where they studied Latin and Greek, and little else, for six years. At the end of that time they were prepared to enter Harvard College, founded by the Massachusetts government in 1636. There, the more ambitious lads studied the same seven arts and three philosophies as at Oxford, using the same Latin manuals of logic and metaphysics, Hebrew and Greek texts. Nor were the fine arts neglected. Seventeenth-century New Englanders had good taste in house design and village layout; artisans fashioned beautiful articles of silver for home and communion table; writers such as Anne Bradstreet produced poetry of great charm. Thus the classical and humanist tradition of the English was carried into the clearings of the New England wilderness.

Three more Puritan colonies, which later formed two states of the Union, sprang up before 1640. Under the lead of the Rev. Thomas Hooker,

the first westward migration in the English colonies took place in 1636, to the Connecticut river, where a Bible Commonwealth was organized on the Massachusetts model. New Haven, founded by a London merchant, Theophilus Eaton, and his pastor the Rev. John Davenport, maintained a separate existence from Connecticut until 1662, and spread along both shores of Long Island Sound. Both these colonies were like-minded with the Bay Colony and Plymouth; but Rhode Island, the creation of four separate groups of Puritan heretics, was distinctly otherwise-minded. Anne Hutchinson of Boston, who set up as a prophetess, and the Rev. Roger Williams, who differed with Bay authorities on many matters, were banished, and on Narragansett Bay formed settlements which federated as Rhode Island and Providence Plantations in 1644. Williams denied the authority of civil or ecclesiastical hierarchy over a man's conscience. 'Forced worship,' he asserted, 'stinks in God's nostrils.' Imbued with the spirit of Christian love, he treated Indians as brothers. Under Williams, Rhode Island became a haven for the persecuted, and the ideas of this seventeenth-century Puritan have inspired secular twentieth-century civil libertarians, even though their views of the universe differ greatly from those of this remarkable divine.

One thing these New England colonies had in common until 1680: all were virtually independent, acknowledging allegiance to whatever authority had control in England, but making their own laws, trading where they pleased, defending themselves without help from home, and working out their own institutions.

New Netherland

Between New England and Virginia the indomitable Dutch, with that uncanny instinct for sources of wealth that has always characterized their commercial ventures, planted a colony that in due time became New York. In 1602 Dutch capitalists organized the Netherlands East Indies Company, a corporation in comparison with which the Virginia Company was a petty affair. Inexorably this company pushed the Portuguese out of most of their trading posts in the Far East, where they

New Amsterdam, 1673. This view of the tip of Manhattan Island, Wall Street south to the Battery, is from Brooklyn Heights, which remained the favored perspective for those seeking to depict the city. The engraving, from Carolus Allard, *Orbis Habitablis*, published in Holland, represents the dying gasp of the Dutch empire in North America. The Dutch recaptured the city in 1673 but it was returned to England by treaty the following year. (*Stokes Collection, New York Public Library*)

created a rich empire. The East Indies Company, seeking a shorter way to the Orient than the dangerous Cape route, made several efforts to find a northwest passage. That is what Henry Hudson was looking for in 1609 when he sailed the *Half-Moon* up the noble river that shares his name with the mighty bay where he met his death. The Hudson river proved to be a passage indeed, to the heart of the Iroquois Confederacy and the richest fur-bearing country south of the St. Lawrence. After skippers Block and May had explored the coast from Maine to the Delaware Capes, Dutch fur traders began to frequent the rivers and trade with the natives.

New Netherland began as a trading-post colony in 1624, with the foundation of Fort Orange (Albany) up the Hudson. Fort Amsterdam on the tip of Manhattan Island was permanently established in 1626, Fort Nassau at the site of Gloucester, N.J., in 1623, and Fort Good Hope on the Connecticut river, near Hartford, in 1633. New Netherland was governed much as Virginia had been before 1619, by a governor and council appointed by the company, without representative institutions. As early as 1630 New Amsterdam was a typical sailormen's town, with numerous taverns, smugglers, and illicit traders, as well as a Dutch Reformed Church, and a number of substantial houses. When in 1638 the States General threw open the seaborne trade of New Netherland to all Dutch subjects, New Amsterdam became practically a free port. In 1629 the company made a half-hearted attempt to encourage settlement by issuing the Charter of Privileges to Patroons. Anyone who brought out 50 families of tenants at his own expense could have an extensive tract of land, with full manorial privileges, including holding court. The directors of the company, such as Kiliaen Van Rensselaer, promptly snapped up all the best sites, and these privileges, which were confirmed under the English regime, meant that the most valuable land in the Hudson valley was held in vast estates on a feudal basis. A certain number of Dutchmen and Walloons acquired 'bouweries' (farms) outside the wall on Manhattan, or in the pretty villages of Haerlem, Breucelen on Long Island, or Bergen across the North (as the Dutch called the Hudson) river; a few hundred New England Puritans spilled over into Westchester County and Long Island. Yet New Netherland did not prosper; it was the neglected child of a trading company whose main interests were in the East.

'Diedrich Knickerbocker' (Washington Irving) created a myth of New Netherland that will never die; the jolly community of tipplers and topers, of waterfront taverns, broad-beamed fraus, and well-stocked farms. The actual New Netherland was a frustrated community. The successive governors, of whom Irving drew comic pictures, were, in reality, petty autocrats and grafters who ruled New Amsterdam with a rod of iron, used torture to extract confessions, and mismanaged almost everything. The peg-legged Peter Stuyvesant enlarged New Netherland at the expense of his neighbors. In 1655 he annexed the colony of New Sweden that centered about Fort Christina (Wilmington) on the Delaware. But on the other side, Fort Good Hope on the Connecticut river was squeezed out by English settlers.

When a small English fleet appeared off New Amsterdam one summer's day in 1664 and ordered the Dutch to surrender, Governor Stuyvesant stomped his wooden leg in vain, and New Netherland became New York without a blow or a tear. The population of the city had then reached only 1500, and that of the colony less than 7000; New England outnumbered New Netherland ten to one. But the Dutch stamp was already placed indelibly on New York, and most of the Dutch families, such as the Van Rensselaers, Van Burens, and Roosevelts, prospered under English rule.

Two Decades of Neglect

That 'salutary neglect' by England, which Edmund Burke later asserted to be one of the main reasons for American prosperity, was never more evident than in the twenty years between 1640 and 1660. The civil war and other commotions, lasting from 1641 to 1653, when Oliver Cromwell became Lord Protector of the English Commonwealth, afforded all three groups of colonies a chance to grow with a minimum of interference; and Oliver, too, decided to let well enough alone. When interference was threatened, colonies as far apart as Massachusetts and Barbados stood stiffly on their privileges. The Virginia Assembly, which proclaimed Charles II king after hearing of the execution of Charles I, capitulated without a blow to a parliamentary fleet in 1652, and in return was allowed to elect the governor and council. In Maryland, the only colony where English events touched off a civil war, Lord Baltimore triumphed in the end.

Perhaps the most significant colonial development of the period was the formation of the New England Confederacy in 1643, largely for defense against the Dutch, the French, and the Indians. A board of commissioners representing Plymouth, Massachusetts, Connecticut, and New Haven, the 'United Colonies of New-England,' established a 'firm and perpetual league of friendship and amity, for offense and defense, mutual advice and succor upon all just occasions.' Several boundary controversies between the member colonies and one with the Dutch were settled, provision was made for the return of runaway servants, contributions were taken up for Harvard College, and an English fund for the conversion of the Indians was administered. In several respects the New England Confederacy anticipated the Confederation of 1781; and the league held together long enough to direct military operations during the Indian war of 1675–76.

New France

New France, too, took on substance in this period. Samuel de Champlain, who unfurled the lilies of France on the rock of Quebec in 1608, protected missionaries and attempted, with but a handful of soldiers, to defend the beaver line of his Huron allies to Quebec from Iroquois assaults. But the companies that employed him, up to his death in 1635, were even less interested in settlement than was the Dutch West India Company. Not a furrow was plowed or a seed planted in Canada until 1628. Shortly after, the Company of the Hundred Associates, which then ruled New France, began establishing seigneuries, not unlike the Dutch patroonships, though smaller and more numerous, along both banks of the St. Lawrence. Each seigneur was supposed to bring out a certain number of habitants, or settlers. But the system caught on very slowly. There were two main interests in New France, conversion of the Indians and conversion of beaver into peltry. The French Crown, which wished Canada to be a country of peasant farms like Normandy, abolished the company regime in 1663, and Canada became a Crown colony under the direct government of Louis XIV. But even *Le Grand Monarque* was unable to make his transatlantic empire change character.

Thus, in little more than half a century after the founding of Jamestown, the French, English, and Dutch had a firm foothold on the shores of five American areas—the St. Lawrence, New England, the Hudson, the Delaware, Chesapeake Bay—and the West Indies. They had planted those attitudes, folkways, and institutions which were destined to endure and to spread across the North American continent.

3

The Empire Comes of Age

*

1660–1763

The Acts of Trade and Navigation

Although the English colonies were by this time conscious of themselves, England was not very conscious of them. Every English colony except Virginia had grown up through the uncoordinated efforts of individuals and small groups. The home government as yet had no clear policy about the connection between colonies and mother country.

With the restoration of the monarchy in 1660 came a perceptible drift into something that may be called a colonial policy. Charles II conquered New Netherland, and filled the gap between New England and Maryland with four new English colonies. He extended the southern frontier by founding the Carolinas. Parliament laid down a definite economic policy in the Acts of Trade and Navigation. After James II tried to consolidate all continental settlements into two vice-royalties, Spanish style, a scheme thwarted by his expulsion from England, William and Mary, more tactfully, brought all their American colonies under some measure of control. And England began a protracted struggle with the French and Spanish for North America.

By 1660 the doctrine known as mercantilism, the pursuit of economic power in the interest of national self-sufficiency, was taken for granted by all European states. Even colonists admitted that the profits of an empire should center in the mother country. Spain and Portugal had seen to that since the beginning; but England, what with haphazard colonization and civil tumults, had allowed her overseas subjects to trade with foreign countries in almost everything except tobacco, and even tobacco was often carried abroad in foreign ships. Now, through a series of Acts of Trade and Navigation (1660–72), an effort was made to make the English empire self-sustaining and to confine profits to English subjects.

These acts embodied three principles. All trade between England and her colonies must be conducted by English- or English-colonial-built vessels, owned and manned by English subjects. All European imports into the colonies, save for perishable fruit and wine from the Atlantic Islands, must first be 'laid on the shores of England'—i.e., unloaded, handled, and reloaded—before being sent to the colonies, some of the duties being repaid on re-exportation. And, finally, certain colonial products 'enumerated' in the laws must be exported to England only. In the seventeenth century the enumerated products were tobacco, sugar, cotton, and tropical commodities grown only in the West Indies. Rice and molasses, furs, and naval stores (tar, pitch, turpentine, ships' spars) were added between 1705 and 1722.

Opinions still differ about the effect of this system on the colonies. It certainly did not stop growth in the century after 1660. But the cutting off of direct tobacco exports to the European continent helped to depress the price of tobacco in Virginia. As time went on, more and more colonial products were added to the enumerated list, until, on the eve of the American Revolution, the only important non-enumerated article was salt fish. The enumerated principle was not too severe, as proved by the fact that Americans after independence continued to use England as an entrepôt for rice and tobacco. Nor should it be forgotten that Parliament paid bounties to colonial producers of naval stores and indigo, prohibited the growing of tobacco in England, and laid preferential duties which excluded Cuban and other Spanish-American leaf from the English market. There was no legal bar to the colonists' trading with the French and other foreign West Indies. In fact a large part of the specie circulating in the continental colonies until the Revolution consisted of French and Spanish coins which were procured in the islands in exchange for the products of northern farms, forests, and fisheries. However, skilled artisans were forbidden to leave England for the colonies, and in the last third of the century, English emigration to her colonies dwindled to a mere trickle. A leading English interest was supplying the colonies with slaves, a traffic in which colonial ships and merchants participated to a limited extent.

In the mercantilist perspective the most valuable colonies were those from the Chesapeake south, which produced tropical or semi-tropical raw materials that England wanted, and imported almost every luxury and necessity from home. And the least valuable colonies were those of New England, which were Old England's competitors rather than her complements. In 1698 seven-eighths of England's American trade was with the West Indies, Virginia, Maryland, and the Carolinas. As time went on, and the Northern Colonies acquired wealth through the West Indies trade, this unequal balance was redressed. By 1767, two-thirds of England's colonial exports were to colonies north of Maryland.

Founding of the Carolinas

After 1660 the impulse toward colonial expansion came mainly from three sources: English merchants and shipowners who wanted new areas for trade and exploitation, courtiers and politicians who planned to recoup their shattered fortunes with great colonial estates, and religious dissenters who sought a refuge for members of their faith.

Restoration of the Stuart monarchy set all doubtful English colonial claimants polishing up their old claims and seeking validation from Charles II. The Carolina Proprietors, a group of eight promoters and politicians, obtained from Charles II a proprietary patent to all North America between the parallels of 31° and 36° N (and the next year had this enlarged to embrace all the territory between Daytona, Fla., and the Virginia-North Carolina boundary). This they named Carolina. The two leading spirits among the proprietors were Sir John Colleton, a wealthy Barbadian planter who sought new homes for the surplus white population of Barbados, and Anthony Ashley Cooper, better known by his later title of Earl of Shaftesbury, Chancellor of the Exchequer. Shaftesbury, in collaboration with John Locke, wrote a charter for the colony, the 'Fundamental Constitutions of Carolina' in 120 articles; an extraordinary document which attempted to provide for this pioneer colony a revived feudalism, with five 'estates,' eight supreme courts, a chamberlain and lord high admiral, and native titles of baron, cacique, and landgrave, depending on the amount of land one bought. After several false starts, a small number of colonists from England and several hundred Barbadians founded Charleston in 1670.

Ten years later the proprietors obtained a group of French Huguenots, and in 1683 Scots began arriving; thus South Carolina was racially heterogeneous from the first. By 1700 the population of the colony was about 5000, half of them black slaves; the principal exports were provisions for the West Indies trade, naval stores, and peltry. These early South Carolinians were as expert fur-traders as the French Canadians, sending agents around the southern spurs of the Appalachians into the future Alabama in search of deerskins; and they followed the Spanish example of enslaving Indians. At the turn of the century the cultivation of rice and indigo began on the low coastal plain and along the rivers; and these gradually replaced the more pioneer pursuits. By 1730 South Carolina was a planting colony like Virginia, with different staples, and a centralized instead of a dispersed social and political system. There were no county or local units of government. Every leading planter had a town house near the battery in Charleston where he spent the summer months, when river plantations were unhealthful. The French Huguenots, the most important element in the ruling class, imparted a high-spirited and aristocratic tone to the colony; they quickly adopted the English language and joined the Established Church of England.

In the meantime a wholly different society was developing in the section of the province which became North Carolina. There the original settlers had been adventurers from New England and poor whites from Virginia. The proprietors granted them a separate governor and assembly. Apart from the Swiss-German settlement of New Bern there were few foreigners before 1713, and still fewer colonists of means. The principal products were tobacco and naval stores; and lack of harbors suitable for seagoing vessels meant heavy transportation costs. North Carolina was poor, turbulent, and democratic, with relatively few slaves, and, unlike South Carolina, few plantations. In 1736 the white population was estimated to be one-third greater than that of the southern colony, but the production very much less.

On the whole, the proprietors of Carolina did a good job in planting these two colonies, but they reaped more headaches than profit. All except Lord Granville sold out to the Crown in 1729,

when the two halves became the royal provinces of North Carolina and South Carolina.

New York and the Jerseys

The Duke of York's brief and unsuccessful reign as James II should not blind us to the fact that he was an excellent seaman and an able administrator. His brother Charles II appointed him Lord High Admiral at the age of 26. As head of the navy he wished to deprive the Dutch of their base at New Amsterdam, and as an impecunious member of the House of Stuart he needed a profitable colony. With parliamentary approval the king conferred on his brother in 1664 the most extensive English territorial grant of the century: the continent between the Connecticut and Delaware rivers, together with the islands of New England and Maine east of the Kennebec. When Stuyvesant surrendered New Netherland, the Duke of York, aged 30, gained possession of a section of America destined to be the wealthiest area in the world. As Lord Proprietor, he was absolute master of this domain, under the king.

The Duke's rule of New York, as he renamed the Dutch colony, was fairly enlightened. He summoned no assembly, but ordered his governor to treat the Dutch with 'humanity and gentleness,' and made no effort to impose on them the English language or his own religion. But he intended to make money out of the colony, and drew up his own schedule of customs duties, quit-rents, and taxes. That made trouble. There were already too many English in the colony for any proprietor to raise taxes without representation. After two decades of resistance, the Duke's governor summoned a representative assembly in 1683.

Realizing that he had bitten off a little more than he could chew, the Duke began giving away slices of his grant as early as 1664. To his friends Lord John Berkeley and Sir George Carteret he ceded all land between the Hudson and the Delaware as the 'Province of Nova Caesaria or New Jersey.' A few hundred Dutch and English Puritans from New England were already there, and, in order to attract more, Berkeley and Carteret granted freedom of conscience, liberal terms for land, and an assembly. In 1674 Berkeley sold out his half share in New Jersey to two Quakers, who took the southwestern half of the province, while Carteret kept the northeastern part. Carteret's widow in 1680 sold out East New Jersey to a group of proprietors, and the two Quakers let William Penn in on West New Jersey. The net result was a heterogeneous population, little social cohesion, and confused land titles.

Penn's Holy Experiment

The founding of Pennsylvania, more so than any other American commonwealth, is the lengthened shadow of one man and of his faith in God and in human nature.

Out of the religious ferment of Puritan England came the Society of Friends, commonly known as Quakers. They believed that religious authority rested neither in the Bible nor in a priestly hierarchy but in the Inner Light of Jesus Christ in the soul of every man. A mystical faith, Quakerism encouraged not quietistic contemplation but an 'enthusiastic' crusade to persuade their fellow men that they could enter a 'paradise of God' on earth. Since every man had some of God's spirit, all men were brothers and all were equal; they addressed one another as 'thee' and 'thou,' and observed literally the divine command 'thou shalt do no murder,' even under the name of war. Like the early Christians they gathered strength from oppression. Over 3000 Quakers were imprisoned in England during the first two years of the Restoration; yet the sect spread like wildfire. In 1652 the first Quaker missionaries appeared in the English colonies. Severe laws were passed against them in every colony but Rhode Island, and in Boston three were hanged; but finally by passive resistance they wore down the authorities and won a grudging toleration. In England, George Fox and his courageous missionaries converted thousands, especially among the poorer country people and the workingmen of London and Bristol. As Puritanism had been in 1600, and as Methodism would be in 1770, so Quakerism became the dynamic form of English Protestantism from about 1650 to 1700.

With William Penn the Quakers obtained one of the greatest colonies. The founder of Pennsylvania, born in 1644, was the son of Admiral Sir William Penn, conqueror of Jamaica. Young William was converted to Quakerism in 1667, when he listened to the sermon of a Friend on the text 'There is a Faith that overcometh the World.' And for the remaining 51 years of his life, William Penn was steadfast in that faith. The Admiral, who swore great oaths when he heard this news, became reconciled before his death and left his Quaker son a considerable fortune. What the young man wanted was a proprietary colony of his own, where he could experiment with political as well as religious liberty. The Friends no longer needed a refuge; but, like the Puritans of half a century before, they wanted a colony where they could live their ideal of the New Testament life, free from the pressure of bad example and worldly corruption. In 1677 in Germany Penn met members of several sects, some akin to the Quakers in doctrine, who were eager to leave. That tour enlarged his conception of a colony to that of a refuge for the persecuted of every race and sect.

Fortunately, Penn's conversion had never caused him to break with his father's friends, among whom was counted the Duke of York, who owed the Admiral £16,000. The cancellation of that bad debt secured for William and his heirs in 1681 a generous slice of the Duke's grant. The king implemented this grant by a charter creating 'Pennsylvania' a proprietary province on the model of Maryland.

Settlement began without delay. In 1681 Penn published in English, French, German, and Dutch *Some Account of the Province of Pennsylvania.* He urged peasants and artisans to come, and get-rich-quick adventurers to stay away; he gave instructions for the journey, and promised political and religious liberty. Even more persuasive were the easiest terms for land yet offered in North America: a 50-acre head-right free; 200-acre tenant farms at a penny an acre rent; estates of 5000 acres for £100, with a city lot thrown in. In three months Penn disposed of warrants for over 300,000 acres, and in 1682 he came over himself.

Neither the banks of Delaware Bay nor the

lower reaches of the rivers were a wilderness in 1682. About a thousand Swedes, Finns, and Dutch survivors of the colonies of New Sweden and New Netherland were already there. These were given free land grants, and proved useful in providing the first English colonists with food, housing, and labor. Choosing an admirable site for his capital, Penn laid out Philadelphia between the Delaware and the Schuylkill rivers in checkerboard fashion—which had a permanent and pernicious effect on American city planning—and undertook the government himself.

William Penn liked to allude to his province as the 'Holy Experiment,' and he made religious liberty and trust in humanity its cornerstones. Though his tastes were those of the English aristocracy, he believed in the traditional liberties of Englishmen, and intended that they should be respected in his province. Yet Penn was no nineteenth-century democrat. He favored government for the people, by liberally educated gentlemen like himself. And the first *Frame of Government* that he issued for Pennsylvania in 1682 reflected this idea. He appointed himself governor. A small council was elected by taxpayers from landowners 'of best repute for wisdom, virtue and ability,' to initiate bills, and a large elective assembly to accept or reject them— but if the assembly 'turn debaters, you overthrow the charter,' said he. Such a system was unpalatable to discussion-loving Englishmen. It worked fairly well when Penn was in his province, but when he returned to England, his government almost blew up. His too great trust in human nature led him to make unsuitable appointments of land agents who robbed him, and of deputy governors who antagonized or scandalized the people.

Penn returned to Philadelphia in 1699 and issued a Charter of Privileges, which remained the constitution of the colony until 1776. It provided the usual set-up of a governor and council (appointed by the proprietor but confirmed by the king), and an assembly composed of four representatives for each county, elected by a property franchise. The three 'Lower Counties,' as the future state of Delaware was then called, acquired an assembly of their own in 1702, but the Charter of Privileges was their charter too, and the governor of Pennsylvania was their governor.

Pennsylvania began with the most liberal and humane code of laws in the world. Capital punishment, which existed for a dozen different offenses in the other English colonies and for more than twenty in England, was inflicted in Pennsylvania only for murder. But a crime wave at the turn of the century caused the criminal code to be stiffened to such a point that the Privy Council in England rejected half the new laws. Accordingly, by 1717, there was little difference between Pennsylvania and other colonies in the rigor of their laws. However, their severity was mitigated by Quaker compassion. Philadelphia had the most humane prisons in the English colonies.

Pennsylvania prospered as did no other early settlement. Two years after its foundation Philadelphia boasted 357 houses; in 1685 the population of the province was little short of 9000. Germans of the Mennonite sect settled Germantown in 1683; Welsh Quakers founded Radnor and Haverford; a Free Society of Traders, organized by English Quakers, started fisheries and established brick kilns, tanneries, and glass works. Penn could state without boasting in 1684, 'I have led the greatest colony into America that ever any man did upon a private credit, and the most prosperous beginnings that were ever in it are to be found among us.'

William Penn himself fell on evil days at the turn of the century. His business affairs went from bad to worse. He had a protracted boundary controversy with Lord Baltimore—eventually settled in 1763–67 by the Mason-Dixon Line.[1] His eldest son, the second proprietor, turned out a spendthrift and a rake. The quarrels among council and governor and assembly distressed him; 'For the love of God, me, and the poor country,' he once wrote to the leader of the opposition, 'do not be so litigious and brutish!' But he never lost

1. The Mason and Dixon Line lies along latitude 39° 43' 26.3" N between the southwestern corner of Pennsylvania and the arc of a circle of twelve miles' radius drawn from New Castle (Delaware) as a center; and along that arc to the Delaware river. It was run by two English surveyors, Mason and Dixon, in 1750. But there have been interstate controversies about parts of it even in the present century.

faith in the Holy Experiment, or in human nature. Pennsylvania was a portent of America to be; the first large community in modern history where different ethnic groups and religions lived under the same government on terms of equality. Pennsylvania interested eighteenth-century philosophers as a successful experiment in the life of reason; Voltaire never tired of holding it up as proof that man could lead the good life without absolute monarchy, feudalism, or religious and ethnic uniformity.

Time of Troubles in Virginia and New England 1675–92

Virginia, ever loyal to the House of Stuart, suffered grievously from its restoration. Charles II appointed Sir William Berkeley governor of Virginia, and in a wave of loyalty the people elected a house of burgesses in 1661 which proved so pliant that Berkeley kept this 'long assembly' going for fifteen years by successive adjournments, and managed to get the whole machinery of government in his hands.

More serious for the Old Dominion were overproduction and low prices for tobacco. The Acts of Trade and the Dutch wars curtailed the foreign market and raised the cost of transportation. In 1662 Governor Berkeley reported the price of tobacco to be so low that it would not pay the cost of freight. 'Forty thousand people are impoverished,' he wrote, 'in order to enrich little more than forty merchants in England.' In 1668 tobacco prices in Virginia reached an all-time low of a farthing a pound, one-quarter of the customs duty on it in England. The assembly for ten years made attempts to curtail production and peg prices; these were thwarted partly by Maryland's refusal to come in, and partly because the English merchants raised prices of goods sent in exchange when they could not make their usual profit. Fifteen years after the Restoration, Virginia, the land of opportunity for poor and industrious Englishmen, had become a place of poverty and discontent. There the first serious rebellion in North American history broke out.

The immediate cause of Bacon's Rebellion was the Indian question. At this time the Indians were restive all along the rear of the English colonies. The Susquehannock, forced south to the Potomac by the Seneca, broke up into small bands and began harrying the Virginia-Maryland frontier in the summer of 1675. Governor Berkeley, hoping to avoid a general Indian war (such as had already broken out in New England), decided on a defensive policy, building a chain of mutually supporting forts around the settled part of Virginia. That infuriated the frontier planters, who believed the Berkeley clique had put the planters' lives in jeopardy in order to profit from the Indian trade. Nathaniel Bacon, an impetuous 28-year-old gentleman fresh from England whose plantation had been attacked, protested: 'These traders at the head of the rivers buy and sell our blood.' As leader of discontented planters, Bacon commanded an unauthorized military force which slaughtered the peaceful Oconeechee tribe, and then advanced on Jamestown. Bacon is said to have exclaimed, 'Damn my blood, I'll kill Governor, Council, Assembly and all!' As this improvised rebel army approached Jamestown, Berkeley decided to dissolve his 'long assembly' and issued writs for a new one, which met shortly and passed some important bills for relief, reform, and defense. What had begun as a sectional quarrel over Indian policy had developed into an assault on political privilege, although in this confused upheaval the poorer farmers had as many grievances against the Bacon faction as against the Berkeley circle.

For a time, Bacon ruled most of Virginia. But Berkeley plucked up courage, called out the loyal militia of the Eastern Shore, and civil war began. Exactly how far Bacon intended to go is not clear, but there is some evidence that he hoped to unite Virginia, North Carolina, and Maryland as a 'free state.' He did set up a government of his own, but cavalier feeling in Virginia was still too strong to support a rebellion against royal authority. After Bacon's premature death (26 October 1676), the rebellion collapsed. Berkeley rounded up the leaders and had twenty-three of them executed for treason. 'That old fool has hanged more men in that naked country than I have done for the murder of my father,' exclaimed Charles II.

Captain Thomas Smith, self-portrait, *circa* 1690. A mariner who arrived in New England in 1650, Captain Smith was a self-taught artist who developed enough proficiency to be commissioned by Harvard in 1680 to paint a portrait. No doubt because he traveled widely, as the naval scene suggests, his work is closer to the more ornate style of Europe than that of his contemporaries in New England, but there is an authentic Puritan emphasis in the skull and the lines beneath it, which bid farewell to a 'World of Evils.' (*Worcester Art Museum*)

New England under the Stuart Restoration not only flourished economically, but preserved its right of self-government. Massachusetts Bay was allowed to continue for a quarter-century longer under her corporate charter, and Connecticut and Rhode Island obtained similar charters from the Crown in 1662 and 1663, with complete self-government. The Connecticut charter included the old New Haven Colony in its boundaries.

Nevertheless, New England, too, had its time of troubles. In 1675–77 broke out the most devastating war in her entire history. King Philip's War it was called, after the Wampanoag chief who began hostilities. The natives were reacting desperately against their diminishing power. Now skilled in the use of firearms, they were able to attack frontier settlements at will, destroy crops, cattle, and houses, and endanger the very existence of white New England. A dozen villages were leveled, and the casualties were distressingly high. But the Puritans had the New England Confederacy, while the Indians were not united; some 2500 converts remained loyal to the whites; and gradually the New England militia, accompanied by loyal Indian scouts, broke up Indian concentrations, destroyed their food supply, and hunted down their bands. With the death of King Philip in August 1676 the rebellion collapsed, and Philip's wife and son were sold into slavery in the West Indies. The power of the natives in southern New England was broken forever; but the Abnaki of Maine and New Hampshire turned to Canada for aid, and kept the English at bay in northern New England for another seventy-five years. Not until 1720 did New England recover the frontier thrown back by this fierce war.

The royal government chose this time to bring the Bay Colony to book for her recalcitrance. Massachusetts offended Charles II by coining the pine-tree shilling, and by purchasing from the Gorges proprietors the Province of Maine, which the king intended to buy for one of his bastards. The province refused to obey the Navigation Acts on the ground 'that the subjects of his majesty here being not represented in Parliament, so we have not looked at ourselves to be impeded in our trade by them.' It declined to allow appeals to English courts, or to grant freedom of worship and the franchise to Anglicans. Consequently, in 1684, the High Court of Chancery declared the old Massachusetts Bay charter to be 'vacated, cancelled and annihilated.' The government was now in the king's hands to do as he saw fit.

James II found the colonial situation disquieting. There were three separate colonies in New England and four in the middle region, each with its own assembly, all of them flouting the Acts of Trade and Navigation as much as they dared. At the same time French Canada seemed menacing again. A great administrator, Count Frontenac, sent explorers like Joliet, Marquette, and La Salle down the Mississippi, and attempted to break the

Anglo-Iroquois alliance. Consolidation was the royal solution. Between 1685 and 1688 the New England colonies, New York, and the Jerseys were combined into one viceroyalty called the Dominion of New England. It was ruled by an appointed governor (Sir Edmund Andros) and council, but had no representative institutions. Andros and his council questioned the validity of land titles, which alarmed every farmer in New England, and they taxed without a legislative grant.

When James II was expelled from England in the 'Glorious Revolution' of 1688, which brought in William III and Mary II as joint sovereigns of the British Isles, a succession of popular revolutions overthrew dominion authorities and put the several colonies back where they had been before 1685. The only conspicuous leader in these revolts was Jacob Leisler, a New Yorker of German birth. Leisler, by antagonizing the patroons and other important groups in his colony, and by firing on royal troops sent to take over the government, placed himself in a position where he could be accused of treason. He was judicially murdered in 1691. Elsewhere the Dominion of New England fell apart with scarcely a blow.

By that time King William's War with the French was going full blast, no English frontier farm was safe; and to cap the catalogue of woes in this seventeen-year period of terror and trouble, a witchcraft scare broke out in Massachusetts. To the already vast literature on witchcraft the Reverend Cotton Mather, boy wonder of the New England clergy, contributed a book entitled *Memorable Providences*. In it he described a case of alleged witchcraft in Boston for which a poor old woman was executed, and how he had handled the accusing children to prevent a witch-hunting epidemic. The second edition of this work (1691) got into the hands of a group of young girls in a suburb of Salem. More or less as a prank, they accused a half-Indian, half-Negro family slave of being a witch. Flogged by her master into confessing, to save her skin she accused two respectable goodwives of being her confederates. The 'afflicted' children, finding themselves the objects of attention, persisted in their charges for fear of being found out, and this started a chain reaction. A special court was set up to try the witches. The

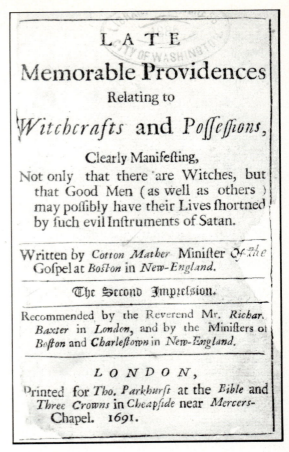

When a copy of this work by the noted Puritan divine Cotton Mather (1663–1728) fell into the hands of some young Massachusetts girls, they made an accusation of witchcraft against a family slave that led to the Salem hysteria of 1692. Before it was over, five men and fourteen women had been hanged and one man pressed to death. (*Library of Congress*)

innocent people whom the girls accused implicated others to escape the gallows, confessing broomstick rides, flying saucers, witches' sabbaths, sexual relations with the devil, and everything which, according to the book, witches were supposed to do. Honest folk who declared the whole thing nonsense were cried out upon for witches. The vicious business continued through the summer of 1692, until nineteen persons, including a Congregational minister and fourteen women, had been found guilty of witchcraft and hanged; and one man pressed to death. About 55 more had pleaded guilty and accused others, 150 of whom were in jail awaiting trial. The frenzy

was only halted because the witch-finders were beginning to go after prominent people. On the tardy advice of Increase Mather and other clergymen, the assembly dissolved the special court and released all prisoners.

As a witchcraft scare, the Salem one was small compared with others at the time in Europe; and it had a few redeeming features. The condemned witches were hanged, not burned to death as elsewhere. Almost everyone concerned in the furor later confessed his error (Judge Sewall doing so in open church meeting), and twenty years later the Massachusetts courts annulled the convictions and granted indemnity to the victims. But the record reveals an appalling moral cowardice on the part of ministry and gentry, and credulity and hatred among the people at large. It was one of those times which unfortunately have occurred more frequently in the present century, when evil is given full sway.

Colonial Reorganization

Colonial reorganization took place gradually by a series of typical English compromises. Rhode Island and Connecticut were allowed to keep their corporate charters; New York, and later the Jerseys and Carolinas, became royal provinces; Pennsylvania and Maryland were restored to their proprietors. A part of the Dominion of New England was salvaged by creating the royal province of Massachusetts Bay, including the old Bay colony, the Plymouth colony, and Maine. In all these units, representative institutions were confirmed or granted. By an act of Parliament of 1696, a new system of admiralty courts, requiring no jury trial, was instituted to enforce the Acts of Trade and Navigation. The new system succeeded in suppressing the grosser forms of piracy and smuggling, and stopping direct importations from continental Europe. Submission of all acts of colonial assemblies to the Privy Council for possible disallowance was insisted on, and appeals from colonial courts to the Privy Council were encouraged.

The Crown could balk colonial legislation that it considered undesirable, both by the royal governor's veto which could not be overridden, and by the royal disallowance. About 2½ per cent of all acts passed by colonial assemblies were disallowed by the Privy Council. Most of those thrown out deserved it; for instance, discriminatory legislation against religious minorities, or laws discriminating against ships, products, or subjects of neighboring English colonies. But some good ones, restricting the slave trade, were also nullified. These colonial laws were disallowed after investigation and report by the Board of Trade and Plantations. That body, appointed by the king under an act of 1696, was the nearest thing to a colonial office in the English government; but its powers were only advisory. Most colonial matters were routed through the Board, which meant a certain uniformity in administration, but decisions were made either by the king, the lords of the admiralty, or the war department. This imperial system, as it existed to 1776, would have been cumbrous and inefficient even if competently and honestly administered, as it was not.

The principal officials in the colonies who were expected to enforce English laws and regulations were the royal and proprietary governors. The former were appointed by the king during his good pleasure; the proprietary governors had to be acceptable to the Crown. They had not only an absolute veto over legislation, but the authority to prorogue and dissolve the lower houses in most colonies, and the power to dismiss judges. Nonetheless, most were dependent on the assemblies for their salaries. Executive patronage, which might have been an important lever, was taken away from them both by the English secretary of state, who needed it for his own henchmen, and by the assemblies, which generally elected the colonial treasurer and other minor officials. The royal governors on the whole were honest and able men, and no small number of them were colonists; but they had an unhappy time, for they were expected to enforce the regulations of an overseas government without the power to do so. The assemblies, representing local interests, demanded greater control than the governors' instructions permitted; the governors demanded more power for their royal and proprietary masters than the people were disposed to admit; and distance, as well as the power of the purse, tended to keep the governor's power at a low ebb.

Imperial Wars

William III brought the English colonies into the orbit of world politics. As stadholder of the Netherlands he had organized a league of European states to resist the pretensions of Louis XIV to the hegemony of Europe. Having obtained the English crown, he made that league into the Grand Alliance, which brought the English and French colonies to blows. There then began the

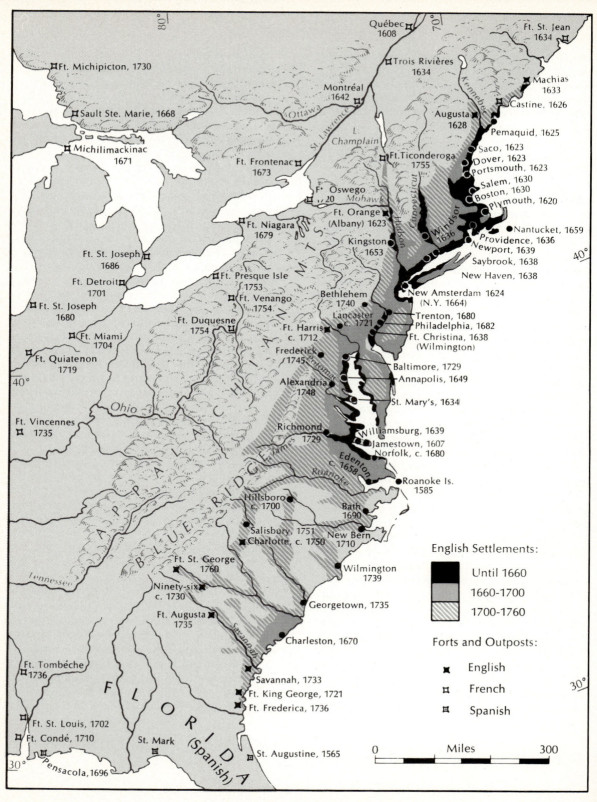

English settlements, 1607–1760

first of the international colonial wars,[2] which took up a large part of colonial energy, and which ended with the complete overthrow of French power in North America.

Informal hostilities between England and Spain on the southern border had been going on for years, and a clash between English and French on the northern border was inevitable because of the menace of the Iroquois Confederacy to Canadian trade. Every young Canadian of spirit became an explorer or a coureur de bois, and the more adventurous of these traveling salesmen of the fur business had reached the Dakotas before Englishmen had attained the crest of the Appalachians. The Iroquois Confederacy, whose sphere of influence covered upstate New York, most of Pennsylvania, and the old Northwest, remained faithful to their alliance with the Dutch and the English, who could provide them with cheaper blankets and liquor than did the French. The Iroquois occasionally raided the canoe fur route of the St. Lawrence basin, forcing Canadian fur traders to travel north of and around the Iroquois country in order to reach the upper Mississippi valley, which by 1715 had become a more valuable source of fur than the basin of the Great Lakes.

In the summer of 1682 the Sieur de La Salle, greatest of French explorers, sailed and rowed down the Mississippi, planted the white banner of St. Louis on its banks below New Orleans, and named the region Louisiana. On his next voyage La Salle reached the Gulf coast of Texas, where he was killed by his own men, who were then finished off by the Comanche. These remarkable expedi-

2. The colonial wars may be summarized as follows:

Colonial Name	European Name	Dates	Peace Treaty
I King William's	League of Augsburg	1689–97	Ryswick
II Queen Anne's	Spanish Succession	1702–13	Utrecht
III King George's	Austrian Succession	1745–48	Aachen
IV Old French and Indian	Seven Years War	1754–63	Paris

King George's War began in the Southern Colonies and Caribbean in 1739 as the 'War of Jenkins' Ear' between England and Spain.

tions so little affected French policy that in 1696 Louis XIV actually issued an edict ordering the Canadian coureurs de bois to take wives, settle down, and cease exploring the wilderness in search of fur! For Louis was entering his pious old age, and the Church objected that these adventurers ruined the work of the missionaries. Governor Frontenac, hand in glove with the fur-trading interests, largely ignored his sovereign's orders.

Louis XIV had no objection to Count Frontenac's using coureurs de bois and friendly Indians to raid the frontiers of New England and New York. So King William's War, as well as that of Queen Anne, took the character of a series of winter attacks on English frontier settlements. Schenectady, New York, was the first place to be destroyed, in February 1690. Other raids followed against the Maine and New Hampshire frontiers, while Canadian privateers from L'Acadie (Nova Scotia) preyed on Yankee fishermen and traders. New England's reply (1690) was to capture Port Royal on the Bay of Fundy, and to send an unsuccessful expedition against Quebec. King William's War ended in Europe with the Treaty of Ryswick (1697), which did not change a single colonial boundary. In New England the war dragged along until 1699. By that time there was hardly a white settler left in the future state of Maine.

During the interval between King William's and Queen Anne's wars, England's rivals in the New World strengthened their positions. In 1696 Spain, which was England's enemy in the next three colonial wars, founded Pensacola. That same year, Father Kino founded the Spanish mission of San Xavier near Tucson, Arizona, and by 1700 the Spanish had reoccupied New Mexico, whence the Pueblo Indians had driven them out in the 1680's. About the same time French Canadians founded three posts—Kaskaskia, Cahokia, and Vincennes—in the Illinois country, partly as a check to Iroquois influence, and partly as connecting links between Canada and Louisiana.

In 1700 came a shifting of European alliances. The king of Spain died without issue, Louis XIV claimed the throne for his grandson, the Grand Alliance supported a rival claimant, and the War

The marriage of a Frenchman and an Indian woman, probably an Iroquois. The bridal couple perform a marriage dance, a volume published in London explains, as 'the relations of each party assemble in the hut of the most ancient person among them' where 'they make an entertainment, after the Canadian fashion.' (*Rare Book Division, New York Public Library*)

of the Spanish Succession broke out—Queen Anne's War the colonists called it after their new sovereign. France and Spain now became allies, and the feeble little colonies of Louisiana and Florida became friends. They found a common enemy in the vigorous young English colony of South Carolina, which had developed much the same sort of fur-trading frontier as had the Canadians. By 1700 the Carolinian traders were even obtaining deer and buffalo skins from across the Mississippi. Queen Anne's War on this southern border was a preliminary skirmish in the contest for mastery of the Mississippi. On the northern frontier, Queen Anne's War began with border raids by the French and Indians, including one which wiped out Deerfield, Mass. After two failures, Massachusetts captured Port Royal, this time permanently; it became Annapolis Royal, Nova Scotia.

The Treaty of Utrecht (1713), which ended this war, was a significant event in the territorial history of North America. Great Britain obtained French recognition of her sovereignty over Nova Scotia and Hudson's Bay, where the great fur-trading corporation of that name had been operating since 1670. But the value of Nova Scotia was largely nullified by allowing France to retain Cape Breton Island, where she later constructed Louisbourg, the 'Gibraltar of the New World.' The negotiators at Utrecht paid no attention to the southern frontier. There the Tuscarora Indians in North Carolina rose against the English in 1711. South Carolina came to the aid of her neighbor, defeated the Tuscarora tribe, and carried a large part of it off to be sold as slaves; the remnant withdrew to the Iroquois country and became the sixth nation of that confederacy. Aside from this exception and the brief King George's War, the Treaty of Utrecht marked the beginning of a generation of peace in which the English colonies expanded westward, drew on new sources for their population, diversified their economy, and began to enjoy the fruits of the century of enlightenment.

New Lands, New People

The Treaty of Utrecht opened the last half-century of the old British empire, a period marked by widespread change. Only two new continental colonies, Nova Scotia and Georgia, were founded; but immigrants poured into the other twelve, and the frontier marched westward, creating a new section along the back-country from New Hampshire to South Carolina. Population and trade increased manyfold, and began to strain at the bonds of the Acts of Trade and Navigation. Religion took a new turn with the Great Awakening; new schools and colleges were founded; and in the East an upper class, growing in wealth and in self-confidence, acquired the refinements and the sophistication of eighteenth-century Europeans. Increasingly, the colonists felt that they were Americans as well as Englishmen. In 1713 nobody predicted or suspected that the English colonies would ever seek union, unless in an imperial war, much less free themselves from English rule; in 1763 union and independence were distinct possibilities.

In 1713 the population of the twelve continental colonies was nearly 360,000; in 1760, with Georgia added, it approached 1.6 million, a fourfold increase. Since 1713 the area of settlement had tripled. Whence came this vast increase, propor-

tionally greater than that of any subsequent half-century of our history? Both from large families and from immigration. The two most important contributions were German and Scots-Irish. Discontented Germans came to English America because the German states had no overseas possessions, and no colonies except those of the English would admit foreigners. Many were assisted by the English government; thousands of others were 'redemptioners,' people given free transportation from Europe by shipowners, who recouped themselves by selling their passengers as indented servants. Most Germans entered America at Philadelphia, whence they spread out fanwise into the back-country and became the most prosperous farmers in North America. They brought their own language and culture, established printing presses and newspapers, and at Bethlehem, a musical tradition that eventually flowered into the annual festival devoted to the works of Johann Sebastian Bach.

Equal in importance were the English- (and sometimes Gaelic-) speaking Scots-Irish from Ulster. These were largely descendants of the Scots who had colonized Northern Ireland when the English were first settling Virginia. After 1713 the pressure of the native Catholic Irish and the restrictive legislation of the British Parliament forced them to emigrate in droves. As land was dear in the Eastern colonies, these fighting Celts drifted to the frontier. By 1763 they formed the outer belt of defense against the Indians all the way from Londonderry, New Hampshire, to the upper country of South Carolina. A considerable number of southern Irish, mostly Protestants but including Catholic families like the Carrolls of Maryland, came at the same time; these were mostly men of property who invested in land and remained in the older-settled regions.

A third non-English strain was the French Protestant. In 1685 the revocation of the Edict of Nantes destroyed their religious liberty, and tens of thousands of the most solid and enterprising French subjects fled. Comparatively few Huguenots, as they were called, came to America; but those who did acquired an influence out of proportion to their numbers. They were particularly prominent in South Carolina (Huger,

Ivory-billed woodpecker by Mark Catesby. This engraving of what Catesby called a 'White Bill'd Woodpecker' was first published in 1731–32, twenty years after the English naturalist arrived in America. It is from his seminal work *The Natural History of Carolina, Florida, and the Bahama Islands. (Rare Book Division, New York Public Library)*

Petigru), Virginia (Maury), Massachusetts (Revere), and New York (Jay, De Lancey).

About 1726 Germans and Scots-Irish began to pour into the Shenandoah valley. Their motive was to acquire cheap land; for William Penn's heirs, reversing his policy, charged £10 for a hundred acres, as against 10s by some of the Virginia speculators. The 'Old Wagon Road' up the valley became a veritable funnel of the frontier. Some settlers sprinkled the Shenandoah valley with log cabins and German names; others turned south, through one of the many gaps in the Blue Ridge, into the piedmont of Virginia and the Carolinas. In North Carolina the defeat of the Tuscarora opened up not only the coastal plain but part of the piedmont, and that colony increased sixteenfold in population between 1713 and 1760. By then it had more people than New York, where Iroquois mastery of the Mohawk valley and the feudal institutions of the Hudson river patroons retarded settlement.

This settlement of the Old West built up new internal tension. South of New York, the older-settled region was English in race and Anglican or Quaker in religion; the West was a mixture of German, Scots-Irish, and English, who were either Presbyterian, Baptist, or German sectarian in religion. People of the eastern belt of settlement controlled the assemblies, which often discriminated against the frontier, building up a West-East antagonism that broke out later in movements like the Paxton Boys, the Regulators, and Shays's Rebellion.

Georgia

The eighteenth century is full of contradictions. This happens in every age when new modes of thought and action, new forms of society and industry, are struggling to emerge from the womb of the past. On the one hand, this was an era of formalism, indifference, and decay in the established churches; on the other, it saw the birth of new religious and philosophical movements, such as Methodism in England, Jansenism in France, the 'natural religion' that stems from Newton, the idealism associated with Berkeley, and the rational philosophy that prepared the way for the French Revolution. In England the age was one of social smugness, brutality, and complacency toward poverty and other evils; yet it was also an age of benevolence, when the first effective protests were made against the slave trade, high infant mortality, and imprisonment for debt. While the colonies as a whole were exploited for the benefit of mercantile classes in England, charitable funds flowed to America from England for the foundation of libraries, schools, and colleges, and for the conversion and education of Indians and Negroes.

The new colony of Georgia was the result of a combination of several charitable individuals and forces for a single well-defined object. James Edward Oglethorpe, a young gentleman of rank and fortune, left Oxford to fight under Eugene of Savoy against the Turks, and then entered Parliament where, 'driven by strong benevolence of soul' (as Alexander Pope wrote of him), he served on a committee to inquire into the state of jails. That state was bad indeed. A debtor once committed to jail could not be released until his debt was paid, and in jail he had no means of discharging it; if released by charity after many years, he was usually incapable of supporting himself. It occurred to Oglethorpe that the way to meet this social evil was to assist poor debtors to emigrate to America under conditions that would enable them to start afresh and lead happy and useful lives. At his instance the Associates of Dr. Bray, an energetic Anglican clergyman who had initiated several benefactions, obtained a proprietary grant, with limited tenure, of the land between the Savannah and the Altamaha rivers, under the name of Georgia. As several of the trustees of Georgia were members of Parliament, they were able to obtain grants of public money to transport and settle the deserving poor. Georgia began as a colony de luxe, the pet project of wealthy and powerful philanthropists.

General Oglethorpe, appointed the first governor, came out with the first shipload of settlers in 1733 and founded Savannah. In the next eight years the trustees sent over 1810 charity colonists, of whom almost half were Germans, Scots, and Swiss, and the rest English. In the same period 1021 persons arrived on their own; 92 of these were Jews. Each settler received 50 acres free, and

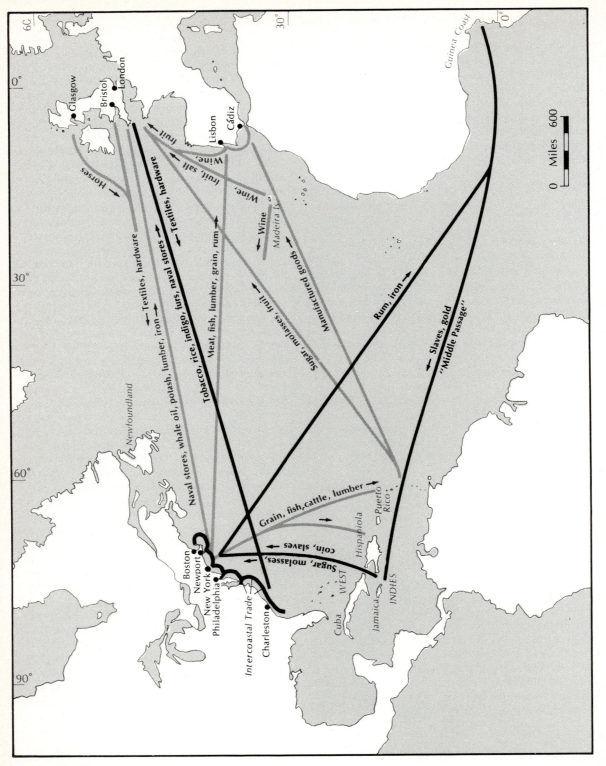

Colonial Trade Routes

Guinea Coast

Glasgow
Bristol
London
Lisbon
Cádiz

Madeira Is.

Newfoundland

Boston
Newport
New York
Philadelphia
Intercoastal Trade
Charleston

Cuba
Jamaica
Hispaniola
Puerto Rico
WEST INDIES

Horses

Textiles, hardware

Textiles, hardware

Naval stores, whale oil, potash, lumber, iron

Tobacco, rice, indigo, furs, naval stores

Meat, fish, lumber, grain, rum

fruit

fruit, salt

Wine, fruit

Wine

Wine, salt

Sugar, molasses, fruit

Manufactured goods

Rum, iron

Slaves, gold
"Middle Passage"

Grain, fish, cattle, lumber

coin, slaves

Sugar, molasses,

0   Miles   600

60°
0°
30°
90°
60°
30°
0°
30°
0°

the trustees forbade the importation of slaves and rum. The charity settlers were not all poor debtors or jailbirds; many were small tradespeople and artisans, for the trustees wished to establish a colony in which many occupations were represented.

Georgia did not prosper under this benevolent despotism. The settlers found it impossible to live off 50 acres; and with no quinine, rum became a necessity in the malarial lowlands. The contrast with South Carolina, where colonists were growing rich through applying slave labor to rice and indigo plantations, attracted the more ambitious to the older colony. The trustees gradually liberalized the conditions of land-owning, removed the slavery and liquor prohibitions, and granted an assembly in 1751; but the colony lost many people through fever and removal—the population was only 1735 whites and 349 blacks in 1752. In that year, when the twenty years' proprietorship lapsed, the trustees were glad to turn Georgia over to the Crown. Gradually the economy of Georgia was assimilated to the rice-plantation pattern of South Carolina, and eventually it received an up-country population by way of the intermountain trough. Yet at the outbreak of the Revolution Georgia was still the weakest and least populous of the Thirteen Colonies. Still, the enterprise did assist several thousand people, whose lives would have been wasted in England, to a new life in the New World.

Industry and Commerce

Despite the tightened controls of the imperial system—perhaps to some extent because of them—the colonial economy prospered as never before during the half-century following the Treaty of Utrecht. The key to this prosperity was a rise in prices for colonial produce. The increased European demand for colonial produce hit first the West Indies; and West Indian prosperity almost automatically affected the continental colonies. The French West Indies were an important source of cheap molasses, which New England and the Middle Colonies made into rum. The British West Indies, annoyed by this competition, induced Parliament in 1733 to pass the Sugar or Molasses Act,

charging a prohibitory duty on foreign molasses and sugar entering English colonies. By that time, rum distilleries had become so numerous in towns from Portsmouth to Philadelphia that the French Antilles were necessary as a source of molasses. So the act was simply ignored.

So brisk was the demand for flour in the West Indies that within a few years the export of grain and flour from Chesapeake Bay ports pushed tobacco for first place. Baltimore was founded in 1729, largely because Jones Falls turned mills which ground the wheat of Pennsylvania and up-country Maryland into flour. However, Philadelphia remained the principal place of export for grain and other provisions. Virginia recovered her ancient prosperity with a rise in the price of tobacco and shared in the flour trade as well. And, as in the previous century, the West Indies trade was vital for southern New England, the islands importing more and more salt fish, wood for boxes, barrels, and house construction, work horses, salt meat, and ground vegetables.

The Carolinas shared in the general prosperity. For North Carolina, the export to England of ship timber and pitch and tar was of great importance. In South Carolina fortunes were built out of rice and indigo. In 1731, over 200 vessels cleared from Charleston, carrying 42,000 barrels (about 21 million pounds) of rice, 14,000 barrels of pitch, tar, and turpentine, about 250,000 deer skins, and a large quantity of provisions. Parliament in 1729 allowed rice to be sent directly to all European ports south of Cape Finisterre, and by 1771 South Carolina's rice exports were threefold what they had been in 1731. Indigo, stimulated by a production bounty from Parliament, was introduced about 1740, and quickly produced a crop of 'indigo millionaires.' Both rice and indigo required a large labor force for profitable cultivation, thus accelerating the growth of slavery and the African slave trade.

Although England did not object to the colonists' indulging in crude manufacturing, such as milling grain and distilling molasses into rum, it attempted to suppress competition with leading English industries. Two acts of Parliament were aimed at protecting English staples. On complaint of London's Worshipful Company of Hatters that the colonists were beginning to make up furs into the wide-brimmed beaver hats of the era, instead of importing headgear from England, a law of 1732 limited the number of hatter apprentices and banned exports of hats from one colony to another. In 1750 British iron interests induced Parliament to remove British duties from colonial pig and bar iron, in the hope of encouraging Americans to supplant importations from Sweden to England. The same act forbade the establishment of new slitting mills (which slit bar iron into nail rods) or plating forges using a trip hammer, or steel tool furnaces, in order to protect the export of English ironmongery and steel. But this law was so flagrantly disregarded that Pennsylvania, New Jersey, and Massachusetts even granted bounties for new plants after the law was on the statute books! By 1760 there was a thriving colonial iron industry wherever a combination of surface iron ore, wood for smelting, and water power was found. So, though the acts restraining manufactures were restrictive in motive, they were hardly so in practice.

Far more serious than all Acts of Trade and Navigation as brakes on colonial enterprise were English restrictions on the colonial use of money, and attempts of colonial assemblies to get around them. Nothing that a colonial assembly did in the way of fiat money could legally discharge debts due to English merchants; hence it was the country storekeeper or seaport merchant who suffered from this sort of restriction and sought redress in England. Royal governors were always instructed to veto paper-money laws unless they provided for prompt redemption out of taxes; and when the governor was forced by political pressure to disobey his instructions, the law was disallowed by the Privy Council. Although few colonial assemblies showed sufficient wisdom and restraint to be entrusted with so dangerous a power as the issuance of paper money, the British government did nothing to provide a substitute. By forbidding the colonies to import English coin, or to mint the bullion they acquired from the Spanish West Indies into coin, they made some other form of currency necessary, and inflation inevitable.

Society and Religion

While the Thirteen Colonies were expanding trade and developing a more heterogeneous population, their social and intellectual ties with England were becoming closer. Every royal governor's mansion provided a little court where the latest European fashions were displayed and London coffee-house gossip was repeated. Transatlantic travel, except during winter months, was relatively safe in the small packet ships and 'constant traders' of the day. Merchants in the seaport towns made a point of visiting London every few years, and sent their sons on long voyages as supercargoes; many sons of rich Southern planters attended school in England; or, if they studied at a colonial college, took a medical course at the University of Edinburgh or read law in the Inns of Court. Between 1713 and 1773, thirteen colonial Americans were accorded the highest scientific honor in the English-speaking world, a fellowship in the Royal Society of London.

Professional architects were few. When Harvard College wanted a new building in 1764, Governor Bernard obligingly drew the plans. Local builders, with the aid of books of design from England, erected mansions in the well-proportioned Georgian style and churches modeled on those of Sir Christopher Wren in London. After 1720 paint was used freely to preserve the exterior and adorn the interior of wooden dwelling houses, and white paneled doors surmounted by graceful fanlights replaced the massive nail-studded oak portals that were designed to resist Indian tomahawks. In the South we have the first colonnaded porches, as at Mount Vernon, a balanced layout with detached offices and kitchen, and landscaped grounds. In the back-country and new settlements from Maine to Georgia the log cabin, made either of round logs or of squared timbers well mortised together and chinked with chips and clay, became universal.

Even colonial towns of 2000 or 3000 inhabitants afforded more amenities in the eighteenth century than do American cities today of tenfold times their population. There would always be a market house and merchants' exchange, a tavern where the latest English gazettes were taken in and where clubs of gentlemen or tradesmen met to talk, smoke, drink, and sing; a dancing assembly for the elite; a circulating library; and, in five or six places, a musical society. Philadelphia had a theater as early as 1724, and in 1749 an English company of players began trouping through the colonies south of New England; for in the Puritan colonies only private theatricals were permitted. Fairs gave entertainment to everyone. Williamsburg established semi-annual fairs for livestock, goods, and merchandise, with foot races, horse races, greased pigs to be caught.

The period from 1740 to the French and Indian War was the golden age of the Old Dominion. Peace reigned, high prices ruled for tobacco, immigrants thronged the back-country; and the Virginia of Thackeray and Vachel Lindsay—'Land of the gauntlet and the glove'—came into being. Living in Virginia at that time was like riding on the sparkling crest of a great wave just before it breaks and spreads into dull, shallow pools. In that wholesome rural society with lavish hospitality and a tradition of public spirit was bred the 'Virginia dynasty' which (with some help from elsewhere, one must admit!) would guide the destinies of the young republic yet unborn.

By mid-century, religious dissenters in every colony had made tremendous gains among the common people through the religious revival known as the Great Awakening. This was the first spontaneous movement of the entire English colonial population. The Great Awakening began in three different colonies. The Reverend Theodore Frelinghuysen of the Dutch Reformed Church started a revival in the Raritan valley, New Jersey, in 1719. William Tennent, a Presbyterian Scot, in 1736 established the Log College for revivalists at Neshaminy, Pa. In 1734 Jonathan Edwards, graduate of Yale and minister of Northampton, Mass., began his imprecatory sermons to recall the people to a sense of sin and bring them to that feeling of communion with God which evangelicals call conversion. His description of this revival, *A Faithful Narration of the Surprising Work of God in the Conversion of Many Hundred Souls in Northampton* (Boston, 1737), was promptly reprinted in London and Edinburgh, translated into German and Dutch, and became, as it still is, a classic. John Wesley read it afoot between London and Oxford. 'Surely this is the Lord's doing,' he wrote in his journal; presently he began to obtain the same effects from his own preaching, and in a little while the Methodist Church was born. George Whitefield, an eloquent young minister sent out to Georgia by the trustees, read *A Faithful Narration* in Savannah, and his amazing career as a revivalist dates from that hour.

Whitefield began the second phase of the Great Awakening by preaching at Philadelphia in 1739, and touring New England in 1740. In 73 days he rode 800 miles and preached 130 sermons. His voice could be heard by 20,000 people in the open air. He made violent gestures, danced about the pulpit, roared and ranted, greatly to the delight of the common people who were tired of unemotional sermons from college-bred ministers. He introduced the stage of revivalism with which many parts of America are still familiar—sinners becoming vocally 'saved.' Gilbert Tennent, son of the proprietor of the Log College, and several score of lay exhorters and itinerant preachers followed Whitefield. The 'New Lights,' as their followers called themselves, proved to be the first blossom of that amazing tree that was to bear the Shakers and the Mormons, Holy Rollers and the Millerites, and a score of other sects. Not one colony or county was unaffected by the Great Awakening.

Jonathan Edwards stayed with the movement, although he deplored its excesses; but the backwash of reaction drove him from the pleasant Connecticut valley. He became a missionary to the Indians in Stockbridge, and there, in the solitude of the wilderness, wrote three of his greatest works—*The Nature of True Virtue, Original Sin,* and *Freedom of the Will.* Edwards faced, as few modern men have dared or cared to face, the problem of evil and the problem of free will. The system of Calvinist theology that he and his disciple Stephen Hopkins worked out emphasized the splendid but terrible omnipotence of Almighty

Jonathan Edwards (1703–58), the brilliant Calvinist theologian. This contemporary engraving by Jocelyn shows him in the last year of his life when he agreed to become president of the College of New Jersey at Princeton, only to die within two months as a consequence of a smallpox inoculation. (*Library of Congress*)

God and the miserable impotence of sinful man. And certain passages in his works express more effectively the beauty of holiness and the supreme importance of man's relation to God than any other in American literature.

Although the more extreme religious enthusiasts were anti-intellectual, and even encouraged book-burning, the Great Awakening gave to the colonies three new colleges; for the 'New Lights' soon perceived that without seminaries to educate an evangelical ministry, their movement would be killed by ignorant hot-gospelers. The College of New Jersey at Princeton (1746), the first colonial school of higher learning to be founded since Yale (1701), was the Presbyterian seminary; Dartmouth (1769) was founded by

Eleazar Wheelock, a disciple of Edwards and Whitefield, ostensibly for training Indian preachers; and the Baptists, who hitherto had been without an educated ministry, were driven by competition to build the College of Rhode Island (later Brown University) at Providence in 1764. King's College (Columbia University), founded in New York City in 1754, was Anglican; Queen's College (Rutgers University), founded at New Brunswick, N.J., in 1766, was Dutch Reformed. The Philadelphia Academy (University of Pennsylvania), founded as a secondary school in 1740, was the only colonial college whose impetus and control were wholly non-sectarian.

All these colleges were very small by modern standards; the record colonial graduating class numbered 63. Princeton, Yale, and Harvard offered graduate training in theology; Philadelphia and King's established medical schools in 1765 and 1767. In the two decades before the Revolution, increasing emphasis was given to modern languages and science. But the great majority of undergraduates followed a prescribed course in rhetoric, philosophy, mathematics, and the ancient classics (including a good deal of political theory), which proved an excellent preparation for public life. Most of the important framers of state and federal constitutions were college-trained.

Nevertheless, only one of the three greatest Americans of the age, Jonathan Edwards, was a college graduate. George Washington (born 1732) attained his superb poise, self-discipline, and character that met every test, partly through manly sports, and partly through contact with his gentle neighbors, the Fairfaxes of Belvoir, who employed him as a surveyor in his young manhood. They introduced him to the Stoic philosophy that breathes through Plutarch's *Lives*, Seneca's *Dialogues*, and Addison's *Cato*. Benjamin Franklin, three years younger than Edwards, was the very antithesis of New England's saint. Essentially worldly and practical, he found little time for theology or philosophy, and none for sports. Yet his moral maxims in *Poor Richard's Almanack* provided ethics for the unchurched, and he organized schools and libraries that others might learn. His industry enabled him to accumulate a competence early, after which the applica-

tion of his inquiring mind to problems made him a leading scientist. His pioneer work on electricity was of the highest significance, and his passion for improvement made him the first inventor of his time. Finding that most of the heat from open fireplaces went up the chimney, he designed the Franklin stove in 1740. Worried by the fires set by lightning, he invented the lightning rod. And during long ocean passages under sail he thought up improvements in the mariner's art, many of which have since been adopted. Franklin loved music, played four different instruments, and invented a fifth, the glass harmonica, for which even Mozart and Beethoven composed music. The most eminent statesmen, scientists, and men of letters in England and France valued his conversation; yet he never ceased to be a good democrat.

Franklin's college was the newspaper office. Colonial journalism began with the colorless *Boston News-Letter* of 1704; within twenty years James Franklin, with teen-aged Ben as printer's devil and anonymous contributor, brought out *The New-England Courant*. 'Mr. Coranto,' as this paper called itself, was a sprightly sheet that attacked Harvard College and the Mather dynasty, even when those clerical autocrats, far ahead of public opinion, were advocating inoculation for smallpox. But when Mr. Coranto attacked the Massachusetts assembly, he got in trouble; and Ben left Boston for Philadelphia. There and in London, Franklin continued his trade of printer; and he was one of the first to sense the use of almanacs to enlighten farm folk who could not afford a newspaper. In 1725 there were only five newspapers in the continental colonies; by 1765 there were twenty-five, two of them in German. All were four-page weekly journals, filled largely with foreign news clipped from London papers, but carrying a certain amount of local items, assembly debates, advertisements of runaway slaves, and 'fine assortments' of English and West Indian goods for sale.

Libel laws in all the colonies were severe, and governments had to be criticized by innuendo rather than directly; yet one of the landmarks in the long struggle for the freedom of the press was the Zenger case. John Peter Zenger, publisher of *The New-York Weekly Journal*, lent his columns

to criticism of the governor, who haled him into court for false and scandalous libel. Andrew Hamilton, an aged Philadelphia lawyer who defended Zenger, offered the unheard of defense that the articles complained of told the truth! Chief Justice De Lancey rejected this contention and insisted on the English common law rule that the greater the truth the greater the libel. Hamilton countered with a ringing appeal to the jury, declaring that the cause of English liberty, not merely the liberty of a poor printer, was at stake, and won a verdict of 'not guilty' in August 1735. Although the Zenger verdict failed either to alter the common law or to provide the basis for a fully developed philosophy of freedom of expression, it encouraged editors to criticize governors. Gouverneur Morris called the Zenger case 'the morning star of that liberty which subsequently revolutionized America.'

It also marked the rise of a lawyer class. In the seventeenth century practitioners were regarded with contempt, and usually deserved it. The increase of commerce brought more litigation and the need for skilled lawyers; and the men of best repute who had defended clients in the courts formed a bar, with rules of entry and of conduct that had the force of law. Prominent lawyers naturally were elected to the assemblies, where they were very clever in tying up the royal governors in legal knots, and making every local dispute a matter of the 'liberties of Englishmen.' So, when weightier matters were at issue in the 1760's, the legal profession as well as the press was prepared.

The Last Colonial Wars, 1739–63

The last colonial war began in 1739 with the 'War of Jenkins' Ear' between England and Spain,[3] which was fought on the Georgia-Florida border and in the Caribbean. There the principal events were raids on Porto Bello and Cartagena by Admiral Vernon, with thousands of volunteers from the continental colonies, nine-tenths of whom succumbed to yellow fever. One survivor was

Benjamin Franklin (1706–90). This engraving, after Mason Chamberlain, shows him with his lightning detector. An avid scientific researcher, the many-sided Franklin set forth the fruits of his work, including the invention of the lightning rod, in *Experiments and Observations on Electricity* (1751–54). (*Metropolitan Museum of Art*)

3. So called because Parliament declared war after being outraged by a smuggler named Jenkins having his ears cropped by a Spanish coast guard.

George Washington's elder brother, who named Mount Vernon after the popular but unlucky admiral.

In 1744 the Anglo-Spanish conflict merged into the War of the Austrian Succession, and France again came to grips with England in North America, where the conflict was called King George's War. Again there was *la petite guerre* along the New York-New England border; and *la grande guerre* but not according to the book. The New Englanders' attack on Acadian Louisbourg, planned by Governor Shirley and led by a Maine merchant, Sir William Pepperell, was one of the maddest schemes in the history of modern warfare, a sort of large-scale 'commando'; but it worked. The Yankee yokels who pitched camp before the 'impregnable' fortress refused to obey any of the rules of war, and so baffled the French governor by their odd antics that he surrendered (1745). By the Treaty of Aachen, which ended this war in 1748, the English restored Louisbourg to France in return for Madras; the disappointment of New England was assuaged by the Crown's paying the entire expenses of the expedition.

This treaty was only a truce in the final conflict for mastery in North America. In Virginia companies were organized with the object of opening a route from the Potomac to the Ohio for Indian trade, and making a profit from Western land. These ventures constituted a threat to communications between Canada, the Illinois country, and Louisiana, which the French could not afford to ignore. In 1749 the governor of Canada sent Céloron de Blainville with several hundred Canadians and Indians in a fleet of bateaux and canoes to take possession of the Ohio valley. This expedition was followed up in 1753 by Marquis Duquesne, who established a chain of log forts on the Allegheny and upper Ohio.

French Canada had a population of only 50,000 or 60,000 farmers and fur-traders in 1750 when the English colonies numbered 1.25 million, and the pretension of France to reserve for herself the unsettled parts of North America was one that the English could hardly be expected to admit. In 1753 Governor Dinwiddie of Virginia commissioned George Washington (aged 22) lieutenant-colonel of Virginia militia, and the next year sent him with 150 men to forestall the French at the forks of the Ohio. But the French had arrived first, and built Fort Duquesne on the site of Pittsburgh. At Great Meadows in western Pennsylvania, the young lieutenant-colonel fired a shot on a French force that began the last and greatest of the colonial wars. The enemy rallied and Washington's troops had to capitulate and go home; for this was only a cold war—not declared for two years more. Both Virginia and New England were eager to call it a hot war and get going. Virginia wished to preserve her ancient charter rights to all the territory west and northwest of her settled area; Massachusetts was still aiming to clear the French out of Canada. But the governments of George II and Louis XV hoped to localize hostilities. So in the fall of 1754 George II sent General Braddock to America with only two regiments, and the powers of commander in chief.

In the meantime eight of the Thirteen Colonies had made an attempt to agree on a plan for common defense. Out of the Albany Congress of June 1754 came the Albany Plan of Union, the work of Benjamin Franklin and Thomas Hutchinson. There was to be a president-general appointed by the Crown, and a 'grand council' appointed by the colonial assemblies, in proportion to their contributions to the common war chest—a typical bit of Ben Franklin foxiness, to ensure that taxes were really paid. The president, with the advice of the grand council, would have sole jurisdiction over Indian relations and the Western territory. The Union would have power to build forts, raise armies, equip fleets, and levy taxes. This plan showed far-sighted statesmanship, in advance of its time, but was a closer union than the Thirteen Colonies were willing to conclude. Whether the British authorities would have accepted it is doubtful; but they never had a chance to express their views. Not one colonial assembly ratified the Plan. Every one refused to give up any part of its exclusive taxing power, even to a representative body. So the ensuing war was carried through under the old system. No British commander had authority to raise troops or money from a colony without the consent of its assembly. As in previous wars, the assemblies of provinces that were not directly menaced, and also some of those that were, like Pennsylvania, refused to make any substantial contribution to the common cause.

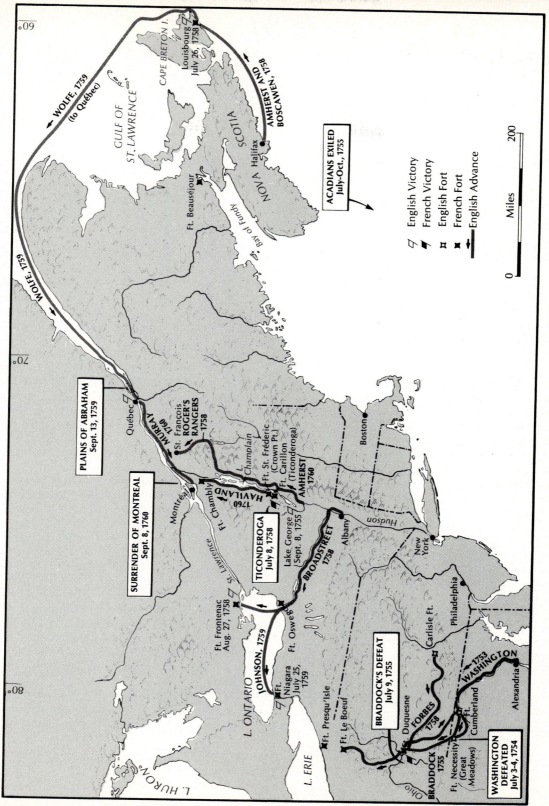

French and Indian War, 1754–1763

Map labels:

WOLFE, 1759 (to Québec)

WOLFE, 1759

GULF OF ST. LAWRENCE

CAPE BRETON I.

Louisbourg July 26, 1758

AMHERST AND BOSCAWEN, 1758

SCOTIA

Ft. Beauséjour

Bay of Fundy

NOVA

Halifax

ACADIANS EXILED July–Oct. 1755

Legend:
- English Victory
- French Victory
- English Fort
- French Fort
- English Advance

Miles
0   200

PLAINS OF ABRAHAM Sept. 13, 1759

Québec

MURRAY 1760

St. Francois ROGER'S RANGERS 1758

L. Champlain

Ft. St. Frédéric (Crown Pt.)

Ft. Carillon (Ticonderoga)

AMHERST 1760

Boston

SURRENDER OF MONTREAL Sept. 8, 1760

Montreal

Ft. Chambly

HAVILAND 1760

TICONDEROGA July 8, 1758

Lake George Sept. 8, 1755

BROADSTREET 1758

Albany

Hudson

St. Lawrence

Ft. Frontenac Aug. 27, 1758

Ft. Oswego

New York

L. ONTARIO

JOHNSON, 1759

Ft. Niagara July 25, 1759

Ft. Presqu'Isle

Carlisle Ft.

Philadelphia

BRADDOCK'S DEFEAT July 9, 1755

Ft. Le Boeuf

Ft. Duquesne

FORBES 1758

1753 WASHINGTON

Ft. Cumberland

BRADDOCK 1755

Ft. Necessity (Great Meadows)

Alexandria

WASHINGTON DEFEATED July 3-4, 1754

L. ERIE

L. HURON

Ohio

Although the Seven Years War (1756–63) was not formally declared for two more years, it was already being hotly waged in America, where it was called the French and Indian War. The haughty Braddock's march against Fort Duquesne ended in total defeat only a few miles from the site of Pittsburgh, lost him his life, brought the Indians of the Northwest over to the French side, and exposed the western settlements of Pennsylvania, Maryland, and Virginia to a series of devastating attacks. The other operations of the English in 1755 were inept, though not disastrous. Governor Shirley failed to take Fort Niagara, the French gateway to the West. William Johnson, a clever Irishman of the Mohawk valley who kept the Six Nations quiet, defeated the French on Lake George and was rewarded with a baronetcy for having gained the only English victory that year. But he was unable to capture Crown Point on Lake Champlain, and the French built Fort Ticonderoga to back up Crown Point.

Before the war was over it had extended to every European power and to all parts of the world. There was naval warfare in the Atlantic, the Mediterranean, the West Indies, and the Indian Ocean; battles on the Asiatic continent between Dupleix and Clive and their East Indian allies, and in the Philippines, where the English captured Manila after hostilities were over in Europe.

The years 1756–57 were disastrous for England. Oswego, the English fort on Lake Ontario, was captured by the French General Montcalm, who then advanced down Lake Champlain to Lake George, and captured Fort William Henry. Admiral Byng lost Minorca in the Mediterranean to the French, and was court-martialed and shot for cowardice, 'pour encourager les autres,' as Voltaire quipped. In India, the British lost Calcutta. On the European continent, Frederick the Great was defeated by the French and Austrians, and an Anglo-Hanoverian army surrendered. At the end of 1757 military experts confidently predicted that France would win hands down and would get all North America.

Yet the whole complexion of the war changed in 1758 when William Pitt, the future Earl of Chatham, became head of the ministry and virtual dictator of the English empire. Pitt had a genius for organization, a knack for grand strategy, and a knowledge of men. While most Englishmen regarded America as a secondary theater, Pitt saw that the principal object for England should be the conquest of Canada and the American West, thus carving out a new field for Anglo-American expansion. Pitt's policy was simple and direct: subsidize Frederick the Great to carry on warfare in Europe; use the navy to command the high seas and contain the French fleet in port; and concentrate the military might of England in America, under young and energetic generals.

James Wolfe, son of a country squire, was a tall, lanky, narrow-shouldered young man with vivid red hair. Ambition, audacity, genius, and a fierce concentration on becoming master of his profession made Wolfe the most Napoleonic soldier in English history. He was only thirty-one in 1758, when Pitt made him first brigadier general under General Jeffrey Amherst, whom Pitt had selected as commander in chief by passing over whole columns of senior officers. These two formed a perfect team with Admiral Boscawen in assaulting Louisbourg, which, though infinitely better fortified than in 1745 and more skillfully defended, was captured in 1758. That same year a force of New Englanders captured Fort Frontenac at the site of Kingston, Ontario; and General Forbes, with George Washington as his right-hand man, seized Fort Duquesne, renaming it Pittsburgh after the great war minister. Clive won the upper hand in India, and Frederick the Great broke out from his encirclement of French, Russian, and Austrian enemies. Then came 1759, England's *annus mirabilis*—the acme of the old empire, when England reached a pinnacle of glory that she had never touched before, and, as Horace Walpole wrote, the very bells of London were worn threadbare pealing out victories. Off the coast of France, Admiral Hawke won the battle of Quiberon Bay, which rendered the French incapable of sending reinforcements to Canada; in the West Indies, a combined naval and military expedition conquered Guadeloupe; in North America, Sir William Johnson captured Fort Niagara, key to the West.

Yet the greatest campaign that year was the one for Canada. Wolfe's army advanced in transports up the St. Lawrence river to Quebec. There Gen-

QUEBEC, *The Capital of* NEW-FRANCE, *a Bishoprick, and Seat of the Soverain* COURT.

1. The Citadel. 2. the Castle.
3. Magazine. 4. y' Recolets.
5. Ursulines. 6. Jesuits. 7.

7. Cathedral of Our Lady.
8. The Palace 9. y' Seminary.
10. The Hôtel Dieu.

11. S.t Charles River.
12. The Common Hospital.
13. The Hermitage of the Recolets.

14. The Bishop's House. 15. The
Parish Church of the Lower Town.
16. The Upper Town 17. y' Lower Town.
18. The Platform & Battery of Cannon
19. The Isle of Orleans. 20. Point Lievi.

Quebec in 1758, a year before the climactic battle in which the capital of New
France fell to the British. Notice how many of the structures in this Thomas
Johnston engraving house Catholic institutions. (*Stokes Collection, New York
Public Library*)

eral Amherst with a land force was supposed to
co-operate with him. Amherst captured Crown
Point and Ticonderoga, but never got within striking distance of Quebec. Thrice in previous wars
this failure in co-ordination had meant that the
great fortress-city remained French. But Wolfe's
forces carried on. After abortive attacks on Quebec
from two sides, Wolfe worked out a ruse for placing a force on the plains above the city. And with a

single concentrated volley on the Plains of Abraham, Wolfe won Quebec on 13 September
1759—as he learned just before his death on the
battlefield.

After the surrender of Quebec in 1759 and
Montreal in 1760, French power ceased on the
North American continent. War continued only
in the West, where after a last flare-up, the conspiracy of Pontiac, the conflict in America flick-

ered to a close. In Europe, Spain came in and the war dragged on. But the new king, George III, dismissed Mr. Pitt, who was becoming altogether too powerful for royalty, and purchased peace by renouncing a number of the conquests. By this Peace of Paris (1763), French Canada and the Spanish Floridas were ceded to Great Britain; while France, in order to compensate Spain for her losses, ceded Louisiana and all French claims to the west of the Mississippi to Spain.

The British empire bestrode the world like a colossus; India gained, all North America to the Mississippi won, and the best of the West Indies; supremacy of the seas confirmed. As the historian Seeley wrote, 'long it continued to be the unique boast of the Englishman,

That Chatham's language was his mother tongue
And Wolfe's great name compatriot with his own.'

English, Scots, Irish, and colonists spilled over with expressions of loyalty; and at a meeting in Boston to celebrate the peace, James Otis declaring that the true interests of Britain and her colonies were identical, warned, 'What God in his providence has united, let no man dare attempt to pull asunder!' Yet the war was not paid for, and the price of glory comes high. The French menace was ended forever; but a flock of new problems within the empire clamored for solution.

4

The Revolution Precipitated

*

1763–1776

Liberty and Authority

The American generation that came to maturity between the Peace of Paris and the inauguration of President Washington lived in an era that was revolutionary and destructive for the old British empire, but creative and constructive for the United States. This period from 1763 to 1789 has a singular unity. We must not let the rush of events and the din of arms hide from us its real meaning. Just as the Greek tragedies of the Periclean Age are concerned not merely with the conflicts of gods and heroes, but with the depths of human nature, so we may discern, behind the noisy conflict of the American Revolution, the stirring of a political problem older than recorded history: the balancing of liberty with authority. This ancient question resolves itself into two: the federal problem of distributing power between one central and many regional governments; and the democratic one of how far the masses of mankind shall be entrusted with control. These two problems are the warp and woof of American history through the Civil War; and the circumstances of our own time have simply restated these ancient issues.

By excluding the French from continental North America, the British took over more responsibility than they could handle. Baffling questions of Indian relations, fur trade, land policy, and military and political administration were created. For the next twenty-five years, Great Britain attempted unsuccessfully to solve the great riddle of imperial organization. And the new American government found itself confronted with the same difficulties.

The immense acquisitions of the Seven Years War persuaded British statesmen that their bigger empire required more ships and soldiers. These would cost money; and unless the British taxpayer supplied it all, the colonies, which also benefited, should contribute to the cost. Revenue could be extracted from the colonies only through a stronger central administration, at the expense of colonial self-government. As Governor Hutchinson wrote in a sentence that lost him his job, 'There must be an abridgement of so-called English Liberties in America.' Furthermore, the Acts of Trade were strengthened to an extent that began to impose real hardships on important colonial interests.

During the half-century since 1713 the lower

61

houses of the colonial assemblies had managed to seize control of the purse and patronage and had taken advantage of the Seven Years War to transform themselves into 'miniature parliaments.' The British government by veto or disallowance was able to prevent things, such as abuse of paper money, that it did not like; but it was unable to get positive things done, such as full co-operation in time of war, or a financial contribution to imperial defense. Despite a panoply of executive powers, the colonial governors were weak. The Board of Trade reported in 1754, with truth, that members of the New York Assembly 'have wrested from Your Majesty's governor, the nomination of all offices of government, the custody and direction of the public military stores, the mustering and direction of troops raised for Your Majesty's service, and in short almost every other part of executive government.' South Carolina even pushed encroachment to the extent that the Anglican churches of the colony were instructed to pray for the assembly instead of the governor!

By 1763 there had been worked out a compromise between imperial authority and colonial self-government. King and Parliament had undisputed control of foreign affairs, war and peace, and overseas trade. Parliament directed colonial trade into channels that it deemed profitable to the empire, colonies included. In almost every other respect the Americans had home rule. They had acquired far more autonomy than Ireland then enjoyed, and infinitely more than the colonies of France, Spain, or any other country had before the next century. So, apart from minor discontents, the Americans were fairly well satisfied with this compromise in 1763. But the government of George III was not. It had devised no method of exacting a uniform contribution from the colonies for defense. And there were still leaks in the enforcement of the Acts of Trade and Navigation. This situation had points of friction, but was not explosive. 'The Abilities of a Child might have governed this Country,' wrote Oliver Wolcott of Connecticut in 1776, 'so strong has been their Attachment to Britain.' But the Americans were a high-spirited people who claimed all the rights for which Englishmen had fought since Magna Carta, and would settle for nothing less.

Make no mistake; the American Revolution was not fought to *obtain* freedom, but to *preserve* the freedom that the colonies already had. Independence was no conscious goal, but a last resort, reluctantly adopted, to preserve 'life, liberty, and the pursuit of happiness.'

The West

The West created the most pressing problem of imperial reorganization. This problem had many strands: the international and military question, the Indians, the fur trade, the dilemma of territorial administration and land policy, and the political issue, particularly with reference to French Canadians.

The international question was whether the West would be won by France, Spain, or Great Britain, or partitioned among them. This was only partially solved by the Seven Years War. To the south and west of the new British possessions lay the rich Spanish empire. Spain was still a power to be reckoned with, still the largest empire in the New World, embracing most of South America and all Central America, together with California, Texas, and everything west of the Mississippi. In spite of her acquisition of a new bulwark in the shape of Louisiana, she was eager to recover the two Floridas which had gone to England, and the east bank of the Mississippi as well. Although the Peace of 1763 presumably disposed of the French danger, the English colonies by no means felt safe. Napoleon's recovery of Louisiana in 1800 may be said to have vindicated English fears in 1770. The French government continued mischievous intrigues with its former Indian allies, and kept its finger on the pulse of colonial discontent.

The Indian danger was more immediate. Pontiac's conspiracy of 1763 was the most formidable Indian outbreak of the century. Goaded to desperation by the tactics of the English traders and trappers, affronted by the refusal of the English to continue the French practice of annual gifts, and foreseeing the future crowding by English settlers, the Indians of the Ohio valley formed a grand confederacy under the leadership of Pontiac, chief of the Ottawa. Every Western fort except Detroit and Pittsburgh was captured, and the frontier from Niagara to Virginia was ravaged. Virginia and Maryland struck back, but Pennsylvania, the worst sufferer, failed to provide adequate defense for her frontiersmen. The uprising was not crushed by Americans, but by British red-coats. If the colonies could not even cooperate for their own defense against the Indians, could there be any doubt that stronger imperial control was needed?

Nor was the Indian question merely one of suppressing a rebellion. How were Indians to be treated after being brought to terms? Should their hunting grounds be reserved for them in the interests of humanity and the fur trade, or, if not, by what means were they to be secured against speculators and land-hungry frontiersmen? It was imperative to provide not only for present emergency but for future developments, a task necessitating centralized control.

Closely connected with the Indian problem was the fur trade. Peltry still dominated the economies of Canada and West Florida, and was a leading interest in New York, South Carolina, and Louisiana. This fur trade was not merely an international rivalry, but a ruthless competition among people of the same country, in a business which knew no ethics. As fast as the peltry of one region was exhausted, the trappers and traders moved further west, where they competed with the Spaniards for an Indian clientele; or by their aggressiveness they stirred up the nearer Indians, who retaliated on the closest white family. Here was another ungrateful task for the harassed officials in London: regulation of a group of unprincipled traders who by antagonizing the Indians endangered frontiersmen and jeopardized the supply of fur.

Even more perplexing was the problem of territorial administration and land policy. Should the extensive domain acquired from France be conserved as an Indian reserve, or opened in whole or part to white settlement? If the latter, should land be regarded as a source of revenue, and assessed with quit-rents, or should quick settling be encouraged? And if so, how? By ceding it to land companies in large tracts, or in small farms to individual settlers? Furthermore, almost every colony had claims. The rights of some, such as

Virginia, were well-founded; those of others, such as New York, were tenuous. Any policy Great Britain adopted would step on someone's corns. But the land question was essentially imperial; land policy had to be administered by a central authority.

Finally, there was the political problem. If new settlements were to be established in the West, what degree of self-government should be permitted them, and what should be their relation to the older colonies and to the mother country? The Treaty of 1763 had also given England jurisdiction over some 60,000 French Canadians, men alien in race and faith, and unaccustomed to English traditions of law and administration. Some general scheme of government had to be provided for these habitants and some method discovered to gain the support of their Church.

The Colonies in 1763–73

Let us now briefly survey the British continental colonies, starting at the southern end. West Florida, defined in 1763 as old Spanish Florida west of the Apalachicola and a section of French Louisiana including Mobile, Biloxi, and Natchez, had very few European inhabitants. But an energetic governor set up civil government at Pensacola, summoned an elective assembly in 1766, and advertised for English settlers; within ten years the population had risen to 3700 Europeans and 1200 slaves. The only settlements in East Florida in 1763 were St. Augustine and St. Marks at the mouth of the Apalachicola. The people of St. Augustine, though granted toleration, chose to leave when England took over; no Spaniard could imagine living under alien heretics. South of St. Augustine lived only Indians, mostly of the Seminole branch of the Creek nation; no white man had yet penetrated the Everglades. One Robert Turnbull recruited 1500 settlers from Minorca, Greece, and Italy, and established them at New Smyrna to grow indigo; and their descendants are still there, known as 'Minorcans.' In addition to these, the census of 1771 showed only 288 whites and 900 Negroes in all East Florida, not enough to warrant the calling of an assembly.

Charleston, South Carolina. Though by 1783 it had a population of only 16,000, Charleston was regarded as a 'metropolis' as early as 1762, when this engraving was published, for, with the finest harbor between Chesapeake Bay and the Gulf of Mexico, it was the leading city in the South. (*Library of Congress*)

Georgia had passed her heroic period. No longer was General Oglethorpe drilling kilted Highlanders to pounce on the dons; evangelists like Whitefield and Wesley had gone on to richer fields. An estimated population of 10,000, including a good proportion of slaves, was scattered along or near the coast, planting indigo and rice. However, South Carolina, having gone beyond the 100,000 mark, had become very prosperous. The powerful Cherokee nation, decisively beaten when they went on the warpath in 1759, had been forced to cede more land, and the back-country was opened to settlement. Charleston had become a gay little city, the only town in America north of Mexico that had a permanent theater. North Carolina, by contrast, seemed more of a social democracy, though its democratic manners concealed the fact that there was a large proportion of landless whites.

The more patrician colony of Virginia was still a congeries of individual plantations. Towns there were none, except Williamsburg and the growing seaport of Norfolk. With only 200 houses and fewer than 1000 permanent residents, Williamsburg was a capital of distinction, with a brick state house, governor's palace, and William and Mary

College. While the assembly was in session, Williamsburg was gay with balls, dinners, and assemblies; and the taverns did a roaring business. During the rest of the year most Virginians lived on their plantations. The Virginia aristocracy, now fairly stable, dominated the politics of the province. Political power was diffused among the members of the leading families by intermarriage. As Bernard Bailyn has written, 'The unpruned branches of these flourishing family trees, growing freely, met and intertwined until by the Revolution the aristocracy appeared to be one tangled cousinry.' Three families—Robinson, Randolph, and Lee—provided most of the leaders of the House of Burgesses.

From Baltimore to Philadelphia, travelers found the aspect of the country changing. In Delaware, fifteen or twenty miles from Philadelphia, farms became smaller, more frequent, and better cultivated. An Englishman crossing the Schuylkill and entering Philadelphia felt at home; the capital of Pennsylvania, remarked Lord Adam Gordon, was 'a great and noble city,' like one of the larger towns in England, but with a Quaker primness and regularity. Some of the neatly laid-out streets were paved, lined with sidewalks, lighted by whale-oil lamps, and policed at night. Philadelphia, with 18,766 people in 1760, was the largest and most prosperous town in English America. In another ten years it increased by another 10,000 and acquired some fine public buildings, including the handsome Carpenters' Hall, where the First Continental Congress would meet in 1774, and the Old State House, where independence was declared and the Federal Constitution drafted.

Pennsylvania had always been faithful to the religious liberty ideas of her founder, but the 'brotherly love' idea had not worked very well. There were many tensions between the English Quakers, who had the highest social standing, the Germans, whom they regarded as uneducated boors, and the tough Scots-Irish of the back-country, who had not been given their due weight in the assembly. Philadelphia was run by an oligarchy of lawyers and merchants, kept in power by a high property qualification for voting which shut out the lower middle class and the working people.

Proceeding northeastward across New Jersey, our traveler of 1763 would reach New York City, a compactly built little town, third in population in the English colonies, still bearing marks of the Dutch regime. A few blocks away from the stately mansions of merchants facing the Bowling Green or the river were evil slums where day laborers, dockhands, and free blacks lived. There were already enough Irish in New York to celebrate St. Patrick's Day, enough Jews to maintain a synagogue, enough Scots to support a Presbyterian church, and enough Germans to maintain four churches with services in their language. The two Anglican churches, Trinity and St. Paul's, worshipped according to the Book of Common Prayer, praying daily for 'George, our most gracious King and Governour.' In the Province of New York, most aristocratic of the continental colonies, the landed gentry controlled politics. Up-river the Livingston and Van Rensselaer manors comprised almost a million acres; four families owned 200 square miles of Long Island, and on Manhattan Island, hundreds of acres were owned by the Stuyvesant, Bayard, De Lancey, and De Peyster families, to the subsequent enrichment of their descendants.

The New England colonies owed their prosperity largely to fishing, shipbuilding, and maritime commerce. Boston with 17,000 inhabitants was the largest town, but no metropolis; there were a dozen little seaports along the coast from Bridgeport to Portland, each with some maritime specialty; and off-shore Nantucket had already gone in for deep-sea whaling in a big way. All these towns had comfortable brick and wooden houses built in the Georgian style, with excellent interior decoration and well-kept gardens. The shipowning merchants who owned them shared top status with the clergy, a few lawyers, and the physicians. New England as yet had no landed aristocracy. New Englanders were mostly members of one of the Congregational churches. Some were strictly Calvinist, having been stirred up during the Great Awakening; others, especially in the larger towns, had become liberal almost to the point of Unitarianism. Every village had a meetinghouse which served as town hall and church; and all churches, except in Boston and in Rhode Island, were supported by public taxation. In addition, there were in 1763 about a hundred Anglican and Baptist churches and Quaker meetings in New England. Every village had a free school, the towns supported grammar schools (roughly equivalent to our present high schools), and most of the people knew how to read and write.

New England had a more democratic social and political organization than any other section, in large part because land was distributed more equally. In the average country town, almost every adult male could participate in town government. The tory governor of Massachusetts, Thomas Hutchinson, complained of his own colony: 'In most of the public proceedings of the town of Boston persons of the best character and estates have little or no concern. They decline attending town meetings where they are sure to be outvoted by men of the lowest order, all being admitted and it being very rare that any scrutiny is made into the qualifications of voters.' Yet even in New England, the electorate deferred to the leading personages who held offices almost as though they were hereditary prerogatives. Despite Connecticut's republican form of government, two-thirds of the top offices were held by men bearing but twenty-five surnames of 'ancient' families, precisely the same pattern as in 'aristocratic' Virginia.

British Politics and George III

British politics were important in the American Revolution because Parliament initiated the new colonial policy and passed the laws which precipitated the War of Independence. In 1760–70 whigs had successfully eliminated tories by fastening on them the stigma of rebellion in 1745. Even King George called himself a whig, and all the ministries with which the colonists had to deal were whig ministries. But the dominant party was breaking up into factions.

Of the different whig factions, the one which showed most sympathy for the Americans was the 'old whig,' so called because its members claimed to inherit the traditions of 1688. These included the Duke of Richmond, General Conway, the Marquess of Rockingham, his secretary Edmund Burke, Lord Camden, and Isaac Barré; names given to American towns and counties in recognition of their efforts. Usually allied with them were the 'Pittites,' William Pitt and his large personal following. These were the most liberal groups in British politics, and also the most conservative; they opposed taxation of the colonies as much because it was new as because it was unfair. Pitt's following included the Duke of Grafton, who succeeded him as Prime Minister in 1767, and Lord Shelburne, who had a broader vision of colonial problems than any English statesman of his time, especially of the Western question. Unfortunately the old whigs, though rich in talents, were poor in leadership. Rockingham, a young man better known on the turf than in politics, was well-meaning but weak, and a halting speaker in the Commons. Pitt, a peerless leader in time of war, became inept in time of peace; and some strange malady thrust him out of the picture in 1767 almost as soon as he became premier. Next, there were a number of factions following such political free-lances as George Grenville and the Duke of Bedford, whose 'Bloomsbury gang' was notorious for being on hand when the plum-tree was shaken;

and finally there was the king, and his friends.

George III, only 22 years old at his accession in 1760, had been brought up under the tutelage of his mother, a strong-minded German princess. 'George, be a *king!*' was his mother's frequent injunction, which he appears to have interpreted as 'George, be a politician!' The young man knew what he wanted, and got it, though it cost him an empire. He wished to beat the whigs at their own game, and restore the power of the Crown by creating and eventually governing through a party of his own. After ministries under men who would not do his bidding had crumbled, George III obtained exactly the government he wanted under his subservient friend, Lord North; and it was this ministry that drove the colonists into revolt, and lost the war.

For the first ten years of his reign, George III was conciliatory toward the colonists. He ordered his friends in Parliament to vote for the repeal of the Stamp Act. When Lord Hillsborough in 1769 proposed to punish Massachusetts by altering her charter, the king refused. But the Boston Tea-Party, the first challenge to his personal rule, aroused his liveliest resentment. In great measure he may be held responsible for the Coercive Acts of 1774, and for the inefficient conduct of the war. If George III, for all his private virtues and well-meaning patriotism, is a pitiable figure in history, it is largely for the opportunities he lost. He might have been a patriot king indeed, by reaching out over the heads of the politicians to his colonial subjects, who were devotedly loyal and attracted by his youth and personality. He did his best for the empire according to his lights; but his lights were few and dim.

George III's ministers were no gang of unprincipled villains, subservient to a royal tyrant. Lord Dartmouth, for instance, who sponsored the Coercive Acts, was a kind and pious gentleman, patron of Dartmouth College and protector of the poet Cowper. Almost every ministry meant well toward the Americans, but almost all were incompetent. The situation called for statesmanship of the highest order; and the political system which George III manipulated to his advantage put statesmanship at a discount, political following at a premium. In the end it was ignorance, confusion, and unresponsiveness to crying needs, rather than corruption or deliberate ill will, which convinced the Americans that their liberties were no longer safe within the British empire. And these three factors—ignorance, confusion, and irresponsiveness—have brought down more governments than we can count, and will continue to do so in the future unless replaced by knowledge, order, and sensitivity.

The Organization of the West

The chain of events that led to the American rebellion began with the situation confronting the Crown in 1763. To cope with the immediate task, the administration and defense of new acquisitions, the Grenville ministry adopted emergency measures for what was thought to be a temporary situation. The ministry decided that settlers must be excluded from the trans-Allegheny country until the Indians were pacified, and a definite land policy worked out. The Royal Proclamation of 7 October 1763 reserved all lands between the Appalachians, the Floridas, the Mississippi, and Quebec for the Indians. Thus at one stroke the Crown swept away every Western land claim of the Thirteen Colonies, and drew a 'Proclamation Line' along the crest of the Appalachians.

In the following year, 1764, an elaborate plan for the regulation of Indian affairs was advanced. As early as 1755 General Braddock had laid the foundations of an imperial Indian policy by appointing two highly capable colonists, Sir William Johnson and John Stuart, superintendents respectively of the Northern and Southern Indians. The 'Plan of 1764' recommended a well-organized Indian service under the control of these superintendents; licenses, regulations, and fixed tariffs for traders; and repeal of all conflicting colonial laws. This was too ambitious a program for immediate fulfillment, but it looked in the right direction.

Before opening the country west of the Proclamation Line to white settlement, it was necessary to purchase territory from the Indians and establish a new boundary west of the Alleghenies. In 1763 Stuart negotiated with the Cherokee nation a treaty establishing the Indian boundary line west of Georgia and the Carolinas. A 1768 treaty extended this boundary north to the Ohio at the confluence of that river with the Great Kanawha. This line called forth a storm of protest from Virginia land speculators and was subsequently adjusted to meet their views. In the same year, Johnson established the line north of the Ohio when by treaty the Iroquois ceded for some £10,000 their rights to a large part of central New York and Pennsylvania as well as their claims to territory south of the Ohio.

Intimately associated with Indian affairs was the pressing question of defense. 'What military establishment will be sufficient? What new forts to be erected?' inquired the secretary of state of the Board of Trade. Pontiac's rebellion made the issue acute. The Board of Trade proposed establishing a chain of garrisons from the St. Lawrence to Florida, and from Niagara to Michilimackinac, with 10,000 soldiers required to garrison these forts and maintain the military establishment in America. An effort to force the colonies to pay for this costly, in fact excessive, military establishment, met stout resistance. But for the time being adequate defense had been provided, the frontiers sufficiently garrisoned, the Indians pacified, the malpractices of Indian traders stopped, and an Indian demarcation line drawn.

Colonial fur traders and British military men wished to keep the West beyond the treaty lines an Indian reservation for the use of the fur traders. Opposed to this policy were the promoters of several big speculative companies. Of these the most important was the Vandalia Company, promoted by Benjamin Franklin, George Croghan, and Thomas Wharton of Philadelphia. The Vandalia aimed to acquire 10 million acres in the Ohio valley, for which it proposed to pay the Crown £10,000. It did, to be sure, promise to assume the cost of administration, and of satisfying the Indians, who of course were not consulted. The Vandalia let in leading English politicians on the ground floor to enlist their active interest, and bribed freely when it thought bribery would do good. Another scheme pressing for a Crown grant was 'Charlotiana,' embracing most of Illinois and Wisconsin, promoted by Franklin and Sir William Johnson. But the Board of Trade and Plantations reported against big land companies on the ground that they would make trouble with the Indians, and that 'inland colonies in America' were contrary to British interests. Let the restless Americans fill up Nova Scotia and the Floridas, where they will export directly to England, and buy British goods! This policy became official in a Royal Proclamation of 1774. It doubtless contributed toward making the big land speculators favor an independent America, which might look more kindly on their schemes, and did.

Two Attempts To Tax the Colonies

The annual cost to Great Britain of maintaining the civil and military establishments in America had risen from some £70,000 in 1748 to well over £350,000 in 1764. In the light of this situation, George Grenville, Chancellor of the Exchequer, felt that it was both necessary and just to extract revenue from the colonies. Parliament greeted this proposition with enthusiastic approval, and even the level-headed Franklin anticipated no trouble from America.

The exact extent of colonial contributions to the upkeep of the empire is not easy to determine. English landowners, paying an income tax of 20 per cent, felt that the colonists could well afford to shoulder some of their burden. But the Americans insisted that they were already carrying their full share, and contributing, directly and indirectly, to the maintenance of the imperial government to the limit of their capacities. The colonies had incurred a debt of over £2.5 million for the prosecution of the war, and, notwithstanding the generosity of Parliament in assuming a part of that debt, a large portion remained. Indirect contributions in the form of English port duties and the monopoly of colonial trade were considerable; William Pitt estimated that colonial commerce brought an annual profit of not less than £2 million to British merchants. Whatever the right of these new revenue measures may have been, events proved their inexpediency quickly enough.

The Revenue Act of 1764—often known as the Sugar Act—was the first of these measures. The preamble stated frankly its purposes: 'That a revenue be raised in your . . . Majesty's dominions in America for defraying the expenses of defending, protecting and securing the same.' It was also designed to plug leaks in the Acts of Trade and Navigation. The law cut the duty on foreign molasses in half, but levied additional duties on foreign sugar and on luxuries such as wine, silk, and linen. It 'enumerated' more colonial products such as hides, which could be exported only to England; and it withdrew some earlier exemptions that the colonies had enjoyed, such as free importation of madeira. That favorite beverage of well-to-do Americans now became subject to a duty of £7 per double hogshead, as against 10s on port wine imported through England—an obvious attempt to change the drinking habits of the colonial aristocrats to profit the British exchequer. Colonial leaders promptly seized on the declared revenue-raising purpose of this act as a constitutional point. If Parliament got away with taxing their trade for revenue purposes, it might proceed to tax their lands, or anything. This seemed prophetic when Parliament on 22 March 1765 passed the Stamp Act.

The Stamp Act levied the first direct, internal tax ever to be laid on the colonies by Parliament; indeed, the first tax of any sort other than customs duties. It provided for revenue stamps to be affixed to all newspapers, broadsides, pamphlets, licenses, commercial bills, notes and bonds, advertisements, almanacs, leases, legal documents, and a number of similar papers. All the revenue was to be expended in the colonies, under the direction of Parliament, solely for the purpose of 'defending, protecting and securing the colonies.' Offenses against the law were to be tried in admiralty courts with no jury. As a sugar-coating to the pill only Americans were to be appointed as agents, and a number of unsuspecting colonials such as Richard Henry Lee applied for such positions.

The reaction to the Stamp Act everywhere in the Thirteen Colonies was violent, for it was the peculiar misfortune of the Act to offend the most powerful and articulate groups in the colonies: the merchants and businessmen, lawyers, journalists, and clergymen. Business came to a temporary standstill; trade with the mother country fell off £300,000 in the summer of 1765. Respectable men organized as 'Sons of Liberty' coerced

The Stamp
(*Library of Congress*)

stamp distributors into resigning, burned the stamped paper, and incited people to attack unpopular local characters. On the very day (1 November 1765) that the Stamp Act came into operation, a howling New York mob forced Lieutenant-Governor Colden to take refuge on board a British warship. The mob then attacked the fort at the Battery, broke into the governor's coach house, destroyed his carriages, and compelled the officer in charge of stamped paper to burn the lot. In Charleston, Henry Laurens, wrongly suspected by the local mob of hiding stamped paper in his house, was pulled out of bed at midnight while the house was searched by his friends, whom he recognized under black-face and sailor disguise. In Boston a mob turned its attention to the royal customs collectors and Chief Justice Hutchinson, gutting their houses, burning their furniture, and tossing their books and papers into the street.

The law was completely nullified by violence. Courts reopened, vessels cleared and entered, and business resumed without the use of stamps. All this on the assumption that the law was unconstitutional and void. Virginia led the way in expressing that view. On 30 May, Patrick Henry made his 'Caesar had his Brutus, Charles I his Cromwell' speech, after which the assembly passed a set of resolves declaring that it had 'the only and sole exclusive right and power to lay taxes... upon the inhabitants of this Colony,' who were 'not bound to yield obedience to any law' of Parliament attempting to tax them.

A few days after Henry had stirred up Virginia, Massachusetts invited all continental colonies to appoint delegates to a congress to consider the Stamp Act menace. This congress, which met at New York in October 1765, drew delegates from nine colonies. Christopher Gadsden of South Carolina sounded the keynote: 'We should stand upon the broad common ground of natural rights.... There ought to be no New England man, no New Yorkers, known on the continent, but all of us Americans.' After the debate the congress adopted a set of resolutions asserting once more that 'no taxes ever have been, or can be constitutionally imposed on them, but by their respective legislatures.'

In August 1765, even before the Stamp Act Congress met, the Grenville ministry fell. An 'old whig' ministry led by the Marquess of Rockingham now came into power. Parliament, encouraged by the king, repealed the Stamp Act in mid-March 1766. The law was repealed simply because it could not be enforced against united opposition, and because English merchants and manufacturers suffered from a boycott of British goods promoted by the Sons of Liberty. Parliament did not thereby renounce the right to tax the colonies, as proved by the fact that on almost the same day as the repeal, it passed a Declaratory Act affirming Parliament's right, as the sovereign legislature of the British empire 'to bind the colonies... in all cases whatsoever.' Americans showed their fundamental loyalty to the Crown by taking no notice of the fact that the Revenue Act of 1764 was not repealed, and no notice of the Declaratory Act. Although the colonists rejoiced in their victory, in reality the British government had taken three steps forward—Proclamation of 1763, Revenue Act, Declaratory Act; and only one back, repeal of the Stamp Act.

The Townshend Acts

During the jubilation that followed repeal of the Stamp Act, no serious effort was made by the British government to find out what, if anything, could be done to raise defense funds through colonial assemblies. No royal commission was sent to America to study and report. Instead, a fresh attempt was made by Parliament to tax the colonists, and a plan of imperial reorganization was placed in effect without consulting them.

The audacious new British initiative came from Charles Townshend, brilliant, ambitious, and unprincipled, who, taunted by George Grenville in the Commons that he dared not try to tax America, retorted, 'I will, I will!' and did. He proposed to reduce the British income tax by one-quarter and meet part of the resulting deficit by obtaining revenue from the colonies. This was to be done by collecting import duties in the colonies on English paint, lead, and paper; and on tea. As the colonies had always paid some customs

duties, how could they object to these? For more efficient collection a Board of Commissioners of the Customs was established at Boston, and new vice-admiralty courts were created. Writs of assistance, whose legality had been challenged by James Otis in 1761, facilitated entry into private premises. Most important of all, the money thus raised in the colonies, instead of going to support the garrisons, was to be used to pay the salaries of royal governors and judges and thus render them independent of colonial assemblies.

The Townshend Acts took Americans by surprise, but colonial leaders were hard put to find a legal argument against the duties. They wished to deny Parliament's power to tax them, yet to acknowledge Parliament's power to regulate their commerce, for they were not prepared to break loose from the protective system of the Acts of Trade and Navigation.

The colonial leader who came closest to resolving this dilemma was John Dickinson of Pennsylvania, who styled himself 'the Pennsylvania Farmer,' but actually was a conservative Philadelphia lawyer. Neither agitator nor politician, Dickinson was a public-spirited citizen, devoid of ambition or vanity, who abhorred violence and hoped to settle all pending disputes with England by persuasion. His twelve 'Farmer's Letters,' which began coming out in colonial newspapers at the end of 1767, were exactly what Americans wanted; and the loyal, respectful tone of them appealed to many in England. Dickinson conceded that Parliament had the right to regulate, even to suppress commerce, but he denied that it had the right to levy internal taxes or even port duties. Nonetheless, he counselled restraint:

Let us behave like dutiful children, who have received unmerited blows from a beloved parent. Let us complain to our parent; but let our complaints speak at the same time the language of affliction and veneration.

Samuel Adams of Boston, boss of the town meeting and leader in the assembly, had already reached conclusions that went well beyond those of Dickinson. He believed that Parliament had no right to legislate for the colonies on any subject. But he was too clever a politician to let that out now. An austere, implacable member of Boston's

Samuel Adams (1722–1803), firebrand of the American Revolution. This 1771 portrait by his fellow Bostonian John Singleton Copley (1738–1815), often regarded as the first important American painter, was commissioned by John Hancock. Pointing to the Massachusetts charter, Sam Adams protests to the lieutenant-governor of the colony against the stationing of red-coats in Boston. (*Museum of Fine Arts, Boston*)

middle class, this 'Matchiavel of Chaos' was a typical revolutionary. A master of propaganda, he realized that people want entertainment with their politics, and Adams provided it in highly agreeable forms. There was dancing around the Liberty Tree, a big elm near Boston Common selected for that purpose; unpopular characters were hanged in effigy from its branches, and those whom the radicals wished to become popular were serenaded. His favorite motto was *principiis obsta*, 'Take a stand at the start,' lest by one appeasement after another you end in complete subjection. No orator, Adams let other Sons of Liberty like Joseph Warren and the firebrand Otis make the speeches while he wrote provocative articles for the newspapers and organized demonstrations.

In February 1768 Adams and Otis drafted (and the Massachusetts assembly adopted) a circular letter to the lower houses of all continental colonies to call their attention to the Townshend laws. The assembly, stated this letter, has 'preferred a humble, dutiful and loyal petition to our most gracious sovereign . . . to obtain redress.' The language of this circular letter was as moderate and loyal as that of Dickinson, but the Grafton ministry decided to make it the occasion for a showdown. Lord Hillsborough, the new secretary for the colonies, ordered the Massachusetts assembly to rescind the letter, and Governor Bernard to dismiss them if they refused. The assembly did refuse, by a vote of 92 to 17. And it was supported by a set of Virginia resolves introduced by the burgess from Fairfax County, Colonel George Washington, and signed, among others, by the new burgess from Albemarle County, Thomas Jefferson. Adams and the Sons of Liberty everywhere made heroes of the patriotic '92,' who refused to rescind.

In Boston the chief contributor to the Sons of Liberty war chest for free rum at Liberty Tree rallies was a 31-year-old merchant, John Hancock. The new Commissioners of the Customs therefore determined to put him out of business. He was 'framed' by a prosecution of his sloop *Liberty*, falsely charged with smuggling madeira. A Boston mob rescued him and his vessel, and

gave the royal customs officials a very rough time. Governor Bernard asked for protection, and two regiments of the Halifax garrison were sent to Boston.

The presence of British red-coats in Boston was a standing invitation to disorder. It did not take long for antagonism between citizens and soldiery to flare up. In the so-called 'Boston Massacre' of 5 March 1770, snowballing of the customs house guard swelled into a mob attack, someone gave the order to fire, and four Bostonians, including a black named Crispus Attucks, lay dead in the snow. Although provocation came from civilians, Samuel Adams and Joseph Warren seized upon the 'massacre' for purposes of propaganda. The British soldiers were courageously defended by young John Adams, Sam's cousin, and Josiah Quincy, and acquitted of the charge of murder; but the royal governor was forced to remove the garrison from the town to the castle, and the strategic advantage lay with the radicals.

On the very day of the 'Boston Massacre,' the new British ministry headed by Lord North repealed all the Townshend duties except the one on tea. A tax of three pence per pound was kept on this article primarily as an assertion of parliamentary authority. 'A peppercorn in acknowledgment of the right is of more value than millions without it,' George Grenville had said; and easy-going Lord North acquiesced in this glib fallacy.

Except for that teasing little duty on tea, all outward grievances of the colonists had been removed by the summer of 1770. The radicals found themselves without an issue. Sam Adams did his best to keep up the agitation, with annual exhibits of bloody relics of the 'Boston Massacre,' but the people showed what they thought of him by defeating him for registrar of deeds in his home county. In New York soldiers of the garrison could promenade their girls on the Battery without being insulted. Prosperity reigned, imports into New England alone jumping from £330,000 to £1.2 million. It looked as if colonial agitation were at an end.

But Sam Adams was simply waiting for some unwise move by the North ministry to revive it.

Back-country Turmoil

Parts of the 'back-country' were full of turmoil during the years of agitation against the Stamp and Townshend Acts; but this turmoil had nothing to do with the America versus England controversy. It was caused by discontent with local governing classes. In Pennsylvania, in 1764, a band of frontier hoodlums known as the 'Paxton Boys,' furious at their lack of protection during Pontiac's rebellion by the Quaker-dominated assembly, took a cowardly revenge by massacring some peaceful members of the Conestoga tribe in Lancaster County. The 'Paxton Boys' then threatened to wipe out the so-called Moravian Indians, an Algonquian tribe which had been converted by Moravian missionaries and settled on a reservation near Bethlehem. These Indians fled to Philadelphia where the government quartered them in barracks, protected by British regulars. The 'Boys,' 1500 strong, heavily armed and uttering 'hideous outcries in imitation of the war whoop,' marched on the capital in February 1764, bent on killing every redskin refugee. Philadelphia was in a panic, and it took Ben Franklin to talk the ruffians into returning home, by promising more frontier protection and legislative bounties for scalps. The Pennsylvania back-country then quieted down, but bided its time to obtain more weight in the assembly.

This situation became most explosive in the Carolinas, where back-country society differed in origin, religion, and even race from that of the seaboard. In North Carolina the separation between coastal region and interior was very sharp. Here the Western grievances were not lack of government, but bad government—unequal taxation, extortion by centrally appointed judges and corrupt sheriffs, greedy lawyers, uncertainty of land titles, scarcity of hard money to pay taxes, refusal of the assembly to provide paper money or to allow taxes to be paid in produce, consequent tax levies 'by distress,' and sheriffs taking over poor men's farms.[1] A particular complaint was a prov-

1. Note similarity of these grievances to those of Shays's rebels in Massachusetts in 1786. And it is significant that Herman Husband, leader of the North Carolina Regulators, turns up 25 years later as a Whiskey rebel in Pennsylvania.

ince law which allowed only Anglican clergymen to perform marriage ceremonies, when there were no such clergy in the back-country! The Regulators marched on Newbern, site of the royal governor's palace, but being untrained and partly unarmed, they were easily defeated by half their number of loyal militia, 16 May 1771, at the so-called Battle of the Alamance. Casualties were only nine men killed on each side, since the Regulators ran away after the first volley. But fifteen of them were captured and tried for treason, and six were hanged. Governor Tryon and his army then made a triumphal progress through Regulator country and exacted an oath of allegiance from every male inhabitant.

That was the end of the 'War of the Regulation,' the most serious internal rebellion in the English colonies since Nat Bacon's. It was put down largely by whigs who later became patriots, though Martin Howard, the hanging judge, became a prominent loyalist. The next assembly passed some remedial legislation, but the North Carolina back-country was still so full of discontent in 1776 that many former rebels emigrated to Tennessee to avoid taking part in the war, and others became tories.

Back-country brawls from New Hampshire to South Carolina seem never to have interested the British government, which thereby missed a golden opportunity to win support from frontiersmen against the silk-stockinged Sons of Liberty and their 'wharf-rat' confederates. But London was involved in another Western problem. In 1774 the British government ordered royal governors to grant no land, and permit no new settlements, except after prior survey, allotment, and sale by auction. Although not put into effect outside Canada, this order called forth Thomas Jefferson's bold *Summary View of the Rights of British America*, denying the Crown's right to dispose of any Western land. It furnished one more grievance for the Declaration of Independence. Yet the United States public land system was based on exactly the same concept.

The Issue Joined

Samuel Adams's genius was for agitation and destruction. Yet he was no mere rabble-rouser, greedy for power. He believed (and the Lees of Virginia, the New York Sons of Liberty, and Gadsden of South Carolina agreed) that 'every day' in the calm period of 1770–73 'strengthens our opponents and weakens us.' They were right. Prosperity dulled vigilance, and the efficiency of the Commissioners of the Customs brought in such ample revenue even after the Townshend duties were repealed that the British government put one royal governor and judge after another on the Crown payroll. The radicals fumed against this in vain—the average colonist thought it fine to be relieved of paying his governors and judges! Adams felt that if this system were allowed to go on, Americans would wake up some day and find that they were helpless under royal officials. But he needed a spectacular, emotional issue to bring home this danger before it was too late. In the tea affair, he found it.

The powerful East India Company, being in financial straits, appealed to the British government for aid and was granted a monopoly on all tea exported to the colonies. The Company decided to sell tea through its own agents, thus eliminating the independent merchants, and disposing of the tea at less than the usual price. This monopoly aspect aroused the colonial merchants and threw them again into alliance with the radicals. Burke, in his speech on conciliation, gauged well the American temper. 'In other countries, the people . . . judge of an ill principle in government only by an actual grievance; here they anticipate the evil. . . . They augur misgovernment at a distance, and snuff the approach of tyranny in every tainted breeze.'

Colonial reaction to the tea monopoly took various forms. In Charleston the tea was landed, but not offered for sale; at Philadelphia and New York the consignments were rejected and returned to England. But in Boston the ingenious Sam Adams brought about a dramatic showdown. Here, on the night of 16 December 1773, Sons of Liberty disguised as Mohawks boarded the three tea ships and dumped the offending leaves into the water. The radicals had called the ministerial bluff. They had refused even the peppercorn in acknowledgment of right.

The Boston Tea-Party accomplished just what Sam Adams wanted. The destruction of property—and tea at that—aroused John Bull more than mobbing officials and beating up redcoats. 'The die is now cast,' wrote George III to Lord North. 'The Colonies must either submit or triumph.' The House of Commons, now obedient to the king and Lord North, passed in May-June 1774 a series of Coercive Acts. These closed the port of Boston until the tea was paid for, drastically changed the provincial government in Massachusetts, and provided for the transportation of certain offenders to England for trial. These laws threatened the very life of Boston. To exclude her from the sea, the element that made her great, was a punishment comparable to the destruction of Carthage.

These 'Intolerable Acts,' as the colonists called them, were quickly followed by the Quebec Act of 1774. This statute of Parliament, the outcome of a carefully thought-out plan to give a permanent government to Quebec, was received by the colonists as yet another punitive measure. They viewed the provisions of the law, which extended the boundaries of Quebec to embrace the vast country west of the Appalachians and north of the Ohio, as a deliberate attempt to discourage expansion by the colonists beyond the mountains and to ignore their land claims. They were even more disturbed by a statement of the privileges of the Catholic Church in Canada. Young Alexander Hamilton warned that 'priestly tyranny' might 'find as propitious a soil in Canada as it ever has in Spain and Portugal.' The Quebec Act, aimed at conciliating the French habitants, had the unanticipated consequence of feeding North American rebellion, and the Coercive Acts rallied the other English colonies to Massachusetts. On 27 May 1774 members of the Virginia Assembly, meeting in the Raleigh Tavern at Williamsburg, called for a congress of all continental American colonies. 'Clouds, indeed, and darkness,' said Edmund Burke, 'rest upon the future.'

The First Continental Congress which as-

Americans throwing the Cargoes of the Tea Ships into the River, at Boston

(Library of Congress)

sembled in Carpenters' Hall, Philadelphia, on 5 September 1774, had been summoned not for independence but for liberty, as Americans understood that word. They expected Congress to take steps to ward off parliamentary wrath, vigorously to assert colonial rights, and happily to restore imperial relations to their former agreeable status. The Continental Congress was an extra-legal body chosen by provincial congresses, or popular conventions, and instructed by them. This meant that the patriot party was in control of the situation, and that extreme conservatives who would have nothing to do with resistance to the laws were not represented. Otherwise, the membership of the Congress was a fair cross-section of American opinion. Here were extremists like the Adamses of Massachusetts, Richard Henry Lee and Patrick Henry of Virginia, and Christopher Gadsden of South Carolina; moderates like Peyton Randolph (chosen president of the Congress) and George Washington of Virginia, John Dickinson of Pennsylvania, and the Rutledges of South Carolina; conservatives like John Jay of New York and Joseph Galloway of Pennsylvania. Every colony except Georgia sent at least one delegate, and the total number was fifty-five—large enough for diversity of opinion, small enough for genuine debate and effective action.

Able as this Congress was, it faced a distressing problem. It must give an appearance of firmness to persuade or frighten the British government into concessions, but at the same time avoid any show of radicalism that might alarm conservative Americans or encourage the spirit of lawlessness and leveling that was already abroad in the country.

Lawlessness, as the conservatives called it, got in the first lick. While Congress was discussing a statesmanlike plan of union presented by Joseph Galloway, Paul Revere came galloping from Boston to Philadelphia with the radical Suffolk Resolves in his saddlebags. These resolutions, as drafted by Joseph Warren and adopted by a convention of the towns around Boston, declared the Coercive Acts to be unconstitutional and void, urged Massachusetts to arm and act as a free state until these 'attempts of a wicked administration to enslave America' were repealed, and called on Congress to adopt economic sanctions against Great Britain. Congress, by a majority of one colony, shelved Galloway's plan (similar to the Albany Plan of 1754) and endorsed the Suffolk Resolves, which Galloway considered 'a declaration of war against Great Britain.' Congress then proceeded to adopt new and more stringent non-importation, non-exportation, and non-consumption agreements. In practice, by denying the colonists needed supplies, these sanctions hurt the Americans more than the British.

Having agreed upon this counteroffensive, Congress passed a Declaration of Rights and Grievances addressed to the people of Great Britain and the colonies; and, as a sop to the moderates, a petition to the king. These papers, taken together, led the Earl of Chatham to declare in the House of Lords: 'For genuine sagacity, for singular moderation, for solid wisdom, manly spirit, sublime sentiment and simplicity of language . . . the Congress of Philadelphia shines unrivalled.' The Declaration of Rights anticipated in many particulars the Declaration of Independence, but did concede parliamentary regulation of commerce.

This concession did not please the radicals. Independently of one another, James Wilson of Pennsylvania, Thomas Jefferson, and John Adams had reached the conclusion that Parliament had no rightful jurisdiction over the colonies. 'All the different members of the British Empire,' said Wilson, 'are distinct States, independent of each other, but connected together under the same sovereign in right of the same Crown.' Wilson's *Considerations on the Authority of Parliament*, Jefferson's *Summary View*, and Adams's *Novanglus* papers published this startling theory between August 1774 and February 1775. Historically they found no ground for Parliament's authority, although they admitted that the colonies had weakly accepted it; logically there was no need for it, since the colonial legislatures were competent. The colonists should honor and obey the king, follow his lead in war, observe the treaties he concluded with other princes; but otherwise govern themselves. They demanded for the Thirteen Colonies the same dominion status which is now the official basis of the British Commonwealth of Nations. But these doctrines had no remote chance of acceptance. Very few Englishmen could understand how a community could be in the empire, unless parliamentary authority over it were complete.

The most important work of the Congress was an agreement called 'The Association.' This provided for committees of inspection in every town or county, whose duties were to supervise the non-importation, non-exportation, and non-consumption agreements. The Association was charged to publish the names of merchants who violated these sanctions, to confiscate their importations, and to 'encourage frugality, economy, and industry.' Congress also voted to give up imported tea and wines. Rum, however, was still a patriotic beverage. Thus the Congress called to protest against parliamentary usurpation ended by creating extra-legal machinery for supervising American daily life. The Association caused many moderates to draw back in alarm. 'If we must be enslaved,' wrote the loyalist Samuel Seabury, 'let it be by a king at least, and not by a parcel of upstart, lawless committeemen.' Having done all this, Congress rose on 22 October 1774, resolving to meet again the following May if colonial grievances had not been redressed by then.

Hostilities Begin

Before Congress reconvened, fighting broke out. Inevitably, when war came, it began in Massachusetts. Since the previous autumn Massachusetts, as suggested by the Suffolk Resolves, had become

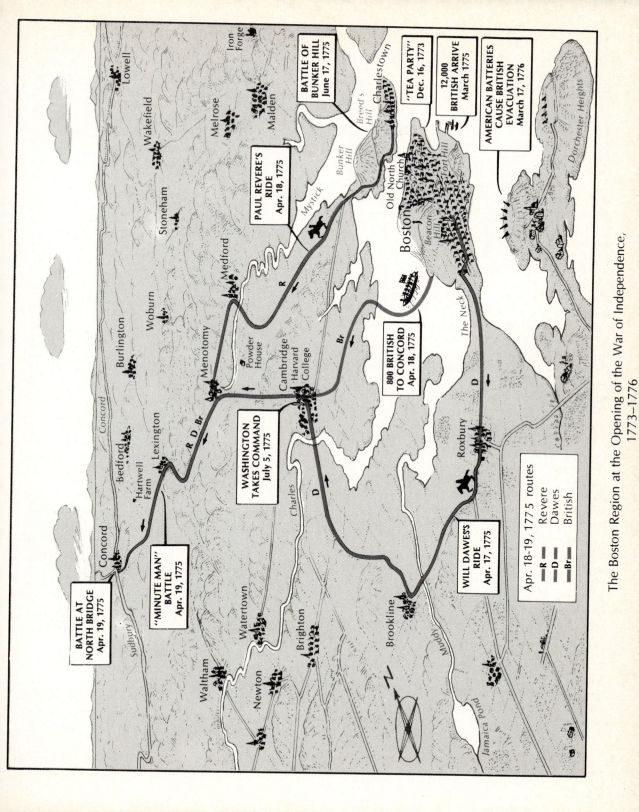

BATTLE AT
NORTH BRIDGE
Apr. 19, 1775

"MINUTE MAN"
BATTLE
Apr. 19, 1775

WASHINGTON
TAKES COMMAND
July 5, 1775

WILL DAWES'S
RIDE
Apr. 17, 1775

PAUL REVERE'S
RIDE
Apr. 18, 1775

800 BRITISH
TO CONCORD
Apr. 18, 1775

BATTLE OF BUNKER HILL
June 17, 1775

"TEA PARTY"
Dec. 16, 1773

12,000
BRITISH ARRIVE
March 1775

AMERICAN BATTERIES
CAUSE BRITISH
EVACUATION
March 17, 1776

Lowell
Iron
Forge
Wakefield
Melrose
Malden
Stoneham
Charlestown
Bunker
Hill
Breed's
Hill
Mystick
Old North
Church
Boston
Beacon
Hill
Fort Hill
Dorchester Heights
Medford
Woburn
Burlington
Menotomy
Powder
House
Cambridge
Harvard
College
Bedford
Hartwell
Farm
Lexington
Concord
The Neck
Roxbury
Charles
Watertown
Waltham
Newton
Brighton
Brookline
Sudbury
Muddy
Jamaica Pond

R D Br
R D Br
R
Br
D

Apr. 18-19, 177 5 routes
R   Revere
D   Dawes
Br   British

The Boston Region at the Opening of the War of Independence,
1773–1776

a free state, governed by a popularly elected provincial congress and a committee of safety which organized armed resistance. On 18 April 1775, the British general, Thomas Gage, on hearing that the revolutionary committee was collecting military stores at Concord, sent a strong detail of his garrison to destroy them. A rude surprise awaited the red-coats, for sounding the alarm 'through every Middlesex village and farm,' Paul Revere and Will Dawes aroused the whole countryside. When Major Pitcairn, after a night of marching, led his column of light infantry into the village of Lexington, he saw through the early morning mists a grim band of minute-men lined up across the common. There was a moment of hesitation, cries and orders from both sides, and in the midst of the confusion somebody fired. Then firing broke out along both lines and the Americans dispersed, leaving eight of their number dead on the green. The first blood of the War for American Independence had been shed. Who first fired, American or Englishman, is one of the unsolved riddles of history; but the patriots managed to circulate their own view of it as a brutal and wanton attack on peaceful villagers.

The British continued their march to Concord, where the 'embattled farmers' at the bridge 'fired the shot heard round the world.' Their purpose partially accomplished, the British regiments began their return march. All along the road, behind stone walls, hillocks, and houses, the minute-men made targets of the bright red coats. When the weary column finally stumbled into Boston it had lost 247 in killed and wounded. Inside of a week Boston was a beleaguered city.

On 10 May 1775, while the country was still resounding with the 'atrocities' of Lexington and Concord, the Second Continental Congress assembled in Philadelphia. The prophetic words of Patrick Henry were still ringing in the ears of the delegates: 'It is vain, sir, to extenuate the matter. Gentlemen may cry "peace, peace" but there is no peace. The war is actually begun! The next gale that sweeps from the north will bring to our ears the clash of resounding arms! Our brethren are already in the field! Why stand we here idle?' Even as Congress met questions, Ethan Allen and his Green Mountain Boys were crashing into Fort Ticonderoga and raising the standard of revolt in the North. Control of events was rapidly drifting out of the hands of law-abiding men, and Congress was forced to recognize accomplished facts.

The delegates to this second Congress, a very distinguished group, have achieved historical immortality as the 'signers.' John Hancock, the wealthy Boston merchant, was chosen president after the death of Peyton Randolph. Young Thomas Jefferson was there, fresh from composing his *Summary View*; and the venerable Dr. Franklin, so discouraged by his vain search for conciliation in London as to have become an exponent of independence. Yet the radicals did not push through their program of accepting war and declaring independence without a severe struggle. John Dickinson again raised his voice in favor of conciliation, and persuaded his reluctant colleagues to adopt another petition to the king.

Even as Congress was debating, it took the militia besieging Boston into its service, and then appointed Colonel George Washington commander-in-chief of the armed forces of the United Colonies. On 23 June Washington rode off from Philadelphia to take charge of the army. En route he heard the stirring story of Bunker Hill. On 17 June 1775 the British garrison in Boston made a frontal assault on a hill in near-by Charlestown, which the patriot militia had fortified. They won the hill, but it cost them 1054 killed and wounded out of 2200 troops engaged. As the first real stand-up battle between New England troops and British red-coats, it was a strategic victory for the Americans. Shortly after, Congress authorized a project which the British could only consider wantonly aggressive: an overland expedition to Quebec under Benedict Arnold, to bring Canada into the Union as the fourteenth colony. In October 1775 Congress began organizing a navy, in November it created the Marine Corps, and in December it sent the Continental fleet of eight converted merchantmen to raid Nassau in the Bahamas.

Independence

Nevertheless, over a year elapsed after Bunker Hill before Congress could make up its mind to declare independence. The very idea was repug-

BOSTON

CHARLES TOWN

The Battle of Bunker Hill, 17 June 1775. Historians have yielded to the popular impression in identifying this encounter which actually took place not on Bunker's Hill but on Breed's Hill on Charlestown peninsula. This illustration shows the Hill raked by British ships and land batteries. (*National Gallery of Art*)

nant to many members of Congress and to a large part of the American people. Magna Carta, Drake, Queen Elizabeth, the Glorious Revolution, the Bill of Rights, Marlborough, Wolfe—these were British memories in which the colonies had shared. Must they break with all that?

On 8 July 1775, after the news of Bunker Hill had reached Philadelphia, Congress adopted, at Dickinson's urgent request, the 'Olive Branch Petition' to George III, assuring His Majesty in most loyal and respectful terms of the 'ardent' desire for 'a happy and permanent reconciliation.' This petition was signed by almost every subsequent signer of the Declaration of Independence. As late as the autumn of 1775, the legislatures of North Carolina, Pennsylvania, New Jersey,

New York, and Maryland went on record against independence, and in January 1776 the king's health was toasted nightly in the officers' mess presided over by General Washington.

Yet the colonies could not forever remain half in, half out of the empire, professing allegiance while refusing obedience. The popular theory that they were not fighting the king or the mother country but a 'ministerial' army made little sense. Many, however, still hoped for a political crisis in England that would place the friends of America in power. But King George refused to receive the 'Olive Branch Petition,' and proclaimed the colonies to be in a state of rebellion (23 August 1775). On 22 December 1775, Parliament interdicted all trade and intercourse with the Thirteen Colonies.

Early in January 1776, before news of that vital step toward severance reached America, Thomas Paine's pamphlet *Common Sense* presented in popular form the natural rights philosophy that was to be embodied in the Declaration of Independence. 'Society in every state is a blessing, but Government, even in its best state, is but a necessary evil; in its worst, an intolerable one.' With ruthless disregard for tradition and sentiment Paine attacked the monarchy and the British Constitution. Monarchy, he argued, was a ridiculous form of government; one honest man worth 'all the crowned ruffians that ever lived'; and 'the Royal Brute of Great Britain,' George III, the worst of the lot. How absurd, too, that a continent should be governed by an island! This unnatural connection subjected the colonies to exploitation, and involved them in every European war. Independence would bring positive benefits, such as a world market for American trade. Anticipating the policy of isolation, Paine announced it to be 'the true interest of America to steer clear of European contentions, which she can never do while, by her dependence on Great Britain, she is made the make-weight in the scale of British politics.' Thus with persuasive simplicity Paine presented the alternatives: continued submission to a tyrannical king, an outworn government, and a vicious economic system; or liberty and happiness as a self-sufficient republic. Within a month this'

amazing pamphlet had been read by or to almost every white American. It rallied the undecided and the wavering. 'Every Post and every Day rolls in upon us Independence like a Torrent,' observed John Adams exultantly.

In each colony a keen struggle was going on between conservatives and radicals for control of its delegation in Congress. As yet only a few delegations were definitely instructed for independence; it was the task of the radicals to force all into line. In Pennsylvania the struggle was particularly bitter, coinciding with the ancient feud of Scots-Irish frontiersmen and city artisans against Quakers and the wealthier Germans. The radicals here achieved success by overthrowing the old government, establishing a new one with full representation of their frontier counties, and drawing up a new constitution. This new government promptly instructed the Pennsylvania delegates for independence. The effect on the Congress sitting in Philadelphia was overpowering.

Events now moved rapidly toward independence. In January 1776 patriots burned Norfolk to prevent its falling into the power of Governor Dunmore. In March the North Carolina legislature instructed its delegates to declare independence and form foreign alliances. Congress then threw American ports open to the commerce of the world, and sent an agent to France to obtain assistance. In early May news arrived that George III was sending over 12,000 German mercenaries to dragoon his American subjects. On 10 May, Congress advised the colonies to establish independent state governments; Virginia and others proceeded to do so. On 7 June Richard Henry Lee rose in Congress and moved 'That these United Colonies are, and of right ought to be, Free and Independent States.' After a terrific debate, Lee's motion carried on 2 July. In the meantime Congress had appointed a committee which consisted of Thomas Jefferson, John Adams, Benjamin Franklin, Roger Sherman, and Robert Livingston to prepare a formal declaration 'setting forth the causes which impelled us to this mighty resolution.' This Declaration of Independence, written by Thomas Jefferson, was adopted 4 July 1776.

The Great Declaration

The Declaration of Independence announced not only the birth of a new nation; it expressed a theory which has been a dynamic force throughout the world. Out of a 'decent respect to the opinions of mankind,' Jefferson summed up, not only the reasons which impelled Americans to independence, but the political and social principles upon which the Revolution itself rested. The particular 'abuses and usurpations' charged against the king are not advanced as the basis for revolution, but merely as proof that George III's objective was 'the establishment of an absolute tyranny over these states.' The Declaration rests, therefore, not upon particular grievances but upon a broad basis which commanded general support in Europe as well as in America. Some of the grievances, examined in the candid light of history, seem distorted, others inconsequential. One of the strongest, an indictment of British support of the African slave trade, was struck out at the insistence of Southern and New England delegates. But Jefferson was not writing history; he was trying to influence its course.

The indictment is drawn against George III. The only reference to Parliament is in the clause, 'He has combined with others to subject us to a jurisdiction foreign to our constitution and unacknowledged by our laws, giving his assent to their acts of pretended legislation.' Thus the odium of parliamentary misdeeds is transferred to the hapless George III. The main reason for fixing all the blame on poor George was to undermine traditional American loyalty to the Crown. Government, according to the theory which almost everyone then believed, was the result of a compact between ruler and people to protect 'life, liberty, and the pursuit of happiness.' And, to quote the Declaration, 'Whenever any form of government becomes destructive to these ends, it is the right of the people to alter or abolish it, and to institute new government, laying its foundation on such principles and organizing its powers in such form, as to them shall seem most likely to effect their safety and happiness.' By breaking the compact, the king had released his subjects from their allegiance.

Whatever the origin of government may have been in prehistoric times, in America it often arose just as Jefferson described. As in the Mayflower Compact of 1620, so in countless frontier settlements from the Watauga to the Willamette, men came together spontaneously and organized their own governments. Jefferson's philosophy seemed to them merely the common sense of the matter.

The Loyalists

The Declaration of Independence divided those who hoped to solve the problem of imperial order by evolution from those who insisted on revolution. By calling into existence a new nation it made loyalty to King George treason; and in most colonies patriot committees went about forcing everyone, on pain of imprisonment and confiscation of property, to take an oath of allegiance to the United States. Thus it gave to the loyalists or tories the unpleasant alternative of submission or flight.

There were loyalists in every colony and in every walk of life. In New York, New Jersey, and Georgia they probably comprised a majority of the population. Although it is impossible to ascertain their number, the fact that some 80,000 loyalists left the country during the war or after, and that everyone admitted these to be a minority of the party, gives some index of their strength. Most loyalists took the required oaths and paid taxes, while praying for the defeat of the American cause, simply because they had no place to go. As late as 1830 there were old ladies in New York and Portsmouth, N.H., who quietly celebrated the king's birthday, but drew curtains and closed shutters on the Fourth of July.

The American Revolution was a civil rather than a class war, with tories and whigs finding supporters in all classes. Outside Virginia and Maryland, most of the greatest landowners were tory, although many remained passive during the war to save their property. Yet the loyalists also won the allegiance of many back-country farmers in New York and the Carolinas. Officials went tory as a matter of course; so, too, most of the Anglican clergy, whose church prescribed loyalty to one's lawful sovereign as a Christian duty. The merchants in the North, except in Boston and the smaller New England seaports, were pretty evenly divided; and many lawyers remained faithful to the Crown. In general the older, conservative, established, well-to-do people were inclined to oppose revolution, but there were countless exceptions. Jonathan Trumbull, though an arch-conservative, was nonetheless the only colonial governor to repudiate his oath of allegiance to the king and throw in his lot with the rebels. Many families were divided. Gouverneur Morris's mother was a tory; so too was Benjamin Franklin's son, William, the royalist governor of New Jersey.

Although most of the prominent leaders of the Revolution were gentlemen, they could not carry their entire class into a revolution which involved not merely separation from the mother country but the stability of society. The question of home rule in the empire could not be divorced from the question of who would rule in America. When the conservatives realized that liberty could be won only by opening the floodgates to democracy, many drew back in alarm. Even some of the radical patriots had their bad moments. John Adams, riding home from the Continental Congress, was accosted by a horse-jockey, who declared that he hoped there would never be another court of justice in Connecticut. 'Is this the object for which I have been contending? said I to myself. . . . If the power of the country should get into such hands, and there is a great danger that it will, to what purpose have we sacrificed our time, health and everything else?' To what purpose indeed! This question forced itself upon the consideration of every thoughtful man, and when independence was achieved, it became a burning question.

The loyalist minority played a variety of roles in the war. Some did very effective fighting for the king. New York furnished more soldiers to George III than to George Washington. Loyalist marauders quartered in New York City frequently harried the shores of Long Island, and tory 'partisans,' often allied with Indians, committed atrocities on civilians of the other side. But for the most part the loyalists were good people of respectable principles. The attitude of those Americans who fought to hold the empire together in 1776 was no different from that of Southern Unionists like General Thomas and Admiral Farragut in 1861; and the difference between success and failure, more than that of right and wrong, explains the different 'verdict of history' toward these two great civil wars.

5

The War of Independence

*

1775–1783

A Divided Effort

The surprising thing about the War of Independence when you compare it with other wars of liberation is not that the Americans won, but that they did not win more easily. All they had to do to gain independence was to hold what they had. The British, on the contrary, had to reconquer a vast territory in order to win. To get troops in action against the 'rebels' of 1775–83, the British government had to send them by bulky, slow-moving sailing vessels which never took less than four weeks (and often ten) to cross the Atlantic. Moreover, those who 'came three thousand miles and died, to keep the Past upon its throne,' had to be armed, clothed, and even partly fed from England, which meant more shipping, more delays, more losses at sea, and such expense as had never been known in English history.

The direction of the war came under the Colonial Secretary of the North ministry, Lord George Germain, who is represented in the savage political cartoons of the day as wearing a white feather. He had been dismissed from the army after the Battle of Minden for something that looked like cowardice, yet had risen in politics through a combination of personal effrontery, family influence, and royal favor. His field commanders objected that he issued fussy orders but would not accept responsibility. 'For God's sake, my Lord, if you wish me to do anything, leave me to myself,' protested Sir Henry Clinton. 'If not, tie me down to a certain point and take the risk of my want of success.' Yet Germain's real shortcoming was that he never grasped the revolutionary character of the uprising.

However, the Revolutionary War was fought with such peculiar want of enthusiasm that in America it took the form of civil war. Many people were loyalists, many were simply apathetic. Washington wrote in the fall of 1775, 'Such a dearth of public spirit, and want of virtue, such stock-jobbing, and fertility in all the low arts to obtain advantages of one kind or another... I never saw before and pray God I may never witness to again. ... Could I have foreseen what I have, and am likely to experience, no consideration upon Earth should have induced me to accept this command.' He was to experience less virtue and more politics as the war went on; but his own steadfast patriotism never wavered.

83

Raising an army presented formidable difficulties. Americans were not eager for sustained warfare. They preferred turning out under a popular local leader like John Stark or Francis Marion to repel an invasion or do a little bushwhacking, then go home to get in the hay. Steady service in an army so ill-fed, paid, and clothed was distasteful; and the average American, though he wished his side to win, saw no need of continuous fighting. When New England was cleared of the enemy, it was difficult to get Yankees to go to the aid of the Middle States or the South; after the first enthusiasm of 1775 it was equally difficult to get Southerners to serve in the North; and the people of the Middle States, where most of the fighting occurred, hung back even there. It proved necessary to offer bounties to raise troops, and the value of the bounties had to be increased steadily. The total who served and counted as veterans, and as ancestors for members of patriotic societies, was several hundred thousand. But Washington's army reached its peak of strength with a little over 20,000 in mid-1778. No provision was made for the families of men in service, and no pensions were paid to the dependents of those who fell; so enlistments were largely restricted to the very young, the adventurous, the floating population, and the super-patriotic.

Although the spokesmen of Irish-Americans, German-Americans, and other minorities like to claim that the American army was largely composed of themselves, there is no evidence of ethnic groups favoring either side. Negroes served in every line regiment of the Continental army and in John Paul Jones's ships. Virginia slaves in the armed forces were liberated at the end of the war. Yet the large numbers of blacks who escaped to British lines to gain their freedom gave a note of doubt to the claim of the patriots that they were fighting for liberty. After the war the British refused to repatriate refugee slaves, and it is possible that as many blacks as white tories departed America.

The weakness of the American government contributed to slackness in the fight. The Continental Congress had no legal authority. It passed resolutions, not laws; it issued requisitions, not orders. In providing arms and munitions, Congress did rather well, but in raising troops and in coping with feeding and clothing the army, it did very ill. War finance was so unstable that by 1780 Continental currency was worth only one-fortieth of its specie value; within a year it ceased to pass. 'Not worth a Continental' was a phrase for complete worthlessness well into the nineteenth century. The government depended heavily on loans from Europe, especially from France, but also in later years from Spain and private bankers in the Netherlands. There was great improvement after February 1781, when Congress appointed Robert Morris, a wealthy Philadelphia merchant, superintendent of finance. He stopped waste and corruption in spending, placed government finances on a specie basis, organized the first American bank of deposit and issue (the Bank of North America), and reformed military purchasing; during the last year of the war, after Yorktown, the army was much better paid, clothed, and fed. But he did not and could not improve revenue; and a financial collapse was just around the corner when the war ended.

Military Operations, 1775–77

Even before the Declaration of Independence there were military operations which affected the outcome of the war. The colonists did not hesitate to assume the offensive. Richard Montgomery, with a little over a thousand men, taking the classic route of the Hudson and Lake Champlain, captured Montreal on 12 November 1775. About six hundred of Benedict Arnold's equal force got through the wilderness of Maine to Quebec, after incredible hardships. They poled, pushed, and dragged their way in flat-bottomed boats up the Kennebec, across a twelve-mile carry, through a complicated chain of ponds and small streams, across a snow-covered mountain pass, and — those who had boats left — down the rapids of the Chaudière river, while the rest, cold and starving, stumbled north along deer trails. Rendezvous was made with Montgomery near Quebec. As many of the troops' terms of enlistment expired on New Year's Day 1776, Montgomery and Arnold delivered a premature assault on Quebec, the strongest fortress in America, in a blinding snowstorm on

Phillis Wheatley. This engraving is the frontispiece of *Poems on Various Subjects, Religious and Moral,* published in London in 1773. A Senegalese-born slave, she was encouraged by her master, a Boston tailor, to pursue her talent for writing verse. Doubts were raised about whether work of such high quality could have come from a black woman, and Jefferson had to vouch for the originality of her poetry. But instead of being resentful at her plight, Phillis Wheatley was thankful that 'young in life, by seeming cruel fate [she] was snatched from Africa's fancy'd happy state.' (*Library of Congress*)

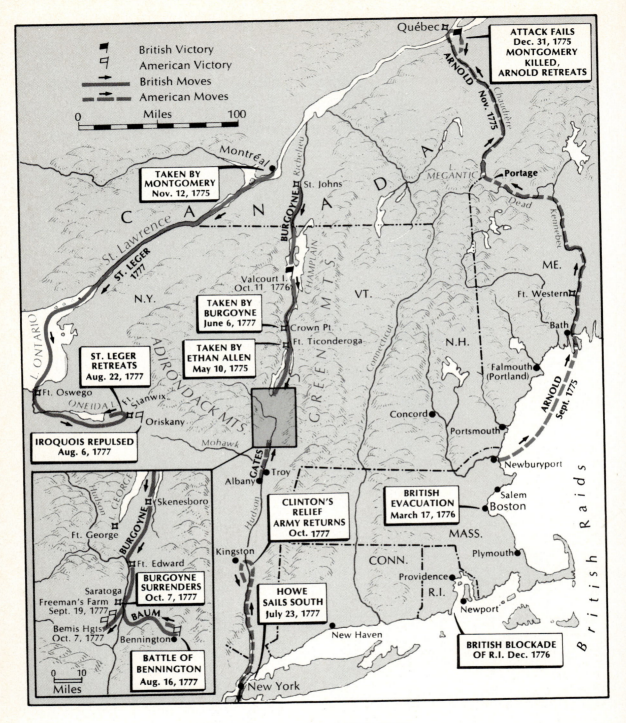

The Northern Campaign of 1775–1777

the last night of 1775. Montgomery was killed, Arnold wounded; and although Congress sent reinforcements, the expeditionary force was compelled to retreat, and Canada remained British. The Arnold-Montgomery campaign had an important bearing on the war. It alarmed the British government for the safety of Canada and caused it to divide the largest force of regulars yet dispatched across the Atlantic and to send almost half of it to Quebec. This ultimately would result in the most decisive American victory of the entire war at Saratoga, but the immediate impact was disheartening.

The colonists had better success in defensive actions. At Moore's Creek Bridge in North Carolina on 27 February 1776 patriot militia badly defeated a band of loyalists led by Donald McDonald, kinsman of Bonnie Prince Charlie's guide Flora, who tried to cut their way through to the coast with a great skirling of pipes and flashing of claymores. A new expeditionary force from Ireland commanded by Lord Cornwallis, with a detachment of British regulars from Boston under Sir Henry Clinton, was forced to try Charleston, S.C., instead. Charleston is a remarkably hard nut to crack, as Spaniards, British, and Yankees have discovered to their cost. Local patriots drove off the ships, and Clinton and Cornwallis, baffled, retired. So the British were denied a Southern base in 1776. About the time of the Moore's Creek fight, Washington, still besieging Boston, resolved to finish up. Seizing and fortifying Dorchester Heights, he placed his artillery in a position to blast the enemy out of Boston. General Billy Howe decided it was time to leave, and, happily for modern Boston, chose St. Patrick's Day 1776 to evacuate his army.

Howe arrived at his next objective, New York, on 2 July 1776. The Howe brothers, liberal in politics and friendly to America, brought an olive branch as well as a sword. All they had to offer (so Ben Franklin drew from them at a conference on Staten Island) was royal clemency to the rebels if they would stop fighting. Franklin refused to negotiate except on the basis of independence. It would have been well for both countries if the British had accepted this condition then, instead of six years later. But national honor forbade the

British to relinquish the Thirteen Colonies without a fight, and with 30,000 men and a navy to oppose Washington's land force of 18,000, it seemed as if the contest would soon be over.

Washington, on his side, felt that he could not honorably abandon New York City without a struggle. He promptly fortified Brooklyn Heights, and prepared to defend them; but Howe quickly shifted his army to the Americans' rear. In the ensuing Battle of Long Island (27 August 1776) Washington's plan was faulty, his generals did not carry out their assignments, all the breaks went against him, and British numbers were overwhelming. On 29 August Washington executed a masterly retreat in small boats to the Manhattan shore. Howe now occupied New York City, and during the remainder of the war that city remained a British base and a tory refuge.

Washington, his army weakened in morale and in men, retreated into New Jersey. This strategy was to save the army to save the cause. By the end of 1776 his army was hardly five thousand strong. The rest had simply dwindled away: deserted, gone absent without leave, or left when terms of enlistment were up. These were 'the times that try men's souls,' wrote Tom Paine. Howe, in that dreary autumn, lost several chances to capture Washington's army; for Howe waged war in the dilatory manner of European campaigns. There seemed to be no hurry. Every month the Americans grew weaker; Jersey loyalists were hospitable; gentlemen did not fight in winter. So Washington reached the far bank of the Delaware before Howe's outposts reached the near bank. But in March 1777, when the roads began to thaw, Washington had only 4000 men, and the British appeared to have everything their way. They could even contemplate an ambitious grand strategy to extinguish the rebellion.

General Burgoyne now mounted his bold tripartite campaign to cut off New England from the rest of the states, and seize Philadelphia. His idea was to march south by the line of Lake Champlain and the Hudson to Albany. Sir John Johnson, son of old Sir William of the Mohawks, promised to bring thousands of Mohawk valley tories and Iroquois braves to help. Howe, after detaching a force to meet Burgoyne up-river,

The red-coats march through New York City, 1776. This *vue d'optique*, or 'peep-show' print, was shown in Europe as a sort of newsreel in mirrored boxes; hence the reverse title at the top of the picture. (*Eno Collection, New York Public Library*)

would himself capture Philadelphia, and perhaps proceed farther south. The weakness of the plan lay partly in the difficulty of obtaining coordination at such a distance. Howe did not learn that he was expected to help Burgoyne until 16 August, when the bulk of his force was embarked in transports in Chesapeake Bay. But the fatal British mistake was to ignore the conditions of warfare in America. The several transfers between Lake Champlain, Lake George, and the Hudson meant an enormous apparatus of baggage and portable boats, ample delays, and plenty of warning to the enemy. European tactics were helpless against a countryside in arms: for the countryside in

Europe never rose; warfare there was a professional game.

In the summer of 1777, General Howe advanced on Philadelphia. All Washington could do against greatly superior forces was to retard his advance at the Brandywine Creek (9 September 1777). Howe occupied Philadelphia on 26 September, and Washington's gallant attack on the British forces at Germantown (3–4 October) failed completely. The British settled down to a comfortable winter at the former seat of Congress, while Washington went into desolate winter quarters at Valley Forge, only a few miles away.

In the meantime the greatest American victory

of the war had been won, on the line of the Hudson. The British army in Canada, some seven thousand strong with a thousand Canadian militia and Indians, jumped off from the St. Lawrence on 1 June, and advanced southward with bright prospects. On 6 July, Burgoyne took Fort Ticonderoga. By 29 July he had reached Fort Edward on the upper Hudson. Here he waited for more supplies from Canada. 'Gentleman Jack' Burgoyne would make no concession to wilderness conditions; he must have his service of plate, his champagne, and thirty wagons for his personal baggage. Burgoyne imagined it would be an easy matter for a raiding force to march across Vermont to Bellows Falls, down the Connecticut river to Brattleboro, and back 'by the great road to Albany' in two weeks. For this exploit he chose 375 dismounted German dragoons, the slowest marchers in his army, and about 300 tories, Canadians, and Indians. They did not even reach the Vermont line. John Stark and his Green Mountain Boys marched out from Bennington to meet them; and after that battle, on 16 August, very few of the Germans returned. Much the same fate met Colonel Barry St. Leger, who commanded a raid from Oswego to Fort Stanwix. He and Sir John Johnson's forces were no match for the Mohawk valley militia under General Herkimer, when reinforced by a column under Benedict Arnold; St. Leger retreated to Canada on 22 August.

In militia fighting, nothing succeeds like success. The Battle of Bennington brought a general turnout of the fighting population of northern New England, and Burgoyne's delay at Fort Edward enabled Washington to dispatch regulars from the lower Hudson. When in early September Burgoyne finally got his unwieldy force in motion, he marched into a hornets' nest of Yankee militia, flushed with the success of their fellows, and stiffened by regulars. The American Northern army, which now outnumbered Burgoyne's two to one, was commanded by Horatio Gates, a timid general who fortunately had Benedict Arnold as his second in command. At Freeman's Farm (19 September) Arnold's audacious leadership and tactical skill won the day. On 7 October Burgoyne lost another fight at Freeman's Farm,

and retreated to Saratoga. Americans were now in front, rear, and flank in overwhelming numbers. So on 17 October 1777, at Saratoga, Burgoyne surrendered his entire army, still over five thousand strong, to General Gates.

This was the decisive blow of the war, for it brought England's hereditary enemy to the American side.

Enter France

France had been waiting for *revanche* since 1763, and America provided the occasion. In the spring of 1776 Congress sent Silas Deane to France to procure clothing, munitions, and supplies. These he obtained secretly from the government of Louis XVI. After July 1776 Franklin and Arthur Lee were sent to join Deane, with instructions to obtain covert or open assistance, and to offer a treaty of amity and commerce. John Adams then, and always, was against an 'entangling alliance,' but the American military situation became so desperate toward the close of 1776 that Congress authorized Franklin to conclude an alliance if necessary to obtain France as a full-fledged ally.

Here indeed was a spectacle to delight the gods—smooth Ben, sleek Silas, and suspicious Arthur selling a revolution to the most absolute monarch in Europe. Actually the sale was not difficult. The French intellectual world hated feudalism and privilege, and admired republican simplicity. Washington seemed a new Cincinnatus; and ardent young men, of whom the Marquis de Lafayette was easily the first, hastened to place themselves under his command.[1] Moreover, the government had practical reasons. England must be humbled and the balance of power redressed in favor of France. French manufacturers were eager for a new market in America, closed to

---

1. Other foreign officers who greatly helped the American cause were Baron von Steuben, who introduced a modified Prussian drill and discipline in the Continental army; Thaddeus Kosciuszko of Poland, an admirable artillery officer; Count Casimir Pulaski of Poland, mortally wounded at Savannah; the Baron de Kalb, who died of his wounds at the Battle of Camden; and the Chevalier du Portail, an accomplished officer of engineers.

them by the British Acts of Trade. Still, though the French gave the United States unneutral aid in the shape of munitions and supplies, and welcomed Yankee privateers to French seaports, Vergennes shrank from the expense of direct intervention.

This 'short of war' policy lasted until after the news of Burgoyne's surrender at Saratoga. It then changed because Vergennes feared lest this disaster induce the English government to make such liberal concessions as would reunite the empire. He was not far wrong. Lord North was eager to recognize American independence as soon as he heard of the defeat at Saratoga; but the king refused, though he would concede everything short of independence in order to keep the American states nominally under his sovereignty. A bill introduced by North appointed a peace commission with authority to make an amazingly broad offer: parliamentary taxation of the colonies to be renounced; no military forces to be kept in the colonies without their consent; the Coercive Acts of 1774 and all other Acts of Parliament to which Congress objected—even the Acts of Trade—to be repealed, if America would but acknowledge the sovereignty of the king; these concessions to be guaranteed by treaty. This was more than Congress had wanted in 1775, all that Adams, Wilson, and Jefferson suggested in their pamphlets, almost all that Canada enjoys today. If the peace commission had reached America before news of the French alliance, its terms might well have been accepted; but, as usual, the British offer came too late.

On 6 February 1778, eleven days before the conciliatory bill passed Parliament, Franklin signed treaties of commerce and of alliance with Vergennes. Each nation promised to make common cause with the other until American independence was recognized. It was a generous treaty, in which America obtained everything and promised nothing except to defend French possessions in the West Indies. Great Britain promptly declared war on France, and the War of Independence became world-wide. Spain entered as an ally of France in 1779, and proved useful by opening New Orleans as a base for privateers and by capturing British posts in West Florida.

So, by 1780 there were naval operations on the Atlantic Ocean, the Mediterranean, the Caribbean, the North Sea, the English Channel, even the Indian Ocean. The shot at Concord bridge literally had been heard around the world.

Military Operations 1778–82

The year 1778 was one of incompetence and failure on both sides, redeemed only by the indomitable patriotism of Washington. While his troops suffered in frigid Valley Forge, Sir William Howe's men reveled in Philadelphia. Howe was recalled in the spring of 1778, and his successor, Sir Henry Clinton, was ordered to evacuate the city and to concentrate on New York in preparation for a new campaign. On 28 June, Washington attacked Clinton's retiring army at Monmouth Court House, New Jersey, a confused battle in which an American disaster was barely averted by Washington. Clinton's army reached New York safely; and all that Washington could do was to encamp at White Plains, fortify West Point, and look on. The only successful American campaign of 1778 was that of George Rogers Clark, acting for the state of Virginia. He shot the rapids of the Ohio, and led his little force across the wilderness to take the British post of Kaskaskia in Illinois, first in a series of bloodless victories. When the British struck back, the intrepid Clark in the dead of winter marched his men 180 miles through icy floods, until sick, sodden, and weary they arrived at Vincennes to surprise the disbelieving British.

At the end of that dismal year, the British turned the war in a new direction. An amphibious operation captured Savannah from its weak Continental garrison on 29 December 1778, then overran the settled part of Georgia, reinstated the royal governor, summoned an assembly, and virtually restored that state to the British empire. From Savannah an augmented force marched overland against Charleston, burning plantations and kidnapping slaves en route. Charleston was successfully defended by its small Continental garrison, and Savannah was attacked by a formidable expedition under the commander of the French fleet, Admiral the Comte d'Estaing. But in

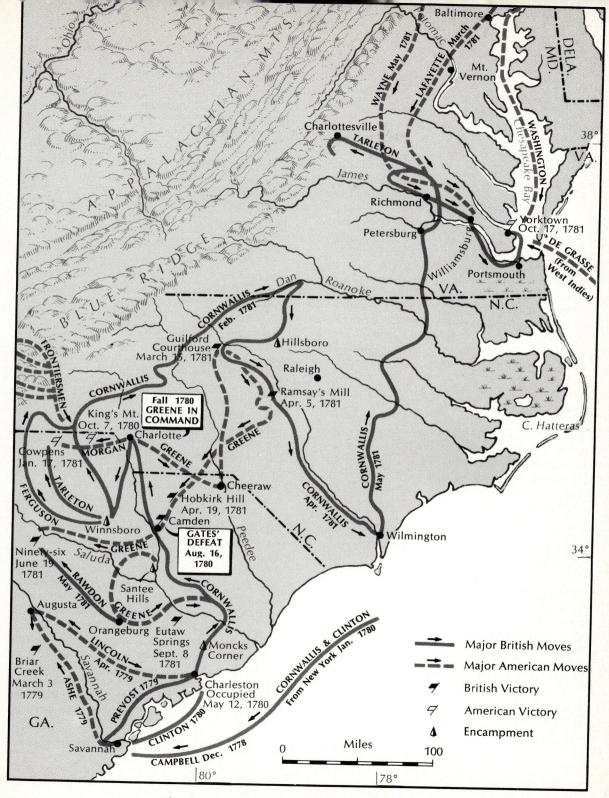

The Seat of War in the South, 1779–1781

the assault (9 October 1779) Count Pulaski was killed at the head of his legion. D'Estaing, twice wounded, re-embarked his landing force and sailed for France. A year and a half had elapsed since the French alliance, and so far it had produced little but disappointment.

The recovery of Georgia and the repulse of D'Estaing gave the British a bold strategic idea: a big amphibious expedition to capture Charleston, and with the aid of local tories set up loyal governments in the Carolinas, roll up all American fighting forces into Virginia, then secure that pivotal state, and Chesapeake Bay. There was nothing wrong with the plan, but the Carolina tories were not formidable enough, the British army treated the people so savagely as to drive even loyal men into rebellion, and the French navy intervened at a crucial moment. The Southern campaign opened brilliantly for Britain when a massive amphibious operation compelled the surrender on 12 May 1780 of Charleston and 5500 men, the worst disaster of the war for American arms. Washington now detached all Southern line regiments from his army which was watching New York, and sent them on the long march south, to stiffen local militia and form a new army. However, Congress, against Washington's advice, appointed to this command Horatio Gates and placed him over the able and courageous Baron de Kalb. Lord Cornwallis, an excellent soldier, beat Gates badly at Camden, S.C., on 16 August, Gates leading the rout on his fast thoroughbred. And Baron de Kalb was mortally wounded.

Cornwallis now had South Carolina pretty well in hand, but cavalry leader Patrick Ferguson went a bit too far when he threatened the 'hillbillies' of the Watauga country to pay them a visit and hang their leaders. They completely wiped out his tory force at its position on Kings Mountain on 7 October 1780. Kings Mountain proved that the British were not invincible, and thousands of small farmers enlisted under partisan leaders like Francis Marion, 'the swamp fox,' Andrew Pickens, and Thomas Sumter.

Congress now shelved galloper Gates for good, and let Washington choose a general for the Southern army, Nathanael Greene. This gifted son of a Rhode Island farmer, generally conceded to be the ablest general officer after Washington on the American side, found the defeated army in a terrible state. 'Nothing can be more wretched and distressing than the condition of the troops,' he wrote to Washington, 'starving with cold and hunger, without tents and camp equipage. Those of the Virginia line are literally naked, and a great part totally unfit for any kind of duty.' Only about a thousand men were effective. Somehow, Greene instilled a new spirit in them, obtained food and clothes (not uniforms, nobody ever saw a Continental uniform on anyone under a colonel in the Carolina campaign) from the countryside; and in a brilliant, shifty campaign inflicted so many losses on Cornwallis at Cowpens (17 January 1781) and Guilford Courthouse (15 March) that the British army had to retire to the coast.

However, after being reinforced and refreshed by his ocean supply line at Wilmington, N.C., Cornwallis marched north into Virginia. On 1 August 1781 Cornwallis occupied Yorktown and began turning that little town into a military base, to help the Royal Navy control Chesapeake Bay, Maryland, and Virginia.

Sea power was decisive in the War of Independence, but it was not until 1780 that the allies were able to challenge British sea supremacy. An American navy was improvised from Marblehead fishing schooners during the siege of Boston, and at least 2000 privateers were commissioned. The most successful warships were those fitted out or operated in European waters with the co-operation of French and Spanish authorities. Captain John Paul Jones raided English shipping in the narrow seas, and spiked the guns at Whitehaven near his old home in Scotland. Subsequently Franklin got him command of a small fleet in France, of which the flagship was an old French Indiaman, which Jones renamed *Bonhomme Richard*. She won a desperate battle with H.M. frigate *Serapis* off Flamborough Head on 23 September 1779. Jones's exploits made him the hero of countless ballads, chapbooks, and folk tales. Yet the Royal Navy continued to command American waters and enabled the British army to be moved from place to place by sea at will, while Washington's army had to walk if it wanted to get any-

Commodore John Paul Jones (1747–92). This bust of America's greatest naval hero was executed by Jean Houdon, the foremost French sculptor of the eighteenth century. Houdon's talent won wide recognition when he was only twelve, and at twenty he was awarded the coveted Prix de Rome. Houdon made busts of Rousseau, Voltaire, and Napoleon and carved 'Diana the Huntress' for Empress Catherine of Russia. In 1785 Franklin brought him to America where he did a bust of Washington that has been widely reproduced. (*Museum of Fine Arts, Boston*)

where. Fortunately for America, the French navy was at a high point of morale and efficiency, whilst the British navy was full of dry rot and grossly mismanaged.

When the French decided to intervene, they did so in grand style. Persuaded by Lafayette to make a real effort to bring the war to an end, Louis XVI sent over a splendid expeditionary force of 6000 men under General Rochambeau, which occupied Newport in the summer of 1780. For a year, in want of naval support, it did nothing except enrich Rhode Island farmers and amuse their daughters. But in May 1781 a powerful fleet under the command of a first-rate seaman, Admiral Grasse, arrived at Cape Haitien. The military-naval campaign of Yorktown was one of the most smoothly executed operations in the history of warfare, considering that it involved co-ordinated movements between two French fleets, an American and a French army, all widely separated, and with no faster means of transport or communication than sailing ships and horses.

In July 1781 Grasse decided to strike Cornwallis's army at the Chesapeake. On 5 August he sailed with his grand fleet and 4000 men of the Haiti garrison under General the Marquis de Saint-Simon. Precisely one month later, as the forces of Washington and Rochambeau were marching southward to join him, Grasse inflicted a bad beating on a portion of the British fleet in the Battle of the Capes of the Chesapeake. The French were now masters of Chesapeake Bay and able to boat Washington's and Rochambeau's armies to positions about Yorktown. The combined allied armies under Washington, Rochambeau, and Saint-Simon, together with Virginia militia, totaled 15,000 men; Cornwallis had about half that number, but his position was well fortified. Two of his redoubts were carried by American and French assaulting parties, and an attempt to escape across the York river was unsuccessful. On 17 October 1781 Cornwallis surrendered his entire force. As the British passed through the allied lines to stack arms, the military bands played 'The World Turned Upside Down.'

Lafayette joyfully wrote the news to Paris, concluding, 'The play is over; the fifth act has just come to an end.'

It was not quite that simple. Grasse's fleet sailed for the Caribbean (where it was badly beaten by the British on 12 April 1782); Rochambeau's army went to the West Indies; and Washington at the close of 1781 found himself back at White Plains watching Clinton, with no French allies at hand. During the summer of 1782 British warships and privateers based in New York were sweeping the waters off the coast. Washington felt this to be the most critical moment of the war. On 18 July he wrote, 'At present, we are inveloped in darkness.' Fortunately, the British will to victory, feeble at best, had completely evaporated. The only fighting on American soil in 1782 was in the West. British-allied Indians raided deep into Pennsylvania, western Virginia, and Kentucky. But George Rogers Clark collected 1100 mounted riflemen and on 10 November 1782 routed the Shawnee near Chillicothe, Ohio. That was the last land battle of the War of American Independence.

The Peace of Paris

If the soldiers had spoken all their parts, the sailors still had something to say; and the diplomats were just warming up behind the scenes.

Before Cornwallis's surrender, it rather looked as if the United States could only obtain peace and independence on the basis of an *uti possidetis* truce—'keep what you have'—which would have meant that Great Britain would retain the principal seaports from New York to Savannah, and Spain (France's ally but not ours) would hold both banks of the Mississippi and the shores of the Gulf of Mexico. No progress had been made toward peace when news of the victory at Yorktown reached Europe. George III still insisted he would never sanction 'getting a peace at the expense of a separation from America.' When Lord North finally threw in the sponge, George III went so far as to draft a message of abdication. But he thought better of it, and in March 1782 called Rockingham to form a ministry, together with Shelburne, Charles James Fox, and others who were traditional friends of America. Shelburne at once sent Richard Oswald to Paris to sound out Dr. Franklin.

Franklin was not to be the sole negotiator, only one of a commission of five appointed by Con-

Washington as lackey. In this contemporary British cartoon, the leader of the American rebellion is depicted in a servile role. (*Library of Congress*)

Washington as victor. This nineteenth-century American lithograph presents him as the triumphant commander, 'first in war' as well as 'first in peace and first in the hearts of his countrymen.' (*Library of Congress*)

95

gress. Their instructions were intended to place the United States completely under the guidance of Vergennes in the negotiations, but John Jay, one member of the peace commission, was by nature suspicious and had witnessed intrigues of the French minister at Philadelphia. John Adams shared his suspicions. Franklin, too, was converted to a separate negotiation with England, though this was contrary to the instructions from Congress. On 30 November 1782 the preliminary treaty was signed with the proviso that it not take effect until France reached agreement with Great Britain. Definitive peace was only concluded on 3 September 1783.

This Peace of Paris gives the lie to the epigram that 'America never lost a war, or won a peace conference.' Considering that the British still held New York, Charleston, Savannah, Detroit, and several other posts in the Northwest, that Washington's army was almost incapable of further effort, and that the British navy had recovered command of the sea, it is surprising what wide boundaries and favorable terms the United States obtained, though precise location of boundaries occasioned controversy for a long time. Americans also retained fishing privileges in the territorial waters of British North America. Article IV provided that 'creditors on either side shall meet with no lawful impediment' to the recovery of pre-war debts, including several million pounds owed by Americans to English merchants, but this article the United States found itself powerless to enforce for many years. Nor did the agreement that Congress should 'earnestly recommend' to the several states to restore tory property amount to much. Despite all these disadvantages from a British perspective, George III brought himself to accept 'the dismemberment of America from this Empire.' But he remained in character to the last. He would be even more miserable about the loss of America, he wrote to Shelburne, 'did I not also know that knavery seems to be so much the striking feature of its Inhabitants.'

6

From Colonies to Confederation

*

1775–1789

Forming New Governments

At the same time that the Americans were winning independence from Great Britain they were transforming colonies into commonwealths. The Revolution furnished Americans an opportunity to give legal form to their political ideals, or, as John Adams put it, to 'realize the theories of the wisest writers.' As James Madison could write, 'Nothing has excited more admiration in the world than the manner in which free governments have been established in America; for it was the first instance, from the creation of the world . . . that free inhabitants have been seen deliberating on a form of government, and selecting such of their citizens as possessed their confidence, to determine upon and give effect to it.' Americans are so accustomed to living under written constitutions that they take them for granted; yet the institution of a written constitution came out of America.

As early as 10 May 1776 Congress passed a resolution advising the colonies to form new governments 'such as shall best conduce to the happiness and safety of their constituents.' Some, such

as New Hampshire and South Carolina, had already done so, and Massachusetts had established a provisional government in the fall of 1774. Within a year after the Declaration of Independence every state except Massachusetts, Connecticut, and Rhode Island had drawn up a new constitution. Massachusetts labored under her provisional government until 1780, while the two others retained their colonial charters, with a slight change in the preamble, until well into the nineteenth century.

The Pennsylvania constitution thanked God for 'permitting the people of this State, by common consent, and without violence, deliberately to form for themselves such just rules as they shall think best for governing their future society.' Yet a method of adopting new constitutions was not easily found. Three were framed by legislative bodies without any specific authorization, and promulgated by them without popular consent. In five others, the legislative bodies or provincial congresses which framed the constitutions did so by express authority, but failed to submit the finished product to popular approval. In Maryland, Pennsylvania, and North Carolina the constitutions framed by authorized legislatures were in some manner ratified by the people. Only Massachusetts (1780) and New Hampshire (1784) had constitutional conventions specifically elected for that purpose, and a popular referendum on the result. This has become the standard method of constitution making.

Massachusetts illustrates the most deliberate and effective transition from colony to commonwealth. The process took five years and the delay was fortunate, for in Massachusetts the sort of people who made John Adams wince by shouting 'no courts, no taxation' were numerous. The first step was for the colonial assembly to resolve itself into a provincial congress. On 5 May 1775 this congress deposed Governor Gage and ordered the election of a new assembly, which drafted a state constitution and submitted it to the people. It was a poor sort of constitution and the voters showed good sense in rejecting it by a five-sixths majority. The chastened assembly then put into effect a new method, which asked the people to decide in town meetings whether or not they wanted a constitutional convention. They so voted. The convention, its delegates elected by manhood suffrage, chose a committee to draft a constitution; on that committee John Adams did almost all the work. His draft, adopted by the convention, was submitted to the people. Citizens were invited to discuss the constitution in town meeting, to point out objections and suggest improvements, to vote on it article by article, and to empower the convention to ratify and declare it in force if two-thirds of the men aged 21 and upward were in favor. This complicated procedure was followed. After town meetings discussed the constitution clause by clause, and voted a two-thirds majority for every article, the convention declared the entire constitution ratified and in force on 15 June 1780.

It would be difficult to devise a more deliberate method of securing a government by popular consent. At every step the rights of the people were safeguarded, and their views consulted. By the constitutional convention, the written constitution, and popular ratification, Americans had discovered a way to legalize revolution.

Most of the new constitutions showed the im-

pact of democratic ideas, but none made any drastic break with the past, and all but two were designed to prevent a momentary popular will from overriding settled practices and vested interests. They were built by Americans on the solid foundation of colonial experience, with the timber of English practice, using Montesquieu as consulting architect. A few men did the main work of drafting. That of New York, one of the best, was written by three young graduates of King's College: John Jay, Robert Livingston, and Gouverneur Morris, of whom the first two were just over 30 and the third, 24 years old.

Most of the constitutions began with a 'Declaration' or 'Bill' of Rights. That of Virginia, framed by George Mason of Gunston Hall, served as a model. It enumerated the fundamental liberties for which Englishmen had been struggling ever since Magna Carta—moderate bail and humane punishments, militia instead of a standing army, speedy trials by law of the land with judgments by one's peers, and freedom of conscience—together with others, based on recent experience, which Englishmen had not yet secured: freedom of the press, of elections, of the right of a majority to reform or alter the government, and prohibition of general warrants. Other states enlarged the list by drawing upon their own experience, or upon English documents such as the Bill of Rights of 1689—freedom of speech, of assemblage, of petition, of bearing arms, the right to a writ of habeas corpus, inviolability of domicile, equal operation of the laws. State governments were generally forbidden to pass *ex post facto* laws, to define treason in such a way as to 'get' undesirables, to take property without compensation, to imprison without warrant, to apply martial law in time of peace, or to force people to testify against themselves.

In other respects, too, the Americans had long English memories. The English people in the seventeenth century had tasted absolutism under Charles I, the Long Parliament, Cromwell, and James II. This experience impressed the English mind with the need for a balance among those who make laws (the legislative), those who execute the laws (king, governor, or executive council), and those who interpret the laws (the judiciary). Accordingly, all state constitutions paid allegiance to the theory of separation of powers brilliantly expounded by Montesquieu's *Spirit of Laws*. But this principle was less well observed in the first round of constitution-making in 1776. The Virginia framers, impressed by Locke's dictum, 'The legislative is the supreme power of the commonwealth,' allowed the legislature to elect governor, council, and all judges except justices of the peace. The classical education of leading men, who knew what Julius Caesar did to the Roman Republic, was reflected by a weakening of the executive power in every state but three. The judiciary in most states was appointed by the legislature, and in three states for a limited term; but every state endeavored to make the judiciary independent by protecting the judges from arbitrary removal or pressure through reduction of salaries.

Although the people were everywhere recognized as sovereign, every constitution but that of Vermont attempted to place control of the government in the hands of persons possessing more or less property. It was accepted that the body politic consisted of those who had a 'stake in society.' Even the democratic Franklin declared that 'as to those who have no landed property . . . the allowing them to vote for legislators is an impropriety.' There were property qualifications— usually meager—for voting, and proportionately higher ones for office-holding. In most states, too, religious qualifications for office-holding or test oaths of office were designed to keep out former loyalists and Roman Catholics. But these state constitutions were incomparably the most liberal and democratic of any in the eighteenth-century world and provided for a degree of self-government unknown elsewhere.

In spite of the haste with which many were drafted, five of these constitutions lasted over half a century, and that of Massachusetts is still in effect, although amended out of all resemblance to John Adams's constitution of 1780. Mistakes were made; but these amateur constitution-makers fully proved themselves worthy of their trust, and their states ripe for self-government.

In most of the states a struggle between democratic and conservative elements started during the war, but did not break out in the open until after it was over. In states such as New York, Massachusetts, South Carolina, and Maryland, where the conservative classes had taken the lead before 1775, they were in a position to direct the course of events and stem the democratic tide. In Pennsylvania and Georgia, where the initial decision in favor of independence had been a radical victory, the democratic elements had things much their own way.

The constitutional history of three typical states, Pennsylvania, Virginia, and South Carolina, illustrates the clash of classes and the essential continuity of this period with the pre-war years.

In the Quaker commonwealth the struggle between east and west culminated early in 1776 in a reapportionment of representation, a smashing victory for the western counties. The radicals then produced a democratic constitution that did away with governor and upper chamber, and provided for a council of censors to examine the operation of the government every seven years. There were no qualifications for voting or for office-holding, except the payment of a state tax and the touching proviso that membership in the House should consist of 'persons most noted for wisdom and virtue.' Vermont copied this constitution almost verbatim, and in that frontier democratic community it worked well enough. But in Pennsylvania, where there were deep class, ethnic, and religious divisions, it established the nearest thing to a democracy anywhere on the globe. 'You would execrate this state if you were in it,' wrote a Pennsylvanian to Jefferson. 'The supporters of this government are a set of workmen without any weight of character.' During the war, the Assembly expended more energy in plundering tories, cracking down on profiteers, and persecuting conscientious objectors than in supporting the Revolution. James Wilson made himself so unpopular by opposing the state constitution that his house was attacked by a radical mob. The legislature annulled the charter of Philadelphia College, the most liberal in the United States, because the provost and trustees were anti-constitutionalists, and handed over the college property to the University of Pennsylvania, but gave that university very little support. Eventually the people of Pennsylvania turned against this constitution, and in 1790 obtained the election of a convention which drafted a new one with a bicameral legislature.

In Virginia the gentry who led the patriot party wanted a conservative constitution but got a moderate one. Modest property qualifications for voting and office-holding remained unchanged, and the eastern counties retained their control of the legislature through the device of giving each county exactly two members. As the western counties were large, populous, and growing fast, this disproportion became greater every year. In 1790 the five valley counties with an average white population of 12,089 had two representatives each; so did five tidewater counties with an average white population of 1471. Yet the Virginia constitution was distinguished for its noble Declaration of Rights, which served as a model for other states and even for France. Although the Virginia gentry were unyielding in matters threatening their political supremacy, they went further in reform legislation than the governing class of any other state, not excepting Pennsylvania. Within a few years, under the driving leadership of Jefferson, Madison, and Mason, quit-rents, primogeniture, and entail were abolished, church and state separated, the legal code revised, and the slave trade abolished.

The South Carolina constitution of 1778 continued those class and sectional inequalities that made trouble in the colonial period. Suffrage was limited to men with a 50-acre freehold, and property qualifications for office-holding were almost prohibitory. A state senator had to hold an estate worth £2000, while the governor, lieutenant governor, and councillors had to own property to the value of £10,000. The coastal region continued to be grossly over-represented. The Anglican Church was disestablished, but only Protestants were guaranteed civil rights. Much of this was abandoned or liberalized in the constitution of 1791. Yet even this constitution left the state under the control of low-country planters, who made it the stronghold of Southern conservatism until it blew up in 1865.

Social Progress

Although democracy had little to do with starting hostilities, the war released it as a major force in American life. Tory estates were confiscated, land reforms adopted, and relics of feudalism such as titles of nobility, quit-rents, and tithes swept away. Progress was made in achieving an incomparably greater degree of religious freedom and separation of church and state than anywhere else in the world, and a concerted attack was made on slavery and the slave trade.

During the Revolution the Crown lands, extensive domains of proprietors such as the Penns and Calverts, and the princely estates of loyalists such as Lord Fairfax of Virginia were confiscated. This was done not to equalize landholding but to punish the recalcitrant and to raise money. Confiscated lands were sold to the highest bidder. In cities like New York and Annapolis, speculators acquired most of the valuable property. Rural estates, however, were frequently subdivided so that in areas like Dutchess County, New York, manor tenants were able to become freeholders. The abolition of entail and primogeniture, chiefly of symbolic importance, indicated a determination to wipe out the remnants of feudalism and create a more egalitarian society.

The fight for separation of church and state won a series of notable victories. In Maryland, the Anglican Church was separated from the state in 1776 and in North Carolina the feeble establishment completely disappeared. In South Carolina, though the Church was firmly entrenched in the affections of the ruling class, the constitution of 1778 provided that all Protestant churches should enjoy equal liberties. The Middle Colonies, where religious liberty already existed, embodied the principle in the new constitutions as a matter of course. In Virginia the arduous struggle against religious privileges took ten years. Not until 1786 did the legislature enact the Statute of Religious Liberty which Jefferson had introduced seven years earlier, and which he accounted one of his three great contributions, the others being the Declaration of Independence and the establishment of the University of Virginia. The statute roundly declares that 'No man shall be compelled to frequent or support any religious worship, place or ministry whatsoever.'

Only in New England did this principle fail of complete recognition. Here the Congregational clergy had been early and eloquent on the winning side; the Reverend Thomas Allen of Pittsfield even led his parishioners into action at Bennington. It was argued that the town church, like the town meeting and the town school, had made New England great. Rhode Island had always enjoyed religious liberty, Vermont adopted it at once; but the other three states set up a sort of quasi-establishment, according to which everyone had to pay a religious tax to the Congregational church of the parish within which he lived, unless he belonged to a recognized dissenting church. In that case the dissenting pastor received the tax. This system lasted in New Hampshire until 1817, in Connecticut until 1818, and in Massachusetts until 1833.

Several sects seized the opportunity afforded by the war to sever ties with churches in Europe. Francis Asbury, who had been John Wesley's superintendent before the war, organized the Methodist Episcopal Church of America in 1784, with himself as first bishop and premier circuit rider—his horseback mileage averaged 5000 annually for the next five years. The Anglican communion organized itself as the Protestant Episcopal Church of America at a series of conventions between 1784 and 1789. A constitution giving far more power to the laity than in England was adopted, and references to English royalty were deleted from the Book of Common Prayer. At a series of synods between 1785 and 1788 the Presbyterian Church in the United States approved a form of government and discipline, a confession of faith, a directory of worship, and two catechisms. The several German and Dutch sects also broke loose from their old-world organizations.

There was a lively struggle among English, French, and Irish Roman Catholics for control of that Church in the United States, which in 1785 counted only 24 priests and as many thousand souls, mostly in Maryland and Philadelphia. The London vicar apostolic made no effort to exercise jurisdiction after 1776; but in France a movement led by that Bishop of Autun who is better known in history as M. de Talleyrand sought to place American Catholics under a French vicar apostolic and provide a seminary at Bordeaux for training American priests. This did not please the faithful in America, who persuaded Pope Pius VI to grant them episcopal government. The Reverend John Carroll was consecrated Bishop of Baltimore, a diocese that covered the entire country until 1804.

The inconsistency of demanding life, liberty, and happiness for themselves while denying those 'natural rights' to a half million Negro slaves was apparent to Americans even before unfriendly English criticism called it to their attention.[1] The first point of attack was the African slave trade. Time and again the American colonies had protested against this traffic, maintained chiefly for the benefit of the Royal African Company, but their protests had been in vain and their prohibitory laws had been disallowed by the Privy Council. Even the pious Lord Dartmouth denounced the colonies for their attempts 'to check or discourage a traffic so beneficial to the nation.' One of the first acts of the Continental Congress was to conclude a non-importation agreement interdicting the slave trade. Soon the states took separate ac-

1. It is impossible to ascertain the exact number of slaves in the American colonies in 1776. The table below gives the approximate number in 1776 and the actual number according to the census of 1790.

	1776	1790
New Hampshire	700	157
Rhode Island	4,000	958
Connecticut	6,000	2,648
Massachusetts	5,249*	0
New York	20,000	21,193
New Jersey	10,000	11,423
Pennsylvania	6,000	3,707
Delaware	?	8,837
Maryland	70,000	103,036
Virginia	200,000	292,627
North Carolina	70,000	100,783
South Carolina	100,000	107,094
Georgia	10,000	29,264
Kentucky	?	12,440
Southwest Territory	?	3,417
	501,949	699,374

*Including free Negroes.

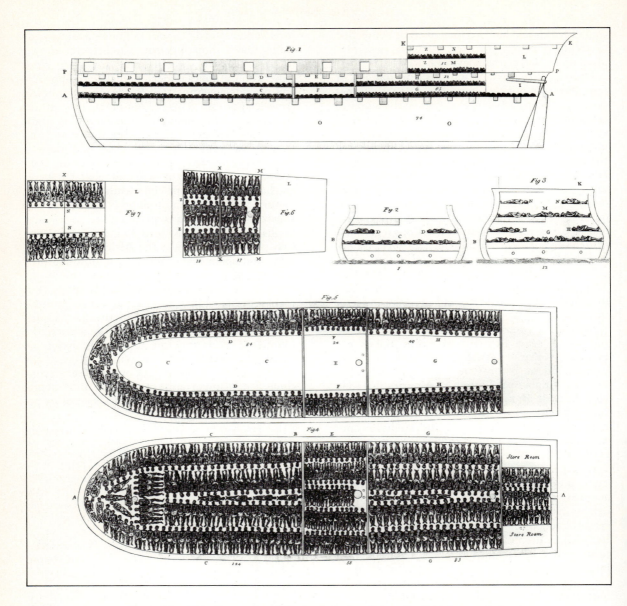

Slave ship. This diagram is of the loading plan for an English slave vessel on a voyage in the late eighteenth century. On its previous run it carried 609 passengers; a reform reduced the number this time to 'only' 450 passengers, but the ship was still so crowded that in some sections the headroom was less than three feet. (*New York Public Library*)

tion. Within ten years after independence every state except Georgia had banned or severely restrained the traffic, and Georgia followed tardily in 1798 with an absolute prohibition. But a good many ships from New York and New England continued to bring slaves illegally from Africa and sell them in the West Indies and the lower South.

The struggle for Negro emancipation proved more difficult. The Revolution and its aftermath put slavery well on the way to extinction north of the Mason-Dixon Line, but in the South slaves were so numerous that to free them would have shaken the economic and social system. 'I tremble for my country,' Jefferson wrote, 'when I reflect that God is just; that his justice cannot sleep forever.' Yet proposals for gradual emancipation were defeated in Virginia and every Southern state. Several states, however, encouraged voluntary manumission by the masters, and thousands of Negroes obtained their freedom by this means. Practically every Southern gentleman looked upon slavery as an evil, but a necessary one; in time it seemed so necessary that it ceased to appear evil.

An unintended consequence of the Revolution was to diffuse political power. Rarely has a revolution been led by men so conservative. James Otis responded to a call for reform of the Massachusetts government in 1776 by sneering: 'When the pot boils, the scum will rise.' Yet the Revolutionary era saw a modest growth in political democracy. To emphasize the right of the electorate to supervise legislators, New Hampshire and Massachusetts erected public galleries in their assemblies. In Williamsburg in 1774, the electors ended the patrician practice of being treated to strong drink by the candidates, and announced that, as befitted free men, they would entertain the candidate instead. In 1775, New Hampshire and Georgia abolished the freehold qualification for voting.

If the American Revolution had some social consequences, its main significance was unquestionably political. Although there had been small-scale revolts earlier in Geneva and Corsica, it was the American rebellion that touched off the explosion that shook the world. A war of liberation, it set an example of how to achieve both

decolonization and constitutional republican government, and the force of it is not yet spent. In a Fourth of July address in 1787 Benjamin Rush declared: 'There is nothing more common than to confound the terms American Revolution with those of the late American War. The American War is over, but this is far from being the case with the American Revolution. On the contrary but the first act of the great drama is closed.'

Arts, Letters, and Education

The American Revolution also stimulated intellectual movements. The Presbyterians founded at least four new colleges in the 1780's, including Transylvania Seminary, the first institution of secondary education beyond the mountains. The Lutherans and Dutch Reformed Church established the German-speaking Franklin College at Lancaster, Pa., in 1787; and the Protestant Episcopal Church between 1782 and 1785 founded Washington College at Chestertown, Maryland, St. John's at Annapolis, and the 'Citadel' at Charleston. Bishop Carroll opened Georgetown, the first Roman Catholic college, in 1789. Within the same period the legislatures of Georgia, Maryland, and North Carolina took the initiative in providing state universities. All the older colleges were injured by the war, but most of them picked up rapidly thereafter. King's College, closed during the British occupation of New York, reopened as Columbia College in 1784, and Benjamin Rush made the Pennsylvania Medical School the best in the country. It was also during the war that William and Mary students founded the Phi Beta Kappa Society.

In other branches of arts, letters, and learning this era was prolific. The versatile Judge Francis Hopkinson, signer of the Declaration of Independence, also excelled as poet, painter, pamphleteer, musician, organist of Christ Church, Philadelphia, and designer of the American flag—even though Betsy Ross may have put it together. David Rittenhouse, a Philadelphia mathematician and astronomer, was the first man of science in America at this time; but everywhere ingenious people were seeking out the secrets of nature. In Massachusetts the Rev. Manasseh Cutler during

Cessions of State Claims, 1783–1802

the war prepared the first systematic account of New England flora, measured (very inaccurately) the height of Mt. Washington, and observed eclipses. Philadelphia even before the war had her learned academy, the American Philosophical Society; in 1780 Boston and Salem virtuosi founded the American Academy of Arts and Sciences.

A 25-year-old schoolmaster named Noah Webster declared in 1783, 'America must be as independent in *literature* as she is in *politics,* as famous for *arts* as for *arms.*' He did more than his share to make her so. His blue-backed speller, the first edition of which appeared in 1783, sold over 15 million copies in the author's lifetime, 60 million in a century. Joel Barlow, who was Webster's classmate at Yale, wrote his epic *Vision of Columbus* in the intervals of preaching, fighting, and teaching. John Trumbull, son of the governor of Connecticut but educated at Harvard, served in the war, studied painting at London under the expatriated Pennsylvanian Benjamin West, and there in 1786 completed his paintings, *The Battle at Bunker's Hill near Boston,* and *The Death of General Montgomery.* St. John de Crèvecœur's *Letters of an American Farmer* were published in 1782; and four years later appeared the first collected edition of the poems of Philip Freneau. The concluding stanzas of one of them, 'On the Emigration to America and Peopling the Western Country,' well express the spirit of this age:

> O come the time, and haste the day,
> When man shall man no longer crush,
> When Reason shall enforce her sway,
> Nor these fair regions raise our blush,
> Where still the *African* complains,
> And mourns his yet unbroken chains.
>
> Far brighter scenes a future age,
> The muse predicts, these States will hail,
> Whose genius may the world engage,
> Whose deeds may over death prevail,
> And happier systems bring to view,
> Than all the eastern sages knew.

Western State-Making

While the thirteen seaboard colonies were being metamorphosed into states, new commonwealths were being created in Vermont and in the trans-Appalachian country.

Ethan Allen was the first leader of the Vermonters. Patriot and speculator, he typified those frontier leaders who directed the expansive forces of that era. Defying a pre-war decision of the British Privy Council allotting the Green Mountain country to New York, defying also Congress and Governor Clinton and General Washington, who regarded this decision as valid, the Allens and their party created and defended the independent commonwealth of Vermont. Although the Allen brothers used the language of patriotism, they were primarily interested in land. To keep control of over 300,000 acres in central Vermont, they carried on intrigues with the Governor of Canada, looking to a guarantee of independence in return for neutrality during the war, or even to a return to the British empire after the war. The people of Vermont, who knew naught of these intrigues, actively supported the American cause, but Congress was estopped from recognizing their claims to statehood in fear of antagonizing New York. In 1790 New York finally relinquished her claims, and on 18 February 1791 Congress admitted Vermont as the fourteenth state.

The creation of new commonwealths west of the Appalachians was attended with even greater difficulties than in Vermont. Lured by the finest hunting and some of the richest land yet spied out in America, the pioneers poured into the 'dark and bloody ground' of Kentucky and Tennessee. As early as 1769 settlers from western Virginia, defying the royal proclamation, established a small community on the upper waters of the Watauga. In the following years James Robertson and John Sevier led a body of 80 men from North Carolina to the Watauga settlements; by 1775 several thousand settlers were west of the mountains. In 1784, frontier leaders organized the state of Franklin, elected John Sevier governor, and adopted a constitution. Taxes were payable in beaver skins, well-cured bacon, clean tallow, rye whiskey, or peach and apple brandy. After a few years Franklin became part of the state of Tennessee, which was admitted to the Union in 1796.

Central Kentucky, the blue-grass country, began to be settled shortly after the Watauga. This region was the scene of a colossal land speculation that assumed the full panoply of sovereignty—the

Daniel Boone (1734–1820). This nineteenth-century engraving from a painting suggests the romantic manner in which the Kentucky backwoodsman came to be perceived. An Indian fighter and trail blazer of the 'dark and bloody ground,' he served as the prototype for James Fenimore Cooper's Leather-Stocking and was apostrophized in Byron's *Don Juan*. (*New York Public Library*)

Transylvania Company, of which the leading spirit was Judge Richard Henderson of North Carolina. On 17 March 1775 this company purchased from the Cherokee for a few thousand pounds all lands lying between the Kentucky, the Ohio, and the Cumberland rivers, although they had no authority from king or colony, and the Cherokee had no right to make the sale. A few bold pioneers had already found their way into the blue-grass and founded Harrodsburg. Henderson and the celebrated scout Daniel Boone now conducted a few dozen more men to a place on the Kentucky river that they named Boonesborough; and there in May 1775, under a great elm in the clover-carpeted meadow, a meeting of delegates from all settlements in the Transylvania domain organized Transylvania Colony, and petitioned the Continental Congress for recognition. But not for another fourteen years was Virginia ready to surrender jurisdiction over her Western territory. On 1 June 1792 Kentucky was admitted to the Union as the fifteenth state.

At the end of the war the Kentucky and Tennessee settlements attracted a flood of emigration from the older states. Settlers from North Carolina and Virginia pressed through the Cumberland Gap, while another stream of settlers from Maryland and Pennsylvania sailed down the Ohio river into the promised land. The trans-Appalachian population, only a few thousand on the outbreak of the war, numbered well over 120,000 by 1790. In the year ending November 1788, some 967 boats containing 18,370 men, women, and children floated down the Ohio, while almost equal numbers were spilling over the mountain barriers to the South.

The most striking features of this migration were its spontaneity and the intense individualism of its members. No government provided the pioneers means of transport, or protected them at their destination. Liberty was restrained only by voluntary organizations to secure defense, and to protect property from the lawless. Some twenty or thirty families lived within a wood palisade, with blockhouses at the corners, encircled by a swath cleared from the surrounding forest as a precaution against surprise. Thus, ten centuries before in England, countless 'stokes' had looked out on unbroken fen and forest. But the American 'stations' were fortuitous and temporary. Some vague instinctive fear, perhaps, that village life would mean serfdom to them as to their Saxon ancestors, broke up the stations before it was safe to do so, and each pioneer made haste to satisfy his ambition for a wilderness farm with log cabin. Nor were the instinct for self-government and the yearning for improvement ever lost. It was typical of West as well as East when the Watauga leaders of 1784 declared: 'If we should be so happy as to have a separate government, vast numbers from different quarters with a little encouragement from the public, would fill up our frontier, which would strengthen us, improve agriculture, perfect manufactures, encourage literature and everything laudable.'

Articles of Confederation

The Articles of Confederation and Perpetual Union, drafted by John Dickinson but altered by Congress, were adopted by that body on 15 November 1777. All states but one had ratified by early 1779. Maryland held out for two years more, until the states which had Western land claims ceded them to the United States. After Virginia made a tentative cession of her claims, Maryland ratified the Articles of Confederation on 1 March 1781, and the same day Congress proclaimed that they were in effect.

The change of government did little more than legalize what Congress had been doing since 1775. The Congress of the Confederation was organized in the same way and had the same powers as the Continental Congress. Each state had one vote. The new provisions were these: (1) assent of nine out of thirteen states was required for decisions in important matters such as making war or concluding treaties, borrowing money, raising armed forces, and appointing a commander-in-chief. (2) Congress acquired the power to appoint executive departments, and shortly created five—foreign affairs, finance, war, a board of admiralty, and a post office department. (3) The Articles provided for a Committee of the States, consisting of one delegate from each state, to sit between sessions of Congress and exercise all powers except those that required the consent of nine out of the thirteen. The essence of federalism is the distribution of national and local powers between governments, and in the Articles of Confederation this distribution was not well done. But the Articles did outline a federal system, and marked an improvement over the constitution of any previous confederation in modern history.

The Articles of Confederation sought to preserve the sovereignty of the states. The Federal Government received only those powers which the colonies had recognized as belonging to king and parliament. Thus, Congress was given all powers connected with war and peace, as well as power to establish post offices and charge postage, to set standards of weights and measures, and to coin money. These were powers which the king had exercised without question. But it lacked power of taxation to support a war, and it could conclude no commercial treaty limiting the states' rights to collect customs duties. The main defects in the Articles—failure to give Congress control over taxation and trade, want of a national executive or judiciary, and lack of any sanction for national powers—resulted from the unwillingness of the states to grant to a national legislature what they had refused to Parliament. Even when the inadequacies of the Articles became glaringly apparent, unanimous consent for amendments was impossible to obtain. Rhode Island defeated a proposal in 1781 to provide Congress with a 5 per cent customs duty; and when Rhode Island was later induced to part with this 'most precious jewel of sovereignty,' the proposal was rejected by the New York Assembly.

Requisition worked as ill as under the colonial system. Payments were to be apportioned according to the value of real estate in each state, but as Congress never had the money to make any property assessment, requisitions were allocated by guess-work. Naturally some states claimed they were unfairly treated and refused to pay, and several used their requisition money to meet federal debts due to their own citizens, leaving little or nothing for the Federal Government. Thus, it was not so much *powers* that the Confederation wanted as *power*. Requisitions might have served in lieu of taxes had Congress possessed authority to enforce them. As James Madison observed in a paper written in 1787:

> A sanction is essential to the idea of law, as coercion is to that of government. The federal system being destitute of both, wants the great vital principles of a political constitution. Under form of such a constitution, it is in fact nothing more than a treaty of amity of commerce and of alliance, between independent and Sovereign States.

A New Colonial System

Despite its circumscribed power, Congress coped remarkably well with all those pesky Western problems of land, Indians, fur trade, settlement, and government of dependencies which had troubled British ministers for half a century. In view of the land cessions by the states to Congress, a strange oversight was the failure to give the new government power over federal territories; but as somebody had to see to that, Congress went ahead and did, and the greatest permanent success of the Confederation was in working out a new territorial policy.

A good precedent had been created by the Continental Congress's passage of a resolution on federal lands in October 1780:

> The unappropriated lands that may be ceded or relinquished to the United States . . . shall be disposed of for the common benefit of the United States, and be settled and formed into distinct republican States, which shall become members of the Federal Union, and have the same rights of sovereignty, freedom and independence as the other States.

By virtue of successive state cessions, Congress by 1786 was in possession of all land south of Canada, north of the Ohio, west of the Alleghenies, and east of the Mississippi. This common possession of millions of acres was the most tangible evidence of nationality that existed during these troubled years.

Though Congress got into bitter strife with frontiersmen and Indians over Western land claims, it made a notable contribution with the Land Ordinance of 1785, reported by Thomas Jefferson, chairman of a committee of Congress. This Ordinance provided for a rectangular survey of public lands and a division into townships six miles square, each to consist of 36 sections of 640 acres each. Land offices were to be established at convenient points in the West and lands sold in orderly progress at a price of not less than one dollar an acre. Four sections of every township were to be set aside for the United States government, and one section reserved for the maintenance of public schools. This land system, largely modeled on that of New England, looked forward to using the national domain as a source of revenue rather than granting it free, or on easy terms, to settlers. And as no less than one section could be sold, and $640 was too much for a pioneer farmer to pay, private land companies did most of the land-office business for many years. Although there were numerous changes in detail in later years, the Ordinance of 1785 remained the basis of public land policy until the Homestead Act of 1862.

The activities of private land companies forced Congress to make provision for the political administration of its Western territory. In the summer of 1787 General Rufus Putnam and the Reverend Manasseh Cutler appeared before Congress requesting the sale of millions of acres north of the Ohio river on highly favorable terms. The prospect of money for the impoverished federal treasury attracted Congress, and the purchase was agreed upon at a bargain price. The Ohio Company of Associates obtained 1.5 million acres at an average price of less than nine cents an acre, reserving one section in each township for education and one for religious purposes. With this immediate prospect of settlement in the Ohio country, Congress had to make some provision for government.

The Northwest Ordinance of 13 July 1787, the most momentous act in the Confederation's history, bridged the gap between wilderness and statehood by providing a system of limited self-government, the essence of which has been repeated for all continental and most insular possessions. The Northwest Territory was first organized as a single district and ruled by a governor and judges appointed by Congress. When this territory should contain 5000 free male inhabitants of voting age it could elect a territorial legislature, with the status of a subordinate colonial assembly, and send a non-voting delegate to Congress. No more than five nor less than three states were to be formed out of the Northwest Territory, and whenever any part had 60,000 free inhabitants it could be admitted to the Union 'on an equal footing with the original States in all respects whatever.' Six 'articles of compact' guaranteed the customary civil rights and liberties, and declared 'Religion, morality, and knowledge, being necessary to good government and the happiness of mankind, schools and the means of education shall forever be encouraged.' Further, 'There shall be neither slavery nor involuntary servitude in the said territory.'

Thus the time-honored doctrine that colonies existed for the benefit of the mother country and were politically subordinate was repudiated. In its stead was established the principle that colonies were but extensions of the nation, entitled, not as a privilege but by right, to equality. The Ordinance of 1787 is one of the great creative contributions of America, for it showed how to get rid of friction in the relations of colony to metropolis. The enlightened provisions of the Land Ordinance of 1785 and the Northwest Ordinance of 1787 enabled the United States to expand westward to the Pacific, and from thirteen states, with relatively little trouble.

Liquidating the Treaty of Paris

The terms of the Treaty of Paris provoked quarrels between England and the United States over several issues, especially the vexing problem of treatment of the loyalists. Congress in January 1783 made the required 'earnest recommendation' to the states to restore confiscated loyalist estates, and a few complied to some extent. Pennsylvania, for instance, paid the Penn family $650,000 in compensation for their proprietary rights, but most of the states failed to act. The treaty requirement that loyalists should be free to reside for a year in any part of the United States, in order to endeavor to recover their property, was not always respected; tory raiders or partisan troops who returned to the districts they had ravaged were fortunate to get off with a term in jail. The treaty requirement, 'that there shall be no future confiscations made,' nor fresh prosecutions commenced against loyalists, was generally obeyed, however. American tories were less harshly treated than royalists in the French Revolution, or than bourgeois, Jew, Catholic, and other dissidents in more recent upheavals. And the 80,000 tories who departed during the war, or left voluntarily afterwards, were but a minority of the loyalist party. None was forcibly expelled after 1776. Even in New York most of the tories remained, and many of the exiles drifted back—men such as Henry Cruger, elected to the New York senate while still a member of Parliament.

The obligation placed on the Thirteen States by the peace treaty to open their courts freely to British subjects seeking to recover their pre-war debts was violated blatantly. Virginia, where the debts were heaviest, led the way in passing laws hampering the recovery of British debts. Congress sent a circular letter to the states, requesting the repeal of these acts, and most had complied by 1789, when the Constitution superseded all state laws contrary to treaty obligations and opened the new federal judiciary to British litigants. The matter, however, was not finally resolved until 1802.

The treaty of peace required all British garrisons on American soil to be withdrawn 'with all convenient speed.' New York was completely evacuated by December 1783, but seven military and fur-trading posts on the American side of the new Canadian boundary remained. The British claimed they were retaining the posts because the United States had not complied with the peace treaty. In fact, they were motivated by desire to control the fur trade and manipulate the Indians. Within a decade of the Quebec Act of 1774, Scots-Canadian fur merchants had so developed the fur trade that peltry to the annual value of £200,000 passed through Montreal on its way to London. In the peace treaty, this immense imperial asset, the land between the Lakes and the Ohio river, was ceded to the new republic, and when Canadian fur merchants remonstrated, the Home Office gave orders to retain the Northwest posts until further notice. This decision exacerbated Anglo-America relations until 1815.

The war also ended America's favored economic position within the British empire. Lord Sheffield argued that England could now absorb the commerce of America without the expense of governing her.

Parliament should endeavor to divert the whole Anglo-American trade to British bottoms. America cannot retaliate. It will not be an easy matter to bring the American States to act as a nation. . . . We might as reasonably dread the effects of a combination among the German as among the American States.

By a series of orders in council of 1783 American vessels were excluded absolutely from Canada and the West Indies. In British ports they were placed on the same footing as the ships of any European country, in carrying the produce of other European countries. American raw materials, provided they came directly from America, were admitted to British ports in American or British bottoms, practically on a colonial footing. This privilege was a great concession: no European country enjoyed as much from Great Britain. It was, however, revocable at pleasure. Anglo-American trade was so largely triangular that the exclusion of American vessels from the West Indies, and from all but a direct trade in American products with England, threw the traffic into British bottoms. The Confederation of 1781–89 had no jurisdiction over commerce, and all efforts of the states to retaliate separately were completely futile. For all its apparent liberality, the orders in council of 1783 were carefully designed for 'strangling in the birth' American shipping, as its loyalist author boasted. It might well have done so, if the American states had not formed an effective combination somewhat more promptly than those of Germany.

American relations with Spain were no more satisfactory than those with Great Britain. Alarmed by the expansive tendencies of the United States, and the danger of republican institutions to the Spanish empire, Spain sought to acquire a satellite state between the Appalachians and the Mississippi. To accomplish this, Spain retained posts on United States territory, choked the southern outlet of the West, corrupted some of its leading citizens, and allied with near-by Indian nations.

Natchez, on the left bank of the Mississippi and within the boundary of the United States as recognized by Great Britain, had been captured in 1779 by the Spaniards, who now refused to give it up to the United States. Natchez and New Orleans gave Spain control of the lower Mississippi—a powerful means of pressure on the West. The people of Kentucky, Tennessee, western Virginia, and even western Pennsylvania, discovered that the long river journey south was their only practical way to market. Their cheap and bulky products could not stand the cost of being sweated over the Appalachian passes. The Mississippi led to natural markets in lower Louisiana, and New Orleans was the natural port of trans-shipment for the New York and European markets. Permission to navigate the lower Mississippi, and to enjoy a 'right of deposit' or free trans-shipment at New Orleans, was for the West a question of life and growth, or strangulation.

Although formally denied to the United States as a right, both navigation and deposit were frequently accorded as a privilege, by the dispensing power of the Spanish governor, in favor of such Westerners as would promise to serve Spain's ambition to detach their communities from the United States. General James Wilkinson of Kentucky, who accepted favors and bribes to make his state a 'bastion of Mexico,' was the most notorious of these conspirators. When John Jay, secretary of the Confederation for foreign affairs, proposed in 1786 to waive the right of deposit temporarily in return for privileges to American shipping in Spanish ports, Spain's Western following increased. A surprising number of backwoods politicians accepted Spanish gold and intrigued for secession because they had lost hope of obtaining their outlet from the United States. To make matters worse, many leading Easterners, disliking frontiersmen as political bedfellows, wished the West well out of the Union.

The Day of the Debtor

The radical weakness of the Confederation was its complete dependence upon the good will of member states. Government starved upon the meager rations delivered by state legislatures. The sum paid into the federal treasury by the states was hardly sufficient to meet the running ex-

penses of government, let alone war costs and the interest on foreign loans. So hopeless had the financial situation become by 1783 that Robert Morris, the able finance minister, resigned in despair, confessing 'it can no longer be a doubt . . . that our public credit is gone.'

At the close of the war most of the states tried to collect long over-due taxes, at a time when districts were burdened by an increase in debt to merchant-bankers and storekeepers. A currency famine made matters worse. Debtors began to press state legislatures for relief in the form of 'tender acts' making land or produce at fixed prices a legal discharge, 'stay laws' postponing the collection of debts, and laws providing cheap money. Seven states issued paper money in 1786, when the depression, brought on by the loss of markets, was at its worst. This virtual confiscation seemed intolerable to creditors. 'They are determined,' wrote General Knox to Washington, 'to annihilate all debts, public and private, and have agrarian laws, which are easily effected by the means of unfunded paper money.' North Carolina purchased tobacco from farmers at double its sale value. In Charleston young radicals formed the Hint Club, which made a practice of sending sections of rope to planters who would not receive state paper for their rice. Rhode Island, where the debtors put through their whole program, furnished an example of what gentlemen might expect elsewhere. The state lent large sums of paper money to landowners, and forced it on others by heavy penalties. If a creditor refused to accept state paper, the debtor could discharge his obligation by depositing the currency with the nearest judge. Hundreds of creditors fled the state to escape implacable debtors seeking to make the legal proffer of paper money! It was this radical movement within the states, threatening the property interests, which, according to James Madison, 'contributed more to that uneasiness which produced the Constitution, and prepared the public mind for a general reform' than any political inadequacies of the Articles of Confederation.

In Massachusetts, where desperate farmers lacked the political power to obtain relief, civil war broke out. Farm produce was a glut on the market, owing to the stoppage of West Indian trade, and

John Jay (1745–1829). The foremost diplomatist of his generation, Jay served as peace commissioner to England, minister to Spain, and secretary of foreign affairs under the Articles of Confederation, and wrote five of the Federalist papers, mainly dealing with foreign policy. While first Chief Justice of the United States, he negotiated Jay's treaty. This portrait was painted in 1786 by Joseph Wright, son of a waxworks proprietress and a secret American agent in Europe during the Revolution. Wright's career was tragically cut short when he and his wife died during the yellow fever epidemic of 1793 in Philadelphia. (*New-York Historical Society*)

taxes were heavier than elsewhere. Courts were clogged with suits for debt, the cost of justice was exorbitant, and lawyers were grasping. All through the summer of 1786 popular conventions and town meetings petitioned in vain for reform in the state administration, the removal of the capital from Boston, and an issue of fiat money as in Rhode Island. Some yeomen faced debtors' prison, many others were sold into servitude for a term to pay off their debt. That many resorted to violence is not so surprising as the sense of law and order that prevented the majority of sufferers from following them.

In the autumn of 1786 mobs of farmers, under the unwilling lead of a former army captain, Daniel Shays, began forcibly to prevent the county courts from sitting. The object appears to have been to prevent further judgments for debt, pending the next state election. They met with stout resistance from the state government. The mobs were ordered to disperse, the leaders declared outlaws, and a price placed upon their heads. Shays and his comrades then resolved to become rebels indeed. For a few days there was danger that the state government might be besieged in Boston by an infuriated yeomanry, as had happened to the last royal government in 1775. But the rebels lacked firearms, and their attempt to capture the federal arsenal at Springfield was repulsed with grape-shot. Loyal militia, financed by forced contributions of merchants, was set in motion from the eastern counties, and college boys formed a cavalry regiment to terrify the country folk. The rebel bands, armed for the most part with staves and pitchforks, were scattered into the barren hills of central Massachusetts, where they were hunted like game in the heavy snow. Many fled to the western wilderness; cold and hunger forced the remnant to surrender.

Fortunately the state government acted with wisdom and mercy. Fourteen leaders were captured and sentenced to death, but all were either pardoned or let off with short prison terms. The newly elected legislature, in which a majority sympathized with the rebels, granted some of their demands, such as allowing soldiers' notes to be tendered for taxes. And the return of prosperity in 1787 caused the eruption to simmer down.

Nevertheless, Shays's Rebellion had a great consequence. 'But for God's sake tell me what is the cause of all these commotions?' Washington implored. 'I am mortified beyond expression that in the moment of our acknowledged independence we should by our conduct verify the predictions of our transatlantic foe, and render ourselves ridiculous and contemptible in the eyes of all Europe.' When Massachusetts appealed to the Confederation for aid, Congress was unable to do a thing, since it had neither armed forces nor money. That was the final argument to sway many in favor of a stronger federal government. Thus, the net effect of Shays's Rebellion was to arouse an emotional surge—without which nothing great can be accomplished in America—toward a new Federal Constitution.

7

The Federal Convention and Constitution

*

1786–1789

The Philadelphia Convention

Though it would be too much to say that the Confederation was falling apart in 1786, there was enough evidence of growing disunion to alarm thinking men. George Washington, John Adams, and others of the generation who had won independence had come to the conclusion that the Union of the States could not endure without a major operation. All attempts to give the government a limited taxing power by amendment had failed. In foreign affairs, an offer by John Adams to the British to negotiate a new treaty which would settle disputes left over in 1783 was met by the sarcastic comment that, since the Confederation was unable to enforce existing treaties, His Majesty's government could only negotiate with each of the Thirteen States. Individual states could not cope with a depression caused largely by the dislocation of foreign trade, and the credit of the Confederation was at a low ebb. Shays's Rebellion revealed the impotence of Congress. Finally, there was grave disquiet concerning interstate brawls over commerce. This last consideration led Virginia's assembly to invite all the states to send delegates to a convention at Annapolis, 'to take into consideration the trade of the United States.'

Only five states sent delegates to the Annapolis Convention, which met in September 1786. Two of its youngest members, Alexander Hamilton and James Madison, took the lead in persuading their colleagues that nothing could be accomplished by so slim a body, and to adopt a report which Hamilton drafted. This report proposed that all thirteen states choose delegates to a convention, 'to devise such further provisions as shall appear to them necessary to render the constitution of the federal government adequate to the exigencies of the Union.'

That was the genesis of the Federal Convention. On 21 February 1787, Congress invited the states to send delegates to a convention at Philadelphia in May, 'for the sole and express purpose of revising the Articles of Confederation,' to 'render the federal constitution adequate to the exigencies of government, and the preservation of the Union.'

Twelve states (Rhode Island having sulkily declined) were represented in the Federal Convention by 55 delegates. Of these, thirty-one, including all who took leading parts in the debates, were college-educated. Two were college presidents; three were or had been professors, and a dozen or more had taught school. Four of the delegates had read law at the Inns of Court in London; nine, including James Wilson, the most useful member after Madison, were foreign-born. Twenty-eight had served in Congress, and most of the others in state legislatures. The surprising thing about the delegates, however, was their youthfulness. Five members, including Charles Pinckney, were under thirty; Alexander Hamilton was thirty-two or thirty-three; and the next oldest group, James Madison, Gouverneur Morris, and Edmund Randolph, were within a year of thirty-five. Practically every American who had useful ideas on political science was there. Notable exceptions were John Jay, busy with the foreign relations of the Confederation; and John Adams and Thomas Jefferson, absent on foreign missions. Samuel Adams, Patrick Henry, and others whose political talents had proved to be on the destructive side were not elected.

It is always a temptation to read present interest into past events. Richard Hildreth, when writing about the Federal Convention in 1849, featured the slavery issue. George Ticknor Curtis and George Bancroft, writing in 1854 and 1882, stressed state rights against nationalism. Charles A. Beard's *Economic Interpretation of the Constitution* (1913) sounded the note of economic determinism; and several writers of that school, with even less reverence for fact than Beard showed, have pictured the Convention as preoccupied with the protection of property and the exploitation of the common people. Another school, building upon Jefferson's qualification of the framers as 'demi-gods' (a phrase he lived to regret), regards the document as almost of divine sanction. A careful reading of Madison's and Yates's notes on the debates—an exercise in which popular writers seldom indulge—reveals that slavery interested the members only as an aspect of sectional balance and that there was substantial agreement on the extent to which the states should yield powers to the Federal Government. The determining consideration throughout the debates was to erect a government that would be neither too strong nor too shocking to popular prejudices for adoption, and yet be sufficiently strong and well-contrived to work.

The temper of the Convention, in marked contrast to that of the French Constituent Assembly of 1789, was realistic rather than theoretical. 'Experience must be our only guide. Reason may mislead us,' was the keynote struck by Dickinson. Most of the members were public creditors, who stood to lose personally by a dissolution of the Union, and to gain by a restoration of public credit; but it would be unjust to attribute their views to property alone, as it is absurd to pronounce them superior to forces that move the best of men. All hoped to remedy the proved defects of the Articles of Confederation. A few saw that something more was at stake. As Madison said from the floor, 'They were now to decide the fate of republican government.' No fair-minded person can read their debates without wonder that a country of just 4 million people could produce so many men of vision.

The Convention opened on 25 May 1787 in the Old State House in Philadelphia. Though the Convention had been authorized merely to draft amendments to the Articles of Confederation, the well-prepared nationalists decided to bring in a plan for a new national government. On the 29th Randolph presented the Virginia or large-state plan. It provided a 'National Executive,' a 'National Judiciary,' and a 'National Legislature' of two branches, with members of both House and Senate apportioned according to population, empowered 'to legislate in all cases to which the separate States are incompetent.' As to the basic question of how the states could be persuaded to abide by these Articles of Union, the Virginia plan offered three solutions: an oath of office, a negative on all state laws contravening the Constitution, and power to call forth the forces of the Union to coerce recalcitrant states. All this was not essentially different from the methods that prevailed under the British connection. The Virginia plan did not get at the root of the problem of maintaining a federal state.

After two weeks of discussion, William Paterson presented a counter-project, the New Jersey or small-state plan, containing almost every feature of the Articles of Confederation that made for weakness and uncertainty. Yet it did contain one clause of far-reaching importance. 'All Acts of the United States in Congress made in pursuance of the powers hereby and by the articles of confederation vested in them, and all Treaties made and ratified under the authority of the United States shall be the supreme law of the respective States . . . and the Judiciary of the several States shall be bound thereby in their decisions, anything in the respective laws of the individual states to the contrary notwithstanding.' Here we see the germ of the doctrine that the Constitution is supreme law, that acts contrary to it are void, and that the courts are the proper agents to enforce it.

By using their superior voting power, the large states were able to shelve the New Jersey plan on 19 June and make that of Virginia again the order of the day. But the small states were unappeased. July brought hot weather, bad temper, and deadlock. Dr. Franklin was moved to suggest that the sessions be opened henceforth with prayer; his motion was lost, not because the members disbelieved in prayer, but because the Convention had no money to pay a chaplain! Fortunately the large states met the small ones halfway. After all, it was not the best possible constitution that must be drafted, but the best that the people would be likely to accept. The same practical consideration ruled out Hamilton's plan for a centralized unitary constitution that would have made the states mere counties—a plan that revealed how completely Hamilton failed to grasp the value of federalism. The deadlock was finally broken by the appointment of a grand committee of one member from each state to deal with the vexatious problem of representation. This committee brought in a report distinctly favorable to the small states. By the terms of this Connecticut or Great Compromise (adopted 16 July), every state was conceded an equal vote in the Senate irrespective of its size, but representation in the House was to be on the basis of the 'federal ratio'—an enumeration of the free population plus three-fifths of the slaves. At the same time it was also provided that all money bills should originate in the popularly elected House of Representatives.

Other questions raised new disputes. Certain members wished no branch of the Federal Government to be popularly elected, whilst others, like Wilson, thought that the 'federal pyramid' must be given as broad a basis as possible in order that it might be 'raised to a considerable altitude.' In the end the qualifications for voting for the House of Representatives were left to each state to decide for itself. Gouverneur Morris struggled to exclude the growing West from statehood, arguing that 'if the Western people get the power into their hands they will ruin the Atlantic interests.' Fortunately, others had a vision of future expansion, and eventually Congress was given full discretion in the matter.

But there was a distinct balancing of sectional economic interests. Charles Pinckney remarked that there were five distinct commercial interests. (1) The fisheries and West Indian trade, which belonged to the New England states. (2) Foreign trade, the interest of New York. (3) Wheat and flour, staples of New Jersey and Pennsylvania. (4) Tobacco, the staple of Maryland and Virginia, and partly of North Carolina. (5) Rice and indigo, the leading exports of South Carolina and Georgia. Madison, in reply to the South Carolinian's contention that a two-thirds majority must be required for all commercial subjects to avoid sectional discrimination, made one of the most prophetic speeches. He observed that the larger the political unit the less likelihood of class or sectional injustice; he pointed out that Rhode Island was the place where one class and interest had been riding roughshod over the others. 'All civilized Societies,' he said, were 'divided into different sects, factions, and interests, as they happened to consist of rich and poor, debtors and creditors, the landed, the manufacturing, the commercial interests, the inhabitants of this district, or that district. . . . The only remedy is to enlarge the sphere, and thereby divide the community into so great a number of interests and parties, that . . . a majority will not be likely . . . to have a common interest separate from that of the whole or of the minority.' Nevertheless, the Southern delegates long contended for a two-thirds majority of both houses for laws such as a navigation act or regulating commerce. They were persuaded to abandon this demand by the Northern states' agreeing to prohibit export taxes (which would have fallen largely on the South) and to cease meddling with the slave trade for twenty years. The only two-thirds requirements embodied in the Constitution were for overriding a presidential veto, for proposing constitutional amendments, and for senatorial consent to treaties.

On 17 September 1787, the finished Constitution was engrossed and signed. The members 'adjourned to the City Tavern, dined together, and took a cordial leave of each other.' Yet the crucial part of the struggle for a more perfect union had not begun. For the document upon which the Federal Convention had expended so much thought and labor required the consent of popularly elected conventions in at least nine states to become a constitution.

The Nature of the Federal Constitution

The essence of the Constitution, and a secret of its success, was the complete and compulsive operation of the central government upon the individual citizen, within the scope of its limited powers. Whereas the old government depended upon the sanction of state governments, and, in the last resort, upon the coercion of sovereign states by force of arms, the new Federal Government could create its own sanctions and enforce them by its own courts and officials and, in the last resort, by the coercion of individuals.

Congress shall have power . . . to make all laws which shall be necessary and proper for carrying into execution the . . . powers vested by this constitution in the Government of the United States. (Art. I., Sec. viii, § 18.)

This Constitution, and the laws of the United States, which shall be made in pursuance thereof, and all treaties made, or which shall be made, under the authority of the United States, shall be the Supreme Law of the land; and the judges in every State shall be bound thereby, anything in the Constitution or laws of any State to the contrary notwithstanding. (Art. VI, § 2.)

Further, state legislators and executive and judicial officers are 'bound by oath or affirmation to support this Constitution' (Art. VI). Thus, the police power of every state is required to enforce the laws of the Union as well. State authorities, in these national aspects, are under the oversight of the federal courts, which have jurisdiction over 'all cases . . . arising under this Constitution, the laws of the United States, and treaties made . . . under their authority.' As a last resort, Congress has power 'to provide for calling forth the militia' under the President's command 'to execute the laws of the Union.'

These are the central clauses of the Constitution. They went far to solve the more perplexing problems of the period following the Revolution. They provide the Federal Government with means for a peaceful enforcement of its laws in normal times, and for coercion of organized law-breaking in abnormal times.

Yet the system is not a unitary one, for although the national government is supreme within its sphere, that sphere is defined and limited. As the Tenth Amendment made clear in 1791, 'The powers not delegated to the United States by the Constitution, nor prohibited by it to the States, are reserved to the States respectively or to the people.' And the supremacy of federal laws is limited to such as 'shall be made in pursuance of the Constitution.' The states are in no legal sense subordinate corporations. To the states belong, not by virtue of the Federal Constitution but of their own sovereign power, control of municipal and local government, chartering of corporations, administration of civil and criminal law, supervision of religious bodies, control of education, and general 'police power' over the health, safety, and welfare of the people. Nor can the Federal Constitution be amended without the consent of three-fourths of the states.

Article IV of the Constitution, copied almost word for word from the Articles of Confederation, has an international flavor. Each state shall give 'full faith and credit' to the public acts, records, and judicial proceedings of its sister states, shall extend to their citizens every privilege of their own, shall extradite criminals and return fugitive slaves. The United States guarantees to every state its territorial integrity, a republican form of government, and protection against invasion or domestic violence—another reflection of Shays's Rebellion. The Supreme Court is open to suits by states and has appellate jurisdiction over disputes between citizens of different states. As the Supreme Court later held, 'For all national purposes embraced by the Federal Constitution, the States and the citizens thereof are one, united under the same sovereign authority, and governed by the same laws.' In all other respects the States are necessarily foreign to and independent of each other.'

In conferring powers on the new government, the Convention included all those of the Confederation, such as the conduct of war, foreign and Indian relations, and administering the Western territories. To these were added a limited taxing power, the judiciary, general supervision over state militia, copyright, patent, naturalization, and bankruptcy laws, and regulation of foreign and interstate commerce. The power to pass all necessary and proper laws for executing these defined powers rendered the Federal Government sufficiently elastic to meet the subsequent needs of a greatly expanded body politic.

Some aspects of the Constitution are antimajoritarian. The Senate was intended both to defend the interests of the small states and to protect property against numbers, as Madison freely admitted, and the six-year term of senators, expiring biennially by thirds, was meant to be a brake on hasty action. It is not, however, correct to say that the sentiment of the Convention was 'undemocratic.' Members insisted on giving democracy its share in what they intended to be a 'mixt' government, with the democratic, aristocratic, and authoritative elements properly balanced. That was the recipe of all leading political writers since Polybius for the successful constitution of a state, whether republican or monarchical. There was no question that the United States should be a republic. Hamilton might think monarchy the best form of government, but he realized that it was wholly unsuited to America. Washington, it was believed, had refused to assume a crown during the war, and who could be king if not Washington?

Apart from setting up the Senate, as Madison said, 'to protect the minority of the opulent against the majority,' the delegates did not insert any safeguards to property in the Constitution. Certain confiscatory practices of the states during the immediately preceding years, for example, breaking contracts and issuing paper money, were forbidden to them, but not to the Federal Government—as the Civil War period and our own have learned. The Constitution gave Congress power to pay the national debt but did not require it to do so, as Elbridge Gerry and others demanded it should. And in one respect the Constitution was more democratic than that of any state except Pennsylvania. No property qualifications were imposed for any federal office, although George Mason wished congressmen to have the same landed requirements as those imposed on members of the House of Commons during the reign of Queen Anne and Charles Pinckney wanted a property qualification of at least $100,000 for the President, and $50,000 for federal judges, congressmen, and senators.

The curious method adopted of indirectly choosing a President of the United States was the result of several compromises, especially between the large and small states. It was assumed that Washington would be the first President, and the number of presidential terms was not limited; but the Convention, not anticipating the rise of a two-party system, expected each state to vote for a 'favorite son,' so that seldom would one candidate obtain a majority of electoral votes. That is why it provided for a final election by the House of Representatives where the voting would be by states, a majority of states being necessary to elect. Thus, the large states would nominate popular leaders, but the small states would have a preponderant share in electing them. Madison thought this would happen 'nineteen times out of twenty'; but the two-party system has allowed it to occur but twice, in 1801 and 1825. Political parties have made the nominations since 1792, and presidential electors almost always merely register the will of the state pluralities.

If the method of electing the President was clumsy, his powers were clean-cut. This was the boldest feature of the new Constitution, for most of the states had a mere figurehead of a governor, chosen by the legislature. The example of Massachusetts, where a strong and popularly elected chief magistrate had put down rebellion, encouraged the Convention to clothe the President with ample powers. He is not only the responsible head of the executive branch but also supreme war chief. He has the power to appoint all federal judges, and by virtue of his suspensive veto over acts of Congress, is a part of the legislative process too.

However, in keeping with the principles of the separation of powers and of checks and balances, Congress is also independent of him. He cannot dissolve Congress, and the Constitution requires Congress to assemble every year, whether the President wants it or not. Congress may re-enact laws over his veto, and the Senate has a check on his appointing and treaty-making powers. Both houses share the power of impeachment and removals of officials, including the Chief Executive.

Article III on the judiciary does not explicitly stipulate the power of the Supreme Court to declare acts of Congress unconstitutional, but this power of judicial review is implied. Article III, sec. 2 declares that the judicial power shall extend to all cases arising under the Constitution and the laws and treaties of the United States; and Article VI, sec. 2 declares that the Constitution, laws 'made in pursuance thereof,' and treaties 'shall be the Supreme Law of the land.' Though President and Congress have a number of ways of shaping the judiciary to their will, including altering the size of the Supreme Court, life tenure for judges has been an important guarantee of the independence of the judicial branch.

The Ratification Contest

The Convention, anticipating that many state politicians would be hostile, provided for the ratification of the Constitution by a popularly elected convention in each state. Suspecting that Rhode Island, if not other states, would prove recalcitrant, it declared that the Constitution would go into effect as soon as nine states ratified. The convention method had the further advantage that judges, ministers, and others ineligible to state legislatures could be chosen to such a body. The nine-state provision was, of course, mildly revolutionary. But the Congress of the Confederation, still sitting in New York to carry on federal government until relieved, formally submitted the new Constitution to the states and politely faded out before the first presidential inauguration.

In the contest for ratification the Federalists (as the supporters of the Constitution called themselves) had the assets of youth, intelligence, something positive to offer, and, absolutely invaluable, the support of Washington and Franklin. However, only 39 of the 55 delegates signed the Constitution, and all delegates who opposed, except Randolph, who changed his mind, took leading parts against the Constitution. The Federalist-Antifederalist lineup was not by class, section, or economic interest. Some of the wealthiest men were in opposition. George Mason, who looked down his nose at Washington as an upstart surveyor, and James Winthrop, scion of New England's most aristocratic family, wrote pamphlets against the Constitution. Delegates to the Virginia ratifying convention from the old tidewater region were mostly Antifederalist; those from the recently settled valley, Federalist. Among the Antifederalists were Patrick Henry and the Lees of Virginia, George Clinton of New York, and (for a time) Samuel Adams and John Hancock of Massachusetts. The warmest advocates of the Constitution were eager young men such as the thirty-two-year-old Rufus King.

Opponents of the Constitution appealed to the popular sentiment, announced by Tom Paine: 'That government is best which governs least.' They viewed with alarm the fact that two popular principles, annual elections and rotation in office, were not embodied in the Constitution. Old radicals such as General James Warren and his gifted wife Mercy, who thought that the states were the true guardians of 'Republican Virtue,' predicted that the Constitution would encourage speculation and vice, and that America would go the way of imperial Rome.

The Federalists, however, believed that the slogans of 1776 were outmoded; that America needed integration, not state rights; that the immediate peril was not tyranny but disorder or dissolution; that certain subjects such as commerce were national by nature; that the right to tax was essential to any government; and that powers wrested from king and parliament should

Portrait of Chief Justice Oliver Ellsworth and his wife Abigail Wolcott. As one of Connecticut's original senators, Ellsworth was mainly responsible for the act organizing the federal judiciary, and from 1796 to 1799 he served as Chief Justice of the United States. This painting by Ralph Earl suggests the wealth and social position of the squire of Windsor who, as a leader of the Connecticut bar, accumulated a sizable fortune. A conservative Federalist, he held his opinions tenaciously. Aaron Burr said of him, 'If Ellsworth had happened to spell the name of the Deity with two d's, it would have taken the Senate three weeks to expunge the superfluous letter.' (*Wadsworth Atheneum, Hartford*)

not be divided among thirteen states, if the American government were to have any influence in the world. Most effective of the Federalist presentations was the series of essays that came out in a New York newspaper, written by Madison, Hamilton, and Jay over the common signature 'Publius,' later republished as a book under the title *The Federalist*.

Despite the power of this remarkable treatise, the struggle for ratification was tough. There is little doubt that most sentiment was Antifederalist. Only in the small state of Delaware was there no contest, since their leaders knew that with an equal vote in the Senate and two extra votes for presidential electors they had got more than their fair share. The Delaware convention ratified unanimously in December 1787. In Pennsylvania, supporters of the Constitution rushed through approval before the Antifederalists could organize. Next came Massachusetts, where the situation was critical, since Shays's Rebellion had only lately been suppressed. Shortly after the ratifying convention met on 9 January 1788, a straw vote polled 192 members against the Constitution and only 144 in favor. But Samuel Adams was reached through a backfire kindled by the Federalists among his old cronies, the ship caulkers of Boston. After some leading merchants had promised to build new ships as soon as the Constitution was ratified, the shipwrights and other artisans passed strong Federalist resolutions, and Sam listened to *vox pop*.

The most important piece of strategy by the Bay State Federalists was to propose a bill of rights to supplement the Constitution. This had not been provided by the Federal Convention, partly because the Constitution was one of limited and specific powers for which it was felt no bill of rights was necessary; but mostly because when the members got around to the subject, they were worn out and wanted to go home. Lack of a bill of rights, however, was a strong Antifederalist talking point. After the Federalists agreed to support one to be recommended to the states as a set of amendments, the Massachusetts convention ratified, 6 February 1788, by the close vote of 187 to 168. The Maryland convention, also proposing bill-of-rights amendments, ratified on 28 April by an emphatic vote; partly, it seems, because the members became weary of listening to Luther Martin's three-hour Antifederalist speeches. In South Carolina Charles Pinckney made strong arguments in favor of union, which he lived long enough to regret; and on 23 May his state ratified the Constitution by a strong majority. New Hampshire had the honor of being the ninth state, whose ratification put the Constitution into force.

But four states, with about 40 per cent of the total population, were still outside, including Virginia without whom no union could be a success. Here took place the most ably and bitterly contested struggle. On the Antifederalist side were George Mason, Richard Henry Lee, and Patrick Henry, who objected that the new Constitution 'squints toward monarchy.' Their withering blasts of oratory were patiently met with unanswerable logic by Madison, Edmund Pendleton, and thirty-two-year-old John Marshall. The Virginia convention ratified unconditionally on 23 June by a vote of 89 to 79. At the same time it adopted a list of amendments similar to those proposed by Massachusetts, which the new Congress and the states were asked to ratify.

Virginia made the tenth state, but New York was still out, and in New York, as Washington remarked, there was 'more wickedness than ignorance' in Antifederalism. The party led by Governor Clinton opposed the Constitution, as did most of the big landowners, who feared heavier land taxes if the state lost her right to levy customs duties. John Jay and Alexander Hamilton led the Federalist forces in the state convention with great skill; but it was only through their threat that if New York as a state failed to ratify, New York City would secede and join the Union as a separate state, that the convention finally voted to ratify by the narrow margin of three, out of 57 voting. Only two states remained outside. The North Carolina convention refused to take a vote at its first session, but met again in November 1788 and decided to join. Rhode Island, still controlled by the debtor element, called no convention until 1790, when it tardily came into the Union.

The Congress of the Confederation, still sitting in New York, declared the new Constitution duly

Hail Columbia. In the Federal Procession, 23 July 1788, by which New York celebrated the ratification of the Constitution, the Society of Pewterers carried this silk banner. (*New-York Historical Society*)

ratified, arranged for the first elections, and decided on New York as the first capital of the new government. Under the heading 'Ship News—Extra,' the New York *Public Advertiser* noted the entrance of the good ship *Federal Constitution*, Perpetual Union master, from Elysium. Her cargo included thirteen large parcels of Union, Peace, and Friendship; on her passenger list were Messrs. Flourishing Commerce, Public Faith, and National Energy. Below is noted the clearance of *Old Confederacy*, Imbecility master, with a cargo

of paper money, legal-tender acts, local prejudices, and seeds of discord; and the total loss with all hands of the sloop *Anarchy*, wrecked on the Rock of Union.

The Young Republic

America was attempting simultaneously three political experiments, which the accumulated wisdom of Europe deemed likely to fail: independence, republicanism, and federal union. While the British and the Spanish empires touched the states on their north, west, and south, it looked as if independence could only be preserved with more of that European aid by which it had been won, perhaps even by becoming a satellite state. Since the Renaissance, the uniform tendency in Europe had been toward centralized monarchy; federal republics had maintained themselves only in small areas, such as the Netherlands and Switzerland.

Even with the Mississippi as its western boundary, the United States equaled the area of the British Isles, France, Germany, Spain, and Italy. The population of a little less than four million, including 700,000 Negro slaves, was dispersed over an expanse of coastal plain and upland slightly more extensive than France. Agriculture was the main occupation of nine-tenths of the people, and in 1790 only six cities (Philadelphia, New York, Boston, Charleston, Baltimore, and Salem) had a population of 8000 or more; their combined numbers included only 3 per cent of the total. Americans had not yet conquered the forest. Volney wrote that during his journey in 1796 through the length and breadth of the United States, he scarcely traveled for more than three miles together on open and cleared land. The difficulties of communication were so great that a detour of several hundred miles by river and ocean was often preferable to an overland journey of fifty miles. It was almost as difficult to assemble the first Congress of the United States as to convene church councils in the Middle Ages. Twenty-nine days were required for the news of the Declaration of Independence to reach Charleston from Philadelphia. Less than half of the national territory had yet come under the effective jurisdiction of the United States or of any state. But if the trans-Appalachian country were ever settled, it would surely break off from the Thirteen States. So at least believed the few Europeans who gave the matter a thought.

Yet Americans dwelt in a land of such plenty that possibilities seemed infinite. There was nothing to match the poverty of a European city; and even the slave population of the Carolina rice-fields was less wretched than the contemporary Russian peasant. The ocean and its shores yielded an abundance of fish; the tidal rivers teemed with salmon, sturgeon, herring, and shad, and the upland streams with trout; game ranged from quail and raccoon to wild turkey and moose; and flights of wild pigeon darkened the air. Cattle and swine throve; Indian corn ripened quickly in the hot summer nights; even sugar could be obtained from the maple, or honey from wild bees. The American of the interior, glutted with nature's bounty and remote from a market, had no immediate incentive to produce much beyond his own actual needs; yet the knowledge that easier life could be had often pressed him westward to more fertile lands. Hence the note of personal independence that was, and in the main still is, dominant in American life. Although the ordinary American recognized the claims of social rank, he was no longer so willing to defer to the gentry. 'The means of subsistence being so easy in the country,' wrote an English observer in 1796, 'and their dependence on each other consequently so trifling, that spirit of servility to those above them so prevalent in European manners, is wholly unknown to them; and they pass their lives without any regard to the smiles or the frowns of men in power.' Yet however independent of those above him the average American might be, he depended on those about him for help in harvest, in raising his houseframe, and in illness. In a new country you turn to your neighbors for many things that, in a more advanced community, are performed by the government or by specialists. Hence the dual nature of the American: individualism and community spirit, indifference and kindliness.

The United States of 1789 was not, by any modern standard, a nation. Materials of a nation were present, but cohesive force was wanting. The English origin of the bulk of the people made for cultural homogeneity; the Maine fisherman could understand the Georgia planter much more readily than a Kentishman could understand a Yorkshireman, or an Alsatian a Breton. Political institutions were fairly constant in form through the land. But there was no tradition of union, and it was difficult to discover a common interest upon which union could be built. Most citizens, if asked their country or nation, would not have answered

American, but Carolinian or Jerseyman, or the like. A political nexus had been found, but unless a national tradition were soon established, the states would develop rivalries similar to those of the republics of Latin America. It would require the highest statesmanship to keep these new commonwealths united. The Federal Constitution made it possible; but few observers in 1789 thought it probable.

Still, if most European commentators believed that the history of the American Union would be short and stormy, the friends of liberty in Europe had high expectations. The French statesman Turgot wrote in 1778:

> This people is the hope of the human race. It may become the model. It ought to show the world by facts, that men can be free and yet peaceful, and may dispense with the chains in which tyrants and knaves of every colour have presumed to bind them, under pretext of the public good. The Americans should be an example of political, religious, commercial and industrial liberty. The asylum they offer to the oppressed of every nation, the avenue of escape they open, will compel governments to be just and enlightened; and the rest of the world in due time will see through the empty illusions in which policy is conceived. But to obtain these ends for us, America must secure them to herself; and must not become, as so many of your ministerial writers have predicted, a mass of divided powers, contending for territory and trade, cementing the slavery of peoples by their own blood.

Yet there was one dominant force in United States history that neither Turgot nor anyone foresaw in 1785: expansion. For a century to come, the subduing of the temperate regions of North America was to be the main business of the United States. In 1790 the boundaries of the republic included 800,000 square miles, in 1860 3 million. In 1790 the population was 4 million; in 1970 203 million. This folk movement, comparable in modern history only with the barbaric invasions of the Roman Empire, gives the history of the United States a different quality from that of Europe; different even from that of Canada and Australia, by reason of the absence of exterior control. The advancing frontier, with growing industrialism, set the rhythm of American society, colored its politics, and rendered more difficult the problem of union.

8

The Federalist Era

*

1789–1801

Organizing an Administration

The prospect for America seemed fair enough on that bright morning of 30 April 1789, when Washington, a picture of splendid manhood, stepped out onto the balcony overlooking Wall Street, New York, and took the oath: 'I do solemnly swear that I will faithfully execute the office of President of the United States and will, to the best of my ability, preserve, protect, and defend the Constitution of the United States.' His progress from Mount Vernon to New York had been a triumphal procession. His reception in the federal capital was tremendous—ships and batteries firing salutes, militia parades, civilians' cheers, triumphal arch, houses decorated. Not a single untoward note—no unrepentant tory raised a cheer for the king, no Antifederalist spat in the gutter as the President passed, no students paraded with signs saying 'George, go home!'

Yet Washington faced formidable problems. Every revolutionary government of Europe, even the Communist ones, has taken over a corps of functionaries and a treasury; but the Confederation left nothing but a dozen clerks, an empty treasury, and a burden of debt. No monies were coming in, no machinery for collecting taxes existed. The new Congress quickly imposed a customs tariff; but months elapsed before an administration could be created to collect it. Until a federal judiciary could be established, there was no means of enforcing any law. England and Spain controlled spheres of influence on United States territory, and a secession movement in the West threatened to split the Union along the crest of the Appalachians. The American army consisted of 672 officers and men; the navy had ceased to exist. However, economic conditions were vastly improved since the panic year 1786; and though that had been effected by good fortune and individual energy before the new government came into operation, the Federalists were quick to claim credit for the tide on which their ship was launched.

It is unlikely that the Constitution would have so soon acquired American loyalty if Washington had not consented to serve. The qualities that made him the first farmer and the first soldier in America also made him the first statesman. As landed proprietor no less than as commander-in-chief, he had shown executive ability; but we shall

George Washington (1732–99), by Edward Savage. On 21 December 1789, Washington wrote in his diary: 'Sat from ten to one o'clock for a Mr. Savage, to draw my Portrait for the University of Cambridge, in the State of Massachusetts.' (*Courtesy of Harvard University*)

underestimate the difficulties of his task if we forget that his superiority lay in character, not in talents. He had the power of inspiring trust, but not the gift of popularity; fortitude rather than flexibility; the power to think things through, not quick perception; dignity, but none of that brisk assertiveness which has often given inferior men political influence. The mask of reserve that concealed his inner life came from humility and stoical self-control, but a warm heart was revealed in numerous kindly acts. And beneath his cool surface there glowed a fire that under provocation would burst forth in immoderate laughter, astounding oaths, or Olympian anger.

Washington's character and prestige counted heavily in establishing the relationships of executive departments, a matter the Constitution purposely left vague. The heads of departments had to be appointed by the President with the consent of the Senate. But Congress, according to colonial usage, might have made them responsible to itself, and removable by the Senate. Instead, it made the secretaries of state and of war responsible to the President alone. Moreover, the Senate admitted that the President could remove officials without its consent. The effect was to make the entire administrative force and diplomatic service responsible to the chief magistrate.

For Secretary of State, Washington chose Thomas Jefferson, who had been a superb minister to France, and for the treasury Alexander Hamilton. Henry Knox, Washington's chief of artillery and Secretary of War under the Confederation, continued as such; and Governor Edmund Randolph of Virginia was appointed Attorney-General. The first President was unwilling to come to any vital decision without taking the advice of people in whom he had confidence. Hence arose the American cabinet. In 1793 there were some 46 meetings of the three secretaries and the Attorney-General at the President's house. These officials were already known collectively as the President's cabinet; but not until 1907 was the cabinet officially recognized as such by law. Washington made minor appointments conscientiously too. The federal civil service began with principles of efficiency and honesty that were in sharp contrast to the jobbery and corruption in Europe and in several states.

Although the first Senate of only 22 members was friendly to the administration, their chamber early developed that *esprit de corps* which has been the bane of willful presidents. 'Senatorial courtesy,' the practice of rejecting any nomination not approved by the senators from the nominee's own state, soon began. In the matter of treaties, however, the Senate's sense of its own dignity defeated its ambition. The Constitution grants the President power, 'by and with the advice and consent of the Senate, to make treaties, provided two-thirds of the senators present concur.' On one memorable occasion Washington appeared before the Senate, like the Secretary of Foreign Affairs in the House of Commons, to explain an Indian treaty and see it through. Hampered in freedom of debate by the august presence, the senators voted to refer the papers in question to a select committee. The President 'started up in a violent fret.' 'This defeats every purpose of my coming here,' he said. After that he dispensed with advice until a treaty was ready for ratification, a practice generally followed by his successors.

The Constitution left the judicial branch even more inchoate than the others. It remained for Congress to create and organize the inferior federal courts, to determine their procedure, and to provide a bridge between state and federal jurisdiction. All this was done by the Judiciary Act of 24 September 1789, the essential part of which is still in force. It provided for a Supreme Court consisting of a chief justice and five associate justices, for thirteen district courts, each consisting of a single federal judge, and three circuit courts, each consisting of two Supreme Court justices and the federal judge of the district where the court sat. One section of the law stipulated that a final judgment in the highest court of a state where the constitutionality of a treaty or statute of the United States is questioned 'may be re-examined and reversed or affirmed in the Supreme Court of the United States.' Without this section, every state judiciary could put its own construction on the Constitution, laws, and treaties of the Union. On 2 February 1790 the Supreme Court opened its first session, at New York. The judges assumed gowns of black and scarlet, but honored Jefferson's appeal to 'discard the monstrous wig which makes the English judges look like rats peeping through bunches of oakum.' Under Chief Justice John Jay the federal judiciary assumed its place as the keystone to the federal arch.

Hamilton's System

To attend to his relations with Congress, Washington found the right man, Alexander Hamilton, in the right office, the treasury. For the primary problems of Washington's first administration were fiscal. If the character of Washington fortified the new government, the genius of Hamilton enabled it to function successfully. No American equaled him in administrative genius; few surpassed him in maturity of judgment. As an undergraduate at King's (Columbia) College he had brilliantly defended the rights of the colonists. At 22 he had earned a place on Washington's staff. In his twenty-sixth year he wrote a remarkable treatise on public finance and commanded a storming party at Yorktown. Admitted to the New York bar at the conclusion of peace, he quickly rose to eminence in the law. With Madison he dominated the Annapolis convention; in the Federal Convention he played a spectacular though hardly a useful part. His contributions to *The Federalist* helped to obtain the ratification of a constitution in which he did not strongly believe. One of the greatest of Americans, he was the least American of his contemporaries: a statesman rather of the type of the younger Pitt, whose innate love of order and system was strengthened by the lack of those qualities among his fellow citizens. Intellectually disciplined himself, Hamilton was eager to play political schoolmaster.

The Constitution, he believed, could only be made an instrument for good and a guarantee of order by 'increasing the number of ligaments between the government and interests of individuals.' The old families, merchant-shipowners, public creditors, and financiers must be welded into a loyal governing class by a straightforward policy favoring their interests. As Thomas Cromwell fortified the Tudor monarchy by distributing confiscated land, so Hamilton would strengthen the Federal Government by giving the people who then controlled the country's wealth a distinct interest in its permanence. The rest, he assumed, would go along, as they always had.

In September 1789, ten days after he took office, the House of Representatives called upon Hamilton to prepare and report a plan for the 'adequate support of public credit.' The report was laid before the House at its next session in January 1790. Based on the tried expedients of English finance, it was worthy of an experienced minister of a long-established government. Hamilton first laid down principles of public economy, and then adduced arguments in support of them. America must have credit for industrial development, commercial activity, and the operations of government. Her future credit would depend on how she met her present obligations. Precise recommendations followed. The foreign debt and floating domestic debt, with arrears of interest, should be funded at par, and due provision should be made by import duties and excise taxes to provide interest and amortization. The war debts of the states should be assumed by the Federal Government in order to bind their creditors to the national interest. In a subsequent report, he urged the creation of a Bank of the United States, on the model of the Bank of England, but with the right to establish branches in different parts of the country.

This daring policy could not have been carried out by Hamilton alone. Every proposal was matured by the cool judgment of the President; and in House and Senate he found eager co-operation. Congress had already passed a customs tariff, with tonnage duties discriminating in favor of American shipping—both essential parts of Hamilton's system—and his other projects were altered and in some respects improved in the process of legislation. The foreign and domestic debt was funded at par, largely through loans from Dutch bankers. Most of the debts of the states were assumed by Congress, after a bitter struggle not unmixed with intrigue. The Bank of the United States was chartered, and its capital subscribed in four hours after the books were open. By August 1791, United States 6 per cents were selling above par in London and Amsterdam; and a wave of development and speculation had begun. 'Our public credit,' wrote

Alexander Hamilton (1755–1804). This portrait is by John Trumbull (1756–1843), son of a Connecticut governor and aide to Washington in the Continental army, who studied art in London under Benjamin West. He painted Hamilton several times. (*Library of Congress*)

Washington, 'stands on that ground, which three years ago it would have been considered as a species of madness to have foretold.'

At the end of that year Hamilton presented to Congress his Report on Manufactures. Alone of his state papers, this report fell flat; later it became an arsenal of protectionist arguments on both sides of the Atlantic. Hamilton believed that the government should intervene to strengthen the economy by fostering industry. He was addressing a country preponderantly rural, where manufactures were still in the household or handicraft stage, where only a few experimental factories existed, and not a single steam engine. Free trade, in view of the dearness of labor and the scarcity of capital, would mean very few American manufactures. Hamilton wished the government to protect infant industries, in order to induce artisans to emigrate, cause machinery to be invented, and employ woman and child labor. His aim here, too, was to brace the new republic by giving yet another interest group a stake in the government. He perceived that merchants and public creditors were too narrow a basis for a national governing class. He believed that manufactures might prosper in the South as well as in the North; the report was a distinct bid for Southern support over the heads of Jefferson and Madison. The South, however, regarded protection as another tax for Northern interests. Hamilton's argument would have been sound, nevertheless, had not Eli Whitney's invention of the cotton gin the following year made the culture of upland cotton a far more profitable employment for slave labor than manufactures.

All Hamilton's other plans were adopted. He turned dead paper into marketable securities and provided for their redemption by taxes that the nation was well able to bear. He set standards of honesty and punctuality that were invaluable for a people of crude financial conceptions. His youthful country, so lately on the verge of bankruptcy, acquired a credit such as few nations in Europe enjoyed. Yet Hamilton failed to achieve his ultimate end of consolidating the Union. Although he created an interested government party, his measures encountered a dangerous opposition. Instead of attaching new interests to the Federal Government, he endowed with fresh privileges those who were already attached to it.

To understand wherein Hamilton failed, we have only to glance at the effect of his measures on two commonwealths: Massachusetts and Virginia. The interests of Massachusetts were primarily maritime: fishermen who benefited by new bounties on dried codfish; foreign traders who benefited by the low tariff; and shipyards which were favored by discriminating tonnage duties. Merchants had invested heavily in government paper that gained enormously in value by the funding system. Since Massachusetts had the largest war debt of any state, she profited most from the assumption of state debts by the Federal Government. Maritime prosperity, percolating from the market towns to the interior, raised the price of country produce and healed the wounds of Shays's Rebellion. Boston, once the home of radical mobs, was now carried by the new Federalist party. The 'Essex Junto' of Massachusetts— Cabots, Higginsons, Lowells, and Jacksons, who had been to sea in their youth and viewed politics as from a quarter-deck—hailed Hamilton as their master and kept his flag flying in the Bay State long after his death. Allied with them were the solid men of Connecticut, New York City, and seaports to the southward. But Hamilton's policy did not touch the great mass of the American people. It would have been otherwise had the public debt remained in the hands of its original possessors; but farmers, discharged soldiers, petty shopkeepers, and the like who held government securities had been forced to part with them at a ruinous discount during the hard times that followed the end of the war. By 1789 the bulk of the public debt was held by the 'right people' at Philadelphia, New York, Charleston, and Boston; and the nation was taxed to pay at par for securities purchased at a tremendous discount.

By the same economic test, a system that appeared statesmanlike in Massachusetts seemed unwarranted in Virginia. The Virginia planter knew little of business and less of finance. A gentleman inherited his debts with his plantation, why then should debt trouble the United States? Why not pay it off at market value, as a gentleman compounds with his creditors? Some Virginians had sold their government I.O.U.'s as low as 15; why should they be taxed to pay other states' debts at 100? To men such as these, in love with 'republican virtue' and ignorant of the simplest principles of accounting, Hamilton's system looked like jobbery and corruption, as in England; might not it lead to monarchy as in England?

Patrick Henry drafted a remonstrance against the federal assumption of state debts which the Virginia Assembly adopted. Therein were expressed the misgivings of plain folk throughout the country, as well as those of the Virginia gentry:

In an agricultural country like this, . . . to erect, and concentrate, and perpetuate a large monied interest, is a measure which your memorialists apprehend must in the course of human events produce one or other of two evils, the prostration of agriculture at the feet of commerce, or a change in the present form of federal government, fatal to the existence of American liberty. . . . Your memorialists can find no clause in the Constitution authorizing Congress to assume the debts of the States!

A vision of civil war flashed across Hamilton's brain as he read this remonstrance. 'This is the first symptom,' he wrote, 'of a spirit which must either be killed, or will kill the Constitution of the United States.'

Virginia could hardly form an opposition party without aid from some of her citizens who were highly placed in the Federal Government. Washington, national in his outlook, signed every bill based on Hamilton's recommendations. Richard Henry Lee, elected to the Senate as an Antifederalist, became a convert to Hamilton's views. Thomas Jefferson, Secretary of State, and James Madison, leader of the House, wavered—but found the Virginia candle stronger than the Hamiltonian star.

Enter Jefferson

When Jefferson took up his post as Secretary of State, ambition to found a political party was remote from his mind. 'If I could not go to heaven but with a party, I would not go there at all,' he wrote. Yet his name and reputation are indissol-

ubly bound up with the party that he was destined to lead.

Jefferson was twelve years older than Hamilton, much more experienced, and far more versatile. He was easily the first American architect of his generation. Monticello, his Virginia mansion, designed by him and superbly located on a hill-top facing the Blue Ridge, has remained one of the most admirable country estates in America. The best group of collegiate buildings in the country, at nearby Charlottesville, was designed by him. Jefferson wrote upon Neo-Platonism, the pronunciation of Greek, Anglo-Saxon, the future of steam engines, archaeology, and theology. But there was one subject of which he was ignorant, and that was Hamilton's specialty, finance.

Hamilton wished to concentrate power; Jefferson, to diffuse it. Hamilton feared anarchy and cherished order; Jefferson feared tyranny and cherished liberty. Hamilton believed republican government could only succeed if directed by a governing class; Jefferson, that republicanism required a democratic base. Hamilton took the gloomy Hobbesian view of human nature; Jefferson, a more hopeful view: the people, he believed, were the safest and most virtuous, though not always the wisest, depository of power; education would perfect their wisdom. Hamilton would encourage shipping and manufactures; Jefferson would have America remain a nation of farmers. All those differences were bracketed by two opposed conceptions of what America was and might be. Jefferson shared the idealistic conception of the new world to which Turgot had paid homage—an agrarian republic of mild laws and equal opportunity, asylum to the oppressed and beacon-light of freedom, renouncing wealth and commerce to preserve simplicity and equality. To Hamilton this was mischievous nonsense. Having assimilated the traditions of the New York gentry into which he had married, he believed that the only choice for America lay between a stratified society on the English model and a squalid 'mobocracy.' Jefferson, who knew Europe, where every man was 'either hammer or anvil,' wished America to be as unlike it as possible; Hamilton, who had never left America, wished to make his country a new Europe.

Their appearance was as much of a contrast as their habits of mind. Hamilton's neat, lithe, dapper figure, and air of brisk energy, went with his tight, compact, disciplined brain. He could not have composed a classic state paper such as the Declaration of Independence; yet Jefferson's mind in comparison was somewhat untidy, constantly gathering new facts and making fresh syntheses. 'His whole figure has a loose, shackling air,' wrote Senator Maclay in 1790. 'I looked for gravity, but a laxity of manner seemed shed about him.' His discourse 'was loose and rambling and yet he scattered information wherever he went, and some even brilliant sentiments sparkled from him.' His sandy complexion, hazel eyes, and much-worn clothes played up this impression of careless ease; whilst Hamilton glowed with vigor and intensity. Women found him irresistible, but they did not care much for Jefferson.

Jefferson assumed his duties as Secretary of State in March 1790, when Hamilton's financial policy was almost a year old and government circles were ringing with his praises. Jefferson approved the payment of the domestic and foreign debt at par, and he secured adoption of Hamilton's program for the assumption of the state debts by making a deal by which the federal capital would be removed southward to the new city of Washington, after a ten-year interval at Philadelphia. Jefferson persuaded two Virginia congressmen to vote for assumption, and Hamilton rounded up Yankee votes for the Potomac. But from the date of Hamilton's report recommending a national bank (13 December 1790), Jefferson's attitude began to change. When the President called on his cabinet for opinions on the constitutionality of the bank bill, Jefferson, foreshadowing the 'strict construction' school, declared that it was unconstitutional. He contended that the congressional power 'to make all laws necessary and proper for carrying into execution' its delegated powers did not include laws merely convenient for such purposes. A national bank was not strictly necessary—the existing state bank at Philadelphia could be used for government funds. Hamilton replied with a nationalistic, 'loose construction' interpretation:

Every power vested in a government is in its nature sovereign, and includes by force of the term, a right to employ all the means requisite . . . to the attainment of the ends of such power. . . . If the end be clearly comprehended within any of the specified powers, and if the measure have an obvious relation to that end, and is not forbidden by any particular provision of the Constitution, it may safely be deemed to come within the compass of the national authority.

A bank, he said, has a relation to the specified powers of collecting taxes, paying salaries, and servicing the debt. This opinion satisfied Washington, and he signed the bank bill; it only needed the clarifying process of Chief Justice Marshall's brain to become the great opinion of 1819, which read the doctrine of implied powers into the Constitution.

Jefferson was neither silenced nor convinced. The Federal Constitution, from his point of view and Madison's, was being perverted into a consolidated, national government. To what end? Before many months elapsed, the two Virginians thought they knew. Hamilton was simply juggling money out of the pockets of the poor into those of the rich, building up through financial favors a corrupt control of Congress; and 'the ultimate object of all this was to prepare the way for a change from the present republican form of government to that of monarchy, of which the English constitution is to be the model.' Jefferson's suspicions were deepened by the brisk speculation in lands, bank stock, and government funds that began in 1790. Northern speculators combed the countryside for depreciated paper, and several associates of Hamilton's were implicated in shady transactions. Jefferson did not, however, create an opposition; he joined and organized the elements of opposition.

The Birth of Parties

Political parties were in bad odor at the end of the eighteenth century. No provision for party government had been made in the Constitution, although parties or factions existed in all states as in all the colonies. Ought Jefferson to resign from the cabinet, leaving Hamilton in undisputed con-

Thomas Jefferson (1743–1826). This portrait is by the English-born Thomas Sully (1783–1872), who studied with the great American artist Gilbert Stuart. Sully, who not only painted four American Presidents but Queen Victoria, was said to perceive an aristocrat in every subject who sat for him. (*American Philosophical Society*)

trol? Was it proper for him openly to support opposition to a policy that Washington had accepted? The President, believing that every month and year the government endured was so much gained for stability, endeavored to keep the smouldering fire from bursting forth. Both were entreated to remain in office, and both consented. But Jefferson, believing Hamilton's policy to be dangerous, used every means short of open opposition to check it; while Hamilton spared no effort to thwart Jefferson.

The first national parties developed out of contests in Congress over Hamilton's financial program. Hamilton's partisans became known as 'Federalists.' (They should not be confused with the Federalists who had supported the Constitution in the ratification struggle; divisions over Hamilton's policies did not coincide with those over ratification.) Madison raised an opposition to Hamilton's system, and for the next seven years Madison, not Jefferson, would lead the 'Republican' interest. Disagreement over the Hamiltonian program broke on sectional lines. On the proposal to establish the Bank, southern members of the House voted 19–6 against, northern members 33–1 for. In February 1791, Jefferson wrote: 'There is a vast mass of discontent gathered in the South, and how and when it will break God knows.' Yet if Madison and Jefferson hoped to build an effective opposition, they needed backing outside their section.

A very important step toward forming an opposition party was an understanding between Virginia malcontents and those of New York. That large state was still divided into two factions. The one that interested Jefferson was led by Governor George Clinton (son of an Irish immigrant), the Livingston clan, and Attorney-General Aaron Burr. Opposed was the 'aristocratic' party of De Lanceys, Van Rensselaers, and General Schuyler, whose daughter Hamilton had married. Clinton, having bet on the wrong horse in opposing the Federal Constitution, obtained neither the vice-presidency, to which he felt he was entitled, nor any federal patronage. He wanted Virginia's support, and the Virginians needed his. On a 'botanizing excursion' that led Jefferson and Madison up the Hudson in the

summer of 1791, they undoubtedly found occasion to study *Clintonia borealis*. In 1792 Republican leaders took a significant stride toward party organization in agreeing on Clinton as their vice-presidential choice, and Virginia, North Carolina, and New York gave their second electoral votes to him for Vice-President, as against John Adams. In that same election, the President was unanimously re-elected.

Washington began his new term in March 1793, in the shadow of the revolution in France, which soon precipitated all floating elements of political dissension into two national parties. For a long time America looked upon the French Revolution with the keenest sympathy. Lafayette, Tom Paine, and the Declaration of Rights seemed to make that revolution a continuation of ours. But in April 1793 came long-delayed news that brought the danger of war to America's shores and made the French Revolution an issue in American politics. France had declared war on Great Britain and Spain; the king had been guillotined; and Citizen Genet was coming over as minister plenipotentiary of the French Republic. America was still, formally, an ally of France. In the treaty of 1778 the United States had guaranteed France possession of her West Indian islands. As the British navy was certain to attack them, it was difficult to see how America could honorably refuse to defend them, if France demanded it. But how defend them without a navy? And did one want to?

On 18 April 1793 the cabinet met at Philadelphia. Washington, though dismayed at the turn of events, still wished the French well, but thought of his own country first. Hamilton loathed the French Revolution. It was disconcerting, just when there seemed some hope of America's settling down, to have America's favorite nation blow up and invite everyone else to follow suit! He wished to declare the treaty of 1778 in suspense now that the king was dead, declare American neutrality, and reject the French minister. Jefferson considered the French Revolution 'the most sacred cause that ever man was engaged in,' but was equally anxious to keep America out of the war. However, he opposed an immediate declaration of neutrality, mainly because he regarded

American neutrality, without some equivalent, as a free gift to England that she would receive only with contempt. To Washington such bargaining seemed unworthy of a self-respecting nation. Accordingly, on 22 April 1793, the President issued a neutrality proclamation. It declared the 'disposition of the United States' to 'pursue a conduct friendly and impartial toward the belligerent powers,' and warned citizens that 'aiding or abetting hostilities,' or unneutral acts committed within the country, would render them liable to prosecution.

In the meantime Citizen Genet, quaintest of the many curious diplomatists sent by European governments to the United States, had landed at Charleston. Genet's instructions called upon him to use the United States as a base for privateering; and before presenting his credentials he undertook to fit out privateers against British commerce. He was instructed to recruit forces for the conquest of Florida and Louisiana, 'and perhaps add to the American constellation the fair star of Canada.' Several land speculators like George Rogers Clark, who had some dubious claims to Western land still held by Spain, showed great enthusiasm for war with that country. To them Genet distributed military commissions, forming the nucleus of an *Armée du Mississippi* and an *Armée des Florides.* In other words, France expected the same sort of aid from her sister republic that she herself had given, aid which was as certain to embroil the giver with Britain. But even Jefferson, though he welcomed the arrival of Genet as a sort of refresher for the opposition party, enforced Washington's neutrality policy with even-handed justice.

When Genet found he could do nothing with the government, he conceived the brilliant notion of turning it out. His official notes became inconceivably truculent. In Charleston he had presided at the birth of a local Jacobin club, whose legitimacy was recognized by the parent organization at Paris; and his progress through the states was marked by similar progeny. After a few weeks of him, Jefferson concluded that Genet was likely to become the Jonah of the Jeffersonian party. In August 1793 the cabinet unanimously voted to request his recall. Robespierre gladly consented,

and in return asked for the recall of Gouverneur Morris, whose intrigues at Paris had been almost as mischievous as Genet's in Philadelphia. Early in 1794 a new French minister arrived in the United States, with an order for his predecessor's arrest. Instead of returning to feed the guillotine, Genet married the daughter of Governor Clinton and settled down to the life of a country gentleman on the Hudson.

That year, 1794, witnessed a marked acceleration in the trend toward the emergence of two national parties, a development which almost everyone viewed with dismay. Each party thought the other seditious, and even treasonable, because in a well-ordered society there could be no place for a party system. The nation was alarmed at feelings so intense that congressmen would not live in the same boarding house with a member of the opposite party, and a Republican had to take care not to stop at a Federal tavern. Not for a generation would the country recognize that parties were a medium for the expression of the popular will, that they encouraged voters to make use of the franchise, and that they enabled groups out of power to channelize their grievances.

Party divisions sharpened in Congress before they did in the states, where in 1792 party organization was still so rudimentary that only New York and Pennsylvania offered slates. But in Congress, party discipline was much more marked. In January 1793 the Federalist Fisher Ames wrote: 'Virginia moves in a solid column, and the discipline of the party is as severe as the Prussian. Dissenters are not spared. Madison is become a desperate party leader.' At the end of 1793, Jefferson retired, pleased to be rid of the 'hated occupations of politics,' and Madison, 'the great man of the party,' now took full responsibility for leading the opposition. In 1794, John Taylor of Virginia observed: 'The existence of two parties in Congress, is apparent. . . . Whether the subject be foreign or domestic—relative to war or peace—navigation or commerce—the magnetism of opposite views draws them wide as the poles asunder.'

By 1794, party warfare, which had originated over the domestic problem of Hamiltonian finance, was coming increasingly to center on for-

Thomas Paine (1737–1809), the revolutionary pamphleteer. This portrait, by A. Millière after George Romney, includes, lower left, two of Tom Paine's most influential works, *Common Sense* (1776) and *The Rights of Man* (1791–92). (*National Portrait Gallery, London*)

eign affairs. The French Revolution seemed to some a clear-cut contest between monarchy and republicanism, oppression and liberty, autocracy and democracy; to others, simply a new breaking-out of the eternal strife between anarchy and order, atheism and religion, poverty and property. The former joined the Republican party; the latter, the Federalist. In reverse order to expectation, democratic New England and the Eastern seaports, rivals to Liverpool and Bristol, became the headquarters of pro-British Federalists; whilst the landed interest, particularly in

136

slave-holding communities, became gallo-maniacs. For in New England the clergy had been worrying over the younger generation: students who preferred Voltaire to Jonathan Edwards. Tom Paine's *Age of Reason* appeared in 1794. That scurrilous arraignment of the Bible sent liberal Christians hotfoot to the standard of reaction, eager for anything to exclude 'French infidelity.' Paine himself, by a nasty attack on Washington the next year, completely identified Jeffersonianism with Jacobinism in the mind of the average New Englander and Middle-State Presbyterian.

Federalism flourished in sight of salt water. In the older seaboard communities, social cleavages were more marked. Moreover, to merchant shipowners of the coastal towns, British capital was indispensable and commerce with Britain the first condition of prosperity. Like Hamilton, they did not care to risk a quarrel with the power that could give or withhold credit. During the entire period of the French war, shipowners could make immense profits by submitting to British sea-power when they could not evade it; whilst French attacks on neutral commerce tended to destroy the only traffic that the British navy permitted.

Thus it came about that great Virginia planters of English race and tradition—men like John Randolph of Roanoke who would wear no boots unless made in London and read no Bible printed outside Oxford, men whose throats would have been the first cut and whose lands the first divided if Jacobinism had really infected America—screamed for the Rights of Man and railed at Britain. Thus it came about that Boston Unitarians, like William Ellery Channing, whose creed was more subversive of traditional Christianity than the crude outbursts of the Paris commune, rang the tocsin against French impiety and anarchy. Around these two poles American opinion crystallized in 1793–95. It was not Britain and France corrupting American opinion, but American merchants and farmers stretching out to Europe for support. As a French observer wrote, 'Each party will use foreign influence as it needs, to dominate.'

Neutral Rights, the West, and Jay's Treaty

Late in 1793, just as Genet's antics had cooled American ardor for France, Britain took two actions that threw fresh, dry timber on the hot embers of Anglo-American relations. Lord Grenville informed the American minister in London that the British government proposed to hold the Northwest posts indefinitely, abandoning all pretense that they would be evacuated when the United States gave full satisfaction for the debts. Washington's patience, Jefferson's forbearance, and Hamilton's long, uphill pull toward good understanding had apparently come to naught. What was left but war? At the same time the burning issue of Atlantic commerce was flaring a like signal. The weaker naval powers had long endeavored to safeguard neutral rights in wartime, with the doctrines of effective blockade, limited contraband, and 'free ships make free goods.' As a neutral in the war of the French Revolution, America hoped to benefit by these principles. But on 6 November 1793 a British order in council of unprecedented severity directed the detention and adjudication of all ships laden with French colonial produce, whether French or neutral property, and all vessels carrying provisions to the French colonies. If a Maine schooner laden with lumber and salt fish ventured into the harbor of St. George's, Bermuda, she would be boarded by a gang of ruffians, stripped of her rudder and sails, her seamen consigned to a calaboose or impressed into the Royal Navy, and the vessel condemned.

Incensed at these developments, Congress began preparations for war. In the midst of the crisis, news leaked of a truculent speech by Governor Lord Dorchester of Canada to an Indian delegation, encouraging them to look for the king's aid shortly in driving the 'long knives' across the Ohio for good and all. In Congress the Republican party was not eager for war, but favored Jefferson's and Madison's favorite plan of commercial retaliation, which would surely have led to war. Matters were prevented from going further by a timely British gesture—revocation of the order in council. This information was communicated to Congress on 4 April 1794; and on the 16th, Washington nominated Chief Justice Jay as envoy extraordinary to Great Britain.

An American military victory expedited the achievement of a main object of Jay's mission: to obtain British evacuation of the Northwest posts. In August 1794 at the Battle of the Fallen Timbers, United States forces under 'Mad Anthony' Wayne overwhelmed an alliance of Indians, who had been incited by the British. Fort Wayne was built at the forks of the Maumee, and on 3 August 1795 the General signed the Treaty of Greenville. By this treaty the Indians ceded the southeastern corner of the Northwest territory, together with sixteen enclaves such as Detroit, and the site of Chicago, in return for annuities to the value of some $10,000. So ended almost twenty years of fighting—the last phase of the War of Independence. Peace came to the border from the Genesee country of New York to the Mississippi. Pioneers began to swarm up the valleys of the Scioto and the Muskingum, and in ten years' time their insatiable greed for land made the Treaty of Greenville a scrap of paper.

The Battle of the Fallen Timbers occurred while John Jay was negotiating in London. Jay's treaty, signed on 19 November 1794, obtained the prime objects of the mission—a promise to evacuate the Northwest posts by 1796, and a limited right of American vessels to trade with the British West Indies. It preserved the peace, secured America's territorial integrity, and established a basis for Western expansion. Other pending questions were referred to mixed commissions, in accordance with which a beginning was made of settling the Maine-New Brunswick boundary. Some £600,000 was eventually paid by the United States in satisfaction of pre-war debts, and £1,317,000 by Great Britain for illegal captures of American ships.

Yet when the terms of this treaty were printed in Philadelphia (March 1795) a howl of rage went up from all sections, especially from the West, that Jay had sold them down-river. It is difficult now to understand why, unless the treaty provided an emotional outlet for varied discontents. A good part of the opposition was simply the French 'party line' being repeated by Republican journals, for the pact prevented a war on which the

French were counting. A bare two-thirds majority for the treaty was obtained in the Senate, but the House of Representatives threatened to nullify it by withholding funds for the mixed commissions.

The fight over appropriations for the Jay Treaty in the House marked the crystallization of the party system. The Federalist administration appealed to the more substantial classes to bring pressure on their representatives, and petitions from merchants in support of the treaty had a telling effect. Washington's popularity also served the Federalists well. A member of the Virginia legislature cried: 'Gracious heaven, is this the return which you are about to make to a man who has dedicated his whole life to your service?' By the narrow vote of 51–48, the House agreed to carry out the treaty, and Michilimackinac, the last frontier post, was evacuated on 2 October 1796, thirteen years after the treaty of peace.

Jay's treaty also came as a clearing breeze to American relations with Spain, which had been carrying out intrigues in the West. In the Treaty of San Lorenzo (27 October 1795), known as Pinckney's treaty after the American minister, His Catholic Majesty granted the right to navigate the lower Mississippi, as well as the 'right of deposit' at New Orleans so ardently desired by the West; and recognized the thirty-first parallel to the Chattahoochee as the southern boundary of the United States. In 1798, after exhausting all its rich resources in procrastination, Spain evacuated the posts it held north of lat. 31°. Thus, fifteen years in all elapsed before the United States obtained control of her own territories from European powers.

The Whiskey Rebellion

In the very week that Wayne crushed the Indians, President Washington was calling out 15,000 militia to put down pale-faced rebels in western Pennsylvania. This 'Whiskey Rebellion' of 1794 tested the ability of the Federal Government to enforce federal law. Hamilton's Excise Act of 1791 appeared as tyrannical to the Westerners as had the Stamp Act to the colonists. Beyond the mountains distillation was the practical way to dispose of surplus corn. Whiskey also did duty as currency—one-gallon jugs of 'moonshine' passing for a quarter in every store on the western slope of the Alleghenies. Covenants were formed never to pay the hated tax. Led by two backwoods firebrands, the people appointed a committee of public safety and called out the militia of the four western counties to protect spirituous liberties. The governor of Pennsylvania, an old Antifederalist, minimized the affair and long refused to lend the aid of state forces.

Washington, on Hamilton's urgent plea, decided to make a test case of the defiance of federal law. Everything worked smoothly. The militia of four states, including Pennsylvania, turned out upon the President's proclamation. They were given a good stiff hike across the Alleghenies in the glorious Indian summer. The more violent leaders of the rebels fled, and the covenanters promptly caved in. Two of the ringleaders were apprehended and convicted of treason. But they were pardoned by the President, thereby ending the final episode in the only armed challenge to the authority of the new government.

Public Land Act of 1796

Now that Jay's treaty and Wayne's victory had caused the gates of the frontier to swing open, it was time to decide how land ceded by the Indians should be disposed of. An American colonial policy had been determined once and for all by the Northwest Ordinance of 1787, but the land policy blocked out in the Ordinance of 1785 was not binding on the Federal Government. Hamilton wanted to slow migration to the West because you could not develop manufactures with labor running off to the backwoods. If the demand for Western land could not be resisted, speculators wished to have it sold in large blocks. But others urged that land be within the reach of all, and that an orderly system of disposition be established to encourage compact settlement that would enable pioneers to obtain good schools and social intercourse. For the most part, those who favored the pattern of the Ordinance of 1785 prevailed.

In the Public Land Act of 1796 the township, six miles square, surveyed in compact 'ranges' or columns, starting on the western boundary of Pennsylvania, became the standard unit of public land, divided into thirty-six sections of one square mile (640 acres) each, no land to be surveyed prior to extinguishing the Indian title of occupancy, or placed on sale until surveyed. This system set the pattern of the American West. Ranges, townships, and sections marched across the continent with the pioneer, imposing their rigid rectangles on forest, plain, and mountain. The question of whether to sell the land in large plots or small was determined by a compromise. The Act of 1796 required alternate townships to be sold in blocks of eight sections each, intervening townships in single sections of 640 acres each. Both large and small lots were sold at public auction for the minimum price of two dollars an acre and one year's credit. The smallest unit, 640 acres, turned out to be too large and the minimum price too high for the ordinary pioneer. So Congress lowered the unit of sale in certain areas to 320 acres (in 1804 to 160 acres), and gave four years' credit. As thus amended the 1796 law was copied for every new acquisition from the Indians in the Northwest Territory until 1820. When Ohio, the first 'public land state,' was admitted in 1803, the Federal Government adopted the precedent of retaining title to all ungranted land within the state boundaries, excepting a donation of one section in each township to a state fund for education.

Until 1825 the Northwest frontier was advanced not so much by settlers as by adventurers. The pioneers seldom acquired a land title, and remained in one spot only long enough to kill off the game, or exhaust their clearings by crude cropping with rude implements, before moving farther west. They acted as a shock battalion for the permanent settlers who followed and provided the trained scouts and sharpshooters for Indian wars. Their wild, free life gave America much of its gusto and savor. They left two legacies—a taint of lawlessness and violence, and the robust tradition of individual prowess which has created America's favorite 'image' of herself.

Pater Patriae

Organizing a government, establishing national credit, fostering maritime commerce, recovering territory withheld under the Confederation, crushing red rebels and white, creating a land policy which set the rhythm of American society, and preserving peace: these were the notable achievements of the two administrations of President Washington. By refusing to run for a third term he established the two-term tradition, and on 17 September 1796, he summed up his political experience in a farewell address to his countrymen. An eloquent plea for union was followed by a pointed exposition of disruptive tendencies, including the 'baneful effects of the spirit of party.' As to foreign policy, the United States should not indulge 'habitual hatred or an habitual fondness' toward any nation and ought to 'steer clear of permanent alliances, with any portion of the foreign world.'

Washington's valedictory, which Hamilton had played an important part in drafting, served as a Federalist campaign document in 1796. For all his abhorrence of parties, Washington was a shrewd political strategist, and the passages in the Address on foreign affairs were aimed at the Republicans' fondness for the French alliance. To succeed Washington, the Federalists informally settled on Vice-President John Adams. Early in 1796, Adams wrote to his wife: 'I am, as you say, quite a favorite. . . . I am heir apparent you know, and a succession is soon to take place.'

The national leaders of the Republican party, centered in Congress, nominated Thomas Jefferson as their standard bearer, without consulting him. Jefferson reported: 'My name . . . was again brought forward, without concert or expectation on my part; (on my salvation I declare it).' Most of the Republicans' second choice votes went to Aaron Burr, but party lines were still so slack that ballots for the second place were widely scattered. Republicans, many of whom wore the tricolored cockade, sought to rally pro-French sentiment in a campaign in which the French ministry actively intervened. The result was a narrow Federalist victory, with the Federalists strong in the Northeast and the Republicans in the South. Adams obtained the Presidency with 71 electoral votes. Jefferson's 68 votes made him Vice-President by the curious method of choice that prevailed prior to the adoption of Amendment XII. After the election, Federalists rejoiced that the 'French party is fallen.' How wrong they were!

'Washington and Liberty.' As this primitive oil painting of the first decade of the nineteenth century reveals, Washington had already become an icon. Miss Liberty places a wreath upon his bust as she treads on the crown, symbol of the old monarchical order. (*New York State Historical Association*)

A generation passed before Washington's services in time of peace were adequately appreciated. As his personality faded into legend, it became clothed in military uniform. Yet Washington's unique place in history rests not only on his leadership in war and his influence in organizing the Federal Government; not merely on his integrity, good judgment, and magnanimity, but also on his courageous stand for peace when his countrymen were clamoring to embark on an unnecessary war with England. This quiet, plain-speaking gentleman of Virginia glimpsed a truth hidden from more talented contemporaries: that the means by which a nation advances are as important as the ends which it pursues.

The Quasi-War with France

Washington left the country one final legacy: an example of the peaceful transfer of power in a new nation. After the inauguration of John Adams on 4 March 1797, a South Carolinian wrote: 'The change of the Executive here has been wrought with a facility and a calm which has astonished even those of us who always augured well of the government and the general good sense of our citizens. . . . John Adams was quietly sworn into office, George Washington attending as a private citizen. A few days after he went quietly home to Mt. Vernon; his successor as quietly took his place.'

This peaceful transition contrasted especially favorably with the turbulence in France, where all political leaders friendly to the United States had been guillotined or were in exile. The Directory, a five-headed executive, regarded Jay's treaty as evidence of an Anglo-American entente; for by accepting the British view of neutral rights, the United States had to order French privateers out of her harbors and to permit the British to capture provision ships destined for France. In retaliation, the Directory loosed its corsairs against the American merchant fleet, refused to receive the new American minister, and employed insolent official language toward the United States. President Adams declared that he would submit to no further indignities, but hoped to maintain Washington's policy of neutrality. To assure the Repub-

licans that he was not seeking a quarrel, Adams appointed Elbridge Gerry to a mission to France; and in order to keep Gerry out of mischief, John Marshall and C. C. Pinckney were joined with him.

In the meantime, party cleavage deepened. When Jefferson arrived in Philadelphia to take the oath of office as Vice-President in March 1797, he noted that party animosity was so intense that 'men who have been intimate all their lives, cross the streets to avoid meeting, and turn their heads another way, lest they should be obliged to touch their hats.' Jefferson, who had played a relatively passive role in party contests since 1794, now took over the reins of party leadership from Madison and Gallatin. Fearing that Adams intended war with France, he used his influence in Congress to frustrate the President.

While the Republicans refused to believe that the French government had changed its character since 1792, the Federalists regarded France as a menace, subversive to moral order and aggressive in intent. Though the fears of the Federalists were exaggerated, French designs on Canada, Louisiana, and Florida were actually more dangerous than even the Federalists suspected. The Directory sought to surround the United States with French territory and push back her boundaries to the Appalachians by coercing Spain to cede the Floridas and Louisiana to France and by seizing Canada. Not only the Federalists but Republicans too were outraged by the French response to Adams's diplomatic mission. When the American peace commission arrived in Paris, Talleyrand, the Directory's minister of foreign affairs, sent some hangers-on (referred to in dispatches as X, Y, and Z) to play on the fears of the American envoys and sound their pockets. A substantial bribe for Talleyrand and a $10 million loan on doubtful security as compensation for President Adams's 'insulting' message were prerequisites to negotiation. Pressed for an alternative, Monsieur Y hinted at the power of the French party in America, and recalled the fate of other recalcitrant nations.

The envoys' dispatches, rendering a detailed account of their Paris contacts, were submitted by President Adams to Congress and published in April 1798. On the Republicans the effect was

stupefying. 'Trimmers dropt off from the party like windfalls from an apple tree in September,' wrote Fisher Ames. Jefferson 'thought it his duty to be silent.' 'Millions for Defence, but not One Cent for Tribute' became the toast of the day.

President Adams's object was to teach the Directory good manners. He would accept war if declared by France, but hoped to avoid it. The bulk of his party agreed. Hamilton and the New England Federalists, on the contrary, regarded the French imbroglio not as an affair to be wound up, but as a starting-point for spirited measures that would strengthen the Federal Government, discipline the American people, and discredit the Republicans. For this reason, no less than to meet an expected French invasion, the regular army was increased, and Washington was appointed Lieutenant-General, with Hamilton his second in command. Congress created a navy department, and in a quasi-war at sea the French picaroons were fairly swept out of West Indian waters.

Repression and High Ambition

While organizing defense and drumming up war enthusiasm, the Federalists did not neglect their enemies at home. The Naturalization, Alien, and Sedition Acts of 1798 were aimed at domestic disaffection as much as at foreign danger. These laws provoked the first organized state-rights movement under the Constitution and helped promote the election of Jefferson to the presidency.

Gouverneur Morris had remarked in the Federal Convention that he wanted none of 'those philosophical gentlemen, those citizens of the world as they call themselves, in our public councils.' The French Revolution, however, sent a good many of them to America; and one who came earlier, Albert Gallatin of Geneva, was leading the congressional minority in 1798. Dr. Joseph Priestley, accused of trying 'to decompose both Church and State' with his chemical formulas, had found refuge in Pennsylvania after being mobbed as pro-French in England. Thomas Cooper, who followed him, founded a Republican newspaper. At the height of excitement in 1798, the Directory requested passports for a delegation

John Adams (1735–1826). He had the honor of serving as the first Vice-President of the United States, but, with characteristic acerbity, he wrote his wife Abigail: 'My country has in its wisdom contrived for me the most insignificant office that ever the invention of man contrived or his imagination conceived.' This portrait is by Mather Brown (1761–1831), a descendant of the Puritan Mathers who won renown in England as well as in America. (Boston Athenaeum)

from the Institute of France under Du Pont de Nemours to visit the United States 'with the view of improving and extending the sciences.' John Adams replied, 'We have too many French philosophers already, and I really begin to think, or rather to suspect, that learned academies . . . have disorganized the world, and are incompatible with social order.' As these were the persons whom super-patriots wished to expel in 1798, it is interesting to note that Gallatin became one of our greatest statesmen, Priestley a notable figure in the history of science, Cooper a college president; whilst the Du Ponts settled in Delaware and have since engaged in the highly respectable manufacture of plastics and explosives.

Immigrants who were neither philosophers nor gentlemen troubled the Federalists even more. French agents were stirring up sedition in the West, and Irish refugees from the rebellion of '98 lost no time in becoming citizens and joining the anti-British party. Congress responded with the Naturalization Act of 1798, which increased the required period of residence for citizenship from five to fourteen years, and the Alien Act, which gave the President power to expel foreigners by executive decree. Adams never availed himself of the privilege; but two shiploads of Frenchmen left the country in anticipation that he would.

The Sedition Act of 1798 declared a misdemeanor, punishable by fine or imprisonment, any speech or writing against President or Congress 'with the intent to defame' or to bring them 'into contempt or disrepute.' Federalists never recognized the legitimacy of party opposition; from their quarterdeck view the Republicans were little better than mutineers. In the Sedition Act prosecutions, every defendant was a Republican, every judge and almost every juror a Federalist. About twenty-five persons were arrested and ten convicted, most of them Republican editors who were conveniently got out of the way by heavy fines or jail sentences.

Akin to the sedition prosecutions was the severe action taken against John Fries, a Pennsylvania German auctioneer who headed an 'insurrection' against the direct tax. This real estate tax, laid to pay for the new army and navy, was the most unpopular feature of the Federalist defense program. 'Captain' Fries, armed with sword and pistol and wearing a French tricolor cockade, led a company of about fifty countrymen who chased all the federal tax collectors out of Bucks County and liberated prisoners from the Bethlehem jail. He was tried for treason in Philadelphia and sentenced to death, but pardoned by the President.

All this was labeled by the Jeffersonians 'The Federalist Reign of Terror.' Looked at in the perspective of history, it was nothing of the sort; the phrase itself was mere humbug. Nobody was drowned, hanged, or tortured, nobody went before a firing squad. A few scurrilous journalists were silenced, a few received terms in jail; but the rest went right on attacking the government, defending the French, and sneering at the United States Navy. Nobody was prevented from voting against the Federalists in the next elections, state or national.

Two startling protests to the Alien and Sedition Acts came from state legislatures: the Virginia Resolves drafted by Madison, and those of Kentucky drafted by Jefferson. Both declared the objectionable laws unconstitutional. As to the Alien Act, undoubtedly the power of expelling aliens belongs to the Federal Government, not to the states. The Sedition Act stands in a different light, for the Constitution (Amendment I) forbids Congress to pass any law abridging the freedom of speech, or of the press. The Resolves developed the 'compact' or 'state rights' theory of the Constitution that Jefferson had adumbrated in his opinion on the bank bill in 1792. Kentucky declared that whenever Congress palpably transcends its powers, as in the Sedition Act, each state 'has an equal right to judge for itself, as well of infractions as of the mode and measure of redress.' She called upon her 'co-states' to 'concur . . . in declaring these acts' void, and to unite 'in requesting their repeal.' Virginia hinted at 'interposing' state authority between the persecuted citizen and his government. Exactly what Madison meant by 'interposing' is uncertain; he later explained that he meant nothing more than strong protest.

In the spring of 1799 Adams made a startling move to ease the crisis by attempting to bring the quasi-war with France to an end. The President had become increasingly alarmed by the acts and the ambitions of Hamilton and the 'High' Federalists. Hamilton, the power behind Adams's administration, was mulling over a grandiose plan. He would lead the new American army over-land against New Orleans and march into Mexico while the South American patriot Miranda, helped by the British, would liberate the Spanish Main. Hamilton would return laurel-crowned, at the head of his victorious legion, to become the First Citizen of America, as Bonaparte was already the First Citizen of France. But the Hamiltonians reckoned without the President. John Adams, in no sense a democrat, regarded Jefferson's belief in the common man's innate virtue as sentimental nonsense; but he was equally hostile to anything resembling plutocracy or militarism. In March 1799 he suddenly awoke to the dangers into which the ship of state was drifting; and, taking the country completely by surprise, the President nominated a minister plenipotentiary to France. Little came of the mission, which ultimately involved three envoys, but, to the fury of Hamilton and the High Federalists, Adams's move stalled the war program completely.

The Election of 1800–1801

If the French had been so accommodating as to land even a corporal's guard on American soil, or a 'seditious alien' had been caught in a real plot, the presidential election of 1800 might have gone very differently; but as time went on, and no enemy appeared, and the new direct tax was assessed, the patriotic fervor of 1798 faded. As a result, the Republican ticket of Jefferson and Burr triumphed over the Federalist slate of John Adams and Charles Cotesworth Pinckney of the XYZ mission. However, since not one of the electors dared

throw away his second vote, Jefferson and Burr tied for first place with 73 votes each, as against 65 for Adams and 64 for Pinckney. The tie vote was an unwelcome tribute to the degree of party regularity that had been achieved by 1800.

In 1801 the House of Representatives, voting by states, had to choose between Jefferson and Burr, a majority of one state being necessary for election. The Federalists saw an opportunity to thwart their enemies by supporting Burr, thus electing a cynical, pliant, and corrupt politician over a 'dangerous radical.' Party division was so close that during thirty-five ballots, and until 17 February 1801, the House was deadlocked. There was talk of civil war. Not until two weeks before the inauguration did several Federalists cast blank ballots, which led to Jefferson's being elected.[1] In the congressional elections of 1800, the Republicans obtained emphatic majorities in House and Senate. Thus, in 1801 the Federalists went out of power in every branch of government except the judiciary, an exception that proved very important.

So passed into minority the party which contained more talent and virtue, with less political common sense, than any of its successors. The character of Washington, the genius of Hamilton, and the disciplined, intelligent patriotism of their colleagues and lieutenants saved the American union from disintegration before its colors were set; but the events of 1798–1800 proved that the Federalists had little more to contribute. Their chosen basis, an oligarchy of wealth and talent, had helped to tide over a crisis, but was neither broad nor deep enough for a permanent polity.

1. The Twelfth Amendment to the Constitution (1804) removed the possibility of a tie between two candidates on the same ticket.

9

Jeffersonian Democracy

*

1801–1809

The 'Revolution of 1800'

Thomas Jefferson, ruminating years later on the events of a crowded lifetime, thought that his election to the Presidency marked as real a revolution as that of 1776. He had saved the country from monarchy and militarism, and brought it back to republican simplicity. But there never had been any danger of monarchy; it was John Adams who saved the country from militarism; and a little simplicity more or less cannot be deemed revolutionary. Fisher Ames predicted that, with a 'Jacobin' President, America would be in for a reign of terror. Yet the four years that followed were one of the most tranquil of olympiads, marked not by radical reforms or popular tumults, but by the peaceful acquisition of territory as large again as the United States. The election of 1800–1801 brought a change of men more than of measures. For the next quarter of a century, a Virginian would rule in the White House; Jefferson, Madison, and Monroe each served eight years, and each was succeeded by his Secretary of State.

Yet if it marked no revolution, the election of Jefferson did harbinger the beginning of an era of greater democracy. Although in the Federalist period the right to vote was widely held, many had not chosen to exercise it, and politics were largely controlled by the gentry. In the Jeffersonian era, an astonishing expansion of the electorate took place in part because to many Jefferson symbolized the striving for liberty and equality. In the last letter of his life, he wrote: 'The mass of mankind has not been born with saddles on their backs, nor a favored few booted and spurred, ready to ride them legitimately, by the grace of God.'

Jefferson was no social democrat, but a slaveholding country gentleman with a classical education, exquisite taste, a lively curiosity, and a belief in the perfectibility of man. His kind belonged to the eighteenth rather than the nineteenth century. Christian but no churchman, he had the serenity of one to whom now and then the Spirit has not disdained to speak. The hold that he enjoyed on the hearts of plain people was attained without speech-making, military service, or catering to vulgar prejudice. The secret of Jefferson's power lay in the fact that he appealed to and expressed America's better self: her idealism, simplicity, youthful mind, and hopeful outlook, rather than the material and imperial ambitions

146

which Hamilton represented. 'We are acting for all mankind,' Jefferson wrote to Priestley. 'Circumstances denied to others, but indulged to us, have imposed on us the duty of proving what is the degree of freedom and self-government in which a society may venture to leave its individual members.'

Jefferson's inaugural address of 4 March 1801 was eighteenth-century idealism rubbed through the sieve of practical politics. Instead of denouncing the Federalists as monarchists, he invited them to rejoin the true republican church: 'We are all republicans—we are all federalists. If there be any among us who wish to dissolve this Union, or to change its republican form, let them stand undisturbed as monuments of the safety with which error of opinion may be tolerated where reason is left free to combat it.' This government, 'the world's best hope,' must not be abandoned 'on the theoretic and visionary fear' that it is not strong enough. 'Sometimes it is said that Man cannot be trusted with the government of himself. Can he, then, be trusted with the government of others?' 'Separated by nature and a wide ocean from the exterminating havoc of one quarter of the globe,' 'possessing a chosen country, with room enough for our descendants to the hundredth and thousandth generation' practicing the social virtues, the only thing 'necessary to close the circle of our felicities' is 'a wise and frugal government, which shall restrain men from injuring one another, shall leave them otherwise free to regulate their own pursuits of industry and improvement.'

The new capital city of Washington, to which the Federal Government had been transferred from aristocratic Philadelphia, offered an appropriate setting for Republican simplicity. Washington was still little more than a cleared space with scattered buildings between wilderness and river. Members of Congress, forced to leave their wives at home and live in crowded boarding houses, finished the public business in annual sessions of three to five months. Written presidential messages were substituted for the annual 'speech from the throne,' and the answers from both houses were omitted. Jefferson also established a new code of republican etiquette. Anthony Merry, in full uniform as British minister plenipotentiary,

was received by the President in morning undress of faded threadbare coat, red waistcoat, corduroy breeches, and slippers.

Jefferson's inaugural pledges to pay the public debt, and to preserve 'the general government in its whole constitutional vigor,' created joy in the Federalist camp. Hamilton viewed the inaugural message 'as virtually a candid retraction of past misapprehensions, and a pledge to the community that the new President will not lend himself to dangerous innovations, but in essential points will tread in the steps of his predecessors.' That, in the main, was what Jefferson did. Both he and his Secretary of the Treasury, Albert Gallatin, regarded the national debt as a mortgage to be paid off without delay. Gallatin would even have retained the excise on distilled liquors, which his former constituents in Pennsylvania had resisted; but Jefferson insisted on removing this detested relic of Federalism, and so made his name immortal in the mountains. This rendered the government even more dependent than formerly on customs revenues, so that the stoppage of foreign trade seriously embarrassed federal finances on the eve of the War of 1812.

The new administration made other changes too. Jefferson signified the coming of party government when he replaced the whole Adams cabinet with prominent Republicans. In his appointments to higher federal offices, Jefferson made a modest departure in the direction of naming men of merit irrespective of social class, although most of them were from the 'top drawer' socially. Jefferson also carried into practice the Republican dislike of a standing army and a large navy. The army was reduced by a 'chaste reformation,' as Jefferson called it, and all new naval construction was stopped. Yet, strangely enough, the most brilliant achievements of Jefferson's first administration were in war and diplomacy.

A Small War and a Big Purchase

By the time Jefferson became President, almost $2 million had been paid for gifts, ransom, and tribute to the Moslem states of Morocco, Algiers, Tunis, and Tripoli, in order to permit American merchant ships to sail in the Mediterranean. Jefferson, after reducing the navy, looked around for

Building the *Philadelphia*. In 1798, during the undeclared war with France, construction was begun in a Philadelphia yard on this frigate, a type of vessel smaller and less heavily armed than a ship of the line but swifter. When Tripolitan pirates captured the *Philadelphia*, Stephen Decatur, in a daring raid in 1804, recaptured her and burned her so that she could not be used by the enemy. (*Prints Division, New York Public Library*)

profitable employment of warships remaining afloat. He found it against the Bashaw of Tripoli, who, feeling he was not getting enough cut on the tribute money, declared war on the United States in May 1801. This naval war dribbled along until 1804, when Commodore Edward Preble appeared off Tripoli in command of a respectable task force, U.S.S. *Constitution* flagship, which delivered a series of bombardments. Before his arrival, frigate *Philadelphia* had grounded on a reef off Tripoli, from which the enemy floated her free. The Bashaw imprisoned Captain Bainbridge and his crew and would have equipped the frigate for his own navy, had not Lieutenant Stephen Decatur, in a captured lateen-rigged schooner named *Intrepid,* entered the harbor at night, boarded and captured *Philadelphia,* and, after setting fire to her, made a safe getaway. Thanks to such exploits by Decatur and others, the war ended in a favorable treaty with Tripoli.

While Tripoli was being taught a lesson, the boundary of the United States advanced from the Mississippi to the Rocky Mountains. The whole of that vast territory, Louisiana, had been under Spanish sovereignty since the peace of 1763, and the retrocession of this great province from Spain to France, in October 1800, completed a policy aimed at creating a new French empire in North America and checking the expansion of the United States. In May 1801 Jefferson got wind of the secret treaty of retrocession, and another event revealed its implications. Bonaparte dispatched an expeditionary force to Hispaniola, with orders to suppress the Negro insurrection there, and then to take possession of New Orleans and Louisiana. The prospect of a veteran French army at America's back door was not pleasant. On 18 April 1802 Jefferson wrote the American minister at Paris: 'The day that France takes possession of New Orleans . . . we must marry ourselves to the British fleet and nation.' Astounding as this letter may appear, it was a logical development of Jefferson's policy for the preceding twelve years. The President's earlier experience convinced him that as long as a foreign country controlled the mouth of the Mississippi, the United States was in danger of being drawn into every European war. Isolation was not a fact but a goal; and to attain it Jefferson was ready to adopt Washington's formula of 'temporary alliances for extraordinary emergencies.'

Late in 1802 the Spanish governor at New Orleans, who still exercised authority, withdrew the 'right of deposit' from American traders. This privilege had been guaranteed only for three years by Pinckney's treaty of 1795; but the indignant inhabitants of the Ohio valley, who were annually trans-shipping a million dollars' worth of produce at New Orleans, believed they had secured it forever. The West exploded with indignation, and

Congress voted $2 million for 'expenses in relation to the intercourse between the United States and foreign nations.' Jefferson remained unperturbable, but in March 1803 he commissioned James Monroe as envoy extraordinary to France, with interesting instructions to himself and to the resident minister, Robert Livingston.

First they were to offer anything up to $10 million for New Orleans and the Floridas, which would give the United States the whole east bank of the Mississippi, and the Gulf coast to the eastward. If France refused, three-quarters of the sum should be offered for the Island of New Orleans alone; or space on the east bank should be purchased for an American port. Failing here, they must press for a perpetual guarantee of the rights of navigation and deposit. That was Jefferson's ultimatum. If this were refused, Monroe and Livingston were ordered to 'open a confidential communication with ministers of the British Government,' with a view to 'a candid understanding, and a closer connection with Great Britain.' A mutual promise not to make a separate peace with France could not 'be deemed unreasonable.' More than even Hamilton had dared suggest!

Livingston began the negotiation before Monroe sailed, and for a time made little progress. But on 11 April 1803, when Livingston approached the minister of foreign affairs to repeat his usual offer for New Orleans, Talleyrand suddenly asked, 'What will you give for the whole of Louisiana?' On 30 April the treaty of cession was signed. Twelve million dollars was paid for Louisiana. The United States guaranteed the inhabitants the rights of American citizens and eventual admission to the Union.

We owe this amazing opportunity to two factors—the blacks of Haiti and the British navy. Napoleon had poured 35,000 troops into Hispaniola, the Vietnam of 1800, and lost almost all; the natives under Toussaint l'Ouverture killed those who invaded the interior, and yellow fever finished off the rest. Without Haiti, Louisiana lost most of its value to France. Second, Napoleon had decided to renew war with England, whose navy would certainly blockade and probably capture New Orleans. So Napoleon deemed it best to sell the whole of Louisiana to fatten his war chest.

UNDER MY WINGS EVERY THING PROSPERS

New Orleans, 1803. Everything was indeed prospering in the Crescent City in the year of the Louisiana Purchase, which had a galvanizing effect on commerce. Flatboat trade with the Ohio valley increased sharply, dockhands unloaded cargoes from ocean-going vessels, and above the *vieux carré* a new business center began to emerge. (*Chicago Historical Society*)

This greatest bargain in American history, the Louisiana purchase, put a severe strain on the Constitution, which said nothing about acquiring foreign territory, much less promising it statehood. Jefferson at first wanted an amendment to the Constitution, but decided to take a broad view when Livingston warned him that Napoleon might change his mind. The Senate promptly consented, not without sarcastic grumblings by the Federalists, and on 20 December 1803 the French prefect at New Orleans formally transferred Louisiana to the United States.

Even before the purchase, Jefferson had ordered

his secretary, Captain Meriwether Lewis, and Lieutenant William Clark, officers of the regular army, to conduct an exploration. Their first object was to find 'water communication across this continent' in United States territory. Other aims were to secure American title to the Oregon country, and impress upon the Sioux and other Indians that their 'Great White Father' lived in Washington, not Windsor. The expedition started from St. Louis on 14 May 1804 with 32 soldiers and ten civilians, embarked in a 55-foot keelboat and two periaguas. These, propelled by sails and oars, took them up the Missouri as far as the South Fork, in

This sketch from Clark's journal shows the way Chinook Indians flattened the skulls of their infants in order to achieve the straight line from the top of the head to the tip of the nose that they admired in both men and women as an indication of a cultured upbringing. In the midst of these drawings, the explorer has taken advantage of unused space to record information on the tides at Fort Clatsop on the Oregon coast. (*Missouri Historical Society*)

The Lewis and Clark expedition came upon this canoe of the Columbia river tribes, with grotesque figures at each end. This sketch is from the journal of William Clark. (*Missouri Historical Society*)

what is now Montana. The winter of 1804–5 they spent among the Mandan in North Dakota. A fleet of dugout canoes took them to the foothills of the Rocky Mountains in what is now Idaho, where their interpreter, the Snake Indian girl Sacajawea, made friendly contact with the Shoshone. These furnished horses for the men and squaws to carry the baggage. In the Nez Percé country the expedition reached the Clearwater, a turbulent but navigable branch of the Snake, flowing westward. They entered the Columbia river, and after many difficulties with rocks and rapids, reached tidewater on 7 November 1805. 'Great joy in Camp,' wrote Clark in his diary, 'we are in view of . . . this great Pacific Ocean which we have been so long anxious to see.' And they built Fort Clatsop within sound of the great Pacific surges, there to spend another winter.

Lewis and Clark learned that New England trading vessels had visited the Columbia, through the coastal Indians' use of such elegant phrases as 'heave the lead' and 'sun-of-a-pitch.' But as months passed and no ship called, the explorers decided to return overland. The expedition reached St. Louis 23 September 1806. They had found no water route through the Rockies, since there was none; but the land and river route they discovered served later pioneers, and their Indian relations were beyond praise.

'Never was there an administration more brilliant than that of Mr. Jefferson up to this period,' said John Randolph in later years. 'We were indeed in the "full tide of successful experiment." Taxes repealed; the public debt amply provided for, both principal and interest; sinecures abolished; Louisiana acquired; public confidence unbounded.'

Crumbling Federalism

Even in this euphoric period, there was one group that could not abide Jefferson's success—the leaders of New England Federalism. Jefferson's reign, they believed, would lead to terror, atheism, and autocracy. Their power was waning, and they knew it. Ohio, admitted to the Union in 1803, looked to Virginia for guidance, although largely settled by Yankees. New states to be formed from

Louisiana would follow the same light; and their political weight would be increased by the federal ratio of representation. The annexation of Louisiana, upsetting the balance of power within the Union, absolved New England from allegiance to the Union; at least so the Federalists reasoned. Before 1803 was out the 'Essex Junto' of Massachusetts and the 'River Gods' of Connecticut began to plan a Northern Confederacy with New England as a nucleus. The British minister at Washington gave this conspiracy his blessing, but Hamilton would have none of it.

The conspirators then turned to Aaron Burr. He had carried New York for Jefferson in 1800, and without that state Jefferson would not have been elected. Yet Jefferson, once safe in office, ignored the Vice-President in distributing patronage and dropped him from the presidential ticket in 1804. Burr then decided to contest the governorship of New York with the regular Republican candidate. In return for Federalist aid, Burr appears to have agreed, if successful, to swing New York into a Northern Confederacy and become its president. But most Federalist leaders opposed the scheme, Burr was defeated, and the Federalist conspiracy dissolved. How remote was its chance of success the presidential election of 1804 proved. Jefferson carried every state but Connecticut and Delaware, with 162 electoral votes to 14 for Pinckney.

At the age of forty-eight, Burr was a ruined politician. He had broken with the Republicans and failed the Federalists. Hamilton was responsible. It was not the first time that Hamilton had crossed his path; it must be the last. On 18 June 1804, six weeks after the New York election, Burr wrote to his rival, demanding 'a prompt and unqualified acknowledgment or denial' of a slur upon his character reported in the press. Hamilton refused to retract, and answered, 'I trust on more reflection you will see the matter in the same light with me. If not, I can only regret the circumstances, and must abide the consequences.' According to the 'code of honor' observed by the gentry of the South and of New York, such language was an invitation to a challenge; and the challenge came quickly. Hamilton had no business to accept. He did not need to prove his courage;

he had a wife and a large family dependent on him. Moreover, he believed it murder to kill an adversary in a duel. Yet the infirmity of a noble mind forced him to accept the challenge.

Poor Hamilton had become enmeshed in a double net of theory and ambition. He might differ from the New England Federalists as to the cure for democracy, but he judged the future by their gloomy formula. A crisis was impending, he thought. The year 1804 in America corresponded to 1791 in France. Jefferson would disappear like Mirabeau and Lafayette, dissolution and anarchy would follow; then America would demand a savior. Hamilton intended to be ready at the call—but no one under suspicion of cowardice could save his country. So Hamilton resolved to prove his courage and yet not to kill, to reserve and throw away his first fire, in the hope that Burr would miss and honor be satisfied. Aaron Burr did not intend to miss.

At six o'clock on a bright summer morning, 11 July 1804, Hamilton and his second were ferried across the Hudson to a grove of trees under the Palisades. The distance agreed upon was ten paces. When the signal *present* was given, the Vice-President raised his arm slowly, took deliberate aim, and fired. Hamilton fell mortally wounded. So perished one of the greatest men of the age, for his little faith in the government he had helped to form and in the people he had served so well.

The Assault on the Judiciary

Aaron Burr fled to Washington, where the President received him amiably and conferred upon his friends the three best offices in Louisiana Territory. It was not that Jefferson wished to reward the slayer of Hamilton, but that he wanted something of Burr. For as Vice-President he must preside over the United States Senate, sitting as a court of impeachment to try Justice Chase of the Supreme Court.

This trial was part of a Republican attempt to rid the federal judiciary of partisan Federalists. Under Chief Justice Jay the federal courts had exercised their constitutional powers without much opposition. They had, however, made two false steps. In Chisholm v. Georgia (1793), a case involving con-

fiscations contrary to the peace treaty, the Supreme Court ordered that state to appear before the bar as defendant and entered judgment against it by default. State susceptibilities, thus aroused, produced the Eleventh Amendment, forbidding suits against states by citizens of other states or nations. It was ratified in 1798. That same year certain federal judges, excited by the supposed Jacobin menace, enforced the Sedition Act with unholy zeal and delivered political harangues to grand juries. In February 1801, when Congress increased the number of federal courts, President Adams filled the new places with members of his party and conferred the chief justiceship on John Marshall, a kinsman whom Jefferson hated bitterly and wished to humiliate.

The feud was intensified when Chief Justice Marshall defied the new President in the case of Marbury v. Madison. Marbury was a justice of the peace for the District of Columbia, a 'midnight appointment' by President Adams in the last hours of his administration. Madison, the new Secretary of State, refused to deliver his commission to Marbury, who applied to the Supreme Court for a writ of mandamus, under section 13 of the Judiciary Act of 1789. Chief Justice Marshall, delivering the opinion of the Court (February 1803), stated that Madison had no right to withhold the commission of a properly appointed official. But Marbury's hopes were dashed by the rest of the opinion. The Federal Constitution, in defining the original jurisdiction of the Supreme Court, had not included the issue of writs to executive officers. Hence, section 13 of the Judiciary Act was unconstitutional and the Court could not take jurisdiction. A nicer sense of propriety might have suggested to Marshall that if the Court had no jurisdiction it should not announce how it would have decided the case if it had. But Marshall was bent on rebuking Jefferson and Madison for what he considered an arbitrary act. In so doing, he firmly enunciated the doctrine of judicial review—the right, indeed the duty, of the Supreme Court to invalidate statutes that are 'contrary to the Constitution.'

Jefferson now incited some of his henchmen in the House to move against certain federal judges. A district judge who had become intemperate to

Aaron Burr (1756–1836). Although some historians believe that Burr's contributions to the republic merit greater recognition, the third Vice-President of the United States seems doomed to be remembered as an intriguer and as the man who killed Alexander Hamilton in a duel. Grandson of the Puritan divine Jonathan Edwards, Burr has been chided by biographers for his 'ingrained amatory habits.' This portrait is by Burr's protégé, John Vanderlyn, the first American to study painting in Paris. Vanderlyn's nudes were so realistic that viewers were shocked, but Napoleon was so impressed by his work that he had a gold medal conferred on him. (*New-York Historical Society*)

the point of insanity was impeached and removed. The next victim was to be Justice Samuel Chase, a signer of the Declaration of Independence, who on the bench had made himself peculiarly obnoxious to the Republicans. By a straight partisan vote, the House of Representatives impeached him on several counts. But since there was no evidence to substantiate the serious charges against him, enough Republican senators joined the Federalists to acquit the Justice of 'crimes and misdemeanors.'

Had Chase been found guilty, the entire Supreme Court would have been purged. As it was, this trial proved to be the high-water mark of Jefferson's radicalism. Under Chief Justice Marshall conservatism rallied, and the Supreme Court mounted a subtle offensive of ideas—the supremacy of the nation and the sanctity of property. 'The Federalists,' wrote Jefferson bitterly, 'defeated at the polls, have retired into the Judiciary, and from that barricade they hope to batter down all the bulwarks of Republicanism.' To a large measure they succeeded.

Domestic Intrigue and Foreign Complications

Thomas Jefferson, returned to the presidency by an overwhelming majority, started his second term on 4 March 1805, expecting to pursue the 'wise and frugal' policy of 1801 to its logical conclusion. But peace in Europe had been the condition of Jefferson's earlier success, and there was to be no peace in Europe for ten years. His second term was compared by John Randolph to Pharaoh's dream of the seven lean kine that ate up the seven fat kine. Many old Virginia Republicans like Randolph felt that Jefferson had deserted his own principles. In his first term he had broken with strict construction to acquire Louisiana, and in his second inaugural address, he recommended spending federal money on internal improvements. In Jefferson's second term, trouble accumulated. He confronted not only the defection of Old Republicans but something much more serious—nothing less than a threat to dismember the country in the shape of the Burr conspiracy.

Before leaving Washington at the expiration of his term as Vice-President, Burr approached the British minister with an offer to detach Louisiana from the Union for half a million dollars, provided the Royal Navy would co-operate. Mr. Merry thought well of it and urged his government to pay, but Downing Street was not interested in promoting American secession. Burr then proceeded to the headwaters of the Ohio and, with a few friends, sailed down-river in a luxury flatboat, stopping here and there to propose a different scheme. The Westerners, duelers themselves, were charmed by the polished gentleman from New York. Harman Blennerhasset, a romantic Irish exile, was fascinated with a plan to conquer Mexico, make Burr emperor and himself a grand potentate. General Wilkinson, still in Spanish pay while governor of Louisiana Territory and ranking general of the United States Army, had already discussed with Burr a project to 'liberate' Mexico from Spain and make Louisiana an independent republic. At New Orleans Burr got in touch with certain creoles who disliked being sold by Napoleon and with an association of American filibusters who were eager to invade Mexico. The Catholic bishop of New Orleans and the mother superior of the Ursuline convent gave him their blessing. Returning overland, Burr found Westerners everywhere eager for war with Spain. In Washington again, Burr obtained $2500 from the Spanish minister, ostensibly for the purpose of capturing the United States naval vessels then in the Potomac and embarking a filibustering expedition to 'liberate' Louisiana!

In the summer of 1806 the former Vice-President established headquarters at Lexington, Ky., and began active recruiting. What was his real object? Ostensibly it was to take up and colonize an enormous land claim he had purchased in western Louisiana. Those supposedly 'in the know' expected him to move into Texas and 'liberate' Mexico. Evidence is strong that Burr did have his eye on Mexico, but that, first, he would promote a secession of Louisiana Territory and become its president. At this juncture General Wilkinson, deciding that Burr was worth more to betray than to befriend, sent a lurid letter to President Jefferson denouncing 'a deep, dark, wicked, and wide-spread conspiracy' to dismember the Union. Similar warnings reached Washington from loyal Westerners. In the late autumn of 1806 the President issued a proclamation ordering the arrest of Burr. He was brought to Richmond for trial, on a charge of treason.

Fortunately for the prisoner, Chief Justice Marshall, who presided at his trial, took care that the constitutional definition of treason, 'levying war against the United States or adhering to their enemies,' and the constitutional safeguard of 'two witnesses to the same overt act,' should be strictly observed. Hence it followed that merely recruiting with treasonable intent was not treason. Burr was acquitted and sought exile in France. In 1812 he managed to obtain a passport and return to New York, where he built up a good law practice; and in 1833, at the age of 77, he married an attractive widow, Madame Jumel, who used to boast that she was the only woman in the world who had slept with both George Washington and Napoleon Bonaparte.

No sooner had the Burr trial ended than Jefferson faced a no less vexing problem in Europe, where Napoleon and Britain sought to starve or strangle each other by continental or maritime blockade and to levy tolls on neutral traders. Furthermore, as soon as the Royal Navy considered the renewal of war with France inevitable, it resumed the practice of impressing British subjects from American vessels on the high seas; men were plucked off American ships even outside New York harbor. Britain never claimed the right to take native-born Americans, but to impress her own subjects from foreign vessels wherever found. British seamen were constantly deserting. The U.S.S. *Constitution* in 1807 had 149 avowed British subjects, and only 241 who claimed American citizenship, in her crew of 419. And neither country then admitted the right of expatriation. When a short-handed man-of-war visited an American merchantman, the boarding officer was apt to impress any likely looking lad who had the slightest trace of an Irish or English accent. Mistakes were difficult to rectify, and there were enough instances of brutality and injustice to create indignation.

An impressment outrage brought the two coun-tries to the verge of war. A British squadron, stationed within the Capes of the Chesapeake to watch French frigates up the Bay, lost many men by desertion, and had reason to believe that Jenkin Ratford, the ringleader, had enlisted in the United States frigate *Chesapeake*. That was true; and she had other British-born tars too. On 22 June 1807 the *Chesapeake*, flying the pennant of Commodore Barron, encountered H.M.S. *Leopard* about ten miles outside the Capes. When the *Leopard* signaled 'Dispatches,' Barron supposed that she wished him to carry mail to Europe, a common courtesy between the two navies, so he invited the British captain to board his vessel. But the dispatches proved to be an order to search for and remove deserters. Barron, ignorant of Ratford's presence, replied that the only deserters from the Royal Navy in his crew were three Americans who had escaped after impressment, and that he would permit no search. *Leopard* fired three broadsides into the *Chesapeake*, which had few of her guns mounted. After three men had been killed, Barron struck his flag. His crew were then mustered by the *Leopard*'s officers, and three Americans and Ratford were impressed.

News of this insult to the flag brought the first united expression of American feeling since 1798. Even the Federalists, who had hitherto defended every move of British sea power, were confounded. If Jefferson had summoned Congress to a special session, he could have had war at the drop of a hat. Instead, he instructed Monroe to demand apology and reparation in London, and ordered British warships out of American territorial waters. But no suggestion of war, or of preparation for war, came from the President. For he imagined that he had England by the throat and could strangle her by a mere turn of the wrist.

Jefferson's Embargo

For years Jefferson had been wanting an opportunity to try commercial exclusion as a substitute for war. He reasoned that since the United States was the world's largest neutral carrier and the chief market for British manufactures, Britain could be brought to terms. The President urged: 'Let us see whether having taught so many other useful lessons to Europe, we may not add that of showing them that there are peaceable means of repressing injustice, by making it to the interest of the aggressor to do what is just.' Under the Embargo Act of December 1807, American or other vessels were forbidden to sail foreign, all exports from the United States whether by sea or land were prohibited, and certain specified articles of British manufacture were refused entrance.[1] For fourteen months every American ship that was not already abroad, or could not escape, lay in port or went coasting.

The embargo struck a staggering blow to foreign trade, the most important source of America's economic growth in these years. After the outbreak of war in Europe in 1793, ships of every belligerent save England had vanished from the seas, leaving the enormous colonial trade of Europe to neutrals, and especially the United States. To avoid being intercepted, ships with tropical products—sugar, coffee, tea, pepper, cocoa—sailed to the United States, and their cargoes were then reshipped. From 1790 to 1807 domestic exports had doubled; re-exports in that same period grew from $300,000 to more than $59 million. The war also proved a boon for grain and cotton growers when Europe's sources of these staples were cut off. During this period of flourishing commerce, the population of Philadelphia more than doubled, Boston nearly doubled, and Baltimore and New York almost tripled. Much of the increase came from shipping and shipbuilding, and their effect on dependent industries such as ropewalks, sailmaking, lumbering, provisioning, marine insurance companies, and even banks. The embargo snuffed out this profitable trade and threw thousands of sailors and shipwrights out of jobs. To the Yankees it seemed as outrageous for Congress to decree 'Thou shalt not sail!' as it would have to the South, had Congress said 'Thou shalt not plant!'

It is true that between British orders in council and French decrees, American vessels could visit no part of the world without rendering themselves liable to capture by one belligerent or the other. But the American merchant marine throve on such treatment; shipowners wanted no protection other than that which the British navy afforded them. European restrictions merely increased the profit with the risk. Hence the embargo was detested by the very interest it was supposed to protect. Many small shipowners were ruined, and some of the lesser seaports such as Newburyport and New Haven never recovered their earlier prosperity. The embargo also hurt the South, where cotton prices were almost halved, but New England spoke out most loudly against the policy, because it was the stronghold of the Federalists, who viewed the embargo as a sectional and partisan conspiracy.

To succeed as a weapon of diplomacy, commercial retaliation requires an unusual combination of circumstances—which very seldom occurs, and did not occur in 1807-9. The embargo caused a shortage of provisions in the French West Indies and of colonial produce in France; but Napoleon confiscated every American vessel that arrived at a French port, on the ground that he was helping Jefferson to enforce the measure! In the English manufacturing districts the embargo caused some distress, but the usual exports soon found their way into the United States through Canada, and British shipowners loved a measure that removed American competition.

Jefferson's mistake was the Federalists' opportunity. Their strength had been dwindling, even in New England, where in 1807 every state government except Connecticut's went Republican. The Federalists had been unable to overcome the stigma of monarchism and militarism the Republicans had fastened on them, and they were handicapped by a late start in developing effective party organization. Now, unexpectedly, Jefferson had handed them an issue on which they might make a popular appeal. The Federalists approached the 1808 election with high hopes. Northern Republicans were restive under a measure that turned their constituents Federalist; and in New York City the embargo produced a schism in the Republican party. When Madison was nominated for the presidential succession by a congressional caucus, the New York legislature placed George Clinton in

1. The last measure was not, strictly speaking, a part of the embargo of December 1807, but the Non-importation Act of 16 April 1806, which did not go into effect until the embargo was adopted.

Salem sea captain. In the generation after the American Revolution, brightly painted ships from the little Massachusetts port of Salem sailed to every quarter of the globe, and prosperous captains commissioned leading artists to depict them and their handsome vessels. The identity of the painter of this portrait of John Carnes is unknown, but many of the best works of the period came from the brush of George Ropes, the deaf and dumb son of a Salem mariner who was taught by a refugee from the Napoleonic wars. (*Peabody Museum of Salem*)

nomination as an anti-embargo Republican. In Virginia John Randolph's sect of 'pure Republicans' nominated Monroe. If a union could have been effected between these factions and the Federalists, Madison might have been defeated. But the Federalist candidate, C. C. Pinckney, carried little but New England, save Vermont, and Delaware, and Madison was elected President by a comfortable majority, 122–47.

Jefferson intended to maintain the embargo until the British orders or the French decrees were repealed. In January 1809 Congress passed the 'Force Act,' permitting federal officials without warrant to seize goods under suspicion of foreign destination and protecting them from legal liability for their actions. Watchmen patrolled Atlantic wharves, and revenue officers seized sails and unshipped rudders. George III and Lord North had been tender in comparison. The people of New England, now in their second winter of privation and distress, began to look to their state governments for protection; and by this time all state governments of New England were Federalist again. The legislatures hurled back in the teeth of Jefferson and Madison the doctrines of the Kentucky and Virginia Resolves of 1798. Connecticut resolved that 'whenever our national legislature is led to overleap the prescribed bounds of their constitutional powers,' it becomes the duty of the state legislatures 'to interpose their protecting shield.' Northern Republicans revolted; and Jefferson was shaken by a volley of protests from New England town meetings, some of them threatening secession. A bill for the repeal of the embargo was rushed through Congress and, on 1 March 1809, approved by Jefferson. Three days later his term ended and he retired to Monticello.

The embargo was intended to be the crowning glory of Jefferson's second administration, as Louisiana had been of his first, but it proved a dismal failure. It neither influenced the policy of Britain or of Napoleon nor protected the merchant marine. It wasted the fruit of Jefferson's first administration: the creation of a broad, countrywide party in every state of the Union. It convinced many good people that the 'Virginia dynasty' was bound to that of Bonaparte, that the Republican party was a greater enemy than British sea power to American shipping. Whatever President Madison might do or neglect to do, he would never have such united support as Jefferson had enjoyed in 1807.

Yet despite the failure of the embargo, Jefferson was one of the greatest of Presidents and the most tolerant of revolutionists. Few men have combined in like degree a lofty idealism with the ability to administer a government. He preferred the slow process of reason to the short way of force. By his forbearance, even more than by his acts, Jefferson kept alive the flame of liberty that Napoleon had almost quenched in Europe.

10

The Second War with Great Britain

*

1809–1815

The Coming of War

Owing to James Madison's labors on the Federal Constitution he must be accounted a great statesman, but he was a very poor politician; and a poor politician usually makes a bad President, although a good 'pol' does not necessarily make a good chief magistrate. Slight in stature and unimpressive in personality, eager to please but wearing a puzzled look as though people were too much for him, 'Jemmy' Madison had few intimate friends, and among the people at large he inspired little affection and no enthusiasm. He had a talent for writing logical diplomatic notes; but logic was not much use in dealing with Europeans locked in a deadly struggle. He was negative in dealing with Congress, allowing Jefferson's system of personal influence with members to fall apart. And Madison was stubborn to the point of stupidity.

Yet, within six weeks of his inauguration on 4 March 1809, Madison was being greeted as a great peacemaker. Congress, when repealing Jefferson's embargo, substituted a non-intercourse act aimed at both Britain and France, with the promise of recommencing commercial relations with

whichever nation first repealed its decrees injuring American commerce. Madison, eager to reach an understanding with England, arranged a treaty with David Erskine, the British minister in Washington, by virtue of which His Majesty's government would rescind orders against American shipping, and the United States would resume normal trading relations with Britain but maintain non-intercourse against France. Touchy subjects such as impressment and the *Chesapeake* affair were postponed. If this draft treaty had been accepted by George Canning, the British minister of foreign affairs, there would have been no second war with England. But Canning brutally repudiated both Erskine and the treaty, and Aglo-American relations returned to a state of mutual recrimination.

The Congress that assembled in December 1809 had no idea what to do, and received no lead from Madison. On 16 April 1810 it voted to reduce both the army and the navy, weak though they already were. And on 1 May Congress reversed the principle of the earlier Non-Intercourse Act by passing Macon's Bill No. 2. This law restored intercourse with both Britain and France, but promised to the first power which recognized neutral rights to stop trading with her enemy. American ships promptly resumed making juicy profits under British license, and merchant tonnage reached figures that were not again attained for another twenty years.

Madison took advantage of this interlude in commercial warfare to take a bite out of West Florida. In 1810 the inhabitants of that portion of West Florida bordering on the Mississippi 'self-determined' for the United States and seized Baton Rouge. Madison promptly incorporated them, by presidential proclamation, into the Territory of Orleans, which two years later became the state of Louisiana. In May 1812 a second bite was taken, when the district between the Pearl and Perdido rivers was annexed to Mississippi Territory.

While Madison was devouring West Florida, Napoleon was becoming aware that Macon's Act offered him an opportunity to incorporate the United States into his Continental system, a scheme for getting the European continent under his control in order to impoverish England. America could help this strategy by adding a sea-power component. For five years Napoleon had treated American shipping harshly, but in the summer of 1810 Napoleon's minister of foreign affairs informed the American minister to France that 'His Majesty loves the Americans,' and as proof of his solicitude had declared that his decrees against neutral shipping after 1 November would be revoked; 'it being understood that the English are to revoke their orders in council.'

John Quincy Adams, minister to Russia, warned Madison that this note was 'a trap to catch us into a war with England.' But the President, searching desperately for an effective policy, fell into the trap. By proclamation on 2 November 1810 he announced that France had rescinded her anti-neutral system, hence non-intercourse would be revived against Britain, if within three months she did not repeal the orders in council. Almost every mail for the next two years brought news of fresh seizures and scuttlings of American vessels by the French. But Madison, having taken his stand, obstinately insisted that 'the national faith was pledged to France.' On 2 March 1811 he forbade intercourse with Great Britain, under au-

thority of Macon's Act. This time, economic sanctions really worked against England—but too late to preserve the peace. The winter of 1811–12 was the bitterest that the English people experienced between the Great Plague of 1665 and the German blitz of 1940–41. Warehouses were crammed with goods for which there was no market, factories were closing, workmen rioting. Deputations from the manufacturing cities besought Parliament to repeal the orders in council to recover their American market.

During these critical months several accidents postponed repeal, which, had it taken place in time, would have maintained peace. Spencer Perceval, the prime minister, was assassinated just after he had made up his mind to repeal the orders in council, and the business of finding a successor brought another and fatal delay. Finally on 16 June 1812, Castlereagh announced that the orders in council would be suspended immediately. If there had been a transatlantic cable, this would not have been too late. But Congress, having no word of the concession, declared war against Great Britain on 18 June 1812.

Congress so acted in response to a message from President Madison recommending war with Britain on four grounds—impressment of seamen, repeated violations of American territorial waters by the Royal Navy, declaring an enemy coast blockaded when it was not blockaded in fact, and the orders in council against neutral trade. Yet six senators and a large majority of the congressmen from the New England states, and a majority in both houses from New York, New Jersey, and Maryland voted against the declaration of war; whilst representatives of the inland and Western states from Vermont to Tennessee, and of the states from Virginia south, were almost solidly for war. New England, where three-quarters of American shipping was owned, and which supplied more than that proportion of American seamen, agitated against war to the brink of treason; whilst back-country congressmen who had never smelled salt water screamed for 'Free Trade and Sailors' Rights.'

The explanation? Republican party leaders believed that they had tried to prevent war by diplomacy and economic sanction and, since both had failed, they had no choice left but capitulation or war. If they did not choose war, they feared they would jeopardize both the confidence of the nation in the strength of republican institutions and the future of the Republican party. The South and West also had economic grievances. Worried over the declining prices of staple exports like cotton, tobacco, and hemp, they blamed their troubles, unjustifiably, on the British.

Some of the newer Republican leaders were much more ardent for war than was Madison. The elections of 1810–11 had sent to Congress a remarkably able group of newcomers, who quickly assumed positions of leadership. There were thirty-four-year-old Henry Clay and Richard M. Johnson from Kentucky; equally young Felix Grundy and aged but very bellicose John Sevier from Tennessee; Peter B. Porter, also in his thirties, from Buffalo, N.Y.; and twenty-nine-year-old John C. Calhoun from the back-country of South Carolina. These men, dubbed 'war hawks' by John Randolph, combined with other new members to elect Henry Clay Speaker of the House; and Clay named his friends chairmen of the important committees. The war hawks believed that national honor demanded a fight. Furthermore, they sought to conquer Canada, end the Indian menace on the Western frontier, and throw open more forest land for settlement. John Randolph of Roanoke, leader of the 'pure' Republicans who wished to keep the peace, poured his scorn on this 'cant of patriotism,' this 'agrarian cupidity,' this chanting 'like the whippoorwill, but one monotonous tone—Canada! Canada! Canada!'

Western concern over the Indian menace was a major cause of war. The 1795 Treaty of Greenville ended a period in which the Northwest Indians had usually been the aggressors, and put them on the defensive. Although the Indians faithfully fulfilled their treaty stipulations, whites in the Northwest committed the most wanton murders of Indians, for which it was almost impossible to obtain a conviction from a pioneer jury. From time to time a few hungry and desperate chiefs were rounded up by government officials and plied with oratory and whiskey until they signed a treaty alienating forever the hunting grounds of their tribe, perhaps of other nations as well. Jefferson encouraged this process; and William Henry Harrison, superintendent of the Northwest Indians and governor of Indiana Territory, pushed it so successfully that during the fourteen years following the 1795 treaty the Indians of that region parted with some 48 million acres. In 1809 this process came to a halt, owing in part to renewed efforts by British authorities in Canada to stiffen Indian resistance. Their efforts, as much as land hunger and far more than indignation over sailors' rights, contributed to war fever west of the Appalachians.

The determination of Indians not to yield to white expansionism actually owed less to the British than to the leadership of the twin brothers Tecumseh and Tenskwatawa, sons of a Shawnee chief. The former, a lithe, handsome, and stately warrior, had been one of those who defeated St. Clair in 1791; Tenskwatawa, better known as The Prophet, was a half-blind medicine man who won ascendancy over his people by such simple means as foretelling an eclipse of the sun. The two, around 1808, bravely undertook the task of saving their people. They sought to reform their habits, stop the alienation of their land, keep them apart from the whites, and to weld all tribes on United States soil into a confederacy. It was a movement of regeneration and defense, a menace indeed to the expansion of the West but not to its existence. The Indians has so decreased in the last decade that scarcely 4000 warriors could be counted on in the region bounded by the Great Lakes, the Mississippi, and the Ohio. Opposed to them were at least 100,000 white men of fighting age in the Ohio valley.

For a time the partnership of warrior and priest was irresistible. The Prophet kindled a religious revival among the tribes of the Northwest, and induced them to give up intoxicating liquor. All intercourse with white men, except for trade, ceased. In 1808 the two leaders, forced from their old settlement by the palefaces, established headquarters at a great clearing in Indiana, where Tippecanoe creek empties into the Wabash river. The entire frontier was alarmed, for The Prophet's moral influence extended as far south as Florida, and northwest to Saskatchewan. Governor Harrison met the situation with an act that Tecumseh could only regard as a challenge. Rounding up a few score survivors of tribes whom he frankly described as 'the most depraved wretches on earth,' the governor obtained from them several enormous tracts cutting up both banks of the Wabash into the heart of Tecumseh's country. This deprived Tecumseh of his remaining hunting grounds and brought the white border within fifty miles of the Tippecanoe. With justice Tecumseh declared this treaty null and void. In July 1811, Governor Harrison decided to force the issue by encamping hard by Tecumseh's village. The Prophet had been strictly enjoined by his brother to avoid hostilities; but instead of retiring he allowed himself to be maneuvered into battle by a few reckless young braves. Harrison drove the Indians into a swamp and destroyed their village. This Battle of Tippecanoe (7 November 1811) made Harrison a hero of the West and helped to elect him President in 1840.

Throughout the West it was believed that Britain had backed Tecumseh's confederacy. In fact, Tecumseh's league was the result of two Indian leaders trying to counteract an American policy which threatened to wipe out their people; as eventually it did. After Tippecanoe, however, the new governor general, Sir George Prevost, decided that war with the United States was inevitable, and his agents welcomed Tecumseh and 1800 warriors in June 1812. Thus many, if not most, Westerners were keen for war with England in order to annex Upper Canada and wipe out the assumed source of Indian troubles.

The War of 1812

Everyone knew that this war for 'Free Trade and Sailors' Rights' would be fought largely on land, preferably in Canada, the only part of the British empire that Americans could get at dry-shod. The population of British North America was less than half a million; that of the United States, by the census of 1810, 7.25 million. In the States the enrolled militia totaled about 700,000; and the regular army, by the time war broke out, had been recruited to about 7000 officers and men. There were fewer than 5000 British regulars in North America, and little chance that Britain, deeply engaged in the Peninsular Campaign, could spare reinforcements. Canada, however, could count on Tecumseh's braves.

Moreover, the war was far from popular in the United States. Every Federalist vote in Congress was cast against the declaration of war, which was greeted in New England by mournful tolling of church bells. Federalists approved neither the Westerners' land-hunger for Canada, nor the Southerners' lust for the fertile acres of the Creek nation. Jefferson's embargo had convinced them of the administration's insincerity in claiming to protect commerce; and Madison's acquiescence in Napoleon's deceptive diplomacy suggested that the Emperor had nudged America into war. And the fact that the British offered an unconditional armistice which Madison contemptuously refused convinced doubters in the party that the administration was bent on conquest. Federalists were incensed when Cognress adjourned 6 July 1812 without making any provision to increase the navy. To refuse to increase one's naval force in a war with the world's greatest sea power for 'Free Trade and Sailors' Rights' seemed gross hypocrisy. The governors of Massachusetts, Rhode Island, and Connecticut refused to call state militia into national service, and Federalist merchants would neither subscribe to war bonds nor fit out privateers. Opponents of the war sometimes met with violence. At Baltimore the plant of a Federalist newspaper was demolished by a mob. The friends of the editor, lodged for safety in the city jail, were dragged out by a waterfront mob and beaten to a pulp; the editor and General Henry Lee were badly injured, and General James M. Lingan, another Revolutionary veteran, was killed.

Chief Justice Marshall wrote that he was mortified by his country's base submission to Napoleon and that the only party division henceforth should be between the friends of peace and the advocates of war. That was indeed the division in the presidential election of 1812. The Federalists supported De Witt Clinton, who had been placed in nomination by an anti-war faction of the New York Republicans, and carried every

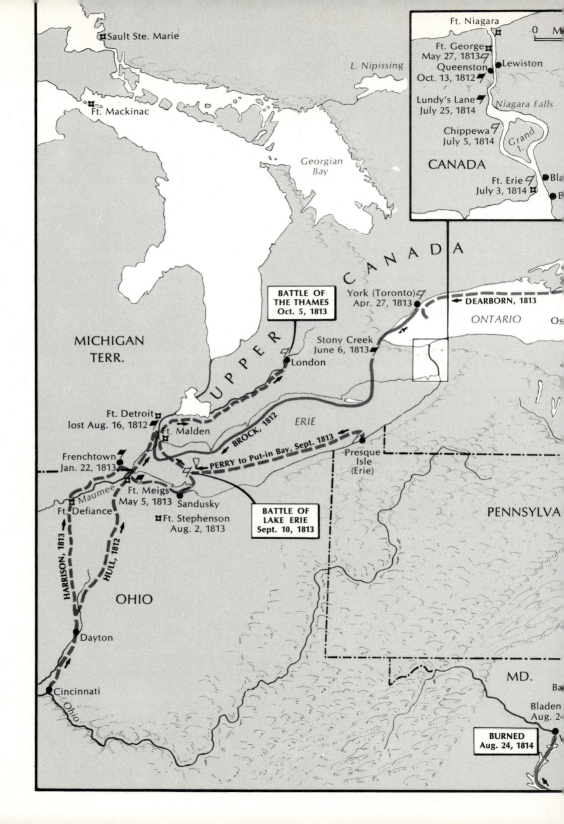

Sault Ste. Marie

L. Nipissing

Ft. Mackinac

Georgian Bay

MICHIGAN TERR.

U P P E R

C A N A D A

BATTLE OF THE THAMES
Oct. 5, 1813

York (Toronto)
Apr. 27, 1813

← DEARBORN, 1813

ONTARIO   Os

London

Stony Creek
June 6, 1813

Ft. Detroit
lost Aug. 16, 1812

Ft. Malden

BROCK, 1812

ERIE

PERRY to Put-in Bay, Sept. 1813

Presque
Isle
(Erie)

Frenchtown
Jan. 22, 1813

Maumee

Ft. Meigs
May 5, 1813   Sandusky

Ft. Defiance

Ft. Stephenson
Aug. 2, 1813

**BATTLE OF
LAKE ERIE
Sept. 10, 1813**

PENNSYLVA

HARRISON, 1813

HULL, 1812

OHIO

Dayton

Cincinnati

Ohio

MD.

Ba

Bladen
Aug. 2-

**BURNED
Aug. 24, 1814**

Inset (top right):

Ft. Niagara

0   M

Ft. George
May 27, 1813   Lewiston

Queenston
Oct. 13, 1812

Lundy's Lane
July 25, 1814

Niagara Falls

Chippewa
July 5, 1814

Grand I.

CANADA

Ft. Erie
July 3, 1814   Bla

B

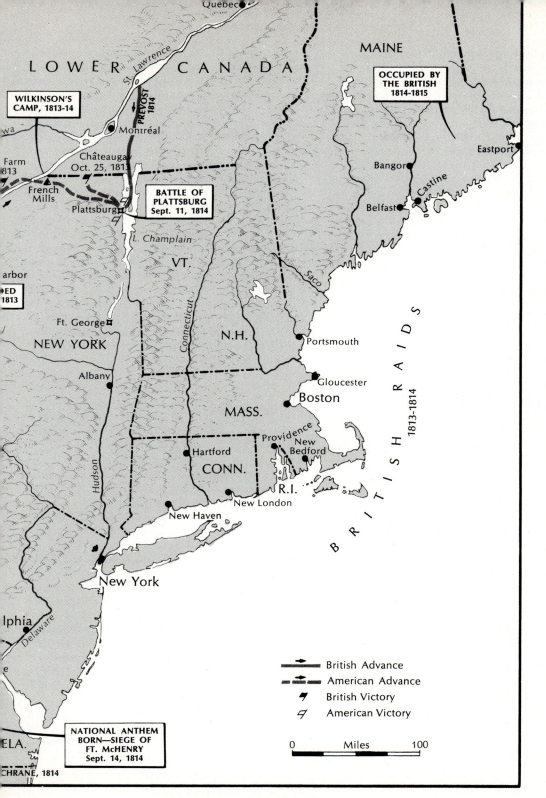

LOWER   CANADA

MAINE

St. Lawrence

OCCUPIED BY THE BRITISH 1814-1815

WILKINSON'S CAMP, 1813-14

PREVOST 1814

Montréal

Eastport

Châteauga
Oct. 25, 181

Bangor

Farm
813

Castine

French
Mills

Belfast

BATTLE OF PLATTSBURG Sept. 11, 1814

Plattsburg

L. Champlain

Saco

VT.

arbor

ED
1813

Connecticut

Ft. George

N.H.

Portsmouth

NEW YORK

Albany

Gloucester

Boston

MASS.

Hudson

Providence

Hartford

New
Bedford

CONN.

R.I.

New London

New Haven

B R I T I S H   R A I D S

1813-1814

New York

Iphia

Delaware

→ British Advance

━ ▶ American Advance

⚡ British Victory

⚡ American Victory

NATIONAL ANTHEM BORN—SIEGE OF FT. McHENRY Sept. 14, 1814

0   Miles   100

ELA.

CHRANE, 1814

War of 1812 in the North

state north of the Potomac except two. But Madison was re-elected.

In addition to having to cope with internal disaffection, the United States had a further disadvantage: the administration's military strategy was stupid. Instead of striking at Montreal or Quebec and severing the St. Lawrence, Madison attempted several feeble blows at less important points. Three weeks before war was declared, Governor William Hull of Michigan Territory, a sixty-year-old veteran of the War of Independence, was ordered to invade Upper Canada. Hull crossed into Canada on 12 July, but the British capture of the American post at Michilimackinac caused him to fall back on Detroit. Hull ordered the American commander at Fort Dearborn (Chicago) to come to his assistance; but the Indians captured a part of that small force and massacred the rest. General Isaac Brock, the British commander in Upper Canada, having transported to Detroit the few troops he could spare from the Niagara front, paraded them in red coats in sight of General Hull and summoned him to surrender. A broad hint in Brock's note, that the Indians would be beyond his control the moment the fighting began, completely unnerved the elderly general. Dreading massacre and deserted by some of his militia, Hull surrendered his army on 16 August 1812. So ended the first invasion of Canada. The effective military frontier of the United States was thrown back to the Wabash and the Ohio.

On 13 October 1812 the Americans crossed into Canada again, on the Niagara front. Captain John E. Wool led a small detachment to a successful attack on Queenston heights, in which General Brock was killed. But the New York militia under General Stephen Van Rensselaer refused to support him. They had turned out to defend their homes, not to invade Canada. In vain the Patroon exhorted them. They calmly watched their countrymen on the other bank being enveloped, shot down, and forced to surrender.

On the ocean there was a different story. The United States Navy was vastly outnumbered, but the Royal Navy was so deeply engaged in war with France that at first it could spare few vessels for this war. The pride of the United States Navy were frigates *Constitution*, *United States*, and *President*, which threw a heavier broadside than the British frigates, and were so heavily timbered and planked as to deserve the name 'Old Ironsides'; yet with such fine, clean lines and great spread of canvas that they could outsail almost anything afloat. The crews were volunteers, and the officers, young and tried by experience against France and Tripoli, were burning to avenge the *Chesapeake*. On the other hand, the compatriots of Nelson, conquerors at Cape St. Vincent, Trafalgar, and the Nile, were the spoiled children of victory, confident of beating any vessel not more than twice their size. Hence, when U.S.S. *Constitution* (Captain Isaac Hull, a nephew of the General) knocked H.M.S. *Guerrière* helpless in two hours and a half on 19 August 1812; when sloop-of-war *Wasp* mastered H.M.S. *Frolic* in 43 minutes on 17 October; and U.S.S. *Hornet* (Captain James Lawrence) in a hot fight off the Demerara river, on 24 February 1813, sank H.M.S. *Peacock* in fifteen minutes, there were amazement and indignation in England, and rejoicing in the United States. The moral value of these victories to the American people, following disaster on the Canadian border, was beyond all calculation, but the military value was slight. Most of the American men-of-war that put into harbor during the winter of 1812–13 never got out again because of the British blockade, and the British were able to raid the Chesapeake country at will.

In the meantime, naval history was being made on the Great Lakes. During the winter of 1812–13, Captain Oliver H. Perry constructed a fleet of stout little vessels. That same winter, General William Henry Harrison advanced from the Ohio river toward Detroit, in three divisions. The British General Procter did not wait for them to unite, but beat two separately in fierce wilderness fights in which the American wounded were massacred by Indian auxiliaries. Harrison then decided to await a naval decision on Lake Erie. On 10 September 1813, at Put-in-Bay among the islands at the western end of the lake, Perry won a notable victory. His laconic report, 'We have met the enemy, and they are ours,' was literally true. It was the only surrender of a complete squadron in British naval history.

The prudent course for General Procter was to abandon Detroit and fall back on the Niag-

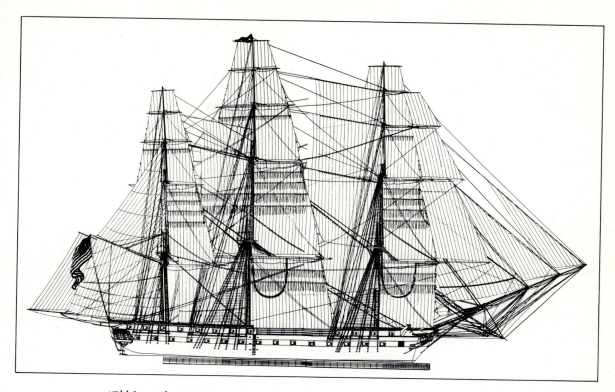

'Old Ironsides.' A 44-gun frigate launched at Boston in 1797, the U.S.S. *Constitution* earned her official nickname in a battle with the British vessel *Java* off Brazil. Oliver Wendell Holmes's poem 'Old Ironsides' sparked a campaign in 1830 that saved her from dismantling, and she is today, at Boston, the oldest ship in the American Navy still in commission. (*Library of Congress*)

ara front. But Tecumseh persuaded his ally to make a stand at an Indian village near the center of the Ontario peninsula. Thither General Harrison pursued him. The Battle of the Thames (5 October 1813) was a victory for the Kentucky mounted rifles. Tecumseh died on that field, his Indian confederacy broke up, Procter fled, and the American military frontier in the Northwest was re-established.

Perry's squadron had obtained valuable cannon from a raid on York (Toronto), the tiny capital of Upper Canada, on 27 April 1813. When the Americans were advancing into the village, a large powder magazine exploded, killing General Zebu-lon M. Pike and about 300 men. As a result of this incident, or of general indiscipline, the American troops got out of hand after the British surrendered the town, and burned the two brick parliament houses, the governor's residence, and other buildings. The Americans also burned Newark and as much as they could of Queenston, turning the inhabitants out of their houses on a cold winter's night. For this act the innocent inhabitants on the United States side paid dear. On 18 December Fort Niagara was taken by surprise, the Indians were let loose on the surrounding country, and the villages of Black Rock and Buffalo were destroyed. The second year of war closed with Canada cleared of American troops, and the Canadians in possession of Fort Niagara and ready to assume the offensive.

After Napoleon's abdication on 6 April 1814, Britain was able to provide Canada with an adequate army to carry the war into the United States and to intensify the naval blockade. The war office planned to invade the United States from three points successively: Niagara, Lake Champlain, and New Orleans; and simultaneously to raid the Chesapeake.

On the Niagara front America took the initiative before British reinforcements arrived. On 3 July 1814 General Jacob Brown boated his army of about 5000 men across the Niagara river and forced Fort Erie to capitulate. On the 5th, his subordinate, Winfield Scott, after giving his brigade a Fourth of July dinner that they had been too busy to eat the day before, was about to hold a holiday parade on a near-by plain when three regiments of British regulars appeared. The parade became the Battle of Chippewa, a European-style stand-up fight in open country. Both lines advanced in close order, stopping alternately to load and fire; when they were about 60 paces from each other, it was the British who broke. On 25 July, in the Battle of Lundy's Lane, the most stubbornly contested fight of the war, both American generals were badly wounded, and the casualties were very heavy for a battle in that era: on the American side, 853 out of fewer than 2000 engaged; on the British side, 878 out of a somewhat larger force. These actions prevented an invasion of the United States from the Niagara front and gave the United States Army a new pride and character.

By mid-August General Sir George Prevost commanded some 10,000 British veterans encamped near Montreal, ready to invade the United States by the classic route of Lake Champlain and the Hudson. It was the strongest, best equipped army that had ever been sent to North America. Prospects for the United States were grim. Prevost's army reached Plattsburg on 6 September 1814. Facing them were only 1500 American regulars, and a few thousand militia. Before attacking, Prevost wished to secure control of the lake. Early in the morning of 11 September there began a murderous engagement between two freshwater fleets, which anchored gunwale to gunwale at pistol range and attempted to pound each other to pieces. After the British flagship had killed one-fifth of the crew of the American flagship *Saratoga*, Captain Thomas Macdonough forced the British flagship and three other vessels to surrender. Prevost was so discouraged by the loss of this supporting fleet that he retreated to Canada. This naval Battle of Plattsburg—'Macdonough's Victory' it was then called—proved to be decisive. But it was not the last battle of the war.

In June 1814 a British expeditionary force had begun a diversion in the Chesapeake. The campaign that followed reflected little credit to the one side, and considerable disgrace on the other. General Robert Ross, British commander of the land forces, was instructed by Admiral Cochrane 'to destroy and lay waste such towns and districts upon the coast' as he might find assailable. A fleet of American gunboats, retreating up the Patuxent river, led Ross's army from Chesapeake Bay to the back door of Washington. For five days the British marched along the banks of the Patuxent, approaching the capital of the United States without seeing an enemy or firing a shot. In Washington about 7000 militia, all that turned out of 95,000 summoned, were placed under an unusually incompetent general and hurried to a strong position behind the village of Bladensburg, athwart the road over which the invaders must advance. President Madison and some of the cabinet came out to see the fight. After the militia had suffered only 66 casualties they broke and ran, and Ross pressed on to Washington (24 August 1814). Some officers arrived at the White House in time to eat a dinner that had been prepared for the President, who fled to the Virginia hills. Most of the public buildings of the capital were deliberately burned, partly in retaliation for the American burning of York and Newark, partly to impress the administration with the uselessness of further resistance. General Ross personally superintended the piling up of furniture in the White House before it was given to the flames.

Fortunately, the destruction of Washington only illustrated the strategic truth that hit-and-run raids achieve little. The British army withdrew to its transports, and proceeded to the next objective, Baltimore. Here the Maryland militia showed a very different spirit. A naval bombardment of Fort McHenry accomplished nothing for the British, but gave America a stirring national anthem. Francis Scott Key, a prisoner on board one of the bombarding vessels, gained his inspiration for 'The Star Spangled Banner' from seeing the flag still flying over Fort McHenry 'by the dawn's early light.' General Ross fell at the head of a landing party (12 September) one day after 'Macdonough's Victory,' and that ended the Chesapeake campaign.

Before the third British expeditionary force reached New Orleans, the West had produced a great military leader, General Andrew Jackson. He had emigrated to Tennessee as a young man, represented that state in the United States Senate, and as commander of its militia had been winning laurels in warfare against the Upper Creeks. That Indian nation endeavored to remain neutral, but some of Tecumseh's warriors stirred it up. A series of raids took some 250 white scalps. This news found Andrew Jackson in bed at Nashville, recovering from a pistol wound received in a street brawl with Thomas H. Benton, the future senator from Missouri. Within a month Jackson at the head of 2500 militia and a band of Choctaw and Lower Creek auxiliaries was in the Upper Creek country. The Tennessee militia showed the same disposition to panic and flee as their Northern brethren, but after Jackson had executed a few militiamen to encourage the others, discipline improved. At the Tohopeka or Horseshoe Bend of the Tallapoosa river (27 March 1814), the military power of the Creek nation was broken; 557 warriors were left dead on the battlefield, while Jackson lost only 26 of his own men and 23 Indian allies. This campaign not only had immediate strategic impact in depriving the British of a powerful ally; the subsequent treaty with the Upper Creek nation opened an immense territory— about two-thirds of Alabama, the heart of the future cotton kingdom—to white settlement and Negro slavery. In early August, a small British force landed at Pensacola in Spanish Florida; its leader proceeded to drill Creek refugees with a

view to renewing the war in that quarter. Jackson invaded Florida on his own authority and crushed this diversion by taking Pensacola in November.

Two months later, the most formidable British expedition of the war threatened New Orleans. On the morning of 8 January 1815 Major General Sir Edward Pakenham directed a foolhardy frontal assault of some 5300 men in close column formation against Andrew Jackson's 3500 on a parapet so well protected that the British could not get at them. The result was more of a massacre than a battle. General Pakenham and over 2000 of all ranks were killed, wounded, or missing. Exactly thirteen Americans were killed and 58 wounded before the attacking columns melted. Ten days later the only surviving British general officer withdrew the army to its transports.

This Battle of New Orleans had no military value, since peace had already been signed at Ghent on Christmas Eve; but it made a future President of the United States, and in folklore wiped out all previous defeats, ending the 'Second War of Independence' in a blaze of glory.

Disaffection and Peace

One of the many anomalies in this curious war is the bitter opposition by the New England states, despite the fact that war built up their economy. Permanently important for New England was the war's stimulus to manufacturing. Unreliable estimates of the number of cotton mills in New England range from 57 in 1809 to as many as 113 in 1810. While John Lowell, leader of the extreme Federalist Essex Junto, was advocating a New England Confederation, his brother Francis C. Lowell was picking up information in England about power looms. After his return to the United States in 1814, Lowell invented a new power loom with which, at Waltham, Massachusetts, he equipped the first complete American cotton factory, where every process of manufacture from the raw material to the finished cloth was performed under one roof.

Though the War of 1812 was enriching New England, Federalists cried that their section was being ruined and complained that the Republican administration left it defenseless against raids by the Royal Navy. On 5 October 1814 Massachusetts summoned a New England Convention at Hartford, for the express purpose of conferring upon 'their public grievances and concerns,' upon 'defence against the enemy . . . and also to take measures, if they shall think proper, for producing a convention of delegates from all the United States, in order to revise the Constitution thereof.' This language showed a compromise between the moderate and the extreme Federalists. The former, led by Harrison Gray Otis, were not disunionists, but wished to obtain concessions for their section. Alarmed by the rising tide of secession sentiment, they hoped the Convention would act as safety valve; their desire to concert defensive measures against the enemy was sincere. But the violent wing of the Federalist party, led by Timothy Pickering and John Lowell, had other objects in view. It was their belief that the British invasion of New Orleans would succeed, and that Aaron Burr's secession plot for Louisiana and the West would then bear fruit. They wished the Hartford Convention to draft a new federal constitution, with clauses to protect New England interests, and present it as a pistol to the original Thirteen States only, not to the democratic West. If these accepted, well and good; if not, New England would make a separate peace and go it alone.

At the Hartford Convention, meeting in secret session on 15 December 1814, the moderates gained control and issued a calm report on 5 January 1815. An element of their caution was the strength of the Republican party in New England; the Federalists controlled all five states, but only by small majorities outside Connecticut, and there would probably have been civil war had the extremists persuaded the states to adopt ordinances of secession. Madison's administration and the war were severely arraigned by the Convention; 'but to attempt upon every abuse of power to change the Constitution, would be to perpetuate the evils of revolution.' Secession was ruled out as unnecessary, since the causes of New England's calamities were not permanent but the result of bad administration and of partisanship in the European war. The New England states were invited to nullify a conscription bill then before

Congress, if it should pass, and it was suggested that the administration might permit them to assume their own defense, applying to that purpose the federal taxes collected within their borders. But there was no threat of a separate peace.

Presently the good news from Ghent and New Orleans put Madison's administration on a high horse, and made New England the scapegoat for government mismanagement of the war. A stigma of unpatriotism, from which it never recovered, was attached to the Federalist party, and rightly so, since the leaders could not or would not see that the war had become defensive. Yet no stigma was attached to the doctrine of state rights; and within a few years it was revived by states like Virginia, which with one voice had denounced the Hartford Convention as treasonable.

In the Treaty of Ghent, signed on Christmas Eve 1814, both sides agreed to disagree on everything important except the conclusion of hostilities, and restoring pre-war boundaries. Madison's announced reasons for declaring war— impressment and neutral rights—were not even mentioned. But the treaty did bear good fruit in the shape of four boundary commissions to settle the line between Canada and the United States. And, before the next maritime war broke out, impressment had been given up as a means of recruiting for the Royal Navy.

So ended an unnecessary war, which might have been prevented by a little more imagination and broader vision. Casualties at least were relatively 'light'—1877 American soldiers and sailors killed in action. Moreover, the war had a good effect on relations between the two governments. The United States was never again denied the treatment due an independent nation, and Americans began to grasp a basic fact of North American sovereignty: that Canada was in the British empire for as long as she wanted, not as long as we wanted. The war had yet another important consequence—Jackson's incursion into Florida indicated that the Spanish empire in North America was ready to fall apart, and the United States had an opportunity to expand to the southeast.

Most of the wartime fleet was maintained after peace, and within three months of the Treaty of Ghent it found profitable employment. The Dey

HARTFORD
CONVENTION
CANDIDATE.

The People's
RIGHTS
No BRIBERY.
No Corruption

In this contemporary cartoon, the Hartford Convention Federalists are identified with Lucifer, incendiarism, and the British crown while their opponents associate themselves with the pristine symbols of the young republic. (*Prints Division, New York Public Library*)

of Algeria had taken advantage of hostilities to capture American merchant ships. On 2 March 1815 Congress declared war on Algeria, and in May Commodore Decatur commanded a squadron that captured the pirates' 44-gun flagship, then sailed to Algiers, where the Dey signed a treaty at gun-point. This time *he* had to pay. Similar 'stick-up' negotiations were held at Tunis and Tripoli. From that time on, the United States has maintained a naval squadron in the Mediterranean.

For the United States, it had been for the most part an inglorious war. Part of the nation's capital lay in ashes, and the President had had to flee. Two days before the treaty of peace, Daniel Webster, noting that the administration could not re-

cruit troops, collect taxes, or borrow money, wrote: 'The Govt. *cannot last,* under this war & in the hands of these men, another twelve month.'

Yet, paradoxically, the country came out of the war with an exhilarating sense of the triumph of republican institutions. It had dared a second time to wage war with the mightiest power on earth, and it had come out whole. Humiliating setbacks were quickly forgotten in the recollection of thrilling victories. One ironic consequence of this divisive war was to intensify American nationalism. With national honor vindicated, with a new conviction of national power, the young republic now looked toward the vast continent to the west which, as Henry Adams wrote, lay before the American people 'like an uncovered ore-bed.'

11

Good Feelings and Bad

*

1815–1829

A Nationalist Era

The year 1815 is a turning-point in American as in European history; and a point of divergence between the two. Hitherto the development of the United States had been vitally affected by Old World brawls. With the Peace of Vienna, Europe turned to problems that had little interest for America; and with the Peace of Ghent, America turned her back on Europe—although she kept looking at the Old World over one shoulder, as the Monroe Doctrine indicates. Most of the difficulties under which the republic had labored since the War of Independence now dropped out of sight, and there opened a serene prospect of peace, prosperity, and social progress. No one suspected that expansion would also bring its problems, and that within half a century Americans would be slaughtering one another.

The nationalism kindled by the war shaped the direction of politics in the next decade. In 1815 Madison startled the country by calling for adequate military and naval forces, direct internal taxation, a protective tariff, and a new national bank. The Federalists were astonished by this volte-face, since the Republicans had long de-plored peacetime armies and internal taxes and had let the first national bank expire in 1811. In his final annual message in December 1816, Madison recommended both a 'comprehensive system of roads and canals' and the creation of a national university in Washington. A Federalist governor wrote: *'The Administration have fought themselves completely on to federal ground.'*

The Republicans encountered little partisan opposition to their program, not only because the Federalists had long espoused such nationalist doctrine, but even more because the party had been all but destroyed by its role in the war. The Federalists, who lacked an appreciation of the importance of the presidential contest in party warfare, ran electoral slates in only three states in 1816. The Republicans further weakened the Federalists by denying their rivals any public office under their control. James Monroe, once the turbulent crown prince but now the accepted heir of the Virginia dynasty, succeeded to the presidency in 1817 almost unopposed, and in 1821 obtained every electoral vote but one. Contemporaries called this period the 'era of good feelings,' but it was, in fact, an interval of stagnant politics in which it became increasingly hard for the Republicans to maintain party discipline and party zeal, and in which voting in presidential elections declined precipitously.

Politics did not long continue in this placid pattern. New forces were transforming the sections; and while readjustment was taking place, everyone acquiesced in nationalism of a sort. Manufacturing was becoming the dominant interest in New England and Pennsylvania; democracy had invaded New York; King Cotton's domain was advancing into the new Gulf states; and the Northwest acquired new aspirations. By 1830 the sections had again become articulate, defining the stand they were to take until the Civil War.

With new interests came a complete reversal in sectional attitudes toward the Constitution. Daniel Webster of Massachusetts, who in 1814 had warned Congress that his state would not obey conscription, in 1830 was intoning hymns to the Union; whilst John C. Calhoun of South Carolina, leader of the war hawks in 1812 and of nationalist legislation after the war, began in 1828 to write textbooks of state rights. Of all publicists and statesmen whose careers bridged the War of 1812, only five were consistent, and three were Virginians: Chief Justice Marshall refused to unlearn the nationalism he had been taught by Washington; John Taylor and John Randolph went on as if nothing had happened since 1798. Clay and Adams never changed their nationalist ideas of 1812.

Both Clay and Calhoun, the nationalist leaders in Congress at this period, feared the growing particularism of the sections. Like Hamilton, they could imagine no stronger binding force than self-interest; and their policy was but a broader version of his reports on public credit and manufactures. Their formula, which Clay christened the 'American System,' was protection and internal improvements: a protective tariff for the manufacturers, a home market and better transportation for the farmers.

It was a propitious moment to raise the tariff. National pride had been wounded by dependence on smuggled British goods. After 1815, infant industries sustained a setback when British manufactures flooded the American market. As a consequence, the 1810–20 decade was the only one in our history in which urbanization declined. Cries from industries for protection came from interests in almost every section: New England cotton mills, experimental mills in the Carolinas, Pittsburgh iron smelters, Kentucky's new industry of weaving hemp into cotton bagging, the shepherds of Vermont and Ohio, and the granaries of central New York. Even Jefferson wrote 'We must now place the manufacturer by the side of the agriculturist.' Congressmen from states that a generation later preferred secession to protection eagerly voted for the tariff of 1816; maritime New England voted against it. Webster was 'not in haste to see Sheffields and Birminghams in America.' Yet New England and Pennsylvania were destined to pocket the earliest benefits of protection.

'Internal improvements'—public works at federal expense—complemented protection. Immediately after the War of 1812 emigrants rushed to the West, eager to exploit the lands conquered from Tecumseh and from the Creek nation. Between 1810 and 1820 the population west of the Appalachians more than doubled. Four new states, Indiana (1816), Mississippi (1817), Illinois (1818), and Alabama (1819), were admitted, as well as Louisiana in 1812. Owing to the difficulty of ascending the Mississippi and Ohio rivers, Western supplies of manufactured goods came by wagon road from Atlantic seaports. But in 1817 a steamboat managed to reach Cincinnati from New Orleans, and two years later 60 light-draught stern-wheelers were plying between New Orleans and Louisville. Their freight charges were less than half the cost of wagon transport. To preserve and expand their stake in the Western trade, Eastern states set out to forge new East-West links; most notable was New York's decision to construct the Erie Canal, which was started in 1817.

Clay and Calhoun, believing that improved transportation was a responsibility of the federal government, induced Congress to push through a national road from Cumberland on the upper Potomac to Wheeling on the Ohio.[1] Connected with Baltimore by a state road, this 'national pike' became the most important route to the Northwest until 1840. In 1817 Congress proposed to

---

1. This National or Cumberland road was later built to Vandalia, Illinois, by successive appropriations between 1822 and 1838; but the Federal Government relinquished each section, upon its completion, to the state within which it lay.

Chicago in 1820. This lithograph reveals the primitive quality of the settlement at that date. Four years before, the United States army had rebuilt Fort Dearborn here, but as late as 1833, when Chicago was incorporated as a village, it had about 200 inhabitants. Within a generation it would be a city of 300,000. (*Stokes Collection, New York Public Library*)

earmark certain federal revenues for bolder projects. Madison so far had accepted every item in the nationalist program; but here he drew the line, and vetoed this internal improvement bill. Monroe had similar constitutional scruples; and by the time J. Q. Adams reached the White House, with even more ambitious plans, Congress proved disappointingly stubborn. The Appalachians were destined to be crossed and tunneled by private enterprise under state authority.

To provide the financial ligaments for the American system, Congress in 1816 chartered a Second Bank of the United States. The B.U.S. began operations in 1817 as a bank of deposit, discount, and issue, with the government as principal client and holder of one-fifth of the capital stock, differing from the Bank of England mainly in the power to establish branches. This feature, necessary for the fiscal operations of a federal government, hampered lesser banks operating under state charters. In Maryland the legislature levied a heavy tax on the notes issued by the Baltimore branch of this 'foreign corporation.' When the B.U.S. refused to pay, McCulloch *v.* Maryland reached the Supreme Court.

Chief Justice Marshall's opinion became a milestone in American nationalism. First, he offered a classic definition of national sovereignty that undercut the argument that the general government held only such power as the states vested in it. Secondly, the Court disposed of the argument that the act was unconstitutional since the power to charter corporations is not expressly granted to Congress by the Constitution and cannot be inferred from the 'necessary and proper' clause. A national bank, Maryland argued, was not necessary, as the want of one since 1811 proved. 'The government of the Union, though limited in its powers, is supreme within its sphere of action,' Marshall responded. 'Let the end be legitimate, let it be within the scope of the Constitution, and all means which are appropriate, which are plainly adapted to that end, which are not prohibited, but consist with the letter and spirit of the Constitution, are constitutional.' Finally, Marshall denied that a state might, by virtue of its reserved power of taxation, levy a tax upon the operations of the B.U.S.

During Marshall's thirty-four-year tenure as Chief Justice, the Supreme Court handed down a number of other rulings giving judicial sanction to the doctrine of centralization of powers at the expense of the states. In Martin v. Hunter's Lessee (1816), the Court upheld the constitutionality of the Judiciary Act of 1789 that gave it the power to review and reverse decisions of state courts where they conflicted with rights guaranteed by the Constitution. In Cohens v. Virginia (1821) Marshall not only vigorously reasserted this principle, but partially nullified the purpose of the Eleventh Amendment by accepting appellate jurisdiction over a suit against a state provided the state had originally instituted the suit. In Martin v. Mott (1827) the Court denied to a state the right, which New England had asserted during the previous war, to withhold militia from the national service when demanded by the President. In Gibbons v. Ogden (1824), perhaps the most far-reaching of his decisions, Marshall mapped out the course that Congress would follow most of the time from that day to this in regulating interstate commerce. In speaking for the Court in a decision which smashed a state-chartered monopoly of steamboat traffic, Marshall boldly insisted that Congressional power over commerce 'is not to be confined by state lines, but acts upon its subject matter wherever it is to be found.'

During these same years, another historic line of decisions by the Marshall Court threw the protective veil of the Constitution over property interests. In Fletcher v. Peck (1810), the so-called Yazoo land fraud case, Marshall prohibited the state of Georgia from rescinding a grossly corrupt sale of Western lands on the principle that such action impaired the obligation of a contract. In the Dartmouth College case of 1819 the Court invalidated a New Hampshire statute abolishing the pre-revolutionary charter of the college and placing it under state control. Marshall's decision that a charter to a corporation was a contract within the meaning of the Constitution, and so beyond the control of a state, was of far-reaching importance, both for good and ill. On the one hand, it protected privately endowed colleges, schools, and the like from political interference, and encouraged endowments for education and charity. On the other, in conjunction with the Yazoo decision, it gave corporations an immunity from legislative interference that was only gradually modified through judicial recognition of the police power of the states. Marshall's opinions, and those of Associate Justice Joseph Story (Martin v. Hunter's Lessee and Martin v. Mott), worked with the spirit of the times in fostering nationalism, but worked against it in opposing democracy and majority rule.

Western Panic and Missouri Compromise

The West, which deeply resented the McCulloch opinion, found other occasions for grievances with the B.U.S. The new settlers, tempted by rising crop prices, purchased land far beyond their capacity to pay; for the Public Land Act of 1800 extended long credit. Much of the best land was engrossed by speculators. When cotton rose to 34 cents a pound in 1818, planters paid up to $150 an acre for uncleared land in the black belt of Alabama. All this led to a wide dispersal of settlers, instead of the orderly progression along a definite frontier that the Act of 1796 had planned. Until vacant spaces were settled, the scattered frontier farmers found themselves without

schools, means of communication, or markets, yet deeply in debt to the Federal Government or to 'wild-cat' Western banks. These in turn were indebted to the B.U.S. and to Eastern capitalists, who at the same time were setting up new corporations far in advance of the country's needs. The Bank of the United States, which might have put a brake on inflation, encouraged this mad scramble, until late in 1818, when the directors took steps to curtail credit. This hastened the inevitable panic, and in 1819 it broke. Many state banks collapsed, and enormous amounts of Western real estate were foreclosed by the B.U.S. in the very year that the McCulloch decision forbade the states to tax the 'Monster.' The West raged against the Eastern money power, and hard times, which lasted until 1824, afforded an ideal culture-bed for the movement afterwards known as Jacksonian Democracy.

While debt, deflation, and hard times were producing these preliminary symptoms of a vertical cleavage between East and West, another Western question, that of slavery extension, threatened to cut the Union horizontally into North and South. Ever since the Federal Convention of 1787 there had been a tacit political balance between these great sections. In 1789 North and South were approximately equal in numbers; but in 1820 the free states had a population of 5,152,000 with 105 members in the House of Representatives, while the slave states had 4,485,000 people with 81 congressmen. An even balance had been maintained in the Senate by the admission of free and slave states alternately; the admission of Alabama in 1819 gave eleven to each.

In the territory of the Louisiana purchase, Congress had done nothing to disturb slavery as it existed by French and Spanish law. Consequently, in the westward rush after the War of 1812, several thousand slaveowners with their human property emigrated to the Territory of Upper Louisiana, establishing plantations in the rich bottom lands of the lower Missouri river, or on the west bank of the Mississippi near St. Louis. When the people of this region demanded admission to the Union as the state of Missouri, slavery was permitted by their proposed state constitution.

In 1819 the House approved a bill admitting

John Marshall (1755–1835). Chief Justice of the United States from 1801 to 1835, he did more than anyone in the nation's history to give stature to the Supreme Court and to shape constitutional jurisprudence. Of the 11,000 opinions of the Court during his long tenure, Marshall wrote no fewer than 519. Chester Harding, a self-taught American artist who executed this portrait, said, 'I had such great pleasure in painting *the whole* of such a man.' (*Boston Athenaeum*)

Missouri but with an amendment prohibiting the further introduction of slaves into Missouri, and requiring that all children subsequently born therein of slave parents should be free at age 25. The bill was put down in the Senate, and a bitter national debate ensued concerned not with the morality of slavery but with sectional power. Northerners regarded the proposed admission of Missouri, which lay almost wholly north of the then dividing line between freedom and slavery, as an aggressive move toward increasing the voting strength of the South; and many threatened secession if slavery were not defeated. Southerners did not yet defend the rightfulness of slavery, but asserted their right to enjoy human property in the trans-Mississippi West, and threatened secession if that were denied. When Congress again took up the question, in January 1820, enough Northern Republicans were detached from the anti-slavery bloc by fear of a Federalist renaissance to get a compromise measure through. Missouri was admitted as a slave-holding state, but slavery was prohibited in United States territory north of lat. 36° 30'. As part of the compromise, Maine, which had detached herself from Massachusetts, was admitted as a free state, making twelve of each.

This Missouri Compromise put the question of slavery extension at rest for almost a generation, but a veil had been lifted for a moment, revealing a bloody prospect ahead. 'This momentous question, like a fire bell in the night, awakened and filled me with terror,' wrote Jefferson. 'I considered it at once as the knell of the Union.' And J. Q. Adams recorded in his diary: 'I take it for granted that the present question is a mere preamble—a title-page to a great, tragic volume.'

Anglo-American Adjustments

While Monroe was coping with the explosive slavery issue he also had to contend with portentous questions in diplomacy that would affect American foreign affairs for generations to come. Almost a century of diplomacy was required to clear up all controversies between Britain and America left by the Treaty of Ghent. J. Q. Adams wrote before the year was out that the treaty was 'a truce rather than a peace' because nothing was settled. 'All the points of collision which had subsisted . . . before the war were left open.' In particular, Canada, with a long and vague boundary, rival peltry and fishing interests, and a fresh-water naval force, promised many points of friction between the two countries.

The three statesmen who did most to preserve peace were Presidents Madison and Monroe, and Lord Castlereagh, the first British statesman since Shelburne to regard friendship with America as a permanent British interest. Madison and Monroe met him halfway, but not John Quincy Adams. He, too, hoped to preserve the peace, but he was suspicious and irascible; as Monroe's Secretary of State his notes needed softening by the now mellow President. But Adams's perception was abnormally keen, and alone of contemporaries in either hemisphere he foresaw his country's future place in the world, and the independence of colonies everywhere.

Disarmament on the Great Lakes was the first fruit of Anglo-American diplomacy after the war, and the most lasting. Peace found each side feverishly building ships against the other on Lake Ontario. The Canadians, apprehensive of further American aggression, looked for large outlays by the British treasury to complete this building program. The Americans, on the contrary, hoped to avoid a fresh-water building contest. In 1815 Congress provided for the sale or laying up of all the Lake fleet not necessary for enforcement of the revenue laws. The army was reduced to 10,000 men, and in 1820 to 6000. But it was President Madison who made the momentous proposal of naval disarmament on the Lakes, and in 1817 an agreement was effected by an exchange of notes at Washington. The Rush-Bagot agreement, named for the American and British ministers, limited naval force on the Lakes, an agreement still in operation, although modified in detail. Not until the 1840's was the boundary line finally settled, but despite periods of severe friction, mutual respect and good will have kept the American-Canadian border undefended and unfortified.

The Treaty of Ghent also provided that the contracting parties 'use their best endeavors' to

SLAVE-BRANDING.

(Library of Congress)

abolish the African slave trade. Congress had outlawed the traffic in 1808, and in 1820 declared it to be piracy, punishable by death. But the United States refused to enter any international agreement for joint suppression, because, owing to recent memories of impressment and the like, Adams refused to allow American ships to be searched for slaves by British men-of-war. A squadron of the United States Navy was maintained off the African coast, to watch for slavers flying the American flag; but plenty of 'black ivory' got by under the flag of freedom, into Cuba or the Southern states.

Meantime, on the southeastern border, Anglo-American amity was gravely endangered. East Florida was a Spanish province, but Spanish authority was little exercised beyond the three fortified posts of Pensacola, St. Marks, and St. Augustine. On the American side of the boundary, there was meddling with Indians, not by Spaniards but by two British traders, an elderly Scot named Arbuthnot, who cultivated the Seminole, a branch of the Creek nation, and a young adventurer named Ambrister, who joined a group of Seminoles under a chief whom the whites called Billy Bow-legs. In 1817 the Seminoles on the American side of the border defied settlers to enter upon the Creek lands which had been ceded three years before, and scalped some of those who did. General Andrew Jackson was ordered by President Monroe to raise a force of Tennessee militia, chastise the offenders, and pursue them into Spanish Florida if necessary. While Jackson was destroying Seminole villages, an army detachment on the way to join him, with women and children, was ambushed by other Seminoles and destroyed. Jackson burst into Florida like an avenging demon. Two Seminole chiefs fled to St. Marks, where they were relieved to find a gunboat flying the Union Jack. With mock honors they were received, and promptly clapped into irons. The gun-boat was American and the Union Jack a ruse. Next day (7 April 1818) Jackson entered St. Marks against the protest of the Spanish governor, hauled down the Spanish flag, hanged the two chiefs without trial, and arrested Arbuthnot. But when he pushed eastward to surprise

Billy Bow-legs, the Seminole chief eluded him. Furious and baffled, Jackson learned the cause of his escape when Ambrister blundered into his camp. On one of his men was found a letter from Arbuthnot, warning Billy of Jackson's approach, and offering him ten kegs of gunpowder. Following a quickly constituted court-martial, Arbuthnot and Ambrister, both British subjects, were put to death.

Jackson was not through yet. After overcoming the Seminoles, he took Pensacola, ejected the Spanish governor, and garrisoned the fortress with Americans. On his return, he was acclaimed once more a hero by the West, but in Washington, Henry Clay reminded the Senate that 'it was in the provinces that were laid the seeds of the ambitious projects that overturned the liberties of Rome.' In Monroe's cabinet, Adams alone insisted that Jackson's every act was justified by the incompetence of Spanish authority to police its own territory; and Adams had his way. When the news reached London in the autumn of 1818, the press rang with denunciation of America and the 'ruffian' who had murdered two 'peaceful British traders.' War would have been declared 'if the ministry had but held up a finger,' wrote the American minister, Richard Rush; but Lord Castlereagh's firmness preserved the peace.

From Madrid came a response of long-lasting significance. Fearful that Jackson's invasion portended an American seizure of Florida, Spain resigned herself to getting out with something to show for it. In 1819 Spain sold all her lands east of the Mississippi, together with her claim to the Oregon country, in return for $5 million. In addition, the boundary between the United States and Mexico was defined. Two years later ratification of the treaty filled out the southeastern domain of the United States to the farthest reach of the Florida Keys.

Canning Proposes, Monroe Disposes

Important as was the acquisition of Florida, Monroe had an even more historic role to play in Latin America. In 1815, two years before he took office, there were only two completely independent nations in the New World, the United States and Haiti. The next seven years saw an eruption of new republics in Latin America. By the autumn of 1822, continental America from the Great Lakes to Cape Horn was independent. European nations maintained sovereignty only in Belize, Bolivia, and the Guianas. In 1822 the United States extended formal recognition to the new republics, but the Continental powers would not accept the outcome as final. After France invaded Spain in 1823, with the avowed object of delivering Ferdinand VII from a constitution that had been forced upon him by the liberals, it was common talk that a Franco-Spanish expeditionary force to South America would follow, with the blessing of the Holy Alliance.

In London George Canning, who had succeeded Castlereagh, sought a way out of a dilemma. Despite substantial interest in South American trade, Britain was not ready to admit rebel republican colonists to the family of nations. On the other hand, if England did not do something, Canning feared that Monroe and Adams would obtain exclusive commercial advantages, and a Pan-American republican alliance. He came up with a brilliant plan. A joint Anglo-American protest against intervention would thwart the Holy Alliance, maintain England's new markets, establish England as co-protector of Latin America and, at the same time, throw America's weight onto the British scale of power. So, on 16 August 1823, the British foreign minister put a question to Richard Rush, American minister at London. What would he say to joining England in warning France to keep hands off South America?

Canning's astounding overture appealed to a number of American leaders, but J. Q. Adams knew that there was slight danger of armed intervention in Latin America, and that the British navy had the power to prevent it in any case. What could be Canning's game? The clue, he thought, was a proposed pledge, in Canning's note of 20 August, against either power's acquiring a part of Spanish America. That pledge might be inconvenient if Cuba voted herself into the United States. Furthermore, Canning was unwilling to deny Spain the right to reconquer its former colonies.

At the next cabinet meeting Adams declared, 'It would be more candid, as well as more dignified, to avow our principles explicitly to Russia and

France, than to come in as a cockboat in the wake of the British man-of-war.' For Adams, moreover, the question had a larger aspect. While the Holy Alliance seemed to threaten South America, Russia was pushing her trading posts from Alaska southward even to San Francisco Bay. In September 1821 Emperor Alexander I issued a ukase extending Alaska to latitude 51° N, well within the Oregon country and declaring *mare clausum* the waters thence to Bering Strait. Adams believed that the New World should be considered closed to further colonization by European powers.

Monroe vacillated between the extremes of doing nothing, for fear of the Holy Alliance, and of carrying the war into Turkey to aid Greece, whose struggle for independence had been followed in the United States with an even greater interest than was shown for South America. Against this meddling in European affairs Adams argued for the better part of two days, and in the end had his way. The passages on foreign relations in Monroe's annual message of 2 December 1823, although written by the President in more concise and dignified language than Adams would have used, expressed exactly the concepts of his Secretary of State. We may summarize the original Monroe Doctrine in the President's own words:

Positive principles: (*a*) 'The American continents . . . are henceforth not to be considered as subjects for future colonization by any European powers.' (*b*) 'The political system of the allied powers is essentially different . . . from that of America. . . . We should consider any attempt on their part to extend their system to any portion of this hemisphere as dangerous to our peace and safety.'

Negative principles: (*a*) 'With the existing colonies or dependencies of any European power we have not interfered and shall not interfere.' (*b*) 'In the wars of the European powers in matters relating to themselves we have never taken any part, nor does it comport with our policy so to do.'

Monroe's message was well received, but few appreciated its significance. Polk was the first President to appeal to Monroe's principles by name; and not until after the Civil War did these principles become a doctrine. Critics of Monroe have pointed out that his message was a mere declaration; that European intervention had already been thwarted by the threat of the British navy; that in view of the exclusive power of Congress to declare war, a mere presidential announcement could not guarantee Latin American independence. True, but irrelevant. What Adams accomplished was to raise a standard of American foreign policy for all the world to see, and to plant it so firmly in the national consciousness that no later President would dare to pull it down.

The Second President Adams

In December 1823 America was much more interested in the coming presidential election than in Latin America. The large number of candidates in 1824 signified the collapse of the old party system. With no outstanding member of the Virginia dynasty available, the burden of finding a nominee proved too much for the congressional caucus at a time when party discipline was weak. William H. Crawford, Secretary of the Treasury, was heir apparent of the Virginia dynasty, but he had suffered a paralytic stroke, and, as an Old Republican, he did not command a national following. A congressional caucus dutifully nominated him, but only one-quarter of the Republicans attended. Two other members of Monroe's cabinet also aspired to the succession. John Quincy Adams was the most highly experienced, but Henry Clay, 'Gallant Harry of the West,' made a wide appeal as an advocate of the American system. However, Clay had a Western rival, General Andrew Jackson, now Senator from Tennessee. All the candidates were Republicans. Jackson carried Pennsylvania, the Carolinas, and most of the West, with a total of 99 electoral votes. Adams took New England, most of New York,[2] and a few districts elsewhere, making 84. Crawford was a poor third, and Clay last. Since no candidate had a majority of the electoral vote, the choice among the top three went to the House—the only such instance since the adoption of the Twelfth Amendment.

---

2. There was no uniformity at this time in methods of choosing presidential electors. In eleven states the voters chose them on a general ticket, as nowadays. In seven states they were chosen by the voters in districts; in eleven by state legislatures.

When Congress convened in January 1825, backers of Jackson and Adams tried to work up a majority for their candidates. Jackson would presumably hold the eleven states which had declared for him in November, but he needed two more for a majority. Adams had only seven states secured, and needed six more. Clay, no longer a candidate, controlled the votes of three states. He opposed the elevation to the presidency of a military leader like Jackson, because he doubted 'that killing two thousand five hundred Englishmen at New Orleans' qualified a man for the chief magistracy. After it was half understood, half promised, that if Adams were elected he would appoint Clay Secretary of State, Clay threw all three of his states to Adams. The lone congressmen who represented Missouri and Illinois, states which had voted for Jackson, were 'conciliated' (Jackson men said 'bought') by Adams. New Yorkers and doubtful Marylanders who still called themselves Federalists were assured that Adams, if elected, would not take revenge on that dying party for what it had done to him and his father. And so it was that on 9 February 1825 the House on its first ballot elected John Quincy Adams President of the United States, by a majority of one state.

It was a barren victory, although perfectly legal. The charge of robbery at once went up from the Jackson forces, and active electioneering for 1828 began. Adams's election, said Senator Benton, with a wild plunge into what he believed to be Greek, violated the *demos krateo* principle. When Adams defiantly gave Clay the state department, the cry 'corrupt bargain' was raised. Jackson wrote: 'So you see the *Judas* of the West has closed the contract and will receive the thirty pieces of silver.'

John Quincy Adams was a lonely, friendless figure, unable to express his burning love of country in any way that would touch the popular imagination. Short, thick-set, with a massive bald head and rheumy eyes, his port was stern and his manners unconciliatory. A lonely walk before dawn, or an early morning swim across the Potomac in summer, fitted him for the day's toil, which he concluded by writing in his diary. The uncomfortable labor of compiling a massive report on weights and measures during a hot summer in Washington, when he might have been playing with his children on the coast of Massachusetts, was a relaxation to Adams. 'I am a man of reserved, cold, austere and forbidding manners,' he once wrote. 'My political adversaries say a gloomy misanthrope; and my personal enemies an unsocial savage. With a knowledge of the actual defects in my character, I have not the pliability to reform it.'

As President, Adams was not only so anxious to be upright that he was often disagreeable, but he made the grave political error of trimming his sails to the nationalism of 1815 after the wind had changed. He would transcend the nationalism of Hamilton and use the ample revenues of the Federal Government to increase the navy, build national roads and canals, send out scientific expeditions, and establish institutions of learning and research. Unhappily, Adams presented his ideas at a time of anti-national reaction, especially in the South which feared that a strong national government might meddle with slavery, and he offered them maladroitly. He antagonized Old Republicans by stating that he hoped no 'speculative scruple' about constitutional limitations would trouble them, and he told Congress not to give the world the impression 'that we are palsied by the will of our constituents.' Adams made many sound recommendations—a national astronomical observatory, a naval academy—that were adopted years later, but they were rudely rejected by Congress at the time.

The Second Party System

As a consequence of the renewal of the contest for the Presidency in 1824, political leaders created a new party system. Unlike the first party system, it did not originate in Congress. Nor was it the result of a popular groundswell. The new two-party system was the deliberate creation of politicians who built cross-sectional alliances in order to capture the presidency. Established not at one time but over a period of some sixteen years, it appeared first in the Northeast, then in the Old South, and finally in the new states. The second party system did not continue the political align-

General Jackson. In this painting by Ralph E. W. Earl in 1833, the year Jackson began his second term, the President's military glory is accentuated. The son of one of the most prominent artists of the late eighteenth century, Earl, who married Mrs. Jackson's niece, lived at the White House, and, in the age of 'King Andrew,' was called 'the King's painter.' Old Hickory was a favorite subject of artists of this generation; Hawthorne, standing before a representation of Pope Julius, regretted that Raphael was not alive to do justice to Jackson. (*Brooks Memorial Art Gallery, Memphis*)

Helpless orphans piteous cries
Scalding tears from widows eyes
Cools with tyrants deadliest pand
Murder'd soldiers clotted blood

Methought the souls of all that I had murder'd, came to my tent. Act 5 Sc 3.

RICHARD III.

Jackson as Richard III. In this engraving D. C. Johnston, called 'the American Cruikshank,' draws upon episodes from the General's military past to liken him to the English monarch, accused of murdering the two young princes in the Tower. (*American Antiquarian Society*)

ments of the Jeffersonian era. Republicans and Federalists could be found in both the new parties: the 'friends of the Administration' who subsequently became the National Republicans and then the Whigs, and the 'Jackson men,' who would later call themselves Democrats. If Daniel Webster won former Federalists to the Adams-Clay 'Coalition,' Martin Van Buren commissioned Alexander Hamilton's son to write campaign tracts for the Jackson-Calhoun alliance. In New England, Federalists joined Adams's party; in the South, Jackson's; in the Middle States, they divided.

Changes in voting procedures and the expansion of the suffrage helped shape the second party system. In 1800, only two states chose electors by popular vote; by 1832, voters cast ballots for electors in every state but South Carolina. By 1824, almost every adult white male could vote in presidential elections, save in Rhode Island, Virginia, and Louisiana. Since parties had to mobilize not a few legislators but a mass electorate, these changes revolutionized political warfare. In 1824, voting increased 130 per cent over the previous national election; in 1828, it jumped another 133 per cent. This growth resulted less from the abolition of suffrage restrictions than from the stimulus of the renewal of party competition. The transportation revolution made it possible to organize politics on a national basis, with wide-ranging campaign tours and 'monster' rallies, and the proliferation of newspapers enhanced the role of the partisan editor who fanned the flames of party feeling. As the new party system spread, the gentry yielded to professional politicians who viewed party management as a vocation.

In 1828 national leaders of the Jackson forces mobilized support for the Hero. Although the new party contained elements of a South-West alliance, the most important aspect of the future Democratic party was the renewal of the New York-Virginia understanding. The Jackson forces in 1828 tended to be more suspicious of centralized government and more favorably disposed toward unhampered capitalism than were their rivals. The South, now in full tide of reaction against nationalism, was assured that Jackson would defend state rights. For the first time, a majority of states held conventions which endorsed a national candidate, but politicians in 1828 seemed less interested in democratizing politics than in manipulating the electorate. General Jackson's frontier brawls and alleged premarital relations with Mrs. Jackson were described in detail. Nonetheless, Jackson polled 56 per cent of the popular vote; no candidate would do so well for the rest of the nineteenth century.

John Quincy Adams never understood why he was spurned by the country he loved with silent passion. In the four sad months between the election and the end of his term, there kept running through his head the refrain of an old song he had first heard at the court of Versailles:

O Richard, O mon Roi,
L'univers t'abandonne.

Yet the noblest portion of his long career lay ahead.

12

The Jacksonian Era

*

1829–1844

Jacksonian Democracy

We are now in an age of great political figures. Adams, Clay, Webster, Van Buren, and Calhoun were statesmen of whom any country could be proud; but the man who towered above them in popularity and gave his name to an era was Andrew Jackson. Old Hickory 'reigned,' as his enemies said, for eight years. He practically appointed his successor, Martin Van Buren; and, after one term of Whig opposition, Jacksonian Democracy returned to the saddle in the person of James K. Polk, 'Young Hickory.' After another brief interim came two Democratic Presidents who had been spoon-fed by Jackson—Franklin Pierce and James Buchanan. Thus Andrew Jackson and the brand of democracy associated with him dominated the political scene for a third of a century, from 1828 to the Civil War.

Jacksonian Democracy was a national movement in that it opposed disunion and knew no geographical limits; Jackson men in Maine and Louisiana uttered the same clichés. But it was anti-national in rejecting Clay's 'American System.' The Democracy wanted roads, canals, and (in a few years) railroads to be chartered and aided by the states, but no Federal Government messing into the operations. Jacksonians spoke for the men on the make who resented government grants of special privileges to rival entrepreneurs and who distrusted the positive state. Opponents of artificial distinctions and advocates of greater popular participation in politics, the Jackson men identified themselves with the movement toward more equality. Yet they believed in equality only for white men; they were far less charitable toward the Indian and the Negro than their 'aristocratic' foes. Jacksonian Democracy was not 'leveling' in the European sense, having no desire to pull down men of wealth to a common plane; but it wanted a fair chance for every man to level up. In the states, Jackson Democrats sometimes, but not invariably, favored free public education and a somewhat cautious humanitarianism, but dissociated themselves from most of the 'isms' of the period, such as abolitionism and feminism. In general, they shared that contempt for intellect which is one of the unlovely traits of democracy. There was no contact between political democrats like Jackson and democratic philosophers such as

Emerson, and Old Hickory cared not a whit. The jackass as symbol of the Democratic party was first used by the Whigs as a satire on Jackson's supposed ignorance; the party not only joyfully accepted this emblem, but has retained it to this day.

Andrew Jackson was no champion of the 'common man,' but they loved him because he proved that a man born in a log cabin could get rich and become President; and, perhaps most of all, because his victory at New Orleans transformed the War of 1812 from a rout to a glorious vindication of American valor. Washington had never held such crowds as assembled there on 4 March 1829 to see the people's champion installed. General Jackson, a tall, lean figure dressed in black, with the hawk-like frontier face under a splendid crest of thick white hair, walked from Gadsby's Hotel up Pennsylvania Avenue, unescorted save by a few friends, to the Capitol. There, at the top of a great stone stairway, he took the presidential oath and read his inaugural address. With difficulty he pushed through the shouting masses, all eager to shake his hand, to where his horse was waiting; then rode to the White House at the head of an informal procession of carriages, farm wagons, people of all ages, colors, and conditions. The White House was invaded by a throng of men, women, and boys who stood on chairs in their muddy boots, fought for the refreshments, and trod glass and porcelain underfoot. 'The reign of King "Mob" seemed triumphant,' said one observer.

Jackson felt that his first task was to 'cleanse the Augean stables,' for even frontier-educated boys in those days knew about the labors of Hercules. Long before Jackson, the Republicans had followed the principle of rotation in office. In a democratic nation it served a number of commendable purposes: denying the claims of officeholders to consider their posts private property; replacing superannuated officials; preventing holdovers from frustrating the policies of a new administration; and affording the citizenry greater direct participation in government. In eight years in office, Jackson removed only a small number of federal officeholders, and his own appointees were mostly college graduates at a time when comparatively few Americans attended college. Yet

there is no doubt that Jackson, by stepping up the tempo of removals, seriously impaired the politically neutral career system which had developed in the first forty years of the republic and fastened the spoils system on the Federal Government, from which, despite civil service reform, it has never been wholly eradicated.

Eaton Malaria

A woman made the first and the most lasting trouble for Jackson. She was Mrs. John H. Eaton, wife of the Secretary of War. Born Peggy O'Neale, daughter of the principal tavern keeper at the Georgetown end of Washington, she was a luscious brunette with a perfect figure and a come-hither in her blue eyes that drove the young men of Washington wild, and some of the old ones too. Married at an early age to a purser in the navy, she became, during his long absences at sea, the mistress of John H. Eaton, bachelor senator from Tennessee and her father's star boarder. At least so 'all Washington' said, except Jackson. The Senator even bought the tavern when Papa O'Neale went broke, in order to continue this pleasant arrangement, and persuaded the navy department to give the purser plenty of sea duty. About the time of the presidential election, the complaisant cuckold, caught short some $14,000 in his accounts, died or committed suicide, nobody quite knew which; and shortly after the news arrived, on New Year's Day 1829, his bonny widow, still only thirty-two years old, married Eaton.

Scandal made Jackson the more determined to champion Mrs. Eaton, and to insist that official society should receive her, but Mrs. Vice-President Calhoun and the other secretaries' wives would give the 'hussy' no countenance. They refused to call, and at official receptions or White House dinners failed to speak. Neither would the ladies of the diplomatic corps, nor the wives of senators and congressmen. The President refused to surrender. He scoffed at the rumors about Peggy; after all, both Eaton and the purser had been Masons, and neither could have had 'criminal intercourse with another mason's wife, without being one of the most abandoned of men.'

Jackson actually held a cabinet meeting about Mrs. Eaton, where he pronounced her 'as chaste as a virgin'; but the female rebellion continued. This 'Eaton malaria,' as Van Buren and the gossips called it, was not only making a breach between the administration and respectable society, but making a fool of the President.

Still, there was some use to be made of the affair by Van Buren, who coveted the presidential succession. This sly fox from New York was burrowing into the heart of the old hero. As a widower, he could afford to show Peggy marked attention, which was not difficult, for she had both wit and beauty. And it was 'little Van' who bound up the wounds of the disappointed office-seekers, who arranged the diplomatic appointments, and directed the negotiations which brought prestige to the administration. His plump figure could be seen every fair day bobbing up and down on horseback, beside the lean, easy-seated President, on his daily constitutionals. Many a time they must have discussed the Eaton affair. Jackson, unable to account for the solid female phalanx against Mrs. Eaton, was sure there must be politics behind it. And we may be sure that Van Buren, oh! so gently and discreetly, would have eliminated one plotter after another until Jackson burst out, 'By the e-tar-nal! it's that proud aristocrat Calhoun' (for did not Mrs. Calhoun start the snubbing game, and were not all the recusant ministers Calhoun's friends?). And how Van Buren would protest that it could never, never be that high-souled pattern of chivalry! And how, if Jackson seemed too easily convinced, he would remind him of an ugly rumor that in Monroe's cabinet, at the time of the Arbuthnot and Ambrister affair, it was Calhoun who said General Jackson should be arrested and tried for insubordination! Calhoun, it will be remembered, was in his second term as Vice-President, and heir apparent.

Were all this merely a question of whether Martin or John should succeed Andrew, it would not be worth our attention. But the 'Eaton malaria,' as treated by Dr. Van Buren, was a symptom of the sectional and economic ills that presently isolated Calhoun and his adherents in a state-rights ward.

The Nullification Controversy

Andrew Jackson's high place in history derives from the way he confronted the two great issues of his presidency: the nullification that threatened the Union and the war on the Bank of the United States that arrayed the Jacksonians against the 'money power.' The first issue arose in South Carolina, a state that had changed from ardent nationalism to extreme wariness of the Federal Government. The protective tariff of 1816 was largely the work of two South Carolinians, Lowndes and Calhoun. Like New England, their native state had water-power, and unlike New England she had cotton; then why not manufactures? But the next few years proved these expectations hollow. Competent managers were rare in the South, and Yankee mill superintendents were unable to handle slave labor, which could be employed with more immediate profit in growing cotton. While the benefits of protection went to Northern manufacturers, Southern planters bore the burden of higher prices. As tariff schedules rose by successive acts of Congress, and the country as a whole grew richer, South Carolina declined in wealth. When the cotton-growing area expanded into the black belts of Alabama and Mississippi, cotton which had sold for 31 cents a pound in 1818 fetched only 8 cents in 1831. Actually, the tariff only aggravated distress for which the land-destroying system of cotton culture was fundamentally responsible; but the planters would not accept this. Furthermore, the South Carolina aristocracy was beginning to squirm over race relations, and rice planters joined cotton growers in wanting to curb the power of the national government.

In 1828 Congress gave new cause for grievance with the 'tariff of abominations.' It was a politicians' tariff, concerned mainly with the manufacture of a President. Pro-Jackson congressmen had introduced a bill with higher duties on raw materials than on manufactures, hoping that New England votes would help defeat it and the onus fall on Adams, but the strategy misfired, to the South's chagrin. At a great anti-tariff meeting in Columbia, S.C., President Cooper of South Carolina College asked, 'Is it worth our while to continue this Union of States, where the North demands to be our masters and we are required to be their tributaries?' More and more South Carolinians answered this question with a thumping 'No!'

Calhoun, once an enthusiastic nationalist, now believed that he had made a grave mistake, for protection had turned out to be an instrument of class and sectional plunder. In a document called the South Carolina Exposition, approved in 1828 by the legislature of that state, he set forth a new doctrine—nullification, though his authorship was secret. The Constitution, he asserted, was established not by the American people, but by thirteen sovereign states. Sovereign in 1787, they must still be sovereign in 1828. Since the Federal Government was merely the agent of the states, a state convention, the immediate organ of state sovereignty, could take measures to prevent the enforcement within state limits of any Act of Congress it deemed unconstitutional. Calhoun, however, recognized one constitutional authority superior to the interpretation of a single state, an interpretative federal amendment adopted by three-fourths of the states. Under the nullification doctrine, South Carolina insisted on the right to disobey the laws of the Union while claiming the privileges of the Union. Calhoun's sincerity and intelligence cannot be doubted, but as the aged Madison declared, 'For this preposterous and anarchical pretension there is not a shadow of countenance in the Constitution.'

A ringing rebuttal to Calhoun's dialectic came two years later in the midst of a classic debate over Western lands, when on 26 January 1830 Daniel Webster of Massachusetts replied for the second time to Senator Hayne of South Carolina. Webster was the most commanding figure in the Senate, a swarthy Olympian with a craggy face and eyes that seemed to glow like dull coals under a precipice of brows. It has been said that no man was ever so great as Daniel Webster looked. Ponderous he was at times, but he carried to perfection the dramatic, rotund style of oratory that America learned from the elder Pitt.

In his historic response to Hayne, Webster, in blue-tailed coat with brass buttons and buff waistcoat, speaking hour after hour, thrilled his audience with rich imagery, crushed his opponents with a barrage of facts, passed from defense of his state to criticism of the 'South Carolina doctrine,' and concluded with an immortal peroration:

I have not allowed myself, Sir, to look beyond the Union, to see what might lie hidden in the dark recess behind. I have not coolly weighed the chances of preserving liberty when the bonds that unite us together shall be broken asunder. . . . Nor could I regard him as a safe counsellor in the affairs of this government, whose thoughts should be mainly bent on considering, not how the Union may be best preserved, but how tolerable might be the condition of the people when it should be broken up and destroyed. While the Union lasts we have high, exciting, gratifying prospects spread out before us, for us and our children. Beyond that I seek not to penetrate the veil. God grant that in my day at least that curtain may not rise! God grant that on my vision never may be opened what lies behind! When my eyes shall be turned to behold for the last time the sun in heaven, may I not see him shining on the broken and dishonored fragments of a once glorious Union; on States dissevered, discordant, belligerent; on a land rent with civil feuds, or drenched, it may be, in fraternal blood! Let their last feeble and lingering glance rather behold the gorgeous ensign of the republic, now known and honored throughout the earth, still full high advanced, its arms and trophies streaming in their original lustre, not a stripe erased or polluted, not a single star obscured, bearing for its motto, no such miserable interrogatory as 'What is all this worth?' nor those other words of delusion and folly, 'Liberty first and Union afterwards'; but everywhere, spread all over in characters of living light, blazing on all its ample folds, as they float over the sea and over the land, and in every wind under the whole heavens, that other sentiment, dear to every true American heart,—Liberty *and* Union, now and forever, one and inseparable!

That peroration, declaimed from thousands of school platforms by lads of the coming generation, established in the hearts of the Northern and Western people a new, semi-religious conception of the Union. One of its earliest readers was a dreamy, gangling youth on the Indiana frontier, Abraham Lincoln.

Webster's reply to Hayne went home instantly to the old patriot in the White House. Jackson counted himself a state-rights man, but he never doubted the sovereignty of the nation. At a Jefferson's birthday dinner on 13 April 1830, when his turn came for a toast, the old soldier arose to his

Daniel Webster (1782–1852). This portrait from the studio of Mathew Brady, America's premier photographer, conveys 'Black Dan's' scowling mien, his piercing eyes, and the majestic presence of the 'god-like Daniel.' (*Library of Congress, Brady Collection*)

full height, fixing his glaring eyes on Calhoun, and flung out a challenge:

Our Federal Union—it must be preserved!

Calhoun took up the challenge with another:

The Union—next to our liberty, the most dear!

For two years after the dinner, Calhoun and the nullifiers were held in check by the unionists of their own state, and Jackson reconstituted his entire cabinet, thereby ridding the administration of the Calhoun influence. But in 1832 Clay precipitated a showdown. With the aid of Western votes, attracted by his scheme to forge a North-West alliance by distributing the proceeds from land sales to the states, Clay pushed through a new tariff bill. Some of the 'abominations' of the 1828 tariff were removed, but high duties on iron and textiles were maintained; and the new act had an air of permanence which acted upon South Carolina as a challenge. In November 1832 the South Carolina legislature declared that the tariff act was 'null, void, and no law, nor binding upon this State, its officers or citizens.' This nullification ordinance forbade federal officials to collect customs duties within the state after 1 February 1833, and threatened instant secession from the Union if the Federal Government attempted to use force. Jackson gave a prompt answer. Forts Moultrie and Sumter were reinforced, revenue cutters were ordered to collect the duties if the customs officials were resisted, and on 10 December the President issued a ringing proclamation calling 'the power to annul a law of the United States, assumed by one State, incompatible with the existence of the Union,' and attacking Calhoun's theory of the 'right of secession.'

South Carolina could not be cowed by proclamation. Her legislature hurled defiance at 'King Jackson' and raised a volunteer force to defend the state from 'invasion.' The President, in turn, prepared to throw an army into South Carolina at the first show of resistance to the customs officers. But could he afford to? Though Virginia regarded nullification as a caricature of her Resolves of 1798, the majority in all the Southern states probably believed in the constitutional right of secession.

Extremists aside, everyone wished to avoid bloodshed. Jackson understood the need to mix conciliation with firmness, and what the nullifiers really wanted was to reduce the tariff. Within three weeks of the President's proclamation, the House committee on ways and means proposed to lower duties. Charleston then resolved to suspend the nullification ordinance until the new tariff bill became law, and not to molest the federal customs officials. On 2 March 1833 Jackson signed two bills—the Force Act, authorizing him to use the army and navy to collect duties if judicial process were obstructed, and Clay's compromise tariff, providing a gradual scaling down of all schedules.

The South Carolina convention then reassembled, repealed the nullification ordinance, but saved face by nullifying the Force Act, for which there was no longer any need. South Carolina had proved that a single determined state could have her way, but Jackson saw that beyond nullification lay secession. The 'next pretext,' he predicted, 'will be the Negro, or slavery question.'

The U.S. Bank and Biddle

In the midst of these alarums and excursions came the presidential election of 1832, memorable in the history of political organization. Jackson men, now organized as the Democratic party, sent delegates to a national party convention which renominated Old Hickory for the presidency and Martin Van Buren for the vice-presidency. The opposition, organized as the National Republican party (for which the name Whig, of happy memory, was shortly substituted), nominated Henry Clay.

The Democrats and Whigs were the two major parties of the future, but in 1832 a third party took the field. The Anti-Masonic party arose in 1826, out of the disappearance of a New York bricklayer named Morgan, who had divulged the secrets of his lodge. A corpse found floating in the Niagara river could not be proved to be Morgan's; but, as a politician said, it was 'good enough Morgan until after election.' Both the event and the Masons' efforts to hush it up revived an old prejudice against secret orders, which in a mobile, swiftly changing society appeared especially threatening to democratic institutions.[1] Furthermore, the Masons seemed to stand for all the forces of special privilege that might thwart the aspirations of ordinary men. Several young politicians, such as William H. Seward, Thurlow Weed, and Thaddeus Stevens, threw themselves into the Anti-Masonic movement. In 1831 it held a national convention and nominated William Wirt of Maryland, who next year robbed Henry Clay, a Mason,

---

1. One aspect of this feeling was the suppression of all fraternities in American colleges except Phi Beta Kappa, which became an 'honor' organization to save its life. Not until after the Civil War did college fraternities revive.

of thousands of votes, and carried Vermont. In a few years the Anti-Masons faded out; but the sort of people who were quick to believe that democracy was being subverted by foreign conspirators were later to be found in another one-idea party, the anti-Catholic Know-Nothings.

This presidential election decided the big issue of 1832: Andrew Jackson *v*. the Bank of the United States. Since 1819 the Bank had been well managed, to the profit alike of the government whose funds it handled, the business community which it served, and the stockholders; but it was unpopular in the South and Southwest. Jackson shared this dislike, together with a conviction that the money power was the greatest enemy to democracy. As the election of 1832 approached, Nicholas Biddle, president of the B.U.S., believing that Jackson would not dare risk making an issue of the Bank in an election year, precipitated a 'war' by asking for recharter immediately, four years before expiration. Biddle's action demonstrated to the President that he had been right in believing that the Bank was meddling in politics, and that, as a consequence, the 'Monster of Chestnut Street' constituted a menace to democracy. When Congress voted a recharter bill in July 1832, Jackson vetoed it. The bill, he declared, was not only an unconstitutional invasion of state rights; it proposed to continue a monopoly, the profits of which must come 'out of the earnings of the American people,' in favor of foreign stockholders and 'a few hundred of our own citizens, chiefly of the richest class.' Biddle called Jackson's message 'a manifesto of anarchy such as Marat or Robespierre might have issued to the mobs.' After a fiercely fought campaign, in which the Bank was the outstanding issue, Jackson won an emphatic electoral victory with 219 votes to Clay's 49.

The election persuaded Jackson that he had to go farther than the veto and deprive the Bank of federal money. One Secretary of the Treasury got himself promoted to the state department in order to duck the issue; his successor was dismissed by Jackson for refusing to obey, but a third Secretary, Roger B. Taney, did; and after 1 October 1833 no more government money was deposited in the expiring 'Monster.' Biddle refused to admit defeat. 'This worthy President thinks that because he has scalped Indians and imprisoned judges, he is to have his own way with the Bank. He is mistaken.' By constricting bank loans, Biddle helped to precipitate a panic. Yet once again his actions succeeded only in demonstrating that his enemies were correct in believing he wielded too much power.

This financial war came in the midst of a period of unparalleled speculation. Clay contributed to it by winning enactment of his 'distribution' scheme in 1836. Some states used the money from the federal surplus for public works, others as a fund for education, one even made a *per capita* distribution; but mostly the money fed speculation. Jackson then administered a severe astringent; the 'specie circular' of 1836 ordered the treasury to receive no 'folding money' for public lands. Shortly after, the panic of 1837 burst upon the country; and Van Buren's four years were spent in seeking a substitute for the B.U.S.; none was found comparable with it for service and efficiency until the Federal Reserve system was established in 1913.

Although Democracy won the battle with the Bank, it lost the war. Jackson, who was right in thinking no private institution should have so much uncontrolled power as this 'hydra-headed monster' held, failed to appreciate the economic functions the Bank performed and the kind of vacuum its departure would create. Out of the war the poor farmer, mechanic, and frontiersman gained nothing. Wall Street picked up the pieces of the shattered institution on Chestnut Street, Philadelphia; and a new 'money power' in New York soon had more money and power than Nicholas Biddle ever dreamed of.

Indian Removal

Presidents of a liberal persuasion have often in our history disregarded the interests of men of a different race, as Jackson demonstrated by carrying out a policy suggested by Jefferson: the removal of all Indian tribes to the West. Between 1829 and 1837, many thousand Indians were more or less unwillingly transferred west of the Mississippi. Tribesmen with well-developed farms, especially influential half-breeds, were given the option of

Les Natchez by Delacroix. The scene derives from Chateaubriand's tale *Atala*, subtitled *Les amours de deux sauvages dans le désert*. In Chateaubriand's work, published in the first year of the nineteenth century, the Indian is depicted in the romantic mode as the melancholy victim of the march of progress, and Delacroix expands upon this theme. Hugh Honour has observed: 'This great painting, with its exquisitely tender figures by a wide expanse of river inexorably flowing past them, even goes beyond Chateaubriand to become a poignant lament for the passing of a whole race.' The experience of the Natchez, who in the eighteenth century were decimated by the French in the Mississippi valley, served as a prelude to the dispersal of the Cherokee and other tribes during the Age of Jackson, the period when Delacroix was painting this canvas. (*Collection Lord Walston*)

staying where they were and becoming American citizens. Those who preferred to leave exchanged their property for new lands in the West, and were promised travel expenses and the value of improvements on their relinquished property. The 'assent' of the Indians was often nominal; federal officials stole what was due to the Indians; and on the journey west thousands died.

Most of the tribes were too feeble to resist, but at three points there was trouble. Chief Black Hawk of the Sauk and Fox tried to retain his ancient tribal seat at the mouth of Rock river, Illinois, but squatters encroached on his village, enclosed the Indians' cornfields, and even plowed up the graves of their ancestors. So in 1831 Black Hawk withdrew into Missouri Territory. There famine followed, and hostile Sioux threatened. Hoping to find a vacant prairie in which to plant a corn crop, Black Hawk returned the following spring with about a thousand of the tribe. Misinterpreting this move as a hostile expedition, the Illinois militia turned out—Abraham Lincoln commanding a company—and pursued the starving Indians up the Rock river into the Wisconsin wilderness. It was a disgraceful frontier frolic, stained by a wanton massacre of Indians, including women and children, when they attempted to recross the Mississippi. The only redeeming feature was the chivalrous consideration of Black Hawk by Lieutenant Jefferson Davis of the regular army, when the captured chief was placed in his charge. Forty years later, Davis referred to Black Hawk's rear-guard action at Wisconsin Heights as the most gallant fight he had ever witnessed.

In the South the Creek, Chickasaw, and Choctaw nations, after much prodding, removed to the Indian Territory (Oklahoma), where the descendants of their survivors still live, but the Cherokee and Seminole were refractory. It had always been a grievance against the Indians that they would not settle down to civilized ways, but in Georgia the Cherokee had built neat houses and good roads, preserved the peace, received Christian missionaries, published books in an alphabet invented by their tribesman Sequoya, and adopted a national constitution. However, in plain derogation of treaty rights, the state of Georgia claimed the Cherokee as her subjects and tenants-at-will.

An unfortunate discovery of gold in the Cherokee country in 1828 brought in a rough class of whites. By violating a treaty, Georgia raised as clear a challenge to federal supremacy as had South Carolina; but President Jackson let Georgia have her way. Regulars sent in by President J. Q. Adams to protect the Indians were withdrawn; and when the Supreme Court decided in Worcester v. Georgia that the laws of Georgia had no force in Cherokee territory, Jackson probably never said 'John Marshall has made his decision. Now let him enforce it,' but these sentences, often attributed to him, did reflect his views. A portion of the Cherokee were bribed to exchange the lands of the whole for a section of the Indian Territory, and $5 million. The rest held out for a few years; but in 1838 they too were driven westward from the lands of their ancestors. The Cherokee lost one-quarter of their number in the removal. Emerson protested in vain: 'Such a dereliction of all faith and virtue, such a denial of justice, and such deafness to screams for mercy were never heard of in time of peace and in the dealing of a nation with its own allies and wards, since the earth was made.'

A similar controversy with the Seminole of Florida had an even more tragic outcome. A tricky treaty of removal, negotiated in 1832 with a few chiefs, was repudiated by the greater portion of the tribe, led by its brave chieftain Osceola. Secure in the fastnesses of the Everglades, Osceola baffled the United States Army for years, and was only captured by treachery when bearing a flag of truce. His people kept up the fight until 1842, costing the United States some $20 million and 1500 lives. A few thousand remained in the Everglades, where their descendants are waging a losing battle against 'progress,' represented by the bulldozer.

By the end of Van Buren's administration all but a few tribes of Eastern Indians had been removed beyond a 'permanent' barrier that ran from Lake Superior to the Red river. A chain of military posts, garrisoned by the regular army, was established to keep whites and reds apart. Jackson declared in 1835 that the nation was pledged to keep this barrier permanent. All but the southern limb of it was torn up within twenty years.

President Jackson

Andrew Jackson, by word and action, expanded the importance of the presidential office. He vetoed more bills than his predecessors had in forty years. He was the first President to insist on his right to disallow bills not for constitutional reasons but simply because he disapproved of them, and he was the first to use the pocket veto. He refused to permit the Senate to encroach on his powers, and he strengthened the unity of the executive branch by ending the ambiguous status of the Secretary of the Treasury, who, he made clear, was in no way an agent of Congress but merely a subordinate of the President. He conducted an aggressive foreign policy, and in concluding agreements with the king of Siam and the sultan of Muscat, his administration negotiated the first treaties between the United States and an Asiatic nation. Jackson also enhanced the political prestige of the presidency by leading a national party with a mass appeal. Although after he left office no President until Lincoln, save Polk, proved a strong executive, Jackson left an indelible mark on the office.

Yet Jackson had so many limitations that it is doubtful whether he should be included in the ranks of the really great Presidents. His approach to problems was too personal and instinctive; his choice of men, at times, lamentably mistaken; and, unlike the Roosevelts, who have been compared with him, he had little perception of underlying popular movements. Still, he also had admirable qualities, and he dealt swiftly and severely with the one disruptive movement whose significance he did perceive.

The Expansion of the Second Party System

The controversies that revolved around Andrew Jackson stimulated the formation of a new party system. In the second year of Jackson's presidency the National Republicans joined with dissenting Democrats to create the Whig party. The name suggested that, as the Whigs of the 1770's had stood up against King George, so the Whigs of the 1830's were fighting for liberty against 'King Andrew I.' The new party appealed to disparate elements united only by their opposition to Jackson: Bank Democrats and others hurt by the war with the B.U.S.; old-fashioned state-righters offended by Jackson's stand on nullification; New England and Middle State Yankees; owners of factory stock who wanted more protection; and Westerners attracted by Clay's economic policies.

The Whigs wished to use the national government to further capitalistic enterprise. They favored internal improvements, rechartering the Bank, and a protective tariff. Somewhat paradoxically, although advocates of strong national government, they believed in weak Presidents, in part as a consequence of their struggle with 'King Andrew.' Yet many who gravitated to the Whigs did so for non-ideological reasons. As the Democrats attracted Irish Catholic immigrants, the Whigs drew British Protestants. While free-thinkers flocked to the Democrats, the Whigs made a home for Protestant clerics who wished to use the State to wipe out 'moral' blemishes like the liquor traffic.

If the Democrats had the 'best principles,' wrote Emerson, the Whigs had the 'best men,' notably Henry Clay. Intelligent, upright, magnetic, and with a quarter-century's experience of Congress, Clay ran for the White House more often than any major party candidate in history, but never successfully. Lincoln called Clay 'my beau ideal of a statesman, the man for whom I fought all my humble life.' Dennis Hanks, Lincoln's illiterate cousin, explained that Lincoln became a Whig because he 'always Loved Hen Clays Speaches I think was the Cause Mostly.' The insouciant 'Prince Hal' gambled for high stakes, fought a duel, enjoyed good whiskey, and attracted women. Presented by Whig orators as 'the mill-boy of the Slashes,' Clay was in fact a prosperous Kentucky planter, identified with conservative interests. 'I would rather be right than President,' he said in a speech in 1850, and he had to be content with being right.

In 1836 the Whigs by-passed Clay to run three candidates, each strong in his own section: Webster in New England, General William Henry Harrison in the West, and Hugh White in the South. They expected that these three 'favorite sons' would carry enough states to deny any one candidate a majority in the electoral college and thus throw the election into the House, where the Whigs might prevail. To counter the Whig strategy Jackson placed Democratic party fortunes in the hands of the affable Martin Van Buren. Never before had a professional politician reached so high; for thirty years, from the age of 25, he had lived largely by politics. His home, at Old Kinderhook near Albany, in its abbreviated form 'O.K.' gave a new word to the language.[2] 'Little Van' earned the nickname 'The Red Fox' from his slyness, and 'The Little Magician' from his ability to turn everything into gold.

The two-party system now took hold in areas of the South, which in recent years had been a one-party (Democratic) reserve, and in the New West, which had been conducting politics on a 'no party' basis. Since Van Buren lacked Jackson's regional appeal, the South split. Yet Van Buren did well enough. With less than 51 per cent of the popular vote, he captured 170 electoral votes to 124 for his three rivals. Harrison polled 73 electoral votes, but the regional strategy broke down, for White carried only Tennessee and Georgia, and Webster only the Bay State. Van Buren thereby became the first President born under the Stars and Stripes, the first of Dutch stock, the first from New York, and the first to step from the governor's mansion at Albany into the White House at Washington.[3]

In 1835 Tocqueville wrote that 'the political activity which pervades the United States must be seen in order to be understood. No sooner do you set foot upon American ground, than you are stunned by a kind of tumult . . . almost the only pleasure which an American knows is to take a part in the government, and to discuss its measures.' The national party organization quickly reflected constitutional developments in the states. Between 1830 and 1850 religious tests and property qualifications for office were generally swept away, manhood suffrage was adopted, and many appointive offices became elective. These constitutional changes were effected by the democratic method initiated by Massachusetts in 1780: a popularly elected constitutional convention, with a popular referendum on the result. Both parties used the device of the nominating convention, which may have increased popular control, but also made possible greater party discipline.

National politics had another important consequence—muffling the growing divergence between North and South. Churches might split, social differences might deepen, and extremists revile one another; but, so long as the Whig and Democratic parties remained national in scope, the Union was safe.

The Panic of 1837

Van Buren in the White House reaped the whirlwind that Jackson had helped to sow. The twelve-year boom in the West resulted in over-extension of credit, to which Jackson unwittingly contributed by putting government deposits in 'pet banks' which used them as a base for further speculation. When English banks insisted on payment in gold of short-term loans to American enterprises, these demands precipitated a panic, for they came at an unpropitious time. In pursuance of Jackson's specie circular, banks had been depleted of hard money to pay for purchases of government land in the West. In addition, the price of cotton fell from 20 to 10 cents and the wheat crop of 1836 failed.

Van Buren was no sooner in the White House than mercantile houses and banks began to collapse, and there were riots in New York over the high cost of flour. In the panic of 1837 almost every bank in the country suspended specie payments, and the government lost $9 million on deposit in 'pet banks.' A severe four-year depression caused widespread suffering, with no government assistance other than the town or

2. O.K., meaning Old Kinderhook (the home of Van Buren), was the secret name for Democratic clubs in New York in the campaign of 1840. The Whigs, unable to penetrate the meaning, invented this conversation between Amos Kendall and Jackson. ' "Those papers, Amos, are all correct. I have marked them O.K. (oll korrect)." The Gen. never was good at spelling.'

3. Since his running mate, Richard M. Johnson, failed to obtain a majority in the electoral college, he was chosen Vice-President by the Senate, according to Amendment XII of the Constitution—the only time that has been done.

county poorhouse for the desperate; cold and hungry people in the cities had to depend on private charity for fuel and food. A special session of Congress accomplished nothing except to authorize a large issue of temporary treasury notes, which started the national debt once more. It has been growing ever since. As a permanent fiscal measure Van Buren proposed an 'independent treasury,' a depository for government funds located in several cities, devised to divorce government from private banking interests so that no one group or class would enjoy an advantage. Not until 1840 did it become law. The Independent Treasury Act was repealed by the Whigs the next year, re-enacted under Polk, and remained the basis of the federal fiscal system until the Civil War.

The Taney Court

Van Buren inherited a virtually new Supreme Court. A number of deaths, including that of Chief Justice Marshall, disposed of all but two of the judges appointed by John Adams and the Virginia dynasty. Jackson was able to designate a new Chief Justice and four associate justices and Van Buren named three more in 1837. This new blood dominated the Court until the Civil War. Marshall's successor, Roger B. Taney, came from a Federalist family, but Jackson's war with the B.U.S. taught him the potential danger of organized finance, and his first service to the country was to provide an important limitation on Marshall's definition of the contract clause in the Dartmouth College case.

An old corporation which operated a toll bridge leading out of Boston sought to invalidate a recent state law which had provided a rival and parallel free bridge. Justice Story, following what would probably have been the opinion of his former chief, believed the state's action to be confiscatory and a breach of contract; the new Chief Justice, speaking for the majority, upheld Massachusetts, on the ground that no corporate charter could confer implied powers against the public. In addition to stating the modern doctrine of the social responsibilities of private property, the Charles River Bridge decision of 1837 helped expedite the

transportation revolution by freeing railroads of the obligation to buy up every competing stagecoach, canal, or turnpike company.

Taney also limited the consequences of earlier decisions related to interstate commerce. Marshall had implied that federal power to regulate commerce was not only full but exclusive, voiding state regulations even if they filled a need that the Federal Government had not yet recognized. Taney posted a different thesis in the license cases (1847):

The controlling and supreme power over commerce with foreign nations and the several states is undoubtedly conferred upon Congress. Yet, in my judgment, the state may nevertheless, for the safety or convenience of trade, or for the protection of the health of its citizens, make regulations of commerce for its own ports and harbors, and for its own territory; and such regulations are valid unless they come in conflict with a law of Congress.

Though in many respects, the Taney Court reflected the reaction in favor of state rights, the new Court had the same views, in general, of the relation between state and nation as its predecessor. Despite the egregious mistake he would later make in the Dred Scott case, Taney, for luminous perception of those social and economic realities upon which judicial statesmanship rests, must be considered one of the three or four really great Chief Justices of the United States.

Tippecanoe and Tyler Too

In 1840 the Whigs fought the Democrats by their own methods. They adopted no platform, nominated a military hero, and ran a jolly campaign that ignored real issues. Clay, the logical Whig candidate, did not get the nomination, which went to old General Harrison, the 'Hero of Tippecanoe.' Harrison was not politically inexperienced, having served as congressman and senator from Indiana, but unlike Clay he was not associated with any particular measures. Harrison's nomination set the pattern that Jackson's had begun—a nationally known figure, uncommitted on controversial issues. The Whig convention even appointed a committee to supervise the General's correspondence lest he write something incau-

In this Whig campaign song of 1840, a soldier, symbolic of General Harrison, is employed for the treble clef while the bass signature is a barrel, to represent the theme of hard cider. (*Library of Congress*)

tious and be quoted! For Vice-President the Whigs named John Tyler, twenty years younger than Harrison but with views as old-fashioned as those of the late John Randolph.

'Tippecanoe and Tyler too' was the slogan. The Whigs had so far abandoned patrician values that Van Buren was pictured with cologne-scented whiskers, drinking champagne out of a crystal goblet at a table loaded with costly viands and massive plate. An unlucky sneer in a Democratic newspaper, to the effect that Harrison would be content with a $2000 pension, a log cabin, and plenty of hard cider, gave opportunity for effective contrast. It became the log-cabin, hard-cider campaign. Huge balls, supposed to represent the gathering majority, were rolled by men and boys from village to village and state to state, singing as they rolled:

> What has caused this great commotion, motion, motion,
> Our country through?
> —It is the ball a-rolling on, for

(*Chorus*) TIPPECANOE AND TYLER TOO:—
> Tippecanoe and Tyler too.
> And with them we'll beat little Van, Van, Van,
> Oh! Van is a used-up man.

Tippecanoe and Tyler rolled up 234 electoral votes, a four-to-one majority, but the popular vote was much closer, Harrison winning less than 53 per cent in an election in which almost four-fifths of the eligible electorate went to the polls.

By 1840, American politics had reached a remarkable equilibrium in which every state boasted a competitive two-party system. For the next twelve years, and for the only time in our history, both parties were national organizations with strong followings everywhere. This unusual situation could persist only at the expense of ignoring divisive sectional feelings.

On 4 April 1841, after one month in office, the Hero of Tippecanoe died, and John Tyler succeeded him. By his actions Tyler established the precedent that a Vice-President in such a situation inherits all the powers, as well as the title, of President. His administration also had one notable achievement. Tyler signed the 'log cabin' bill which made permanent in public land policy the pre-emption principle first incorporated in an Act of 1830. Any American not already an owner of 320 acres or more could now buy 160 acres in the public domain, and pay later at the rate of $1.25 an acre. This Pre-emption Act of 1841 was probably the most important agrarian measure ever passed by Congress.

But in most respects, the Tyler administration broke down in political squabbling, for the new President was a state-rights ideologue who disapproved of a strong Democratic chief executive like Jackson and who was out of place at the head of a Whig government. To be sure he fulfilled Whig expectations by taking over Harrison's cabinet intact and accepting an upward revision of the tariff as a necessary measure for the revenue. But whereas Clay, who expected to be 'mayor of the palace,' wished to cater to substantial interests, Tyler believed it his mission to strip the Federal Government of its 'usurped' power. He vetoed all bills for internal improvements and harbor works, and vetoed Clay's bill for a new bank as well as a second bill especially drafted to meet his constitutional scruples. From that date (9 September 1841) there was open warfare between Tyler and Clay. Four days later the cabinet resigned—except Webster who wished to appear independent of Clay—and the President was read out of the Whig party.

Here was Calhoun's chance to count in the sectional balance of power. For three years (1841–43), while Tyler attempted to form a party with a corporal's guard of faithful Whigs, Calhoun played a waiting game, repressing a secession movement among his hot-headed followers in South Carolina, intriguing to obtain the Democratic nomination for the presidency in 1844. Webster left the cabinet in 1843; and in March 1844 Calhoun became Tyler's Secretary of State. The new combination was extraordinary. Tyler had gone over to the Democrats, and Calhoun had returned to the fold. The loss of Tyler inclined the internal balance of the Whig party slightly, but definitely, northward; Calhoun tipped the internal balance of the Democratic party very definitely southward. Significantly, the Democrats, in adopting their 1844 platform, neglected to reaffirm their faith, as had been their wont, in the principles of the Declaration of Independence.

Anglo-American Relations

Both Van Buren and Tyler faced a troublesome situation on the northern border. In the autumn of 1837, rebellion broke out in Canada. Van Buren issued a neutrality proclamation, but most Americans hailed the uprising as a new American Revolution. For over a year, the Ontario rebel William L. Mackenzie and his followers were able to recruit money, supplies, and men in the United States and return to loot and burn in Canada. In response, on the night of 29 December 1837, a picked band of loyal Canadians performed the hazardous feat of rowing across the Niagara river to the United States side just above the head of the falls and setting afire the *Caroline*, an American steamer that had been supplying the rebels. In 1840, a Canadian named McLeod boasted in a New York barroom that he had killed an American in the affray; he was promptly indicted for murder. Prime Minister Palmerston, while belatedly admitting that the *Caroline* had been destroyed under orders, as a necessary means of defense against American 'pirates,' demanded the immediate release of McLeod. His execution, so he wrote to the British minister at Washington, 'would produce war, war immediate and frightful in its character, because it would be a war of retaliation and vengeance.' Tyler, now President, was as eager as Van Buren had been to preserve the peace, but Governor Seward of New York insisted that the justice of his state should take its course. In the trial, fortunately, McLeod sober found an alibi for McLeod drunk, and was acquitted.

Lord Durham, who had been sent to Canada to report on conditions, saw the real significance of the crisis. Protracted discontent in Canada must lead to Anglo-American war, or to liberals in Canada seeking annexation to the United States. At his suggestion, the British government granted responsible government to Quebec and Ontario in 1841, and to Nova Scotia and New Brunswick several years later. Canada owes this, in some measure at least, to the disturbing presence of her neighbor.

Tyler, who did especially well in foreign rela-

tions, not only finished the work that Van Buren had begun of pacifying the New York-Ontario border, but he and Secretary Webster settled the smoldering Northeastern boundary dispute. The Webster-Ashburton treaty of 1842 established the present boundary between Maine and Canada; rectified the frontier on Lake Champlain, where the United States had inadvertently built a fort on Canadian territory; and extended the international lake and river boundary from Sault Ste. Marie to the Lake of the Woods. Skillful diplomacy thereby averted war between the United States and Great Britain at two points on the Canadian-American border, but one final test of wills between the great powers remained to be resolved—in the Oregon country.

13

The Two Sections

*

1820–1850

The Cotton Kingdom

South of the border states of Delaware, Maryland, Virginia, and Kentucky, cotton ruled from 1815 to 1861; and the principal bulwark of his throne was slavery. Almost 60 per cent of the slaves in the United States in 1850 were employed in growing cotton. In 1820 the cotton crop of 160 million pounds was already the most valuable Southern interest. As more and more people in the Western world switched from linen and wool to cotton, its production doubled by 1830, and more than doubled again in the next decade. New Orleans, which in 1816 received 37,000 bales of cotton, counted almost a million in 1840. By 1850 the crop had passed a thousand million pounds; and the crop of 1860 was almost 2300 million pounds in weight, and in value two-thirds the total exports of the United States.

This growth was brought about by a rapid extension of the cotton-growing area. Like typical pioneer farmers, exploiters rather than conservers of the soil, the cotton planters advanced from South Carolina and Georgia across the 'black belts' and Indian cessions of Alabama and Mississippi, occupied the great valley up to Memphis, pushed up the Red river of Louisiana to the Indian Territory, and passed the boundary of Mexico into Texas. On the march King Cotton acquired new subjects: moneyed immigrants from the North, and ambitious dirt farmers who purchased a slave or two on credit and with luck became magnates. The white population of Arkansas jumped from 13,000 in 1820 to 324,000 in 1860; the number of slaves rose from 1600 to 111,000. The richest lands were sooner or later absorbed by planters, while poor whites settled on pine barrens, abandoned fields, and gullied hillsides.

Cotton plantations differed greatly both in size and character. One of the better sort in Mississippi, described by Olmsted, covered several square miles. The mansion house, which the absentee owner had not seen for two years, was four miles distant from the nearest white neighbor. The cleared portion, about 1400 acres, was tilled by a plough-gang of 30 men and a larger hoe-gang, mainly women, who were encouraged by a black driver, whip in hand. Enough corn and pork were usually raised to feed the cattle and the 135 slaves, who included three mechanics, two seamstresses, four teamsters and cattle-tenders, a mid-wife, and a nurse who had charge of a day nursery. The overseer also maintained a pack of hounds to hunt runaways. He kept the field hands working from sun to sun, but gave them most of Saturday as well as Sunday off, except in the picking season. They cut their fuel in the master's woods and were allowed to make boards for sale in their free time. Everywhere in the South slave families were allotted land to raise vegetables and poultry to eke out their rations of corn and pork.

A 'middle-class plantation,' which did not produce enough surplus to enable the owner to travel or reside elsewhere, would have 100 to 400 acres under cultivation and 10 to 40 slaves. A planter of this class might be a younger son, a self-made pioneer, an ex-overseer, or a professional man using his plantation to enhance his dignity in the community. In few instances did he enjoy comforts or amenities superior to those of the poorest farmers in the North: a bare house without conveniences, a diet largely of 'hog and hominy,' no literature but a weekly paper, no diversion but hunting and an occasional visit to the county seat. That sort of planter belonged to the governing class and had things much his own way in Alabama, Mississippi, and Arkansas.

A large part of the cotton crop was made by small farmers with one to half a dozen slaves, and below these yeomen farmers came a class called 'pore white trash,' 'crackers,' 'peckerwoods,' and other opprobrious nicknames. Constituting less than 10 per cent of the white population, these sallow, undernourished illiterates, whose only pride was their color, envied successful white men and hated the blacks. Very different were the mountain men, the 'hillbillies' who lived in the secluded valleys and on the steep slopes of the Appalachians and the Ozarks. These upstanding, independent people were expert hunters and fishermen. Almost isolated from the rest of the South, they were encountered only when they drove ox teams to market to sell moonshine whiskey made in illicit stills, and pork cured from acorn-fed pigs.

For more than a century writers have carried on a strenuous debate over the profitability of slavery, and the argument is as vigorous today as ever. Some historians contend that as a result of the high cost of slaves even planters opulent in nominal wealth found it difficult to keep out of debt, and the poorer ones depended on the money-lender for maintenance between crops. Thus, it is said, the system was uneconomical even for large planters in the long run; and for small farmers the first cost of labor became prohibitive. Furthermore, it has been argued that slavery retarded industrialization because the purchase of slaves absorbed an inordinate amount of capital; because slavery limited the development of a home market with widespread purchasing power; and because, by keeping the bondsmen in ignorance, the South denied itself the benefits of an educated, skilled working class. Other historians question whether the slow pace of industrialization was the consequence of slavery or of the fact that the South was an agricultural society in which capital could be more profitably employed in planting. Moreover, some historians who concede that slavery was not viable as an economic system argue that it was often very profitable as a business enterprise. There is no reason to suppose that slavery would have died out if it had not been ended by war, since even the most hopelessly inefficient master acquired status from owning slaves, even if the slave did not earn his keep.

It is often forgotten that the slave trade was begun by Negroes in Africa before Europeans reached the 'Dark Continent,' that every black bought by a slave trader was sold by one of his own race, and that victims of the system who were shipped to North America were better off than those who remained in bondage in Africa;[1] better off, in some respects, than many poor workers and peasants in Europe. John Randolph's slave valet, who accompanied his master to Ireland in 1827, 'looked with horror upon the mud hovels and miserable food' of the Irish peasantry. But these 'white slaves,' as the scornful Virginian called them, could emigrate to America as free men, their sons could become congressmen and

---

1. Compare Saint-Exupéry's account in *Wind, Sand and Stars* (1939) of an old and useless slave being turned out in the desert by his Moslem master to die of starvation—this around 1928.

In this unusual photograph, slaves are arranged by order of rank. They stand at the rear of the house on the occasion of Captain James Rembert's seventy-fifth birthday. The foreman, Nero, is at the left of the group of field hands; the second yard boy is middle front, the first yard boy middle forefront, the cook right forefront. The picture was taken at Stirrup Branch Plantation, Bishopsville, South Carolina, in 1857. (*Library of Congress, Courtesy Frank Des Champs, Bishopsville, S.C.*)

bishops, and their grandsons governors and even Presidents; whilst the children of Negro slaves were born into bondage.

Social gradations divided the slaves. Between a Virginia slave major-domo, whose ancestors had been American for two centuries, and a Gullah Negro of the Carolina sea islands who had been smuggled over from Africa within a year, there was an immense gap. Many a black butler or maid occupied a status similar to those confidential slaves that we meet in Greek and Roman literature, but field hands constituted the majority of slaves. A third and intermediate class were those who learned a trade such as carpentry, and often were hired out by their masters. In 1820 slaves made up 20 per cent of the population of Southern cities; by 1860, a half million slaves labored in factories or in pursuits like railroad construction.

The distinctive aspect of slave society in the United States was the resistance offered to the bondsman who sought to escape the system. The master who contemplated freeing his slaves faced unusually great impediments. To a far less extent than in countries like Brazil, some slave artisans were allowed to purchase their freedom out of earnings; but state laws made that increasingly difficult, since every successful free black was a living argument against keeping the rest of his race enslaved. The Romans usually freed their talented slaves, and in any case their progeny went free. But America subjected a writer like Frederick Douglass to the caprice of a white owner who might be his inferior in every respect.

Until around 1822 the planter class apologized for slavery as something forced on them by circumstances, but thereafter there was a defiant adoption of the theory that slavery was a positive good, sanctioned by history and the Bible. The starting point for this change of sentiment was the report that Denmark Vesey, a free mulatto, with the help of Gullah Jack, an aged African witch doctor, had hatched a plot in Charleston in 1822 involving thousands of blacks bent on slaughter and rape. In retrospect it appears that the plot was at most a vague notion in the minds of a few men given to loose talk, and it is possible that no conspiracy existed. But in a city in which Negroes outnumbered whites, and in which, as urban blacks, they were more advanced, less servile, and free from constant surveillance, rumors of insurrection bred panic. Betrayed by one of the 'conspirators,' loyal to a kind master, the 'revolt' was suppressed before it really started, and 37 blacks, including Vesey, were executed. A system of control, then adopted in the Lower South, gradually spread to Virginia and the border states. Blacks were forbidden to assemble or circulate after curfew, and night patrols policed the roads. Whites were forbidden to teach slaves to read or write in every Southern state except Maryland, Kentucky, and Tennessee. Nonetheless, in tidewater Virginia in 1831, a pious slave named Nat Turner enlisted a number of others who in August killed 57 whites before they were rounded up; between 40 and 100 Negroes were killed, and Turner was hanged.

Southern Society

Slavery and cotton preserved in the South a rural, almost feudal, society.[2] The eighteenth-century social contempt for trade persisted. Agriculture, the army, the church, and the law were the only proper careers for a planter's son. Northern and

2. The following statistics roughly indicate the social classes in the South as a whole (including the District of Columbia) and in the cotton states (South Carolina, Georgia, Florida, Alabama, Mississippi, Louisiana, Arkansas, and Texas) in 1850:

	All Slave States	Cotton States
Number of slaveholding families	347,525	154,391
Number of families owning 1 to 9 slaves	255,258	104,956
Number of families owning 10 to 49 slaves	84,328	43,299
Number of families owning 50 or more slaves	7,939	6,144
White population	6,242,418	2,137,284
Free Negro population	238,187	34,485
Slave population	3,204,077	1,808,768

Century of Population Growth, p. 136; J. D. B. De Bow, *Statistical View of the U.S.* (1854), pp. 45, 63, 82, 95, 99. Slaveholding families are counted more than once if they owned slaves in different counties.

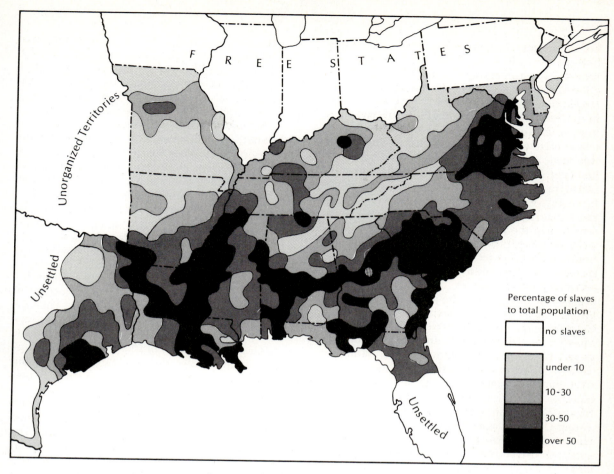

Percentage of slaves
to total population

no slaves

under 10

10-30

30-50

over 50

Proportion of Slaves in 1850

European merchant-bankers and shipowners handled the cotton crop, and kept most of the profits. Shopkeepers in the market towns were often Yankees, Germans, or Jews. Of the 15 largest cities in 1860, only one (New Orleans) was in the South. European immigrants, overwhelmingly from Northern countries, shunned a region where manual labor was regarded as unfit for a free man, and where the warm climate made adjustment difficult. Frontier conditions still prevailed through the greater part of the Lower South in 1850, combined with a turbulence and ignorance that seldom lingered in the Northern frontier beyond the first generation.

Theology, which had been neglected in the South when the section was liberal and anti-slavery, was much cultivated after it became conservative and pro-slavery. The influence of the evangelical sects among the planters increased in proportion as their ministers 'discovered' pro-slavery arguments in the Bible. The Catholic and Episcopalian churches remained neutral on the slavery question, and stationary in numbers. Thomas Jefferson, dying, saluted the rising sun of Unitarianism as destined to enlighten the South; but it sent only a few feeble rays beyond the Mason-Dixon Line. Horace Holley, the gifted young Unitarian who had made of Transylvania University in Lexington, Ky., a southern Harvard, was driven from his post and the university almost completely ruined by an alliance between Presbyterian bigotry and Jacksonian Democracy. Thomas Cooper, a victim of the 1798 Sedition Act, who had moved south, was 'tried' for atheism, and ejected, at the age of 75, from the presidency of South Carolina College.

The dominant religious mode was evangelical. Presbyterians and Episcopalians appealed to the upper classes, but Methodists and Baptists were more successful among middle classes, poor whites, and blacks. For a time these churches were a bond of union between North and South; but when the Northern Methodists unreasonably insisted that a Southern bishop emancipate slaves which he had inherited and could not conscientiously get rid of, the Southern members seceded and formed the Methodist Church South (1844). The Baptists followed, and doubled their membership in fifteen years. Though these Southern evangelicals condoned slavery, they banned card-playing and dancing; by 1860 the bastard puritanism of the age was more prevalent in Alabama and Mississippi than in Massachusetts and Connecticut.

The finest product of the plantation regime was the Southern gentleman. Numbering but few, the gentry ruled the older Southern states by virtue of personality even more than property, and governed them honorably and efficiently, although not with enlightenment. Discriminatingly hospitable, invariably gracious to women, endowed with a high sense of personal honor and civic virtue, they yet lacked the instinct for compromise that, time and again, has preserved the English aristocracy from annihilation.

Of this ruling class, only a small fraction belonged to the eighteenth-century aristocracy of Maryland, Virginia, and the Carolinas. The type of colonial gentleman that Washington was, appeared undiminished in his Lee kinsmen; but the old Huguenot families of Charleston were declining, and the creoles of Louisiana were easy-going and unambitious. Apart from these three persistent types, the mass of the greater planters in 1850 were self-made men like Jefferson Davis, whose parents had lived in log cabins. If not well educated themselves, their sons and daughters were. The South, despite poverty in elementary education, had good secondary schools, especially of the military type, and more students in college than the North.

Life on a resident plantation of the better sort was neither sordid as the abolitionists asserted, nor splendid as the novelists have depicted it. The mansion house, seated on rising ground, was generally a well-proportioned wooden building of neo-classic style, with a columned portico or veranda that gave dignity to the elevation and afforded shade to the ground floor and front chambers. The rooms, seldom more than fifteen in number, were high-ceiled and simply furnished. There were plenty of flowers, and masses of native flowering shrubs. Simplicity rather than ostentation was the dominant note in the planter's life. He enjoyed little leisure. On a Virginia plantation visited by Olmsted, not ten consecutive minutes

'Leaving the Manor House.' This canvas, painted on the eve of the Civil War, gives a stylized and romanticized view of the Southern plantation gentry. (*National Gallery of Art*)

elapsed even during dinner when the proprietor was not interrupted by a servant. The owner's wife had to guard against pilferers, serve out supplies, bind up wounds, and nurse the sick.

Such a life was a continuous exercise of tact, self-control, and firmness; yet the condition of unlimited power was a constant temptation to passion. The sort of bluster considered gentlemanly in the eighteenth century remained so in the South at a time when smoother and more reticent manners had become the mark of good breeding in England and the North. Alexander H. Stephens, future Vice-President of the Confederacy, was unable to take part in the political campaign of 1848 because he had been disabled by stabs received in an 'affray.'

The 'Southern chivalry' tradition was created in the generation of 1820 to 1850. In *Ivanhoe* and the flood of imitative literature that followed, the cotton lord and his lady found a romantic mirror of their life and ideals. A generalizing French traveler, Michel Chevalier, assumed that all Northerners were descended from Cromwell's Roundheads, and all Southern whites from King Charles's Cavaliers. Every owner of two Negroes, however dubious his origin or squalid his existence, became a 'cavalier,' entitled to despise the low-bred shopkeepers, artisans, and clerks of the North. The rage to establish *Mayflower* ancestry in the North, 50 years later, was a compensation of the same sort for descendants of colonial families who were being crowded by newcomers.

To comprehend the psychology of the Southern planter we must remember that his social system was on the defensive against most of the Western world. Under the leadership of Wilberforce and Clarkson in England, Parliament in 1833 passed an act emancipating all slaves in the British West Indies, allowing compensation to the owners. The Second Republic did the same in the French West Indies in 1848; Denmark and all other colonial powers in the West Indies, with the important exception of Spain, had already done so. The white Southerner's proud assertiveness was the sign not of confidence but of fear. Just as New England in 1800 refused every quickening current from France or Virginia, for fear it might bear the seeds of Jacobinism, so the South, a generation later, rejected a literature and philosophy which might conceal abolitionist sentiment. At a time when Bryant, Longfellow, and Whittier were redeeming Northern materialism with cheerful song, Southern silence was broken only by the gloomy and romantic notes of Edgar Allan Poe. The most distinguished and prolific man of letters of the antebellum South, William Gilmore Simms, wrote in 1855, 'All that I have [done] has been poured to waste in Charleston.'

Southern men of letters were compelled to write in glorification of the 'Southern way of life.' A pro-slavery theory of society was provided by Thomas R. Dew, a bright young Virginian who returned from study in Germany to a chair at William and Mary College. In a pamphlet of 1832, he argued that slavery had been the condition of classical culture, that the Hebrew prophets and St. Paul admitted its moral validity, that civilization required the many to work and the few to think. George Fitzhugh, in a tract entitled *Cannibals All*, argued that the Negro was something less than man, and in his *Sociology for the South* scoffed at the 'glittering generalities' of a century of enlightenment.

John C. Calhoun gave pro-slavery doctrine the sanction of his name and character, and so cunningly combined it with American prepossessions that slavery appeared no longer the antithesis, but the condition, of democracy. Calhoun began with the axiom that no wealthy or civilized society could exist unless one portion of the community lived off the labor of others. Chartism in England and trade-unionism in the United States proved that social stability could not be maintained where labor was free. It was too late to re-establish serfdom in Europe and the North. But to the South a beneficent providence had brought a race created by God to be hewers of wood and drawers of water for His chosen people. In return, kind masters provided for all reasonable wants of their slaves, and saved them from the fear of destitution that haunted the white proletariat. The masters themselves, relieved from manual labor and sordid competition, would reach that intellectual and spiritual eminence of which the founders of the Republic had dreamed.

Such was the nonsense that became orthodox in the South by 1850. Yet it is doubtful how wide or deep this folly really went. It was never accepted by the great Virginians who fought so valiantly for the Confederacy.[3] There was no place in the system for poor whites, from one of whom, Hinton R. Helper, came the first prophecy of disaster: *The Impending Crisis* (1857) which was suppressed throughout the South. Still, many non-slaveholding whites who disliked slavery agreed with the planters that it would never do to eman-

---

3. Robert E. Lee emancipated the few slaves he inherited from his mother, and owned no others. Stonewall Jackson purchased two slaves at their own request, and allowed them to earn their freedom. J. E. Johnston and A. P. Hill never owned a slave, and disliked slavery. J. E. B. Stuart owned but two slaves, and disposed of them for good reasons, long before the war. M. F. Maury, who called slavery a 'curse,' owned but one, a family servant.

New York in 1849. At the birth of the republic, it was already regarded as a metropolis, though it had but 33,000 souls. By the 1850 census, New York numbered 515,000, crowded into the southern sector of Manhattan Island, with settlement extending northward only to about 20th Street. In the year of this illustration, a free academy was chartered that became the City University of New York, and an argument over whether an English tragedian or the native-born Edwin Forrest was the better actor led to a nativist riot that resulted in 200 casualties. (*Eno Collection, New York Public Library*)

cipate the slave, since the South must be kept a 'white man's country.' By 1850 the Cotton Kingdom, closing in on itself, had excluded every means of saving reform, and had resolved to make Negro slavery, in an ever-increasing radius, a permanent basis of American society.

The Industrious North

Though statesmen and parties had done much in these years to preserve the Union, social and economic forces were pulling North and South apart.

Both were progressing, but divergently. To be sure, both North and South were affected by common experiences: nationalism, capitalism, evangelicalism, and the westward movement. But Northern society was being transformed by the industrial revolution, by cheap transportation, and by educational, humanitarian, and migratory movements that touched the border slave states very little, and the Lower South not at all. In this same period Southern society was readjusting itself to the cotton plantation, tilled by slaves. By 1850 two distinct civilizations had evolved.

The most striking aspect of Northern society was egalitarianism, a feature that some foreign observers approved and others lamented. Harriet Martineau noted that in America 'the English insolence of class to class, of individuals toward each other, is not even conceived of, except in the one highly disgraceful instance of people of colour.' The 'sweet temper' of Americans she attributed to the 'practice of forbearance requisite in a republic.' Yet forbearance Americans carried to excess in their uncritical attitude toward their own books, customs, institutions, and abuses. Almost every European visitor denounced their acceptance of majority opinion and deplored their fear of expressing unpopular notions, for Americans were becoming less independent and more gregarious. On the other hand, so complex was the American character that the excess of one quality was balanced by its reverse. Intolerance appeared in the persecution of unpopular groups such as blacks, immigrants, abolitionists, and Catholics; and in hot resentment of unfavorable criticism. Nor was distinction wanting in a country that produced in one generation Clay, Calhoun, Webster, Poe, Hawthorne, and Irving; and in the next, Emerson, Longfellow, Whitman, Lee, and Lincoln.

It was a busy age. Each Northern community was an anthill, intensely active. Every man worked, or at least made a semblance of it. The Northern American had not learned how to employ leisure; his pleasure came from doing things. Yet the Northern and Western states were a land where dreams of youth came true; where the majority were doing what they wished to do, without class or official restraint. 'We were hardly conscious of the existence of a government,' wrote a Scandinavian immigrant in New York. The fun of building, inventing, creating, in an atmosphere where one man's success did not mean another's failure, gave American life that peculiar gusto that Walt Whitman caught in his poetry. And the resources of a new country, exploited by the inhabitants under laws of their own making and breaking, had brought a degree of comfort and security to the common man that he had not known since the days of good Queen Bess.

Transportation and Migration

The westward movement developed new momentum in the age of Jackson. New Englanders, who a generation before had settled the interior of New York and Ohio, were pressing forward into the smaller prairies of Indiana and Illinois, where the tough sod taxed their strength but repaid it in the end with bountiful crops of grain; where shoulder-high prairie-grass afforded rich pasturage for cattle, and groves of buckeye, oak, walnut, and hickory furnished wood and timber. A favorite objective was southern Michigan, a rolling country of 'oak openings,' where stately trees stood well-spaced as in a gentleman's park. Others were hewing farms from the forests of southern Wisconsin and venturing across the Mississippi into land vacated by Black Hawk's tribe.

Improved transportation was the first condition of this quickening life. Canals, roads, and railways took people west, and connected them with a market when they got there. By bringing the Great Lakes within reach of a metropolitan market, the Erie Canal, completed in 1825, opened up the hitherto neglected northern regions of Ohio, Indiana, and Illinois and made New York City the principal gateway to the farther West. Ohio linked the Great Lakes with the Mississippi valley by canal in 1833–34. By 1850 Cleveland rose from a frontier village to a great lake port; Cincinnati, at the other end of the state canal system, sent pickled pork down the Ohio and Mississippi by flatboat and steamboat, shipped flour by canal boat to New York, and in 1850 had a population of 115,000—more than that of New York City in 1815. Three hundred lake vessels arrived at Chicago in 1833, although its permanent population was about 200. An English traveler pronounced Chicago in 1846 to be a city of 'magnificent intentions,' and predicted that after being burned down once or twice it might amount to something. In 1856 the city was connected by railway with New York, and by 1860 it was almost as large as Cincinnati. During the 1840's, while the population of the United States increased 36 per cent, that of towns and cities of 8000 or more grew 90 per cent. Measured by numbers, the urban movement was stronger than westward migration, and its effect on the American character equally important.[4]

Only gradually did railroads replace the canals. In 1828 the first spadeful was turned on the Baltimore and Ohio, but the line did not reach the Ohio river until 1853. In the early '50's the completion of the Hudson River Railway from New York to Albany (where it was connected with the New York Central for Buffalo) and of the Pennsylvania Railroad from Philadelphia to Pittsburgh caused such an astounding transfer of freight from canals to railroads, particularly in the winter season, as to prove the superiority of rail for the long haul, and to suggest that the steam locomotive was the proper instrument for penetrating the continent.

Though American shipbuilders lagged behind England in applying steam to ocean navigation, their sailing vessels largely captured the freight and passenger traffic between Liverpool and New York. 'The reason will be evident to any one who will walk through the docks at Liverpool,' wrote an Englishman in 1824. 'He will see the American ships, long, sharp built, beautifully painted and rigged, and remarkable for their fine appearance and white canvas. He will see the English vessels, short, round and dirty, resembling great black tubs.' One consequence of the transportation revolution was the development of a safe and inexpensive ocean crossing. Shippers encouraged the emigrant trade in order to have a return freight on their westward voyage.

In the century after 1815 some 30 million people migrated from Europe to America. The country was staggered by the wave of nearly 600,000 immigrants in the 1830's, four times as

many as in the previous decade, but in the 1850's a startling 2,314,000 newcomers would step ashore. The number of immigrants who came to the United States between 1815 and 1860 was greater than the total population of the country in 1790. Americans liked to believe that migrants were attracted to their country by admiration for the unique political institutions of the United States, but, in truth, most came for economic reasons. Cycles of prosperity in America drew them; periods of depression discouraged their coming. They responded both to the 'pull' of the burgeoning American economy and the 'push' of the population explosion and hard times in Europe. After the terrible Great Famine due to the potato blights of 1845–49, the Irish peasant came to view migration as a release instead of a banishment. Many arrived penniless; others often fell prey to waterfront sharpers. But as soon as they recovered their shore legs the immigrants were well able to defend themselves. As early as 1835 Irishmen were driving the Whigs from the polls in New York with showers of 'Irish confetti.' Despite suffering and homesickness, most of the immigrants prospered and sent for their friends.

Almost all of the 5 million immigrants in these years came from northwestern Europe, two million from Ireland, over a million and a half from Germany, three-quarters of a million from England, Scotland, and Wales. All but a small fraction of the newcomers arrived in seaports in the Northeast and settled in the northern half of the country. Although mostly country folk, the Irish congregated in cities where thousands of them were recruited for construction work and domestic service. The impoverished Irishman lacked the cash to acquire land, had no experience of farming other than potatoes, and distrusted the land after

4. Table showing populations of principal cities:

	1790	1800	1810	1820	1830	1840	1850
Boston	18,038	24,937	33,250	43,298	61,392	93,383	136,881
New York	33,131	60,489	96,373	123,706	202,589	312,710	515,547
Philadelphia	42,520	69,403	91,874	112,772	161,410	220,423	340,045
Baltimore	13,503	26,114	35,583	62,738	80,825	102,313	169,054
Charleston	16,359	20,473	24,711	24,780	30,289	29,261	42,985
New Orleans			17,242	27,176	46,310	102,193	116,375

his bitter experience in Ireland. He was too gregarious for life on the isolated American farm, and needed a community large enough to support a Catholic Church. Peasant also were a majority of the Germans, but not in like degree; among them were thousands of artisans, a few thousand political refugees from the revolutions of 1830 and 1848 such as Carl Schurz, and a sprinkling of intellectuals. German colonies were formed in cities such as Milwaukee, but the greater number acquired Western land, as did the Scandinavians.

This wave of immigration enhanced the wealth of the country, yet encountered bitter opposition. In part, the antagonism was religious, since most of the Irish and many of the Germans were Roman Catholics. In part it was political, for most immigrants to the cities became Jackson Democrats, largely because the politicians of that party were the first to give them help. In part it was due to the widespread belief among native Americans that the immigrants were paupers. Most immigrants only wanted an opportunity to work, but their need for jobs was so desperate that by cutting wages they displaced some laborers, especially free Negroes. Yet the main consequence of immigration was an acceleration of economic growth that benefitted native Americans as well as the newcomers.

Factory and Workshop

In the generation after 1815, textiles propelled the American economy. The South grew cotton, the Northeast converted it into cloth and supplied manufactured goods to the South, which obtained a large part of its food from the Midwest. From 1820 to 1840, the number of cotton spindles increased from 191,000 to two and a quarter million, two-thirds of them in New England. Farmers' daughters were attracted to the new factory city of Lowell by relatively high wages, and the scruples of their pious parents were overcome by the provision of strictly chaperoned boarding houses. For a generation the Lowell factory girls, with their neat dresses, correct deportment, and literary weekly, were a wonder. Never, unfortunately, were they typical. Yet it is also true that because of wide opportunities in a new country, no permanent proletariat was created. Lawrence, a woolen

counterpart to Lowell, was established on the Merrimack, the same river, in 1845. The woolen industry developed more slowly, but by 1850 the Northern states boasted over 1500 woolen mills.

Of the many industries that were still in the domestic stage at this period, the most significant was shoemaking, for which no machine process of any importance was invented until 1850. In New England it was a winter occupation of farmers and fishermen, who, when the harvest was gathered, or the vessel hauled out for the winter, formed a 'crew' to make boots and shoes in a neighborhood workshop, from stock put out by some local merchant. Every man was master of his own time, and there was no clatter of machinery to drown discussion. A boy was often hired to read to the workers. It was said that 'every Lynn shoemaker was fit to be an United States Senator'; and Henry Wilson 'the cordwainer of Natick' became Vice-President. The shoemakers of New York and Philadelphia, more hard-pressed than their Yankee brethren by the capitalist and the immigrant, were pioneers in the first political labor movement in America.

In England the industrial revolution turned mainly on coal and iron; not so in the United States, where the iron industry lagged. Suitable coal for coking was not found east of the Appalachians, but wood for making charcoal was abundant. Even Pittsburgh used charcoal for smelting prior to 1840, rather than the bituminous coal which was plentiful in the neighborhood. And Pittsburgh, although it commanded the iron market of the Mississippi valley, could not sell its products in the East until it obtained through railroad connection with Philadelphia. Eastern Pennsylvania was the principal coal- and iron-producing region until 1860. The production of pig-iron increased from 54,000 tons in 1810 to 564,000 tons in 1850; but by that time Great Britain's output was almost 3 million tons. Very little steel was produced in America before 1870, and the engineering trades were undeveloped.

Textiles and iron do not exhaust the list of factory industries in the United States at this time, nor had mass production become a necessary condition of American industrial success. Connecticut, in particular, was famous for small, water-driven workshops where specialized articles were produced by native ingenuity. Connecticut

Passenger Pigeon by John James Audubon (1785–1851). Audubon, who arrived in America from France in 1803, painted in the 1820's in Pittsburgh this watercolor and pastel of a male passenger pigeon being fed by his mate. When Audubon's work was exhibited in Europe, critics were astonished by the fidelity to detail and by the vivid sense conveyed of the creatures of the New World. 'Who would have expected such things from the woods of America?' asked a Parisian artist. So plentiful were passenger pigeons that in 1813 in Kentucky Audubon estimated that a billion birds passed overhead in three hours, and they were but a small segment of a three-day migration. 'The air was literally filled with pigeons,' he wrote; 'the light of noon-day was obscured as by an eclipse.' But so great was the slaughter of these birds that by the end of the century they were nearly extinct, and in 1914 the last known passenger pigeon died. (*New-York Historical Society*)

tinware and wooden clocks were carried by Yankee peddlers far and wide. One of the most popular exhibits at London's Crystal Palace in 1851 was the array of reapers, ranges, sewing machines, and other 'Yankee notions.'

Science, Technology, and Education

Comparatively little scientific advance was made in the United States during this era because the stress was on practice rather than theory. Benjamin Franklin started the trend; his American Philosophical Society was dedicated to 'useful knowledge,' and his loyalist contemporary Benjamin Thompson founded the Rumford professorship at Harvard in 1816 'on the Application of Science to the Useful Arts.' Alexis de Tocqueville, in his *Democracy in America* (1835), observed that in a democratic society short cuts to wealth, labor-saving gadgets, and inventions catering to the comfort of life 'seem the most magnificent effort of human intelligence.'

The one American 'pure' scientist of this era was Joseph Henry. After inventing the electromagnet, he produced a rudimentary motor which he regarded as 'a philosophical toy.' His studies of induced currents, begun independently of his English contemporary Michael Faraday who first announced the discovery, led Henry to discover step-up and step-down transformers and to formulate theories of intensity (voltage) and quantity (amperage) of currents. In 1846 Henry became the first director of the Smithsonian Institution at Washington. This earliest American foundation for scientific research was established by a bequest of over £100,000—greater than the then endowment of any American university—from a British chemist named James Smithson, for founding at Washington 'an Establishment for the increase and diffusion of knowledge among men.' Congress expected the Institution to comprise a library, art museum, and collection of scientific curiosities that would amuse congressmen and their friends, but Henry saw to it that the Smithsonian became an indispensable agency for the financing and wide distribution of original research. Henry also helped Samuel F. B. Morse to invent the electric telegraph in 1837.

It was typical of mid-century piety that the first message sent over this line on 24 May 1844 between Morse in the Supreme Court chamber in the Capitol, and Alfred Vail in Baltimore, was 'What hath God wrought!' (Numbers xxiii:23).

The branches of science that made good progress in the generation after 1830 were natural history, chemistry, and geology. John Audubon had to visit England in order to obtain subscriptions for his classic *Birds of America* (1827), but he was acclaimed a hero on his return. In 1835 Benjamin Silliman of Yale, who founded and edited the first American scientific periodical, delivered a series of lectures at Boston on geology which, pious Congregationalist though he was, made the first important dent on the Biblical account of creation. A year or two later his friend the Reverend Edward Hitchcock, a science professor of Amherst College, discovered dinosaur tracks in the red sandstone of the Connecticut valley: a new proof of the antiquity of life on this planet. When in 1848 Louis Agassiz left his native Switzerland and occupied a chair of zoology and geology in the new scientific school at Harvard, America found a leader in natural science who was at once an original investigator, a great teacher, and one who could appeal to the popular imagination. No American, native or adopted, was Agassiz's equal in stimulating both popular and scholarly interest in that segment of natural science which stretched from biology to paleontology.

The most tangible social gain during this period of ferment was in popular education. Since the Revolution, education had been left largely to private initiative and benevolence, but almost all secondary academies charged fees. Most of the Northern states had some sort of public primary school system, but only in New England was it free and open to all. In some instances only parents pleading poverty were exempted from fees. Consequently a stigma was attached to free schools. In New York City, around 1820, nearly half the children went uneducated because their parents were too poor to pay fees and too proud to accept charity.

Opposition to free public education came from people of property, who thought it intolerable that they should be taxed to support schools to which they would not dream of sending their children. To this argument the poor replied with votes, and reformers with the tempting argument that education was insurance against radicalism. New York City in 1832, and Philadelphia in 1836, established elementary public schools free from the taint of charity; but the growth of public schools did not keep pace with the increase of population by birth and immigration. There were half a million white adult illiterates in the country in 1840; almost a million in 1850.

In the New England states free elementary schools, maintained by the townships and taught by birch-wielding pedagogues or college students during their vacations, were much in need of improvement. When Horace Mann became chairman of the Massachusetts Board of Education (1837), he insisted that control of the schools should rest not with professional schoolmen but with popularly elected legislatures and school committees composed of laymen. At Lexington, in 1839, the first American teachers' college was established. After a struggle with the older teachers, who insisted that mental discipline would be lost if studies were made interesting, the elementary school ceased to be a place of terror. New England also set the pace in free public high schools; but until after the Civil War most pupils following a secondary course attended an endowed academy.

Outside New England, public schools were generally supported by the interest on a fund set up out of the proceeds of public lands or earmarked taxes, administered by a specially appointed state board. In Pennsylvania a terrific fight took place over free schools which were opposed by not only the well-to-do but the Germans, who feared the loss of their language and culture. Ohio was fairly well provided with free public elementary schools by 1830, and six years later the state sent Calvin E. Stowe, professor of Biblical literature in Lane Theological Seminary at Cincinnati (better known as husband of the author of *Uncle Tom's Cabin*) to Europe to investigate public school systems. His *Report on Elementary Instruction in Europe* (1837) had an influence not inferior to the reports of Horace Mann. Among other things, it resulted in dividing public education in Ohio into elemen-

tary, grammar, and high school grades. By 1850 the modern system of grades one through twelve had been adopted in places where the number of pupils allowed it. Indiana established a free public school system in 1848, but opposition of the Southern element in the population prevented the Illinois legislature from enacting a state-wide public school law until 1855. However, by 1860, the Midwest had a larger proportion of its children in public schools than any other region.

It was long before the free blacks of the North had any benefit from free public education. Philadelphia opened the first school for black children in 1822 with an apology for doing something for 'this friendless and degraded portion of society.' In northern New England where blacks were few, they were admitted to the public schools without question; but in urban centers both reformers and the blacks themselves favored separate schools, to avoid the stigma of charity and give the children more congenial companionship. The move against segregation began with the anti-slavery agitation of the 1830's. Massachusetts in 1855 was the first state to enforce integration of all races and religions in her public schools, but segregation was not legally ended in New York City schools until 1900.

American schools of the nineteenth century reflected Protestant thinking. They aimed to cultivate qualities of character, such as thrift and industry, appropriate to the Puritan tradition and the cult of the self-made man, and William H. McGuffey's moralistic readers reflected the values of evangelical ministers. Increasingly the community expected the school to take over the roles of church and family. As the school committee of Springfield, Massachusetts, explained: 'The school-master is for the time being during school hours *in loco parentis*; sustaining a relation to his pupils parallel to that of a father to his children.'

This period saw an amazing multiplication of small denominational colleges; and a somewhat less surprising mortality among them. In sixteen Eastern and Midwestern states (both North and South) 516 colleges and 'universities' were founded before the Civil War; but only 104 of these were still in existence in 1929. Yale alone begat sixteen Congregationalist colleges before

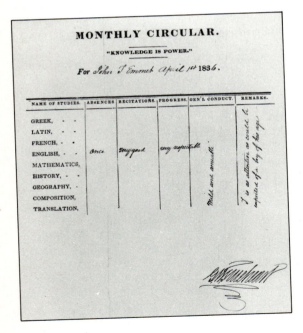

Report card. His mother wrote of the recipient of this assessment, who would grow up to be a West Point cadet and a physician: 'Little John is at my elbow and expressly desires me to tell you that he is a very good boy, that he has gotten a new spelling book from his Grandmother Patten, and that he will take care and get his lessons well. All this I am sure he has sincere intentions of performing tho I must confess that in his old spelling book he is not very brilliant.' Still, she added of John Patten Emmet's schooling, 'he does not learn any bad habits and is fond of it. At home he would be apt to grow sluggish.' *(Henry E. Huntington Library)*

1861, and Princeton 25 Presbyterian ones. It was the heyday of the small, rural college with six to a dozen professors and 100 to 300 students. During a good part of this period, Amherst, Dartmouth, and Union colleges had as many or more students than Harvard, Yale, and Princeton. The average statesman and professional man of the Northern states completed his formal education at a small college.[5]

In the same period the movement for public and secular state universities, which had begun just before the Revolution, received a new impetus, in part from the founding of the University of Virginia. The earliest of the Western state universities was founded at Detroit in 1817, but the University of Michigan remained a mere secondary school until 1837, when it was rechartered and removed to Ann Arbor. The University of Wisconsin, second of the state universities to become famous, was founded at Madison in 1848, on a wilderness site crossed by Black Hawk's warriors only sixteen years before.

Harvard was the first of the older universities after the War of 1812 to feel the new spirit of progress; and the source of her inspiration was Germany. Between the years 1815 and 1820 four young Harvard graduates—George Ticknor, Edward Everett, Joseph G. Cogswell, and George Bancroft—studied at the Universities of Göttingen and Berlin. The young Americans admired the boundless erudition, critical acumen, and unwearied diligence of German scholars, marveled at the wealth of the university libraries, and envied the *Lernfreiheit* or academic freedom. They returned with an ambition to transform their little brick colleges into magnificently equipped universities. All four upon their return received posts at Harvard. Everett gave prestige, by his graceful delivery and easily worn mantle of scholarship, to the lecture method of instruction; Bancroft applied German thoroughness to early American history; Cogswell is memorable in library history; and Ticknor remained professor of belles lettres long enough to establish a worthy school of Romance and Germanic languages, and to secure the principle that undergraduates might elect them as a substitute for traditional subjects. And it was in part the influence of American scholars who had caught the flame in Germany, in part the liberal tendency of Unitarianism, that made Harvard, as early as the 1830's, a steadfast defender of the scholar's freedom from political and religious pressure.

Though many of the colleges of mid-century had high standards in the subjects they professed to teach, the university law and medical schools of the period were not even respectable. Yet the application of anesthesia to surgery was discovered independently by three graduates of American medical schools around 1842. And, just as Jefferson wished to live as the founder of a university, so Dr. O. W. Holmes, author of *The Autocrat of the Breakfast Table*, considered his best title to fame the discovery in 1843 that puerperal fever could be prevented by the use of antiseptics.

Adults were not neglected in this educational awakening. Mechanics' institutes provided vocational courses and night schools; free public libraries were widespread; and lyceums offered popular lectures, scientific demonstrations, debates, and entertainments. Mechanical improvements in printing made possible the penny press; the New York *Tribune*, Baltimore *Sun*, and Philadelphia *Ledger* began as penny newspapers in the 1840's. The *Tribune*, under Horace Greeley's editorship, became a liberal power of the first magnitude.

By 1850, then, in the Northern and Western states there had been formulated, and to some extent established, the basic principles of American education today: (1) that free public primary and secondary schools should be available for all children; (2) that teachers should be given professional training; (3) that all children should attend school up to a certain age, but not necessarily the free public school, religious and other bodies having complete liberty to establish their own educational systems at their own cost; (4) that a liberal higher education, and professional training schools for law, medicine, divinity, and engineer-

5. Oberlin in Ohio became the first co-educational college in 1833, but had very few imitators. Wesleyan College in Georgia was the first college to give degrees to women. Mary Lyon established Mount Holyoke Female Seminary in Massachusetts in 1836, but it was some years before it offered a course of college grade.

ing be provided. However, the research function of modern universities was hardly yet thought of.

Reformers, Revivalists, and Utopians

'The ancient manners were giving way. There grew a certain tenderness on the people, not before remarked,' wrote Emerson of these years. 'The key to the period appeared to be that the mind had become aware of itself. . . . The young men were born with knives in their brain.' One of these young men was Thomas H. Gallaudet, who before he was 30 established the first American school for the deaf at Hartford, Connecticut. Samuel Gridley Howe of Boston fought for Greek independence in his early twenties, and returned to found the Perkins Institute for the Blind. Elihu Burritt, the 'learned blacksmith' of New Britain, Conn., in his early thirties threw himself heart and soul into the peace movement. Neal Dow, a prominent Maine businessman with Quaker antecedents, started a brisk campaign against Demon Rum.

Young women, too, were 'born with knives in their brain.' In 1848 Elizabeth C. Stanton and Lucretia Mott launched at Seneca Falls, N.Y., a movement for women's suffrage, which, carried forward by the eloquence of Lucy Stone and the energy of Susan B. Anthony, eventually bore fruit in Amendment XIX to the Constitution (1920).

Most remarkable of these pioneer women was Dorothea Lynde Dix, a New England gentlewoman who at the age of 33 began a life-long crusade on behalf of the insane. These unfortunates were then largely treated as criminals, 'chained, naked, beaten with rods and lashed into obedience,' as she described their plight in her *Memorial to the Legislature of Massachusetts* (1843). This amazing woman—beautiful, naturally timid and diffident—visited all parts of the United States on behalf of the mentally ill. She persuaded Congress to establish St. Elizabeth's Hospital, and, the only New England reformer to penetrate the South, secured the establishment of public hospitals for the insane in nine Southern states. Off then she went to Europe, where she enlisted the support of the Duke of Argyll and Queen Victoria, and in Rome told Pope Pius IX that the local asylum was 'a scandal and disgrace';

the Pope listened to her and did something about it.

The great breeding ground of mid-century 'isms' was not New England itself, but an area peopled by Yankees in the rolling hills of central New York and along the Erie Canal. These folk were so susceptible to religious revivals and Pentecostal beliefs that their region was called 'The Burned-over District.' Anti-Masonry began there, and, at Palmyra, N.Y., Mormonism. At Hampton, N.Y., William Miller evolved the theory that the Second Coming of Christ would take place on 22 October 1843. The Millerite or Adventist sect persuaded thousands to sell all their

"BLOOMERISM,"
OR THE
NEW FEMALE COSTUME OF 1851.

As it has appeared in the various Cities and Towns.

BOSTON. S. W. WHEELER, 66 Cornhill—1851.

Dorothea Dix (1802–87). The outstanding humanitarian reformer of the nineteenth century, she left home at ten, was teaching school at fourteen. 'I never knew childhood,' she said. She worked indefatigably on behalf of the insane, who as she told Congress, she had seen 'bound with galling chains, . . . lacerated with ropes, scourged with rods, and terrified beneath storms of profane execrations and cruel blows.' Her intercession brought changes on two continents, including new mental hospitals in Scotland and in Italy. Not until she was eighty did she retire, and in her last years she was saying, 'I think even lying in my bed I can still do something.' (*Library of Congress*)

goods and, clothed in suitable robes, to await the Second Coming on roofs, hilltops, and haystacks, which they felt would shorten their ascent to Heaven. Mother Ann Lee (at New Lebanon, N.Y.) and Jemima Wilkinson (at Jerusalem, N.Y.) attempted to sublimate sexual urges by founding Shaker and 'Universal Friend' communities on the basis of celibacy. John H. Noyes, on the contrary, sought catharsis in sexual indulgence at his Oneida Community. It seemed appropriate that spirits from the other world seeking means to communicate with this should have chosen Rochester, metropolis of the Burned-over District. There the Fox sisters' spirit-rappings and table-turnings had the whole country agog in 1848. Out of their performances issued the cult of spiritualism which within ten years had 67 newspapers and periodicals devoted to culling messages from 'angel spheres.'

This exuberant generation believed a man could take action not only to change society but to save his soul. Charles Grandison Finney, probably the greatest American evangelist, carried out most of his work in the final decade of the Second Great Awakening that began in 1795 and ended about 1835. Finney, who had felt God come to him 'in waves of liquid love,' struck one of the last blows at orthodox Calvinism and helped substitute a liberal Calvinism which found a place for man's effort to achieve his own salvation. By 1855 the evangelical Methodists and Baptists accounted for nearly 70 per cent of all Protestant communicants. Both sects rebelled against such Calvinist ideas as man's depravity, predestination, and unconditional election. Although evangelical Protestantism eventually tended to be conservative in political outlook and divided in its attitude toward slavery, in the years of the Second Great Awakening it gave powerful support to the thrust for social reform.

The first labor movement in America was initiated by urban handicraftsmen rather than factory operatives. When merchant-capitalists organized trades such as tailoring on a larger scale, with long credits, division of labor, and wholesale marketing, the master workman who employed a few journeymen and apprentices was degraded to a foreman under an entrepreneur. Minute specialization broke down the apprentice system. With the introduction of gas in the cities, the old working hours of sun to sun were lengthened in the winter, making a twelve-hour day the year round. The ranks of labor were so constantly replenished by immigrants and women[6] that native male artisans were alarmed over their declining status. In 1828 a group of Philadelphia artisans organized a 'Workingmen's party,' and parties with the same name sprang up in other Eastern cities. They were not proletarian, but largely middle-class. Mechanics and small shopkeepers wanted local and practical reforms like free schools and laws giving workers such as carpenters liens on buildings to prevent their being cheated by contractors. The Workingmen's parties, with their moderate programs of social betterment, were making progress in the cities of Pennsylvania and New York when they made a costly alliance with utopian idealists.

Robert Owen, the earliest foreign radical who imagined that because America had achieved political liberty she would be receptive to every type of libertarianism, came to reform, and remained to scold. In 1825 he purchased a settlement at New Harmony, Indiana, and experimented in a form of communism. His son Robert Dale Owen took it over, and in two years New Harmony became new discord. Young Owen then joined forces with Frances Wright (Madame d'Arusmont), a vigorous Scotswoman who had founded a community in Tennessee for the purpose of emancipating slaves. When that, too, came to an untimely end, 'Fanny' Wright became a lecture-platform apostle of woman's rights, free inquiry in religion, free marital union, birth control, and a system which she called 'National, Rational, Republican Education, Free for All at the Expense of All, Conducted under the Guardianship of the State,' apart from the contaminating influence of parents.

These 'Free Enquirers' had already attracted much unfavorable attention from the Northern press in 1829, when the artisans of New York City

---

6. Although women were not generally employed in shops or in offices until after the Civil War, they were in over a hundred different occupations in 1835, even in trades such as printing from which the unions later excluded them.

New Harmony, Indiana. *Above,* as it was envisioned by British mill-owner Robert Owen (1771–1858). But the reality fell well short of this architect's fantasy of turreted towers, and an enclosed botanical garden. Owen did attract about a thousand settlers to his communal experiment, but, his son later reflected, they turned out to be 'a heterogeneous collection of radicals, enthusiastic devotees of principle, honest latitudinarians and lazy theorists, with a sprinkling of unprincipled sharpers thrown in.' (*Library of Congress*). *Below,* New Harmony, as it actually was. This sketch by Lesueur, a French naturalist who spent ten years at the colony, makes it possible to contrast New Harmony with the original ideal. (*Muséum d'Histoire Naturelle, Le Havre*)

organized a Workingmen's party. Grateful for intellectual leadership, they accepted the aid of George Henry Evans, a young editor recently arrived from England, who was also an ardent admirer of Owen and of Fanny Wright, both of whom promptly joined the workingmen in the hope of capturing their support for 'National, Rational Education.' To the consternation of conservatives, the 'Workies' polled 30 per cent of the city vote in the autumn election. A press campaign then began, denunciatory toward Fanny Wright, the 'bold blasphemer and voluptuous preacher of licentiousness.' The printers' union repudiated this 'band of choice spirits of foreign origin,' and

led a secession from the party, which promptly broke up. Small groups of the party joined the Democrats, who rewarded them by obtaining a mechanics' lien law and the abolition of imprisonment for debt.

In 1833, when a period of prosperity began, the labor movement abandoned politics in favor of trade organization, the closed shop, and the strike. Trades' unions—federations of all the organized trades in a single community—were formed in twelve Northern cities; and in 1837 delegates from these cities organized a National Trades' Union. Strikes on several occasions included not only the organized workers but the unskilled

A shoemakers' strike in Lynn, Massachusetts. Eight hundred women operatives march in a snowstorm, followed by four thousand workmen and preceded by the band of the Lynn City Guards. (*Collection Judith Mara Gutman*)

laborers of an entire city. Wages improved, and the ten-hour day was established in several cities for municipal employees, and in the navy yards by order of President Jackson. Harriet Martineau, visiting the Northern states at that time, took note of the well-dressed, well-fed, and even well-read 'dandy mechanics.'

But the panic of 1837 brought unemployment and misery to the landless artisans. Wages fell 30 to 50 per cent and the 'dandy mechanics' were glad to sell their 'gay watch guards and glossy hats' for a bit of bread. A promising labor movement collapsed; the 300,000 trade unionists of 1837 (about half the urban skilled workers in the United States) could no longer pay their dues. Hard times followed, with long hours; the Lowell factory girls petitioned the Massachusetts legislature in vain to reduce their twelve-hour day to ten. Immigrants took their places, and by 1850 these show workers, with their white gowns and literary journal, were no longer found in the cotton mills.

Disappointed in his experience both with political action and with unionization, the artisan once again lent an ear to the utopians. Almost every known panacea was applied, with meager or negative results. Robert Owen in 1845 summoned a 'World Convention to Emancipate the Human Race from Ignorance, Poverty, Division, Sin, Misery.' Josiah Warren, the first American anarchist, devised a system of 'time stores' and 'labor notes,' inspired by Owenite 'labor bazaars.' Many unions went in for producers' co-operation; others began consumers' co-operatives. The typical experiment was some sort of association or community. Brook Farm, the transcendentalist community described in Hawthorne's *The Blithedale Romance*, became one of forty Fourierite 'phalanxes' in the Northern states.

Horace Greeley kept the columns of the New York *Tribune* hospitable to all these movements; but his best advice was: 'Go West, young man, go West!' Here was a point of contact with national politics. Public land at $200 the quarter-section was not for those who needed it most, but for those who had the price, or for squatters who defied all comers to dislodge them. Greeley insisted that every man had the same natural right to a bit of land as to air and sunlight. George Henry Evans advocated a free homestead from the public domain to every settler; limitation of individual holdings; and no alienation of the homestead, voluntary or otherwise. 'Vote yourself a farm' was his slogan. In 1846 Andrew Johnson introduced the first free homestead bill in Congress, but Northern Whigs and Southern Democrats combined to defeat it.

For all the paucity of results, the labor movement did score some modest gains. Unionization made a beginning, and in 1842 Chief Justice Lemuel Shaw of Massachusetts, in the memorable case of Commonwealth *v.* Hunt, declared that a trade union was a lawful organization, the members of which were not collectively responsible for illegal acts committed by individuals. Yet there was still no national federation of labor, and the first state provision for factory inspection did not come until 1867. Instead of trying to humanize the new industrial order, both workers and thinkers had dissipated their energy in efforts to escape it.

Transcendentalism and Literature

Transcendentalism, which coursed through the Northern states between 1820 and 1860, embraced so wide a spectrum of ideas that the term almost defies definition. Optimistic about human nature, these romantic 'enthusiasts' deplored religious and literary formalism and believed that by relying on intuition Man and Society could be renovated. The new spirit appeared in some men as intense individualism, in others as a passionate sympathy for the oppressed. It gave to Hawthorne his deep perception of the beauty and the tragedy of life, to Walt Whitman his robust joy in living. But it was Emerson who perfectly embodied the essential spirit, a belief in the soul's inherent power to grasp the truth. Remarkably, this outburst of intellectual activity occurred largely within a 50-mile radius of Boston during a single generation.

The soil had been prepared by Unitarianism, which with its sister Universalism took a great weight off the soul of New England. The Unitarians not only denied that God was a member of a trinitarian Godhead but had an optimistic faith in man's capacity for good and rejected the Calvinist

The New England literati. In this clever composite photograph, the great figures of nineteenth-century letters are grouped as though actually in the same library. From left to right, they are John Greenleaf Whittier, Oliver Wendell Holmes, Ralph Waldo Emerson, John Lothrop Motley, Bronson Alcott, Nathaniel Hawthorne, James Russell Lowell, Louis Agassiz, and Henry Wadsworth Longfellow. (*Concord Free Public Library*)

view that men predestined for damnation cannot achieve salvation. Longfellow's *Psalm of Life*, which seems so trite nowadays,

> Life is real! life is earnest!
> And the grave is not its goal;
> Dust thou art, to dust returnest,
> Was not spoken of the soul.

came as a message of hope to thousands of young people reared in the fear of everlasting damnation. Yet something was lacking in mere Unitarianism. A faith in the essential goodness of human nature might be a theological counterpart to democracy; but it failed to supply the note of mysticism that democrats no less than aristocrats seek in religion.

Emerson in 1832, at the age of 29, gave up his pastoral office in a Unitarian church because it no longer interested him. In his next four years of reading and travel, he found God again in nature; and settled down as 'lay preacher to the world' in the placid village of Concord, which harbored during one generation Emerson, Hawthorne, Thoreau, and the Alcotts. If Jefferson was the prophet of democracy, and Jackson was its high priest, Emerson was its high priest. Like Jefferson, he believed ardently in the perfectibility of mankind; but he knew what Jefferson never learned, that free institutions would not liberate men not themselves free. His task was to induce Americans to cleanse their minds of hatred and prejudice, to make them think out the consequences of democracy instead of merely repeating its catchwords, and to seek the same eminence in spirit that they had reached in material things.

Henry Thoreau, whose *A Week on the Concord and Merrimack Rivers* came out in 1849, was the best classical scholar of the Concord group and the most independent of classic modes of thought. Concord for him was a microcosm of the world. Thoreau's *Walden* (1854) has had a pervasive influence on writers as different as Proust and Tolstoy, and translations have appeared from South America to the Orient. When bumbling county commissioners in 1959 tried to turn the shores of Walden Pond into a beach resort, a blast of protests from all over the world halted the desecration. In Emerson, Thoreau, and Haw-

thorne, in Herman Melville, who was half Yankee, and in the timeless Emily Dickinson of the next generation, the New England that had slowly matured since the seventeenth century justified itself.

In New York the 'Knickerbocker School' was declining. Bryant's last spurt of poetical activity ended in 1844; during the rest of his long life he was a leading figure in journalism. Washington Irving's *Sketch Book* came out as early as 1818; seven years later he turned to Spain for inspiration and to history for expression; returning to New York a literary hero, he visited the West for material, but his *Astoria* and *Adventures of Captain Bonneville* lack the authenticity of Francis Parkman's *Oregon Trail* (1849). For the rest of his life, Irving at 'Sunnyside' on the Hudson and at Madrid well played the roles of diplomat, host, and sage. James Fenimore Cooper's 'Leather-Stocking' and 'Sea Tales' started in the 1820's, after which he embarked on a crusade to put everybody right both in England and in America, and succeeded in making himself the most unpopular person in the English-speaking world.

New England intellectuals had more to say than their New York contemporaries, but they, too, conveyed it in traditional forms. 'We all lean on England,' wrote Emerson. Not until 1851 did a distinctive American literature, original both in form and content, emerge, with Melville's *Moby-Dick*. Four years later, with Emerson's blessing, *Leaves of Grass* began to sprout. Walt Whitman, half Yankee, half New York Dutch, had grown up outside the ambit of New England respectability, in intimate contact with the crude realities of American life. In the 'barbaric yawp' that so deeply influenced twentieth-century poetry, Whitman sang of the common American and his life in seaport, farm, and frontier.

Whitman was the poet of democracy, but Henry Wadsworth Longfellow was democracy's favorite poet. Longfellow's verse was tuned to catch the ear of a busy and unlearned people. And, until Lincoln's prose poem, 'The Gettysburg Address,' was delivered, no poem had a greater effect in creating that love of the Union which made young men fight to preserve it than the peroration to Longfellow's 'Building of the Ship' (1849):

Thou, too, sail on, O Ship of State!
Sail on, O Union, strong and great!
Humanity with all its fears,
With all the hopes of future years,
Is hanging breathless on thy fate!

Anti-Slavery and Abolition

Of all reform movements, the one that shook the Union to its foundation sought the abolition of slavery. An earlier anti-slavery agitation won its last victory in 1807 when Congress passed an act against the slave trade, but in 1817 the American Colonization Society was founded with the aim of doing for American Negroes what the Republic of Israel later did for Jews—to give them back a part of their homeland, though with the frank admission that the Negro, free or slave, had no place in American society. To further this enterprise, the A.C.S. purchased from native tribes several tracts along the Grain Coast of West Africa; and several thousand American blacks had been settled by 1847, when they organized the Republic of Liberia, with a capital named Monrovia after President Monroe, and a constitution modeled on that of the United States. However, when the A.C.S., having scraped the barrel of private benevolence, appealed to Congress for federal aid in 1827, Southerners opposed the movement as jeopardizing the supply of slaves and abolitionists denounced it as a subtle attempt to increase the value of the remaining slaves in America. The A.C.S., though discouraged, continued its work to the Civil War, but without congressional backing for colonization, moral suasion against slavery appeared to have spent its force.

Apathy could hardly have been more complete, when on 1 January 1831 the first number of *The Liberator* appeared in Boston, published by William Lloyd Garrison. On the first page he announced:

I shall strenuously contend for the immediate enfranchisement of our slave population. . . . On this subject I do not wish to think, or speak, or write, with moderation. . . . I am in earnest—I will not equivocate—I will not excuse—I will not retreat a single inch—AND I WILL BE HEARD.

Therein spoke the Old Testament, not the New.

Garrison's policy was to hold up the most repulsive aspects of Negro slavery to the public gaze; to castigate the slaveholders and all who defended them as man-stealers, torturers, traffickers in human flesh. He recognized no rights of the masters, acknowledged no racial animosities, tolerated no delay. Blackguarding the slaveholders would have made few converts in the South at any time, but least of all in the very year of the Nat Turner slave insurrection. Prominent Southerners at once asserted that Garrison was responsible (although only four copies of *The Liberator* had reached the South), and demanded that the Northern states, if they valued the Union, suppress this incendiary agitation.

Many efforts short of press censorship were made in the North to satisfy the South on this point. Garrison wrote that he 'found contempt more bitter, opposition more stubborn, and apathy more frozen' in New England than among slave-owners. Elijah Lovejoy, who persisted in printing an abolitionist paper, had his press twice thrown into the river, and in 1837 was murdered by a mob at Alton, Ill. Two years earlier Garrison was paraded around Boston with a rope around his neck, by what was called a 'broadcloth mob'; and on the same day delegates who met at Utica to organize an anti-slavery society were dispersed by a mob of 'very respectable gentlemen' led by a congressman and a judge. Yet the abolition movement grew, and made converts at every mobbing: of Gerrit Smith, for instance, at the Utica affair; of Wendell Phillips in Boston; of Cassius M. Clay, a cousin of Henry Clay, in Kentucky. In 1836 there were more than 500 anti-slavery societies in the Northern states, and by 1840 their membership was over 150,000.

Garrison, driven by a fierce passion for righteousness to write words that cut and burned, personified this new and dreadful force to the white South, but Theodore D. Weld of New York was the most effective abolition leader. A great bear of a man, Weld could subdue a mob or whip an assailant, and often had to. In 1833 Weld and two wealthy New York merchants, Arthur and Lewis Tappan, organized the American Anti-Slavery Society. Weld then tried teaching at Lane Seminary, Cincinnati, and when the trustees or-

Harriet Tubman (1821–1913). Born a slave, she escaped to Philadelphia and became so effective a 'conductor' on the Underground Railroad that John Brown called her 'General Tubman.' (*Schomburg Center for Research in Black Culture, New York Public Library*)

dered discussion of slavery by the students to cease, he and his student converts seceded to Oberlin, which became the first college in the United States to admit both blacks and women. Owing perhaps to their Quaker connection, the abolitionists preceded other reformers in permitting women to address their meetings and serve on committees. Lucretia Mott of Philadelphia, and the Grimké sisters, gentlewomen of South Carolina who freed their slaves and came north to obtain freedom of speech, were counted among the leaders; Angelina Grimké married Weld, and it was perhaps her influence which kept hatred of the slaveholder out of Weld's agitation for freedom and which made him favor gradual, compensated emancipation.

The abolitionists took special pride in the 'Under Ground Railroad' which carried Negroes to liberty. Slaves who had the courage to strike out for freedom would take cover in the woods or swamps near their master's plantation until the hue and cry died down, then follow the North Star to Mason and Dixon's line, or the Ohio river. Once across, the 'U.G.' took them in charge. They were transferred from one abolitionist household to another, hidden by day in attics, haystacks, or corn shocks; piloted by night through the woods, or concealed in farm wagons; sometimes driven in a Friend's carriage, disguised in women's clothes and a deep Quaker bonnet. Others were smuggled north by sea, and made their way into Canada through New England. Most famous of all 'conductors' on the 'U.G.' was Harriet Tubman, an illiterate field hand from the Eastern Shore of Maryland, who not only escaped herself but repeatedly returned southward and guided more than 300 slaves from bondage to freedom, taking some as far as Canada. The number thus rescued in proportion to the total slave population was infinitesimal. Moreover, many of the slaves who escaped did so largely through their own devices; the runaways often fled to other parts of the South where they found refuge in swamps or in cities, among Indians, or as deckhands on ships. Yet if measured by the stimulus it gave the abolitionist cause, the 'Under Ground' was a brilliant success.

By a federal statute of 1793, a master, or his agent, who caught a runaway in a free state could repatriate him forcibly after swearing to his identity before a magistrate. A professional slave-catcher whom the right Negro eluded was apt to conclude that 'any nigger' would answer. Kidnapping became so frequent that Northern states passed 'personal liberty laws' to protect their free colored citizens. The abolitionists cleverly turned local resentment against kidnapping, and Northern dislike of domineering Southerners, into opposition to the return of genuine fugitives. Gradually the personal liberty acts were strengthened to a degree that made a runaway's identity almost impossible to establish. The Supreme Court invalidated such a law in Prigg v. Pennsylvania (1842). But if the states had no right to obstruct, by the same token they had no obligation to assist the federal authorities; and without such assistance the slave-catchers began to receive the attention of mobs. The abolitionists for the first time voiced a popular sentiment when Whittier declared:

No slave-hunt in our borders—no pirate on our strand!
No fetters in the Bay State—no slave upon our land!

The most famous case involving slavery, until eclipsed by Dred Scott's, was that of the *Amistad*, in 1839. She was a Spanish slaver carrying 53 newly imported slaves from Havana to another Cuban port. Under the leadership of an upstanding young Negro named Cinqué, the 'cargo' mutinied and killed captain and crew; but, ignorant of navigation, the mutineers had to rely on the white owners who were on board to sail the ship. The owners stealthily steered north until the *Amistad* was picked up off Long Island by U.S.S. *Washington* and taken into New Haven, where the Negroes were jailed. Spain demanded that they be given up to be tried for piracy, and President Van Buren attempted to do so. Southern senators insisted that, if not surrendered to Spain, the blacks be tried for murder and piracy by a federal court. John Quincy Adams, persuaded by abolitionists to act as attorney for the mutineers, argued for their liberty on the ground that the African slave trade was illegal by Spanish law and by the natural right of mankind to freedom. The Supreme Court, with a majority of Southerners, was so impressed by the old man's eloquence that it ordered the Negroes set free, and they were returned to their native Africa. The ironic epilogue is that Cinqué, once back home, set himself up as a slave trader.

To the right of the abolitionists were the antislavery men. They opposed the extension of slavery into more territories, but did not propose to interfere with slavery in the slave states. However, almost all these moderate anti-slavery men were eventually forced by Southern intransigence into more radical views. The South made three tactical errors in combating abolition. It assumed that every anti-slavery person was an inciter of Negro insurrection. It enacted laws making it increasingly difficult for masters to liberate slaves, and for free Negroes to make a living. And by frantic attempts to suppress all discussion of the subject, and to expand slavery, the South ended in persuading the North that every man's liberty was at stake. William Jay, son of the Chief Justice, said in 1836, 'We commenced the present struggle to obtain the freedom of the slave; we are compelled to continue it to preserve our own.'

The most notorious attempt to suppress discussion of slavery arose from indignation at the slave trade in the District of Columbia. Washington was then a shipping point for slaves from Virginia and Maryland to the cotton states. Even from the windows of the Capitol one could watch coffles of Negroes marching by in clanking chains. Abolitionists protested, but at the insistence of Southern members the House in 1836 adopted a

John Quincy Adams (1767–1848). Denied a second term as President, he humbly sought election to the U.S. House of Representatives where for seventeen years 'old man eloquent' served his constituents in Quincy and fought against the slavocracy. This 1847 daguerreotype captures his forbidding integrity. A year later, at eighty, he collapsed at his desk and was taken to the Speaker's office, where he died. (*Metropolitan Museum of Art*)

'gag resolution,' to the effect that all petitions relating 'in any way' to slavery be laid on the table. John Quincy Adams, now a member of the House, was not an abolitionist; but the gag rule awakened in him ancestral memories of royal tyranny. Session after session he fought for the right of petition. Every attempt short of personal violence was made to silence, to censure, or to expel Adams; but the tough old puritan persisted, and in 1844 the gag rule was finally repealed. It made no difference to the slaves. But on the day when the news reached South Carolina, the leading Whig newspaper of Columbia discontinued printing installments from Washington's Farewell Address, and substituted an appeal for secession.

More than a century has elapsed since Lincoln's Emancipation Proclamation and Amendment XIII to the Constitution destroyed chattel slavery on United States soil. We now know that the slavery question was but one aspect of a race and class problem that is still far from solution. The grapes of wrath have not yet yielded all their bitter vintage.

14

Western Empire

*

1820–1848

The Great Plains

Since 1806, when Lewis and Clark returned from their journey to the Oregon Country, the United States government had not taken much interest in the Far West. Major Long's expedition of 1819 reported the Great Plains 'almost wholly unfit for cultivation,' and laid down on the map of that region, which now supports a thriving population of several millions, the legend 'Great American Desert.'

Over this area of grassland and sagebrush roamed the Kansa, Pawnee, Sioux, Cheyenne, Blackfoot, Crow, and Arapaho. Countless herds of buffalo supplied the plains Indians with every necessity of life, and they had long since domesticated the wild mustang, offspring of those set free by the Spanish conquistadors. These Indians seldom practiced agriculture, and knew little or nothing of pottery, basketry, or weaving; but they were marvelous horsemen and in warfare, once they had learned the use of the rifle, proved more formidable than the Eastern tribes that had yielded so slowly to the white man.

The only whites who penetrated this region before 1830 were explorers, fur traders, and trappers. Every river, valley, mountain, and waterhole of the Far West was known to the trappers before 1830, and without their guidance transcontinental emigration would have been impossible. It was they who discovered the South Pass of the Rockies in Wyoming, a wide valley that takes one to the transcontinental divide by easy gradients. A party of trappers led by Jedediah Smith and William Sublette took the first covered wagons from the Missouri to the Rockies in 1830. Six years later Captain Bonneville, whose adventures provided literary material for Washington Irving, led the first loaded wagons through the South Pass and down the Snake valley to the Columbia river.

The Oregon Country

The climate, timber, and salmon-teeming rivers of the Oregon Country, which included not only the present state of Oregon, but Washington, Idaho, part of Montana, and British Columbia, invited settlement. But how to get at it? And would the pioneer who braved the transcontinen-

231

'Watching the Cargo' by George Caleb Bingham. In 1853 Bingham wrote, 'I am getting quite conceited, whispering to myself . . . that I am the greatest among the disciples of the brush my country has ever produced.' If he was less than that, Bingham undoubtedly ranks as the most important delineator of the American political process of his day, and, as in this 1849 painting, of the Missouri river country. (*State Historical Society of Missouri, Columbia*)

tal journey or the 200-day voyage around Cape Horn find himself on United States soil when he got there?

Every diplomatic negotiation between the United States and Great Britain since 1815 had agreed to disagree on the Oregon question. The only thing settled upon was a temporary joint occupation, north of lat. 42° N, where Spanish California stopped, and south of lat. 54° 40', where Russian Alaska ended. When John Jacob Astor's trading post of Astoria at the mouth of the Columbia river was sold to a Canadian fur trading company, which in 1821 amalgamated with the Hudson's Bay Company, the only American foothold in Oregon was relinquished. Three years later, the Hudson's Bay Company constructed on the north bank of the lower Columbia Fort Vancouver, which Dr. John McLoughlin, the company factor, a shrewd, stalwart, and humane British subject, built up to be an efficient imperial outpost. His hospitality to early American immigrants is memorable, and eventually he became a citizen of the United States; but the flag flown at Fort Vancouver was the company's British banner, not the Stars and Stripes.

In the meantime the Pacific coast was being visited by Boston fur traders and 'hide droghers.' Many of these vessels also traded with Hawaii, where the American Board of Foreign Missions had established a native Congregational church in 1820 under a great missionary, the Reverend Hiram Bingham. He kept urging Easterners to do something about the free-for-all Oregon Country, and in 1831 Hall J. Kelley founded 'The American Society for Encouraging the Settlement of the Oregon Territory.' Kelley stirred up Nathaniel J. Wyeth, a 28-year-old man of action whose zest for oceanic trade had been whetted by successfully exporting ice from Fresh Pond, Cambridge, to the West Indies and South America. Wyeth organized expeditions in 1832 and 1834 that led to the establishment of an American colony in the Willamette valley and did more than anything else to win Oregon for the United States.

In 1842 'Oregon fever' struck the frontier folk of Iowa, Missouri, Illinois, and Kentucky. Backwoodsmen who had no use for treeless prairies or arid high plains, they wanted wood, water, and game, which the Oregon Country had in abundance. Independence, Mo., was their jumping-off place. 'Prairie schooners,' as the canvas-covered Conestoga wagons were nicknamed, converged there in May, when the grass of the plains was fresh and green. Parties were organized, a captain appointed, an experienced trapper or fur trader engaged as pilot; and amid a great blowing of bugles and cracking of long whips, the caravan, perhaps a hundred wagons strong with thousands of cattle on the hoof, moved off up the west bank of the Missouri. At Fort Leavenworth, the emigrants for the last time enjoyed the protection of their flag.

For a long time there was neither road nor trail. Near Council Bluffs, where the Missouri is joined by the Platte, the route to Oregon turned west to follow the Platte over the Great Plains.[1] Until a road had been beaten into the sod, it was easy to lose the way. Numerous tributaries of the Platte, swollen and turbid in the spring, had to be forded or swum, to the great damage of stores and baggage. Every night the caravan made a hollow square of wagons round its fire of cottonwood or buffalo chips. The horses and mules were kept inside, for protection, and the howling of prairie wolves was drowned by a chorus of hymns and old ballads. At dawn the horsekind were let out to graze for an hour or two, the oxen were rounded up and hitched to the wagons, bugles blew, and another start was made toward 'the sunset regions.'

Until the forks of the Platte were reached, near the present northeastern corner of Colorado, the herbage was luxuriant, and the grades easy. Following the north fork, the trail became hilly, then mountainous, as one turned north to avoid a spur of the Rockies. Beyond the South Pass came the worst part of the journey—a hard pull across the arid Wyoming basin, where grass was scanty, and alkali deposits made the water almost undrinkable. Between the Gros Ventre and Teton ranges, the Oregon-bound emigrant found westward-flowing waters, and took heart; but there were still 800 miles to go to the lower Columbia, following the meanderings of the Snake river. As there was no good road in early days through the heavily forested country along the Columbia, wagons were often rafted down the stream; and with fair luck a party that left Independence in May might celebrate Thanksgiving Day in the Willamette valley. But it was a lucky caravan indeed that arrived with the same number of souls that started; and some of the weaker parties disappeared—whether by starvation after losing the trail, or at the hands of Indians, no one ever knew.

This sizable immigration of 1843–45, 4000 to 5000 strong, strained the provisional territorial organization that the settlers established, and convinced Congress that something must be done to

1. Later, the Oregon trail cut straight across the prairie from Independence to the southernmost bend of the Platte, near the site of Kearney, Nebraska.

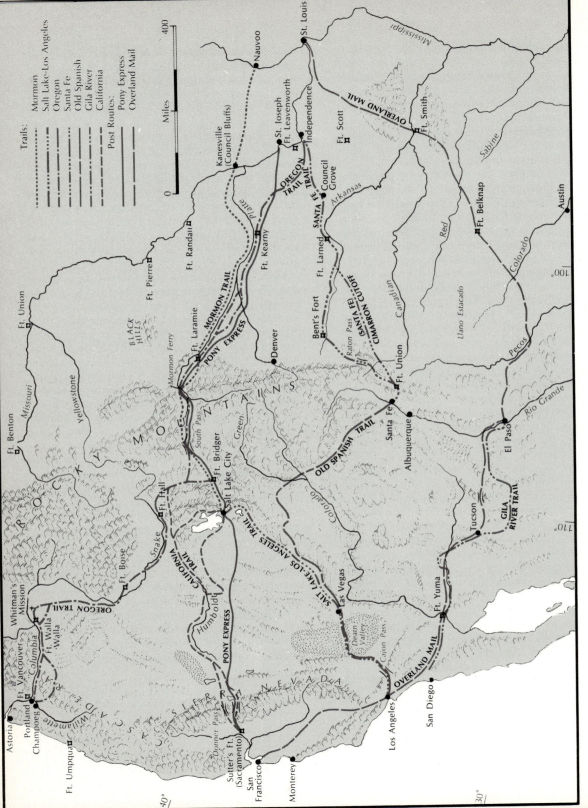

Routes to the West

reach a settlement with Great Britain and provide this remote colony with government, law, and land titles. Secretary Calhoun opened negotiations in 1844 with the British minister at Washington and repeated a proposal, thrice made by J. Q. Adams, to divide the territory along latitude 49°. But Aberdeen, like Castlereagh and Canning, refused to abandon the north bank of the Columbia. If the question were to be decided by extent of actual occupation, the British claim was just; and it would be difficult to discover any other basis of division. North of the Columbia, about Fort Vancouver and along Puget Sound, were living over 700 British subjects, and only half a dozen American citizens. The United States, however, could well afford to wait. A decline in the Columbia river fur trade was making Fort Vancouver unprofitable, and the menacing attitude of the latest American immigrants threatened its security. At Dr. McLoughlin's suggestion the company abandoned Fort Vancouver to the Americans in 1845, and erected a new post at Victoria on Vancouver Island.

By this time the expansionist James K. Polk had become President. He defiantly asserted that the American title to the whole of Oregon, up to lat. 54° 40', was 'clear and unquestionable,' and asked Congress for authority to terminate the joint occupation agreement of 1818. Polk, however, never intended to risk a war to acquire the whole of Oregon. His ambition was to annex California, which probably meant war with Mexico; he did not care to fight England and Mexico at the same time. Thus, when Lord Aberdeen formally proposed to extend the international boundary along latitude 49° N to Puget Sound, thence to the ocean through Juan de Fuca Strait, leaving Vancouver Island to Canada, Polk accepted. He submitted the British offer to his cabinet and to the Senate. During the Senate debate some Western expansionist coined the slogan '54–40 or fight!' but few agreed, and on 15 June 1846 the Oregon treaty was ratified. Thus was completed the last section of the 3000-mile frontier between Canada and the United States.

The Mormons

Before the Oregon question was finally adjusted came the hegira of the Church of Jesus Christ of the Latter-day Saints, commonly called the Mormons, to the Great Salt Lake.

Joseph Smith was the offspring of a family of New England frontier drifters, who had made at least ten moves in nineteen years, ending at Palmyra, N.Y., in the midst of the Burned-over District. At the age of fifteen he began to see visions and dig for buried treasure. An angel of the Lord, he avouched, showed him the hiding-place of a package of inscribed gold plates, together with a pair of magic spectacles which enabled him to read the characters. The resulting Book of Mormon (first printed in 1830), a mixture of personal experiences, religious notions, and disputed history, gave the story of certain Lost Tribes of Israel (the Indians), whom the Saints were commanded to redeem from paganism. Joseph Smith then organized the Church of the Latter-day Saints, a co-operative theocracy in which all power emanated from Smith the Prophet.

Persecutions drove the Mormons to a spot on the east bank of the Mississippi which the Prophet named Nauvoo. The settlement grew rapidly— even faster than Chicago; by 1844, with 15,000 citizens, Nauvoo was the largest and most prosperous city in Illinois. Following Brigham Young's visit to Liverpool, almost 4000 English converts reached Nauvoo. It was at Nauvoo that Joseph Smith received the 'revelation' sanctioning polygamy, which he and the inner circle of 'elders' were already practicing. Although supported by Isaiah iv:1, 'And in that day seven women shall take hold of one man,' this revelation split the church. The monogamous 'schismatics' started a paper at Nauvoo, but Smith caused the press to be broken up after the first issue. He and his brother were then arrested by the authorities for destruction of property and lodged in the county jail, whence, on 27 June 1844, they were pulled out by a mob and lynched. Brigham Young, who succeeded to the mantle of the Prophet, and to five of his 27 widows, directed retaliation; and for two

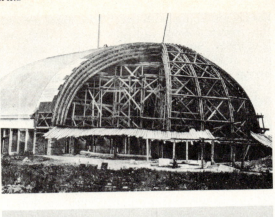

Building the Mormon tabernacle, Salt Lake City. This illustration shows the skeleton turtle above and the completed edifice below. An unusual feature of this structure is that there are no interior supports for the roof. Nor were metal nails used. Workers, supervised by the builder Williams Folsom and the architect Henry Grow, fashioned wooden pegs which they glued into place. The beams are held together by strips of rawhide dipped in water and wrapped around the timbers. (*Utah State Historical Society*)

years terror reigned in western Illinois. The Mormons were a virile, fighting people, but the time had come for them to make another move, before they were hopelessly outnumbered.

Under their new Moses the Mormons abandoned their homes in Nauvoo, and in 1846, several thousand strong, began their westward journey. In July 1847 they reached the promised land, the basin of the Great Salt Lake. By the end of 1848, 5000 people had arrived in the future state of Utah, which Young named Deseret. Young chose this dry and inhospitable land in the hope that his Saints would no longer be molested by Gentiles, and also because it was Mexican territory; but the Mexican War would change that.

The Mormons soon demonstrated that they had resourceful leaders and a genius for disciplined community life. Brigham Young caused irrigation canals and ditches to be dug, and appointed committees to control water for the public benefit. He set up a system of small farms, intensively cultivated and carefully fertilized. He forbade speculation in land, but respected private property. He kept the Indians quiet by a judicious mixture of firmness and justice. He repressed heresy and schism with a heavy hand. He organized foreign and domestic missions and financed migration.

Yearly the community grew in numbers, strength, and wealth, a polygamous theocracy within a monogamous and democratic nation. Congress organized Deseret as Utah Territory in 1850, but since President Fillmore appointed Brigham Young the territorial governor, government in the hands of the Prophet continued. The Latter-day Saints brought comfort, happiness, and self-respect to thousands of humble folk; and Brigham Young must be included among the world's most successful commonwealth builders.

The Spanish Borderlands

While one column of pioneers deployed into the prairies of Illinois and Iowa, and another wound over the Oregon trail, a third crossed into Mexican territory where it came into contact with a proud and ancient civilization, no longer upheld by a dying empire but by the young Republic of Mexico. Upper California, New Mexico, and Texas, frontier provinces of the old viceroyalty, spread out fanwise toward the United States. Explored as early as the sixteenth century by the Spaniards, they had been thinly colonized after a long interval, and in the Roman rather than the English sense. Missions had been planted among the Indians; *presidios* or frontier garrisons established to protect the fathers in their work; and such few colonists as could be persuaded to venture so far were generously endowed by the Spanish government with lands and Indian serfs.

Weak, distracted, lacking expansive energy, the new Mexican government did not know how to use the frontier provinces, and eyed nervously the influx of men of ambition from the United States. Upper California, a province the size of Asia Minor, was sparsely settled by Mexicans, but by 1840, hundreds of Americans had 'left their consciences at Cape Horn' to live and trade in this delightful country, and in that year overland emigrants began to trickle in from a branch of the Oregon trail through the passes of the Sierra Nevada. Each year an armed caravan of American traders assembled at Independence, Mo., and followed the Santa Fe trail with pack-mule and wagon through the country of the Osage and Comanche to the capital of New Mexico, returning with silver and peltry.

But it was in Texas that the first compact wedge of English-speaking people was thrust across Mexico's borders. The tenuous claim of the United States to Texas, a land larger than France, had been renounced in the Florida Treaty of 1819, but both J. Q. Adams and Jackson pressed Mexico to sell the whole or a part of Texas. The mere offer was considered insulting; its repetition aroused suspicion. Yet, with strange inconsistency, Mexico encouraged emigration from the United States to Texas. The most important grant was made in 1821 to Moses Austin, and on his death confirmed to his son in 1823. This gave Stephen F. Austin the privilege of *empresario*. The Austin colony was a great success. By 1834 it comprised 20,000 white colonists and 2000 slaves, outnumbering the native Mexicans in Texas four to one. Austin, a grave and gentle young man, chose recruits for his colony with care, and ruled it with autocratic power until 1829. Texas was more law-abiding and better governed than any nineteenth-century American frontier.

Although anti-slavery by preference, Austin faced the same choice as every colonist with capital: pioneer poverty or using some form of forced labor. There were no Indian peons in that part of Mexico, and Southern planters would not come unless permitted to bring their slaves, and could not prosper without them. Mexico enacted laws or issued decrees abolishing slavery throughout the Republic. But Austin was always able to obtain some 'explanation' which allowed the Americans to hold their slaves in fact, if not by law.

Insecurity of slave property was but one of many factors pulling toward the separation of Texas from Mexico. Austin and the older American *empresarios* tried to be good Mexicans; but it was difficult to respect a government in constant turmoil. The American colonist admired the horsemanship of his Mexican neighbor and adopted his saddle and trappings, but his attitude toward the 'natives' was condescending, and toward their government, impatient. This irritation became mutual. There was trouble about the tariff, representation, and immigration; conflicts with Mexican garrisons whose proud officers resented the crude and boisterous settlers. For in the 1830's, quiet law-abiding pioneers of Austin's type began to be outnumbered by swashbucklers like Sam Houston, former governor of Tennessee, Indian trader on the Texas frontier, and adopted Cherokee; the Bowie brothers of Louisiana, slave-smugglers who designed the long and deadly knife that bears their name; Davy Crockett, a publicity-mad professional backwoodsman from Tennessee; and many others who had left their country for their country's good.

I leave this rule for others
when I am dead Be always sure,
you are right, then go, a head

David Crockett

The Lone Star Republic

The break came in 1835, when President Santa Anna of Mexico proclaimed a unified constitution for Mexico that made a clean sweep of state rights. The American settlers of Texas set up a provisional government and expelled the Mexican garrison from San Antonio. Over the Rio Grande came Santa Anna with 3000 men. In the Alamo, the fortified mission at San Antonio, a garrison of fewer than 200 Texans refused to retreat or to surrender. For ten days, the defenders turned back assaults on the adobe walls. At dawn on 6 March 1836 Santa Anna assaulted the Alamo again, captured it after every Texan, including Crockett, Jim Bowie, and Colonel William Travis, had been killed or wounded, and put the wounded to death.

Already a convention elected by the American settlers had proclaimed the independent Republic of Texas, and adopted a flag with a single star. Santa Anna quickly advanced eastward, and for a few weeks it looked as if the Lone Star Republic would be snuffed out. Generalissimo Sam Houston managed to keep a force together, acquired volunteers from across the border, and awaited the Mexicans in an ilex grove by the ferry of the San Jacinto river, not far from the site of the city that bears his name. On 21 April, shouting 'Remember the Alamo!' the Texans and their allies burst on Santa Anna's army, scattered it, and took the general prisoner. The Battle of San Jacinto proved decisive. The Texans ratified their new constitution, legalized Negro slavery, elected Sam Houston President, and sent an envoy to Washington. On Jackson's last full day of office (3 March 1837), the Lone Star Republic won recognition.

Texas would have preferred annexation to the United States, but annexation would affect the balance of power between the sections. The South was beginning to realize that it had received the thin end of the Missouri Compromise of 1820, which prohibited slavery in federal territory north of 36° 30'. Arkansas and Michigan had just been admitted to the Union, making thirteen free and thirteen slave states. Florida was the only slave territory left; but three free territories, Wisconsin, Iowa, and Minnesota, would soon be demand-

David Crockett (1786–1836). This painting has been dated 'about 1835,' when the 'coonskin Congressman' served his final term in the House. Nettled at being defeated in his bid for re-election, Davy moved to Texas where in the following year he died at the Alamo, and rapidly became a legend. 'Everything here is Davy Crockett,' observed an English visitor in 1839. 'He picked his teeth with a pitchfork—combed his hair with a rake—fanned himself with a hurricane, wore a cast-iron shirt, and drank nothing but creosote and aqua-fortis. . . . He could whip his weight in wildcats—drink the Mississippi dry—shoot six cord of bear in one day—and, as his countrymen say of themselves, he could jump higher, dive deeper, and come up dryer than anyone else.' (*New-York Historical Society*)

ing admission, and more might well follow if the Indian barrier to the Great Plains were broken. Texas, greater in area than nine free states of the Northeast, might be carved into several slave states to balance New England. However, since the North wanted to halt the expansion of slavery, the campaign for annexation foundered.

Southern insistence on annexation became more intense when it appeared that Texas might agree to abolish slavery in return for British support of her independence. The prospect of Texas becoming a second Canada, a refuge for fugitive slaves, alarmed the South to the point of panic. Abel P. Upshur, President Tyler's Secretary of State, at once began to negotiate a treaty of annexation with the Texan minister at Washington, and informed him that the abolition project was inadmissible.

At this juncture there occurred a fatal accident on a United States warship which influenced political history. On a gala trip of U.S.S. *Princeton* down the Potomac on 28 February 1844, with President Tyler, cabinet ministers, diplomats, senators, and numerous ladies on board, one of its 12-inch wrought iron guns, 'Peacemaker,' burst. Secretary of State Upshur, the Navy Secretary, and a New York state senator were killed; Senator Thomas H. Benton and nineteen others were severely wounded. The explosion virtually threw into President Tyler's arms the fair Julia Gardiner, daughter of the slaughtered state senator; shortly she became the second Mrs. Tyler and mistress of the White House. And the loss of the two secretaries gave the President an opportunity to reconstruct his cabinet without a single Northerner or even a Whig, although it was that party which had elected him. John C. Calhoun was brought back as Secretary of State—to put Texas into the Union, and to get Tyler the Democratic (not the Whig) nomination for the presidency in 1844. Like several later Vice-Presidents who have succeeded through death, 'Tyler too' wanted to be elected President 'in his own right.' Calhoun accepted because he hoped to be able to link the Texas question with Oregon, and so forge an alliance of South and West under the Democratic aegis, and become President after Tyler. However, Calhoun's effort to annex Texas got nowhere, because it was perceived as a pro-slavery maneuver.

But President Tyler had another card up his sleeve. After the election of 1844 had 'pronounced' in favor of annexation, he recommended that Texas be admitted to the Union by joint resolution of both houses, which did not require a two-thirds vote. The deed was done on 28 February 1845. President Tyler on his last day of office had the satisfaction of sending a courier to inform President Houston that only the consent of the Lone Star Republic was necessary to make Texas the twenty-eighth state of the Union, and that consent was promptly given.

President Polk and His Maneuvers

While Tyler and Calhoun were rushing Texas into the Union, wiser politicians had been trying to keep it out of politics. In 1842 Martin Van Buren, who expected the Democratic nomination in 1844, and Henry Clay, who had an equally firm expectation for the Whig nomination, agreed to issue a letter opposing the immediate annexation of Texas. Van Buren warned that to rush the affair would mean war with Mexico, and Clay declared that he would welcome Texas to the Union if it could be done 'without dishonor, without war, with the common consent of the Union, and upon just and fair terms.' These praiseworthy efforts to preserve the peace lost Van Buren the nomination and Clay the election.

At the 1844 Democratic convention, Van Buren had a majority of the delegates, but the Southern expansionist delegates put over the two-thirds rule,[2] which Little Van was not strong enough to surmount, and the nomination went to the first 'dark horse' in presidential history: James K. Polk. Clay, now 67 years old, received the Whig nomination by acclamation, and he felt confident of election. But Clay's open letter offended the annexationists and lost him votes in the South. Enough anti-slavery Whigs in New York voted for

2. First adopted in 1836, but not used in 1840; after this it continued in Democratic national conventions until 1936.

Birney, the Liberty party (abolitionist) candidate, to give Polk a slight edge, and New York's electoral vote was pivotal. Save for the unusual four-way race in 1824, the 1844 outcome marked the first time that a President had been elected with less than 50 per cent of the vote. Hence, Polk's triumph was hardly a mandate for expansion. Yet it permitted the Democrats to claim that a firm conviction of America's 'manifest destiny' to extend west to the Pacific and south at least to the Rio Grande lay behind the defeat of the popular Clay.

James Knox Polk, though not yet 50 years of age, looked 20 years older by reason of bad health. He was a stiff, angular person, with sharp gray eyes in a sad, lean face, and grizzled hair overlapping a black coat-collar. He had majored in mathematics and the classics at the University of North Carolina to train his mind, and the event proved that he succeeded. His working day in the White House was nearer eighteen than eight hours, and in four years he was absent only six weeks from Washington. His will controlled a cabinet of experienced and distinguished men. Determined and tenacious, seldom smiling and never relaxing, Polk recalls that other presidential scholar and diarist, J. Q. Adams, rather than Jackson, with whom his political supporters were apt to compare him. Their domestic policies were as wide apart as the poles, but Polk adopted the same foreign policy as Adams, and he had a way of getting things done. He aspired not only to reduce the tariff and re-establish Van Buren's independent treasury, but to settle the Oregon question, and acquire California. Within four years all of his ambitions were fulfilled.

About California almost nothing was known in the United States until after Frémont's exploration of 1843. John C. Frémont, a 28-year-old second lieutenant in the topographical corps of the United States Army, wooed and won sixteen-year-old Jessie, daughter of Senator Thomas Hart Benton. Papa Benton, equally devoted to hard money, western expansion, and daughter Jessie, conceived the idea of sending sonny-boy on an expedition, with competent guides like 'Kit' Carson to take care of him. That was not difficult for

an important senator to arrange. On Frémont's second trip, he struck political pay dirt. Turning south from Oregon into the future Nevada and then into the Sacramento valley, he passed through central and southern California and returned via Santa Fe. His report on this journey (largely written by Jessie), published in the fall of 1844, gave Washington its first knowledge of the feeble Mexican hold on California and the limitless possibilities of that romantic land. Incidentally, it made Frémont a presidential candidate, and, later, one of the most inefficient generals on either side of the Civil War.

War with Mexico

Shortly after Polk entered office, Mexico protested against the annexation of Texas, and broke diplomatic relations. From her point of view, Texas was still a rebellious province. In July 1845 Polk ordered a detachment of the regular army under General Zachary Taylor to take up a position on the Nueces river, the southwestern border of Texas, to protect the new state against a possible Mexican attack. If Polk had been content with Texas and had not reached out for something besides, there is no reason to suppose that Mexico would have initiated hostilities. But Polk desperately wanted to acquire California, because he feared, not without reason, that if the United States did not, England or France would. On 24 June 1845 the Secretary of the Navy sent secret orders to Commodore Sloat, commander of the Pacific station, to seize San Francisco if he should 'ascertain with certainty' that Mexico had declared war on the United States.

On 10 November 1845 the President commissioned John Slidell minister plenipotentiary to Mexico, with instructions to offer that the United States assume the unpaid claims of its citizens against Mexico, in return for Mexican recognition of the Rio Grande as the southern boundary of Texas and of the United States. In addition, $5 million would be paid for the cession of New Mexico, and 'money would be no object' if California could also be bought. Mexico refused to receive Slidell. On 13 January 1846, the day after

A native New Mexican religious figure. (*Index of American Design, Smithsonian Institution*)

he received word of Mexico's decision, Polk ordered General Taylor to cross the Nueces and occupy the left bank of the Rio Grande, though that river had never been the southern boundary of Texas.

On 25 April Polk began to prepare a message to Congress urging war on the sole grounds of Slidell's rejection as minister and the unpaid claims—which amounted to only $3.2 million when adjudicated by a United States commission in 1851. On that very day Mexican cavalry crossed the Rio Grande, engaged in a skirmish with United States dragoons, killed a few troopers, and captured the rest. 'The cup of forbearance has been exhausted,' the President told Congress on 11 May. 'After reiterated menaces, Mexico has passed the boundary of the United States, has invaded our territory and shed American blood upon the American soil.' Two days later Congress declared that 'by act of the Republic of Mexico, a state of war exists between that Government and the United States.' The record is clear: Polk baited Mexico into war over the Texas boundary question in order to get California.

Outside the Mississippi valley the war was highly unpopular. The Whig party opposed the war, although with more shrewdness than the Federalists of 1812 they voted for war credits and supplies in the hope that the Democrats would be hanged if given plenty of rope. Anti-slavery men and abolitionists regarded the war as part of an expansionist conspiracy of slave-owners. Henry Thoreau made his own protest against the war by refusing to pay his state poll tax. After he had spent a night in the Concord lock-up, his aunt paid the tax and he went back to his cabin on Walden Pond. It sounds petty and futile, as one tells it. Yet the ripples from that Concord pebble, like the shot of 19 April 1775, went around the world; Thoreau's *Essay on Civil Disobedience*, which he wrote to justify his action, became the best-known work of American literature to the peoples of Asia and Africa struggling to be free.

Glory and Conquest

California, the main objective, lay beyond the principal seat of war, and became the scene of confusing conflicts. A few dozen American squatters in the Sacramento valley proclaimed the 'Republic of California' and waved a white flag with a bear and star painted on it (14 June 1846). Three weeks later Commodore Sloat raised the Stars and Stripes at Monterey and declared California a part of the United States. The Spanish-speaking Californians rose in arms, but by the end of 1846 resistance had been quelled.

In the main theater of war, General Zachary Taylor pushed across the Rio Grande and captured the Mexican town of Monterrey (21–23 September 1846). Polk was not too pleased. 'Old Rough and Ready' Taylor, blaspheming veteran of the Jackson breed, was becoming dangerously popular, and the Whigs began to talk of running him for President in 1848. So Polk turned to Major General Winfield Scott, a Whig but a dandy swashbuckler whose airs and foibles were unlikely to win golden opinions from democracy. On 27 March Scott captured Vera Cruz, and then started for Mexico City along the route that Cortés had followed three centuries earlier.

It was a brilliant campaign. At the fortified pass of Cerro Gordo, Captain Robert E. Lee found a way to outflank the Mexicans, an impressive operation in which Captain George B. McClellan and Lieutenant Ulysses S. Grant took part. On 10 August Scott's army reached the divide 10,000 feet above sea level, with the wonderful Valley of Mexico stretching before, and the towers of Mexico City rising through the mist. At Churubusco (20 August) the American forces lost one in seven; most of these casualties were inflicted by a Mexican outfit made up of Irish and other deserters from the United States Army. But 3000 Mexican prisoners (including eight generals!) were captured, and the victory was overwhelming.

In the meantime Polk had provided Mexico with a leader. General Santa Anna, in exile at Havana when the war broke out, was able to persuade Polk that, once in possession of the Mexican government, he would be pliable. So he was allowed to enter Mexico City in triumph in September 1846, to assume dictatorship and take command of the army facing Taylor in the north of Mexico. Taylor beat him badly at Buena Vista (22–23 February 1847)—a picture-book battle on a sun-soaked plain; a fight that advanced in politics both General Taylor and his son-in-law, Colonel Jefferson Davis, who distinguished himself and his regiment (uniformed in red shirts, white pants, and slouch hats) by breaking up a Mexican cavalry charge. To the South, Scott's army, refreshed by a fortnight among the orchards and orange groves of the Valley of Mexico, marched forward to a bloodbath at Molino del Rey (8 September), and five days later stormed its last obstacle, the fortified hill of Chapultepec, heroically defended by the boy cadets of the Mexican military school. At dawn 17 September a white flag came out from Mexico City, and a vanguard of doughboys[3] and marines swung along to the main plaza, where they gazed with wonder on the great baroque cathedral and the lofty pink-walled palace—the Halls of the Montezumas at last. In the meantime the Gulf Squadron under Commodore Matthew C. Perry and the Pacific Squadron under Commodore Robert F. Stockton had established a tight block-

3. This term for infantrymen began in the Mexican War and lasted until World War II, when it was replaced by 'GI.'

ade of both coasts of Mexico, preventing munitions and supplies, previously ordered from Europe, from reaching the Mexican army.

Polk attached to the American army as peace commissioner Nicholas Trist, chief clerk of the department of state, and though he was recalled by the President and hence had no authority, and though there was for some time no Mexican government with which he could deal, Trist stayed on and negotiated the Treaty of Guadalupe Hidalgo (2 February 1848) in accordance with his original instructions. Mexico ceded Texas with the Rio Grande boundary, New Mexico, and Upper California to the United States. The region embraced what would become the states of California, Utah, and Nevada, large sections of New Mexico and Arizona, and parts of Colorado and Wyoming. The victor assumed unpaid claims, and paid $15 million to boot. It remained to be seen whether these immense and valuable acquisitions would be settled peacefully, or become a bone of contention between pro- and anti-slavery interests, leading to civil war.

15

Peaceful Interlude

*

1846–1854

The Wilmot Proviso

John C. Calhoun was right, for once. He foresaw that the acquisition of new territory would bring the question of slavery expansion into the open. The man who opened the door was an obscure Democratic congressman from Pennsylvania, David Wilmot. On 8 August 1846, about twelve weeks after the war began, the President asked Congress for a secret appropriation of $2 million as a down payment to bribe Santa Anna into ceding California. Wilmot proposed an amendment to the $2 million bill that in any territory so acquired 'neither slavery nor involuntary servitude shall ever exist,' a phrase copied from the Northwest Ordinance of 1787.

The question of slavery extension was no mere abstract principle, though many believed that the geography of the West erected a barrier against the spread of slavery. 'What do you want?—what do you want?—you who reside in the free States?' Clay would ask shortly. 'You have got what is worth more than a thousand Wilmot provisos. You have nature on your side.' Nor was the question immediately practical; even when they had a legal right to do so, few slaveholders would go West in the next decade. The 1860 census numbered only two slaves in Kansas. Yet, in truth, there was no climatic or natural bar to slavery extension, or to the Negro race—after all, a black was one of the two men who accompanied Admiral Peary to the North Pole in 1909. If slavery could flourish in Texas, why not in New Mexico, Arizona, and points west? In southern California, black slaves, if introduced, would undoubtedly have thrived and multiplied, just as the Chinese and Mexicans did who later filled the demands of ranchers and fruit growers for cheap labor.

The Wilmot proviso provoked bitter sectional animosity. To many Northerners it seemed monstrous for the 'land of the free' to introduce slavery, even in principle, where it had never previously existed. Yet it should be noted that while Northern anti-slavery men were pressing for adoption of the proviso, the Illinois constitution of 1848 excluded free blacks, and Iowa in 1851 stipulated severe penalties for any black who dared enter that state. To Southerners the proviso was alarming. They had watched anxiously as population gains gave the North control of the House;

soon the admission of new free states would upset the balance in the Senate. Now Wilmot was proposing to seal off the South so that it could never hope to add even one more slave state to the Union, unless Texas split up.

The Wilmot proviso did not pass, nor did any measure to organize the newly acquired territory. Settlers in the Far West lacked law and government, because Congress could not decide whether or not they could have slaves. Oregon in 1848 was finally organized as a territorial government without slavery, but Polk's term ended on 4 March 1849 before anything had been done about California, New Mexico, or Utah.

Election of 1848; Gold Rush of 1849

At a time of mounting crisis, both parties in 1848 turned to men with military backgrounds, since generals have a useful talent for blurring issues and winning votes. The Democrats named Senator Lewis Cass of Michigan, an ardent expansionist, veteran of 1812, and Jackson's Secretary of War. The Whigs nominated General Zachary Taylor, hero of the Mexican War. A third party, the Free-Soil, was formed by a coalition of three elements—the abolitionist Liberty party, 'conscience' or anti-slavery Whigs, and Northern Democrats alienated by Polk's policies on patronage, the tariff, or rivers and harbors. 'Free soil, free speech, free labor, and free men' was the slogan. Van Buren, convinced that only slavery restriction could save the Union, accepted the Free-Soil presidential nomination, with the 'conscience' Whig, Charles Francis Adams, as his running mate. Among the former Democrats who rallied to the Free-Soil standard was David Wilmot.

Although the Free-Soil party carried not one state, it rolled up an impressive 10 per cent of the popular vote, and by taking Democratic votes from Cass in states like New York and Pennsylvania, made possible Taylor's victory. Since little was known of Taylor's views, the Whigs had been able to offer him to voters in different sections according to which posture would draw the most support. In the South, they pointed out that 'Old Rough and Ready' was a Louisianan who held more than a hundred slaves on a Mississippi plantation; Northern voters heard that Taylor was friendly to the Wilmot proviso. The strategy worked; Taylor, with only 47 per cent of the popular vote, received 163 electoral votes to Cass's 107. But the Whigs bought victory at too high a cost; for once in office they would inevitably alienate a large section of their followers. The Southern Whigs were especially vulnerable for they were tied to a leader said to be committed to an extreme Northern position. The Whig party was living on borrowed time.

A simple, honest soldier, who detested the sophistries of politicians and regarded the slavery question as an artificial abstraction, Taylor was ready to sign any bill Congress might pass for organizing new territories; but before Congress could resolve the deadlock, California proposed to skip the territorial stage altogether, and to become a free state of the Union. On 24 January 1848, shortly before peace was signed with Mexico, a workman in the Sacramento valley discovered gold in Sutter's millrace. By the end of 1849 thousands of Argonauts from every part of Europe, North America, and the antipodes, had made their way to the gold fields and were living in a state of nature that would have made Rousseau a tory. Owing to neglect by Congress the government was still military in theory, though impotent in fact; *alcaldes* and *ayuntamientos* appointed by the military governor administered any sort of law they pleased—the code of Mexico or of Napoleon, or of Judge Lynch. So California went ahead and made herself a state, with the blessing of President Taylor. A state constitution prohibiting slavery was ratified by a popular vote of over 12,000 ayes to 800 noes. Without waiting for congressional sanction, the people chose a governor and legislature which began to function in 1850. Only formal admission to the Union was wanting; and on that issue the Union almost split.

Up to this time the most extreme Southerners had admitted the right of a state to prohibit slavery—for slavery was emphatically a state matter, but during 1849 the temper of the South had been steadily rising. South Carolina only hesitated from secession because it hoped to unite the entire South on that program. Though the South

Miner at sluice box in California's gold country. This early photograph was taken in Auburn Ravine in 1852, four years after gold was discovered in the Sacramento valley. Only recently have historians recognized the role of blacks in the development of the American West. (*Wells Fargo Bank History Room*)

had achieved disproportionate strength in the national government, it felt insecure. From every side—England and New England, Jamaica and Mexico, Ohio and the Northwest, and now California—abolition seemed to be pointing daggers at her heart. Still, it was not wholly fear that moved the South. What Benét called 'the purple dream,' the vision of a great slaveholding republic stretching from the Potomac into the tropic seas, monopolizing the production of cotton and so dictating to the world, was beginning to lift up the hearts of the younger and more radical Southern leaders.

The Union Preserved

Though Zachary Taylor was a large slaveholder, he saw no reason why the South should be bribed to admit California as a free state. Hence he recommended immediate admission of California with her free constitution and organization of New Mexico and Utah territories without reference to slavery. To protesting Georgia senators, the old soldier declared his determination to crush secession wherever and whenever it might appear, if he had to lead the army personally. Others were less willing to risk war. On 27 January 1850 Henry Clay advanced compromise resolutions: (1) immediate admission of free California to the Union; (2) organization of territorial governments in New Mexico and Utah, without mention of slavery; (3) a new and stringent fugitive slave law; (4) abolition of the domestic slave trade in the District of Columbia; (5) assumption of the Texan national debt by the Federal Government.

These resolutions brought on one of those superb Senate debates that did so much to mold public opinion. Clay defended them in a speech that lasted the better part of two days. Haggard in aspect and faltering in voice, he spoke with such passionate devotion to the Union as to bring back all the charm and fire of 'Young Harry of the West.' He asked the North to accept the substance of the Wilmot proviso without the principle and honestly to fulfill her obligation to return fugitive slaves. He reminded the South of the great benefits she derived from the Union and warned her against the delusion that secession could be peaceful. For Clay was old enough to remember the excitement in Kentucky when Spain and France had attempted to stop the river outlet of the Middle West. 'My life upon it,' he offered, 'that the vast population which has already concentrated . . . on the headwaters and the tributaries of the Mississippi, will never give their consent that the mouth of that river shall be held subject to the power of any foreign State.'

Calhoun, grim and emaciated, his voice stifled by the catarrh that shortly led to his death, sat silent, glaring defiance from his hawk-like eyes, while his ultimatum was voiced for him by Senator Mason of Virginia. The North must 'do justice by conceding to the South an equal right in the acquired territory'—which meant admitting slavery to California and New Mexico—returning fugitive slaves, restoring to the South through constitutional amendment the equilibrium of power she once possessed in the Federal Government.[1] And the North must 'cease the agitation of the slave question.' Note well this imperative as to free speech, even in the North.

Three days later Webster rose for his last great oration. His voice had lost its deep resonance, his massive frame had shrunk, and his face was lined with suffering and sorrow. But in his heart glowed the ancient love of country, and the spell of his personality fell on Senate and galleries with his opening words: 'I speak to-day for the preservation of the Union. "Hear me for my cause."' He attacked both the abolitionists and the Wilmot proviso. 'I would not take pains to reaffirm an ordinance of nature, nor to re-enact the will of God,' he said. Viewing the situation eye to eye with Clay, Webster restated in richer language the points made by his old-time rival. The North could never have been induced to swallow a new fugitive slave law, had not Webster held the spoon, and the Seventh of March speech permitted Union sentiment to ripen until it became irresistible.

Senator Seward of New York, in opposing the compromise, spoke for the 'conscience' Whigs. He admitted that Congress had the constitutional power to establish slavery in the territories. 'But there is a higher law than the Constitution which regulates our authority over the domain': the law of God, whence alone the laws of man can derive their sanction. The fugitive slave bill would endanger the Union far more than any anti-slavery proposal. 'All measures which fortify slavery or extend it, tend to the consummation of violence; all that check its extension, and abate its strength, tend to its peaceful extirpation.'

For all the skill of Clay, the omnibus bill stalemated. Southern firebrands denounced it, and Northern abolitionists called Webster a lackey of the slavehounds; a Mississippi senator confronted Senator Benton with a cocked and loaded revolver. With the older generation stymied, the young men took over. One of the youngest in the Senate was Stephen A. Douglas of Illinois, a sturdy five-footer, chock-full of brains, bounce, and swagger. In August, with the struggle in its eighth month, the 'Little Giant' put together a winning combination; his fellow Democrats proved sturdier than the Whigs.

In early September 1850 the essential bills passed: admission of California; a more stringent fugitive slave law; organization of New Mexico and Utah as territories free to legislate on slavery and to enter the Union with or without slavery when sufficiently populous; curbing of the slave trade in Washington; adjustment of the Texas boundary; assumption of the Texas debt. The Compromise of 1850 did not repeal the Missouri Compromise; the 1820 enactment dealt with the Louisiana purchase land, the 1850 law exclusively with the territory acquired from Mexico. The act

---

1. Calhoun's proposed amendment would have taken the form of a dual executive, one President elected by the North and one by the South, each armed with a veto.

Henry Clay addresses the Senate in the debate on the Compromise of 1850. As 'the Great Pacificator' speaks, Calhoun (standing third from the right, steel-gray hair falling loosely) stares at him intently. Seated two rows behind Clay (front left), Webster, head on his left hand, looks away. The man with the bulbous nose seated second from right is Thomas Hart Benton. (*Library of Congress*)

had some disappointing consequences. The Fugitive Slave Law failed to bring sectional peace; the free state of California added a surprising element to the argument over sectional balance when it sent pro-slavery men to the Senate; and the slave trade continued to flourish in the District. Still, the law gave both North and South something each badly wanted. Once more the Union was preserved by the same spirit of compromise that created it; but for the last time. It took another year to stop the secession movement in the cotton states, and in the North, which was committed by the law to returning runaway slaves to bondage, Emerson, the serene philosopher who had advised the abolitionists to love their white neighbors more and their colored brethren less, wrote in his journal, 'This filthy enactment was made in the nineteenth century, by people who could read and write. I will not obey it, by God!'

The Compromise of 1850 came at a time of transition in American leadership. On 9 July 1850 'Old Rough and Ready' succumbed to a combination of concern over misconduct in his cabinet, Washington heat, and doctors. The death of Taylor, denounced in the South as a Southern man of Northern principles, helped make possible the adoption of the Compromise, for his successor, Vice-President Millard Fillmore, shared the outlook of Webster and Clay. Giants of other days had already passed. Calhoun died on 31 March 1850; Andrew Jackson had died peacefully in his 'Hermitage'; John Quincy Adams, stricken at his seat in the House, had been carried out of the chamber to die. Clay and Webster, the one denounced as traitor by Southern hotspurs, the other compared with Lucifer by New England reformers, had only two years to live; but that was time enough to teach them grave doubts whether their compromise could long be maintained and whether their party could survive their departure. With their death the second generation of independent Americans departed. The galaxy of 1812 that had seemed to bind the heavens together was extinguished.

Calm Before Storm

Passage of the Compromise of 1850 caused the slavery question to subside for a short time, while other matters occupied the nation. Not that slavery was forgotten. *Uncle Tom's Cabin*, published in 1852, served to keep it in the back of people's minds; but everyone save Northern abolitionists and Southern 'fire-eaters' wished to let it remain there.

The country enjoyed the fruits of its flourishing economy. In the 1850's steam engine and machinery output shot up 66 per cent, coal mined 182 per cent, hosiery goods 608 per cent. By 1860 New York City's population would exceed one million.

Craft unions were negotiating agreements with their employers; the National Typographic Union (1852), the United Hatters (1856), and the Iron Moulders' Union of North America (1859) were the first permanent federations. In the Cotton Kingdom, Kentucky backwoodsmen, who in the 1830's had taken up land in the black belts, were now gentleman planters, and their sons were attending the University of Virginia, with hounds and hunters and black servants. Georgia built a railroad across the southern end of the Appalachians, which helped to make Atlanta and Chattanooga great cities, and by 1860 there was through rail connection between New York and New Orleans.

The promise that America would fulfill her destiny through quality rather than quantity was never brighter. Consider the great books of that decade. In 1850–51, Hawthorne's *Scarlet Letter* and *House of the Seven Gables*, Melville's *White Jacket* and *Moby-Dick*, Emerson's *Representative Men* and *English Traits*. In 1852, Melville's *Pierre*; in 1854–56, Thoreau's *Walden*, Whitman's *Leaves of Grass*, and Melville's *Piazza Tales*. In 1857 the *Atlantic Monthly* was founded, with James Russell Lowell, satirist of slavery and the Mexican War, as editor, and Longfellow, Whittier, and Dr. Holmes (whose *Autocrat* appeared in 1858) as contributors. This was Longfellow's most productive decade, with *The Golden Legend* (1851), *Hiawatha* (1855), and *The Courtship of Miles Standish* (1858). Whittier published his *Songs of Labor* in 1850 and his 'Maud Muller' and 'Barefoot Boy' in 1856. And Parkman's *Conspiracy of Pontiac* (1851) opened a great historical series that required 40 years to complete.

The presidential election of 1852 proved that an overwhelming majority of Americans were disposed to regard the Compromise of 1850 as final and that economic questions were predominant once again. Since both parties endorsed the Compromise, party lines were drawn not on slavery but on such old economic issues as the tariff and internal improvements. The Democratic party nominated Franklin Pierce of New Hampshire, whose only apparent qualifications were a winning smile and a fair military record in the Mexican War. No more were needed. The New York 'barnburners,'[2] starved for four lean years with the Free-Soilers, returned to their Democratic allegiance; and thousands of Southern Whigs, disgusted by the anti-slavery tendencies of Northern Whigs, went over to their opponents. Although Pierce won less than 51 per cent of the popular vote, he handed the Whigs a drubbing in the electoral column, where General Winfield Scott carried only four states. The Whigs would never recover from this defeat.

More 'Manifest Destiny'

Republicanism and democracy appeared to be sweeping the western world. After the revolution of 1848, France adopted a constitution which was a centralized edition of that of the United States. Within the Democratic party, a 'Young America' movement sprang up, devoted at first to creating ideals of service and duty, then to enlisting Young America's aid for democrats beyond the seas, and finally to electing Stephen A. Douglas to the presidency. There had been wild talk in 1848 of annexing Ireland and Sicily to the United States, as certain revolutionists in those countries requested; and when the news came that Hungary had fallen and had been forcibly incorporated with Austria, the legislatures of New York, Ohio, and Indiana called for action. Louis Kossuth, brought to New York as guest of the nation in 1851, was given an overwhelming ovation, and a Harvard professor who exposed Hungarian humbug was forced to resign.

American diplomacy was particularly truculent when directed by Southern gentlemen who wanted new slave territory, as compensation for the 'loss' of California. Certain Southern statesmen professed to fear lest Cuba fall to England, or become a black republic like Haiti. Others had an eye on the large and redundant slave population there. Polk, still in the market for new territory after the vast acquisitions from Mexico, proposed to buy Cuba in 1848 for $100 million, but Spain rejected his offer with contempt. Then came filibustering expeditions, frowned upon by

2. The radical wing of the New York Democrats who opposed the expansion of slavery was likened to the Dutchman who set fire to his barn to rid it of rats.

Taylor, tolerated by Fillmore and Pierce; and consequent interference by the Spanish authorities with Yankee traders. One such instance, the case of the *Black Warrior* (1854), seemed a good opportunity to provoke Spain into war. The Secretary of War, Jefferson Davis, urged President Pierce to take that line; but the Secretary of State, William L. Marcy, kept his head; and Spain disappointed the annexationists by apologizing. Nonetheless, in October 1854 the American ministers to Spain, France, and Great Britain, meeting at Ostend, drafted a serious recommendation to Marcy pontificating that if Spain refused to sell Cuba, then, 'by every law, human and divine, we shall be justified in wresting it from Spain if we possess the power.' The New York *Herald* made a 'scoop' of this secret document and published it as the 'Ostend Manifesto.' Its only effect was to lower American prestige in Europe and that of Pierce at home. The Cubans' consent to being annexed was never asked; and it is interesting to reflect whether, if it had been, a José Martí or a Fidel Castro would have arisen to demand *Cuba Libre* from the United States.

In these same years, American diplomacy was crossing the Pacific. In 1844 Caleb Cushing, as the first United States minister to China, negotiated a treaty by which American ships obtained access to certain Chinese seaports, and American merchants acquired extraterritorial privileges. The 'opening' of Japan proved more difficult. Japan had been closed for two centuries to all foreign intercourse, save a strictly regulated trade with the Dutch and Chinese at Nagasaki. Her government was feudal, her economy medieval—no factories, no steamships or steam engines, only small junks allowed to be built in order to keep the Japanese at home. Foreign sailors wrecked on the shores of Japan were not allowed to leave, and Japanese sailors wrecked on foreign coasts were not permitted to return. Commodore James Biddle USN tried to open relations at Tokyo Bay in 1845, but was surrounded by small guard boats and forced to leave.

Largely to protect castaways from the growing American whaling fleet, President Fillmore decided to make another try. He entrusted the mission to Commodore Matthew C. Perry, brother of

北亞墨利加人物

ペルリ像

Commodore Matthew Perry (1794–1858). Japanese officials, including the imperial court of Kyoto and the Shogun's court at Edo, dispatched artists to depict the 'hairy barbarians' from America on parchment scrolls and woodblocks, and news sheets with illustrations of Perry's expedition proved immensely popular. (*Library of Congress*)

the hero of Lake Erie. The Commodore, who had had diplomatic experience dealing with Turkey, Naples, and several African kings, studied every available book on Japan. On 8 July 1853 his armed squadron anchored in the mouth of Tokyo Bay. Perry's orders forbade him to use force, except as a last resort; but the Kanagawa Shogun who then ruled Japan was so deeply impressed by the Commodore's show of force that, contrary to all precedent, he consented to receive the President's letter to the Emperor. Perry tactfully sailed to Macao, in order to give the elder statesmen time to make up their minds; and by the time he returned (February 1854), with an even more impressive squadron, they had decided to yield. At the little village of Yokohama they exchanged gifts: lacquers and bronzes, porcelain and brocades, for a set of telegraph instruments, a quarter-size steam locomotive complete with track and cars, Audubon's *Birds* and *Quadrupeds of America*, an assortment of farming implements and firearms, a barrel of whiskey, and several cases of champagne. Thus old Japan first tasted the blessings of Western civilization! Progressive Japanese leaders, who wished to put an end to isolation, persuaded the Shogun to sign the Treaty of Kanagawa allowing the United States to establish a consulate, assuring good treatment to castaways, and permitting American vessels to visit certain Japanese ports for supplies and repairs. Such was the famous 'opening' of Japan, and it was Perry's proud boast that without firing a shot he had effected what European nations had failed to do by using force.

To shorten the route from Atlantic ports to the Orient and to improve communications between the older United States and her new Pacific territories, the government gave serious consideration to an interocean canal. President Polk in 1846 obtained right of transit over the Isthmus of Panama by treaty with Colombia, in return for guaranteeing to that republic her sovereignty over the Isthmus, and undertaking to defend its neutrality. But an alternative route via Lake Nicaragua brought on a sharp controversy with Great Britain. When the Monroe Doctrine was first announced, the British had two bases in Central America: the old logwood establishment of Belize or British Honduras, and a shadowy protectorate over the Mosquito Indians of Nicaragua. Owing in part to indifference at Washington, British influence in Central America increased between 1825 and 1845. In 1848 the British government declared the sovereignty of 'Mosquitia' over San Juan or Greytown, the eastern terminus of the proposed Nicaragua ship canal.

All this created a very ticklish situation, from which the United States and United Kingdom emerged by negotiating the Clayton-Bulwer treaty in 1850. It was agreed that neither government would ever fortify, or obtain exclusive control over, the proposed Isthmian canal. Later generations of Americans regarded the treaty as a sellout; but at the time it was a fair compromise between the concessions that Britain had obtained in Central America when the American government was indifferent, and the new interest that the United States had acquired by becoming a Pacific power.

As American capitalists showed no enthusiasm for building a ship canal, the Clayton-Bulwer treaty might have caused no embarrassment for many years, but for ambiguous clauses. The United States government supposed that they meant British withdrawal from the Bay Islands, Greytown, and the Mosquito coast. The British government insisted that the treaty merely forbade future acquisitions. This dispute became dangerous in 1854, when President Pierce and the Democrats were looking for an issue to distract the country from the slavery question. The game then began of 'twisting the lion's tail' to cater to native and Irish-American voters. But the game recessed in 1859–60 when Britain ceded the Bay Islands to Honduras and the Mosquito coast to Nicaragua.

In the meantime, a curious episode occurred in Nicaragua. Cornelius Vanderbilt, 'commodore' of the Hudson river steamboat fleet, organized a company to compete with the Panama railway. It ran steamers up the San Juan river and across Lake Nicaragua, whence freight was forwarded to the Pacific by muleback. Wanting political stability in that region, this company financed William Walker, a professional filibuster, to overthrow the existing government of Nicaragua. Walker, 'the gray-eyed man of destiny,' in 1856 succeeded in

Flying Cloud. This splendid clipper ship, launched in 1851 in East Boston, established its designer, Donald McKay, as America's master builder. 'What ships they were!' Alan Villiers has written of these greyhounds of the sea. 'Man had never before and has never since been hurtled along by the elemental force of the wind at sea at such a speed.' In this 1855 Currier lithograph, *Flying Cloud* leaves another clipper ship astern while a flying fish leaps from the water off her port bow. (*Peabody Museum of Salem*)

making himself President of Nicaragua. He planned (with the approval of Pierce's Secretary of War, Jefferson Davis) to introduce Negro slavery and to conquer the rest of Central America. But he had the bad judgment to quarrel with Vanderbilt and seize his ships. The 'commodore' then supported a Central American coalition that invaded Nicaragua, and Walker surrendered. Twice more this prince of filibusters tried; on his last attempt, in 1860, he was seized and executed by a Honduran firing squad.

Midway in the Isthmian negotiations there was established a landmark in North American commerce and diplomacy, the Canadian Reciprocity Treaty of 1854. Britain's repeal of the corn laws had abolished the preference for colonial grain and flour that had given Canada the business of milling American wheat for the British market and prostrated the industry. At the request of the Canadian legislature the British foreign office negotiated at Washington a reciprocity treaty, but it was a difficult matter to put through concurrent acts of Parliament, of Congress, and of four Canadian legislatures, especially since the Maritime Provinces were loath to admit Yankees to their offshore fisheries. Secretary of State Marcy greased the way at Halifax, Fredericton, and St. John by a judicious expenditure of secret service funds; and Lord Elgin, a hard-headed but genial Scot, is said to have floated the treaty through the United States Senate on 'oceans of champagne.' If true, both served their respective countries well. The treaty opened the United States market to Canadian farm produce, timber, and fish, and Canada to American rice, turpentine, and tobacco; the bait for Southern support is obvious. Yankee fishermen got new privileges in Canadian waters, and the American merchant marine obtained the right to navigate the Great Lakes, the St. Lawrence, and their connecting canals. Thus Britain maintained her political dominion over Canada by sanctioning a partial economic union with the United States.

While the diplomats were wrangling over future canals to the Pacific, the shipwrights of New York and New England were engaged in cutting down the time of ocean passage around Cape Horn. In one month of 1850, 33 sailing vessels from New York and Boston entered San Francisco

A clipper ship sailing card. The *Hornet* once raced the redoubtable *Flying Cloud* from New York to San Francisco and, after 105 days out, finished ahead by forty minutes. (*Seamen's Bank, New York*)

bay after an average passage of 159 days. Then there came booming through the Golden Gate the clipper ship *Sea Witch* of New York, 97 days out. At once the cry went up for clipper ships at any price.

This new type of sailing vessel, characterized by great length in proportion to breadth of beam, an enormous sail area, and long concave bows ending in a gracefully curved cutwater, had been devised for the China-New York tea trade. The voyage of the *Sea Witch* showed its possibilities, and in 1851 the *Flying Cloud* of Boston made San Francisco in 89 days from New York, a record never surpassed. As California then afforded no return cargo except gold dust, the Yankee clippers sailed in ballast to the Chinese treaty ports, where they came into competition with the British merchant marine. Crack East-Indiamen humbly waited for cargo weeks on end, while one American clipper after another sailed off with a cargo of tea at double the ordinary freights. When the *Oriental* of New York appeared at London, 97 days from Hong Kong, crowds thronged the dock to admire her beautiful hull, lofty rig, and patent fittings, and *The Times* challenged British shipbuilders to set their 'long practised skill, steady industry and dogged determination' against the 'youth, ingenuity and ardour' of the United States.

Nightingale and *Witch of the Wave*, *Northern Light* and *Southern Cross*, *Young America* and *Great Republic*, *Golden Age* and *Herald of the Morning*, *Red Jacket* and *Westward Ho!*, *Dreadnought* and *Glory of the Seas*—no sailing vessel ever approached them in power, majesty, or speed. Yankee ingenuity, with its latent artistic genius, had at last found perfect and harmonious expression. Yet the clipper fulfilled a very limited purpose: speed to the goldfields at any price or risk. When that was no longer an object, no more were built. Meantime the British, leaving glory to their rivals, were quietly evolving a more useful type of medium clipper and perfecting the iron screw steamer. By 1857 the British empire had an ocean-going steam tonnage of almost half a million tons, as compared with 90,000 under the American flag. England had won back her maritime supremacy in fair competition, and civil war turned the Yankee mind to other objects.

16

The Irrepressible Conflict

*

1854–1861

Prairie Settlement and Pacific Railways

In the 1850's economic change had an enormous impact on political events. Increasingly the lines of force in the economy moved on an East-West axis rather than on a West-South axis. To be sure, the Mississippi trade flourished; the Illinois Central Railroad linked the South and the Northwest; and cotton still played a significant role in North-South trade. But cotton was no longer king. The Northeast, which now did not raise enough food for its own needs, provided the most important market for the Western farmer. And the Northwest, no longer so dependent on the South, turned its gaze away from the slave-tilled plantations and toward the empire of rolling prairie and Great Plains.

In the 1850's the prairie farmer came into his own. New agricultural machinery, especially the reaper, helped to cope with the labor shortage. Even greater impetus to prairie farming came from the rising price of wheat (from $0.93 a bushel in 1851 to $2.50 in 1855 at the New York market) and from the transportation revolution. The value of merchandise shipped to the West over the Erie Canal soared from $10 million in 1836 to $94 million in 1853. Railways linked the East with the farms and burgeoning cities of the Northwest. In 1850 railroads had hardly penetrated the Middle West; by 1860 their network covered it. The prairie farmer, hitherto dependent on long wagon hauls over execrable roads, could at last market his grain and livestock to advantage. As the Illinois prairie filled up, the state moved away from its Southern ties. One Illinois politician ruined his political future in an attempt to preserve the old alliance, and another led a new North-and-West political party which caused the South to seek safety for slavery in secession.

A struggle over the route of the first transcontinental railway promoted the same result. Of the many schemes projected since 1845, the four most important were (1) the Northern, from the upper Mississippi to the upper Missouri and by Lewis and Clark's trail to the Columbia river; (2) the Central, from St. Louis up the Kansas and Arkansas rivers, across the Rockies to the Great Salt Lake and by the California trail to San Francisco; (3) the Thirty-fifth Parallel route from Memphis, up the Arkansas and Canadian rivers, across the

Rockies near Santa Fe, and through the Apache and Mojave country to Los Angeles; (4) the Southern, from New Orleans up the Red river and across Texas and by the Gila valley to Yuma and San Diego.[1] Either of the first two would bind the Far West to the old Northwest; but the unorganized Indian country was an obstacle. The Southern route was the shortest, with the best contours, and led through states and territories already organized.

Congress, in March 1853, authorized surveys of these four routes under the direction of Secretary of War Jefferson Davis of Mississippi. He saw that the Southern route might well be the means of the South's recovering all she had lost by the Compromise of 1850; and, although a state-rights man, he advocated its construction by the Federal Government under the war power. As soon as the survey showed that a Southern railway would have to pass through Mexican territory south of the Gila river, Davis induced President Pierce and Congress to buy the land for $10 million. The Gadsden treaty of 30 December 1853 effected this purchase.

The stage was now set for Congress to sanction the Southern route.

The Kansas-Nebraska Bill

Stephen A. Douglas, the senior senator from Illinois, was the best orator in the Northwest and the idol of Northern Democrats. As an Illinoisan, he was sensitive to the demands of prairie folk for the organization of the trans-Missouri country and opening it to settlement. He wished to erase the 'barbarian wall' of Indian tribes impeding migration to the plains and 'to authorize and encourage a continuous line of settlements to the Pacific Ocean.' A heavy speculator in Western lands, including the city site which he expected to be the eastern terminus of the railroad, he favored a Central route for the transcontinental railway. To contest Davis's Southern route, he had to find a

way to extend law and government over, and invite settlers into, the region through which the Central route must pass. Douglas and fellow Democrats in Washington sought a promising political issue for 1856. For these reasons, and probably for others known to themselves, the 'Little Giant' reported a bill to organize the Great Plains as the Territory of Nebraska, in January 1854. Earlier bills of this nature had been defeated by Southern senators. So Douglas baited this one for Southern votes by incorporating the principle of popular sovereignty. At the insistence of Southern leaders, he made clear that his bill would render the Missouri Compromise 'inoperative and void.' Furthermore, the bill, as amended, divided the region into two distinct territories: Kansas and Nebraska.

Douglas miscalculated grievously. He thought reopening the slavery question a minor matter; personally opposed to slavery, he believed the Plains would be inhospitable to it. But Northerners were incensed at a proposal to permit the slave power to extend its domain into a virgin land which more than 30 years before the Missouri Compromise had closed to the slaveholder 'forever.' Anti-slavery men raged at the Northern apostate; as Douglas himself said, he could have traveled from Boston to Chicago by light of his burning effigies. Nor did Douglas realize how passionate the South had become over maintaining prestige.

For three months the bitter debate dragged on. President Pierce whipped his party into line, except for a few Northern Democrats. Old Sam Houston of Texas reminded the Senate that by solemn treaties it had confirmed most of Kansas and Nebraska to the Indians 'as long as grass shall grow and water run,' but no one else thought of the aborigines. Federal agents were already bullying them into renouncing their 'perpetual' titles. The once powerful Delaware accepted a small reservation with an annual bounty. Others, like the Shawnee and Miami, who had once terrorized the Kentucky frontier and beaten a Federal army, were removed to the Indian Territory, which fortunately lay between the rival railway routes.

Democratic discipline triumphed. On 25 May 1854 the Kansas-Nebraska bill passed the Senate

---

1. These, in order, were followed in part by (1) the Northern Pacific; (2) the Missouri Pacific, Denver & Rio Grande, and Southern Pacific; (3) the Rock Island and the Santa Fe; and (4) the Texas Pacific and Southern Pacific.

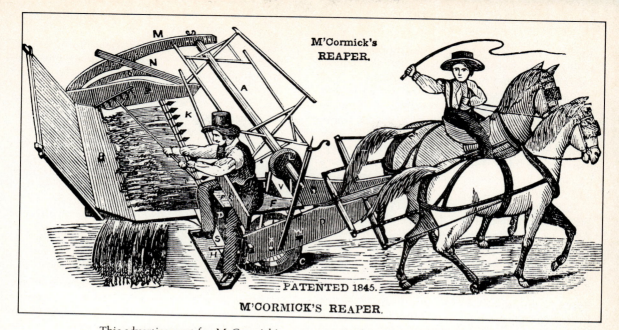

This advertisement for McCormick's reaper appeared in May 1846 in a monthly agricultural journal *The Cultivator*, which explained: 'The machine is warranted to cut from 15 to 20 acres in a day, and at a great saving of expense over the common mode of harvesting.' (*State Historical Society of Wisconsin*)

by a comfortable majority. 'It is at once the worst and best Bill on which Congress ever acted,' declared Senator Charles Sumner. The worst, inasmuch as it is a present victory for slavery. The best, for 'it annuls all past compromises with slavery, and makes all future compromises impossible. Thus it puts freedom and slavery face to face, and bids them grapple. Who can doubt the result?'

'If the Nebraska bill should be passed, the Fugitive Slave Law is a dead letter throughout New England' wrote a Southerner in Boston. 'As easily could a law prohibiting the eating of codfish and pumpkin pies be enforced.' It did pass; and the very next day a Boston mob led by a Unitarian minister tried to rescue a fugitive slave from the courthouse where he was detained for examination. They did not succeed. Anthony Burns, the

slave, was identified by his master and escorted to the wharf by a battalion of United States artillery, four platoons of marines, and the sheriff's posse, through streets lined with silent spectators and hung with crepe, every church-bell tolling a funeral dirge. It cost the United States some $40,000 to return that slave to his master; and he was the last to be returned from Massachusetts.

The Break-up of Parties

The first palpable result of the Kansas-Nebraska Act was the creation of a new anti-slavery party. A convention held under the oaks at Jackson, Mich., on 6 July 1854, resolved to oppose the extension of slavery, and 'be known as "Republicans" until the contest be terminated.' Many places, especially

Ripon, Wisconsin, claim the birthplace of the G.O.P., but Jackson at least made the happy suggestion of adopting Jefferson's old label. The new party, however, was slow in gathering momentum outside the Northwest. Seward sulked in his Whig tent; 'Anti-Nebraska Democrats' were loath to cut all connection with their party; Free-Soilers could not see why a new party was needed. With the old parties breaking up, many people hearkened to a new gospel of ignorance.

Know-Nothingism was a No Popery party. Protestants suspected that the Pope had his eye on America, for who would dwell in decaying Rome when he could live in the Mississippi Valley? Anti-Catholics thrived on volumes like Maria Monk's *Awful Disclosures of the Hotel Dieu Nunnery of Montreal*. Nativists were alarmed too by the rising flood of immigrants. In 1845, the immigrant tide passed the 100,000 a year mark for the first time; only two years later it had reached 200,000 and by 1854 had more than quadrupled. It was charged that the newcomers corrupted the nation's morals; one observer complained, 'They bring the grog shops like the frogs of Egypt upon us.' Even more important, nativists believed that the immigrants were sapping republican institutions. Between 1850 and 1855 in Boston, native-born voters increased 15 per cent, foreign-born 195 per cent. The declining Whigs attributed Pierce's victory in 1852 to the immigrant vote.

Accordingly, native-born Protestants formed a secret 'Order of the Star-Spangled Banner,' with elaborate ritual and rigid discipline. Members, when questioned by outsiders, answered 'I know nothing.' Candidates nominated secretly developed surprising strength at the polls, and many politicians joined up, thinking that this was the wave of the future. In the state elections of 1854 the Know-Nothings almost won New York and did win Massachusetts, electing a new legislature that passed some good reform laws but also conducted a clownish investigation of Catholic schools and convents. The new party sent some 75 congressmen to Washington; especially strong in New England and the border states, it also found a considerable following in the South. At Baltimore where the white working class was still largely native-born, the Know-Nothings organized 'plug-uglies,' gangs who attended the polls armed with carpenters' awls to 'plug' voters who did not give the password, and a series of pitched battles between native Americans and Irish Catholics in St. Louis in 1854 took many lives.

In the summer of 1855 the American party, as the Know-Nothings now called themselves, held a national convention; the Southern members obtained control, passed pro-slavery resolutions, and nominated for the presidency old Millard Fillmore. Northerners then lost interest, and by 1856 the movement was no longer able to offer the nation an escape from the slavery question.

Bleeding Kansas, 'Black' Republicanism

'Bleeding Kansas' soon diverted attention from the 'Popish peril.' Most of the settlers who came to Kansas went there to build a new life and live in peace, not to agitate the slavery question. Yet the new territory also witnessed a savage conflict over slavery which helped to plunge the nation into civil war. In the elections for the territorial legislature in March 1855, several thousand 'border ruffians' crossed over from Missouri to stuff ballot boxes. The legislature elected by such fraudulent means then put through a drastic slave code. The free-state men responded by setting up their own rump government, and by 1856 Kansas had two governments, both illegal. Since popular sovereignty was to settle the question of slavery in Kansas, sectional rivals dispatched settlers into the state. The New England Emigrant Aid Company sent some 1240 migrants. After Missourians had sacked their first settlement at Lawrence, the Company started arming its forces with a new breech-loading weapon, the Sharps rifle, or 'Beecher's Bible,' so called after the abolitionist preacher who advised its use. Parties of Northern 'Jayhawkers' battled with organizations from Missouri and points south. 'Now let the Southern men come on with their slaves,' wrote Senator Atchison of Missouri. 'Ten thousand families can take possession of and hold every acre of timber in the Territory of Kansas, and this secures the prairie. . . . We are playing for a mighty stake; if we win, we carry slavery to the Pacific Ocean.'

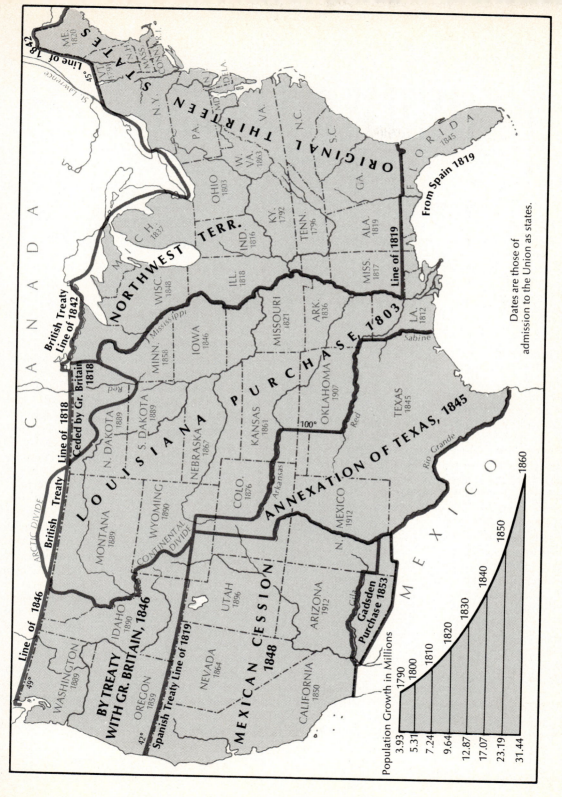

Territorial Growth of the United States

CITIZENS OF LAWRENCE!

☞ **L. Arms, a Deputy U. S. Marshal, has come** into your midst for the avowed purpose of NEGRO HUNTING, and is watching your houses, by his piratical minions, night and day, and will enter and search them for victims. KNOW YOUR RIGHTS, and STAND TO THEM. He has no right thus to INVADE your CASTLES. Do we live on the Guinea Coast, or in FREE America?
The Eldridge House is the head-quarters of the gang. — Mark them well.

(Kansas State Historical Society, Topeka)

Few Southerners, however, cared to risk valuable property in such a region, and free-state settlers came in with the spirit of crusaders. One of the newcomers, a fanatic named John Brown, was responsible for the murder of five men at the 'Pottawatomie massacre.' Such were the workings of popular sovereignty.

On 19 May 1856 Senator Sumner of Massachusetts delivered a speech on 'The Crime against Kansas,' which contained some unpalatable truth, much that was neither truthful nor in good taste, and some disgraceful personal invective against Senator Andrew Butler of South Carolina. Three days later, a kinsman of Butler, Preston Brooks, attacked Sumner as he sat at his desk in the Senate chamber and beat him senseless with a stout cane, while Stephen Douglas and Robert Toombs looked on. He was following the code of a Southern gentleman in dealing with an enemy unworthy of a duel. 'Towards the last he bellowed like a calf,' Brooks reported. 'I wore my cane out completely but saved the Head which is gold.' Returning to South Carolina, the assailant was feted from place to place and presented by admirers with suitably inscribed canes. From Louisiana, Braxton Bragg wrote, 'You can reach the sensibilities of such dogs only through their heads and a big stick.'

A few days after this episode, the new Republi-

can party held its first national convention. The Republicans embraced diverse elements: anti-slavery radicals like Sumner; former Whigs, many of a conservative stripe; Free-Soil Democrats like Chase and Lyman Trumbull; and dissatisfied Know-Nothings. Glamorous John C. Frémont, the 'Pathfinder,' won the first Republican presidential nomination. The platform proclaimed it 'both the right and the duty of Congress to prohibit in the territories those twin relics of barbarism, polygamy and slavery.' The Democratic convention in Cincinnati met for the first time west of the Appalachians. James Buchanan, for twenty-five years disappointed at not getting the Democratic presidential nomination, now wrested it from pleasant Mr. Pierce, the first man elected President to be denied a second term by his own party.

The Republicans conducted a lively campaign for 'Free soil, free speech, and Frémont,' but Buchanan won—though with only 45 per cent of the popular vote. He swept the South and every border state but one, and took five Northern states too. Frémont polled only 33 per cent, not much more than Fillmore received. The ominous aspect to Frémont's 1.3 million votes was that all but 1200 came from non-slaveholding states.

No previous candidate had so nearly united

262

North and West against the South. Party divisions were approaching dangerously close to the Mason-Dixon Line; and the Lower South, even in this campaign, made it perfectly clear that it would secede if a purely Northern party elected its presidential candidate.

Dred Scott

On 6 March 1857, two days after Buchanan's inauguration, the Supreme Court published its decision in Dred Scott v. Sandford. Dred Scott was a slave who had been taken by his master to Illinois, thence to the unorganized territory north of lat. 36° 30', where slavery had been forbidden by the Missouri Compromise, and finally back to Missouri, where he sued for freedom on the ground of having twice been resident of free soil. Chief Justice Taney and the four Southerners among the associate justices hoped through this case to settle the question of slavery by extending it legally to all territories of the United States. President-elect Buchanan slipped a clause into his inaugural address declaring that the Supreme Court was about to determine 'at what point of time' the people of a territory could decide for or against slavery, pledging his support to this decision, and begging 'all good citizens' to do likewise.

Poor, foolish Buchanan! He had hoped for a peaceful term of office, but the Dred Scott case unleashed the worst passions of pro- and anti-slavery when his administration was less than a week old. The nine justices filed nine separate opinions. Taney, speaking for the Court, declared against Scott's claim for freedom on three grounds: (1) as a Negro he could not be a citizen of the United States, and therefore had no right to sue in a Federal court; (2) as a resident of Missouri the laws of Illinois had no effect on his status; (3) as a resident of the territory north of lat. 36° 30' he had not been emancipated because Congress had no right to deprive citizens of their property without 'due process of law.' The Missouri Compromise, it followed, was unconstitutional.

On all these points the Chief Justice's opinion was either vulnerable or mistaken. As Justice Curtis asserted in his vigorous dissent, Negroes had always been considered citizens in most of the Northern states, and thus had the right to sue in the Federal courts. Under the rule of interstate comity, Missouri had in seven earlier cases recognized the claim to freedom of a slave who had resided in free territory. And congressional authority over slavery in the territories had been acknowledged for 70 years. As for 'due process of law,' that term in the Constitution referred to the method of enforcing the law, not to its substance.

Only once before, in Marbury v. Madison (1803), had the Supreme Court declared an act of Congress unconstitutional. In that case the law directly concerned the Federal judiciary; but the Missouri Compromise was a general law, resting on the precedent of the Ordinance of 1787, on the statute books for 34 years. By its ruling the Court had sanctioned Calhoun's doctrine that slavery was national, freedom sectional. Oregon and Nebraska, as well as Kansas, were opened to the slaveholder. Squatter sovereignty thenceforth was no sovereignty; slavery was theoretically legal in every territory.

Buchanan reeled from disaster to disaster. The conclusion of the Crimean War, which deprived the farmer of a prime market in Europe, came at a time when the North was feeling the effects of the collapse of the Western land boom and paying the price for a weak banking structure and an over-built railway system; by October, the panic of 1857 had hit with full force. Congressmen returned to Washington at the end of 1857 to cope with the Kansas question in an atmosphere of anxiety over the economy and in the midst of a religious revival which intensified sectional sensitivity about slavery.

Events in Kansas pointed toward civil war. A convention chosen by a minority of the voters had adopted the 'Lecompton constitution,' an out-and-out pro-slavery charter, subsequently ratified in a bogus referendum. The free-state faction then drafted its own constitution and got it ratified in an extra-legal referendum. Each group appealed to Washington for statehood. Despite the travesty of the fraudulent elections, Buchanan insisted on pushing the Lecompton constitution through Congress. He asserted that Kansas was 'as much a slave state as Georgia,' and warned that refusal to admit Kansas as a slave state would be 'keenly felt' by the South. At this, Stephen Douglas decided he had had enough. Embarrassed by the way popular sovereignty had worked out, he broke with Buchanan and the Southern Democrats and fought the Lecompton proposal. In the end the Democrats were compelled to submit the constitution to a new referendum, and in August 1858 in an honest election the voters of Kansas rejected it overwhelmingly. But by then both sections had found new cause for grievance, and the Democratic party, badly split between the Buchanan and Douglas factions, was rapidly losing its function as a unifier of the nation.

The Lincoln-Douglas Debates

Before the Kansas struggle Abraham Lincoln had been distinguished from hundreds of Northwestern lawyer-politicians only by a high reputation for integrity and a habit of prolonged, abstracted contemplation. Slavery he had long regarded as evil; but the abolitionist agitation seemed to him mischievous and unrealistic.

About the time of the Kansas-Nebraska Act an unseen force began to work on Lincoln's soul and to prepare him for the most arduous and distressing responsibility that has ever fallen to an American. He began to preach a new testament of anti-slavery, without malice or hatred toward slave-owners. In 1858 he had become a rival candidate to Stephen A. Douglas for election to the Senate from Illinois. His opening speech in the campaign gave the ripe conclusions to his meditations during the last four years and stuck the keynote of American history for the seven years to come.

'A house divided against itself cannot stand.'[2]

I believe this government cannot endure permanently half slave and half free.

I do not expect the Union to be dissolved—I do not expect the house to fall—but I do expect it will cease to be divided. It will become all one thing, or all the other.

Either the opponents of slavery will arrest the further spread of it, and place it where the public mind shall rest in the belief that it is in the course of ultimate extinction; or its advocates will push it forward till it shall become alike lawful in all the States, old as well as new, North as well as South.

2. Matthew xii:25.

Lincoln and Douglas engaged in seven joint debates, covering every section of the state, through the summer and autumn of 1858. Imagine some parched prairie town of central Illinois, set in fields of rustling corn; a dusty courthouse square surrounded by low wooden houses and stores blistering in the August sunshine, decked with flags and party emblems; shirt-sleeved farmers and their families in wagons and buggies and on foot, brass bands blaring out 'Hail! Columbia' and 'Oh! Susanna,' wooden platform with railing, perspiring semicircle of local dignitaries in black frock coats and immense beaver hats. The Douglas special train (provided by George B. McClellan, superintendent of the Illinois Central) pulls into the 'deepo' and fires a salute from the twelve-pounder cannon bolted to a flatcar at the rear. Senator Douglas, escorted by the local Democratic club in columns of fours, drives up in an open carriage and aggressively mounts the platform. His short, stocky figure is clothed in the best that Washington tailors can produce. Every feature of his face bespeaks confidence and mastery; every gesture of his body, vigor and combativeness. Abe Lincoln, who had previously arrived by an ordinary passenger train, approaches on foot, his furrowed face and long neck conspicuous above the crowd. Wearing a rusty frock coat the sleeves of which stop several inches short of his wrists, and well-worn trousers that show a similar reluctance to approach a pair of enormous feet, he shambles onto the platform. His face, as he turns to the crowd, has an air of settled melancholy.

In their debates, Douglas accused Lincoln of advocating doctrines which would lead to fratricide, while Lincoln sought to show the inconsistency of the Dred Scott decision and Douglas's popular sovereignty. At Freeport, Lincoln asked Douglas whether the people of a territory could, in any lawful way, exclude slavery from their limits. Apparently, Douglas must either accept the Dred Scott decision and admit popular sovereignty to be a farce, or separate from his party by repudiating a ruling of the Supreme Court. But this clever statesman had already found a way out of the dilemma: the principle of 'unfriendly legislation.' 'Slavery cannot exist a day or an hour anywhere, unless it is supported by local police regulations, said Douglas. If a territorial legislature failed to pass a black code, it would effectually keep slavery out, for no slaveholder would take valuable property into a territory unless he were sure of protection. No doubt Douglas was right. Congress could invalidate a positive enactment of the territorial legislature, but not force it to pass a law against its will. It is probable that this 'Freeport doctrine' won Douglas his re-election to the Senate. But by saying that popular sovereignty gave slaveholders no protection, Douglas, who had already antagonized them by his role in the Lecompton affair, made himself 'unavailable' for the Democratic nomination in 1860.

If Lincoln had the more principled argument, Douglas had a more sensible position at the moment. Kansas was safe for freedom; and if theoretically slavery were legal in all the territories, there was slight chance of any except New Mexico and Arizona, not even a territory until 1863, becoming slaveholding states. Yet the long-run practicality of Douglas's stand hinged on the extreme unlikelihood that the South would rest content with the Dred Scott principle, any more than it had rested content with the compromises of 1787, 1820, and 1850. As early as 1848 four Southern states had endorsed the 'Alabama platform' which called for positive action by Congress to protect slavery in the territories, and the majority platform of the national Democratic convention at Charleston in 1860 would demand that Congress enact a 'black code' and impose it on the Western settlers. The South was becoming increasingly insistent, too, that Northern states silence the abolitionists, and that Congress agree to reopen the African slave trade. Some writers have assumed that the institution of slavery would have withered away because it was unprofitable, and hence regard the Civil War as an unmitigated tragedy. The profitability of slavery is an issue hotly debated by historians. But even if one concludes that slavery was unprofitable, and many historians would disagree, one still confronts the fact that slavery was not merely an economic matter but was valued as a social necessity for keeping the South 'a white man's country.' There is less reason to suppose that slavery would have been abandoned than that the South would have demanded that its 'peculiar institution' be extended further and further afield until the world cried out, 'Away with this foul thing!'

Northern Aggression and John Brown

In 1859 came two startling portents of what Seward called the 'irrepressible conflict.' The Anthony Burns fugitive slave case was followed by a new crop of state 'personal liberty laws.' These penalized citizens for helping federal officials to perform this unwelcome duty. A certain Booth of Wisconsin, convicted in a federal court of having rescued a runaway slave from his captors, was released by the state supreme court on the ground that the Fugitive Slave Act of 1850 was unconstitutional. After the Supreme Court of the United States had reversed this decision, in Ableman v. Booth (1859), the Wisconsin legislature, quoting the Kentucky Resolves of 1798 which Southern men considered canonical, declared 'that this assumption of jurisdiction by the federal judiciary . . . is an act of undelegated power, void, and of no force.' The Federal Government vindicated its power by rearresting and imprisoning Booth; but the deeper significance lies in the fact that Calhoun's nullification had been enunciated in a new quarter.

If the Booth case aroused bitterness, the next episode of the year brought the deeper anger that comes of fear. John Brown, 'of Pottawatomie,' formed a vague project to establish an abolitionist republic in the Appalachians and wage guerrilla war on slavery with fugitive Negroes and a few determined whites. To this wild scheme he rallied support from many of the leading abolitionists. On the night of 16 October 1859, leading an army of thirteen whites and five Negroes, Brown seized the federal armory at Harpers Ferry, Virginia, killed the town's mayor, and took prisoner some of the leading townspeople.

Governor Wise called out the entire state militia and implored the Federal Government for aid. John Brown retreated to the engine-house of the armory, knocked portholes through the brick wall, and defended himself. One of his prisoners has left us a graphic description of the scene: 'Brown was the coolest and firmest man I ever saw in defying danger and death. With one son dead

John Brown of Osawatomie (1800–1859). An avid foe of slavery, Brown viewed himself as an instrument of the Lord's vengeance. In the spring of 1856 in 'bleeding Kansas' he executed reprisal for the sack of Lawrence by pro-slavery elements by leading a party of six, four of them his sons, to the Pottawatomie country where they brutally murdered five men. Though many viewed him as a fanatic, anti-slavery men hailed 'Brown of Osawatomie' as a hero. This photograph was taken in 1856, the year of the 'Pottawatomie massacre.' (*Library of Congress*)

by his side, and another shot through, he felt the pulse of his dying son with one hand and held his rifle with the other, and commanded his men with the utmost composure, encouraging them to be firm and to sell their lives as dearly as they could.' In the evening, when Colonel Robert E. Lee arrived with a company of marines, only four of Brown's men were alive and unwounded. The next day the marines forced an entrance and captured the slender remnant.

Eight days after his capture the trial of John Brown began. From the pallet where he lay wounded the bearded old fighter rejected his counsel's plea of insanity. The jury brought in a verdict of murder, criminal conspiracy, and treason against the Commonwealth of Virginia. John Brown, content (as he wrote to his children) 'to die

for God's eternal truth on the scaffold as in any other way,' was hanged on 2 December 1859.

Southerners thought of Haiti and shuddered, although not a single slave had voluntarily joined their would-be liberator. Keenly they watched for indications of Northern opinion. That Christian burial was with difficulty obtained for John Brown's body they did not know. That every Democratic or Republican newspaper condemned his acts they did not heed so much as the admiration for a brave man that Northern opinion could not conceal. And the babble of shocked repudiation by politicians and public men was dimmed by one bell-like note from Emerson: 'That new saint, than whom nothing purer or more brave was ever led by love of men into conflict and death . . . will make the gallows glorious like the cross.'

The Election of 1860

An unfortunate vote of the Democratic national convention of 1856 had decided on Charleston, the headquarters of secession sentiment, as the seat of the next national convention in 1860. Southern Democrats believed that they had been duped by Douglas. They had 'bought' popular sovereignty in 1854, expecting to get Kansas; but Kansas slipped the other way. Its territorial legislature was now in the hands of anti-slavery men, encouraged by Douglas's Freeport doctrine to flout the Dred Scott decision. Nothing less than active protection for slavery in every territory would satisfy the Southerners. Northerners on the platform committee were willing to go along with Southerners in supporting the Dred Scott decision, condemning personal liberty laws, and proposing annexation of Cuba. But the Southerners insisted that Congress must adopt a black code for all territories to override 'popular sovereignty.' The Democratic party must affirm 'that slavery was right,' said Yancey of Alabama. 'Gentlemen of the South,' replied Senator Pugh of Ohio, 'you mistake us—you mistake us—we will not do it.'

The minority report of the Northern delegates was adopted by the convention on 30 April as the Democratic platform. Thereupon the Alabama delegation, and a majority from South Carolina, Georgia, Florida, Louisiana, and Arkansas, withdrew. This symbolic secession was even more rash and foolish than the actual secession which developed from it as inevitably as vinegar from cider. For the best possible way for the South to protect slavery was to elect a Democrat President; and this split in the party made it impossible to elect any Democrat.

After the Southern rights men bolted the Charleston convention, balloting started for the presidential nomination. Although Douglas led, neither he nor anyone could obtain the required two-thirds majority. So the convention adjourned, to meet again in the calmer atmosphere of Baltimore on 18 June. At Baltimore a second split occurred over re-admitting the bolters. It was decided in the negative, and another secession took place. The convention then nominated Stephen A. Douglas, who thus became the official Democratic candidate. The seceders nominated Vice-President John C. Breckinridge of Kentucky for President, an action later endorsed by the original seceders from Charleston.

In the meantime, old Whigs, Know-Nothings, and moderate men of both North and South had held a convention of what they called the Constitutional Union party, and nominated Senator John Bell of Tennessee for President and Edward Everett of Massachusetts for Vice-President. They avowed no principles other than the Constitution, the Union, and the enforcement of the laws. This praiseworthy attempt to found a middle-of-the-road party, pledged to solve the slavery extension issue by reason rather than violence, came at least four years too late.

The Republicans were no longer a party of one idea, but a party of the North. Their 1860 platform stipulated: no more slavery in the territories, no interference with slavery in the states. So there was no place in the party either for the slavocracy or for the abolitionists. John Brown was condemned in the same breath with the 'border ruffians' of Missouri. The platform also promised settlers a free quarter-section of public land and revived Clay's 'American system' of internal improvements and protective tariff, representing Northern desires that had been balked by Southern interests. Abraham Lincoln received the presidential nomination; not for his transcendent merits, which no one yet suspected, but as a matter of political strategy. His humble birth, homely wit, and skill in debate would attract the sort of Northerners who had once voted for Andrew Jackson; and no one else could carry the doubtful states of Indiana and Illinois.

Lincoln triumphed in the four-way race by capturing every free state, save New Jersey, whose vote was divided. In his camp were two newly admitted free states, Minnesota and Oregon. But in ten Southern states he did not receive one vote. Breckinridge carried every cotton state, together with North Carolina, Delaware, and Maryland. Douglas, although a good second to Lincoln in the total popular vote, won only Missouri and three electoral votes in New Jersey. Virginia, Kentucky, and Tennessee went for Bell, although his popular vote was the least. Lincoln would have won even if

Stephen A. Douglas (1813–61). This illustration, which comes from a 'propaganda envelope,' an artifact of the popular culture of the era, gives a stamp of approval to the 'Little Giant.' In 1860 Douglas ran as the presidential candidate of Northern Democrats. Though he opposed Lincoln in this campaign, as he had for some time before in Illinois, Douglas proved loyal to Lincoln and the Union when war broke out. He traveled through the border states to stir up enthusiasm for the Union cause and sought in other ways to be of service to his country. But two months after Fort Sumter fell, Douglas was stricken with typhoid fever and died. (*Library of Congress*)

John Breckinridge of Kentucky (1821–75). In 1856 he was elected Vice-President of the United States and in 1860 he polled seventy-two electoral votes as the presidential candidate of the pro-slavery Democrats. Although he had resisted disunion before the war, he helped organize a Confederate government in Kentucky after the fighting began. In November 1861 he was indicted for treason in a federal court, and in the following month the Senate formally expelled him. In the North, Breckinridge, as this propaganda envelope indicates, was branded a 'traitor,' but in the South he was respected as a statesman and as a brigadier-general in the Confederate army. (*Library of Congress*)

Cloth banner for the Republican party ticket, 1860. (*Library of Congress*)

the opposition to him had been united, because he rolled up a large majority in the electoral college.[3]

Secession

It was a foregone conclusion that South Carolina would secede if Lincoln were elected. As soon as

the result of the election was certain, the South Carolina legislature summoned a state convention. On 20 December 1860 it met at Charleston and unanimously declared 'that the Union now subsisting between South Carolina and other states under the name of "The United States of America" is hereby dissolved.'

In the other cotton states Union sentiment was strong. Men like Jefferson Davis, who had traveled in the North, wished to give Lincoln's administration a fair trial. Outside South Carolina secession was insisted upon by small planters, provincial lawyer-politicians, journalists, and clergymen, but they met stout opposition. After Mississippi, Alabama, and Florida seceded, the key struggle took place in Georgia, trapped between states which had pulled out of the Union.

3. | Candidates | Popular vote | Per cent | Electoral vote |
|---|---|---|---|
| Lincoln | 1,866,432 | 39.9 | 180 |
| Douglas | 1,375,197 | 29.4 | 12 |
| Breckinridge | 845,763 | 18.1 | 72 |
| Bell | 589,586 | 12.6 | 39 |

These figures include no popular vote in South Carolina, where Breckinridge electors were chosen by the legislature. In the other states that seceded the popular vote was Breckinridge 736,592; Bell, 345,919; Douglas, 72,084.

Alexander H. Stephens declared: 'This government of our fathers, with all its defects, comes nearer the objects of all good government than any other on the face of the earth.' But Senator Robert Toombs cried: 'Throw the bloody spear into this den of incendiaries!' On 19 January 1861 Georgia voted secession by a 2 to 1 plurality at its convention, but only after a motion to defer action had been narrowly defeated.

By 1 February 1861, these five states had been joined by two more: Louisiana, where the vote for secessionist delegates had totalled only 20,448 to 17,296 Unionists, and Texas, over the opposition of old Sam Houston, subsequently deposed as governor for refusing to swear fealty to the Confederacy. On 4 February, delegates from the seven seceded states met at Montgomery, Alabama, and on the 8th formed the Confederate States of America. The next day this Congress elected Jefferson Davis provisional President and A. H. Stephens Vice-President of the Southern Confederacy, and proceeded to draft a constitution.

The causes of secession, as they appeared to its protagonists, were plainly expressed by the state conventions. 'The people of the Northern states,' declared Mississippi, 'have assumed a revolutionary position towards the Southern states.' 'They have enticed our slaves from us,' and obstructed their rendition under the fugitive slave law. They claim the right 'to exclude slavery from the territories,' and from any state henceforth admitted to the Union. They have 'insulted and outraged our citizens when travelling among them . . . by taking their servants and liberating the same.' They have 'encouraged a hostile invasion of a Southern state to excite insurrection, murder and rapine.' To which South Carolina added, 'They have denounced as sinful the institution of slavery; they have permitted the open establishment among them' of abolition societies, and 'have united in the election of a man to the high office of President of the United States whose opinions and purposes are hostile to slavery.' On their own showing, then, the states of the Lower South seceded as the result of dissatisfaction respecting the Northern attitude toward slavery. There was no mention of any other cause, neither the tariff nor state rights. A strong minority regarded Southern independence as an end in itself.

Even for the purpose of protecting slavery, secession was a colossal act of folly. Southerners and Democrats combined would have possessed a majority in both houses of Congress. Lincoln could have done nothing without their consent. At worst Republicans might eventually gain strength to outlaw slavery in the territories, but secession would immediately lose the cotton states all rights of any sort in the territories. Northern states were not enforcing the fugitive slave law, but secession would make that law a dead letter. Abolitionists were disagreeable fellow-countrymen; but their propaganda could not be stopped by international boundaries. And as Lincoln asked, 'Can enemies make treaties better than friends can make laws?' The Republicans contemplated no interference with slavery in the Southern states, and those in Congress early in 1861 actually proposed a constitutional amendment to that effect. Even had they wished, they could not have freed the slaves in unwilling states except as an act of war. To free them by constitutional amendment would have been impossible even today, if the slave states had stayed united.[4]

Confusion and Attempted Compromise

During the awkward four months' interval between Lincoln's election in November 1860 and his inauguration on 4 March, a period in which the Confederacy was formed, the timid Buchanan was President. Buchanan had the same power to defend federal property and collect federal taxes within states that obstructed federal law as President Jackson possessed in 1832, but the President did nothing. 'Vacillating and obstinate by turns, yet lacking firmness when the occasion demanded firmness, he floundered about in a sea of perplexity, throwing away chance after chance.'[5] In his annual message of 8 December, Buchanan had an opportunity to sound the Jacksonian trumpet note to recall loyal citizens to their duty. Instead, he querulously chided the abolitionists for the fact

4. There were fifteen slave states in 1860, enough to prevent the ratification of a constitutional amendment a century later.
5. J. F. Rhodes, *United States*, III, 150.

that 'many a matron throughout the South retires at night in dread of what may befall herself and her children before the morning.' And he did a notable shilly-shally on secession, which Seward not unfairly paraphrased thus: 'It is the duty of the President to execute the laws, unless somebody opposes him; and that no state has a right to go out of the Union, unless it wants to.'

Yet Buchanan confronted a situation which appeared to spell defeat no matter what course he pursued. He hoped by a policy of conciliation to encourage the seceding states to return. But he found little support for his policies in any section. Washington was a Southern city. Congress, cabinet, and all the federal departments were riddled with secessionists. Secretary of the Treasury Howell Cobb resigned in December to organize secession in Georgia. To onlookers like young Henry Adams, the Federal Government seemed to be dissolving; soon there would be nothing left to secede from. Northern opinion was indistinct. Horace Greeley may have struck the key-note with the phrase, 'Wayward sisters, depart in peace!'

'Why not?' we may ask, in an era that has seen more than fifty new nations created. 'Why not have let the cotton states form their own republic?' With the best will in the world, redistribution of federal power would have been difficult,[6] and good will was notably wanting. Peace could not have been maintained for a year between the United States and the Confederacy. Fugitive slaves, adjustment of the national debt, and of each government's share in the territories would have raised problems only solvable by force; once the right of secession had been admitted, other states would have broken away.

The issue came to a head in Charleston harbor. When South Carolina seceded, Major Robert Anderson, who commanded the small U.S. Army detachment at Charleston, shifted his command from the mainland to the incomplete Fort Sumter,

6. The matter of breaking up the federal postal service, for instance, was so difficult that the Confederacy permitted United States mails to run their usual course through the South until 30 June 1861, six weeks after the Civil War had begun, and almost six months after South Carolina had 're-sumed her separate and equal place among nations.'

on an island commanding the harbor entrance. An 'embassy' from South Carolina to Washington almost bullied Buchanan into ordering Major Anderson out, or home; but at the turn of the year Attorney-General Jeremiah H. Black managed to put a little ginger into the President, and he refused. Buchanan also reconstructed his cabinet, with Black as Secretary of State, and made a half-hearted attempt to reinforce Fort Sumter with 200 men and arms and ammunition in an unarmed passenger steamer which retired after gunfire from a fort flying the palmetto flag had straddled her.

Buchanan did not retaliate, because he continued to hope that one of the compromise movements might succeed. None did, though when Senator John J. Crittenden of Kentucky proposed to extend the old 36° 30' line between free and slave territories to the California boundary, the Republicans were willing to go so far as to admit New Mexico as a slave state if the people there chose slavery. A Peace Convention summoned by the Virginia legislature also broke on the rocks of Southern intransigency. Even the adoption of a 'never-never' proposition to the effect that neither by law nor constitutional amendment could Congress ever interfere with slavery in the states or the District of Columbia proved unavailing. All formal compromises failed to bring back the 'wayward sisters.' The repeal by several Northern states of personal liberty laws, and the breaking up of an abolition meeting in Boston to commemorate John Brown, seemed insufficient evidence of a change of heart. Nothing further had been done toward compromise by 4 March 1861, when Abraham Lincoln was inaugurated President of the no longer United States.

Fort Sumter and Seward

Buchanan had flinched from defending those coigns of vantage, the federal forts in the Southern states; and we shall judge him less harshly when we reflect that it took Lincoln a month to meet the issue bravely. By the time he was inaugurated, all the forts and navy yards in the seceded states, except Fort Pickens at Pensacola, Fort Sumter at Charleston, and two minor posts off the

Florida coast, had fallen unresisting to the Confederate authorities. So, too, had a string of post offices and custom houses and the mint at New Orleans. From the extreme Southern point of view, the jurisdiction of such places passed with secession to the states, and their retention by the Federal Government was equivalent to an act of war. Confederate commissioners came to Washington to treat for their surrender, a few days after Lincoln's inauguration. Although Seward refused to receive the gentlemen, he assured them indirectly that no supplies or provisions would be sent to the forts without due notice, and led them to expect a speedy evacuation.

William H. Seward, as Lincoln's chief rival for the nomination, and as the most experienced statesman in the Republican party, had been given the department of state, where he was playing a deep and dangerous game. Lincoln he regarded as an inexperienced small-town lawyer; and Confederate leaders, he thought, were merely using secession as a way of obtaining concessions to Southern rights. If a collision could be avoided, they would sneak back into the Union. If they did not, Seward would rally the Southern people to their old flag by a foreign war. But events were rapidly overtaking him.

Major Anderson, commanding Fort Sumter, notified the war department that his supplies were giving out, and that new Confederate batteries commanded his position. Fort Sumter had no strategic value in case of civil war. Why, then, risk war by holding it? The Confederacy made it clear that any attempt to reinforce or even to supply Sumter would be regarded as a hostile act, which would probably pull Virginia into the Confederacy. In the middle of March, five of the seven members of Lincoln's cabinet opposed supplying Fort Sumter. If, however, the forts were tamely yielded, would not the principle of union be fatally compromised? Could a recognition of the Confederacy thereafter be avoided?

Lincoln delayed decision, not from fear, but because he was watching Virginia. Jefferson Davis, too, was watching Virginia. The Old Dominion was a stake worth playing for. Her sons were the ablest officers in the United States Army, and her soil was almost certain to be the theater of any war between the sections. The 'panhandle' of western Virginia thrust a salient between Pennsylvania and Ohio to within 100 miles of Lake Erie. If Virginia seceded, she must carry North Carolina with her; and other states would probably follow.

Virginia showed her union sentiment in 1860 by voting for Bell rather than Breckinridge; but unionism in Virginia meant a voluntary association of sovereign states. A majority of the delegates to a Virginia state convention that met at Richmond in February were union men, but the secessionist minority was united, aggressive, and clever; it kept the convention in session week after week, until many unionist delegates left for their homes in the western part of the state. Delegations of unionist members besought Lincoln to let Fort Sumter go. Twice the President offered to do so if the Virginia unionists 'would break up their convention without any row or nonsense'; but they were not strong enough to promise that. Finally Lincoln came to see that to yield Fort Sumter would not bring the 'wayward sisters' back; and Virginia would join them the moment he raised his hand to strike. If Virginia would not accept the Union as it was, she must abide the consequences.

Toward the end of March Lincoln, determined to face the issue squarely, ordered a relief expedition to be prepared for Fort Sumter. Seward then showed his hand. On April Fools' Day 1861, he presented Lincoln with a paper, 'Thoughts for the President's Consideration.' The most startling proposal was that the United States should at once pick a quarrel with France and Spain, possibly with England and Russia as well, as a means of reuniting North and South for glory and conquest! And Lincoln was invited to appoint Seward his prime minister to execute this mad policy! Lincoln did not take him up on this wild proposal, but Seward pressed ahead. On 6 April, when the President ordered the Sumter expedition to sail, Seward by deception obtained Lincoln's signature diverting the capital ship of the expedition to Fort Pickens.

Jefferson Davis, who was also troubled by divided counsel, ordered General P. G. T. Beauregard to fire on Sumter only if absolutely necessary to prevent its reinforcement. On the night of 11–12 April Beauregard sent four staff officers to Fort Sumter demanding surrender. Major Anderson, a Kentuckian who loathed the idea of civil war, had no desire for the sort of fame that would come from being the occasion of it. Nothing as yet had been seen or heard of the relief expedition. So, at a quarter past three in the morning, he offered to surrender as soon as he might do so with honor—in two days' time, when the garrison's food would be exhausted. The Confederate staff officers peremptorily refused this reasonable stipulation, and on their own responsibility gave orders to open fire. For, as one of them admitted in later life, they feared that Davis would clasp hands with Seward, and the chance of war would slip away forever.

On 12 April 1861, at 4:30 a.m., the first gun of the Civil War was fired against Fort Sumter. The relief expedition appeared, but for lack of its capital ship was unable to pass the batteries. All day Major Anderson replied as best he could to a concentric fire from four or five Confederate forts and batteries, while the beauty and fashion of Charleston flocked to the waterfront as to a gala. At nine o'clock the next morning, 13 April, the barracks caught fire; in the early afternoon the flagstaff was shot away, and a few hours later, although his situation was by no means desperate, Major Anderson accepted terms of surrender. On the afternoon of Sunday, 14 April, the garrison marched out with drums beating and colors flying.

Walt Whitman caught the spirit of that occasion in his

Beat! beat! drums!—blow! bugles! blow!
Through the windows—through doors—burst like a
    ruthless force,
Into the solemn church, and scatter the congregation,
Into the school where the scholar is studying;
Leave not the bridegroom quiet—no happiness must he
    have now with his bride,
Nor the peaceful farmer any peace, ploughing his field
    or gathering his grain.
So fierce you whirr and pound you drums—so shrill
    you bugles blow.

Secession Completed

On 15 April President Lincoln issued a call for 75,000 volunteers to put down combinations 'too powerful to be suppressed by the ordinary course of judicial proceedings,' and 'to cause the laws to be duly executed.' Already the Virginian secessionists were organizing attacks on the Norfolk navy yard and the arsenal at Harpers Ferry. The state convention was in a state of high-strung emotion bordering on hysteria when Lincoln's call precipitated matters. On 17 April it voted, 88 to 55, to submit an ordinance of secession to the people. Without awaiting that verdict, the governor placed his state under Confederate orders.

The western part of Virginia refused to leave the Union;[7] but three more states did. Arkansas seceded on 6 May; Tennessee on 7 May concluded an alliance with the Confederacy, which a month later the people approved; North Carolina, having previously voted down secession, was in the impossible position of a Union enclave until 20 May, when she ratified the Confederate constitution. The attitude of Maryland was crucial, for her secession would isolate the Federal Government at Washington. The first Northern troops on their way to the capital were mobbed as they passed through Baltimore (19 April), but the danger of disunion in Maryland passed. In Kentucky, opinion was evenly divided, but by the end of the year the state threw in its lot with the Union. Missouri was practically under a dual regime throughout the war; Delaware never wavered in her loyalty. In California Unionists won a fierce struggle with Southern sympathizers; but California was too remote to give the Union cause other than pecuniary aid, in which she was generous. The Indians of the Indian Territory, many of them slaveholders, mostly threw in their lot with the South.

Before Lincoln's call for troops, a number of states in the Upper South had, in different ways, voted their sentiments against secession, but the Upper South was drawn to the Lower by a determination to keep that region a 'white men's country.' This emotion was rationalized by the theory that any state had a right to secede; hence Lincoln's call for coercion was illegal. And it forced the issue: everyone had to choose between defending the Confederacy or helping to put it down.

7. West Virginia was admitted as a state in 1863, but gave comparatively little aid to the Union cause.

Robert E. Lee (1807–70). His nobility of character has made him a hero not just of the former Confederacy but of the nation. 'I have met many of the great men of my time,' Viscount Garnet Wolseley observed, 'but Lee alone impressed me with the feeling that I was in presence of a man who was cast in a grander mold and made of different and finer metal than all other men.' (*Library of Congress, Brady Collection*)

Yet throughout the Civil War, lines were never strictly drawn between the states that seceded and those that did not. The majority of men went with their neighbors, as most people always do. But there were thousands who did not. The Confederate army contained men from every Northern state, who preferred the Southern type of civilization, and the United States Army and Navy contained loyal men from every seceded state, Americans who knew that the break-up of the Union would be the worst blow to the cause of self-government and republicanism since the day that Bonaparte assumed the purple. Samuel P. Lee commanded the Union naval forces on the James river while his uncle, General Robert E. Lee, was resisting Grant in the Wilderness. Senator Crittenden of the attempted compromise had two sons, Major General T. L. Crittenden, USA, and Major General G. B. Crittenden, CSA. Three brothers of Mrs. Lincoln died for the South, whilst near kinsmen of Mrs. Davis were in the Union army. In a house on West 20th Street, New York, a little boy named Theodore Roosevelt prayed for the Union armies at the knee of his Georgia mother, whose brothers were in the Confederate navy. At the same moment, in the Presbyterian parsonage of Augusta, Georgia, another little boy named Thomas Woodrow Wilson knelt in the family circle while his Ohio-born father invoked the God of Battles for the Southern cause.

Robert E. Lee abhorred the methods of the abolitionists, but agreed with them that slavery was wrong and emancipated his few inherited slaves. He did not believe in a constitutional right of secession, and severely criticized the action of the cotton states. In January 1861 Lee wrote to his son, 'I can contemplate no greater calamity for the country than a dissolution of the Union. . . . Still, a Union that can only be maintained by swords and bayonets, and in which strife and civil war are to take the place of brotherly love and kindness, has no charm for me.' To a cousin and brother officer of the United States Army, who determined to remain faithful to the flag, Lee expressed sympathy and respect. But, 'I have been unable to make up my mind to raise my hand against my native state, my relatives, my children and my home.' With deep regret Colonel Lee resigned his commission in the United States Army; a sense of duty induced him to accept a commission in the Confederate cause. What anguish that decision cost him we can never know. What it cost the United States we know too well.

17

The Civil War: An Overview

*

1861–1865

The Union and the Confederacy

From a distance of more than a century many wonder at the rash gallantry of the Southern war for independence. A loose agrarian confederacy of 5 or 6 million whites and 3.5 million slaves challenged a federal union of 19 or 20 million freemen with overwhelming financial and industrial advantages.[1] Yet, futile as the effort proved, the Southern cause was not predestined to defeat.

The Confederacy, in order to win, needed merely to defend her own territory long enough to weary the Northerners of war. The United States, in order to win, had to conquer an empire almost as large as the whole of western Europe and crush a people. A negotiated peace, or any less emphatic result than unconditional surrender of the Southern armies and total collapse of the Confederate government, would have meant some sort of special privilege to the Southern states within the Union, if not independence without the Union: in either event a Southern victory.

These considerations go a long way toward explaining the military advantages of the Confederacy. Since the South would be fighting on home soil, it had all the advantages of familiar terrain. The South was on the defensive, and it takes far larger armies and more formidable equipment to mount an offensive; the North would have to maintain long lines of communication deep into hostile territory. Furthermore, the South had an immense coastline, with innumerable inlets and harbors, and might expect to defy a Northern blockade and import military necessities. As Southerners were more inclined than Northerners to make a profession of arms, the officers with the longest experience were Southern. Finally, Southerners were convinced that 'Cotton was

---

1. By the census of 1860 the white population of the eleven seceded states was 5,449,467; the white population of the nineteen free states, 18,936,579. Both figures leave out of account the white population (2,589,533) of the four border slave states (Delaware, Maryland, Kentucky, and Missouri), which did not secede, but which probably contributed as many men to the Confederacy as to the Union. Subtracting the loyal regions of Virginia and Tennessee would reduce the Confederacy's white population to about 5 million. By the census of 1860 there were 3,521,111 slaves in the Confederate states, and 429,401 in the four border states, and from those the Union recruited about 100,000 troops.

King.' The Confederacy believed that Great Britain and France would be forced to intervene to stop the war or to aid the South in order to keep cotton supplies flowing across the Atlantic. In these circumstances there was a good reason to expect that the South would win. The Thirteen Colonies, the Netherlands, and in recent memory the South American and the Italian states had achieved their independence against great odds.

With the one crucial exception of slavery the moral scales seemed weighted in favor of the South. From their point of view, Southerners were fighting for everything that men hold dear: liberty and self-government, hearth and home. They could abandon the struggle only by sacrificing the very bases of their society; and defeat for them involved the most bitter humiliation. The Northern people, on the contrary, could have stopped the war at any moment, at the mere cost of recognizing what to many seemed an accomplished fact. They were fighting for the sentiment of Union, which, translated into action, seemed to tender souls scarcely different from conquest. Negro emancipation, itself an ideal, came more as an incident than as an object of the war. It was not the abolitionist 'Battle-Hymn of the Republic' that stirred the North in those years of trial, but the simple sentiment of:

The Union forever, hurrah! boys, hurrah!
Down with the traitor, up with the star,
While we rally round the flag, boys, rally once again,
Shouting the battle-cry of Freedom.

When we look to material factors, the position of the South was less favorable. In the secession winter, a Virginia editor had warned, with only some exaggeration, that so dependent was the South on Europe and the North that if secession came, 'we should, in all the South, not be able to clothe ourselves; we could not fill our firesides, plough our fields, nor mow our meadows.' New York state alone turned out manufactures worth four times more than the output of all the seceded states, and the North manufactured 97 per cent of the nation's firearms. The Union commanded an immense superiority in men, money, railroads, industrial potential, navy and merchant marine.

The Confederacy also labored under political disadvantages. Its constitution had one fateful flaw; it took seriously the dogma of state rights.

Bounties, protective tariffs, and 'internal improvements' were forbidden. Federal officials and even judges could be impeached by the legislatures of the state in which their functions were exercised. No 'law denying or impairing the right of property in negro slaves' could be enacted by the Confederate Congress, and in all new territory acquired 'the institution of negro slavery' was protected. The executive branch proved to be distressingly weak. Nor were the other departments more successful. The pull of the army operated to discourage first-rate statesmen from service in the Confederate Congress. Finally, although the Confederate Constitution provided for a Supreme Court, this provision was never implemented, and the Confederacy fought the war without an effective judicial system.

The Southern Confederacy was weakened by faction and shaken by the vice of localism. Davis and most of the Southern leaders had been talking state rights but thinking Southern nationalism; yet many important men loved state rights more than Southern unity and feared a tyranny at Richmond no less than they had at Washington. No Union general ever had to write, as Lee did of the Lower South when contemplating an advance: 'If these states will give up their troops, I think it can be done.' The Confederacy suffered, too, from the absence of a two-party system, which could restrain petty personal politics and link leaders in state and nation.

At the outset of the war few doubted that Davis was abler than Lincoln. Lieutenant of dragoons, colonel of volunteers, congressman, senator, and Secretary of War, Davis brought to his post experience such as Lincoln had never had. Courage, sincerity, patience, and integrity were his; only tact, perception, humility, and inner harmony were wanting. Isolated from the Southern democracy out of which he had sprung, Davis moved as to the manner born among the whispering aristocracy of Richmond; yet he had a perverse knack of infuriating the gentlemen who tried to work under him, in part because of his meddling in military operations. An unstable amalgam, the Davis cabinet in four years had five attorneys-general and six secretaries of war. Nor did Davis win the affections of the plain people as Lincoln did. In the last years of the war his health and nerves gave way, and his state papers show an

Jefferson Davis (1808–89), President of the Confederate States of America. Carl Schurz, who met him when he was Secretary of War in the Pierce cabinet, recalled: 'His slender, tall, and erect figure, his spare face, keen eyes, and fine forehead, not broad, but high and well-shaped, presented the well-known strong American type. There was in his bearing a dignity which seemed entirely natural and unaffected—that kind of dignity which does not invite familiar approach, but will not render one uneasy by lofty assumption.' (*Library of Congress, Brady Collection*)

increasing querulousness which contrasts sharply with the dignity and magnanimity of all that Lincoln wrote.

At the beginning of Lincoln's administration the members of his cabinet showed scant respect for him. After the firing on Sumter, Seward assumed the role of premier—as he liked to be called, and several months elapsed before the President was really master in his own house. However, his feeling for the democratic medium in which he had to work, for its limitations, imperfections, and possibilities, proved to be akin to that of a great artist. If Lincoln was slow to direct the conduct of the war, he never faltered in his conception of its purpose: to preserve the Union. The Union, which for Hamilton was a panoply of social order, had become, in the hands of Jackson, Clay, and Webster, a symbol of popular government. Lincoln drove home this conception in his every utterance, and gave it classical expression in the Gettysburg Address. He made the average American feel that his dignity as a citizen of a free republic was bound up with the fate of the Union, whose destruction would be a victory for the enemies of freedom. Because Lincoln raised the Union standard at the beginning and kept it flying, the Union was preserved. Lincoln never forgot that those whom he liked to call 'our late friends, now adversaries' must, if his object were attained, become fellow citizens once more. He could never bring himself to contemplate the South with feelings other than sorrow and compassion.

The Two Armies

In military preparations the Confederacy had a start of several months. It secured many of the ablest officers of the United States Army then in active service—Lee, both Johnstons, Beauregard, J. E. B. Stuart, and A. P. Hill; as well as Thomas 'Stonewall' Jackson and D. H. Hill, who were teaching in Southern military colleges. While Virginia-born Winfield Scott and George Thomas and David G. Farragut of Tennessee remained loyal to the nation, most Southern officers went with their states. In the regular army of the United States—only 16,000 strong—many brilliant young officers like Philip Sheridan were con-

fined to small units until late in the war. Until mid-April no attempt was made to enlarge or even to concentrate the small United States fleet, for fear of offending the Virginia unionists. In the meantime the Confederate States had seized the United States arsenals and navy yards within their limits, had obtained munitions from the North and from Europe, and had organized state armies; by the end of April 1861 President Davis had called for and quickly obtained 100,000 volunteers for twelve months.

Winfield Scott, general-in-chief of the United States Army, infirm in body but robust in mind, advised the President that at least 300,000 men, a general of Wolfe's capacity, and two or three years' time would be required to conquer even the Upper South. No one else dared place the estimate so high; Seward believed with the man in the street that one vigorous thrust would overthrow the Confederacy within 90 days. The President, in his proclamation of 15 April 1861, called for only 75,000 volunteers for three months. Militia regiments fell over one another in their alacrity to aid the government; within two weeks 35,000 troops were in Washington or on their way. The government should have taken advantage of this patriotic outburst to create a national army for the duration of the war. Instead, Lincoln on 3 May called for 40 more volunteer regiments of 1050 men each and 40,000 three-year enlistments in the regular army and navy, leaving the recruiting, organization, and equipment of all volunteer regiments to the states, as had been done in past wars.

As a basis for the new army, every Northern state had some sort of volunteer militia force which was mobilized for an annual 'muster' and 'Cornwallis' (sham battle)—usually not much better than a frolic. Many militia units volunteered en masse. But for the most part, the volunteer regiments that made up the bulk of the United States Army during the war were created on the spot. A patriotic citizen would receive a colonel's commission from his state governor, and raise and even equip a regiment by his own efforts and by those who expected to be officers under him. When the regiment was reasonably complete and partially equipped, it was forwarded to a training camp and placed under federal control. The Federal Government in practice had to respect state

Confederate soldiers. These are Richmond militiamen of the First Virginia Regiment. Notice the soldier (upper left) brandishing a bowie knife. (*Valentine Museum, Richmond, Virginia*)

appointments until they were found wanting in action; its own were scarcely better. This system did give an unmilitary country a stake in the war. But something better was wanted before a year had elapsed.

By much the same system was the first Confederate army raised, though the Southern respect for caste was more manifest. Indeed the first Southern armies were embarrassed by a plethora of officer material. J. E. B. Stuart remarked of one unit, 'They are pretty good officers now, and after a while they will make excellent soldiers too. They only need reducing to the ranks!' The Southern troops had the advantage of being accustomed to the use of arms—for every slaveholder kept weapons by him in case of insurrection, and the non-slaveholders were good marksmen. Both classes were lovers of horseflesh, and it was a poor white indeed who did not own a horse or a mule. Northern troops, unless from the West, had outgrown the hunting and horseback-riding frontier, and the Northern gentry had not yet adopted field sports or fox-hunting for recreation. Discipline, to which the more primitive individualistic Southerners were averse, soon outweighed these differences. The two armies became as nearly equal in fighting capacity, man for man, as any two in history; and they took an unprecedented amount of punishment. If the Confederates won more battles, it was due to their better leadership, which gave them tactical superiority on the field of battle, against the strategical superiority of their enemies on the field of operations. As the North had the greater immigrant population, it had a far larger proportion of foreign-born soldiers, in particular German, Irish, and Scandinavian.[2] Throughout the war the Union army was the better equipped in shoes and clothing, and more abundantly supplied with munitions. Yet though the Union at all times had greater fire power than the Confederacy, the South never lost a major battle for want of ammunition.

Lincoln had appealed to the states to raise 'three hundred thousand more' on 2 July 1862. The New York abolitionist James Gibbons responded with a

song, 'We are coming, Father Abraham, three hundred thousand more,' but that was almost the only response; for the states, even by drafting from their own militia, produced but 88,000 men. Yet not until 3 March 1863 did Congress pass the first United States Conscription Act. The law was a travesty. All men between the ages of 20 and 45 had to be registered. As men were needed, the number was divided among the loyal states in proportion to population and subdivided among districts, giving credit for previous enlistments. In the first draft (1863) these credits wiped out the liability of most of the Western states, which had been most forward in volunteering. You could commute service in a particular draft upon payment of $300; or evade service during the entire war by procuring a substitute to enlist for three years—no matter if the substitute deserted the next day. The system was inequitable to the poor, and in the working-class quarters of New York the first drawing of names in 1863 was the signal for terrible riots. On 13 July the provost marshal was driven from his office by a mob of irate Irish-Americans, and for four days and nights marauders sacked shops, gutted saloons, burned mansions, and lynched or tortured Negroes who fell into their clutches. Not until troops poured into the city was order restored, after the loss of hundreds of lives.

Conscription provided only a very small proportion of the Union army. In the fall of 1863, of 88,000 men drafted in New York, only 9000 went into the army; more than 52,000 paid fees, the rest hired substitutes. As recruits were credited to the district where they enlisted, and not to that of their residence, several wealthy communities escaped the draft altogether by purchasing cannon-fodder in the poorer country districts. Professional bounty-brokers often induced the recruits they furnished to desert at the first opportunity and re-enlist elsewhere. 'Bounty jumpers' enlisted and deserted, ten, twenty, and even thirty times, before being apprehended. Federal officials were bribed to admit cripples, idiots, and criminals as recruits. The success of conscription, however, is not to be measured by the very small number of draftees or the large proportion of deserters, but by the number of volunteers obtained under pressure. Unquestionably the quality of both armies

---

2. And many foreign-born officers like the Germans Franz Sigel and Carl Schurz, the Irish generals Corcoran and Meagher, the French Philippe de Trobriand, and the Norwegian colonels Hans Christian Heg and Hans Mattson.

deteriorated as the war dragged on; but the men who followed Grant through the Wilderness compare well with any soldiers of modern times.

The slaves were, as Lincoln later said, 'somehow the cause of the war,' but at the beginning they were denied any part in it, as were free Negroes. It is not surprising that until the last days of the war Confederate authorities rejected all proposals to use slaves as soldiers, opening the door to freedom; but it is strange that for almost two years Washington followed much the same policy. Congress was so sensitive to the feelings of the border states, and so indifferent to those of the Negroes, that it refused to enlist even free blacks. And when slaves found their way to the Union armies in Virginia or Tennessee federal officers frequently returned them to their former owners. However, the irrepressible General Benjamin F. Butler decided upon a different course. Commanding in New Orleans in the summer of 1862, he found his ranks depleted and informed the Secretary of War, 'I shall call on Africa to intervene, and I do not think I shall call in vain.' Within a few weeks the First Regiment Louisiana Native Guards was mustered into the federal service. Soon there were Negro regiments in all theaters. The First South Carolina, recruited from fugitive slaves who had escaped to the sea islands, was commanded by the preacher-soldier Thomas Wentworth Higginson, whose *Army Life in a Black Regiment* is one of the classics of Civil War literature.

After the Emancipation Proclamation it was thought logical to let any and all Negroes into the ranks. About 180,000 Negro soldiers enlisted in the Union armies, and almost 30,000 served in the navy; most of these were recruited from among the free Negroes of the North. Boston witnessed the stirring spectacle of the 54th Massachusetts Infantry swinging down its flag-decked streets— William Lloyd Garrison in the reviewing stand— to the very wharf whence less than ten years earlier the fugitive Anthony Burns had been returned to slavery. Some 50,000 of the black soldiers, refugees from slavery, fought under special handicaps. As Higginson tells us:

They fought with ropes around their necks, and when orders were issued that the officers of colored troops

Union volunteer, 1861, photographed by Mathew Brady. When on 15 April 1861, Lincoln issued a call for 75,000 volunteers, the response was overwhelming. In Iowa some men walked for ten days to reach the recruiting center, and twenty times as many volunteers offered themselves as could be accepted. Those who were rejected would not return home, and the state had to plead with Washington to expand its quota. (*Library of Congress, Brady Collection*)

The 107th U.S. Colored Infantry. (*Library of Congress*)

should be put to death on capture, they took a grim satisfaction. It helped their *esprit de corps* immensely.

Black soldiers took part in every theater of the war—at Battery Wagner guarding the harbor of Charleston, where Robert Gould Shaw fell at the head of his regiment; in the bayous of Louisiana; along the Missouri borderlands; and at Nashville, where they helped shatter Hood's command. In part because they were more susceptible to such diseases as dysentery and tuberculosis, their losses—66,000 deaths—were proportionately higher than those suffered by white troops.

Liberty in Wartime

Lincoln wielded a greater power throughout the war than any English-speaking ruler between Cromwell and Churchill. If Lincoln was the ideal tyrant of whom Plato dreamed, he was nonetheless a dictator from the standpoint of American constitutional law and practice. The war power of the President as commander-in-chief of the army and navy is, in practice, limited only by public opinion and the courts. At the very beginning of the war, Lincoln of his own authority called for enlistments not yet sanctioned by Congress, proclaimed the blockade, and suspended the writ of habeas corpus in parts of Maryland. The first assumption of power was shortly legalized by Congress, the second by the Supreme Court; but Chief Justice Taney protested in vain against executive suspension of the writ (*ex parte* Merryman). At the same time military officers, acting under orders from the state or the war department, began to arrest persons suspected of disloyalty or espionage, and to confine them without trial in military prisons for indefinite terms. Lincoln thought it unwise to indulge a meticulous reverence for the Constitution when the Union was crumbling. He asked, 'Must I shoot a simple-minded soldier boy who deserts, while I must not touch a hair of the wily agitator who induces him to desert?' Lincoln himself counseled moderation, but the power he wielded was grossly abused by subordinates.

Simultaneously with the Emancipation Proclamation, the President announced that all persons resisting the draft, discouraging enlistment, or 'guilty of any disloyal practice affording aid and comfort to rebels' would be subject to martial law, tried by court-martial, and denied the writ of habeas corpus. Under this proclamation, over 13,000 persons were arrested and confined by military authority, for offenses ranging from the theft of government property to treason. Earlier in 1862 President Davis, who was open to the same charge of behaving on occasion like a dictator, obtained from his Congress the power to suspend the writ of habeas corpus, and promptly did so in Richmond and other places, where arbitrary and unjust proceedings occurred.

Undoubtedly the provocation was great, especially in the North, where opposition to the war was open and active. The copperheads, as the Northern opponents of the war were called, worked ceaselessly to discourage recruiting and to hamstring the government. In the Confederacy, the 'Heroes of America' gave aid and comfort to the enemy. In Ohio, Indiana, and Illinois, where treason flourished side by side with the most stalwart loyalty, General Burnside attempted repression in 1863 with slight success. For violating Burnside's order against 'declaring sympathy for the enemy,' the prominent copperhead Clement Vallandigham was arrested, tried by a military commission, and sentenced to confinement for the duration of the war. Lincoln altered the sentence by having Vallandigham escorted within the military lines of the Confederacy. He received *in absentia* the Democratic nomination for governor of Ohio and conducted a campaign for peace and reunion from Canadian soil. In 1866 the Supreme Court took cognizance of a similar case (*ex parte* Milligan), and ruled that neither the Constitution nor any custom of war could sanction the military trial of a civilian in districts where the civil courts were open. But this decision, coming after the war, helped nobody.

Owing to unchecked acts of over-zealous military officers, personal liberty was subject to a more arbitrary, if spasmodic, control during the Civil War than during the two world wars. Yet on the whole pacifists, conscientious objectors, and critics of the government fared better under Lincoln than under Wilson, and the 'relocation' of Japanese-Americans in World War II was more outrageous than anything that happened under Lincoln. Throughout the Civil War there was no general censorship of the press, and hardly a Northern community lacked a few 'unterrified Democrats' who maintained with impunity that Jeff Davis was a better man than Abe Lincoln, secession was legitimate, and the Union forever dissolved.

Although in the field of civil and political liberties, the Confederate record was better than that of the Union, the habits of command bred in a slave society expressed themselves in aggravated form. Military commanders like General Braxton Bragg established martial law and ruled their areas with an iron hand. Hordes of provost marshals infested the land, demanding credentials from all who attracted their suspicion. Loyalty oaths were exacted indiscriminately—even from aliens—and neutrals and Unionists were badly treated. These practices, however, proved futile either to put down Unionism or arrest defeatism in the Confederacy.

Northern Industry and Westward Expansion

It was an article of faith among subjects of King Cotton that Northern industry, cut off from its Southern markets and its supply of fiber, would collapse. On the contrary, Northern industry grew fat and saucy during the war. Union sea power maintained the routes to foreign markets; the waste of war stimulated production. The government, generous in its contracts and lavish in expenditure, helped to create a new class of profiteers, who became masters of capital after the war.[3] The North, prepared to endure the deprivation of war, was startled to find it was enjoying a

3. The foundations of the Armour (meat packing), Havemeyer (sugar), Weyerhaeuser (lumber), Huntington (merchandise and railroads), Remington (guns), Rockefeller (oil), Carnegie (iron and steel), Borden (milk), and Marshall Field (merchandise) fortunes were laid during the war.

war-boom, an experience which would be a common phenomenon in the twentieth century. After the middle of 1862 enough cotton was obtained from the occupied parts of the South, and even brought from Liverpool, to re-open many cotton mills. Indeed the only essential Northern industry that suffered from the war was the carrying trade.

In many ways the war served as a stimulus to economic growth in the North. The drain of men into the army and navy was compensated for by immigration, which during the five war years amounted to almost 80,000, and labor-saving devices, invented before the war, were now generally applied. The Howe sewing machine proved a boon to the clothing manufacturer, though a curse to the poor seamstress, and the Gordon McKay machine for sewing uppers to shoe-soles speeded up that process one hundredfold and revolutionized the industry. Petroleum, discovered in Pennsylvania in 1859, developed so rapidly that kerosene lamps had begun to replace candles and whale oil by 1865. New industries sprang up to meet the army's insatiable demand for food: Gail Borden supplied condensed milk, the packing houses of Armour and Morris provided meat, and the Van Camp Company experimented with canned vegetables to frustrate the threat of scurvy.

Like causes speeded up the revolution in agriculture. The mechanical reaper came into general use, giving every harvest hand fivefold his former capacity with scythe and cradle. The annual pork pack almost doubled, the annual wool clip more than tripled between 1860 and 1865. The opening up of new prairie wheatfields was greatly stimulated by the Homestead Act of 1862, which supplemented the Pre-emption Act of 1841 by offering a settler title to 160 acres of public land after five years' residence and use, for a nominal fee. To be sure, the government disposed of most of the best prairie land to corporations and speculators and when the settler reached the Great Plains he usually found that if he wanted to buy a farm with fertile soil and that was near transportation he required to take his crops to market, he had to deal with a land jobber. Nonetheless, the wartime enactment did serve to expedite the advance of the trans-Mississippi frontier.

Development of the West continued. Colorado, the goal of the 'Pikes Peak or Bust' gold rush in 1859, was organized as a territory in 1861; and with the reorganization of Dakota and Nevada territories the same year, no part of the United States, on paper at least, was any longer outside the dominion of law. Kansas became a state in 1861; and Nevada was admitted prematurely in 1864, because the Republicans thought they needed its electoral vote. At least 300,000 emigrants crossed the plains during the war—some to farms, others to seek gold, and many to escape the draft.

The normal growth and activity of a civilized community carried on in the North. Enrollment in the universities hardly decreased beyond the loss of Southern students, although in some of the Western colleges the undergraduates enlisted in a body for short tours of service. Fifteen new institutions of higher learning, including Cornell University, Swarthmore College, and the Massachusetts Institute of Technology, were founded in wartime. The Harvard-Yale boat-races, interrupted in 1861, were resumed in 1864 while Grant was besieging Petersburg, and not a single member of either crew enlisted.

Paying for the War

To finance the war, Secretary Chase resorted to three methods: taxes, loans, and paper money. Congress doubled the customs duties, laid a direct tax of $20 million, and imposed numerous excise taxes. Most important for the future was the decision to levy an income tax. The merchant prince A. T. Stewart paid $400,000 on an income of $4 million, yet the income tax brought in only a meager $55 million during the entire war. And all taxes raised under $675 million in four years, less than the cost of one year of fighting. Inevitably Chase had recourse to borrowing. Altogether the government borrowed some $2.6 billion, enough to pay for three-fourths of the cost of the war. Secretaries Chase and Fessenden (who succeeded Chase when he went to the Supreme Court) relied on banks to take up most of their bonds on terms that brought rich rewards. Even at that Chase had difficulty in disposing of bonds until the Philadelphia banker Jay Cooke—who played a role analogous to that of Robert Morris in the Revolution—undertook to sell them directly to the public.

Casting about for a method of easy financing, Congress, in 1862, authorized the treasury to issue $150 million of legal tender. Before the war was over the treasury had issued some $450 million of these 'greenbacks.' Because they were not redeemable in gold, and the government itself refused to accept them in payment of customs duties, greenbacks speedily depreciated. In mid-summer 1864 they fell to 39 on the gold dollar; and though they rose to 74 after Appomattox it was not until the treasury 'resumed' specie payments in 1879 that they finally reached par.

Chase's banking policy was more constructive. At the beginning of the war some 1500 banks with charters issued by 29 states operated under a bewildering variety of privileges and restrictions. No fewer than 7000 different kinds of bank notes were circulating, alongside another 5000 varieties of fraudulent notes. To bring some order out of this chaos, to provide a national currency, and to assure a regular market for government bonds, Chase recommended a national banking system. Under the National Bank Acts of 1863 and 1864 member banks were required to invest one-third of their capital in government bonds (on which they were paid a handsome interest); they could then issue notes up to 90 per cent of the value of these bonds (on which they could earn handsome profits). The scheme was useful to the government, profitable to the banks, and convenient to the public. Competition from state banks ended in 1865 when Congress taxed their notes out of existence, and by October 1865 over 1500 banks had joined the new national banking system.

The South in Wartime

Compared with the Union, the Confederacy was more nearly a nation in arms. During four years war was its only business. Fighting for independence and the supremacy of the white race, Southerners gave their government more, and asked of it less, than did Northern people. Yet the Southern cause met hostility and indifference too. In the mountainous regions of North Carolina and Tennessee no Confederate conscription officer dared show his face. Much more costly were the inveterate provincialism and widespread ignorance, the stiff-necked insistence on the rights of states and of social position, and withal a certain shrewd instinct on the part of the poor whites that it was 'a rich man's war and a poor man's fight.'

The history of conscription illustrates these attitudes. The Confederate system was, in theory, a mass levy of manhood between the ages of 18 and 35. Yet, instead of prompting solidarity, it fomented class antagonism and doubts about its constitutionality. There was no answer to Senator Foote's question, 'If agents of the Confederate Government had the right to go into any state and take therefrom the men belonging to that state, how were state rights and state sovereignty to be maintained?' The Chief Justice of North Carolina even discharged two deserters who killed a man when resisting capture, on the ground that a state had nothing to do with enforcing Confederate conscription! In Georgia, Governor Joseph E. Brown openly defied conscription, withholding Georgia soldiers for the defense of the state. A week before the fall of Atlanta, as Sherman poised for his march to the sea, Brown recalled 10,000 men he had 'loaned' to General Hood and sent them home for 30 days to harvest the crops. When the Confederate Congress exempted plantation overseers, at the rate of one to every twenty slaves, there arose a great clamor from the democracy. Deeply resented too was substitution, which was stopped toward the close of 1863 when the price of a substitute reached 6000 paper dollars. Though no Southern city was disgraced by draft riots like those of New York, fraud and evasion were widespread, and remoter districts were terrorized by armed bands of deserters and draft-dodgers who waged a successful guerrilla warfare against the troops sent to apprehend them.

Even when the South had resources it was rarely able to exploit them, and as Union armies penetrated ever more deeply, the resource base of the Confederacy shrank dangerously. Union advances imperilled food supplies and cut the Confederacy off from key cities like New Orleans. Inadequate railways also segmented the nation. At the outbreak of the war the Confederacy boasted some 9000 miles of rails, compared to 22,000 miles in the North, turned out only 4 per cent of the country's locomotives, and had in-

'The Walking Wounded' by Winslow Homer. In 1861 *Harper's Weekly* sent the twenty-three-year-old artist to the front, where he was appalled by what he witnessed. This drawing, in pen and brown ink on paper, James Thomas Flexner has observed, 'expressed horror with a spare misery of line that presaged the World War I protests of the Expressionist George Grosz.' (*Cooper-Hewitt Museum, Smithsonian Institution*)

adequate repair facilities. Through traffic hardly existed; at 'bottle-necks' like Knoxville, freight had to be carted from one station to another. Between Danville, Va., and Greensboro, N.C., a 40-mile gap interrupted a main line into the interior. Without an engineering tradition, the Confederacy was unable either to organize the transportation it had or to rebuild it when shattered. That is why there were bread riots in Richmond when the barns of the valley of Virginia were bursting with wheat.

The Confederacy also mismanaged finances. Deluded by faith in the indispensability of cotton, the government deliberately withheld its most valuable single asset from foreign markets, and restricted cultivation. Too late did the government change its policy and buy cotton for export or for security against foreign loans. The Confederacy raised only about one per cent of its revenue from taxation. Tax receipts did not exceed $27 million, while expenditures ran to a couple of billion dollars. The gap between income and outgo was

Clara Barton (1821–1912), in a photograph by Mathew Brady. In 1862 she gained permission 'to go upon the sick transports in any direction, for the purpose of distributing comforts for the sick and wounded, and nursing them.' Though the 'Angel of the Battlefield' won renown for her courage under fire in ministering to the wounded, her significance lies less in her role as a nurse than as an organizer of relief. On returning from the Franco-Prussian war, where her service earned her the Iron Cross of Merit, she led a campaign that resulted in the establishment of the American Red Cross and became its first president. Her experience spanned much of the history of the republic, for her father fought under Mad Anthony Wayne and she lived well into the twentieth century. (*Library of Congress, Brady Collection*)

bridged by bonds and by treasury notes payable in gold on the acknowledgment of independence by the United States. By January 1864 Confederate paper was worth five cents on the dollar, and even before Lee's surrender it had become practically worthless. As a consequence of the resort to paper money and a shortage of certain staples, prices rose to fantastic levels: by 1864 flour was $500 a barrel. The government in vain tried to fix maximum prices, and blockade runners often imported luxuries for profiteers rather than necessities for the army. In desperation the Confederate government resorted to a form of confiscation, bitterly antagonizing the farmers on whom it bore unfairly.

After noting these many instances of selfishness, indifference, incompetence, and defeatism on both sides, we must remember that both the Union and Confederate governments were sustained by popular suffrage in 1862 and 1864, and that no earlier war in modern history drew out so much sacrifice, energy, and heroism. Vice-President Stephens divined the situation in 1863 when he wrote, 'The great majority of the masses both North and South are true to the cause of their side. . . . A large majority on both sides are tired of the war; want peace. . . . But as we do not want peace without independence, so they do not want peace without union.' The average American loathed army life and only acquiesced because of patriotism and social compulsion. Union soldiers sang 'When This Cruel War Is Over,' while their enemies in gray sang the equally sentimental 'Lorena,' and both rejected the 'fighting' ballads printed by patriots behind the lines. Yet both fought gallantly to the end.

Casualties

In the Union army 67,058 were killed on the field of battle, and 43,012 died from wounds; 224,586 died from disease and 25,566 more from accidents and miscellaneous causes—a total of 360,222. Confederate losses from battle probably reached 80,000 or 90,000 and deaths from disease 160,000 to 180,000.

Illness took an appalling toll from both armies. The average soldier was sick enough two or three times a year to be sent to a hospital, which was often more dangerous than the battlefield: deaths from disease were more than twice as high as deaths from battle—but we should remember that in the Mexican War the ratio was ten to one! Poor sanitation, impure water, wretched cooking, exposure, lack of cleanliness, and sheer carelessness exposed soldiers on both sides to dysentery, typhoid, malaria, and consumption—the chief killers. Care for the wounded was haphazard and callous: after Shiloh and Second Bull Run the wounded were allowed to lie for two or three days on the battlefields without relief. Antisepsis was unknown and anesthetics were not always available; abdominal wounds and major amputations meant probable death. Out of a total of 580 amputations in Richmond in two months of 1862 there were 245 deaths. Katherine Wormeley, later a distinguished literary figure, wrote of one of the hospital transports to which the wounded were brought during the Peninsular campaign:

We went on board; and such a scene as we entered and lived in for two days I trust never to see again. Men in every condition of horror, shattered, and shrieking, were being brought in on stretchers borne by contrabands who dumped them anywhere, banged the stretchers against pillars and posts, and walked over the men without compassion. There was no one to direct what ward or what bed they were to go into. Men shattered in the thigh, and even cases of amputation, were shovelled into top berths without thought or mercy.

It was thought not quite respectable for women to nurse soldiers, and the armies relied at first on male nurses and orderlies, mostly untrained. The heroic Dorothea Dix was appointed Superintendent of Nurses at the beginning of the war, and over 3000 intrepid women volunteered to work under her, but the army did not welcome their services. Clara Barton, 'Angel of the Battlefield,' nursed the wounded. Confederate medical skill was no worse than that of the Union, but lack of drugs, anesthetics, and surgical instruments imposed pitiful difficulties and losses.

18

The Civil War: The Test of Arms

*

1861–1865

Terrain, Tactics, and Strategy

Civil War battles were fought in rough, forested country with occasional clearings—Antietam, Gettysburg, Fredericksburg, Shiloh, and Vicksburg were the only big battles in open country. The defending infantry is drawn up in a double line, the men firing erect or kneeling. Preceded by a line of skirmishers, the attacking force moves forward by brigade units of 2000 to 2500 men, covering a front of 800 to 1000 yards, in double rank; captains in the front rank, the other officers and non-coms in the rear to discourage straggling. Normally the attack moves forward in cadenced step and is halted at intervals to fire and reload—a slow business with old-fashioned muzzle-loading rifles—the enemy returning fire until one or the other gives ground. Occasionally the boys in blue, more often the boys in gray, advance on the double-quick, the former shouting a deep-chested 'Hurrah!', the latter giving vent to their 'rebel yell,' a shrill staccato hunting cry. An attack of this sort generally ends in a bayonet encounter; but both sides, ill-trained in bayonet work, prefer to club their muskets. There was slight attempt at concealment, and so little entrenchment until 1863 that the moments of actual combat were more deadly to officers and men than the battles of World War I; but as soon as contact was broken the men were comparatively safe. Between encounters, picket guards, and even whole units of men, fraternized.

Union strategy, aggressive by the nature of the cause, took a form dictated by the geography of the Confederate States. The Appalachians and the Mississippi river divided the Confederacy into three nearly equal parts: the eastern, western, and trans-Mississippi theaters of war. The most spectacular campaign came in that part of the eastern theater bounded by North Carolina, the Appalachians, the Susquehanna, and Chesapeake Bay. Here were the two capitals, Washington and Richmond, and between them a rough wooded country, crossed by numerous streams and rivers. Although destruction of the enemy's army, not occupation of the enemy's capital, is considered the proper object in warfare, in a civil war, especially, possession of the enemy capital is of immense moral value. The Union expended more effort in trying to capture Richmond than on all its

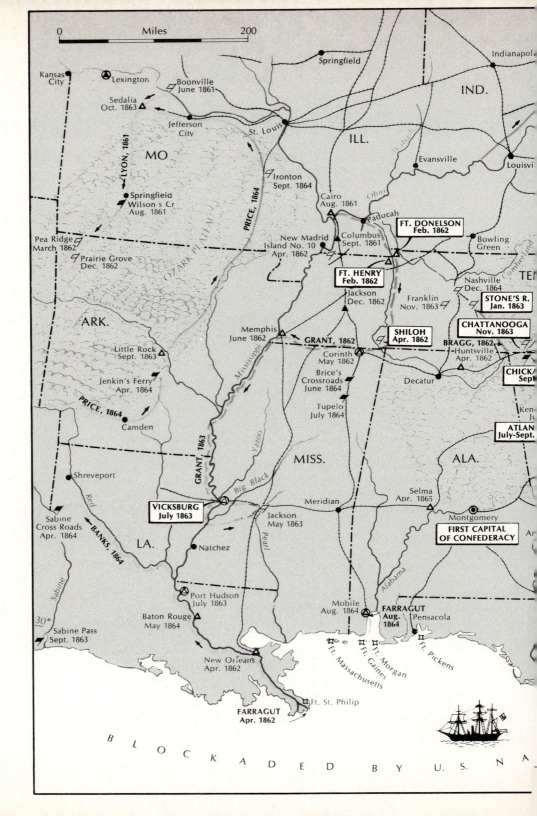

0   Miles   200

Springfield

Indianapol

IND.

Kansas City

Lexington

Boonville June 1861

Sedalia Oct. 1863

Jefferson City

St. Louis

ILL.

Evansville

Louisvi

MO

LYON, 1861

Springfield Wilson's Cr. Aug. 1861

Ironton Sept. 1864

Cairo Aug. 1861

Ohio

Paducah

PRICE, 1864

New Madrid Island No. 10 Apr. 1862

Columbus Sept. 1861

FT. DONELSON Feb. 1862

Bowling Green

Pea Ridge March 1862

Prairie Grove Dec. 1862

OZARK PLATEAU

FT. HENRY Feb. 1862

Nashville Dec. 1864

TEN

Cumberla

Jackson Dec. 1862

Franklin Nov. 1863

STONE'S R. Jan. 1863

ARK.

Arkansas

Memphis June 1862

GRANT, 1862

SHILOH Apr. 1862

CHATTANOOGA Nov. 1863

Little Rock Sept. 1863

Corinth May 1862

Brice's Crossroads June 1864

BRAGG, 1862 Huntsville Apr. 1862

CHICKA Sept.

Jenkin's Ferry Apr. 1864

Decatur

PRICE, 1864

Camden

Tupelo July 1864

Ken Ju

ATLAN July-Sept.

GRANT 1863

MISS.

ALA.

Shreveport

Big Black

Yazoo

Selma Apr. 1865

Red

VICKSBURG July 1863

Jackson May 1863

Meridian

Montgomery

Sabine Cross Roads Apr. 1864

BANKS, 1864

LA.

Natchez

Pearl

Alabama

FIRST CAPITAL OF CONFEDERACY

Ar

Sabine

30°

Sabine Pass Sept. 1863

Port Hudson July 1863

Baton Rouge May 1864

Mobile Aug. 1864

FARRAGUT Aug. 1864

Pensacola

Ft. Pickens

Ft. Morgan

Ft. Gaines

New Orleans Apr. 1862

Ft. Massachusetts

Ft. St. Philip

FARRAGUT Apr. 1862

B L O C K A D E D   B Y   U. S.   N A

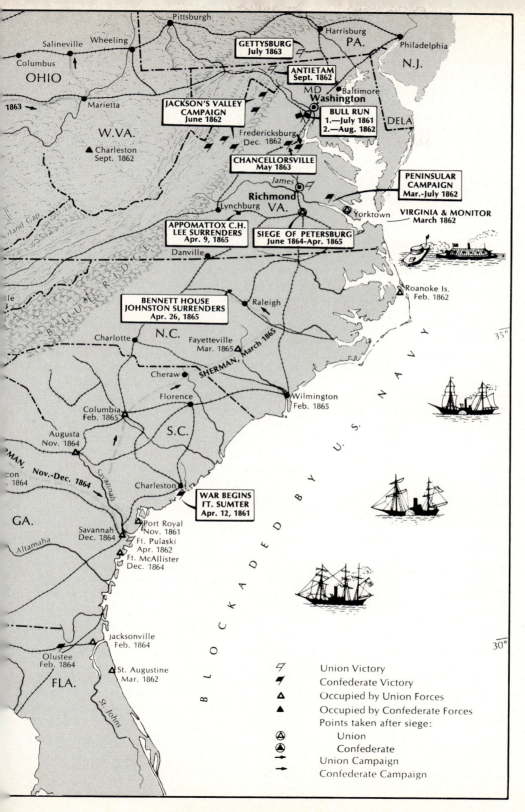

The Civil War, 1861–1865

other operations combined, while the Confederacy in turn allowed its military strategy to be determined by the supposed necessity of defending its capital. In the retaliating threats to Washington, the Shenandoah-Cumberland valley, pointing like a long cannon at the heart of the Union, became the scene of dashing raids and military exploits. Military operations beyond the Mississippi had little effect on the result. But the western theater of war between the Mississippi and the Appalachians was as important as the eastern. Lee might perform miracles in Virginia, and even carry the war into the enemy's country; but when Grant and the gunboats had secured the Mississippi, and Sherman was ready to swing round the southern spurs of the Appalachians into Georgia, the Confederacy was doomed. Control of the sea was a priceless asset to the Union. The navy maintained communications with Europe, cut off those of the South, captured important coastal cities, and on the Western rivers—and as Lincoln put it, 'wherever the ground was a little damp'—co-operated with the army. A threefold task lay before the Union forces: constriction, scission, and defeat of the Southern armies. Both the nature and the magnitude of the task were imperfectly apprehended in 1861, except by Winfield Scott, whose 'anaconda policy' of constriction was dismissed as the ravings of an old fogey, but eventually adopted, in principle, by Grant.

The War in 1861

The Union plan for 1861 was to blockade the Southern coast and occupy strategic points along its edge; to mobilize a volunteer army in regions convenient for invading the South; and to capture Richmond. By July some 25,000 three-month volunteers were at Washington, spoiling for a fight, and the Northern press and people clamored for action. Against Scott's advice, President and cabinet yielded to the cry of 'On to Richmond.' General Irvin McDowell, with a 'grand army' of 30,000, crossed the Potomac to seek out Beauregard's army of some 22,000 near Manassas Junction, Virginia. A throng of newspaper correspondents, sight-seers on horse and foot, and congressmen in carriages came out to see the sport.

On 21 July McDowell attacked Beauregard near a small stream called Bull Run. The troops on both sides were so ill-trained, the officers so unused to handling large numbers, the opposing flags so similar, and the uniforms so varied that extraordinary confusion ensued. For hours it was anyone's battle, but the timely arrival of 9000 Confederate reinforcements and the stand of General Thomas Jackson (who thereby earned the sobriquet Stonewall) won the day. Union retreat turned to rout. All next day, soldiers straggled into Washington, dropping down to sleep in the very streets; rumors were flying that Beauregard was in hot pursuit, that the Capitol would be abandoned; treason was preached openly. But Lincoln did not flinch, and Beauregard did not pursue. 'The Confederate army was more disorganized by victory than that of the United States by defeat,' wrote General Johnston. There was no more talk of a 90-day war. From the dregs of humiliation the Union was nerved to prepare for a long war; while the South, believing her proved superiority would dissolve the Northern 'hordes' and procure foreign recognition, indulged in an orgy of self-applause.

At this point, on 24 July 1861, Lincoln summoned General McClellan to Washington and gave him command of the army in that department. George B. McClellan was only 34, a graduate of West Point on the eve of the Mexican War, in which he had distinguished himself. His subsequent business experience accustomed him to deal with large affairs; his personal magnetism and some easy successes in western Virginia made him a popular hero. The Northern states provided him plenty of three-year volunteers, Congress was generous with money and equipment, and the President supported him fully. No untried general in modern times has had such abundant means as McClellan enjoyed during the nine months that followed Bull Run; and few used them to so little profit when the time came to fight. McClellan's methodical mind, his appetite for work, and his attractive personality and genuine interest in his men were exactly the qualities needed to form an army from a mob. But he lacked perception of the democratic medium. His love of display, the French princes on his staff, frequent mention of 'my army,' a curt way with politicians, and his contempt for Lincoln seemed out of place in a republican soldier. ('Never mind,' said Lincoln of the affronts he received, 'I will hold McClellan's horse if he will only bring us success.') McClellan forever dreamed of the future in terms of self: victorious McClellan, dictator McClellan, President McClellan. Yet no Union general was so beloved by the untrained volunteers whom his talent turned into a superb instrument of war, the Army of the Potomac.

Weeks stretched into months, and 'All quiet along the Potomac' appeared so often in the head-lines as to become a jest. When McClellan esti-mated the enemy's number at 150,000, the Con-federate army in northern Virginia was less than 50,000 strong and wretchedly equipped. Still, Lincoln refused to let the politicians worry him into ordering an advance. In fact on 1 November he appointed McClellan general-in-chief of all the armies of the republic. But McClellan continued to mark time. 'If General McClellan does not want to use the army,' said the President, 'I would like to *borrow* it.' A mere victory, McClellan believed, would be indecisive; but one dramatic coup such as the capture of Richmond, if accompanied by satis-factory assurances as to slave property, would win back the South. 'I shall carry the thing *en grande,* and crush the rebels in one campaign,' he wrote his young and adoring wife. If McClellan's 'one big victory' concept was mistaken, his strategy of delay was correct. The Union needed to postpone offensives until its superior resources were or-ganized for a war of attrition and constriction; the Confederacy needed to force an issue promptly.

On the Confederate side, Lee, and probably J. E. Johnston, had the right instinct of aggression; but they were overruled by President Davis's pol-icy of defense and delay.

Naval Action

In naval strategy, the policy of constriction was so obvious that it was consciously applied from the first. On 19 April 1861, Lincoln proclaimed a blockade of the Southern ports. But the following day brought a naval counterpart to Bull Run. The navy yard at Norfolk, which the United States government had not reinforced for fear of offend-ing Virginia, was captured without a blow by the troops of that state, together with enormous stores of ordnance, munitions, and the hull of the frigate *Merrimac*—promptly rebuilt and chris-tened *Virginia.*

The navy department then awoke, and Gideon Welles gave the navy much more efficient direc-tion than the army received. However, the prob-lem of blockading 3550 miles of coastline seemed at first insoluble. Congress had begun to build a new steam navy in 1850; but as yet only 24 steamers had been placed in commission, and only two were actually available to guard the Atlantic coast in April 1861. Without waiting for Congress to assemble, the administration undertook a large construction program, and side-wheelers, screw steamers, clipper ships, tugboats, and even ferryboats were purchased. Before the end of the war the navy totaled almost 700 ships, manned by over 50,000 seamen. And in David Glasgow Far-ragut, with 50 years of service, the nation found a naval hero in the tradition of John Paul Jones.

It was a paper blockade for two or three months and not wholly effective for more than two years; but by the end of July 1861 four blockading squad-rons were stationed off the seven or eight enemy ports that were commercially important. About 800 vessels entered and cleared from Confederate ports during the first year of the blockade; but the last year of peace had seen more than 6000. In the last half of 1861 the navy captured Cape Hatteras and Hilton Head on the sea islands off Port Royal, S.C., the only important Union victory of that year.

The achievement of the hastily improvised Union navy on inland waters was no less impor-tant. Mississippi and Ohio river steamboats were converted to transports for Union campaigns, and Western energy and ingenuity created an effective fleet suited to the special needs of Western war-fare. James B. Eads, an engineering genius from St. Louis, launched a fleet of armored gunboats, and Charles Ellet built a fleet of ironclad rams which, in the summer of 1862, destroyed the entire Confederate river defense fleet guarding Memphis and captured that city. Captain Andrew H. Foote, commander of naval operations on the

The intrepid Confederate blockade-runner *Nashville* sets afire the *Harvey Birch*, a captured Union merchant vessel, in the English Channel. (*Peabody Museum of Salem*)

Mississippi, built some 40 mortar-boats. These ugly little rafts carrying mortar-guns capable of hurling a 230-pound shell over two miles did terrible damage to the river towns that stood high on the bluffs above the Mississippi.

The Attitude of Europe

The British and French had an avid interest in the Civil War. They divided, on the whole, along class lines. The plain people of Europe for the most part were convinced that destruction of the Union would be a mortal wound to democracy. To the ruling classes, however, the United States had long been obnoxious for the encouragement its success afforded to radicals and democratic reformers. 'An involuntary instinct, all-powerful and unconquerable,' wrote the Comte de Montalembert, 'at once arrayed on the side of the pro-slavery people all the open or secret partisans of the fanaticism and absolutism of Europe.' Many Englishmen even outside that category favored the South for, as Henry Adams wrote, 'the English mind took naturally to rebellion—when foreign.' Most liberals supported the North, but some, like the historian Lord Acton, could see no difference between the Southern struggle for independence and the nationalist movements in

Europe with which they had sympathized. Humanitarians, who would have welcomed a war against slavery, were put off for nearly two years by the repeated declarations of Lincoln and Seward that slavery was not the issue. Shipping interests hoped for the ruin of their most formidable competitor and approved a new cotton kingdom for which they might do the carrying trade. However, the efforts of statesmen like Bright and Cobden, intellectuals like John Stuart Mill, and American emissaries such as Henry Ward Beecher and Archbishop Hughes, as well as the march of events, rallied British opinion eventually to the support of the Union.

Southern expectations of victory were based in good part upon the belief that Britain and France would break the blockade to get cotton. By the decade of the 1850's over 80 per cent of British cotton came from America. No wonder Senator Hammond of South Carolina could boast that 'you dare not make war upon our cotton. No power on earth dares make war upon it. Cotton is King.' Yet, as it turned out, this was short-sighted. By April 1861 there was a 50 per cent oversupply of cotton in the English market. Furthermore Britain was able to get cotton from Egypt and India. So instead of demanding intervention to get more cotton, the big textile interests of England and France welcomed the opportunity to work off surplus stocks and to free themselves from dependence on the American supply. It was the working-men of Lancashire and Yorkshire who suffered most from the cotton blockade; by the winter of 1862 some 330,000 operatives were out of work. The South had assumed that these would join with the manufacturers in demanding that Britain break the blockade, but they rallied instead to the support of the Union. That winter the working-men of Manchester assured President Lincoln that 'our interests are identified with yours. . . . If you have an ill-wishers here, be assured they are chiefly those who oppose liberty at home, and that they will be powerless to stir up quarrels between us.' Moreover, the Civil War years saw poor wheat and corn harvests in Europe and exceptionally good harvests in the United States. If Britain's looms depended on Southern cotton, her dinner tables depended on American grain; British im-

ports of American wheat rose from 17 million bushels in 1860 to 62 million in 1862. It was evident that any attempt to break the blockade, and consequently fight the United States, would bring the British Isles face to face with starvation. 'Old King Cotton's dead and buried, brave young Corn is King,' went the refrain of a popular song.

The South also ignored the traditional British doctrine of naval warfare. As Lord John Russell wrote, the American blockade satisfied principles that the Royal Navy had always observed; and in view of England's dependence on sea power, it would be highly imprudent for her to insist on different principles which might hamper her in the future. Lord Palmerston's government issued a proclamation on 13 May 1861 which declared 'strict and impartial neutrality' in the contest between 'the Government of the United States of America and certain states styling themselves the Confederate States of America.' This proclamation was greatly to the advantage of the Union, but its unprecedented mention of a rebel government by its chosen name seemed unfriendly to the North and raised false hopes of recognition in the South. In fact the British position was, and remained throughout the war, technically correct. There was no recognition of the South; Southern emissaries were never officially received; and delivery of ships built or under construction in British shipyards for the Confederacy was stopped—on protest from the American minister.

Yet there were episodes that threatened a serious break. The first was the *Trent* affair. The British mail steamer *Trent* was conveying to Southampton two Confederate diplomatic agents, J. M. Mason and John Slidell, when on 8 November 1861 she was boarded from the U.S.S. *San Jacinto*, Captain Charles Wilkes commanding, and the two Confederates seized and jailed. When the news reached England, the British clamored for a showdown, the government sent reinforcements to Canada, and Lord John Russell drafted a demand for apology and reparation in terms so offensive as to be unacceptable. Fortunately Prince Albert, then in his last illness, toned down Russell's dispatch, and Queen Victoria made it clear that she wanted peace. And by a notable dispensation of Providence the Atlantic cable had ceased to function. Seward from the first saw that Mason and Slidell must be surrendered; but Lincoln, fearing the political effect of yielding to Britain, required persuasion. Seward's note to the British minister, designed more to placate the American public than the British, contained no apology; but Mason and Slidell were released and forwarded to their uncomfortable posts. In the end the *Trent* episode cleared the air. Seward now appeared in the new role of conciliator—and found that he liked it; an Anglo-American war had been faced and ruled intolerable to both governments; and the British cabinet was stiffened in its policy of neutrality.

Plans and Personalities

Day by day McClellan's inaction increased Lincoln's political difficulties. The united spirit forged by the guns that fired on Fort Sumter had disintegrated. Lincoln was challenged in his own party by conservatives and by the radicals led by 'Ben' Wade, 'Zach' Chandler, and 'Thad' Stevens. A diverse group which differed on many issues, the Radicals were united in their hatred of the insolent slave power. By their zeal they helped transform the war from a struggle to put down an insurrection to a crusade for human rights, but their politics were often maladroit and even nasty. The policy they wished to force upon the President was immediate emancipation and arming of the slaves—a policy which, if adopted in 1861, would have alienated the Northern Democrats and driven the border slave states into secession. General Frémont's pretense to free the slaves in Missouri by proclamation, an act which Lincoln sternly rebuked, received their hearty approbation, whilst McClellan, even more conservative than Lincoln on the slavery question, was the particular object of their jealousy and suspicion.

To the Radical standard surged the uncompromising, who dominated the Joint Committee on the Conduct of the War created by Congress on 20 December 1861. Throughout the war their inquisitorial activities, *ex parte* investigations, and missions to the front hampered the executive, undermined army discipline, and encouraged less

Ulysses S. Grant (1822–85). Critics disparaged his slovenly appearance, and when he came to Washington in 1864 to confer with the President he seemed to Richard Henry Dana 'a short, round-shouldered man, in a very tarnished . . . uniform . . . no station, no manner . . . and rather a scrubby look withal.' But Lincoln said, 'I can't spare this man. He fights.' (*National Archives, Brady Collection*)

competent generals. Yet the Radicals differed in one crucial respect from Jefferson Davis's gadflies. While Davis's opponents often valued particularist interests more highly than winning the war, the Radicals energetically supported the war and indeed wished to enlarge its aims.

Owing to the efforts of another House committee, corruption on a gigantic scale was uncovered in the war department, and the scandal smirched Secretary Cameron. Lincoln sent him on a foreign mission and appointed a 'War Democrat,' Edwin M. Stanton, Secretary of War. Gloomy, ill-mannered, and vituperative, Stanton was another cross for Lincoln to bear. Ignorant of military matters and contemptuous of military science, intolerant of delay and harsh to subordinates, he was hated by almost every officer with whom he came in contact; and with several he dealt injustly. Yet for all that, Stanton's determination and thoroughness made him a fit instrument for Lincoln's purpose.

The first substantial victory for the Union came in an unsuspected quarter, from an unknown general. Ulysses S. Grant, an officer who disliked war and loathed army routine, had fallen on evil days since the proud moment before Mexico City. After promotion to a captaincy he resigned from the army to avoid a court-martial for drunkenness. Unable to extract a living from 'Hardscrabble Farm' near St. Louis, he attempted to sell real estate, and failed again. His father bestowed a clerkship in the family leather store at Galena, Illinois. Brothers condescended, fellow townsmen sneered. Only after many rebuffs did he obtain a colonelcy of volunteers in 1861. His regiment was promptly ordered to dislodge a Confederate regiment under a Colonel Harris. Approaching the reported position, so Grant relates, fear gripped his heart; but he had not the moral courage to halt and consider what to do. Suddenly there opened a view of the enemy's encampment—abandoned! 'It occurred to me at once that Harris had been as much afraid of me as I had been of him. This was a new view of the question I had never taken before; but it was one I never forgot afterwards.'

In August 1861 Grant received a brigadier's commission and in late autumn was stationed at Cairo, Ill., at the junction of the Ohio with the Mississippi. Less than 50 miles up the Ohio from Cairo the Tennessee and Cumberland rivers opened parallel routes into Tennessee, Alabama, and Mississippi. Grant observed that capture of Fort Henry and Fort Donelson, the two Confederate earthworks which closed these rivers, would open navigable waterways into the enemy's center and drive in his flanks. On 7 February 1862 a gunboat flotilla reduced Fort Henry. A week later, Grant made exactly the right tactical disposition in the fierce battle to wrest control of Fort Donelson. The result justified Grant in asking and the Confederate generals in agreeing to 'unconditional surrender'[1] of army and fortress. Grant had practically restored Tennessee to the Union; and, if his victory were followed up, the whole area would be open from Chattanooga to the Mississippi. Equally important was the moral gain to the then dispirited North. The prairie boys of the new Northwest had tried their mettle, and the legend of Southern invincibility collapsed.

But 'Unconditional Surrender' Grant's jealous and pedantic superior, General Halleck, instead of allowing him to pursue Albert Sidney Johnston, held up his advance and withdrew his troops to attack the northernmost Confederate strongholds on the Mississippi. On 6 April Johnston caught Grant napping, encamped in an ill-chosen position at Pittsburg Landing. His rear to the swollen Tennessee and his front unprotected by entrenchments, Grant had the Battle of Shiloh forced upon him. If the Union army was not routed in the first twelve hours, it was due less to Grant's steadfast coolness than to the fiery valor of divisional commanders like William Tecumseh Sherman and to the pluck of individual soldiers. By the end of the day the Confederates had captured a key position and thousands of stragglers were cowering under the bluffs. But Albert Sidney Johnston was mortally wounded, leaving the Confederates leaderless. After ten hours of desperate fighting the next day, the Confederate army withdrew.

Shiloh was a Union victory at a dreadful price. Out of 63,000 Union troops, the loss was 13,000; the Confederates lost 11,000 out of 40,000. Pres-

---

1. Actually it was the astonishing Ben Butler, at Hatteras Inlet in August 1861, who first used this term, which has become a controversial one since World War II.

Sailors on the deck of the U.S.S. *Monitor*, James river, Virginia, July 1862. The cylindrical structure is the revolving gun turret, which was introduced in the first battle between armored naval vessels four months before when the *Monitor* encountered C.S.S. *Virginia*, formerly U.S.S. *Merrimac*, at Hampton Roads. (*Brady Collection, Library of Cognress*)

sure was put upon the President to remove Grant, but Lincoln replied: 'I can't spare this man; he fights.' However, Halleck took command of his army in person, and in consequence little more was accomplished by the army during 1862 in this western theater of the war.

While Halleck temporized, Captain Farragut had to force his way up the Mississippi from the Gulf without a single ironclad, but in the small hours of 24 April Farragut's column of eight steam sloops-of-war and fifteen wooden gunboats, with chain cables secured as a coat of mail abreast the engines, crashed through a log boom and ran a gantlet of armored rams, fire-rafts, river defense fleet, and two forts. Two days later United States forces took possession of New Orleans, largest and wealthiest city of the Confederacy. Farragut then proceeded up-river to join the gunboat fleet above Vicksburg. But as Halleck could not be induced to provide troops for a joint attack on Vicksburg, that 'Gibraltar of the Mississippi' held out for a year longer, enabling Richmond to maintain communication with Arkansas, Missouri, and Texas.

The Confederacy was tightly pinched along its waistline; but the blood could still circulate. Thanks to the fumbling of Halleck the Union offensive in the West had failed in its great purpose, yet thanks chiefly to Grant it accomplished much of value. That was more than could be said of the grand campaigns of this year in the eastern theater of war.

The Peninsular Campaign

'In ten days I shall be in Richmond,' declared General McClellan on 13 February 1862. It was one of those rash boasts that made men doubt either his judgment or his sincerity. All he actually did was march his men to the deserted Confederate headquarters at Manassas, which he found abandoned, then march them back again to Washington. For Lincoln this was all but the last straw. Still, when McClellan proposed a wide flanking movement by the York peninsula, the President reluctantly acquiesced. But he stripped McClellan of his superior command and left him with forces inadequate for his ambitious plans. Nonetheless, the Army of the Potomac, well armed and 110,000 strong, was greatly superior to anything the Confederacy could organize.

McClellan's peninsular plan had one obvious advantage, that it enabled the Union army to be supplied and reinforced by sea. The navy could protect the army's right flank as it advanced up the peninsula. On its left flank the James was a better line of approach; but C.S.S. *Virginia* (ex U.S.S. *Merrimac*) closed it to the Union navy during the first weeks of the campaign. The *Virginia* met her equal in the *Monitor* in Hampton Roads on 9 March 1862, when a new principle of naval armament, the revolving turret, proved its worth. But

so long as the *Virginia* was afloat she protected the mouth of the James.

McClellan intended to take Richmond and crush the rebellion that summer. Splendid visions were in his brain. Himself, on prancing charger, entering Richmond in triumph. Magnanimous terms to the gallant enemy: civil rights restored, slave property guaranteed. Discomfited administration not daring to refuse ratification. Grand review at Washington. Modest savior of his country resigns sword to Congress and returns to wife and baby at Cincinnati. Nominated by acclamation for President in 1864. Yet he did not employ the only methods that had the slightest chance of realizing these dreams: mobility and dash. His caution allowed the Confederates to withdraw in good order to the defense of Richmond.

Still it was difficult to see how Richmond could be saved. McClellan with over 100,000 men would soon be advancing up the York peninsula, and J. E. Johnston had less than 60,000 to oppose him. McDowell with 40,000 was before Fredericksburg with only 11,000 Confederates between him and McClellan's right flank. The repulse of Stonewall Jackson near Kernstown had apparently corked up the Shenandoah valley. Frémont with 15,000 was approaching the upper valley through the Appalachian passes, where only 3000 Confederates faced him. Upon Lee's advice President Davis on 16 April adopted the strategy of delaying McClellan until Jackson could frighten the Union government into recalling McDowell's corps from its advanced position. On the same day the Confederate Congress adopted conscription. Of doubtful constitutionality, this courageous act drove a wedge between Davis and his state-rights critics, who feared that their precious theory was being done to death in the house of its friends. But conscription retained in the ranks the men who saved Richmond.

By 14 May McClellan was within three days' march of Richmond. Lee, instead of recalling the scattered legions of the Confederacy to her capital, had the audacity to use Jackson to break up McClellan's plans by threatening Washington. Jackson returned to the upper valley, got around behind Banks, crushed his outposts (Front Royal, 22 May), administered a stinging defeat at Win-

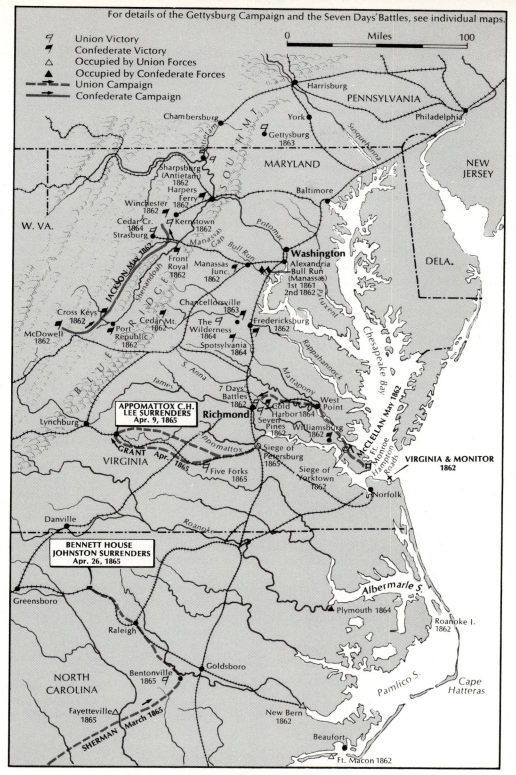

For details of the Gettysburg Campaign and the Seven Days' Battles, see individual maps.

Legend:
- Union Victory
- Confederate Victory
- △ Occupied by Union Forces
- ▲ Occupied by Confederate Forces
- Union Campaign
- Confederate Campaign

0   Miles   100

PENNSYLVANIA

Harrisburg

York

Chambersburg

Gettysburg 1863

Philadelphia

NEW JERSEY

MARYLAND

Sharpsburg (Antietam) 1862

Harpers Ferry 1862

Winchester 1862

Baltimore

Cedar Cr. 1864

Kernstown 1862

Strasburg

DELA..

Manassas Gap

Bull Run

Front Royal 1862

Manassas Junc. 1862

Washington

Alexandria

Bull Run (Manassas) 1st 1861 2nd 1862

JACKSON MAY 1862

Shenandoah

Cross Keys 1862

McDowell 1862

Cedar Mt. 1862

Port Republic 1862

Chancellorsville 1863

The Wilderness 1864

Fredericksburg 1862

Spotsylvania 1864

BLUE RIDGE

SOUTH MT.

Potomac

Patuxent

Rappahannock

Chesapeake Bay

W. VA.

James

S. Anna

7 Days' Battles 1862

Mattapony

West Point

APPOMATTOX C.H. LEE SURRENDERS Apr. 9, 1865

Richmond

Cold Harbor 1864

Seven Pines 1862

Williamsburg 1862

McCLELLAN May 1862

Lynchburg

GRANT Apr. 1865

VIRGINIA

Appomattox

Five Forks 1865

Siege of Petersburg 1865

Siege of Yorktown 1862

Ft. Monroe

Hampton Roads

VIRGINIA & MONITOR 1862

Norfolk

Danville

Roanoke

BENNETT HOUSE JOHNSTON SURRENDERS Apr. 26, 1865

Albermarle S.

Greensboro

Plymouth 1864

Roanoke I. 1862

Raleigh

NORTH CAROLINA

Bentonville 1865

Goldsboro

Pamlico S.

Cape Hatteras

Fayetteville 1865

SHERMAN March 1865

New Bern 1862

Beaufort

Ft. Macon 1862

The Eastern Theater of War, 1862–1865

chester, and sent him whirling north to the safe side of the Potomac (25 May). Washington was panic-stricken by Jackson's rapid advance, although shielded by double his numbers. Lincoln did exactly what Lee intended him to do: on 25 May he recalled McDowell's corps, on the point of marching to join McClellan. Jackson, after winning successive victories on 8 and 9 June, was then ready to transfer his army to the Richmond front, while large Union forces remained immobile in the valley to protect Washington from another attack of nerves.

After this Battle of Fair Oaks (or Seven Pines), McClellan dug himself into a stronger position and waited for fair weather to advance on Richmond under cover of superior artillery. On 1 June Robert E. Lee succeeded Johnston, who had been wounded, and named his force the Army of Northern Virginia. He saw that McClellan must win Richmond if he were permitted to choose his own 'species of warfare' and that the closing cordon must be broken. Lee seized the offensive and threw McClellan upon the defensive.

On 26 June Lee took the initiative, and the great Seven Days' battles[2] began. Lee's strategy was superb, but too ambitious for his army to execute. McClellan, outnumbered in effective force at the beginning of the Seven Days, inflicted a superior loss on his adversaries[3] and executed a brilliant withdrawal to the James river. To be sure, he had to give up his cherished plan to capture Richmond. Yet his army was still full of fight and ready to resume the advance on Richmond if properly reinforced. The summer was still young. McClellan entreated Lincoln to give him an opportunity to attack Richmond via Petersburg. But General Halleck (who had replaced Stanton in control of operations) pronounced this plan, by which Grant subsequently brought the war to an end, impracticable; and Lincoln feared he could no longer carry McClellan. The country could see nothing except

2. Mechanicsville (26 June), Gaines's Mill or first Battle of Cold Harbor (27th), Savage Station (29th), Frayser's Farm or Glendale (30th), Malvern Hill (1 July).
3. Union effectives engaged, 91,169; Union loss (killed, wounded, and missing), 15,849. Confederate effectives engaged, 95,481; Confederate loss, 20,614. T. L. Livermore, *Numbers and Losses*, p. 86.

that Richmond was still in rebel hands after a costly campaign. Accordingly, on 3 August, Halleck ordered the Army of the Potomac back to the river that gave it birth; and all the gains of the Peninsular campaign were thrown away. Not for over two years did another Union army approach so near Richmond.

The Emancipation Proclamation

For Lincoln the slavery question was complicated. He always remembered what it seemed all the world had forgotten, that he was President of the United States—not of the Northern States. His policy was explained in a letter to Horace Greeley, editor of the New York *Tribune*, of 22 August 1862:

As to the policy I 'seem to be pursuing,' as you say, I have not meant to leave any one in doubt. I would save the Union. I would save it the shortest way under the Constitution. The sooner the national authority can be restored, the nearer the Union will be 'the Union as it was.' If there be those who would not save the Union unless they could at the same time save slavery, I do not agree with them. If there be those who would not save the Union unless they could at the same time destroy slavery, I do not agree with them. My paramount object in this struggle is to save the Union, and is not either to save or to destroy slavery. If I could save the Union without freeing any slave, I would do it; and if I could save it by freeing all the slaves I would do it; and if I could save it by freeing some and leaving others alone, I would also do that. What I do about slavery, and the colored race, I do because I believe it helps to save the Union; and what I forbear, I forbear because I do not believe it would help to save the Union.

From the first advance into Southern territory, slaves of rebel owners had flocked into the Union lines, embarrassing both government and commanders, until the ingenious Ben Butler declared them 'contraband of war.' The 'contrabands' were organized in labor battalions, and school teachers were provided to look after their welfare. When Union forces captured the sea islands between Charleston and Savannah in November 1861, the cotton planters fled, and their plantations and some 10,000 slaves came under the jurisdiction of the Treasury, which conducted an 'experiment in

Private Edwin Francis Jennison, Georgia Infantry, killed at Malvern Hill. A Wisconsin soldier wrote of this 1862 engagement in the Seven Days which cost Lee's army more than 20,000 casualties: 'Charge after charge is made on our artillery . . . till they lie in heaps and rows. . . . The slaughter is terrible, and to add to the carnage, our gun boats are throwing their murderous missiles with furious effect.' (*Library of Congress*)

reconstruction.' Betrayed by their enemies and sometimes by their friends, the blacks nonetheless demonstrated that they could participate in a free society in which they owned property and earned wages. After the war some of the returning planters found themselves borrowing money from their former slaves.

Lincoln moved cautiously but deliberately toward emancipation, though against stout resistance. The border states blocked proposals for compensated emancipation on which the President had set his heart, and not until April and June 1862 did Congress finally carry out a party pledge by abolishing slavery in the District of Columbia and the territories. 'The moment came,' said Lincoln, 'when I felt that slavery must die that the nation might live.' In the cabinet meeting on 22 July he proposed to declare that on the next New Year's Day all slaves in rebel territory would be free. Seward pointed out that such a proclamation at such a time would be interpreted as 'our last shriek on the retreat' from Richmond. Emancipation was then put aside to be a crown to the first victory.

Yet if the decisive moment had to be postponed, Lincoln had attained new stature. Resolute in purpose and sure of vision he had always been; but often vacillating and uncertain in performance. From those anxious vigils at the White House during the Seven Days the perplexed, over-advised, and humble Lincoln emerged humble only before God, but the master of men. He seemed to have captured all the better qualities of the great Americans who preceded him, without their defects: the poise of Washington without his aloofness, the astuteness of Jefferson without his indirection, the conscience of J. Q. Adams without his harshness, the forthrightness of Jackson without his ignorance, the magnetism of Clay without his vanity, the lucidity of Webster without his ponderousness; and fused them with a magnanimity peculiarly his own. Lincoln would have full need of all these qualities, for his time of troubles had already begun.

After overwhelming the Army of the Potomac under the headstrong and inept General John Pope at the second Battle of Bull Run, or Manassas (29 August–1 September 1862), thereby undoing the Union gains of an entire year in Virginia, Lee prepared to carry the war onto Northern soil. With Virginia clear of invaders, Lee early in September crossed the Potomac above Washington into Maryland. Of many crises for the Union, this was the most acute. In the West a Confederate offensive was unraveling the work of Grant; if it succeeded, Kentucky would be secured for the Confederacy, and a Southern invasion of Ohio might follow. Lee expected to win Maryland for the Confederacy; but his prime objective was capture of the railway bridge over the Susquehanna at Harrisburg, Pa. That would come perilously near cutting the Union in two, leaving Washington connected with the West only by the roundabout Atlantic Ocean, Hudson river, and Great Lakes route. The victorious Southern army would be in a central position to attack Washington, Baltimore, or Philadelphia. President Davis, on Northern soil, would propose peace on the basis of Southern independence; and if Lincoln's government refused they would have to reckon with the people in the November election and face the likelihood of foreign intervention. On 7 September the French minister at Washington informed Seward that it was time to recognize the independence of the Confederacy. Napoleon III was only waiting for English approval, which might well have come after another Confederate victory.

But Lee underestimated McClellan, whom Lincoln had put in 'command of the forces in the field.' On 13 September a soldier brought McClellan Lee's Order No. 191 setting forth in detail the whole plan of the campaign. It was one of those strokes of chance that changes the course of history. Moving decisively, McClellan caught the outnumbered Confederate forces in a cramped position between Antietam Creek and the Potomac, where Lee had no room to perform those brilliant maneuvers that were his delight and the enemy's confusion. The Battle of the Antietam or Sharpsburg (17 September) exhausted Lee's army, but when McClellan refused to renew the battle the next day, Lee was able to recross the Potomac into Virginia. McClellan had missed the opportunity for a knockout. Yet by restoring morale to the army, and through the lucky break of the lost

Union prisoners at Salisbury, North Carolina, 1862. They are playing baseball, appropriately enough, for the man usually credited with inventing the game, Abner Doubleday, was a Union general who distinguished himself in the first years of the War. *(Stokes Collection, New York Public Library)*

order, he had frustrated Lee's campaign and parried the most serious thrust at his country's heart. Antietam averted all danger of foreign recognition of the Confederacy; and by giving Lincoln the opportunity he sought to issue the Emancipation Proclamation, it brought the liberal opinion of the world to his side.

On 22 September 1862, five days after Antietam, Lincoln opened a momentous cabinet meeting. He had not summoned his cabinet for advice, he said. He had made a covenant with God to free the slaves as soon as the rebels were driven out of Maryland; God had decided on the field of Antietam. Cabinet members from border slave states thought the moment inopportune; the President reminded them that for months he had urged their states to take the initiative in emancipation. In the Preliminary Emancipation Procla-

mation the President, by virtue of his power as commander-in-chief of the army and navy, declared that upon the first day of January 1863 all slaves within any state or district then in rebellion against the United States 'shall be then, thenceforward, and forever free.' This proclamation, potentially more revolutionary in human relationships than any event in American history since 1776, lifted the Civil War to the dignity of a crusade. Though at the outset it did not actually free any slaves—for it did not apply to loyal border states—it did indicate that slavery would not survive Union victory.

Yet it was slow to influence public opinion at home or abroad. The South, indignant at what was considered an invitation to the slaves to cut their masters' throats, was nerved to greater effort. The Northern armies received from it no new impetus. The Democratic party, presenting it to the Northern people as proof that abolitionists were responsible for the duration of the war, made signal gains in the autumn elections. Julia Ward Howe saw in it the glory of the coming of the Lord; but in England and Europe the proclamation was greeted by conservatives with contempt, as a flat political maneuver, though by liberals with joy. However, Antietam and its aftermath did convince Palmerston's ministry that the moment was inopportune for intervention. So passed the second great crisis in foreign relations.

The Diplomatic Front

A third round of foreign crises resulted from the failure of Union generalship. Public opinion in the North was not so much grateful to McClellan for what he had done as indignant because he had let Lee escape. When Lincoln ordered McClellan to 'cross the Potomac and give battle to the enemy, or drive him South,' the General clamored for supplies and clothing and bandied words. The prospect of another winter of bickering and procrastination was more than the President could bear; and the fall elections had begun. Lincoln decided that if McClellan permitted Lee to get between him and Richmond, McClellan must go. Lee did just that; and on 7 November the President relieved McClellan of command of the Army of the Potomac and appointed Burnside in his place.

Distinguished chiefly for his flowing side-whiskers, Burnside proved monumentally incompetent. Learning nothing from experience, he reverted to the old plan of a 'covering advance' on Richmond, only to have Lee post a mighty army of 75,000 men and over 300 guns on the south bank of the Rappahannock, on the wooded heights above Fredericksburg. There, on 13 December, Burnside, with an army of 113,000, ordered a frontal attack on Lee's center, strongly entrenched on Marye's Heights. Six times the Union infantry—long double lines of blue, bright national and regimental colors, bayonets gleaming in the sun—pressed across an open plain completely covered by the Confederate artillery and entrenched riflemen. Six times the survivors were hurled back, leaving the dead and wounded lying in heaps. The slaughter was appalling and one-sided: Burnside lost 12,700 men, Lee 5400. 'It is well that war is so terrible,' said Lee as he watched the battle, 'or we should grow too fond of it.'

The interventionist forces in Europe, encouraged by Fredericksburg, began to make trouble again in 1863. In June a French army took Mexico City, and the next year the unfortunate Maximilian of Austria accepted the imperial crown of Mexico from France. Thus the Civil War gave Napoleon III an opportunity to perform the feat of which Talleyrand had dreamed: to re-establish European influence in North America. Slidell, the Southern agent in Paris, offered Confederate support to the Emperor in Mexico, and in January 1863, Napoleon III proposed a peace conference between North and South, with the object of establishing the Confederacy. Spain in a small way was pursuing a similar policy in Santo Domingo. France in Mexico, Spain in Santo Domingo, meant a counter-stroke of monarchial Europe against republican America, an after-clap of the Holy Alliance. Though the rally of liberal sentiment to the Union in England, France, and Spain as the meaning of the Emancipation Proclamation sank in was a powerful deterrent, Confederate partisans persisted. The British-built *Alabama* and *Florida* were destroying United States shipping; another English-built commerce-destroyer, the *Alexandria*, was almost ready for sea; and the Lairds were building two armored rams to break the Union blockade. But on 4 April Lord Russell ordered the detention of the *Alexandria*, and the prospects of the slave power dimmed.

Vicksburg to Gettysburg

In the end recognition of the Confederacy would be determined by military events. During the winter of 1862–63 all eyes were fastened on the struggle for the Mississippi. At Vicksburg and more than 100 miles to the south at Port Hudson, Louisiana, the Confederates had strongly fortified the bluffs bordering the river, and between them troops and supplies reached the heart of the Confederacy from Arkansas, Louisiana, and Texas.

A Confederate army camp in Louisiana. Note the orderly at the left of the picture approaching with liquid refreshment. (*Louisiana State University Archives, Baton Rouge*)

Vicksburg was a hard nut to crack, but the resolute Grant, with the aid of the audacious fresh-water navy, penned the enemy army. After a six-week siege, the 'Confederate Gibraltar' surrendered on 4 July. Five days later Port Hudson capitulated. Within a week a steamboat arrived at New Orleans from St. Louis, having passed the entire course of the Mississippi undisturbed by hostile shot or challenge. 'The Father of Waters,' Lincoln rejoiced, 'again goes unvexed to the sea.'

In the eastern theater 'Fighting Joe' Hooker, brave, vain, and unreliable, relieved Burnside after the Fredericksburg disaster. One hundred and thirty thousand strong, the Army of the Potomac was indeed 'the finest army on the planet.' Hooker did much to restore its morale, but on 27 April 1863, at Chancellorsville, Lee outsmarted him in one of the bloodiest battles of the war. The South, though, paid a heavy price for this victory—the loss of Stonewall Jackson, mortally wounded by his own men when reconnoitering between the lines. Lee had lost 'his right arm.'

Lee was soon ready for another spring at the enemy's throat, and by 27 June his entire army was in Pennsylvania. Lee anticipated that he could compel Lincoln to open peace negotiations on the basis of independence for the Confederacy. Chance placed the crucial battle where neither Lee nor General George Gordon Meade, who had replaced Hooker, wanted it. On 30 June a Confederate unit happened to come upon a Union cavalry division in a quiet little market town, Gettysburg. There, on 1 July, the great three-day battle began.

The first day went ill for the Union, until in the nick of time Winfield Scott Hancock, the greatest fighting general in the Army of the Potomac, rallied the men in blue on Cemetery Ridge. On the next evening (2 July) the Confederacy had a great opportunity when Jubal Early broke the Union defenses on Cemetery Ridge and Ewell stormed up a slope on the Union right, but both were hurled back. The following afternoon (3 July) Lee, against Longstreet's protest, ordered a direct attack on the strongest part of the Union center with Pickett's, Pettigrew's, and Trimble's divisions, 15,000 strong. Pickett rode up to Longstreet and asked, 'General, shall I advance?' Longstreet, unwilling to give the word, bowed his head. 'Sir, I shall lead my division forward,' said Pickett.

From Cemetery Ridge the Union troops saw three gray lines of battle issue from the wooded ridge three-quarters of a mile away and march with bayonets glittering and the colors of 47 regiments fluttering in the breeze into the valley below. When less than halfway across, the Union artillery opened up on them; a little nearer they

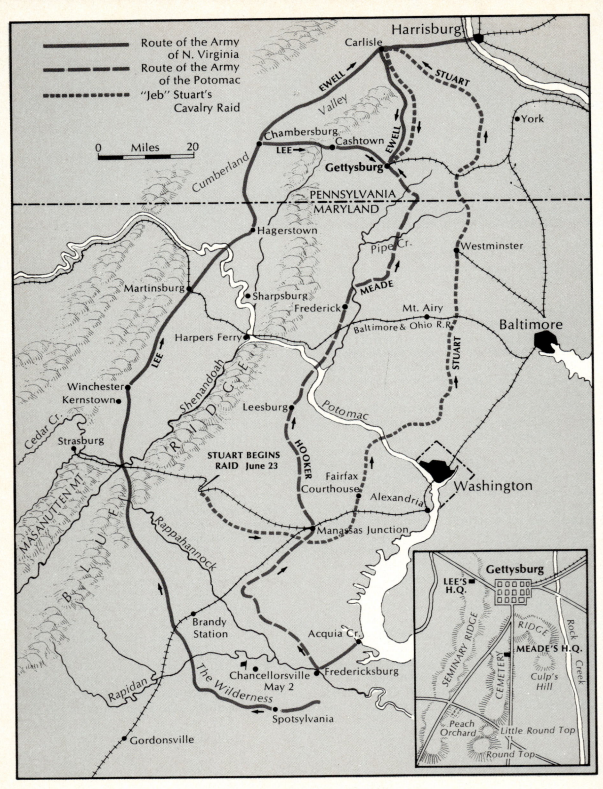

The Gettysburg Campaign, 27 June–4 July

came under raking fire from the batteries on Round Top. The flank divisions melted away; but the Northern troops, peering through the smoke, could see Pickett's men still coming on, merged in one crowding, rushing line. Lost for a moment in a swale, they emerged so near that the expression on their faces could be seen. 'The line springs,' wrote Frank Haskell of Meade's Second Corps. 'The crest of the solid ground with a great roar heaves forward its maddened load, men, arms, smoke, fire, a fighting mass. It rolls to the wall— flash meets flash, the wall is crossed, a moment ensues of thrust, yells, blows, shots, and undistinguishable conflict, followed by a shout universal, and the last and bloodiest fight of the battle of Gettysburg is ended and won.' Two of Pickett's brigadiers and fifteen of his regimental commanders were killed. General Armistead, with cap raised on point of sword, leaped the stone wall into the Union lines, a hundred men followed him, and for a brief moment the battle cross of the Confederacy floated on the crest of Cemetery Ridge. Then the Union lines closed in relentlessly and all Armistead's men were shot down or captured.

The next evening, 4 July, the climactic battle lost, Lee retired to a position west of Sharpsburg. There the flooded Potomac stopped his retreat and gave Meade an opportunity that Lincoln begged him to seize. 'Call no council of war,' telegraphed Halleck. 'Do not let the enemy escape.' Meade called a council of war, the Potomac fell, and the enemy got away. But Lee was too candid to congratulate himself for having escaped. He had seen the flower of his army wither under the Union fire. He knew that all hope for peace that summer was gone, and he must have felt that slight hope for Southern independence remained. Yet his soldiers gathered only confidence and resolution from the placid countenance of their beloved 'Marse Robert.' To President Davis Lee wrote, 'No blame can be attached to the army for its failure to accomplish what was projected by me, nor should it be censured for the unreasonable expectations of the public. I am alone to blame.' On 8 August he submitted his resignation as commander of the Army of Northern Virginia. 'To ask me to substitute you by some one more fit to command,' Davis answered, 'is to demand an impossibility.'

Four months later, when a national cemetery was dedicated on the battlefield of Gettysburg, Lincoln delivered his immortal address:

Fourscore and seven years ago our fathers brought forth on this continent a new nation, conceived in liberty, and dedicated to the proposition that all men are created equal.

Now we are engaged in a great civil war, testing whether that nation, or any nation so conceived and so dedicated, can long endure. We are met on a great battle-field of that war. We have come to dedicate a portion of that field as a final resting-place for those who here gave their lives that the nation might live. It is altogether fitting and proper that we should do this.

But, in a larger sense, we cannot dedicate—we cannot consecrate—we cannot hallow—this ground. The brave men, living and dead, who struggled here, have consecrated it far above our poor power to add or detract. The world will little note nor long remember what we say here, but it can never forget what they did here. It is for us, the living, rather, to be dedicated here to the unfinished work which they who fought here have thus far so nobly advanced. It is rather for us to be here dedicated to the great task remaining before us—that from these honored dead we take increased devotion to that cause for which they gave the last full measure of devotion; that we here highly resolve that these dead shall not have died in vain; that this nation, under God, shall have a new birth of freedom; and that government of the people, by the people, for the people, shall not perish from the earth.

Gettysburg and Vicksburg had momentous consequences. Lord John Russell impounded the Laird armored rams, from which the Confederacy hoped much, and Napoleon III, who now had second thoughts, ordered vessels destined for the Confederacy to be sold to foreign governments. The military results of these two great victories were even more important than the diplomatic. For with Lee's invaders repulsed and the Mississippi liberated, the North could concentrate all of its energies on a final strategy of conquest.

From Chattanooga to the Wilderness

The advance of the Army of the Cumberland toward Chattanooga in July 1863 began a campaign that ended only with Sherman's march to the sea and a division of the Confederacy. Chattanooga, after Richmond and Vicksburg, was the most vital point in the Confederacy—a key railway junction and the place where the Tennessee river breaks through the parallel ridges of the southern Appalachians. Once in possession of Chattanooga, the Union armies might swing round the Great Smoky mountains and attack Atlanta, Savannah, Charleston, or even Richmond from the rear. When Lincoln made Grant supreme commander in the West, Grant ordered the loyal Virginian, George H. Thomas, 'the rock of Chickamauga,' to hold Chattanooga, which had been occupied in September, and on 24 November launched an offensive against the rebels. The capture of Missionary Ridge was perhaps the most gallant action of the war. Thomas's men, after driving the Confederates from the rifle-pits at the foot, were ordered to halt. Refusing to obey, they kept straight on up the steep rocky slope, overrunning a second and a third line of defense, rushed the Confederate guns on the crest, and turned them on the enemy; then, with Phil Sheridan leading, pursued the fleeing gray-coats down the eastern slope.

This Battle of Chattanooga placed the combined armies of the Tennessee and the Cumberland (Sherman and Thomas) in a position to advance into Georgia in the early spring. In May 1864 Sherman, in command of 100,000 men, opened his campaign, and by 2 September had captured Atlanta. On 17 October, after sending Thomas back to Nashville to cope with the fighting John B. Hood, who was imperilling the long, thin line of Union communications, the imperturbable Sherman cut loose in the opposite direction toward the sea, marching 62,000 men without supplies into the 'garden spot of the Confederacy.' The march to the sea was one of deliberate and disciplined destruction. Sherman's army cut a swath 60 miles through central Georgia, destroying stores of provisions, standing crops and cattle, cotton-gins and mills, railways and bridges, everything that could be useful to the Confederacy and much that was not. Many a Georgia family was stripped of its possessions; but outrages on persons were surprisingly few. It was the sort of campaign that soldiers love—maximum of looting and destruction, minimum of discipline and fighting: splendid weather, few impedimenta; broiled turkey for breakfast and fried chicken for supper. For a

month the North lost sight of Sherman. He emerged at Savannah on 10 December 1864 and was able to offer Lincoln the city as a Christmas present. Before the month was out, Thomas had added to the jubilation in the North by inflicting on Hood at Nashville the most smashing defeat of the war.

While Sherman and Thomas were carrying on this brilliant scission of the Confederacy, Grant was having rough going with Lee, whose prowess very nearly conquered the Northern will to victory in the summer of 1864.

On 9 March 1864 Grant was appointed general-in-chief of the armies of the United States. Summoned to Washington, where he had never been, to confer with Lincoln, whom he had never seen, this slightly seedy individual, perpetually smoking or chewing a cigar, caused some misgivings among those used to the glittering generals of the Army of the Potomac. Keener observers were impressed with Grant's rough dignity. He was the first of all the commanders in the East who never doubted the greatness of his President; and Lincoln knew that he had a general at last 'who would take the responsibility and act.'

Grant assumed personal direction of the Virginia campaign against Lee. 'I determined,' wrote Grant himself, 'to hammer continuously against the armed force of the enemy and his resources, until by mere attrition, if in no other way, there should be nothing left to him but submission.' On 4 May 1864 Grant marched his army of 102,000 through the tangled Wilderness. In the first Battle of the Wilderness (5–7 May), which cost Grant 17,700 men, Lee fought him to a draw. Grant then tried to outflank the enemy; but clouds of dust from his marching columns warned Lee of his intention and by the time his van reached Spotsylvania Court House, Lee was there to check him. Both armies threw up field entrenchments, and the five-day battle that followed (Spotsylvania, 8–12 May) was the first based on trench warfare. Grant lost 31,000 more men and a cry went up for his removal. He declared, 'I . . . propose to fight it out on this line if it takes all summer' and Lincoln stood by him. On 1–3 June came the Battle of Cold Harbor, a bloody Union assault upon the entire line of Lee's trenches.

General William Tecumseh Sherman (1820–91). This photograph was taken in 1865, the year of final Union victory following his 'march to the sea' of 1864 that made him a hero to the North but anathema to the South. (*National Archives, Brady Collection*)

Before going over the top the Union soldiers pinned papers on their backs, giving their names and addresses to identify their corpses. Eight or nine thousand men fell in a few hours, but hardly a dent was made on the Confederate lines.

War had now acquired many of the horrors that we associate with World War I. The wounded, unattended between the lines, died of thirst, starvation, and loss of blood. Corpses rotted on the ground. Sharpshooters kept up their deadly work.

Officers and men fought mechanically without hope. The war had begun so long ago that one could hardly remember what it was about.

In one month Grant had advanced from the Rapidan to the Chickahominy, the exact spot where McClellan had stood two years before, and he had lost from 55,000 to 60,000 men as against Lee's 25,000 to 30,000; but he could count on a continuous flow of reinforcements, and Lee could not. On 12 June Grant began a change of base to the James. With immense skill he ferried his vast army across that broad river, unmolested by Lee. But an opportunity to push into undefended Petersburg and thus outflank Richmond was lost. Lee slipped in by the interior lines, entrenched in time, and three assaults cost the Union 8000 more men (15–18 June). Grant's army sat down to besiege Petersburg and remained there for nine months.

A war of position had arrived. Lee, with an army that despised digging as unsoldierly and hated fighting from entrenchments, had developed the technique of trench warfare to a point that Europe reached only in 1916. He had saved his army and saved Richmond. Grant, after making mistakes and suffering losses that would have broken any of his predecessors, was still indomitable. But how long would the country suffer such stupendous losses with no apparent result? The country could not then appreciate what we now know, that Grant had brought the end near and had forced the Confederate government to concentrate its best efforts on supporting Lee, thereby denying Joseph Johnston the necessary reinforcements to stop Sherman's march to the sea. But in the summer of 1864 the appalling toll of casualties seemed to have brought the war no nearer conclusion, and through the presidential campaign that year there ran an undercurrent of doubt and despair.

The Presidential Election

Alone of democratic governments before World War II, the United States carried out a general election in wartime. Lincoln said, 'We cannot have free government without elections; and if the rebellion could force us to forego or postpone a national election, it might fairly claim to have already conquered and ruined us.' In June 1864 Lincoln was renominated for the presidency by acclamation by a National Union convention of Republicans and War Democrats; the 'Union' of the two groups was dramatized by the nomination of Andrew Johnson of Tennessee, a life-long Democrat, to the vice-presidency.

Yet within a few weeks a movement developed against Lincoln within his own party. Sherman was stalled in front of Atlanta; things were going badly in Virginia; Chase resigned from the cabinet and struck an alliance with political adventurers and marplots like General Butler, Roscoe Conkling, and Horace Greeley who had concluded that Lincoln could not win and it was necessary to name another ticket. In July the President and the radicals split over how to reconstruct the Union after the war. When Lincoln pocket-vetoed a bill embodying the radical views of reconstruction, Senator Wade and Representative Henry Davis issued a public manifesto denouncing the President. Greeley published this Wade-Davis Manifesto in the *Tribune* on 5 August; two weeks later, he and the radicals began to circulate a call for a new Republican convention to reconsider Lincoln's candidacy.

It was an alarming situation. Some of Lincoln's staunchest supporters thought the election already lost, and Republican leaders implored the President to make a peace move. Lincoln sent them away satisfied that he cared nothing for himself, but that so palpable a confession of weakness as an overture to Jefferson Davis, at that juncture, would be equivalent to surrender. What Lincoln really thought is clear from the paper he wrote and sealed on 23 August:

> It seems exceedingly probable that this administration will not be re-elected. Then it will be my duty to so co-operate with the President-elect as to save the Union between the election and the inauguration, as he will have secured his election on such ground that he cannot possibly save it afterward.

A week later the Democratic national convention adopted a resolution drafted by the Ohio copperhead Vallandigham calling for an end to hostilities and nominated General McClellan for President. He repudiated the peace plank but was willing to ride into the White House on a wave of opposition to war.

However, the wave soon subsided. Jefferson Davis by bluntly insisting on recognition of Southern independence as the price for peace, the Democrats by their defeatism, and Sherman by capturing Atlanta knocked the bottom out of the schemes of Lincoln's opponents. Lincoln's election, so doubtful in August, was conceded on every side in October. After Sheridan had devastated the Shenandoah valley, the Northern people, on 8 November, chose 212 Lincoln electors and only 21 for McClellan. Still, Lincoln's popular majority was only 400,000 in 4,000,000 votes.

'The election,' said Lincoln two days later, 'has demonstrated that a people's government can sustain a national election in the midst of a great civil war.'

The Collapse of the Confederacy

The re-election of Lincoln, the failure to obtain foreign recognition, the increasing pinch of the blockade, Sherman's march to the sea, and Grant's implacable hammering at the thin lines around Petersburg took the heart out of the South. By the start of 1865 the Confederacy was sinking fast. Even slavery was jettisoned—in principle. President Davis sent an envoy to Europe, in January 1865, to offer abolition in exchange for recognition, and on 25 March the Richmond Congress authorized arming black slaves. Sherman, as he marched northward, was proving his sulphurous synonym for war. 'Columbia!—pretty much all burned; and burned *good.*' Yet the doughty Sherman passed some anxious hours when he learned that Lee and his grim veterans were on the loose again.

For nine months Grant and Lee had faced one another across long lines of entrenchment in the outskirts of Petersburg. At the beginning of the siege their forces were not disparate; but by the middle of March 1865 Grant had 115,000 effectives to Lee's 54,000. Lee had to move out of his trenches before Grant enveloped him, though if Petersburg were abandoned, Richmond must fall. Lee's only hope was to retreat westward and unite

with Johnston, who commanded the remnants of his former army in North Carolina. On the night of 2–3 April Lee's army slipped out of the Petersburg lines; and the next evening the Union forces entered Richmond. Without pause Grant pursued. Sheridan blocked the Confederates' escape southward and westward. Lee's last hope was gone.

Lee ordered a white flag to be displayed and requested an interview with his opponent. The scene that followed, in a house of the little village of Appomattox Court House, has become a part of American folklore. Lee, in new full-dress uniform with jewel-studded sword, Grant in his favorite private's blouse, unbuttoned, and without a sword, 'his feelings sad and depressed at the downfall of a foe who had fought so long and valiantly.'

Formal greetings. Small talk of other days, in the old army. . . .

Grant writes the terms of surrender in his own hand. . . . Officers and men paroled . . . arms and matériel surrendered . . . not to include the officers' side-arms, and—

'Let all the men who claim to own a horse or mule take the animals home with them to work their little farms.'

'This will do much toward conciliating our people.'

The conference is over. Lee pauses in the doorway, looking out over a field blossoming with the stars and stripes. Thrice, and slowly, he strikes a fist into the palm of his gantleted hand. He mounts his horse Traveller and is gone.

A sound of cheering spreads along the Union lines.

Grant orders it to cease:

'The war is over; the rebels are our countrymen again.'

General Joshua Chamberlain, who received the surrender on behalf of Grant, recalled the moving scene:

Before us in proud humiliation stood the embodiment of manhood: men whom neither toils and sufferings, nor the fact of death, nor disaster, nor hopelessness could bend from their resolve; standing before us now, thin, worn, and famished, but erect, and with eyes looking level into ours, waking memories that bound us

A troubled Lincoln. This photograph by Mathew Brady was taken in May 1861, a month when the President felt compelled to call for a huge increase in the armed forces. As Benjamin P. Thomas has written, 'Lincoln's face began to reveal his inner torment as lines of travail etched his features.' (*Library of Congress, Brady Collection*)

together as no other bond;—was not such manhood to be welcomed back into a Union so tested and assured?

When the head of each division column comes opposite our group, our bugle sounds the signal and instantly our whole line from right to left, regiment by regiment in succession, gives the soldier's salutation, from the 'order arms' to the old 'carry'—the marching salute. Gordon at the head of the column, riding with heavy spirit and downcast face, catches the sound of shifting arms, looks up, and taking the meaning, wheels superbly, making with himself and his horse one uplifted figure, with profound salutation as he drops the point of his sword to the boot toe; then facing to his own command, gives word for his successive brigades to pass us with the same position of the manual—honor answering honor. On our part not a sound of trumpet more, nor roll of drum; not a cheer, nor word nor whisper of vain-glorying, nor motion of man standing again at the order, but an awed stillness rather, and breath-holding, as if it were the passing of the dead! . . . How could we help falling on our knees, all of us together, and praying God to pity and forgive us all![4]

The Last Days of Lincoln

. . . With malice toward none; with charity for all; with firmness in the right, as God gives us to see the right, let us strive on to finish the work we are in; to bind up the nation's wounds; to care for him who shall have borne the battle, and for his widow, and his orphan—to do all which may achieve and cherish a just and lasting peace among ourselves, and with all nations.

Thus closed the second inaugural address of President Lincoln on 4 March 1865. The struggle over reconstruction was already on. Truculent Ben Wade with his fierce hatred of the slaveholders, Democrats eager for revenge on the President, Charles Sumner with his passionate conviction that right and justice required the South to pass under the Caudine forks, were certain to oppose the terms with which Lincoln proposed to bind up the nation's wounds. But Congress would not meet until December. It might be confronted with the established fact of a restored nation, if the South were wise, if nothing happened to Lincoln.

On 11 April, two days after Lee's surrender, Lincoln delivered his last public address. In unfolding his reconstruction policy, he announced the most magnanimous terms toward a helpless opponent ever offered by a victor. For Lincoln did not consider himself a conqueror. He was, and had been since 1861, President of the United States. The rebellion must be forgotten, and every Southern state re-admitted to full privilege in the Union as soon as 10 per cent of the whites had taken the oath of allegiance and organized a state government.

On Good Friday, the 14th, the President held his last cabinet meeting. He urged his ministers to turn their thoughts to peace. There must be no more bloodshed, no persecution. Grant, who attended the meeting, was asked for late news from Sherman, but had none. Lincoln remarked that it would soon come and be favorable,[5] for last night he had had a familiar dream. In a strange indescribable ship he seemed to be moving with great rapidity toward a dark and undefined shore. He had had this same dream before Sumter, Bull Run, Antietam, Murfreesboro, Vicksburg, and Wilmington. Matter-of-fact Grant remarked that Murfreesboro was no victory—'a few such fights would have ruined us.' Lincoln looked at him curiously and said, however that might be, his dream preceded that battle.

Secretary Welles, who records this incident, may be our guide to the fearful events of that night. He had gone to bed early and was just falling asleep when someone shouted from the street that the President had been shot. After checking on the condition of Secretary Seward and his son, who had also been shot, he hurried down to 10th Street. The dying President had been carried across that street from Ford's Theatre to a poor lodging-house, where he was laid on a bed in a narrow back room. He never recovered consciousness. 'The giant sufferer,' writes Welles, 'lay extended diagonally across the bed, which was not long enough for him. . . . His slow, full respiration lifted the clothes with each breath that he took. His features were calm and striking.'

A little before half-past seven the great heart ceased to beat.

4. Joshua Chamberlain, *The Passing of the Armies*, pp. 258ff.

5. Johnston surrendered his army to Sherman 26 April. Jefferson Davis was captured 10 May. The last Confederate force surrendered 26 May.

The assassination of Abraham Lincoln, 14 April 1865. After firing his one-shot derringer point-blank at the President, John Wilkes Booth leaps from the balustrade upon the stage of Ford's Theatre and, brandishing a dagger, heads for the wings. In the box above, Lincoln slumps, mortally wounded, while the stunned audience, many of whom recognize Booth, gesticulate at him. (*New-York Historical Society*)

Welles continues, 'I went after breakfast to the Executive Mansion. There was a cheerless cold rain and everything seemed gloomy. On the Avenue in front of the White House were several hundred colored people, mostly women and children, weeping and wailing their loss. This crowd did not appear to diminish through the whole of that cold, wet day; they seemed not to know what was to be their fate since their great benefactor was dead, and their hopeless grief affected me more than almost anything else, though strong and brave men wept when I met them.'

The Heritage of War

Bow down, dear land, for thou has found release!
  Thy God, in these distempered days,
  Hath taught thee the sure wisdom of His ways
And through thine enemies hath wrought thy peace!
  Bow down in prayer and praise!

No poorest in thy borders but may now
Lift to the juster skies a man's enfranchised brow;
O Beautiful! My Country! Ours once more!

Thus James Russell Lowell, at the Harvard commemoration service of 1865, saluted, as he believed, a reunited nation purged by war of all grossness that had accompanied its rise to power. But the fierce passions of warfare had burned good with evil; and in the scorched soil the new growth showed tares as well as wheat. 'The Civil War marks an era in the history of the American mind,' wrote Henry James fourteen years after Appomattox. From the war, the American had gained a sense 'of the world being a more complicated place than it had hitherto seemed, the future more treacherous, success more difficult.'

The North had fought the war for three purposes: Union, freedom, and democracy. At the outset, preservation of the Union had been the main goal, but after 1862 the abolition of slavery came to be a second acknowledged objective. And to many, in Europe as in America, the maintenance of a 'government of the people, by the people, for the people' was a third.

Union had been preserved, but it could not be said that the old Union had been restored. The long dispute over the nature of the Union had been settled, at last, in favor of the nationalist contention, but it had required force to bring that about. Nor had sectionalism disappeared. In the generation after the war, to the North and South was added a third powerful section—the trans-Mississippi West. Until well into the next century American political life was to be conditioned by this division of North, South, and West.

Slavery, to be sure, was gone, but emancipation, too, had been brought about by violence. Perhaps this was the only way slavery could have been ended, but even the most ardent champions of freedom were forced to admit that the method was painful for white and black alike. Moreover, slavery gave way not to freedom but to a kind of peonage. Not for another hundred years after the breakdown of Reconstruction were most Negroes to enjoy even in part those rights which the war and the new constitutional amendments had attempted to assure them.

What shall we say of the third objective—

government of, by, and for the people? Democracy, indeed, had not 'perished from the earth,' yet for a brief interval Americans witnessed what they had never known before: military government in time of peace. The Civil War had destroyed slavery and the slaveholding class; but within a few years corporate industry would wield excessive power. Twenty years after the attack on Fort Sumter the railroads alone represented a greater investment and concentration of power than the slave interest ever had. Justice John M. Harlan of the Supreme Court, looking back upon this period, remembered that 'there was everywhere among the people generally a deep feeling of unrest. The nation had been rid of human slavery . . . but the conviction was universal that the country was in real danger from another kind of slavery, namely the slavery that would result from aggregations of capital in the hands of a few.'

The cost of the war had been colossal. Deaths from all causes in the two armies totaled some 620,000, and thousands more were wounded. How many lives were lost because of malnutrition, disease, and the chaotic conditions of 1865 and 1866, it is impossible to say, nor can we count the lives shattered by destruction and demoralized by defeat. The money cost of the war was staggering; proportionally higher, indeed, than that of World War I. Loans and taxes raised by the Federal Government came to nearly $3 billion, and the interest on the Civil War debt an additional $2.8 billion. The Confederacy floated loans of over $2 billion, but the total financial loss of the South, in property confiscated, depreciated, and destroyed, in the losses of banks and insurance companies and businesses, and in the expense of reconstruction, was incalculable. Many states, North and South, went heavily into debt for the prosecution of the war. And the country continued to pay for the war well into the twentieth century: United States government pensions amounted to almost $8 billion, and Southern states doled out additional sums to Confederate veterans. The total cost of the war to North and South may be estimated at well over $20 billion— five times all the expenditures of the Federal Government from 1789 to 1865!

The material problems of the war could be met;

the moral devastation was never wholly repaired. During the war violence and destruction and hatred had been called virtues; it was a long time before they were again recognized as vices. The war had brutalized combatants and non-combatants alike. Ruthlessness and corruption had accompanied the conflict, and they lingered on to trouble the postwar years. Above all, the war bred animosities that affected men, Northern and Southern, for over a generation.

But the revolution wrought by the war also offered the nation an opportunity to right the grievous wrongs done to the blacks and to make this country one truly dedicated to the principles of equality. In the years after the war, for the first time, the power of the national government was employed to extend the civil rights of the Negro. One may well doubt whether, had it not been for the war and Reconstruction, even a century later there would be constitutional guarantees of these rights. Only at this unique juncture in history, when the South was subjugated and the North felt some of the equalitarian spirit of the war, was it possible to write provisions into the Constitution designed to achieve these ends. If Reconstruction ultimately failed, it at least left a legal foundation for subsequent struggles against inequality.

19

Reconstruction

*

1865–1877

The Prostrate South

Four years of warfare had devastated the South. Over large sections of the country, Union and Confederate armies had tramped and fought. From Atlanta to Savannah and from Savannah to Raleigh, Sherman had left a broad belt of blackened ruin: 'where our footsteps pass,' wrote one of his aides, 'fire, ashes, and desolation follow in the path.' Sheridan had swept down the fertile Shenandoah valley like an avenging fury. 'We had no cattle, hogs, sheep, or horses or anything else,' wrote a native of Virginia. 'The fences were all gone... the barns were all burned; chimneys standing without houses and houses standing without roofs, or doors, or windows... bridges all destroyed, roads badly cut up.' In the West, conditions were just as bad. The Governor of Arkansas wrote of his state: 'The desolations of war are beyond description.... Besides the utter desolation that marked the tracks of war and battle, guerilla bands and scouting parties have pillaged almost every neighbourhood.'

Some of the cities presented a picture as appalling as the countryside. Charleston had been bombarded and partially burned; a Northern visitor painted it as a city of 'vacant houses, of widowed women, of rotting wharves, of deserted warehouses, of weed-wild gardens, of miles of grass-grown streets, of acres of pitiful and voiceless barrenness.' The business portion of Richmond, the capital of the Confederacy, lay in ruins 'all up and down, as far as the eye could reach.... Beds of cinders, cellars half filled with bricks and rubbish, broken and blackened walls, impassable streets deluged with débris.' In Atlanta, brick and mortar, charred timber, scraps of tin roofing, engine bolts and bars, cannonballs, and long shot filled the ruined streets. Mobile, Galveston, Vicksburg, and numerous other cities of the South were in a similar plight.

With the collapse of the Confederacy, civil administration all but disappeared throughout the South. There was no money for the support of government and no authority which could assess or collect taxes. There were few courts, judges, sheriffs, or police officers with any authority, and vandalism went unrestrained except by public opinion or by lynch law. 'Our principal danger,' observed George Cary Eggleston, 'was from lawless bands of marauders who infested the country, and our greatest difficulty in dealing with them

Ruins of Charleston, South Carolina, 1865. (*Library of Congress, Brady Collection*)

lay in the utter absence of constituted authority of any sort.' Fraud and peculation added to the universal distress. United States Treasury agents seized hundreds of thousands of bales of cotton, and other property as well. The Federal Government subsequently reimbursed no fewer than 40,000 claimants because of illegal confiscation of their property.

The economic life of the South was shattered. Manufacturing had been all but destroyed. Few Southern banks were solvent, and it was years before the banking system was even partially restored. Confederate securities into which the people had sunk their savings were now as worthless as Continental currency. Shops were depleted of goods, and almost everything had to be imported from the North on credit. Even agriculture was slow to revive. Not until 1879 did the seceding states raise a cotton crop as large as that of 1860. In 1870 the tobacco crop of Virginia was one-third that of 1860, and the corn and wheat crop one-half. Farm land that had once sold for $100 an acre went begging at $5, and in Mississippi alone almost 6 million acres of land were sold for nonpayment of taxes.

The transportation system had mostly collapsed. Roads were all but impassable, bridges destroyed or washed away, river levees broken. Railroad transportation was paralyzed, and most of the railroad companies bankrupt. Over a stretch of 114 miles in Alabama 'every bridge and trestle was destroyed, cross-ties rotten, buildings burned, water-tanks gone, ditches filled up, and tracks grown up in weeds and bushes.'

The cultural life of the South did not recover for over a generation. Schools, colleges, libraries, and churches were destroyed or impoverished, and the intellectual life of the South was paralyzed by the preoccupation with sheer survival and by obsession with the past and with defeat. 'You ask me to tell you the story of my last year,' wrote the poet Henry Timrod. 'I can embody it all in a few words: beggary, starvation, death, bitter grief, utter want of hope.' Young men of family who had interrupted their education to fight for Southern independence had to labor in the fields to keep their kinfolk from starving; and a planter's family which still had young men was deemed fortunate.

General Anderson worked as a day laborer in the yards of the South Carolina Railroad. George Fitzhugh, the philosopher of slavery, lived in a poor shanty among his former slaves. William Gilmore Simms, the South's leading man of letters, lost not only his 'house, stables, barns, gin house, machine and threshing houses, mules, horses, cattle, wagons, ploughs, implements, all destroyed' but what was probably the finest private library in the South. 'Pretty much the whole of life has been merely not dying,' wrote the Southern poet Sidney Lanier, himself dying.

The fall of the Confederacy dealt an extremely heavy blow to the planter aristocracy that had long guided the destinies of the South. Some of this class was excluded for a time from any participation in the government, and for such able leaders as Davis and Lee the disability was never removed. Slave property valued in 1860 at over $2 billion evaporated, and the savings and sacrifices represented by Confederate securities were lost. A labor system which was the very basis of the Southern economy was overthrown, the agricultural regime which it sreved was disarranged, and a new system, no less wasteful and scarcely less oppressive, was established in its stead.

The planter aristocracy suffered especially severely; for if the war had been 'a poor man's fight,' the poor white had nothing to lose, and his condition was no worse in 1870 than it had been in 1850. Many planters gave up the struggle to maintain themselves on the land. A few fled to England, Mexico, or Brazil; others migrated to the Northern cities or started life anew in the West; many moved to the towns and adapted themselves to business or professional life. The small farmers and poor whites took advantage of this exodus to enlarge their farms and elect men of their own kind to high office. A little while and the Tillmans, Watsons, and Longs would sit in the seats of the Calhouns, the Cobbs, and the Clays.

The Triumphant North

To the North the war brought not only victory but unprecedented prosperity, a sense of power, a spirit of buoyant confidence, and exuberance of energy that found expression in a thousand out-

The Richmond and Petersburg Railroad Depot, 1865. This Mathew Brady photograph of a demolished locomotive and a gutted station in the former Confederate capital of Richmond, Virginia, reveals how little was left of the railroad system of the South after the devastation of the Civil War. (*Brady Collection, Library of Congress*)

lets. To the generation that had saved the Union everything seemed possible. 'The truth is,' wrote Senator Sherman to his brother, the General, 'the close of the war with our resources unimpaired gives an elevation, a scope to the ideas of leading capitalists far higher than anything ever undertaken in this country before. They talk of millions as confidently as formerly of thousands.' Men hurled themselves upon the continent as if to ravish it of its wealth. Railroads were flung across mountain barriers, and settlers crowded into half a continent, while cattle swarmed over the grasslands of the High Plains. Forests were felled, the earth gutted of coal, copper, iron ore, and precious metals; petroleum spouted from untended wells. Telegraph wires were strung across the country and cables stretched from continent to continent; factories sprang up overnight; speculators thronged the floors of stock and produce exchanges, inventors flooded the patent office with applications for new devices with which to conquer nature and create wealth.

The census of 1870 revealed that, despite four years of war, the per capita wealth of the North had doubled in ten years. The war, while depressing some industries, created new opportunities for amassing private wealth. Supplying the armies with food and clothing and munitions proved immensely profitable. More profitable still was the business of financing the war, and many a fortune was founded upon speculation in government bonds and on the banking expansion encouraged by the National Banking Act. Banks which held government bonds received an estimated aggregate of 17 per cent interest annually upon their investment. The rewards of railroad organization, financing, construction, and operation were even greater. In the ten years after the war, the country doubled its railroad mileage, and the profits went, often by devious means, to establish the fortunes of Vanderbilt and Gould, Huntington and Stanford, and other multimillionaires.

No less spectacular was the exploitation of natural resources. After oil was struck in western Pennsylvania in 1859, thousands of fortune-hunters stampeded into the oil-soaked triangle between the Allegheny river and Oil Creek. During the war oil production increased from 21 mil-

lion to 104 million gallons, and the capitalization of new companies was not far from half a billion dollars. In 1860 silver production was a paltry $150,000; by the end of Reconstruction annual output had reached $38 million, and the silver barons of the West had come to exercise an influence in politics comparable to that of industrialists in the East. In the postwar years coal production trebled, and iron ore output in the Lake Superior region alone increased more than tenfold.

In the 1860's the number of manufacturing establishments increased by fully 80 per cent. Four times as much timber was cut in Michigan, four times as much pig iron was smelted in Ohio, four times as much freight was handled by the Pennsylvania Railroad, four times as many miles of railroad track were laid, in 1870 as in 1860. After the war, the woolens, cotton, iron, lumber, meat, and milling industries all showed a steady and even a spectacular development. And while property values in the South were suffering a cataclysmic decline, total property value of the North and West increased from $10 billion in 1860 to over $25 billion a decade later.

Accompanying this extraordinary development of business was a steady rise in the population of cities and in immigration. New York and Philadelphia, Boston and Baltimore, continued the growth which had begun back in the 'forties, and newer cities such as Chicago and St. Louis, Cleveland and Pittsburgh, St. Paul and San Francisco, more than doubled their population in ten years. Even during the war some 800,000 immigrants had entered the United States, and in the ten years after Appomattox some 3.25 million immigrants flooded into the cities and the farms of the North and the West.

These developments all contributed to the growth of income, and observers were already remarking upon the concentration of wealth in certain fortunate areas and favored groups. In 1870 the wealth of New York State alone was more than twice that of all the ex-Confederate states. Every business grew its own crop of millionaires, and soon the names of Morgan and Armour, Swift and Pillsbury, came to be as familiar to the average American as the names of his statesmen. A new plutocracy emerged from the war and Reconstruction, masters of money who were no less self-conscious and powerful than the planter aristocracy of the Old South.

While the old patterns were being rearranged in the South, a different kind of transformation was effected in the North. With the representatives of the planter class out of Congress, the spokesmen of industry, finance, and of free Western lands no longer had to contend with their most powerful opponent. During the war they pushed through legislation to fulfill the arrested hopes of the 'fifties, and after victory they garnered the fruits.

The moderate tariff of 1857 gave way to the Morrill tariff of 1861, and that to a series of war tariffs with duties scaling rapidly upward. By the National Banking Acts of 1863 and 1864, the Independent Treasury system of 1846 was swept away, and an act of 1865 imposed a tax of 10 per cent on all state bank notes, a fatal blow which none would regret. To ensure an ample labor supply, Congress in 1864 permitted the importation of contract labor from abroad, and though this act was soon repealed, the practice itself was not discontinued until the 'eighties. Internal improvements at national expense found expression in subsidies to telegraph and cable lines and in generous grants of millions of acres out of the public domain to railroad promoters.

Western farmers achieved a century-old ambition with the Homestead Law of 1862. This act, limited temporarily in its application to those who 'have never borne arms against the United States Government,' granted a quarter-section (160 acres) of public domain to anyone who would undertake to cultivate it. The Morrill Act, passed the same year, subsidized agricultural education through public lands. At the same time easier access to the West was assured through the government-subsidized railroads. By carrying out the promise of the Republican platform, this legislation strengthened that party in the agricultural West.

Finally, the Civil War had an important political consequence. The Republicans came out of the war with an aura of legitimacy, for they could claim to be the party that had saved the Union, while the Democrats had the odium of secession. For a generation Republican orators rang the changes on Fort Sumter and Andersonville prison, and 'waved the bloody shirt of the rebellion,' and presented themselves as the liberators and defenders of the former slaves.

The Freedman

In Reconstruction the Negro was the central figure. Upwards of a million blacks had in one way or another become free before the end of the war; victory and the Thirteenth Amendment liberated about 3 million more. Never before in the history of the world had civil and political rights been conferred at one stroke on so large a body of men. Many thought that freedom meant no more work and proceeded to celebrate an endless 'day of jubilee'; others were led to believe that the property of their former masters would be divided among them. 'Emancipation having been announced one day,' wrote Tom Watson about his Georgia home, 'not a Negro remained on the place the next. The fine old homestead was deserted. Every house in "the quarter" was empty. The first impulse of freedom had carried the last of the blacks to town.' Thousands took to the woods or to the road, or clustered around the United States army posts, living on doles or dying of camp diseases. As the most famous of black leaders, Frederick Douglass, said, the black 'was free from the individual master but a slave of society. He had neither money, property, nor friends. He was free from the old plantation, but he had nothing but the dusty road under his feet. He was free from the old quarter that once gave him shelter, but a slave to the rains of summer and the frosts of winter. He was turned loose, naked, hungry, and destitute to the open sky.' Deaths among blacks from starvation, disease, and violence in the first two years of freedom ran into the tens of thousands. Yet despite the deprivations of a slave society, the freedmen contributed leaders who faced these harsh realities with uncommon good sense.

To the average Southerner emancipation changed only the legal position of the Negro. Few whites were willing to acquiesce in anything approaching race equality. Some of the former slaveholders tried sincerely and with some success

Frederick Douglass (1817–95). So eloquent was he as a speaker and so independent was his spirit that some who heard him on the lecture platform refused to believe that he had been reared as a slave. He married twice, the second time to a white woman. He answered critics of his second marriage by pointing out that his first wife 'was the color of my mother, and the second, the color of my father.' (*Art Museum, University of New Mexico*)

Freedmen in Richmond, Virginia. (*Library of Congress, Brady Collection*)

to assist the black in adjusting himself to his new status. But the small farmers and the poor whites were determined to 'keep the Negro in his place,' by laws if possible, by force if necessary. J. T. Trowbridge, writing shortly after the war, remarked that 'there is at this day more prejudice against color among the middle and poorer classes . . . who owned few or no slaves, than among the planters, who owned them by the hundred.'

Most planters sought to keep their former slaves as hired help or as tenant farmers, or on the sharecrop system, and every Southern state but Tennessee attempted to assure this by a series of laws collectively known as the 'black codes.' The codes of Virginia and North Carolina, where the whites were in secure control, were mild; those of South Carolina, Mississippi, and Louisiana, where blacks outnumbered whites, severe. These black codes conferred upon the freedmen fairly extensive privileges, gave them the essential rights of citizens to contract, sue and be sued, own and inherit property, and testify in court, and made some provision for education. In no instance, however, were the freedmen accorded the vote or made eligible for juries, and for the most part they were not permitted to testify against white men. Because of their alleged aversion to work they were required to have some steady occupation, and subjected to penalties for violation of labor contracts. The especially stringent vagrancy and apprenticeship laws lent themselves readily to the establishment of peonage. The penal codes provided harsher and more arbitrary punishments for blacks than for whites, and some states permitted individual masters to administer corporal punishment to 'refractory servants.' Negroes were not allowed to bear arms, or to appear in certain public places, and there were special laws governing their domestic relations.

Southern whites, who had never dreamed it possible to live side by side with free blacks, professed to believe that these laws were liberal and generous. But every one of the codes confessed a determination to keep the freedmen in a permanent position of inferiority. This Old South point of view was succinctly expressed in the most influential of Southern journals, *De Bow's Review:*

We of the South would not find much difficulty in managing the Negroes, if left to ourselves, for we would be guided by the lights of experience and the teachings of history. . . . We should be satisfied to compel them to engage in coarse common manual labor, and to punish them for dereliction of duty or nonfulfillment of their contracts with sufficient severity to make the great majority of them productive laborers. . . . We should treat them as mere grown-up children, entitled like children, or apprentices, to the protection of guardians and masters, and bound to obey those put above them in place of parents, just as children are so bound.

It was scarcely surprising that Northerners regarded the black codes as palpable evasions of the Thirteenth Amendment, which had abolished slavery, and conclusive evidence that the South was not prepared to accept the 'verdict of Appomattox.' In response to the black codes the North demanded that the Federal Government step in to protect the former slaves. This object, eventually embodied in the Fourteenth and Fifteenth Amendments and the various civil rights

bills, was first pursued through the agencies of the Freedmen's Bureau and the military governments.

The Freedmen's Bureau of the War Department was created by Congress 3 March 1865, with powers of guardianship over Negroes and refugees, under General O. O. Howard, the 'Christian soldier.' The bureau extended relief to both races, administered justice in cases involving freedmen, and established schools for colored people. During its brief existence the Freedmen's Bureau set up over a hundred hospitals, gave medical aid to half a million patients, distributed over 20 million rations to the destitute of both races, and maintained over 4000 schools for black children. Yet, as the failure of the Freedmen's Bureau Bank—wiping out the savings of thousands of former slaves—revealed, the bureau also offered an opportunity for men of low character to enrich themselves.

The bureau's most important work was educational. As rapidly as schools were provided, the freedmen took advantage of them. 'It was a whole race trying to go to school,' wrote Booker T. Washington. 'Few were too young and none too old to make the attempt to learn. As fast as any kind of teachers could be secured, not only were day schools filled, but night schools as well. The great ambition of the older people was to try to learn to read the Bible before they died.' Most of these freedmen's schools were taught by Northern women who volunteered for what W. E. B. Du Bois called the Ninth Crusade:

Behind the mists of ruin and rapine waved the calico dresses of women who dared, and after the hoarse mouthings of the field guns rang the rhythm of the alphabet. Rich and poor they were, serious and curious, bereaved, now of a father, now of a brother, now of more than these, they came seeking a life work in planting New England schoolhouses among the white and black of the South. They did their work well. In that first year they taught one hundred thousand souls and more.

By the end of Reconstruction there were 600,000 blacks in elementary schools in the South; the Federal Government had set up Howard University in the national capital, and private philanthropy had founded industrial schools like

Freedman's Bureau, Memphis. A long line of blacks wait to hear their cases heard. This particular office of the Bureau distributed more rations than most. (*Library of Congress*)

Hampton Institute in Virginia and Fisk in Tennessee.

Progress in land-ownership, the other great ambition of the freedmen, proved slow and halting, one of the most egregious failures of reconstruction. Northern statesmen had encouraged the Negro to look to the Federal Government to provide 'forty acres and a mule.' But in the end nothing was done to help the black man become an independent landowner. The Federal Government still owned enough public land in the South to have given every Negro family a 40-acre farm,

while the cotton tax of some $68 million would have provided the mule. A Congress that was able to give 40 million acres of land to a single railroad might have done something to fulfill its obligation to the freedmen. Without effective assistance from federal—or state—governments, the vast majority of blacks could not purchase even small farms and were forced to lease land on such terms as whites were prepared to grant. And when the Negro did set up as an independent landowner he was severely handicapped by his unfamiliarity with farm management and marketing, and his lack of capital for farm animals and implements. In 1888 Georgia farmlands were valued at $88 million; the blacks, who were half the population, owned land to the value of $1.8 million.

Emancipation altered the form rather than the substance of the Negro's economic status for at least a generation after Appomattox. The transition from slave to independent farmer was long and painful, made usually through the medium of tenancy, and for many it was never completely made. Without the requisite capital, without credit except such as was cautiously extended by white bankers or storekeepers on usurious terms, and without agricultural skills, most freedmen were unable to rise above the sharecropper or tenant class. They continued to work in the fields, to live in the shacks provided by the former master or by his children, and to exist on credit provided by the same hands. A very few achieved something more—a business or a profession which brought them social standing as well as livelihood. After 1890 some blacks became laborers in the coal mines or steel mills or tobacco factories of the New South; others headed northward to work in industrial centers while their wives and daughters became 'domestics.' But the majority remained on land that belonged to others, plodding behind the plow in spring and picking cotton in the fall, reasonably sure of food and shelter and clothing, a Saturday afternoon in town, a Sunday at revival meetings, continuing in the ways of their fathers.

Reconstruction during the Civil War

Reconstruction had been debated in the North ever since the beginning of the war. As usual with American political issues involving sectional balance, the argument took place on the plane of constitutional theory. It turned largely on two questions: whether the seceded states were in or out of the Union when their rebellion was crushed and whether the prerogative of restoration lodged with President or Congress. From the Northern premise that secession was illegal, strict logic reached the conclusion that former states of the Confederacy had always been and were now states of the Union, with all the rights and privileges pertaining thereto. If, on the contrary, secession

was valid, the South might consistently be treated as conquered territory, without any legal rights that the Union was required to respect. Both sides adopted the proper deductions from the other's premise. Radical Republicans, the most uncompromising nationalists, managed to prove to their satisfaction that the Southern states had lost or forfeited their rights, while former secessionists insisted that their rights in the Union from which they had seceded were unimpaired!

But the question of the status of the Southern states was to be decided in accordance not with theory but with political necessities. Lincoln, with his customary clarity, saw this, and saw, too, how dangerous was any dogmatic approach. In his last speech, on 11 April 1865, he insisted that the question whether the Southern states were in or out of the Union was 'bad as the basis of a controversy, and good for nothing at all—a merely pernicious abstraction.... Finding themselves safely at home, it would be utterly immaterial whether they had ever been abroad.' Obviously, these states were 'out of their proper practical relation with the Union'; the object of all should be to 'get them into their proper practical relation' again.

Lincoln had been pursuing this eminently sensible policy since the beginning of the war. As early as 1862 he had appointed provisional military governors in Tennessee, Louisiana, and North Carolina whose duty it was to re-establish loyal governments. The North Carolina experiment came to naught, but in Tennessee Governor Andrew Johnson and in Louisiana General Banks made impressive progress toward restoring federal authority, and after the fall of Vicksburg, Arkansas was similarly reclaimed. Encouraged by this success, Lincoln, in a proclamation of 8 December 1863, formulated what was to be the presidential plan of reconstruction.

The object of this plan was to get the seceded states back into their normal relations with the Federal Government as quickly and as painlessly as possible; the means was the presidential power to pardon. The plan itself provided for a general amnesty and restoration of property other than slaves to most of those who would take a prescribed oath of loyalty to the Union. Furthermore, whenever 10 per cent of the electorate of 1860 should take this oath, they might set up a state government which Lincoln promised to recognize as the true government of the state.

This magnanimous 10 per cent plan was very promptly adopted in Louisiana and Arkansas. Thousands of voters, many of them cheerfully perjuring themselves, swore that they had not willingly borne arms against the United States; they were then duly registered. They held constitutional conventions, drew up and ratified new constitutions abolishing slavery, and their states then prepared to reassume their place in the Federal Union. But all was not to be such easy sailing. Congress, which was the judge of its own membership, refused to admit the representatives of these reconstructed states, and in the presidential election of 1864 their electoral votes were not counted.

The congressional leaders had a plan of their own which carefully retained control of the entire process of reconstruction in congressional hands. The Wade-Davis Bill of 8 July 1864 stipulated that Congress, not the President, was to have jurisdiction over the processes of reconstruction, and that a majority of the electorate, instead of merely 10 per cent, was required for the reconstitution of legal state governments. When Lincoln averted this scheme by a pocket veto, he brought down upon himself the bitter excoriation of the Wade-Davis Manifesto. 'The President . . . must understand,' said the two Congressmen, 'that the authority of Congress is paramount and must be respected . . . and if he wishes our support he must confine himself to his executive duties—to obey and execute, not make the laws—to suppress by arms armed rebellion, and leave political reorganization to Congress.' Here was the real beginning of the rift between the President and the Radicals. The term refers to those who were determined to employ the power of the national government to ensure the freedmen's rights and establish the supremacy of the Republican party in national politics and of Congress in the federal administration. Though at first small, the Radical faction included such formidable leaders as Thaddeus Stevens of Pennsylvania, Ben Wade of Ohio,

Zachariah Chandler of Michigan, and Charles Sumner of Massachusetts, and it would eventually come to dominate the Republican party.

With the publication of the Wade-Davis Manifesto, an issue had been raised that would not be settled until a President had been impeached, a Supreme Court intimidated, and the Constitution altered. Congressional opposition to Lincoln's plan was due in part to legislative *esprit de corps*, in part to concern for the black, in part to the hatreds engendered by the war, and in part to persuasive constitutional considerations, for it seemed only logical that Congress, which had the power to admit new states and was the judge of its own membership, should control reconstruction. Moreover, the Radicals thought it monstrous that traitors and rebels should be readmitted to full fellowship in the Union they had repudiated and tried to destroy. It would be the Union as in Buchanan's time, administered by 'rebels' and 'copperheads' for the benefit of an unrepentant slavocracy. Even Northerners who were quite willing to admit that Davis and Stephens were honorable men did not care to see them at their old desks in the Senate, shouting for state rights. Moreover, party interests were at stake. As Thaddeus Stevens put it, the Southern states 'ought never to be recognized as capable of acting in the Union, or of being counted as valid states, until the Constitution shall have been so amended . . . as to secure perpetual ascendancy to the party of the Union.' That was the nub of the matter. If the Southern states returned a solid Democratic counterpart to Congress, as appeared inevitable, a reunited Democratic party would have a majority in both houses of Congress. The amendment which Stevens had in mind was that providing for Negro suffrage, which would fulfill the moral obligation to the freedmen and create a flourishing Republican party in the South.

If the partisan considerations seem narrow, we should ask ourselves what other nation in history has ever turned over control of the government and of the spoils of victory to the leaders of a defeated rebellion.

For about six weeks after Lincoln's assassination there was a petty 'reign of terror,' directed by

Secretary Stanton and supported by President Johnson, who had always been in favor of hanging 'traitors.' Only the stern intervention of Grant prevented the seizure of Lee and other Confederate generals. Large rewards for the apprehension of Davis and his cabinet, as alleged promoters of the murder of Lincoln, resulted in their capture and temporary imprisonment. But the charge of complicity in the murder was quickly seen to be preposterous, and it was obviously impossible to get a Virginia jury to convict Davis of treason. Thirst for vengeance appeared to be slaked by the shooting or suicide of the assassin Booth, by hanging his three accomplices and the unfortunate woman who had harbored them, after an extra-legal trial by a military tribunal, and by hanging the miserable Henry Wirz, commander of the infamous Andersonville prison, for the 'murder' of Union prisoners.

All this was cause for shame, but no other great rebellion of modern times has been suppressed with so little loss of life or formal punishment of the vanquished. Not one of the rebel leaders was executed, none was brought to trial for treason. There were no mass arrests, not even of those officers of the United States who took up arms against their government. Even the civil disabilities imposed were mild; by 1872, only some 750 ex-Confederates were still barred from office-holding. For generations Southerners have rung the changes on the theme of Northern ruthlessness during the Reconstruction years, and many historians have concluded that the North imposed upon the South a 'Carthaginian peace.' Yet we have only to recall the suppression of the Peasants' Revolt in Germany in the sixteenth century, the ravages of Alva in the rebelling Low Countries, the punishments inflicted on the Irish by Cromwell and on the Scots after Culloden, or the Russian, Nazi, and Spanish revolutions of our own time, to appreciate how moderate was the conduct of the triumphant North after 1865.

Andrew Johnson Takes Charge

Lincoln's assassination and the accession to the presidency of Andrew Johnson drastically altered the political situation.[1] Like Tyler in 1841, Johnson was the nominal head of a party of which he was not really a member. Of origin as humble as Lincoln's, in early life a tailor in a Tennessee mountain village and unable to write until taught by his wife, he possessed many of Lincoln's virtues but lacked his ability to handle men. Self-educated and self-trained, he had a powerful though not well-disciplined mind. United with these intellectual qualities were the virtues of integrity, devotion to duty, and courage. But at a time when tact was called for, he was stubborn and inflexible; Johnson 'had no budge in him.' And he misunderstood the revolution brought by the war.

No President ever faced a more difficult situation. He had no personal following either in the South or in the North, none of the prestige that came to Lincoln from the successful conduct of the war, and no party organization behind him, for he had broken with the Democrats and had not been accepted by the Republicans. Seward and Welles were loyal to Johnson, but Stanton, with his customary duplicity, used the machinery of the War Department against him and kept the Radicals posted on cabinet secrets. Yet at the outset the Radicals were a minority, and they were generally well disposed toward him. It was Johnson's own blunders that isolated him not only from the Radicals but from the moderates.

At first Johnson appeared to be willing to cooperate with the Radicals. 'Treason is a crime and must be punished,' he said; 'treason must be made infamous, and traitors must be impoverished.' Bluff Ben Wade exclaimed exultantly, 'Johnson, we have faith in you. By the gods, there will be no trouble now in running this government.'

---

1. Some of the Radicals rejoiced in the removal of Lincoln and the accession of Johnson. 'I spent most of the afternoon in a political caucus,' wrote Representative George Julian of Indiana, 'and while everybody was shocked at his murder, the feeling was nearly universal that the accession of Johnson to the Presidency would prove a godsend to the country. Aside from Mr. Lincoln's known policy of tenderness to the Rebels ... his ... views of the subject of Reconstruction were as distasteful as possible to radical Republicans.'

But soon there was trouble enough. When Congress was not in session, Johnson swung around to a sharply different course. He proceeded to appoint provisional civil governors in all Confederate states where Lincoln had not already done so. These governors were enjoined to summon state constitutional conventions, which were to be elected by the 'whitewashed rebels'—former citizens of the Confederacy who took the oath of allegiance required by the presidential proclamation. Fourteen specified classes, assumed to be inveterate rebels, were excluded from this general amnesty and required to make personal application for pardon. Although many of those thus proscribed did receive special pardons from President Johnson, the general effect was to exclude many experienced statesmen from participation in the task of establishing the new state governments. The ensuing constitutional conventions invalidated the ordinances of secession, repudiated the state war debts—which they could not in any event have paid—declared slavery abolished, and wrote new state constitutions. Not one granted the vote to any class of blacks. Elections were promptly held under these new or amended constitutions, and by the autumn of 1865 regular civil administrations were functioning in all former Confederate states except Texas.

This speedy process of reconstruction excited distrust in the North. That distrust was exacerbated by the enactment of black codes, and by the understandable but impolitic alacrity with which Southern voters elected their former Confederate leaders to high offices. As James G. Blaine later wrote, 'If the Southern men had intended, as their one special and desirable aim, to inflame public opinion of the North against them, they would have proceeded precisely as they did.' Many Northerners came to believe that reconstruction had been accomplished before the South had either repented its sins or become reconciled to defeat. To meet this criticism Johnson, in the fall of 1865, sent a number of observers to survey conditions in the South. They returned with reports that the South had fairly 'accepted defeat,' but many continued to doubt that Southerners were willing to accord the Negro equal rights. 'Refusing to see that a mighty cataclysm had shaken the profoundest depths of national life,' says Professor Coulter, Southerners 'did not expect that many things would be made anew but rather looked for them to be mended as of old,—that Humpty Dumpty might after all be put back on the wall.'

Congress Intervenes

The Congress which met for the first time on 4 December 1865 appointed a joint committee of both Houses with authority to investigate and report on the title of Southern members-elect. This Joint Committee of Fifteen, a resurrection of the old Committee on the Conduct of the War, formulated the theory and set the pace of congressional reconstruction. The committee was not controlled by the Radicals, and many of the crucial measures came from moderates like Lyman Trumbull.

The most influential member of the committee was Thaddeus Stevens of Pennsylvania, leader of the Republicans in the House. A sincere democrat, lifelong spokesman for the poor and the oppressed, and tireless champion of public education, Stevens was now an embittered old man of seventy-four nursing an implacable enmity toward the Southern slavocracy and President Johnson, who, he thought, stood between them and their just deserts. 'The punishment of traitors,' he declared, 'has been wholly ignored by a treacherous Executive and a sluggish Congress. To this issue I desire to devote the small remnant of my life.' And he did. 'Strip a proud nobility of the bloated estates,' he demanded; 'reduce them to a level with plain republicans; send them forth to labor and teach their children to enter the workshops or handle a plow, and you will thus humble the proud traitors.' Partly out of passionate devotion to the Negro, partly out of conviction that the welfare of the Union was identical with the triumph of the Republican party, Stevens was determined to impose black suffrage on the South. 'I am for Negro suffrage in every rebel State,' he said. 'If it be just it should not be denied; if it be necessary it should be adopted; if it be punishment to traitors, they deserve it.' He insisted that Congress should treat the Southern states as nothing but conquered provinces.

Charles Sumner of Massachusetts, Republican leader in the Senate, was not on the Joint Committee, but next to Stevens he was the most powerful figure in congressional reconstruction. An idealist by conviction, and a reformer by training, he was a pedantic dogmatist, but in his way quite as sincere as Stevens. Against the ex-Confederates he held no vindictive feelings, but he was committed to giving Negroes the vote. Sumner advanced the theory that the Southern states had committed political suicide, had extinguished their standing as states, and were in the position of territories subject to the exclusive jurisdiction of Congress. Vain, humorless, and irritable, Sumner nevertheless had a distinguished record as a champion of good causes: the New England intellectuals looked to him for leadership, his polished orations impressed the commonalty, and he infused the Radical movement with altruism.

The Joint Committee propounded the theory of reconstruction upon which Congress ultimately acted. It announced that 'the States lately in rebellion were . . . disorganized communities, without civil government and without constitutions or other forms by virtue of which political relation could legally exist between them and the federal government,' that they had 'forfeited all civil and political rights and privileges under the federal Constitution,' and that they could be restored to their political rights only by Congress. In other words, the states were intact, but the state governments were, for most but not for all purposes, in a condition of suspended animation. Under this interpretation it was possible for Congress at once to deny representation to the Southern states and to accept the ratification of the Thirteenth Amendment by the legislatures of these same states.

The Radical program can be summarized:

1. To keep the ex-Confederate states out of the Union until they had set up governments that could be regarded as 'republican' in nature.

2. To require them, as prerequisites for readmission, to repeal their black codes, disqualify those who had been active in rebellion from holding state office, guarantee the Negro his civil rights and give him the right to vote and to hold office. Furthermore, they advocated constitutional amendments to protect the civil rights of the blacks.

3. To ensure a larger role for Congress in the process of reconstruction.

The Radicals did not, as is often said, share a common attitude on economic policy. They frequently held diametrically opposite views on currency and the tariff, and businessmen, who had diverse interests and attitudes, were as likely to be against them as for them. Some of the Radicals, however, wished to assure permanence to that body of tariff, agricultural, and money legislation which had been written into the statute books during the war years, and were prepared to exploit the Reconstruction crisis to achieve their ends.

The bitter conflict between the Radicals and President Johnson erupted over a proposal that represented the ideas not merely of the Radicals but of most Republicans and was, in fact, sponsored by the moderate Lyman Trumbull. Opposition to legislation to enlarge the scope of the Freedmen's Bureau bill centered in the Democrats, who exploited race prejudice; not one Democrat in either house of Congress voted for the bill. But on 19 February 1866 Johnson opened war on the advocates of civil rights by vetoing the measure.[2] In a shocking speech three days later, he denounced the campaign for Negro rights and cried that Stevens, Sumner, and Wendell Phillips were planning to assassinate him. Many Northern Republicans read Johnson out of the party.

Yet most Republicans still wanted conciliation with Johnson, and they hoped to win his approval for a second measure sponsored by Trumbull, a Civil Rights bill which sought to protect the rights of the freedman in the courts rather than through such institutions as the army. Congress enacted the bill, again without a single Democratic vote, but Johnson stunned his party by vetoing this measure too. The President announced that he opposed 'the Africanization of half the United States.' After this veto most Republicans broke with the President, and Congress passed the bill

---

2. A second Freedmen's Bureau bill was subsequently passed over the presidential veto, 16 July 1866.

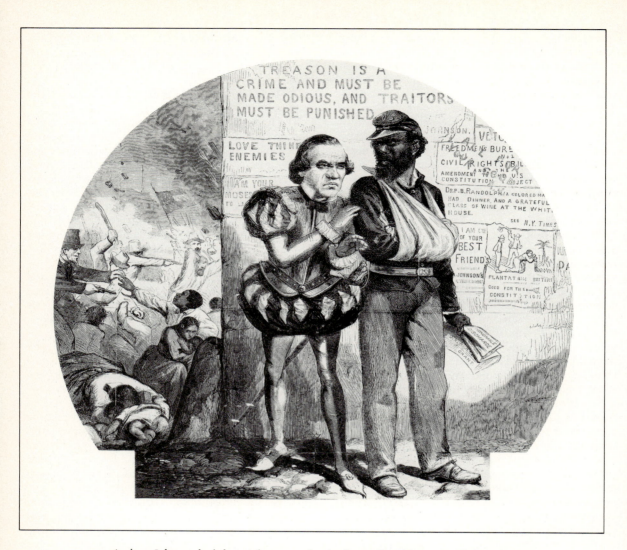

Andrew Johnson had the misfortune to be the first political figure singled out by Thomas Nast, the greatest cartoonist of his day, for caricature. In this illustration (which depicts the atrocities suffered by blacks in the early Reconstruction period), Nast portrays the President as Iago and a wounded but proud black Union veteran as the scornful Othello. (*Harper's Weekly, 1 Sept., 1866*)

over his veto. Not Sumner nor Stevens but Johnson himself had turned the men of moderation in the party against the administration.

By now the Republicans were determined to write new guarantees into the Constitution and to insist that the Southern states accept them before they were readmitted into the Union. On 30 April 1866 the Committee of Fifteen reported the Fourteenth Amendment, the most important ever added to the Constitution. It was designed to guarantee the civil rights of the Negro against unfavorable legislation by the states, reduce congressional representation in proportion to the denial of suffrage to Negroes, disqualify ex-Confederates who had formerly held office, invalidate the Confederate debt, and validate the federal debt. Section I of the amendment was particularly significant. It first defined citizenship, and then provided that 'No State shall make or enforce any law which shall abridge the privileges or immunities of citizens of the United States; nor shall any State deprive any person of life, liberty, or property, without due process of law; nor deny to any person within its jurisdiction the equal protection of the laws.' It thus for the first time clearly threw the protection of the Federal Government around the rights of life, liberty, and property which might be invaded by the states, reversing the traditional relationships between these governments which had from the beginning distinguished our federal system. Designed to protect the Negro, this stipulation came increasingly to be construed as extending the protection of the Federal Government to corporations whose property rights were threatened by state legislation, although the framers of the amendment did not anticipate any such interpretation.

There was ample evidence that the freedman needed national protection. The conservative General Jefferson C. Davis reported that in Kentucky 19 blacks had been killed, 233 maltreated, and none of the offenders had been prosecuted. In Texas, one black was murdered for not doffing his hat; in Louisiana, a black who answered a white boy 'quickly' was 'taken thro' the town and across the Levee, and there stripped and terribly beaten, with raw-hides.' In May 1866 a mob of whites, aided by some of the police, burned and pillaged the Negro quarter of Memphis and killed 46 freedmen. In New Orleans on 30 July, a mob, numbering many police and former Confederate soldiers, assaulted a convention of Negroes and white Radicals, and killed and wounded scores in cold blood.

Everything now turned on the election of a new Congress in the autumn of 1866, one of the most critical contests in our history. A National Union Convention of moderates from both sections pledged support of the President but did not form a new party or create party machinery. Hence in most congressional districts in the North voters had to choose between a Radical Republican and a Copperhead Democrat. Faced with this prospect many moderate Republicans went over to the Radical camp. Johnson apparently sought a political realignment in which, with the Radicals driven from the party, he could lead a union of Republicans with War Democrats and Southern loyalists. Instead, he cut himself off from the mass of his own party. Southerners, he said, 'cannot be treated as subjugated people or vassal colonies without a germ of hatred being introduced, which will some day or other, though the time may be distant, develop mischief of the most serious character.' But the President proved to be an immoderate advocate of moderation. His 'swing around the circle,' a stumping tour of the Middle West, became in many instances an undignified exercise in vituperation. 'I would ask you,' the President shouted on 3 September 1866 in Cleveland, 'Why not hang Thad Stevens and Wendell Phillips?' The outcome was a smashing victory for the Republicans, who picked up a margin in Congress large enough to override a presidential veto.

Johnson saw himself as the champion of the Constitution, and he was a stubborn man, but Congress was no less determined. When ten of the former Confederate states refused to ratify the Fourteenth Amendment, they left Congress with no alternative save more drastic measures or acquiescence in denying equality to the Negro. In February 1867 Congressman James Garfield cried, 'The last of the sinful ten has, with contempt and scorn, flung back into our teeth the magnanimous offer of a generous nation. It is now our turn to act.'

Congressional Reconstruction

The Radicals took the results of the fall elections as a vindication of their 'thorough' policy, and under the implacable leadership of Stevens whipped through a series of measures of far-reaching importance. This program undid the whole of presidential reconstruction, placed the Southern states back where they had been in April 1865, and temporarily revolutionized the political system by substituting a quasi-parliamentary for a presidential system of government.

The most important legislation of the entire period was the First Reconstruction Act of 2 March 1867. This act declared that 'no legal government' existed in any Southern state except Tennessee, and divided the rest of the South into five military districts subject to army commanders. Escape from this military regime and restitution of state rights were promised on condition that a constitutional convention, chosen by universal male suffrage, set up governments based on black and white suffrage and that the new state legislatures ratify the Fourteenth Amendment. Johnson returned the bill with a scorching message, but to no avail.

In March 1867 military rule replaced the civil governments that had been operating in the South for over a year. The military governors ruled with a firm hand, sometimes with flagrant disregard for the rights of white inhabitants, at the same time that they secured rights for Negroes that these whites had denied them. Thousands of local officials were removed to make way for Northern 'carpetbaggers' or Negroes; the governors of six states were displaced and others appointed in their place; civil courts were superseded by military tribunals; the legislatures of Georgia, Alabama, and Louisiana were purged of conservatives; state legislation was set aside or modified; and an army of occupation, some 20,000 strong and aided by a force of Negro militia, kept order. The relatively brief rule of the major generals was harsh but had the merits of honesty and a certain rude efficiency. Particularly important were the efforts to cope with economic disorganization and to regulate the social life of their satrapies. Thus in South Carolina, General Sickles abolished imprisonment for debt, stayed foreclosures on property, made the wages of farm laborers a first lien on crops, prohibited the manufacture of whiskey, and softened racial discrimination.

The main task of the military commanders was to create new electorates and establish new governments. In each of the ten states they enrolled a new electorate; in South Carolina, Alabama, Florida, Mississippi, and Louisiana black voters outnumbered white. This electorate chose in every state a constitutional convention which, under the guidance of carpetbaggers, drafted new state constitutions enfranchising blacks, disfranchising ex-Confederate leaders, and guaranteeing civil and political equality to the freedmen.

These new state constitutions represented, in almost every instance, a definite advance upon the older constitutions. The Constitution of South Carolina, for example, set up a far more democratic, humane, and efficient system of government than that which had obtained during the antebellum regime. In addition to providing for universal manhood suffrage it abolished property qualifications for office-holding, reapportioned representation in the legislature, drew up a more elaborate Bill of Rights, abolished all 'distinctions on account of color,' reformed local government and judicial administration, outlawed dueling and imprisonment for debt, protected homesteads from foreclosure, enlarged the rights of women, and provided—on paper—for a system of universal public education.

By the summer of 1868 reconstructed governments had been set up in eight Southern states: the other three—Mississippi, Texas, and Virginia—were reconstructed in 1870. After the legislatures of the reconstructed states had duly ratified the Fourteenth Amendment, as well as the Fifteenth Amendment which stipulated that 'the right of citizens of the United States to vote shall not be denied or abridged by the United States or by any State on account of race, color, or previous condition of servitude.' Congress formally readmitted them, seated their elected representatives and senators, and, as soon as the new governments appeared reasonably secure, withdrew the army.

Ambitious as their program for Reconstruction

was, the Radicals had an even larger ultimate aim—modifying the American governmental system by establishing congressional supremacy. The majority of Congress, not the Supreme Court, was to be the final judge of the powers of Congress; the President a servant of Congress. This new dispensation was implicit in the Reconstruction Act of 2 March 1867 and in two other pieces of legislation adopted the same day. First, the Command of the Army Act virtually deprived the Executive of control of the army by requiring that he issue all military orders through the General of the Army, who was protected against removal or suspension from office. Second, the Tenure of Office Act, by denying the President the right to remove civil officials, including members of his cabinet, without the consent of the Senate, made it impossible for him to control his own administration. The Radicals put it through in order to prevent Johnson from continuing to wield the patronage weapon against them and to stop him from ousting Secretary of War Stanton, the last Radical sympathizer left in the cabinet. The next move in the game was to dispose of Johnson by the impeachment process, whereupon Benjamin Wade, president *pro tem.* of the Senate, would succeed to his office and title.

Impeachment had been proposed by Benjamin Butler in October 1866, and all through the following year a House committee had been trying to gather evidence which might support such action, but without success. Now Johnson furnished the House with the excuse for which it had waited. Convinced that the Tenure of Office Act was unconstitutional, he requested and then ordered Secretary Stanton to resign. Stanton himself thought the act unconstitutional and had even helped write the veto message, but when General Lorenzo Thomas, the newly appointed Secretary of War, sought to take possession of his office, Stanton barricaded himself in the War Department. On 24 February 1868, the House voted to impeach the President for 'high Crimes and Misdemeanors,' and within a week eleven articles of impeachment were agreed upon by the Radicals. Ten of the articles dealt with the removal of Stanton; the other consisted of garbled newspaper reports from the President's speeches. A monstrous charge to

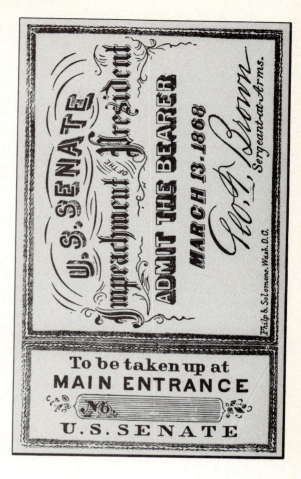

the effect that Johnson was an accomplice in the murder of Lincoln was finally excluded.

The impeachment of Johnson was one of the most disgraceful episodes in the history of the Federal Government, one that barely failed to suspend the presidential system. For had impeachment succeeded, the Radicals would have established the principle that Congress may remove a President not for 'high Crimes and Misdemeanors,' as required by the Constitution, but for purely political reasons. The managers of impeachment themselves admitted this; Johnson's crime, they asserted in their report, was 'the one great purpose of reconstructing the rebel states in accordance with his own will.' The President was defended by able counsel including William M. Evarts, leader of the American bar, and Benjamin R. Curtis, formerly a justice of the Supreme Court. These tore the allegations to shreds, and it was soon apparent to all but the most prejudiced that there was no valid case. Even the Tenure of Office Act charges proved groundless, for the law restrained a President from removing a cabinet officer he had appointed, and Stanton had been named not by Johnson but by Lincoln. Yet the Radicals would have succeeded in their object but for Chief Justice Chase, who insisted upon legal procedure, and for seven courageous Republican Senators who risked their political future by voting for acquittal.[3] One more affirmative vote and Ben Wade—who himself voted for conviction—would have been installed in the White House. Then, in all probability, the Court would have been battered into submission.

President Grant

Even as the Senate sat in solemn judgment on President Johnson, the triumphant Republicans met in party convention to nominate his successor, General Grant. Before the Civil War he had seldom taken the trouble to vote, and such political principles as he professed had inclined him toward the Democrats. He had been to Lincoln a faithful subordinate but to Johnson less than faithful, and after his break with Johnson he had been captured by the Radical politicians who saw in him an unbeatable candidate.

The campaign that followed was bitterly fought. To Republicans success promised an indefinite tenure of power, during which the party might be given a national basis through the extension of suffrage to the Southern blacks. To the Democrats, who nominated the former governor of New York, Horatio Seymour, whose wartime record had associated him with the Copperheads,

victory would spell the end of federal backing for the Negro, and the restoration of the remaining Southern states. The Republicans waved the 'bloody shirt of the rebellion' effectively. Grant carried all the states but eight, although his popular majority was only 300,000. The Negro vote of some 450,000 gave him his popular margin, and the exclusion of three Southern states (Mississippi, Texas, Virginia) and the control of six others assured him his large electoral college majority. With less equipment for the presidency than any predecessor save Harrison and a temperament unfitted for high political office, Grant was unable to overcome his deficiencies. Although a leader of men, he was not a good judge of men, and the very simplicity which had carried him safely through the intrigues of the Civil War exposed him to the wiles of politicians whose loyalty to himself he mistook for devotion to the public weal. It came as a shock that he seemed to have lost the qualities he had shown in the war—a sense of order and of command, resoluteness, and consistency. The magnanimous victor of Appomattox revealed himself in office petty, vindictive, and shifty. He was naïve rather than innocent, and his simplicity, as Henry Adams remarked, 'was more disconcerting than the complexity of a Talleyrand.' He regarded the presidency as a personal prerogative, a reward for services rendered rather than a responsibility.

Grant's only hope lay in the wisdom and integrity of his advisers, but his choices were bizarre. Altogether, during his eight years of office, Grant appointed no less than twenty-six men to his cabinet. Six—Hoar, Cox, Creswell, Jewell, Bristow, and Fish—proved to be men of intelligence and integrity, and of these Grant managed to dismiss all but one, Secretary of State Fish. It was fortunate that Grant was able to command, throughout the eight years of his administration, the talents of Hamilton Fish. A New York patrician, Grant's third choice for the State Department, and relatively unknown when he took office, Fish proved himself one of the shrewdest men who have ever directed the foreign affairs of the nation. He had what most of his colleagues in Grant's cabinet lacked—honesty, disciplined intelligence, learning, experience, urbanity, and a

---

3. Fessenden, Grimes, Trumbull, Ross, Van Winkle, Fowler, and Henderson. Fessenden died in 1869; none of the others was re-elected to the Senate; yet they did not suffer as severely as the legend of their martyrdom would suggest.

tact and patience sufficient to win and retain the confidence of his chief.

Yet for all his defects, Grant retained the devotion of millions. 'The plain man,' as Allan Nevins observes, 'had not elected Grant; he had elected an indestructible legend, a folk-hero.' It was well for Grant that he brought to the presidency this imperishable glamor, for he brought little else.

Radical Reconstruction in the South

The election of 1868 strengthened the position of the Radicals. To be sure, 'Let us have peace,' the concluding phrase of Grant's letter accepting the presidential nomination, had led the country to believe that Grant would abandon Radical reconstruction and adopt toward the white South a more conciliatory policy, and in the beginning this belief seemed justified. The President suggested to his cabinet a sweeping amnesty proclamation and urged Congress to complete the reconstruction process in Virginia, Mississippi, and Texas. By 1870 representatives from these states again sat in Congress. But it was soon clear that Grant was still in the Radical camp. He took the lead in a drastic reconstitution of the legislature of Georgia, and in South Carolina, Alabama, Mississippi, Louisiana, and Arkansas, he authorized the use of federal troops to overthrow duly elected Democratic governments and keep these states in the Radical Republican ranks.

Inevitably Radical reconstruction aroused determined opposition, which took both legal and illegal form. In states such as Virginia and North Carolina, where whites greatly outnumbered blacks, the Democrats recaptured control of the state governments by regular political methods almost at once. Elsewhere it was thought necessary to resort to a much greater degree of intimidation to destroy the combination that made Radical success possible. Whites who took part in Reconstruction soon felt the heavy weight of economic pressure or the sharp sting of social ostracism. Negroes were dealt with more ruthlessly, by employing terror.

Much of this violence was perpetrated by secret societies, of which the most famous, though not the largest, was the Ku Klux Klan. In 1867 a social

kuklos (circle) of young men in Pulaski, Tennessee, organized as the 'Invisible Empire of the South,' with elaborate ritual and ceremonial. The KKK described itself as an institution of 'chivalry, humanity, mercy and patriotism,' but it was in fact simply an institution for the maintenance of white supremacy. During the next three or four years the KKK and other secret societies—notably the Knights of the White Camellia and the White Leagues of Louisiana and Mississippi—policed 'unruly' Negroes in the country districts, discouraged blacks from serving in the militia, delivered spectral warnings against using the ballot, and punished those who disregarded the warnings. The Ku Klux Klan investigation of 1871 reported 153 Negroes murdered in a single Florida county that year; over 300 murdered in parishes outside New Orleans; bloody race riots in Mississippi and Louisiana; a reign of terror in parts of Arkansas; and in Texas, 'murders, robberies and outrages of all kinds.' Not all of this could be laid at the doors of the Klan or the White Leaguers, or even of the whites, but groups like the KKK were responsible for most of the violence that afflicted the South during these turbulent years. Under the impact of all this, Negro participation in politics declined sharply, and the Radical cause was put in jeopardy.

The Radicals had no intention of acquiescing tamely in the undoing of reconstruction. Their answer was first a series of state laws which sought to break up the secret societies and, when these proved unavailing, an appeal to Washington for help. The Grant administration responded with renewed military occupation of evacuated districts, the unseating of Democratic administrations on the ground of fraud, and a new crop of supervisory laws of which the most important were the Force Acts of 1870 and 1871 and the drastic Ku Klux Klan Act of 1871 authorizing the President to suspend the writ of habeas corpus and suppress violence by military force. Altogether some 7000 indictments and over 1000 convictions were found under these acts, but they did not fulfill their purpose. In large areas of the South—notably in South Carolina, Louisiana, and Mississippi—violence flourished throughout the entire reconstruction period.

From 1868 to 1877 the Radicals controlled, for

The KKK. This engraving is from a photograph of Mississippi Klansmen who were caught wearing these disguises after they attempted to murder a family. (*Library of Congress*)

varying periods, most of the reconstructed states of the South, but it was not, as it is sometimes called, 'Black Reconstruction.' In no state did the blacks ever control the government, and only in South Carolina—where blacks outnumbered whites four to three—did they have even a temporary majority in the legislature. There were no black governors, and very few Negroes in high positions in the executive branch or in administration. At no time did Negroes have a representa-tion proportional to their numbers in any branch of any government.

Radical control of Southern states was exercised by an uneasy coalition of three groups—Negroes, 'carpetbaggers,' and 'scalawags.' Both of the latter words are heavily loaded. The one conjures up the image of an impecunious Yankee adventurer descending on a prostrate South with a carpetbag to be stuffed full of loot; the other was a word commonly applied to runty cattle and, by implication, to the lowest breed of Southerner. There were, in truth, disreputable adventurers among the carpet-baggers, but most were Union veterans who had returned to the South to farm, businessmen looking for good investments, government agents who for one reason or another decided to stay on in the South, schoolteachers who thought of themselves as a kind of 'peace corps' to the freedmen. As for the 'scalawags'—the largest single element in the Radical coalition—these were the men who had opposed secession in the first place and were now ready to return to the old Union and to take in the blacks as junior partners in the enterprise of restoration.

The Radical governments were, in many cases, incompetent, extravagant, and corrupt. The corruption was pervasive and ostentatious. In Florida, for example, the cost of public printing in 1869 exceeded the total cost for all of the state government in 1860; in South Carolina the state maintained a restaurant and barroom for the legislators at a cost of $125,000 for a single session, and under the head of 'legislative supplies' provided Westphalia hams, Brussels carpets, and ornamental cuspidors; and in Louisiana the youthful Governor Warmoth managed to garner a fortune of half a million dollars during four years of office, while bartering away state property and dissipating school funds. But corruption did not begin with the advent of the Radicals, nor did it cease when they were forced from office. The land and railroad legislation of some of the 'Redeemer' governments was no less corrupt and considerably more expensive than anything that the Radical governments achieved. Corruption was confined to no class, no party, and no section: larceny by the Tweed Ring in New York City and the Gas Ring in Philadelphia made the Southern Radicals look like feckless amateurs, as most of them were.

Radical reconstruction was expensive, and taxes and indebtedness mounted throughout the South, but we should keep in mind mitigating circumstances. The task of repairing the damages of the war was herculean and made unprecedented demands on government; with emancipation the population requiring public services had almost doubled and Radical governments for the first time tried to set up public schools for all children;

much of the property that had customarily borne the burden of taxation—banks, railroads, and industries—had been destroyed by the war, leaving almost the whole burden to fall on real estate. Some two-thirds of the total new indebtedness was in the form of guarantees to railroads and other industries. In this extravagant and often corrupt policy of underwriting railroads, the conservative governments which succeeded the Radicals spent, or pledged, more money than had the Radicals. Of the situation in Alabama, John Hope Franklin has observed, 'Corruption was bisectional, bipartisan and biracial.'

More important was the constructive side of Radical reconstruction—progressive legislation. In South Carolina the Radical legislature reformed the system of taxation, dispensed relief to the poor, distributed homesteads to Negroes, established numerous charitable and humane institutions, encouraged immigration, and, for the first time in the history of the state, provided free public schools and compelled attendance of all children from six to sixteen. It was in the realm of public education that the Radical governments made their most significant contribution. In general the Radical legislatures advanced political democracy and inaugurated social reforms, and these contributions go far to justify a favorable judgment upon them. So, too, does the consideration that the Radical legislatures enacted no vindictive legislation against the former slaveowners.

Notwithstanding these accomplishments, the Negro was unable to make any serious dent on Southern white hostility or prejudice. Convinced that he was incompetent politically, Southern whites blamed him for all the ills and burdens and humiliations of reconstruction. And because the experiment of black participation in politics had been associated with the Republican party, Southerners concluded that Democrats were the party of white supremacy and fastened upon the South a one-party system. Because some progressive laws were identified with carpetbag and Negro rule, they came to distrust such legislation. Because high taxes had accompanied Radical rule, they concluded that economy and good government were synonymous. Even many of their quondam

Northern champions reached the unhappy conclusion that black participation in politics had been premature.

Reconstruction and the Constitution

At no time in American history has the Constitution been subjected to so severe or prolonged a strain as during the era of reconstruction. There arose at once a number of knotty problems concerning the legal status of the seceded states after Appomattox and the status of persons who had participated in the rebellion. Throughout the war President Lincoln maintained the legal principle that the states were indestructible. This theory, though vigorously controverted by the Radical leaders, received judicial support in *Texas v. White* in 1869, in which Chief Justice Chase, speaking for the majority, said:

The Constitution, in all of its provisions, looks to an indestructible Union composed of indestructible States.... Considered, therefore, as transactions under the Constitution, the ordinance of secession . . . and all the acts of her legislature intended to give effect to that ordinance, were absolutely null. They were utterly without operation in law. The obligations of the State, as a member of the Union, remained perfect and unimpaired.... Our conclusion therefore is, that Texas continued to be a State, and a State of the Union.

Upon what theory, then, could reconstruction proceed? If the states were still in the Union, it was only the citizens who were out of their normal relations with the Federal Government, and these could be restored through the pardoning power of the President. This was Lincoln's theory, and Johnson took it over from him; when, in a series of proclamations, Johnson declared the insurrection at an end, the Supreme Court accepted his proclamations as legally binding.

But if the insurrection was at an end, by virtue of what authority did Congress proceed to impose military government upon Southern states and set up military courts? The Supreme Court had already passed upon the question of military courts in *ex parte Milligan*. In this case involving the validity of military courts in Indiana, the Court laid down the doctrine that 'martial rule can never exist where the courts are open, and in the proper

and unobstructed exercise of their jurisdiction'; and to the argument of military necessity the Court said, 'No doctrine involving more pernicious consequences was ever invented by the wit of man than that any of the [Constitution's] provisions can be suspended during any of the great exigencies of government. Such a doctrine leads directly to anarchy or despotism.' Yet within a year, in clear violation of this decision, Congress established military tribunals throughout the South; and when the validity of this legislation was challenged, in the McCardle case, Congress rushed through a law depriving the Court of jurisdiction over the case, while the Supreme Court sat idly by.

Radical leaders sought to legitimize their policies by relying upon the clause in the Constitution that 'the United States shall guarantee to every State a Republican Form of Government.' For three-quarters of a century this clause had been interpreted to mean that Congress would sustain the pre-existing governments, but now the Radicals insisted that—for the Southern states at least—a 'republican' form of government included Negro suffrage, despite the fact that at the beginning of the Reconstruction era only six Northern states permitted the black man to vote. The Court supported the Radicals to the extent of declaring that 'the power to carry into effect the clause of guarantee is primarily a legislative power, and resides in Congress.'

Some of the reconstruction acts were palpably unconstitutional, but the attitude of the Radicals was well expressed by General Grant when he said of this legislation that 'much of it, no doubt, was unconstitutional; but it was hoped that the laws enacted would serve their purpose before the question of constitutionality could be submitted to the judiciary and a decision obtained.' This hope was well founded, for the validity of some of the reconstruction measures never came before the courts, and others were not passed upon until long after they had 'served their purpose.' When Mississippi asked for an injunction restraining President Johnson from carrying out the reconstruction acts, the Supreme Court refused to accept jurisdiction. Georgia then brought suit against Secretary of War Stanton and General Grant, but once again the Court refused to intervene in what it termed a political controversy.

Individuals fared somewhat better. In *ex parte Garland* the operation of the federal test oath to exclude lawyers who had participated in the rebellion from practicing in federal courts was declared unconstitutional because *ex post facto;* and in *Cummings v. Missouri* similar state legislation was held invalid on the same grounds. For practical reasons it proved almost impossible to challenge the constitutionality of the confiscation of cotton or other property seized from those who were assumed to be rebels, but one notable case vindicated the right of the individual against lawless action even when committed in the name of the United States government. During the war Robert E. Lee's splendid estate at Arlington, Virginia, had been seized for nonpayment of taxes and bid in by the Federal Government, which then used it as a national cemetery. Long after the war the heirs of Lee brought suit. By a five to four vote the Supreme Court held that it would hear a suit against a sovereign—or its agents—and that the original seizure was illegal. Constitutionally, the significance of the decision lies in the assertion that no official of the government may cloak himself in the immunity of sovereignty for his illegal acts.

The Grant Administration

While Grant was wrestling with the difficult problems of Reconstruction he also had to concern himself with diplomatic and economic issues that were often altogether unrelated to the question of what policy to pursue toward the South. Thanks to Seward the Johnson administration was at its best in the realm of foreign affairs. Thanks to Hamilton Fish the Grant administration likewise won its most notable successes in this area. Both administrations had to cope with vexatious foreign questions which had grown out of the Civil War. Seward, by his firm attitude toward the French in Mexico and the Spaniards in Santo Domingo, sustained the Monroe Doctrine, and by strokes of diplomacy advanced imperialism in the Pacific. Spain's attempted conquest of Santo

Domingo broke down of its own accord, but the Spanish withdrawal from the island in 1865 appeared to be a diplomatic victory for Seward. Two years later Seward persuaded Napoleon III he must abandon the Mexican venture: in June 1867 the puppet-Emperor Maximilian slumped before a firing squad and the cardboard empire collapsed. Russia had long been eager to get rid of Alaska, and in 1867 Sumner in the Senate and a well-oiled lobby in the House permitted Seward to buy that rich domain, known at the time as 'Seward's Folly,' for $7,200,000. To round out his expansionist policy Seward annexed the Midway Islands west of Hawaii, and, with a view to the construction of an isthmian canal at some future date, acquired the right of transit across Nicaragua.

President Grant was enormously interested in another of Seward's projects—the annexation of Santo Domingo. This hare-brained proposal had originated with two Yankee fortune-hunters who planned to secure for themselves half the wealth of the island. They managed to draw into their conspiracy powerful economic interests and bought the support of such men as Ben Butler, John A. Rawlins, and Grant's personal secretary, Orville Babcock; these in turn won over the President. But when Grant submitted a treaty of annexation to the Senate, it encountered the implacable hostility of Charles Sumner and Carl Schurz and failed of ratification, a severe defeat for the administration.

The Santo Domingo episode, in itself minor, had important consequences. It revealed how easily Grant could be taken in and how naïve was his understanding of foreign affairs. It led to the deposition of Charles Sumner as chairman of the Senate Committee on Foreign Affairs, which widened the rift in the Republican party. And by distracting the attention of Grant and the Radicals from the Cuban situation, it enabled Fish to preserve peace with Spain.

A Cuban rebellion had broken out in 1868 and dragged on for ten dreadful years before it was finally suppressed. The sympathy of most Americans was with the rebels, but a movement to recognize Cuban belligerency encountered the firm opposition of Fish. Recognition would have been a serious mistake, for it would have gravely com-

A ripening pear. In this 1868 *Harper's Weekly* engraving, a covetous Secretary of State, William H. Seward, advocates annexation of Cuba, which had just raised the standard of rebellion against Spain, while a sage Uncle Sam counsels patience—but with the same end in view. Seward, who roved the Caribbean from Santo Domingo to the Danish West Indies in search of acquisitions, aimed at nothing less than 'possession of the American continent and the control of the world,' but Congress restrained his ambitions. From the presidency of James K. Polk to that of John Fitzgerald Kennedy, 'the Pearl of the Antilles,' only ninety miles off the Florida coast, tempted and vexed American administrations. (*Library of Congress*)

promised pending American claims against Great Britain for premature recognition of the belligerency of the Confederacy. As it was, the United States and Spain came to the very brink of war in 1873 over the curious *Virginius* affair. The *Virginius*, a ship flying the U.S. flag and carrying arms for the Cuban insurgents, was captured on the high seas by a Spanish gunboat; fifty-three of her seamen, including eight Americans, were summarily executed for 'piracy.' When Spain disowned the barbarous deed and paid an indemnity, and when it was discovered that the ship had no right to her American papers or to fly the American flag, the danger of war evaporated.

To the northward, too, relations were strained. During the war Canada had furnished a base for

Confederate raids on Vermont and New York. In time of peace the Fenians, or Irish Revolutionary Brother-Republics, took similar liberties in the United States. Two rival Irish republics were organized in New York City, each with its president, cabinet, and general staff in glittering uniforms of green and gold. Each planned to seize Canada with Irish veterans of the Union army, and hold it as hostage for Irish freedom. The first invasion, in April 1866, was promptly nipped by federal authorities at Eastport, Maine. But the ensuing outcry from Irish-Americans, who carried heavy weight at the polls, frightened the Johnson administration. Before it could decide who should take on the onus of stopping him, 'General' John O'Neil led 1500 armed Irishmen across the Niagara river. The next day, 2 June 1866, the Canadian militia gave battle, and fled; but the Fenians fled farther—to New York State, where they were promptly arrested and as promptly released. In the spring of 1870 tatterdemalion armies moved once more on Canada from St. Albans, Vermont, and Malone, New York. United States marshals arrested the Fenian leaders, and the armies disintegrated. Ridiculous as they were, the Fenian forays caused Canada much trouble and expense for which she was never reimbursed by the United States.

The greatest achievement of the Grant administration was the liquidation of outstanding diplomatic controversies with Great Britain. The sympathy of the English ruling classes for the Confederacy and the lax enforcement of neutrality by the British government had aroused deep resentment in the United States, and for some years no calm adjudication of American claims was possible. The most important of these claims had to do with the alleged negligence of the British in permitting the Confederate cruisers *Alabama*, *Shenandoah*, and *Florida* to be armed in, and escape from, British ports. Seward's persistent advocacy of these claims was finally rewarded in the last months of Johnson's administration by a convention for their adjudication. In April 1869 the Senate rejected this convention as insufficient, after Sumner had charged Great Britain with responsibility for half the total cost of the war: a mere $2,125 million! Sumner's speech shocked

his English friends who so faithfully had sustained the Union cause; nor were they much comforted by his explanation that the cession of Canada would be an acceptable form of payment.

After Sumner was eliminated as a result of his recalcitrance on Santo Domingo, negotiations went forward more successfully, for England was now ready to make amends. So the Canadian Sir John Rose staged with Hamilton Fish a diplomatic play of wooing and yielding that threw dust in the eyes of extremists on both sides. The covenant thus arrived at, the Treaty of Washington (8 May 1871), provided for arbitration of boundary disputes, the fisheries question, and the *Alabama* claims; determined rules of neutrality that should govern the arbitral tribunal (which subsequently assessed the British for damages wrought by the three cruisers); and contained an expression of regret for the escape of the *Alabama*.

Although the United States was thereby vindicated, the greater victory was for arbitration and peace. Never before had questions involving such touchy matters of national honor been submitted to a mere majority vote of an international tribunal. The English accepted the verdict with good grace. Charles Francis Adams never forgot that he was judge not advocate, and President Grant by his unwavering support of peaceful methods showed a quality not unusual in statesmen who know war at first hand. In a later message to the Arbitration Union of Birmingham, Grant set forth his guiding principle: 'Nothing would afford me greater happiness than to know that... at some future day, the nations of the earth will agree upon some sort of congress which will take cognizance of international questions of difficulty, and whose decisions will be as binding as the decisions of our Supreme Court are upon us. It is a dream of mine that some such solution may be.'

If the Grant administration, for all its shortcomings, was at its best in diplomatic affairs, the hero of Appomattox came off most poorly in coping with domestic issues such as the 'money question' and civil service reform. Like the Southern question, the money question was inherited from previous administrations. During the war the government had issued $450 million of legal tender notes, and at the close of the war some $400 million of these 'greenbacks' were still in circulation. The presence of greenbacks gave rise to two divisive issues. The first involved the medium of payment of the interest and principal of government bonds. Since these bonds had been purchased with depreciated greenbacks, farmers and workingmen reasoned that they should be redeemable in greenbacks unless otherwise specified, while bondholders insisted on payment in gold. The Democrats endorsed the proposal to redeem government securities in greenbacks, and Johnson went even further and urged that future interest payments be applied to liquidating the principal of the debt. But in his first inaugural address Grant committed himself to paying all government obligations in gold, and the first measure passed by the new Congress (18 March 1869) pledged the faith of the United States to such payment.

The second question concerned government policy toward the contraction of greenbacks and the resumption of specie payments. The inflation of the currency through greenbacks had tended to raise commodity prices, make credit easier and money cheaper. The farmer and the debtor therefore regarded with dismay any proposal to contract the currency by calling in these greenbacks. Business interests were divided; most wanted a stable currency, and hence opposed both currency expansion and abrupt resumption. But some businessmen, such as those who had gone into debt, favored expansion, while conservative bankers and others of the creditor class demanded that the government pledge itself to redeem greenbacks with gold and thus bring this paper currency to par.

A powerful argument for stabilizing the currency was that constant fluctuation in the value of greenbacks invited speculation. Because greenbacks were not legal tender for all purposes and because it was uncertain whether the government would ever redeem them in gold, they circulated at a discount which varied from month to month. In September 1869 two notorious stock gamblers, Jay Gould and Jim Fisk, took advantage of this fluctuation in the value of money to organize a 'corner' in gold. With the passive connivance of persons high in the confidence of the President and the Secretary of the Treasury, the nefarious scheme almost succeeded. On 'Black Friday,' 24 September 1869, the premium on gold rose to 162, and scores of Wall Street brokers faced ruin. Then the government dumped $4 million in gold on the market, and the 'corner' collapsed. 'The worst scandals of the 18th century,' wrote Henry Adams, 'were relatively harmless by the side of this which smirched executive, judiciary, banks, corporate systems, professions, and people, all the great active forces of society.' Yet the episode reflected not so much upon Grant's character as upon his judgment, which vacillated.

In 1870 the greenback question came before the Supreme Court. When Chief Justice Chase—who as Secretary of the Treasury had originally issued them—announced that greenbacks were not legal tender for obligations entered into prior to the emission of the notes, and even made the alarming suggestion that they were completely invalid,[4] the government promptly moved for a rehearing. Two vacancies on the Supreme Court afforded Grant a propitious opportunity. In Joseph P. Bradley and William Strong, Grant found jurists upon whose faith in the constitutionality of the greenbacks he could rely. He was not disappointed. In the second Legal Tender decision, *Knox v. Lee*, the Court in 1871 reversed itself and sustained the constitutionality of the Civil War greenbacks. Thirteen years later, in an even more sweeping decision, *Juilliard v. Greenman*, it proclaimed the government's right to issue legal tender even in time of peace. When, in 1874, Congress attempted to do this, Grant interposed his veto and the threat of inflation passed. In 1875 Congress finally provided for the resumption of specie payments on 1 January 1879. This act settled, for the time being, the legal tender question, but the money question remained to plague the next generation.

The tariff question also vexed the Grant administration. The skyhigh Civil War tariffs were originally accepted as emergency revenue measures; protected industries soon came to regard them as permanent. After Appomattox, Western farmers

4. *Hepburn v. Griswold* 8 Wallace 603 (1870).

and Eastern reformers joined hands in demanding tariff reduction, but the protected interests would not yield. The Grant administration set itself against tariff reform. Secretary Cox was forced out of the cabinet in part because of his sympathy for it, and David A. Wells, the able economist who was a special commissioner of revenue, had to resign for the same reason.

Nor did civil service reform fare better. In no area was the record of Grant's administration more discreditable. Grant's appointment of Jacob Cox to the Interior Department was a gesture toward reform, and when in 1871 a Civil Service Commission, headed by George William Curtis, submitted a list of desirable reforms, Grant promised a fair trial. But Cox was shoved out, and Grant soon scuttled the commission and packed the civil service with party henchmen. Curtis, wearied of shadow-boxing with the spoilsmen, resigned in disgust, and in 1875 the commission itself was discontinued.

The Liberal Republican Movement

Within less than a year after Grant's assumption of office, a revolt within the Republican party was in full swing. The full measure of administrative corruption was as yet unknown, but enough was suspected to outrage men who cherished standards of political decency. Grant's Southern policy was controversial, his Caribbean policy an affront, while his repudiation of reformers troubled even some of his own followers. Above all there was a growing distrust of Grant himself, which found expression in Senator Sumner's speech of May 1872 scoring him for taking and giving bribes, nepotism, neglect of duty, and lawless interference with the other departments of the government. Grant's abuse of the civil service alienated Cox and Schurz, his Southern policy antagonized Lyman Trumbull and Gideon Welles, his tariff policy cost him the support of David A. Wells, and such men as Chief Justice Chase, Horace Greeley, Charles Francis Adams, and E. L. Godkin came to regard the President as unfit for high office.

This revolt against Grant was started by liberals and reformers, but old-line politicians and disap-

pointed factional leaders soon flocked to it in embarrassing numbers. In the end it consisted of a group even more heterogeneous than usual in American parties. The one idea that animated them was distrust of President Grant. It was a movement of opposition rather than of positive reform; and therein lay its chief weakness. When the Liberal Republican convention met at Cincinnati 1 May 1872, this weakness became apparent. It was impossible for the discordant elements to agree upon a satisfactory platform or a logical candidate. The platform called for the withdrawal of troops from the South, civil service reform, and a resumption of specie payments; as for the tariff, the convention 'recognizing that there are in our midst honest but irreconcilable differences of opinion' remanded 'the discussion of the subject to the people in their congressional Districts.' Nor could the convention unite on a presidential candidate like Charles Francis Adams or Lyman Trumbull, the latter for almost 20 years one of the ornaments of the party. Intrigues and jealousies defeated them, and in the end the convention stampeded to Horace Greeley.

No man in the country was better known than Greeley, for over thirty years editor of the powerful New York *Tribune*, but he was renowned as an editor not as a statesman. A Vermont Yankee who had kept his homespun democracy and youthful idealism, Greeley persistently championed the cause of the underprivileged, the worker, and the farmer. Yet for all his intellectual abilities and idealism, Greeley lacked the first qualifications for responsible political position. He was impulsive, intriguing, vain, and vindictive, and his carefully cultivated idiosyncrasies laid him open to caricature. A familiar figure on the streets of New York, he wore a crumpled white coat, its pockets stuffed with newspapers, and crowning his bewhiskered face was a tall white hat. He reminded some of Mr. Pickwick, others of the Mad Hatter.

The nomination of Greeley came as a shock to the reformers who had organized the Liberal Republican movement. *The Nation* reported that 'a greater degree of incredulity and disappointment' had not been felt since the news of the first battle of Bull Run. But the discomfort of the reformers was as nothing to the dismay of Southern Dem-

Election Night, 1872. A New York City crowd peers up at the rooftop of a building at Broadway and 22nd Street where a stereopticon projects a bulletin showing Pennsylvania giving Grant a 100,000-vote lead. Final returns increased Grant's margin in the Keystone State to a whopping 138,000. Rock-ribbed Republican Pennsylvania voted for Buchanan in 1856 but did not wind up in the Democratic column again until Franklin D. Roosevelt's landslide in 1936. (New-York Historical Society, *Frank Leslie's Illustrated Newspapers, 23 Nov. 1872*)

ocrats. For thirty years Greeley had castigated the South and the Democratic party, and much of the responsibility for anti-slavery, and later for Radical reconstruction, could justly be laid at his door. Yet the Democrats had no choice but to make Greeley their nominee, for he offered the only alternative to the continuation of Radical reconstruction. But it was hard to work up enthusiasm for a candidate who had said: 'May it be written on my grave that I was never the Democratic party's follower and lived and died in nothing its debtor.'

Greeley proved himself an excellent campaigner, but the odds against him were insuperable. Grant could command the support of rank and file Republicans, veterans of the Union armies, the blacks North and South, and most of the German vote alienated by Greeley's temperance views. Grant carried all but six states; Greeley, with less than 44 per cent of the vote, failed to win a single state in the North or West. Three weeks later Horace Greeley died, broken-hearted. The Liberal Republican party did not long survive him, but many of the men who took part in that campaign would be active in the 'Mugwump' wing of the Republican party for the next generation.

Scandal and Stagnation

While the 1872 campaign was still under way, the country was startled by charges of wholesale corruption in connection with the construction of the Union Pacific Railroad, charges which reflected upon men high in Republican councils. The promoters of the Union Pacific, in order to divert the profits of construction to themselves, had organized a construction company, the Credit Mobilier of America. To this company the directors of the Union Pacific awarded fantastically profitable contracts. As a result of this corrupt arrangement the Union Pacific was forced to the verge of bankruptcy while the Credit Mobilier paid in a single year dividends of 348 per cent. Fearing Congress might interpose, the directors placed large blocks of Credit Mobilier stock 'where they would do most good.' Exposure of the scheme brought disgrace to a number of representatives, and to Vice-President Schuyler Colfax,

while others such as Henry Wilson of Massachusetts and James A. Garfield of Ohio were never able to explain away their connection with the unsavory affair.

Scarcely less excusable was the so-called Salary Grab. In 1873 Ben Butler pushed through a bill doubling the President's salary and increasing by 50 per cent the salary of Congressmen. This could be justified; what particularly affronted public opinion was that the increases granted to Congressmen were made retroactive for two years: thus each Congressman voted himself $5000 in back salary out of public funds. The bill was an evasion if not an outright violation of the Constitution, but Grant signed it without demur. A storm of indignation against this 'steal' swept the country, and in the following session Congress hastened to restore the old salary scale.

The Credit Mobilier and the Salary Grab were merely the most sensational of the exposures. In the Navy Department, Secretary Robeson accumulated a fortune of several hundred thousand dollars during his tenure of office. The Department of the Interior worked hand in glove with land speculators. The Treasury farmed out uncollected taxes to one J. D. Sanborn who promptly proceeded to highjack some $425,000 out of corporations, one-half of which he took for himself. The U.S. minister to England, Robert Schenck, lent his prestige to the Emma Mine swindle, and the minister to Brazil, J. W. Webb, defrauded the Brazilian government of $50,000 and fled to Europe, leaving the United States Government to refund the money, with apologies. The Custom House in New York was a sink of corruption, but when Collector Thomas Murphy was finally forced out, Grant accepted his resignation 'with regret.' In the national capital 'Boss' Shepherd ran up a debt of $17 million, a large part of which was graft, and found himself appointed by a grateful President to be chairman of the Board of Public Works. It was Shepherd, too, who was largely responsible for the failure of the Freedmen's Bank, a cruel hardship for thousands of trusting blacks.

Worse was still to come. After the Democrats carried the congressional elections of 1874, a Democratic House, the first since the Civil War, set

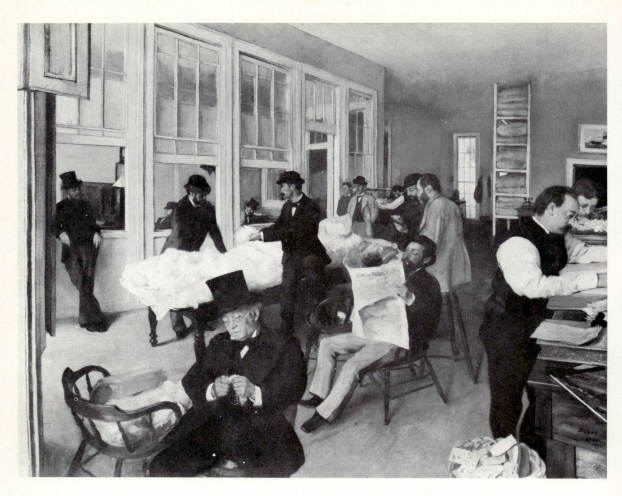

'The Cotton Exchange at New Orleans.' This painting by the French artist Edgar Degas entitled 'Le Bureau de coton de la Nouvelle-Orléans' shows that though the war devastated trade in the South, cotton continued to be 'King.' In 1872 Degas visited the Crescent City, where his brothers were cotton brokers. 'One does nothing here,' he wrote. 'It's in the climate, so much cotton, one lives for and by cotton.' From the sketches he made he painted this picture on his return to France in 1873. The following year he helped organize the first exhibition of the Impressionists. (*Musée des Beaux Arts, Pau. Photo Giraudon*)

The "Brains."

That achieved the Tammany victory at
the Rochester Democratic Convention.

The Tweed Ring. Nast, who invented the tiger as the
symbol of Tammany Hall, caricatured the Tammany
boss, William Marcy Tweed, so effectively that the
Ring's lawyers offered him $500,000 to desist. New
York voters might not be able to read, Tweed said, but
they could 'look at the damn pictures,' in which he was
depicted as obese and corrupt, wearing an ornate
diamond stickpin. To evade imprisonment, Tweed, disguised as a sailor, fled to Spain, but he was identified
from a Nast cartoon, arrested, and returned to America,
where he died in a New York jail. (*Harper's Weekly*,
19 Aug. 1871)

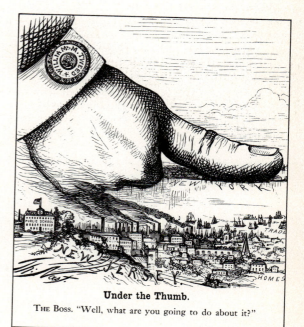

Under the Thumb.

THE BOSS. "Well, what are you going to do about it?"

afoot a series of investigations. In the Treasury and War departments, investigators uncovered sensational wrongdoing. For years a 'Whiskey Ring' in St. Louis had systematically defrauded the government of millions in taxes on distilled whiskey. The Ring had operated with the collusion of Treasury officials and of the President's private secretary, Babcock. When Grant was apprised of the situation he said, 'Let no guilty man escape.' But most of them did escape, Babcock with the President's connivance. No sooner had the 'Whiskey Ring' been exposed than the country confronted a new scandal. Secretary of the Treasury Benjamin H. Bristow found irrefutable proof that Secretary of War Belknap had sold Indian post traderships. Faced with impeachment, Belknap hurried to resign, and his resignation was accepted 'with great regret' by the President whom he had betrayed. Impeachment proceedings were instituted, but the Secretary was finally acquitted on the technical ground that the Senate no longer had jurisdiction over his case.

Corruption was not confined to the national government. It could be found in local governments, in business, and even in the professions. There was almost everywhere a breakdown of old moral standards. The industrial revolution, the building of transcontinental railroads, and the exploitation of new natural resources had called into existence a class of new rich untrained to the responsibilities of their position. Never before and only twice since—after World War I and in the 1970's—have public morals fallen so low.

State legislatures, too, were guilty of gross corruption. In the fierce struggle between Daniel Drew and Cornelius Vanderbilt for control of the Erie Railroad the legislature of New York State was auctioned off to the highest bidder, and both bar and bench proved that they too were for sale. In Pennsylvania the Cameron machine bought and sold legislation with bare-faced effrontery. In Wisconsin, Minnesota, and California, railroads controlled the legislatures; in Iowa the money for the Agricultural College realized from land-grant sales was stolen. Cities also presented a sorry spectacle. The brigandage of the Tweed Ring cost New York City not less than $100 million.

At a time when the Grant administration was reeling from reports of corruption, the panic of 1873 struck an even heavier blow. Reckless speculation and wholesale stock watering helped precipitate the panic. Other causes were perhaps equally important. Europe, too, felt the hard times, and overseas investors proceeded to call in their American loans. The unfavorable balance of trade, which had persisted all through the war and the postwar years, mounted during the early 'seventies. Too rapid expansion of the agricultural West produced surplus crops which could not be marketed abroad at satisfactory prices. Credit was overextended, currency inflated, and public finances deranged by the conflicting claims of greenbacks and of gold. With an immense self-confidence the country had mortgaged itself to the future; now it found itself unable to pay either interest or principal.

The crash came 17 September 1873 with the failure of the great banking house of Jay Cooke and Company—the house that had helped finance the war and the Northern Pacific Railroad. Soon one substantial business firm after another toppled, and the New York Stock Exchange took the unprecedented step of closing its doors for ten days. Industrial plants shut down, railway construction declined sharply, and over half the railroads defaulted on their bonds. Long bread lines began to appear in the larger cities, and tramps swarmed the countryside. Such a crisis was bound to have political consequences; it not only lead to the birth of a farmer-labor party, but put the chances of the Republicans in the 1876 election in serious jeopardy.

The Disputed Election of 1876

Republican defeat seemed certain in 1876 as the bankruptcy of the Grant administration became increasingly apparent. To give the party respectability, the Republicans chose the honest if uninspiring Rutherford B. Hayes, thrice Governor of Ohio. The Democrats, determined to make reform the issue of the campaign, nominated Samuel J. Tilden, who had broken the notorious Tweed Ring and then, as Governor of New York, smashed the 'Canal Ring.'

When the first reports came in, Tilden appeared

to have won a sweeping victory. He carried New York, New Jersey, Connecticut, Indiana, and apparently all the South while piling up a popular plurality of over 250,000. But, scanning the returns, the Republican campaign managers became convinced that the election might yet be swung to their candidate. Four states—South Carolina, Florida, Louisiana, and Oregon—were apparently in doubt. Without these states Tilden had only 184 electoral votes; 185 were necessary to win. On the morning after election Zach Chandler wired each of the doubtful states, 'Can you hold your state?'—and that afternoon he announced, 'Hayes has 185 electoral votes and is elected.'

The situation was highly precarious. In all three Southern states there had been intimidation and fraud on both sides. Hayes appeared to have carried South Carolina, but in Florida and Louisiana Tilden seemed to have a safe majority. Republican returning boards threw out about 1000 Democratic votes in Florida and over 13,000 in Louisiana, and gave certificates to the Hayes electors. In Oregon a Democratic governor had displaced a Republican elector on a technicality and appointed a Democrat in his place. From all four states came two sets of returns.

The Constitution provides that 'The President of the Senate shall, in the presence of the Senate and House of Representatives, open all the certificates, and the votes shall then be counted.' But counted by whom? If the Republican President of the Senate did the counting, the election would go to Hayes; if the Democratic House counted, Tilden would be President. And if the two houses could not agree on the procedure, there would be no President. Was the nation then to drift, distraught and confused, without a chief executive?

Conservatives, North and South, hastened to head off such a crisis. The solution was hinted at by Representative Garfield in a letter to Hayes. Some of the extremists on both sides, he wrote, were prepared to make trouble, but 'in the meantime two forces are at work. The Democratic businessmen of the country are more anxious for quiet than for Tilden; and the old Whigs are saying that they have seen war enough, and don't care to follow the lead of their northern associates.' Garfield suggested that 'if in some discreet way, these southern men who are dissatisfied with Tilden and his violent followers, could know that the South is going to be treated with kind consideration,' they might acquiesce in Hayes's election. If Southern conservatives secured an end to military reconstruction, restoration of 'home rule,' some voice in the Hayes administration, and generous subsidies for internal improvements, particularly railroads, they were prepared to concede the presidency. The Hayes forces were prepared to make these concessions.

With this understanding and with Tilden's reluctant consent, Congress was able to act. On 29 January 1877 it set up an Electoral Commission of fifteen members (five from the House, five from the Senate, and five from the Supreme Court) to pass on the disputed credentials. It was originally planned to appoint to this committee seven Democrats and seven Republicans and, as the fifteenth member, the non-partisan Judge David Davis of Illinois. At the last moment, however—and not by inadvertence—the legislature of Illinois elected Davis to the U.S. Senate and, with the approval of both parties, Judge Bradley was named in his place. As it turned out it was Bradley who named the next President of the United States. For on all questions the Electoral Commission divided along strict party lines, and Bradley voted invariably with the Republicans. By a straight 8-7 vote the Commission awarded all four states to Hayes, and thus the presidency—electoral count: 185 to 184.

Would the Democrats accept a solution which seemed so partisan and so unfair? For a time it was touch and go. Northern Democrats were prepared to filibuster long enough to prevent Congress from opening and counting the votes. But in the end wiser counsels prevailed. With renewed assurances from Hayes that he would abide by the sectional understanding, enough Southern Democrats deserted the Northern intransigents to permit Congress to count the ballots, and on 2 March 1877, only two days before Inauguration Day, Hayes was declared elected. This compromise worked well for those who contrived it. The real victim of the compromise was the Southern Negro, for it had been made at his expense and delayed for three generations the enforcement of those guarantees written into the Fourteenth and Fifteenth Amendments.

The Undoing of Reconstruction

Even before the Compromise of 1877, the country had wearied of the 'Southern question.' No longer would opinion molders in the North sustain military rule. In 1874 the Democrats captured the lower house, and the repudiation of Radicalism was all but complete. Meantime all the Southern states had been readmitted, and by the Amnesty Act of 1872 almost all Southern whites who were still disfranchised were restored to full political privileges. When the Radicals, their power waning, called for more military intervention, Grant rebuffed them. 'The whole public,' he protested, 'are tired out with the annual autumnal outbreaks in the South, and the great majority are ready now to condemn any interference on the part of the government.'

In state after state conservative whites recaptured control of the political machinery, until by the end of 1875 only South Carolina, Louisiana, and Mississippi were still under Radical control, and even in these states that control was precarious. Negores were eliminated from politics, carpetbaggers scared out, scalawags won over— and 'home rule' was restored. The Redeemer governments then proceeded to reduce expenditures and taxes—often at the expense of school children—and to erase a good deal of progressive legislation from the statute books. Acting on the assumption that the Radicals had saddled their states with fraudulent debts, and on the fact that in some instances the railroads, for whose benefit the debts had been contracted, had not carried out their part of the bargains, the Redeemers proceeded to repudiate a good part of the state obligations. By this convenient method Southern states rid themselves of perhaps $100 million of debts.

When Rutherford B. Hayes was inaugurated President, 4 March 1877, the carpetbag regime had been overthrown in all the states save South Carolina and Louisiana, where it was still upheld by federal bayonets. In South Carolina Confederate veterans known as Red Shirts organized white voters, kept blacks away from the polls, and elected the beloved Confederate General Wade Hampton governor and a Democratic legislature. A Republican returning board, however, sustained by federal soldiers, threw out the ballots of two counties, canceled thousands of others, and declared the carpetbag Governor D. H. Chamberlain duly re-elected. The Democratic members then organized their own House, and with Speaker, clerks, and sergeant-at-arms forced their way into the representatives' chamber where the Radicals were sitting. During three days and nights the rival Houses sat side by side, every man armed to the teeth and ready to shoot if the rival sergeant-at-arms laid hands on one of his colleagues. At the end of that time the Democrats withdrew, leaving Chamberlain in possession of the state house, but for four months the people of the state paid their taxes to Hampton's government. Chamberlain hastened to Washington to appeal for aid, but in vain. Faithful to the compromise by which he had been elected, President Hayes broke the deadlock by withdrawing the troops from Columbia, and the Democrats took possession. Two weeks later, when federal troops evacuated New Orleans, conservative white rule was completely restored throughout the South.

The withdrawal of troops by President Hayes in 1877 marked the abandonment not only of reconstruction, but of the Negro, who paid the price of reunion. There were three parts to the unwritten agreement: that President, Congress, and the North generally, would hereafter keep hands off the 'Negro problem'; that the rules governing race relations in the South would be written by whites; and that these rules would concede the Negro limited civil rights, but neither political nor social equality. The principle underlying this relationship was set forth succinctly by Henry Grady of the Atlanta *Constitution*: 'The supremacy of the white race of the South must be maintained forever, and the domination of the Negro race resisted at all points and at all hazards, because the white race is superior.' It was as simple as that.

The Negro's sole remaining hope lay with the courts. When, in 1873, the Supreme Court was called upon for the first time to interpret the phrases of the Fourteenth Amendment, Justice Samuel Miller, speaking for the Court, reviewed the history of the three Civil War Amendments and observed:

No one can fail to be impressed with the one pervading purpose found in them all, lying at the foundation of each, and without which none of them would have been even suggested; we mean the freedom of the slave race, the security and firm establishment of that freedom, and the protection of the newly made freedman and citizen from the oppressions of those who had formerly exercised unlimited dominion over him.

At the time this seemed the common sense of the matter, and no judge challenged this interpretation.

Each of these Amendments contained an unusual provision, 'Congress shall have power to enforce this article by appropriate legislation.' And, beginning with the ill-fated Civil Rights Act of 1866, Congress enacted a series of laws designed to do just that. The most important were the Enforcement Acts of 1870 and 1871 which threw the protection of the Federal Government over the Negro's right to vote; the Ku Klux Klan Act of 1871 which made it a federal offense to conspire to deprive Negroes of the equal protection of the laws; and the Civil Rights Act of 1875 which undertook to secure the Negro 'full and equal enjoyment of the accommodations, advantages, facilities, and privileges of inns, public conveyances on land or water, theatres, and other places of public amusement,' as well as the right to serve on juries.

Abandoned by Congress and the President, the Negro was now repudiated by the courts. If the 'one pervading purpose' of the Amendments was to protect the freedman, then it failed. Beginning with the Slaughterhouse case of 1873 the Supreme Court proceeded systematically to riddle the structure of Negro rights. In the Slaughterhouse case the Court asserted that all the important privileges and immunities derived not from national but from state citizenship and that the Fourteenth Amendment did not extend federal protection over these. The Cruikshank opinion of 1875, which involved a mob attack on blacks who were trying to vote, deliberately restricted the reach of the Fourteenth Amendment to state—not private—interference with rights, and to such interference as was clearly directed against blacks on account of their race or color. When an election official in Kentucky refused to receive a black's vote, the Court held that Congress did not have authority to protect the right to vote generally, but only where that right was denied by the *state*, and on grounds of *race* or *color*. In 1878 the Court provided the legal foundation for segregation by striking down a Louisiana statute forbidding discrimination in transportation as an unlawful interference with congressional authority over interstate commerce! In the *United States v. Harris*, a case in which a Tennessee mob had lynched four black prisoners, the Court returned to the theme that the national government could protect the black only against acts by the state, and that for protection against violence by individuals or mobs the victim must look to state authorities. The crucial test came with the Civil Rights Cases of 1883, where the Court, in effect, wiped off the statute book the Civil Rights Act of 1875.

It would be running the slavery argument into the ground [said Justice Bradley] to make it apply to every act of discrimination which a person may see fit to make as to the guests he will entertain, or as to the people he will take into his coach or cab or car, or admit to his concert or theatre, or deal with in other matters of intercourse or business.

And the Court added, that

When a man has emerged from slavery and by the aid of beneficent legislation has shaken off the inseparable concomitants of that state, there must be some stage in the progress of his elevation when he takes the rank of a mere citizen, and ceases to be the special favorite of the laws, and when his rights as a citizen, or a man, are to be protected in the ordinary modes by which other men's rights are protected.

This was the thesis, too, of the crucial *Plessy v. Ferguson* decision of 1896 which, by accepting the doctrine of 'separate but equal accommodations,' threw the mantle of judicial approval over segregation.[5]

This jettisoning of the civil rights program did not go without protest from within the Court itself. Justice Harlan of Kentucky spoke for a con-

---

5. Reversed some sixty years later in the even more crucial decision of *Brown v. Board of Education of Topeka*.

'Twenty Years After Independence.' This photograph of a Fourth of July celebration in Richmond suggests that two decades after the Emancipation Proclamation blacks still had a long way to go, but it also indicates reverence toward the Great Emancipator. (*Valentine Museum, Richmond, Virginia*)

struction of the Constitution broad enough to embrace the rights of all citizens. And, observing that the 'separate but equal' doctrine of the Plessy case would, in time 'be quite as pernicious as the decision in the Dred Scott case,' Harlan wrote prophetically:

The destinies of the two races in this country are indissolubly linked together, and the interests of both require that the common government of all shall not permit the seeds of race hate to be planted under the sanction of law. What can more certainly arouse race hate, what more certainly create and perpetuate a feeling of distrust between these races, than state enactments which in fact proceed on the ground that colored citizens are so inferior and degraded that they cannot be allowed to sit in public coaches occupied by white citizens.

The end of Reconstruction and the nullification of the Enforcement Acts exiled the Southern Negro to a kind of no-man's land halfway between slavery and freedom. No longer a slave, he was not yet free. He was tied to the soil by the share-crop and crop-lien systems, excluded from most

The Negro exodus. In 1879 some 50,000 blacks from Mississippi and other Deep South states migrated to the Western prairie out of discontent with the violent aftermath of Reconstruction, bad crops, and yellow fever, and with great expectations of 'sunny Kansas.' Many died during the bitter winter of 1879–80, and the 'Exodusters' found that racial discrimination was not confined to the South but was endemic in the old abolitionist havens too. This sketch by James H. Moser depicts a scene on the wharves at Vicksburg. (*Collection Judith Mara Gutman*)

professions and from many jobs, and fobbed off with 'separate' accommodations that were rarely 'equal.' He was expected not only to accept a position of social inferiority without protest, but to rejoice in it by playing the role of 'Uncle Tom.' At first gradually, then with dramatic speed, he was rendered politically impotent: 'grandfather' clauses, literacy tests, poll taxes, and—where these failed—naked intimidation, deprived him of the vote. In 1885 the Louisiana novelist, George Washington Cable, wrote:

One of the marvels of future history will be that it was counted a small matter, by a majority of our nation, for six millions of people within it, made by its own decree a component part of it, to be subjected to a system of oppression so rank that nothing could make it seem small except the fact that they had already been ground under it for a century and a half. . . . It heaps upon him in every public place the most odious distinctions, without giving ear to the humblest plea concerning mental or moral character. It spurns his ambition, tramples upon his languishing self-respect, and indignantly refuses to let him either buy with money or earn by any excellence of inner life or outward behavior, the most momentary immunity from these public indignities.

Southerners generally congratulated themselves that they had persuaded the North to concede them almost complete control of their domestic institutions. Yet the cost of the restoration of white rule was high, for white as well as for black. By sanctioning the use of fraud and coercion to deny the black his legal rights, they weakened moral standards. By restricting Negro voting they limited white suffrage, and thus struck a heavy blow at democracy. By identifying white supremacy with the Democrats they saddled a one-party system upon the South, and threw that party into the hands of the least enlightened elements of their society.

Reconstruction left deep physical and moral scars upon the South. A century later, the apostles of white supremacy were able to ring the changes on the evils of Reconstruction whenever even modest alterations in racial patterns were suggested. For decades after 1877, race relations were poisoned by an annual crop of outrages. Politics were forced into an unnatural groove, and the one-party system, a hostage to white supremacy, proved inhospitable to the introduction of new issues. Southern society remained relatively static, immune to modern movements in education and social regeneration. But Reconstruction also left another legacy: the civil rights amendments to the Constitution. In years to come, although much too tardily, Americans would begin to give to these provisions the meaning their framers intended.

Bibliography

GENERAL WORKS

1. Journals, Encyclopedias, and Reference Books

The American Historical Review (1895–   ); *The Mississippi Valley Historical Review* (1915–   ), now *The Journal of American History*; U.S. Bureau of the Census, *Historical Statistics of the United States; Colonial Times to 1970*, and *Statistical Abstract of the United States* (annual); F. Freidel & R. K. Showman (eds.), *Harvard Guide to American History*; A. Johnson & D. Malone (eds.), *The Dictionary of American Biography* (22 vols.), and supplementary volumes; R. B. Morris, *Encyclopedia of American History*.

2. Collections of Documents and Other Sources

H. S. Commager, *Documents of American History*; R. Leopold, A. Link, and S. Coben (eds.), *Problems in American History*; M. Meyers et al., *Sources of the American Republic* (2 vols.); R. B. Morris (ed.), *Documentary History of the United States*.

CHAPTER 1

1. The Indians and Prehistoric America

W. N. Fenton, *American Indian and White Relations to 1830*; A. M. Josephy, Jr. (ed.), *The American Heri-tage Book of Indians*; G. B. Nash, *Red, White, and Black*; W. T. Sanders, *New World Prehistory*; R. Underhill, *Red Man's Religion*; W. Washburn (ed.), *The Indian and the White Man*; C. Wissler, *Indians of the United States*; H. M. Wormington, *Ancient Man in North America*.

2. Northmen

E. Haugen, *Voyages to Vinland*; H. R. Holand, *Westward from Vinland*; A. M. Reeves, *Finding of Wineland the Good*; E. Wahlgren, *The Kensington Stone, a Mystery Solved*.

3. Exploration

C. H. & K. George, *The Protestant Mind of the English Reformation*; J. H. Hexter, *Reappraisals in History*; H. M. Jones, *O Strange New World*; S. E. Morison, *European Discovery of America*, vol. i: *Northern Voyages*, vol. ii: *Southern Voyages*; J. H. Parry, *The Age of Reconnaissance*, and *The Establishment of European Hegemony, 1415–1715*; J. J. Te Paske, *Three American Empires*.

4. Spanish and Portuguese

H. E. Bolton (ed.), *Spanish Borderlands*, and *Spanish Exploration in the Southwest*; E. G. Bourne, *Spain in America*; C. R. Boxer, *Four Centuries of Portuguese Expansion, 1415–1825*; R. B. Cunninghame Graham,

The Conquest of New Granada; C. H. Haring, The Spanish Empire in America; F. W. Hodge & T. H. Lewis (eds.), Spanish Explorers in the Southern United States; W. Lowery, Spanish Settlements in the United States; D. L. Molinari, Descubrimiento y Conquista de América; S. E. Morison, Admiral of the Ocean Sea (shorter version, Christopher Columbus, Mariner); G. T. Northup (ed.), Vespucci Reprints; J. E. Olson & E. G. Bourne (eds.), The Northmen, Columbus and Cabot; J. H. Parry, The Spanish Seaborne Empire; A. Pigafetta, Magellan's Voyage Around the World (J. A. Robertson, ed.); W. H. Prescott, Conquest of Mexico, and Conquest of Peru; E. Wolf, Sons of the Shaking Earth.

5. English and French
J. B. Brebner, The Explorers of North America; H. S. Burrage (ed.), Early English and French Voyages; Sir William Foster, England's Quest of Eastern Trade; R. Hakluyt (ed.), The Principall Navigations, Voiages, Traffiques and Discoveries of the English Nation; M. Kammen, People of Paradox; W. Notestein, The English People on the Eve of Colonization; F. Parkman, Pioneers of France in the New World (selections in S. E. Morison, ed., The Parkman Reader); J. E. Pomfret and F. M. Shumway, Founding the American Colonies; D. B. Quinn, Raleigh and the British Empire; A. L. Rowse, The Expansion of Elizabethan England, and The Elizabethans and America; H. R. Wagner, Sir Francis Drake's Voyage around the World; D. W. Waters, The Art of Navigation in England in Elizabethan and Early Stuart Times; J. A. Williamson, Voyages of John and Sebastian Cabot, and Age of Drake.

CHAPTER 2

1. Virginia and Maryland
C. A. Andrews, The Colonial Period of American History, vols. i, ii; P. L. Barbour, The Three Worlds of Captain John Smith; P. A. Bruce, Economic History (2 vols.), and Institutional History of Virginia in the Seventeenth Century (2 vols.); W. F. Craven, Dissolution of the Virginia Company, The Southern Colonies in the 17th Century, and White, Red, and Black; C. H. Firth, An American Garland; I. N. Hume, Here Lies Virginia; M. W. Jernegan, Laboring and Dependent Classes in Colonial America, 1607–1783; R. L. Morton, Colonial Virginia, vol. i; H. L. Osgood, The American Colonies in the 17th Century (3 vols.); H. R. Shurtleff, The Log Cabin Myth; A. Smith, Colonists in

Bondage; J. M. Smith (ed.), Seventeenth Century America: Essays in Colonial History; A. Vaughan, American Genesis; L. B. Wright, First Gentlemen of Virginia, and Cultural Life of the American Colonies.

2. The Puritan Colonies
B. Bailyn, New England Merchants in the 17th Century; W. Bradford, Of Plymouth Plantation (S. E. Morison, ed.); J. Demos, A Little Commonwealth; R. S. Dunn, Puritans and Yankees; K. T. Erikson, Wayward Puritans; G. L. Haskins, Law and Authority in Early Massachusetts; W. G. McLoughlin, New England Dissent, 1630–1833; P. Miller, Orthodoxy in Massachusetts, The New England Mind: The Seventeenth Century, Roger Williams (with T. H. Johnson), The Puritans, and From Colony to Province; E. S. Morgan, The Puritan Family, Visible Saints, and The Puritan Dilemma: The Story of John Winthrop; S. E. Morison, The Founding of Harvard College, Harvard in the Seventeenth Century (2 vols.), Builders of the Bay Colony, Intellectual Life of Colonial New England, and Story of the 'Old Colony' of New Plymouth; R. G. Pope, The Half-Way Covenant; S. Powell, Puritan Village; D. B. Rutman, Husbandmen of Plymouth; A. Vaughan, New England Frontier; T. J. Wertenbaker, The Puritan Oligarchy; O. Winslow, Roger Williams; L. Ziff, The Career of John Cotton, and Puritanism in America.

3. New Netherland
J. F. Jameson (ed.), Narratives of New Netherlands; C. Ward, Dutch and Swedes on the Delaware; T. J. Wertenbaker, The Founding of American Civilization: The Middle Colonies.

4. New France
M. Bishop, Champlain; D. Creighton, History of Canada, ch. 1; F. Parkman, Pioneers of France in the New World (selections in S. E. Morison, ed., The Parkman Reader); J. F. Saintoyant, Colonisation française sous l'ancien régime.

CHAPTER 3

1. General
C. A. Andrews, W. F. Craven, and H. L. Osgood, as in ch. 2; G. L. Beer, The Old Colonial System (2 vols.); D. J. Boorstin, The Americans: The Colonial Experience; W. F. Craven, The Colonies in Transition, 1660–

1713; O. M. Dickerson, *American Colonial Government, 1696–1765*; L. A. Harper, *The English Navigation Laws*; R. Hofstadter, *America at 1750*; D. S. Lovejoy, *The Glorious Revolution in America*; J. H. Smith, *Appeals to the Privy Council from the American Plantations*; C. L. Ver Steeg, *The Formative Years*; C. Williamson, *From Property to Democracy*.

2. The Carolinas

L. F. Brown, *The First Earl of Shaftesbury*; V. W. Crane, *The Southern Frontier, 1670–1732*; D. D. Wallace, *History of South Carolina*, vol. i.

3. New York and the Jerseys

A. C. Flick (ed.), *History of the State of New York*, vol. ii; J. H. Kennedy, *Thomas Dongan*; T. J. Wertenbaker, *The Founding of American Civilization: The Middle Colonies*.

4. Pennsylvania

H. Barbour, *Quakers in Puritan England*; W. W. Comfort, *William Penn and Our Liberties*; M. D. Learned, *Francis Daniel Pastorius*; F. B. Tolles, *Meeting House and Counting House*.

5. Virginia and New England

V. F. Barnes, *The Dominion of New England*; R. E. Brown, *Middle Class Democracy and the Revolution in Massachusetts*; R. E. & B. K. Brown, *Virginia: Democracy or Aristocracy?*; N. H. Chamberlain, *Samuel Sewall and the World He Lived In*; D. E. Leach, *Flintlock and Tomahawk*; D. Levin (ed.), *What Happened in Salem*; P. Miller, *The New England Mind: From Colony to Province*; R. L. Morton, *Colonial Virginia*, vol. i; G. W. Mullin, *Flight and Rebellion*; C. S. Sydnor, *Gentlemen Freeholders*; G. B. Warden, *Boston, 1689–1776*; W. E. Washburn, *The Governor and the Rebel*; T. J. Wertenbaker, *Torch-bearer of the Revolution*; L. B. Wright (ed.), *The Secret Diary of William Byrd of Westover, 1709–1712*; R. Zemsky, *Merchants, Farmers, and River Gods*.

6. Canada and the West Indies

V. W. Crane, *The Southern Frontier, 1670–1732*; C. H. Haring, *The Buccaneers in the West Indies in the Seventeenth Century*; L. W. Labaree, *Royal Government in America*; F. Parkman, *Frontenac and New France*, and *La Salle and the Discovery of the Great West* (extracts in S. E. Morison, ed., *Parkman Reader*).

7. Social, Economic, and Religious Development

B. Bailyn, *Education in the Forming of the American Society*, and *The New England Merchants in the 17th Century*; C. Bridenbaugh, *Cities in the Wilderness, Rebels & Gentlemen: Philadelphia in the Age of Franklin, Cities in Revolt, The Colonial Craftsman*, and *Mitre and Sceptre*; L. Cremin, *American Education: The Colonial Experience, 1607–1783*; D. S. Freeman, *George Washington*, vol. i; E. S. Gaustad, *The Great Awakening in New England*; W. M. Gewehr, *The Great Awakening in Virginia, 1740–90*; L. H. Gipson, *The British Empire before the American Revolution* (9 vols.); C. Grant, *Democracy in the Connecticut Frontier Town of Kent*; C. C. Gray, *History of Agriculture in the Southern United States*; P. J. Greven, Jr., *Four Generations*; E. Heckscher, *Mercantilism* (2 vols.); J. B. Hedges, *The Browns of Providence Plantations*; B. Hindle, *The Pursuit of Science in Revolutionary America*; K. A. Lockridge, *A New England Town*; C. H. Maxson, *The Great Awakening in the Middle Colonies*; R. Middlekauff, *Ancients and Axioms*, and *The Mathers*; P. Miller, *Jonathan Edwards*; E. S. Morgan, *The Gentle Puritan: A Life of Ezra Stiles*; R. B. Morris, *Government and Labor in Early America*; L. Morton, *Robert Carter of Nomini Hall*; R. L. Morton, *Colonial Virginia*, vol. ii; R. Pares, *Yankees and Creoles*; A. Simpson, *Puritanism in Old and New England*; A. Smith, *Colonists in Bondage*; W. W. Sweet, *Religion in Colonial America*; F. B. Tolles, *Quakers and the Atlantic Culture*; O. Winslow, *Jonathan Edwards*, and *Meetinghouse Hill*; L. B. Wright, *The Cultural Life of the American Colonies*; M. Zuckerman, *Peaceable Kingdoms*.

8. Georgia

V. W. Crane, *Promotion Literature of Georgia*; J. R. McCain, *Georgia as a Proprietary Province*; A. B. Saye, *New Viewpoints in Georgia History*.

9. Wars

J. S. Corbett, *England in the Seven Years' War* (2 vols.); D. S. Freeman, *Washington*, vol. ii; E. P. Hamilton, *The French and Indian Wars*; J. S. McLennan, *Louisbourg from Its Foundation to Its Fall*; R. Pares, *War and Trade in West Indies, 1739–63*; S. Pargellis, *Lord Loudoun in North America*; F. Parkman, *Half-Century of Conflict*, and *Montcalm and Wolfe* (extracts in Morison, ed., *Parkman Reader*); H. H. Peckham, *The Colonial Wars*; G. A. Wood, *William*

Shirley; G. M. Wrong, *The Fall of Canada*, and *The Rise and Fall of New France*.

CHAPTER 4

1. *Imperial Problems*

C. M. Andrews, *Colonial Background of the American Revolution*, and *The Colonial Period of American History*, vol. iv; G. L. Beer, *British Colonial Policy, 1754–1765, The Old Colonial System* (2 vols.), and *The Origins of the British Colonial System*; O. M. Dickerson, *The Navigation Acts and the American Revolution*; L. H. Gipson, *British Empire before the American Revolution*, vols. ii, iii, and iv; J. P. Greene, *The Quest for Power: The Lower Houses of Assembly in the Southern Royal Colonies*; L. A. Harper, *The English Navigation Laws*; M. Jensen, *The Founding of a Nation*; M. Kammen, *Empire and Interest*; L. W. Labaree, *Royal Government in America*; E. I. McCormac, *Colonial Opposition to Imperial Authority during the French and Indian War*; C. H. McIlwain, *The American Revolution*; P. Maier, *From Resistance to Revolution*; E. S. Morgan, *The Birth of the Republic*; C. Nettels, *The Money Supply of the American Colonies Before 1720*; J. Sosin, *Agents and Merchants*.

2. *The West and the Albany Plan of Union*

S. E. Morison, *Sources and Documents Illustrating the American Revolution*; H. M. Muhlenberg, *Notebook of a Colonial Clergyman*; R. Newbold, *The Albany Congress and Plan of Union*; H. Peckham, *Pontiac and the Indian Uprising*; J. Sosin, *Whitehall and the Wilderness*.

3. *The Colonies, 1763–1773*

C. L. Becker, *The History of Political Parties in the Province of New York*; P. U. Bonomi, *A Factious People*; C. Bridenbaugh, *Seat of Empire*; I. B. Cohen, *Benjamin Franklin*; E. B. Greene, *The Revolutionary Generation*; C. S. Sydnor, *Gentlemen Freeholders*.

4. *The West*

T. P. Abernethy, *Western Lands and the American Revolution*; C. W. Alvord, *The Mississippi Valley in British Politics* (2 vols.); C. Bridenbaugh, *Myths and Realities*; S. E. Morison, *Sources and Documents*, introd. and pp. 1–55.

5. *Revenue and Stamp Acts*

B. Bailyn (ed.), *Pamphlets of the American Revolution*; L. H. Gipson, *The Coming of the Revolution*; B. W. Labaree, *The Boston Tea Party*; J. C. Miller, *Origins of the American Revolution*, and *Sam Adams*; E. S. & H. M. Morgan, *The Stamp Act Crisis*; P. D. G. Thomas, *British Politics and the Stamp Act Crisis*; E. Wright, *Fabric of Freedom*.

6. *Townshend and Coercive Acts*

R. D. Brown, *Revolutionary Politics in Massachusetts*; O. M. Dickerson, *Boston Under Military Rule as Revealed in the Journals of the Times*; M. G. Kammen, *A Rope of Sand*; C. H. Metzger, *The Quebec Act*; R. B. Morris, *Studies in the History of American Law*, and *The Era of the American Revolution*; A. M. Schlesinger, *The Colonial Merchants and the American Revolution*, and *Prelude to Independence: The Newspaper War in Great Britain*; M. C. Tyler, *Literary History of the American Revolution*; H. B. Zobel, *The Boston Massacre*.

7. *Back-country Turmoil*

T. P. Abernethy, *Western Lands and the American Revolution*; J. R. Alden, *John Stuart and the Southern Colonial Frontier*; C. Bridenbaugh, *Myths and Realities*; R. M. Brown, *The South Carolina Regulators*; C. Woodmason, *The Carolina Backcountry*.

8. *Ideology*

R. G. Adams, *Political Ideas of the American Revolution*; B. Bailyn, *Pamphlets of the American Revolution*; C. L. Becker, *The Declaration of Independence*; J. P. Boyd, *Anglo-American Union*; E. C. Burnett, *The Continental Congress*; D. F. Hawke, *Paine*; D. Malone, *Jefferson the Virginian*; R. L. Schuyler, *Parliament and the British Empire*; C. P. Smith, *James Wilson*.

9. *Opening of Hostilities*

J. R. Alden, *General Gage in America*; J. Bakeless, *Turncoats, Traitors, and Heroes*; A. French, *The First Year of the American Revolution*.

10. *The Loyalists*

C. Berkin, *Jonathan Sewall*; J. B. Brebner, *The Neutral Yankees of Nova Scotia*; R. M. Calhoon, *The Loyalists in Revolutionary America, 1760–1781*; L. Einstein, *Divided Loyalties*; A. S. Flick, *Loyalism in New York*

During the American Revolution; P. H. Smith, *Loyalists and Redcoats*; C. H. Van Tyne, *Loyalists in the American Revolution*.

CHAPTER 5

1. *General*

J. R. Alden, *American Revolution, 1775–1783*, and *A History of the American Revolution*; T. S. Anderson, *The Command of the Howe Brothers during the American Revolution*; A. Bowman, *The Morale of the American Revolutionary Army*; H. S. Commager & R. B. Morris (eds.), *The Spirit of 'Seventy-six, the Story of the American Revolution as Told by Participants*; D. S. Freeman, *George Washington*, vols. iii–v; T. G. Frothingham, *Washington, Commander in Chief*; D. Higginbotham, *War of American Independence*; D. W. Knox, *The Naval Genius of Washington*; P. Mackesy, *War for America, 1775–1783*; J. T. Main, *The Sovereign States 1775–1783*; J. C. Miller, *Triumph of Freedom, 1775–1783*; R. B. Morris (ed.), *The Era of the American Revolution*; H. Peckham, *War for Independence*; E. Robson, *American Revolution in Its Political and Military Aspects, 1763–1783*; F. E. Schermerhorn, *American and French Flags of the Revolution*; P. Smith, *A New Age Now Begins*; W. M. Wallace, *Appeal to Arms*; C. Ward, *The War of the Revolution* (2 vols.); G. S. Wood, *The Creation of the American Republic, 1776–1787*.

2. *Supply and Finance*

A. Bezanson, *Prices and Inflation During the American Revolution*; C. J. Bullock, *Finances of the United States from 1775 to 1789*; R. A. East, *Business Enterprise in the American Revolutionary Era*; E. J. Ferguson, *Power of the Purse*; L. C. Hatch, *Administration of the American Revolutionary Army*; C. P. Nettels, *The Emergence of a National Economy, 1775–1815*; C. L. Ver Steeg, *Robert Morris*.

3. *Military Operations, through 1777*

J. R. Alden, *General Charles Lee, Traitor or Patriot?*; G. A. Billias, *General John Glover and His Marblehead Mariners*; G. S. Brown, *American Secretary: The Colonial Policy of Lord George Germain, 1775–1778*; L. Lundin, *Cockpit of the Revolution*; H. Nickerson, *The Turning Point of the Revolution*; J. M. Palmer, *General von Steuben*; H. Swiggett, *War Out of Niagara: Butler and the Tory Rangers*; W. B. Willcox, *Portrait of a General: Sir Henry Clinton in the War of Independence*.

4. *France and Diplomacy*

S. F. Bemis, *The Diplomacy of the American Revolution*; H. Butterfield, *George III, Lord North, and the People*; E. S. Corwin, *French Policy and the American Alliance of 1778*; V. W. Crane, *Benjamin Franklin and a Rising People*; G. H. Guttridge, *David Hartley*; F. Monaghan, *John Jay*; R. B. Morris, *The Peacemakers*; J. B. Perkins, *France in the American Revolution*; P. C. Phillips, *The West in the Diplomacy of the American Revolution*; R. W. Van Alstyne, *Empire and Independence*; C. Van Doren, *Benjamin Franklin*, and *Secret History of the Revolution*; G. M. Wrong, *Canada and the American Revolution*.

5. *Naval War and Military Operations, 1778–1782*

J. R. Alden, *The South in the Revolution*; G. W. Allen, *Naval History of the American Revolution* (2 vols.); W. B. Clark, *Lambert Wickes, Gallant John Barry*, and *Captain Dauntless*; W. M. James, *The British Navy in Adversity*; C. L. Lewis, *Admiral de Grasse and American Independence*; E. S. Maclay, *History of American Privateers*; Admiral A. T. Mahan, *The Influence of Sea-Power Upon History*, and *Major Operation of the Navies in the War of Independence*; S. E. Morison, *John Paul Jones, A Sailor's Biography*; T. Thayer, *Nathanael Greene*.

CHAPTER 6

1. *State Constitutions*

H. J. Eckenrode, *The Revolution in Virginia*; A. C. Flick, *History of the State of New York*, vol. iv; Z. Haraszti, *John Adams and the Prophets of Progress*; A. Nevins, *The American States during and after the Revolution*; J. P. Selsam, *The Pennsylvania Constitution of 1776*.

2. *Reform, Religion, and Slavery*

D. B. Davis, *The Problem of Slavery in the Age of the Revolution*; W. E. B. Du Bois, *Suppression of the African Slave-Trade*; H. J. Eckenrode, *Separation of Church and State in Virginia*; P. Guilday, *Life and Times of John Carroll* (2 vols.); J. F. Jameson, *The American Revolution Considered as a Social Movement*; W. D. Jordan, *White over Black*; G. A. Koch, *Republican Religion*; R. McCormick, *Experiment in Independence: New Jersey in the Critical Period, 1781–1789*; R. J. Purcell, *Connecticut in Transition*; M. Savelle, *Seeds of Liberty*.

3. Arts, Letters, Education

S. J. Buck, *The Planting of Civilization in Western Pennsylvania*; E. Ford, *David Rittenhouse*; N. Goodman, *Benjamin Rush*; S. E. Morison, *Three Centuries of Harvard*, ch. 7; E. C. Shoemaker, *Noah Webster, Pioneer of Learning*; R. E. Spiller, et al., *Literary History of the U.S.*, vol. i; D. J. Struik, *Yankee Science in the Making*, pt. 2.

4. The West and Vermont

G. H. Alden, *New Governments West of the Alleghenies before 1780*; C. A. Hanna, *The Wilderness Trail*; A. Henderson, *Star of Empire*; A. B. Hulbert, *Boone's Wilderness Road*; M. B. Jones, *Vermont in the Making*; L. P. Kellogg, *The British Regime in Wisconsin and the Northwest*; W. S. Lester, *The Transylvania Company*; J. Pell, *Ethan Allen*; F. J. Turner, 'Western State Making in the Revolutionary Era,' in his *Significance of Sections in American History*; S. C. Williams, *History of the Lost State of Franklin*.

5. The Articles of Confederation

L. B. Dunbar, *Study of 'Monarchial' Tendencies in the United States from 1776 to 1801*; M. Jensen, *The Articles of Confederation*, and *The New Nation*; A. C. McLaughlin, *Confederation and the Constitution*; R. B. Morris, *The American Revolution Reconsidered*.

6. Land Policy and the Ordinances

T. P. Abernethy, *Western Lands and the American Revolution*; C. W. Alvord, *The Illinois Country*; K. P. Bailey, *The Ohio Company of Virginia and the Westward Movement*.

7. Foreign Affairs and Commerce

S. F. Bemis, *Jay's Treaty*; F. Gilbert, *To the Farewell Address*; F. Monaghan, *John Jay*; S. E. Morison, *Maritime History of Massachusetts*, chs. 3–7; A. P. Whitaker, *The Spanish-American Frontier*.

8. Debtors and Shays

J. T. Adams, *New England in the Republic*; M. L. Starkey, *A Little Rebellion*.

CHAPTER 7

1. General

I. Brant, *James Madison*, vols. i-iii; R. Brown, *Charles Beard and the Constitution*; M. Farrand (ed.), *Records of the Federal Convention* (3 vols.); G. Hunt & J. B. Scott (eds.), *The Debates in the Federal Convention of 1787 . . . reported by James Madison*; F. McDonald, *E Pluribus Unum*, and *We the People*; A. C. McLaughlin, *Confederation and the Constitution*; J. T. Main, *The Antifederalists*, and *Political Parties Before the Constitution*; C. Rossiter, *Alexander Hamilton and the Constitution*; R. L. Schuyler, *The Constitution of the United States*; C. Page Smith, *James Wilson*; C. Warren, *The Making of the Constitution*.

2. Ratification

F. G. Bates, *Rhode Island and the Formation of the Union*; A. J. Beveridge, *Life of John Marshall*, vol. i; S. B. Harding, *Contest over Ratification of the Federal Constitution in the State of Massachusetts*.

CHAPTER 8

1. General

J. Flexner, *George Washington*; D. S. Freeman, *George Washington*, vol. vi; J. C. Miller, *The Federalist Era*; R. R. Palmer, *Age of Democratic Revolution*; N. Schachner, *The Founding Fathers*.

2. Organization of the Federal Government

E. C. Corwin, *The President, Office and Powers*; R. V. Harlow, *History of Legislative Methods in the Period before 1825*; C. Warren, *The Supreme Court in United States History* (2 vols.); L. D. White, *The Federalists*.

3. Biographies

I. Brant, *James Madison*, vol. iii; G. Chinard, *Honest John Adams*, and *Thomas Jefferson: The Apostle of Americanism*; D. Malone, *Jefferson and the Rights of Man*; J. C. Miller, *Alexander Hamilton*; R. B. Morris (ed.), *Alexander Hamilton and the Founding of the Nation*, and *John Jay, The Nation and the Court*; N. Schachner, *Alexander Hamilton*.

4. The Birth of Parties

W. N. Chambers, *Political Parties in a New Nation*; J. Charles, *Origins of the American Party System*; N. Cunningham, *The Jeffersonian Republicans*; D. Fischer, *Revolution of American Conservatism*; R. Hofstadter, *The Idea of a Party System*.

5. French Revolution and Foreign Affairs

S. F. Bemis, *Jay's Treaty*, and *Pinckney's Treaty*; A. L. Burt, *The United States, Great Britain, and British*

North America; A. De Conde, *Entangling Alliance*; F. Gilbert, *To the Farewell Address*; C. D. Hazen, *Contemporary American Opinion of the French Revolution*; H. M. Jones, *America and French Culture, 1750–1848*; E. P. Link, *Democratic-Republican Societies, 1790–1800*; C. M. Thomas, *American Neutrality in 1793*; A. P. Whitaker, *Spanish-American Frontier*.

6. Whiskey Rebellion, Public Land, the West
C. W. Alvord, *The Illinois Country*; L. D. Baldwin, *Whiskey Rebels*; T. Boyd, *Mad Anthony Wayne*; B. H. Hibbard, *History of Public Land Policies*; F. L. Paxson, *History of the American Frontier*; M. M. Quaife, *Chicago and the Old Northwest*.

7. John Adams's Administration
M. J. Dauer, *The Adams Federalists*; S. G. Kurtz, *The Presidency of John Adams*; C. Page Smith, *John Adams*.

8. French Relations and Naval War
G. W. Allen, *Our Naval War with France*; S. E. Morison, *Harrison Gray Otis*, vol. i; M. de Saint-Méry, *Voyage aux États-Unis, 1793–98*; M. Smelser, *Congress Founds the Navy*; A. P. Whitaker, *The Mississippi Question, 1795–1803*.

9. Alien and Sedition Acts
L. W. Levy, *Freedom of Speech and Press in Early American History*, and *Legacy of Suppression*; D. Malone, *The Public Life of Thomas Cooper*; J. M. Smith, *Freedom's Fetters*; V. Stauffer, *New England and the Bavarian Illuminati*.

CHAPTER 9

1. General
H. Adams, *History of the United States during the Administration of Jefferson* (4 vols., Commager ed. of 2 vols.); S. H. Aronson, *Status and Kinship in the Higher Civil Service*; A. J. Beveridge, *John Marshall*; D. J. Boorstin, *The Lost World of Thomas Jefferson*; N. E. Cunningham, Jr., *The Jeffersonian Republicans in Power*; W. E. Dodd, *Life of Nathaniel Macon*; R. E. Ellis, *The Jeffersonian Crisis*; T. Hamlin, *Benjamin H. Latrobe*; A. Koch, *Jefferson and Madison: The Great Collaboration*; A. T. Mahan, *The Influence of Sea Power upon the French Revolution* (2 vols.); D. Malone, *Jefferson the President*; M. D. Peterson, *The Jeffersonian Image in the American Mind*, and *Thomas Jefferson and the New Nation*; M. Smelser, *The Democratic Republic, 1801–1815*; L. D. White, *The Jeffersonians*; C. M. Wiltse, *The Jeffersonian Tradition in American Democracy*.

2. Tripoli War, Louisiana, Lewis and Clark
J. E. Bakeless, *Lewis and Clark*; E. S. Brown, *Constitutional History of the Louisiana Purchase*; I. J. Cox, *The West Florida Controversy*; G. Dangerfield, *Chancellor Robert R. Livingston of New York*; B. De Voto (ed.), *The Journals of Lewis and Clark*; J. A. Robertson, *Louisiana under the Rule of Spain, France, and the United States* (2 vols.); L. B. Wright & J. H. Macleod, *First Americans in North Africa*.

3. Federalist and Burr Conspiracies
T. P. Abernethy, *The Burr Conspiracy*; H. Adams (ed.), *Documents Relating to New England Federalism*; W. F. McCaleb, *The Aaron Burr Conspiracy*; S. E. Morison, *H. G. Otis*; N. Schachner, *Aaron Burr*.

4. Embargo
S. E. Morison, *Maritime History of Mass.*, chs. 12, 13; B. Perkins, *Prologue to War*; L. M. Sears, *Jefferson and the Embargo*.

CHAPTER 10

1. General
H. Adams, *History of the U. S. during the Administration of Madison* (5 vols.), and *The War of 1812* (reprint of the War chapters); F. F. Beirne, *The War of 1812*; I. Brant, *Madison*, vol. ii; R. H. Brown, *Republic in Peril: 1812*; A. L. Burt, *The United States, Great Britain and British North America*; A. H. Z. Carr, *The Coming of War*; J. P. Cranwell & W. B. Crane, *Men of Marque*; R. Horsman, *The Causes of the War of 1812*, and *The War of 1812*; R. Ketcham, *James Madison*; D. W. Knox, *History of the U.S. Navy*; C. P. Lucas, *The Canadian War of 1812*; A. T. Mahan, *Sea Power in Its Relations to the War of 1812* (2 vols.); B. Mayo, *Henry Clay*; B. Perkins, *Prologue to War*; J. W. Pratt, *Expansionists of 1812*; M. M. Quaife, *Chicago and the Old Northwest*; E. Rowland, *Andrew Jackson's Campaign*; C. M. Wiltse, *John C. Calhoun: Nationalist, 1782–1828*.

2. *Peace of Ghent and Hartford Convention*

J. Banner, *To the Hartford Convention*; S. F. Bemis, *J. Q. Adams and the Foundations of American Foreign Policy*; F. L. Engelman, *The Peace of Christmas Eve*; S. E. Morison, *H. G. Otis*, vol. ii, *Maritime History of Mass.*, chs. 12, 13, and *By Land and By Sea*, ch. 12; B. Perkins, *Castlereagh and Adams*; T. A. Updyke, *Diplomacy of the War of 1812*.

CHAPTER 11

1. *General*

H. Adams, *United States*, vol. ix; J. Q. Adams, *Diary* (selections from 12-vol. *Memoirs*, A. Nevins, ed.); S. F. Bemis, *J. Q. Adams and the Foundations of American Foreign Policy*; W. P. Cresson, *James Monroe*; G. Dangerfield, *The Era of Good Feelings*, and *The Awakening of American Nationalism*; S. Livermore, Jr., *The Twilight of Federalism*; C. Schurz, *Henry Clay*, vol. i; F. J. Turner, *Rise of the New West*.

2. *Marshall and the Judiciary*

A. J. Beveridge, *John Marshall*, vol. iv; E. S. Corwin, *John Marshall and the Constitution*; F. Frankfurter, *The Commerce Clause under Marshall, Taney, and Waite*; J. T. Horton, *James Kent*; R. Pound, *The Formative Era of American Law*; J. Story, *Commentaries on the Constitution of the United States* (2 vols.).

3. *Missouri Compromise*

G. Moore, *The Missouri Compromise*; D. L. Robinson, *Slavery in the Structure of American Politics, 1765–1820*; F. C. Shoemaker, *Missouri's Struggle for Statehood, 1804–1821*; C. S. Sydnor, *Development of Southern Sectionalism*.

4. *Monroe Doctrine*

A. Alvarez, *The Monroe Doctrine*; S. F. Bemis, *J. Q. Adams . . . Foreign Policy*; F. A. Golder, *Russian Expansion on the Pacific*; D. Perkins, *Hands Off: A History of the Monroe Doctrine*; A. P. Whitaker, *The U.S. and the Independence of Latin-America*.

5. *J. Q. Adams's Administration*

S. F. Bemis, *J. Q. Adams and the Union*; C. Eaton, *Henry Clay and the Art of American Politics*; H. E. Putnam, *Joel Roberts Poinsett*.

CHAPTER 12

1. *General*

T. P. Abernethy, *From Frontier to Plantation in Tennessee*; J. S. Bassett, *Andrew Jackson*; Lee Benson, *The Concept of Jacksonian Democracy*; W. N. Chambers, *Old Bullion Benton*; J. C. Curtis, *The Fox at Bay*; W. Hugins, *Jacksonian Democracy and the Working Class*; M. James, *Life of Andrew Jackson*; W. MacDonald, *Jacksonian Democracy*; M. Meyers, *The Jacksonian Persuasion*; E. Pessen, *Jacksonian America*; R. Remini, *Andrew Jackson*; A. M. Schlesinger, Jr., *The Age of Jackson*; J. A. Shackford, *David Crockett*; H. C. Syrett, *Andrew Jackson*; F. J. Turner, *Rise of the New West*, and *The United States, 1830–50*; G. G. Van Deusen, *The Jacksonian Era*; J. W. Ward, *Andrew Jackson, Symbol for an Age*; L. White, *The Jacksonians*.

2. *Political Conditions and Background*

E. M. Carroll, *Origins of the Whig Party*; C. R. Fish, *Civil Service and the Patronage*; D. R. Fox, *Decline of Aristocracy in the Politics of New York*; H. L. McBain, *De Witt Clinton and the Origin of the Spoils System in New York*; R. McCormick, *The Second American Party System*; H. Martineau, *Society in America*, and *Retrospect of Western Travel*; A. Nevins (ed.), *The Diary of Philip Hone*; R. Remini, *The Election of Andrew Jackson*, and *Martin Van Buren and the Making of the Democratic Party*; A. de Tocqueville, *Democracy in America*; F. Trollope, *Domestic Manners of the Americans* (Donald Smalley, ed.).

3. *Webster and the West*

R. N. Current, *Daniel Webster and the Rise of National Conservatism*; C. M. Fuess, *Daniel Webster* (2 vols.); R. G. Wellington, *Political and Sectional Influence of the Public Lands, 1828–42*.

4. *Calhoun and Nullification*

M. L. Coit, *John C. Calhoun: American Portrait*; W. Freehling, *Prelude to Civil War*; D. F. Houston, *Critical Study of Nullification in South Carolina*; D. Malone, *Public Life of Thomas Cooper*; A. G. Smith, *Economic Readjustment of an Old Cotton State*; G. G. Van Deusen, *Economic Bases of Disunion in South Carolina*; C. M. Wiltse, *John C. Calhoun, Nullifier*.

5. Finance and the War on the Bank

R. C. H. Catterall, *The Second Bank of the U.S.*; T. P. Govan, *Nicholas Biddle*; B. Hammond, *Banks and Politics in America from the Revolution to the Civil War*; A. B. Hepburn, *History of Currency in the U.S.*; J. M. McFaul, *The Politics of Jacksonian Finance*; R. C. McGrane, *Foreign Bondholders and American State Debts*; M. G. Madeleine, *Monetary and Banking Theories of Jacksonian Democracy*; W. B. Smith, *Economic Aspects of the Second Bank of the United States*; P. Temin, *The Jacksonian Economy*.

6. Indian Removal

A. Debo, *The Road to Disappearance*; G. Foreman, *Indian Removal*, *The Last Trek of the Indians*, and *The Five Civilized Tribes*; G. D. Harmon, *Sixty Years of Indian Affairs, 1789–1850*; W. Lumpkin, *Removal of the Cherokee Indians from Georgia*; F. P. Prucha, *American Indian Policy in the Formative Years*; R. N. Satz, *American Indian Policy in the Jacksonian Era*.

7. Democrats and Whigs

L. Benson, *The Concept of Jacksonian Democracy*; O. P. Chitwood, *John Tyler*; H. D. A. Donovan, *The Barnburners*; H. R. Fraser, *Democracy in the Making, the Jackson-Tyler Era*; D. B. Goebel, *William Henry Harrison*; R. G. Gunderson, *The Log-Cabin Campaign*; R. C. McGrane, *The Panic of 1837*; J. B. McMaster, *History of the People of the U.S.*, vol. vi; J. C. N. Paul, *Rift in Democracy*; C. Schurz, *Henry Clay*, vol. ii; R. Seager, *And Tyler Too!*; J. Silbey, *The Transformation of American Politics, 1840–1860*; T. C. Smith, *The Liberty and Free Soil Parties in the Northwest*.

8. Taney and the Supreme Court

F. Frankfurter, *Commerce Clause under Marshall, Taney and Waite*; C. B. Swisher, *The Oliver Wendell Holmes Devise History of the Supreme Court of the United States*, vol. v: *The Taney Period, 1836–64*, and *Roger B. Taney*; C. Warren, *Supreme Court*, vol. ii.

9. Anglo-Canadian-American Relations

J. B. Brebner, *North Atlantic Triangle*; H. S. Burrage, *Maine in the Northeastern Boundary Controversy*; W. Kilbourn, *The Firebrand: W. L. Mackenzie*; T. H. Raddell, *Path of Destiny, Canada 1763–1850*.

CHAPTER 13

1. Cotton Kingdom

K. Bruce, *Virginia Iron Manufacture in the Slave Era*; A. Conrad & J. Meyer, *The Economics of Slavery and Other Studies in Econometric History*; A. Craven, *Edmund Ruffin, Southerner*; W. E. Dodd, *The Cotton Kingdom*; J. W. DuBose, *Life and Times of William Lowndes Yancey*; C. Eaton, *A History of the Old South*; J. H. Franklin, *The Militant South*; F. P. Gaines, *The Southern Plantation*; E. D. Genovese, *The Political Economy of Slavery*; L. C. Gray, *History of Agriculture in the Southern States to 1860*; M. B. Hammond, *The Cotton Industry*; O. Handlin, *Race and Nationality in American Life*; F. A. Kemble, *Journal of Residence on a Georgian Plantation*; A. B. Longstreet, *Georgia Scenes*; F. L. Olmsted, *The Cotton Kingdom* (A. M. Schlesinger, ed.); U. B. Phillips, *Robert Toombs*; A. F. Scott, *The Southern Lady*; S. D. Smedes, *Memorials of a Southern Planter*; C. S. Sydnor, *Development of Southern Sectionalism, 1819–1848*; L. White, *Robert Barnwell Rhett*.

2. The Negro

H. Aptheker, *American Negro Slave Revolts*; F. Bancroft, *Slave-Trading in the Old South*; J. W. Blassingame, *The Slave Community*; H. A. Bullock, *A History of Negro Education in the South from 1619 to the Present*; H. T. Catterall, *Judicial Cases concerning American Slavery and the Negro*; D. Davis, *The Problem of Slavery in Western Culture*; C. N. Degler, *Neither Black Nor White*; S. M. Elkins, *Slavery*; R. Flanders, *Plantation Slavery in Georgia*; W. Fogel & S. Engerman, *Time on the Cross*; J. H. Franklin, *From Slavery to Freedom*; E. D. Genovese, *The Political Economy of Slavery*, and *The World the Slaveholders Made*; U. B. Phillips, *Life and Labor in the Old South*, and *American Negro Slavery*; K. M. Stampp, *The Peculiar Institution*; R. S. Starobin, *Industrial Slavery in the Old South*; C. S. Sydnor, *Slavery in Mississippi*; F. Tannenbaum, *Slave and Citizen*; R. C. Wade, *Slavery in the Cities*.

3. Southern Culture

C. H. Ambler, *Thomas Ritchie*; J. J. Audubon, *Birds of America* (William Vogt, ed.); P. A. Bruce, *History of the University of Virginia* (5 vols.); W. J. Cash, *The*

Mind of the South; V. Dabney, *Liberalism in the South*; C. Eaton, *Freedom of Thought in the Old South*, and *The Mind of the Old South*; S. W. Geiser, *Naturalists of the Frontier*; W. S. Jenkins, *Pro-Slavery Thought in the Old South*; T. C. Johnson, *Scientific Interests in the Old South*; E. W. Knight, *Public Education in the South*; V. L. Parrington, *Main Currents in American Thought*, vol. ii; L. Rhea, *Hugh S. Legaré*; C. G. Sellers, Jr., *The Southerner as American*; W. R. Taylor, *Cavalier and Yankee*; W. P. Trent, *William Gilmore Simms*.

4. The North
P. W. Bidwell & J. I. Falconer, *History of Agriculture in the Northern States*; P. W. Gates, *The Farmer's Age*; J. B. McMaster, *History of the People of the U.S.*, vols. v-vii; E. W. Martin, *The Standard of Living in 1860*; T. L. Nichols, *Forty Years of American Life, 1821–1861*; D. C. North, *The Economic Growth of the United States*; R. H. Shryock, *Medicine and Society in America, 1660–1860*; F. J. Turner, *The United States, 1830–50*; N. J. Ware, *The Industrial Worker, 1840–1860*.

5. Transportation and Westward Movement
C. H. Ambler, *History of Transportation in the Ohio Valley*; C. F. Carter, *When Railroads Were New*; A. D. Chandler, Jr., *Henry Varnum Poor*; A. S. Dunbar, *History of Travel in America* (4 vols.); R. W. Fogel, *Railroads and American Economic Growth*; C. Goodrich, *Government Promotion of American Canals and Railroads, 1800–1890*; C. Goodrich, et al., *Canals and American Economic Development*; A. B. Hulbert, *Paths of Inland Commerce*; E. Hungerford, *Story of the Baltimore & Ohio Railroad*; K. W. Porter, *John Jacob Astor*; J. Rubin, *Canal or Railroad?*; G. R. Taylor, *The Transportation Revolution*; R. L. Thompson, *Wiring a Continent*; D. B. Tyler, *Steam Conquers the Atlantic*.

6. Immigration and Packet Ships
E. Abbott, *Historical Aspects of the Immigration Problem*; W. F. Adams, *Ireland and Irish Emigration to the New World from 1815 to the Famine*; R. G. Albion, *Square-Riggers on Schedule*, and *The Rise of New York Port 1815–1860*; R. B. Anderson, *Norwegian Immigration to 1848*; R. T. Berthoff, *British Immigrants in Industrial America, 1825–1850*; R. A. Billington, *The Protestant Crusade, 1800–1860*; J. R. Commons, *Races and Immigrants in America*; R. Ernst, *Immigrant Life in New York City*; A. B. Faust, *The German Element in the United States*; F. E. Gibson, *The Attitudes of the New York Irish toward State and National Affairs, 1848–1892*; O. Handlin, *The Uprooted*; M. L. Hansen, *The Atlantic Migration*, and *The Immigrant in American History*; F. E. Janson, *Background of Swedish Immigration, 1840–1930*; M. A. Jones, *American Immigration*.

7. Manufacturing and Cities
S. Batchelder, *Introduction and Early Progress of the Cotton Manufacture in the United States*; D. H. Calhoun, *The American Civil Engineer*; V. S. Clark, *History of Manufactures in the United States*; A. H. Cole, *The American Wool Manufacture* (2 vols.); P. R. Knights, *The Plain People of Boston, 1830–1860*; K. W. Porter, *The Jacksons and the Lees: Two Generations of Massachusetts Merchants*; J. M. Swank, *History of the Manufacture of Iron*; R. M. Tryon, *Household Manufactures in the U.S.*; R. C. Wade, *The Urban Frontier*.

8. Science and Technology
G. Daniels, *American Science in the Age of Jackson*; A. H. Dupree, *Science in the Federal Government*, and *Asa Gray*; B. Jaffe, *Men of Science in America*; E. Lurie, *Louis Agassiz*; P. H. Oehser, *Sons of Science*; C. Resek, *Lewis Henry Morgan*; R. H. Shryock, *American Medical Research Past and Present*; M. Wilson, *American Science and Invention*.

9. Education
C. Bode, *The American Lyceum*; M. Curti, *Social Ideas of American Educators*; B. A. Hinsdale, *Horace Mann and the Common School Revival in the United States*; R. Hofstadter & W. Metzger, *The Development of Academic Freedom in the United States*; M. A. D. Howe, *Life and Letters of George Bancroft* (2 vols.), and *Classic Shades*; R. A. McCaughey, *Josiah Quincy*; S. E. Morison, *Three Centuries of Harvard*; F. L. Mott, *American Journalism*, and *History of American Magazines*; F. Rudolph, *The American College and University*; S. K. Schultz, *The Culture Factory*; R. Storr, *The Beginnings of Graduate Education in America*; D. G. Tewkesbury, *Founding of American Colleges and Universities before the Civil War*; C. F. Thwing, *The American and the German University*; C. G. Woodson, *Education of the Negro Prior to 1861*.

10. *Reformers and Utopias*

E. Abbott, *Women in Industry*; W. Bennett, *Whittier, Bard of Freedom*; G. Brooks, *Three Wise Virgins*; C. C. Cole, *Social Ideas of the Northern Evangelists, 1826–1860*; W. R. Cross, *The Burned-Over District*; M. Curti, *The American Peace Crusade, 1815–60*, and *The Learned Blacksmith*; W. A. Hinds, *American Communities and Co-operative Colonies*; S. M. Kingsbury (ed.), *Labor Laws and Their Enforcement*; J. A. Krout, *The Origins of Prohibition*; R. W. Leopold, *Robert Dale Owen*; L. Litwack, *The Negro in the Free States, 1790–1860*; G. B. Lockwood, *New Harmony Movement*; W. G. McLoughlin, *Modern Revivalism*; R. A. Mohl, *Poverty in New York, 1783–1825*; R. B. Nye, *Society and Culture in America, 1830–1860*; R. Riegel, *American Feminists*; D. J. Rothman, *The Discovery of the Asylum*; C. E. Sears, *Days of Delusion* (Millerites); T. L. Smith, *Revivalism and Social Reform in Mid-Nineteenth Century America*; L. Swift, *Brook Farm*; A. F. Tyler, *Freedom's Ferment*; N. Ware, *The Industrial Worker, 1840–60*; W. R. Waterman, *Frances Wright*; E. Webber, *Escape to Utopia*.

11. *Literature and Transcendentalism*

G. W. Allen, *The Solitary Singer* (Whitman); N. Arvin, *Longfellow*, and *Herman Melville*; V. W. Brooks, *The Flowering of New England, 1850–65*, and *The World of Washington Irving*; H. S. Canby, *Walt Whitman*; H. S. Commager, *Theodore Parker*; O. B. Frothingham, *Transcendentalism in New England*; W. R. Hutchison, *The Transcendentalist Ministers*; J. W. Krutch, *Thoreau*; F. O. Matthiessen, *American Renaissance*; P. Miller (ed.), *The Transcendentalists, an Anthology*; L. Mumford, *The Golden Day*; B. Perry, *The American Spirit in Literature*, and (ed.), *The Heart of Emerson's Journals*; R. L. Rusk, *Life of Ralph Waldo Emerson*; O. Shepard (ed.), *The Heart of Thoreau's Journals*; R. Stewart (ed.), *American Notebooks, by Nathaniel Hawthorne*; M. Wade, *Margaret Fuller*; R. Welter, *The Mind of America, 1820–1860*; S. Whicher, *Fate and Freedom* (Emerson).

12. *Anti-Slavery and Abolition*

G. H. Barnes, *The Antislavery Impulse, 1830–44*; W. Barney, *The Road to Secession*; M. Duberman (ed.), *The Antislavery Vanguard*; D. Dumond, *Anti-Slavery*; L. Filler, *The Crusade Against Slavery*; G. M. Fredrickson, *The Black Image in the White Mind*; L. Gara, *The Liberty Line*; A. S. Kraditor, *Means and Ends*; G. Lerner, *The Grimké Sisters from South Carolina*; R. B. Nye, *Fettered Freedom*; W. A. Owens, *Slave Mutiny*; B. Quarles, *Black Abolitionists*; G. Sorin, *Abolitionism*; B. P. Thomas, *Theodore Weld*; J. L. Thomas, *The Liberator*; C. Woodward, *American Counterpoint*.

CHAPTER 14

1. *General*

R. A. Billington, *The Far Western Frontier*; H. M. Chittenden, *The American Fur Trade of the Far West* (3 vols.); K. Coman, *Economic Beginnings of the Far West* (2 vols.); B. De Voto, *The Year of Decision, 1846*, and *Across the Wide Missouri*; N. A. Graebner, *Empire on the Pacific*; G. C. Lyman, *John Marsh*; F. Merk, *Manifest Destiny and Mission in American History*; H. N. Smith, *Virgin Land*; R. G. Thwaites, *Early Western Travels*; A. K. Weinberg, *Manifest Destiny*.

2. *Great Plains, Oregon, and Rockies*

H. C. Dale, *The Ashley-Smith Explorations and the Discovery of a Central Route to the Pacific, 1822–29*; D. O. Johansen & C. M. Gates, *Empire of the Columbia*; F. Parkman, *Oregon Trail*, and *Journals* (Mason Wade, ed.), and *Letters* (W. R. Jacobs, ed.); J. Schafer, *History of the Pacific Northwest*; W. P. Webb, *The Great Plains*; D. E. Wood, *The Old Santa Fé Trail from the Missouri River*.

3. *The Mormons*

F. M. Brodie, *No Man Knows My History: The Life of Joseph Smith*; C. A. Brough, *Irrigation in Utah*; B. De Voto, *Forays and Rebuttals*; W. A. Linn, *The Story of the Mormons*; W. Mulder & A. R. Mortensen, *Among the Mormons, Historic Accounts by Contemporary Observers*; T. F. O'Dea, *The Mormons*; G. Thomas, *The Development of Institutions under Irrigation*; M. R. Werner, *Brigham Young*.

4. *Polk and the Texas Question*

E. C. Barker, *Life of Stephen F. Austin*; E. I. McCormac, *James K. Polk*; F. Merk, *Slavery and the Annexation of Texas*; A. Nevins (ed.), *Diary of a President* (1-vol. abridgment of Polk's Diary); J. F. Rippy, *The United States and Mexico*; C. G. Sellers, *James K. Polk*; S. Siegel, *A Political History of the Texas Republic*; J. H. Smith, *The Annexation of Texas*, and *The War with Mexico* (2 vols.); N. W. Stephenson, *Texas and the Mexican War*.

5. The Mexican War

K. J. Bauer, *The Mexican War*; A. H. Bill, *Rehearsal for Conflict*; C. W. Elliott, *Winfield Scott*; H. Hamilton, *Zachary Taylor*; O. A. Singletary, *The Mexican War*; W. P. Webb, *The Texas Rangers*.

CHAPTER 15

1. General

A. C. Cole, *The Irrepressible Conflict, 1850–65*; A. Craven, *The Growth of Southern Nationalism*; E. Foner, *Free Soil, Free Labor, Free Men*; C. B. Going, *David Wilmot, Free-Soiler*; H. Hamilton, *Zachary Taylor*, vol. ii, and *Prologue to Conflict*; G. F. Milton, *The Eve of Conflict* (Douglas); A. Nevins, *Ordeal of the Union*, vol. i; R. F. Nichols, *Franklin Pierce*; J. F. Rhodes, *History of the United States from the Compromise of 1850*, vol. i; T. C. Smith, *Liberty and Free Soil Parties in the Northwest*; biographies of Calhoun, Clay, Rhett, Webster, and others already cited.

2. California and the Gold Rush

J. W. Caughey, *Gold Is the Cornerstone*; R. G. Cleland, *From Wilderness to Empire*, and *History of California*; C. Goodwin, *Establishment of a State Government in California, 1846–1850*; L. R. Hafen, *The Overland Mail, 1849–1869*; O. T. Howe, *Argonauts of '49*; A. Nevins, *Frémont*; R. W. Paul, *California Gold*.

3. Opening of Japan

A. B. Cole, *Yankee Surveyors in the Shogun's Seas*; T. Dennett, *Americans in Eastern Asia*; F. R. Dulles, *The Old China Trade*; W. E. Griffis, *Matthew C. Perry*; S. E. Morison, *Old Bruin* (Perry); I. Nitobe, *Intercourse between the U.S. and Japan*; P. J. Treat, *Diplomatic Relations between U.S. and Japan, 1853–95* (2 vols.); A. Walworth, *Black Ships off Japan*.

4. Isthmian Diplomacy

D. Perkins, *The Monroe Doctrine, 1826–1867*; B. Rauch, *American Interests in Cuba*; W. O. Scroggs, *Filibusters and Financiers*; I. D. Travis, *History of the Clayton-Bulwer Treaty*; M. W. Williams, *Anglo-American Isthmian Diplomacy*.

5. Canadian Relations

C. D. Allin, *Annexation, Preferential Trade and Reci*procity; L. B. Shippee, *Canadian-American Relations, 1849–1874*; C. G. Tansill, *Canadian Reciprocity Treaty of 1854*.

6. The Clipper Ship and Steam

A. H. Clark, *The Clipper Ship Era*; C. C. Cutler, *Greyhounds of the Sea*; C. L. Lewis, *Matthew Fontaine Maury*; S. E. Morison, *Maritime History of Massachusetts*, ch. 22, and *By Land and By Sea*, ch. 2; E. L. Pond, *Junius Smith*; D. B. Tyler, *Steam Conquers the Atlantic*.

CHAPTER 16

1. General

A. Craven, *The Coming of the Civil War*, and *The Growth of Southern Nationalism*; D. E. Fehrenbacher, *Prelude to Greatness*; M. Holt, *Forging a Majority*; P. S. Klein, *President James Buchanan*; G. F. Milton, *The Eve of Conflict*; A. Nevins, *Ordeal of the Union*, vol. ii, and *Emergence of Lincoln*; R. F. Nichols, *The Democratic Machine, 1850–54*, *The Disruption of American Democracy*, and *Franklin Pierce*; J. A. Rawley, *Race and Politics*; K. M. Stampp (ed.), *The Causes of the Civil War*.

2. Prairie Settlement, Kansas, and Nebraska

F. W. Blakmar, *The Life of Charles Robinson*; C. A. Dawson & E. R. Younge, *Pioneering in the Prairie Provinces*; E. Dick, *Vanguards of the Frontier*, and *The Sod House Frontier*; D. Donald, *Charles Sumner and the Coming of the Civil War*; P. W. Gates, *The Illinois Central R. R. and Its Colonization Work*, and *Fifty Million Acres*; H. C. Hubbart, *The Older Middle West, 1840–1880*; W. T. Hutchinson, *Cyrus Hall McCormick* (2 vols.); S. A. Johnson, *The Battle Cry of Freedom*; J. C. Malin, *The Nebraska Question*; M. M. Quaife, *The Doctrine of Non-Intervention with Slavery in the Territories*; P. O. Ray, *Repeal of the Missouri Compromise*; R. Russel, *Improvement of Communication with the Pacific Coast as an Issue in American Politics*.

3. Know-Nothings

R. A. Billington, *The Protestant Crusade*; W. D. Overdyke, *The Know-Nothing Party in the South*; L. F. Schmeckebier, *The History of the Know-Nothing Party in Maryland*.

4. Dred Scott

R. M. Cover, *Justice Accused*; V. C. Hopkins, *Dred Scott's Case*; C. B. Swisher, *The Oliver Wendell Holmes Devise History of the Supreme Court of the United States*, vol. v: *The Taney Period, 1836–1864*, and *Roger B. Taney*.

5. Lincoln-Douglas Debates

P. M. Angle (ed.), *Created Equal?*, and E. E. Sparks (ed.), *Lincoln-Douglas Debates*, for the texts; H. V. Jaffa, *Crisis of the House Divided*; H. V. Jaffa & R. W. Johannsen (eds.), *In the Name of the People*; R. W. Johannsen, *Stephen A. Douglas*; C. Sandburg, *Abraham Lincoln, the Prairie Years*; P. Simon, *Lincoln's Preparation for Greatness*.

6. Secession

W. M. Caskey, *Secession and Restoration of Louisiana*; S. A. Channing, *Crisis of Fear*; A. M. B. Coleman, *The Life of John J. Crittenden*; E. M. Coulter (ed.), *The Course of the South to Secession*; O. Crenshaw, *The Slave States in the Presidential Election of 1860*; R. Current, *Lincoln and the First Shot*; C. P. Denman, *Secession Movement in Alabama*; D. L. Dumond, *The Secession Movement*; N. Graebner (ed.), *The Crisis of the Union*; W. J. Grayson, *James Louis Petigru*; R. Gunderson, *Old Gentlemen's Convention*; P. M. Hamer, *Secession Movement in South Carolina*; J. Hodgson, *The Cradle of the Confederacy*; G. H. Knoles (ed.), *The Crisis of the Union*; E. Merrill, *James J. Hammond*; G. F. Milton, *The Eve of Conflict*; D. M. Potter, *Lincoln and His Party in the Secession Crisis*; P. L. Rainwater, *Mississippi: Storm Center of Secession*; R. R. Russel, *Economic Aspects of Southern Sectionalism, 1840–1861*; H. T. Shanks, *The Secession Movement in Virginia*; E. C. Smith, *The Borderland in the Civil War*; K. Stampp, *And the War Came*; A. H. Stephens, *A Constitutional View of the Late War Between the States*; A. Whitridge, *No Compromise!*; R. A. Wooster, *The Secession Conventions of the South*.

CHAPTERS 17–18

1. General

D. Aaron, *The Unwritten War*; B. Catton (ed.), *American Heritage Picture History of the Civil War*; H. S. Commager, ed., *Official Atlas of the Civil War*; E. M. Coulter, *The Confederate States of America*; D. Donald, *Charles Sumner and the Coming of the Civil War*; C. Eaton, *History of the Southern Confederacy*; C. R. Fish, *The American Civil War: An Interpretation*; E. D. Fite, *The Presidential Campaign of 1860*; J. B. McMaster, *History of the People of the United States During Lincoln's Administration*; B. Mayo (ed.), *The American Tragedy*; A. Nevins, *The War for the Union* (4 vols.), and *The Emergence of Lincoln*, vol. ii, chs. 1–11; T. J. Pressly, *Americans Interpret Their Civil War*; J. G. Randall, *Civil War and Reconstruction*; J. F. Rhodes, *History of the United States*, vols. ii–v; C. P. Roland, *The Confederacy*.

2. Abraham Lincoln

C. R. Ballard, *The Military Genius of Abraham Lincoln*; R. Basler (ed.), *Collected Works of Abraham Lincoln* (8 vols.); R. Bruce, *Lincoln and the Tools of War*; R. N. Current, *The Lincoln Nobody Knows*; D. Donald, *Lincoln Reconsidered*; B. J. Hendrick, *Lincoln's War Cabinet*; W. B. Hesseltine, *Lincoln and the War Governors*; G. F. Milton, *Lincoln and the Fifth Column*; H. Mitgang (ed.), *Lincoln As They Saw Him*; J. G. Nicolay & J. Hay, *Abraham Lincoln* (10 vols.); J. G. Randall, *Constitutional Problems Under Lincoln*, and *Lincoln the President: Springfield to Gettysburg* (2 vols.); J. G. Randall & R. N. Current, *Last Full Measure*; C. Sandburg, *Abraham Lincoln: The War Years* (4 vols.); D. M. Silver, *Lincoln's Supreme Court*; H. Strode, *Jefferson Davis* (2 vols.); B. Thomas, *Abraham Lincoln*; T. H. Williams, *Lincoln and His Generals*; W. F. Zornow, *Lincoln and the Party Divided*.

3. Biographies

R. von Abele, *Alexander H. Stephens*; F. Brodie, *Thaddeus Stevens*; F. Cleaves, *The Rock of Chickamauga* (Gen. Thomas); B. Davis, *Jeb Stuart*; W. C. Davis, *Breckinridge*; D. Donald, *Charles Sumner and the Rights of Man*; G. E. Govan & J. W. Livingood, *A Different Valor* (Joseph E. Johnston); U. S. Grant, *Personal Memoirs* (2 vols.); G. F. R. Henderson, *Stonewall Jackson and the American Civil War* (2 vols.); B. J. Hendrick, *Statesmen of the Lost Cause*; T. Lyman, *Meade's Headquarters*; R. McElroy, *Jefferson Davis* (2 vols.); R. D. Meade, *Judah P. Benjamin*; J. Niven, *Gideon Welles*; J. Parks, *General Edmund Kirby Smith C.S.A.*; R. W. Patrick, *Jefferson Davis and His Cabinet*; W. T. Sherman, *Memoirs of General William T. Sherman* (2 vols.); R. Taylor, *Destruction and Reconstruction*; J. Thomason, *Jeb Stuart*; F. Vandiver, *Mighty Stonewall* (2 vols.); R. F. Weigley,

Quarter-Master General of the Union Army (Montgomery Meigs); K. P. Williams, *Lincoln Finds a General* (U.S. Grant) (5 vols.); J. Wyeth, *Life of General Nathan Bedford Forrest.*

4. Military

G. W. Adams, *Doctors in Blue*; R. Brownlee, *Gray Ghosts of the Confederacy: Guerrilla Warfare in the West*; B. Catton, *A Stillness at Appomattox, Glory Road, Grant Moves South, Mr. Lincoln's Army, Never Call Retreat, Terrible Swift Sword*, and *This Hallowed Ground*; D. T. Cornish, *The Sable Arm*; H. H. Cunningham, *Doctors in Gray*; D. S. Freeman, *Lee's Lieutenants*, and *R. E. Lee*; T. R. Hay, *Hood's Tennessee Campaign*; S. Horn, *The Army of the Tennessee*; R. U. Johnson & C. C. Buel (eds.), *Battles and Leaders of the Civil War* (4 vols.); F. Maurice, *Statesmen and Soldiers of the Civil War*; E. S. Miers, *The Web of Victory: Grant at Vicksburg*; J. Monaghan, *Civil War on the Western Border*; L. V. Naisawald, *Grape and Canister*; B. Quarles, *The Negro in the Civil War*; J. C. Ropes & W. R. Livermore, *The Story of the Civil War* (3 vols.); M. Schaff, *The Sunset of the Confederacy*; F. A. Shannon, *Organization and Administration of the Union Army* (2 vols.); A. Townsend, *Campaign of a Non-Combatant*; B. Wiley, *The Life of Billy Yank*, and *The Life of Johnny Reb.*

5. Naval

D. Ammen, *The Atlantic Coast*; J. P. Baxter, *Introduction of the Ironclad Warship*; F. Dorsey, *Road to the Sea: Story of James B. Eads and the Mississippi River*; H. A. Gosnell, *Guns on the Western Waters*; J. D. Hill, *Sea Dogs of the Sixties*; C. L. Lewis, *David Glasgow Farragut* (2 vols.); A. T. Mahan, *Admiral Farragut*, and *The Gulf and Inland Waters*; J. T. Scharf, *History of the Confederate States Navy*; G. Welles, *Diary* (3 vols.).

6. Foreign Relations

E. D. Adams, *Great Britain and the American Civil War* (2 vols.); H. Adams, *The Education of Henry Adams*; J. O. Bullock, *Secret Service of the Confederate States in Europe* (2 vols.); J. M. Callahan, *Diplomatic History of the Southern Confederacy*; M. Clapp, *Forgotten First Citizen: John Bigelow*; D. Jordan & E. J. Pratt, *Europe and the American Civil War*; J. Monaghan, *Diplomat in Carpet Slippers*; F. L. Owsley, *King Cotton Diplomacy.*

7. Behind the Lines

J. C. Andrew, *The North Reports the Civil War*; R. C. Black, *The Railroads of the Confederacy*; A. C. Cole, *The Irrepressible Conflict*; E. M. Coulter, *The Confederate States of America*; E. Crozier, *Yankee Reporters 1861–65*; E. D. Fite, *Social and Industrial Conditions in the North during the Civil War*; P. Gates, *Agriculture and the Civil War*; W. Gray, *The Hidden Civil War*; W. B. Hesseltine, *Civil War Prisons*; H. Hyman, *Era of the Oath*; E. C. Kirkland, *The Peacemakers of 1864*; F. L. Klement, *The Copperheads in the Middle West*; M. Leech, *Reveille in Washington*; E. Lonn, *Foreigners in the Confederacy*, and *Foreigners in the Union Army and Navy*; W. Q. Maxwell, *Lincoln's Fifth Wheel: The U.S. Sanitary Commission*; A. B. Moore, *Conscription and Conflict in the Confederacy*; F. L. Owsley, *States Rights in the Confederacy*; W. M. Robinson, *Justice in Grey: A History of the Judicial System of the Confederate States of America*; J. C. Schwab, *The Confederate States of America*; L. Starr, *The Bohemian Brigade*; R. C. Todd, *Confederate Finance*; T. Weber, *Northern Railroads in the Civil War*; C. Wesley, *The Collapse of the Confederacy*; B. Wiley, *Southern Negroes 1861–1865*, and *The Plain People of the Confederacy*; W. Yearns, *The Confederate Congress.*

Source Selections

P. M. Angle & E. S. Miers, *Tragic Years* (2 vols.); H. S. Commager, *The Blue and the Gray* (2 vols.), and (ed.), *Documents*, nos. 189–244; F. Moore (ed.), *The Rebellion Record* (12 vols.).

CHAPTER 19

1. General

P. H. Buck, *The Road to Reunion*; J. A. Carpenter, *Sword and Olive Branch: Oliver Otis Howard*; A. Conway, *The Reconstruction of Georgia*; E. M. Coulter, *The South During Reconstruction*; A. Craven, *Reconstruction*; C. Crowe (ed.), *The Age of Civil War and Reconstruction*; R. Cruden, *The Negro in Reconstruc-*

tion; R. O. Curry, *Radicalism, Racism, and Party Realignment*; D. Donald, *The Politics of Reconstruction, 1863–1867*; W. A. Dunning, *Reconstruction, Political and Economic*; R. F. Durden, *James Shepherd Pike*; J. H. Franklin, *Reconstruction*; H. M. Hyman (ed.), *New Frontiers of the American Reconstruction*; A. Nevins, *The Emergence of Modern America*; E. P. Oberholtzer, *History of the United States since the Civil War*, vol. i; O. H. Olsen, *Carpetbagger's Crusade: The Life of Albion Winegar Tourgee*; R. W. Patrick, *The Reconstruction of the Nation*; J. G. Randall & D. Donald, *The Civil War and Reconstruction*; J. F. Rhodes, *History of the United States*, vol. v; R. P. Sharkey, *Money, Class, and Party*; K. M. Stampp, *The Era of Reconstruction, 1865–1877*; A. W. Trelease, *White Terror*; I. Unger, *The Greenback Era*; F. G. Wood, *The Era of Reconstruction, 1863–1877*.

2. The Negro as Freedman

P. A. Bruce, *The Plantation Negro as Freedman*; G. W. Cable, *The Negro Question* (Arlin Turner, ed.); W. J. Cash, *The Mind of the South*; H. H. Donald, *The Negro Freedman*; W. E. B. Du Bois, *Black Reconstruction*, and *The Souls of Black Folk*; F. A. Logan, *The Negro in North Carolina, 1876–1894*; R. W. Logan, *The Negro in American Life and Thought, 1877–1901*; W. S. McFeely, *Yankee Stepfather*; J. M. McPherson, *The Struggle for Equality*; B. Mathews, *Booker T. Washington*; A. Meier, *Negro Thought in America, 1880–1915*; G. Myrdal, *An American Dilemma* (2 vols.); W. Peters, *The Southern Temper*; B. Quarles, *Lincoln and the Negro*; A. Raper, *Preface to Peasantry*; J. M. Richardson, *The Negro in the Reconstruction of Florida, 1865–1877*; O. Singletary, *Negro Militia and Reconstruction*; S. R. Spencer, Jr., *Booker T. Washington and the Negro's Place in American Life*; C. E. Synes, *Race Relations in Virginia, 1870–1902*; G. B. Tindall, *South Carolina Negroes, 1877–1900*; B. T. Washington, *Up from Slavery*; C. H. Wesley, *Negro Labor in the United States, 1850–1925*; V. Wharton, *The Negro in Mississippi*; J. Williamson, *After Slavery: The Negro in South Carolina During Reconstruction, 1861–1877*; C. G. Woodson, *A Century of Negro Migration*.

3. Presidential Reconstruction

H. Beale, *The Critical Year*; L. & J. H. Cox, *Politics, Principle, and Prejudice: 1865–1866*; J. Dorris, *Pardon and Amnesty under Lincoln and Johnson*; W. B. Hesseltine, *Lincoln's Plan of Reconstruction*, and *Lincoln and the War Governors*; C. McCarthy, *Lincoln's Plan of Reconstruction*; E. McKitrick, *Andrew Johnson and Reconstruction*; G. F. Milton, *The Age of Hate*; J. G. Randall, *Constitutional Problems under Lincoln*; W. L. Rose, *Rehearsal for Reconstruction: The Port Royal Experiment*.

4. Congressional Reconstruction

T. B. Alexander, *Political Reconstruction in Tennessee*; M. L. Benedict, *A Compromise of Principle*; G. Bentley, *A History of the Freedmen's Bureau*; W. R. Brock, *An American Crisis: Congress and Reconstruction*; W. M. Caskey, *Secession and Restoration in Louisiana*; W. L. Fleming, *Civil War and Reconstruction in Alabama*; J. W. Garner, *Reconstruction in Mississippi*; W. Gillette, *The Right To Vote: Politics and the Passage of the Fifteenth Amendment*; R. Shugg, *Origins of Class Struggle in Louisiana*; F. B. Simkins & R. H. Woody, *South Carolina during Reconstruction*; D. Y. Thomas, *Arkansas in War and Reconstruction*; C. M. Thompson, *Reconstruction in Georgia*; H. L. Trefousse, *Benjamin Franklin Wade*.

5. Reconstruction and the Constitution

H. Hyman, *A More Perfect Union*, and *The Era of the Oath*; J. B. James, *The Framing of the Fourteenth Amendment*; S. Kutler, *Judicial Power and Reconstruction Politics*; J. M. Mathews, *Legislative and Judicial History of the Fifteenth Amendment*; J. Ten Broek, *Antislavery Origins of the Fourteenth Amendment*; C. Warren, *The Supreme Court in United States History*, vol. ii.

6. Radical Reconstruction

M. L. Benedict, *The Impeachment and Trial of Andrew Johnson*; F. Brodie, *Thaddeus Stevens*; R. N. Current, *Old Thad Stevens*; D. Donald, *Charles Sumner and the Rights of Man*; W. R. Gillette, *The Right to Vote*; H. Hyman & B. P. Thomas, *The Life and Times of Lincoln's Secretary of War*; R. Korngold, *Thaddeus Stevens*; H. L. Trefousse, *Impeachment of a President*, and *The Radical Republicans*; H. White, *Life of Lyman Trumbull*.

7. Grant and Domestic Politics

H. Adams, *The Education of Henry Adams*; D. C. Barrett, *Greenbacks and the Resumption of Specie Payments*; W. A. Cate, *L. Q. C. Lamar*; M. Duberman, *Charles Francis Adams*; W. B. Hesseltine, *Ulysses S. Grant, Politician*; H. Larson, *Jay Cooke, Private Banker*; R. S. Mitchell, *Horatio Seymour of New York*; A. B. Paine, *Thomas Nast, His Period and His Pictures*; E. D. Ross, *The Liberal Republican Movement*; J. Schafer, *Carl Schurz, Militant Liberal*.

8. *Foreign Affairs*

S. F. Bemis (ed.), *The American Secretaries of State and Their Diplomacy*, vol. vii; J. M. Callahan, *The Alaska Purchase*; C. L. Jones, *Caribbean Interests of the United States*; A. Nevins, *Hamilton Fish*; C. C. Tansill, *The United States and Santo Domingo 1789–1873*.

9. *The Election of 1876*

H. Barnard, *Rutherford B. Hayes and His America*; H. J. Eckenrode, *Rutherford B. Hayes*; A. C. Flick, *Samuel Jones Tilden*; P. L. Haworth, *The Hayes-Tilden Disputed Election of 1876*; A. Nevins, *Abram S. Hewitt: With Some Account of Peter Cooper*; J. F. Rhodes, *History of the United States*, vol. vii; L. B. Richardson, *William E. Chandler, Republican*; C. R. Williams, *Life of Rutherford B. Hayes* (2 vols.); C. V. Woodward, *Reunion and Reaction*.

Statistical Tables

Admission of States to the Union
Presidents, Vice Presidents, and Heads of Departments
Population of the United States, 1770–1860
Presidential Vote, 1789–1876
Justices of the United States Supreme Court

ADMISSION OF STATES TO THE UNION

State	Entered Union	State	Entered Union	State	Entered Union	State	Entered Union
Alabama	1819	Indiana	1816	Nebraska	1867	South Carolina	1788
Alaska	1958	Iowa	1846	Nevada	1864	South Dakota	1889
Arizona	1912	Kansas	1861	New Hampshire	1788	Tennessee	1796
Arkansas	1836	Kentucky	1792	New Jersey	1787	Texas	1845
California	1850	Louisiana	1812	New Mexico	1912	Utah	1896
Colorado	1876	Maine	1820	New York	1788	Vermont	1791
Connecticut	1788	Maryland	1788	North Carolina	1789	Virginia	1788
Delaware	1787	Massachusetts	1788	North Dakota	1889	Washington	1889
Florida	1845	Michigan	1837	Ohio	1803	West Virginia	1863
Georgia	1788	Minnesota	1858	Oklahoma	1907	Wisconsin	1848
Hawaii	1959	Mississippi	1817	Oregon	1859	Wyoming	1890
Idaho	1890	Missouri	1821	Pennsylvania	1787		
Illinois	1818	Montana	1889	Rhode Island	1790		

President	Vice President	Secretary of State	Secretary of Treasury	Secretary of War	Secretary of Navy	Postmaster General	Attorney General
George Washington 1789	John Adams	T. Jefferson 1789 E. Randolph 1794 T. Pickering 1795	Alex. Hamilton 1789 Oliver Wolcott 1795	Henry Knox 1789 T. Pickering 1795 Jas. McHenry 1796		Samuel Osgood 1789 T. Pickering 1791 Jos. Habersham 1795	E. Randolph 1789 Wm. Bradford 1794 Charles Lee 1795
John Adams 1797	Thomas Jefferson	T. Pickering 1797 John Marshall 1800	Oliver Wolcott 1797 Samuel Dexter 1801	Jas. McHenry 1797 Samuel Dexter 1800	Benj. Stoddert 1798	Jos. Habersham 1797	Charles Lee 1797 Theo Parsons 1801
Thomas Jefferson 1801	Aaron Burr George Clinton 1805	James Madison 1801	Samuel Dexter 1801 Albert Gallatin 1801	H. Dearborn 1801	Benj. Stoddert 1801 Robert Smith 1801 J. Crowninshield 1805	Jos. Habersham 1801 Gideon Granger 1801	Levi Lincoln 1801 Robert Smith 1805 J. Breckinridge 1805 C. A. Rodney 1807
James Madison 1809	George Clinton Elbridge Gerry 1813	Robert Smith 1809 James Monroe 1811	Albert Gallatin 1809 G. W. Campbell 1814 A. J. Dallas 1814 W. H. Crawford 1816	Wm. Eustis 1809 John Armstrong 1813 James Monroe 1814 W.H. Crawford 1815	Paul Hamilton 1809 William Jones 1813 B. W. Crowninshield 1814	Gideon Granger 1809 R. J. Meigs, Jr. 1814	C. A. Rodney 1809 Wm. Pickney 1811 Richard Rush 1814
James Monroe 1817	D. D. Tompkins	J. Q. Adams 1817	W. H. Crawford 1817	Issac Shelby 1817 George Graham 1817 John C. Calhoun 1817	B. W. Crowninshield 1817 Smith Thompson 1818 S. L. Southard 1823	R. J. Meigs, Jr. 1817 John McLean 1823	Richard Rush 1817 William Wirt 1817
John Q. Adams 1825	John C. Calhoun	Henry Clay 1825	Richard Rush 1825	Jas. Barbour 1825 Peter B. Porter 1828	S. L. Southard 1825	John McLean 1825	William Wirt 1825
Andrew Jackson 1829	John C. Calhoun Martin Van Buren 1833	Martin Van Buren 1829 Edward Livingston 1831 Louis McLane 1833 John Forsyth 1834	Sam D. Ingham 1829 Louis McLane 1831 W. J. Duane 1833 Roger B. Taney 1833 Levi Woodbury 1834	John H. Eaton 1829 Lewis Cass 1831 B. F. Butler 1837	John Branch 1829 Levi Woodbury 1831 Mahlon Dickerson 1834	Wm. T. Barry 1829 Amos Kendall 1835	John M. Berrien 1829 Roger B. Taney 1831 B. F. Butler 1833
Martin Van Buren 1837	R. M. Johnson	John Forsyth 1837	Levi Woodbury 1837	Joel R. Poinsett 1837	Mahlon Dickerson 1837 Jas. K. Paulding 1838	Amos Kendall 1837 John M. Niles 1840	B. F. Butler 1837 Felix Grundy 1838 H. D. Gilpin 1840
William H. Harrison 1841	John Tyler	Daniel Webster 1841	Thos. Ewing 1841	John Bell 1841	George E. Badger 1841	Francis Granger 1841	John J. Crittenden 1841
John Tyler 1841		Daniel Webster 1841 Hugh S. Legaré 1843 Abel P. Upshur 1843 John C. Calhoun 1844	Thos. Ewing 1841 Walter Forward 1841 John C. Spencer 1843 George M. Bibb 1844	John Bell 1841 John C. Spencer 1841 Jas. M. Porter 1843 Wm. Wilkins 1844	George E. Badger 1841 Abel P. Upshur 1841 David Henshaw 1843 Thomas Gilmer 1844 John Y. Mason 1844	Francis Granger 1841 C. A. Wickliffe 1841	John J. Crittenden 1841 Hugh S. Legare 1841 John Nelson 1843

President	Vice President	Secretary of State	Secretary of Treasury	Secretary of War	Secretary of Navy	Postmaster General
James K. Polk 1845	George M. Dallas	James Buchanan 1845	Robt. J. Walker 1845	Wm. L. Marcy 1845	George Bancroft 1845 John Y. Mason 1846	Cave Johnson 1845
Zachary Taylor 1849	Millard Fillmore	John M. Clayton 1849	W. M. Meredith 1849	G. W. Crawford 1849	Wm. B. Preston 1849	Jacob Collamer 1849
Millard Fillmore 1850		Daniel Webster 1850 Edward Everett 1852	Thomas Corwin 1850	C. M. Conrad 1850	Wm. A. Graham 1850 John P. Kennedy 1852	Nathan K. Hall 1850 Sam D. Hubbard 1852
Franklin Pierce 1853	William R. King	Wm. L. Marcy 1853	James Guthrie 1853	Jefferson Davis 1853	James C. Dobbin 1853	James Campbell 1853
James Buchanan 1857	John C. Breckinridge	Lewis Cass 1857 J. S. Black 1860	Hqwell Cobb 1857 Philip F. Thomas 1860 John A. Dix 1861	John B. Floyd 1857 Joseph Holt 1861	Isaac Toucey 1857	Aaron V. Brown 1857 Joseph Holt 1859 Horatio King 1861
Abraham Lincoln 1861	Hannibal Hamlin Andrew Johnson 1865	William H. Seward 1861	Salmon P. Chase 1861 W. P. Fessenden 1864 Hugh McCulloch 1865	S. Cameron 1861 E. M. Stanton 1862	Gideon Welles 1861	Horatio King 1861 M'tgomery Blair 1861 Wm. Dennison 1864
Andrew Johnson 1865		William H. Seward 1865	Hugh McCulloch 1865	E. M. Stanton 1865 Ulysses S Grant 1867 Lorenzo Thomas 1868 J. M. Schofield 1868	Gideon Welles 1865	Wm. Dennison 1865 Alexander Randall 1866
Ulysses S. Grant 1869	Schulyer Colfax Henry Wilson 1873	E. B. Washburne 1869 Hamilton Fish 1869	G. S. Boutwell 1869 W. A. Richardson 1873 B. H. Bristow 1874 Lot M. Morrill 1876	John A. Rawlins 1869 Wm. T. Sherman 1869 Wm. W. Belknap 1869 Alphonso Taft 1876 Jas. D. Cameron 1876	Adolph E. Borie 1869 George M. Robeson 1869	John A. J. Creswell 1869 James W. Marshall 1874 Marshall Jewell 1874 James N. Tyner 1876
Rutherford B. Hayes 1877	William A. Wheeler	William M. Evarts 1877	John Sherman 1877	George W. McCrary 1877 Alexander Ramsey 1879	R. W. Thompson 1877 Nathan Goff, Jr. 1881	David M. Key 1877 Horace Maynard 1880

Attorney General	Secretary of Interior
John Y. Mason 1845	
Nathan Clifford 1846	
Isaac Toucey 1848	
Reverdy Johnson 1849	Thomas Ewing 1849
J. J. Crittenden 1850	Thomas McKennan 1850
	A. H. Stuart 1850
Caleb Cushing 1853	Robert McClelland 1853
J. S. Black 1857	Jacob Thompson 1857
Edw. M. Stanton 1860	
Edward Bates 1861	Caleb B. Smith 1861
Titian J. Coffey 1863	John P. Usher 1863
James Speed 1864	
James Speed 1865	John P. Usher 1865
Henry Stanbery 1866	James Harlan 1865
William M. Evarts 1868	O. H. Browning 1866
Ebenezer R. Hoar 1869	Jacob D. Cox 1869
Amos T. Akerman 1870	Columbus Delano 1870
G. H. Williams 1871	Zachary Chandler 1875
Edward Pierrepont 1875	
Alphonso Taft 1876	
Charles Devens 1877	Carl Schurz 1877

TABLE OF POPULATION OF THE UNITED STATES, 1770–1870

Estimates for 1770 taken from *A Century of Population Growth* (1909), others from the United States censuses

State	1770	1790	1800	1810	1820	1830	1840	1850	1860	1870
New England										
Maine	34,000	96,540	151,719	228,705	298,335	399,455	501,793	583,169	628,279	626,915
New Hampshire	60,000	141,885	183,858	214,460	244,161	269,328	284,574	317,976	326,073	318,300
Vermont	25,000	85,425	154,465	217,895	235,981	280,652	291,948	314,120	315,098	330,551
Massachusetts	265,000	378,787	422,845	472,040	523,287	610,408	737,699	994,514	1,231,066	1,457,351
Rhode Island	55,000	68,825	69,122	76,931	83,059	97,199	108,830	147,545	174,620	217,353
Connecticut	175,000	237,946	251,002	261,942	275,248	297,675	309,978	370,792	460,147	537,454
Middle Atlantic										
New York	160,000	340,120	589,051	959,049	1,372,812	1,918,608	2,428,921	3,097,394	3,880,735	4,382,759
New Jersey	110,000	184,139	211,149	245,562	277,575	320,823	373,306	489,555	672,035	906,096
Pennsylvania	250,000	434,373	602,365	810,091	1,049,458	1,348,233	1,724,033	2,311,786	2,906,215	3,521,951
South Atlantic										
Delaware	25,000	59,096	64,273	72,674	72,749	76,748	78,085	91,532	112,216	125,015
Maryland	200,000	319,728	341,548	380,546	407,350	447,040	470,019	583,034	687,049	780,894
Dist. of Columbia			14,093	24,023	33,039	39,834	43,712	51,687	75,080	131,700
Virginia	450,000	747,610	880,200	974,600	1,065,366	1,211,405	1,239,797	1,421,661	1,596,318	1,225,163
West Virginia										442,014
North Carolina	230,000	393,751	478,103	555,500	638,829	737,987	753,419	869,039	992,622	1,071,361
South Carolina	140,000	249,073	345,591	415,115	502,741	581,185	594,398	668,507	703,708	705,606
Georgia	26,000	82,548	162,686	252,433	340,989	516,823	691,392	906,185	1,057,286	1,184,109
Florida						34,730	54,477	87,445	140,424	187,748
South Central										
Kentucky		73,677	220,955	406,511	564,317	687,917	779,828	982,405	1,155,684	1,321,011
Tennessee		35,691	105,602	261,727	422,823	681,904	829,210	1,002,717	1,109,801	1,258,520
Alabama					127,901	309,527	590,756	771,623	964,201	996,992
Mississippi			8,850	40,352	75,448	136,621	375,651	606,526	791,305	827,922
Arkansas				1,062	14,273	30,388	97,574	209,897	435,450	484,471
Louisiana				76,556	153,407	215,739	352,411	517,762	708,002	726,915
Oklahoma										
Texas								212,592	604,215	818,579

	C1	C2	C3	C4	C5	C6	C7	C8	C9	C10
North Central										
Ohio			45,365	230,760	581,434	937,903	1,519,467	1,980,329	2,339,511	2,665,260
Indiana			5,641	24,520	147,178	343,031	685,866	988,416	1,350,428	1,680,637
Illinois			{	12,282	55,211	157,445	476,183	851,470	1,711,951	2,539,891
Michigan				4,762	8,896	31,639	212,267	397,654	749,113	1,184,059
Wisconsin							30,945	305,391	775,881	1,054,670
Minnesota								6,077	172,023	439,706
Iowa							43,112	192,214	674,913	1,194,020
Missouri				19,783	66,586	140,455	383,702	682,044	1,182,012	1,721,295
North Dakota									4,837	14,181
South Dakota										
Nebraska									28,841	122,993
Kansas									107,206	364,399
Mountain										
Montana										20,595
Idaho										14,999
Wyoming										9,118
Colorado									34,277	39,864
New Mexico								61,547	93,516	91,874
Arizona										9,658
Utah								11,380	40,273	86,786
Nevada									6,857	42,491
Pacific										
Washington									11,594	23,955
Oregon								13,294	52,465	90,923
California								92,597	379,994	560,247
	2,205,000	3,929,214	5,308,483	7,239,881	9,638,453	12,866,020	17,069,453	23,191,876	31,443,321	38,558,371

Year	Candidate	Party	Popular vote	Per cent	Electoral vote
1789	*Washington*	none	————————		69
	J. Adams	none	————————		34
	Jay	none	————————		9
	Harrison	none	————————		6
	Rutledge	none	————————		6
	Hancock	none	————————		4
	G. Clinton	none	————————		3
	Huntington	none	————————		2
	Milton	none	————————		2
	Armstrong	none	————————		1
	Lincoln	none	————————		1
	Telfair	none	————————		1
	Votes not cast	————————	————————		12
1792	*Washington*	Federalist	————————		132
	J. Adams	Federalist	————————		77
	G. Clinton	Democratic-Republican	————————		50
	Jefferson	————————	————————		4
	Burr	————————	————————		1
1796	*J. Adams*	Federalist	————————		71
	Jefferson	Democratic-Republican	————————		68
	T. Pinckney	Federalist	————————		59
	Burr	Anti-Federalist	————————		30
	S. Adams	Democratic-Republican	————————		15
	Ellsworth	Federalist	————————		11
	G. Clinton	Democratic-Republican	————————		7
	Jay	Independent-Federalist	————————		5
	Iredell	Federalist	————————		3
	Washington	Federalist	————————		2
	Henry	Independent	————————		2
	Johnston	Independent-Federalist	————————		2
	C. C. Pinckney	Independent-Federalist	————————		1
1800*	*Jefferson*	Democratic-Republican	————————		73
	Burr	Democratic-Republican	————————		73
	J. Adams	Federalist	————————		65
	C. C. Pinckney	Federalist	————————		64
	Jay	Federalist	————————		1
1804	*Jefferson*	Democratic-Republican	————————		162
	C. C. Pinckney	Federalist	————————		14
1808	*Madison*	Democratic-Republican	————————		122
	C. C. Pinckney	Federalist	————————		47
	G. Clinton	Democratic-Republican	————————		6
	Votes not cast	————————	————————		1
1812	*Madison*	Democratic-Republican	————————		128
	D. Clinton	Fusion	————————		89
	Votes not cast	————————	————————		1
1816	*Monroe*	Republican	————————		183
	King	Federalist	————————		34
	Votes not cast	————————	————————		4

Year	Candidate	Party	Popular vote	Per cent	Electoral vote
1820	*Monroe*	Democratic-Republican	————————	————————	231
	J. Q. Adams	Independent-Republican	————————	————————	1
	Votes not cast		————————	————————	3
1824**	Jackson	No Distinct	152,933	42.2	84
	J. Q. Adams	Party Designations	115,696	31.9	99
	Clay		47,136	13.0	37
	Crawford		46,979	12.9	41
1828	*Jackson*	Democratic	647,292	56.0	178
	J. Q. Adams	National-Republican	507,730	44.0	83
1832	*Jackson*	Democratic	688,242	54.5	219
	Clay	National-Republican	473,462	37.5	49
	Wirt	Anti-Masonic Nullifiers	101,051	8.0	7
	Floyd	Independent	————	————	11
	Votes not cast		————	————	2
1836	*Van Buren*	Democratic	764,198	50.9	170
	W.H.Harrison	Whig	549,508	36.6	73
	White	Whig	145,352	9.7	26
	Webster	Whig	41,287	2.7	14
	Mangum	Anti-Jackson	————	————	11
1840	*W.H.Harrison*	Whig	1,275,612	52.9	234
	Van Buren	Democratic	1,130,033	46.8	60
	Birney	Liberty	7,053	.3	—
1844	*Polk*	Democratic	1,339,368	49.6	170
	Clay	Whig	1,300,687	48.1	105
	Birney	Liberty	62,197	2.3	—
1848	*Taylor*	Whig	1,362,101	47.3	163
	Cass	Democratic	1,222,674	42.4	127
	Van Buren	Free-Soil	291,616	10.1	—
1852	*Pierce*	Democratic	1,609,038	50.8	254
	Scott	Whig	1,386,629	43.8	42
	Hale	Free-Soil	156,297	4.9	—
1856	*Buchanan*	Democratic	1,839,237	45.6	174
	Frémont	Republican	1,341,028	33.3	114
	Fillmore	American	849,872	21.1	8
1860	*Lincoln*	Republican	1,867,198	39.8	180
	Douglas	Democratic	1,379,434	29.4	12
	Breckinridge	National-Democratic	854,248	18.2	72
	Bell	Constitutional Union	591,658	12.6	34
1864	*Lincoln*	Republican	2,219,362	55.1	212
	McClellan	Democratic	1,805,063	44.9	21
	Votes not cast		————	————	1
1868	*Grant*	Republican	3,013,313	52.7	214
	Seymour	Democratic	2,703,933	47.3	80
	Votes not cast		————	————	23

Year	Candidate	Party	Popular vote	Per cent	Electoral vote
1872	*Grant*	Republican	3,597,375	55.6	286
	Greeley	Democratic, Liberal Republican	2,833,711	43.8	—
	Hendricks	Democratic	————	——	42
	Brown	Democratic, Liberal Republican	————	——	18
	Other	———————	————	——	3
	Votes not cast	———————	————	——	17
1876	Tilden	Democratic	4,284,885	50.9	184
	Hayes	Republican	4,033,950	48.0	185
	Cooper	Greenback	81,740	1.0	—
	Smith	Prohibition	9,522	.1	—
	Walker	American	2,636	.0	—

*Candidates for President and Vice-President were not nominated separately, and voting ended in a tie between Jefferson and Burr. The House of Representatives elected Jefferson on the 36th ballot. The Twelfth Amendment, ratified in 1804, provided for separate balloting thereafter.

**No candidate received a majority of the electoral vote, and the election was decided in the House of Representatives. Adams was chosen on the first ballot.

Source: *Historical Statistics of the United States* and *The New York Times Encyclopedic Almanac*

Name and State Appointed from	Service		Name	Service	
Chief Justices in Italics	Term	Yrs.		Term	Yrs.
John Jay, N.Y.	1789–1795	6	George Shiras, Jr., Pa.	1892–1903	11
John Rutledge, S.C.	1789–1791	2	Howell E. Jackson, Tenn.	1893–1895	2
William Cushing, Mass.	1789–1810	21	Edward D. White, La.	1894–1910	16
James Wilson, Pa.	1789–1798	9	Rufus W. Peckham, N.Y.	1895–1910	14
John Blair, Va.	1789–1796	7	Joseph McKenna, Cal.	1898–1925	27
Robert H. Harrison, Md.	1789–1790	1	Oliver W. Holmes, Mass.	1902–1932	29
James Iredell, N.C.	1790–1799	9	William R. Day, Ohio	1903–1922	19
Thomas Johnson, Md.	1791–1793	2	William H. Moody, Mass.	1906–1910	4
William Paterson, N.J.	1793–1806	13	Horace H. Lurton, Tenn.	1910–1914	5
John Rutledge, S.C.	1795–1795		Charles E. Hughes, N.Y.	1910–1916	6
Samuel Chase, Md.	1796–1811	15	Willis Van Devanter, Wyo.	1910–1937	27
Oliver Ellsworth, Conn.	1796–1799	4	Edward D. White, La.	1910–1921	11
Bushrod Washington, Va.	1798–1829	31	Joseph R. Lamar, Ga.	1911–1916	6
Alfred Moore, N.C.	1799–1804	5	Mahlon Pitney, N.J.	1912–1922	10
John Marshall, Va.	1801–1835	34	Jas. C. McReynolds, Tenn.	1914–1941	27
William Johnson, S.C.	1804–1834	30	Louis D. Brandeis, Mass.	1916–1939	23
Brock. Livingston, N.Y.	1806–1823	17	John H. Clarke, Ohio	1916–1922	6
Thomas Todd, Ky.	1807–1826	19	William H. Taft, Conn.	1921–1930	9
Joseph Story, Mass.	1811–1845	34	George Sutherland, Utah	1922–1938	16
Gabriel Duval, Md.	1811–1836	25	Pierce Butler, Minn.	1922–1939	17
Smith Thompson, N.Y.	1823–1843	20	Edward T. Sanford, Tenn.	1923–1930	7
Robert Trimble, Ky.	1826–1828	2	Harlan F. Stone, N.Y.	1925–1941	16
John McLean, Ohio	1829–1861	32	Charles E. Hughes, N.Y.	1930–1941	11
Henry Baldwin, Pa.	1830–1844	14	Owen J. Roberts, Pa.	1930–1945	15
James M. Wayne, Ga.	1835–1867	32	Benjamin N. Cardozo, N.Y.	1932–1938	6
Roger B. Taney, Md.	1836–1864	28	Hugo L. Black, Ala.	1937–1971	34
Philip P. Barbour, Va.	1836–1841	5	Stanley F. Reed, Ky.	1938–1957	19
John Catron, Tenn.	1837–1865	28	Felix Frankfurter, Mass.	1939–1962	23
John McKinley, Ala.	1837–1852	15	William O. Douglas, Conn.	1939–1975	36
Peter V. Daniel, Va.	1841–1860	19	Frank Murphy, Mich.	1940–1949	9
Samuel Nelson, N.Y.	1845–1872	27	Harlan F. Stone, N.Y.	1941–1946	5
Levi Woodbury, N.H.	1845–1851	6	James F. Byrnes, S.C.	1941–1942	1
Robert C. Grier, Pa.	1846–1870	24	Robert H. Jackson, N.Y.	1941–1954	13
Benj. R. Curtis, Mass.	1851–1857	6	Wiley B. Rutledge, Iowa	1943–1949	6
John A. Campbell, Ala.	1853–1861	8	Harold H. Burton, Ohio	1945–1958	13
Nathan Clifford, Me.	1858–1881	23	Fred M. Vinson, Ky.	1946–1953	7
Noah H. Swayne, Ohio	1862–1881	20	Tom C. Clark, Tex.	1949–1967	18
Samuel F. Miller, Iowa	1862–1890	28	Sherman Minton, Ind.	1949–1956	7
David Davis, Ill.	1862–1877	15	Earl Warren, Cal.	1953–1969	16
Stephen J. Field, Cal.	1863–1897	34	John M. Harlan, N.Y.	1955–1971	16
Salmon P. Chase, Ohio	1864–1873	9	William J. Brennan, Jr., N.J.	1956–	
William Strong, Pa.	1870–1880	10	Charles E. Whittaker, Mo.	1957–1962	5
Joseph P. Bradley, N.J.	1870–1892	22	Potter Stewart, Ohio	1959–1981	23
Ward Hunt, N.Y.	1872–1882	10	Byron R. White, Colo.	1962–	
Morrison R. Waite, Ohio	1874–1888	14	Arthur J. Goldberg, Ill.	1962–1965	3
John M. Harlan, Ky.	1877–1911	34	Abe Fortas, Tenn.	1965–1969	4
William B. Woods, Ga.	1880–1887	7	Thurgood Marshall, N.Y.	1967–	
Stanley Matthews, Ohio	1881–1889	8	Warren E. Burger, Minn.	1969–	
Horace Gray, Mass.	1881–1902	21	Harry A. Blackmun, Minn.	1970–	
Samuel Blatchford, N.Y.	1882–1893	11	William H. Rehnquist, Ariz.	1972–	
Lucius Q. C. Lamar, Miss.	1888–1893	5	Lewis F. Powell, Jr., Va.	1972–	
Melville W. Fuller, Ill.	1888–1910	22	John Paul Stevens, Ill.	1975–	
David J. Brewer, Kan.	1889–1910	21	Sandra D. O'Connor, Ariz.	1981–	
Henry B. Brown, Mich.	1890–1906	16			

The Constitution of the United States

We the People of the United States, in order to form a more perfect union, establish Justice, insure domestic tranquility, provide for the common defence, promote the general Welfare, and secure the Blessings of Liberty to ourselves and our Posterity, do ordain and establish this Constitution for the United States of America.

ARTICLE I

Section 1. All legislative Powers herein granted shall be vested in a Congress of the United States, which shall consist of a Senate and a House of Representatives.

Section 2. The House of Representatives shall be composed of Members chosen every second Year by the People of the several States, and the Electors in each State shall have the Qualifications requisite for Electors of the most numerous Branch of the State Legislature.

No Person shall be a Representative who shall not have attained to the Age of twenty-five Years, and been seven Years a Citizen of the United States, and who shall not, when elected, be an Inhabitant of that State in which he shall be chosen.

Representatives and direct Taxes shall be apportioned among the several States which may be included within this Union, according to their respective Numbers, which shall be determined by adding to the whole Number of free Persons, including those bound to Service for a Term of Years, and excluding Indians not taxed, three fifths of all other Persons. The actual Enumeration shall be made within three Years after the first Meeting of the Congress of the United States, and within every subsequent Term of ten Years, in such Manner as they shall by Law direct. The Number of Representatives shall not exceed one for every thirty Thousand, but each State shall have at Least one Representative; and until such enumeration shall be made, the State of New Hampshire shall be entitled to chuse three, Massachusetts eight, Rhode-Island and Providence Plantations one, Connecticut five, New-York six, New Jersey four, Pennsylvania eight, Delaware one, Maryland six, Virginia ten, North Carolina five, South Carolina five, and Georgia three.

When vacancies happen in the Representation from any State, the Executive Authority thereof shall issue Writs of Election to fill such Vacancies.

The House of Representatives shall chuse their Speaker and other Officers; and shall have the sole Power of Impeachment.

Section 3. The Senate of the United States shall be composed of two Senators from each State, chosen by the Legislature thereof, for six Years; and each Senator shall have one Vote.

Immediately after they shall be assembled in Consequence of the first Election, they shall be divided as equally as may be into three Classes. The Seats of the Senators of the first Class shall be vacated at the Expiration of the second Year, of the second Class at the Expiration of the fourth Year, and of the third Class at the Expiration of the sixth Year, so that one-third may be chosen every second Year; and if Vacancies happen by Resignation, or otherwise, during the Recess of the Legislature of any State, the Executive thereof may make temporary Appointments until the next Meeting of the Legislature, which shall then fill such Vacancies.

No Person shall be a Senator who shall not have attained to the Age of thirty Years, and been nine Years a Citizen of the United States, and who shall not, when elected, be an Inhabitant of that State for which he shall be chosen.

The Vice President of the United States shall be President of the Senate, but shall have no Vote, unless they be equally divided.

The Senate shall chuse their other Officers, and also a President pro tempore, in the Absence of the Vice President, or when he shall exercise the Office of President of the United States.

The Senate shall have the sole Power to try all Impeachments. When sitting for that Purpose, they shall be on Oath or Affirmation. When the President of the United States is tried, the Chief Justice shall preside: And no Person shall be convicted without the Concurrence of two thirds of the Members present.

Judgment in Cases of Impeachment shall not extend further than to removal from Office, and disqualification to hold and enjoy any Office of honor, Trust or Profit under the United States: but the Party convicted shall nevertheless be liable and subject to Indictment, Trial, Judgment and Punishment, according to Law.

Section 4. The Times, Places and Manner of holding Elections for Senators and Representatives, shall be prescribed in each State by the Legislature thereof; but the Congress may at any time by Law make or alter such Regulations, except as to the Places of chusing Senators.

The Congress shall assemble at least once in every Year, and such Meeting shall be on the first Monday in December, unless they shall by Law appoint a different Day.

Section 5. Each House shall be the Judge of the Elections, Returns and Qualifications of its own Members, and a Majority of each shall constitute a Quorum to do Business; but a smaller Number may

adjourn from day to day, and may be authorized to compel the Attendance of absent Members, in such Manner, and under such Penalties as each House may provide.

Each House may determine the Rules of its Proceedings, punish its Members for disorderly Behavior, and, with the Concurrence of two thirds, expel a Member.

Each House shall keep a Journal of its Proceedings, and from time to time publish the same, excepting such Parts as may in their Judgment require Secrecy; and the Yeas and Nays of the Members of either House on any question shall, at the Desire of one fifth of those present, be entered on the Journal.

Neither House, during the Session of Congress, shall, without the Consent of the other, adjourn for more than three days, nor to any other Place than that in which the two Houses shall be sitting.

Section 6. The Senators and Representatives shall receive a Compensation for their Services, to be ascertained by Law, and paid out of the Treasury of the United States. They shall in all Cases, except Treason, Felony and Breach of the Peace, be privileged from Arrest during their Attendance at the Session of their respective Houses, and in going to and returning from the same; and for any Speech or Debate in either House, they shall not be questioned in any other Place.

No Senator or Representative shall, during the Time for which he was elected, be appointed to any civil Office under the Authority of the United States, which shall have been created, or the Emoluments whereof shall have been encreased during such time; and no Person holding any Office under the United States, shall be a Member of either House during his Continuance in Office.

Section 7. All Bills for raising Revenue shall originate in the House of Representatives; but the Senate may propose or concur with Amendments as on other Bills.

Every Bill which shall have passed the House of Representatives and the Senate, shall, before it becomes a Law, be presented to the President of the United States; If he approves he shall sign it, but if not he shall return it, with his Objections to that House in which it shall have originated, who shall enter the Objections at large on their Journal, and proceed to reconsider it. If after such Reconsideration two thirds of that House shall agree to pass the Bill, it shall be sent, together with the Objections, to the other House, by which it shall likewise be reconsidered, and if approved by two thirds of that House, it shall become a Law. But in all such Cases the Votes of both Houses shall be determined by Yeas and Nays, and the Names of the Persons voting for and against the Bill shall be entered on the Journal of each House respectively. If any Bill shall not be returned by the President within ten Days (Sundays excepted) after it shall have been presented to him, the Same shall be a Law, in like Manner as if he had signed it, unless the Congress by their Adjournment prevent its Return, in which Case it shall not be a Law.

Every Order, Resolution, or Vote to which the Concurrence of the Senate and House of Representatives may be necessary (except on a question of Adjournment) shall be presented to the President of the United States; and before the Same shall take Effect, shall be approved by him, or being disapproved by him, shall be repassed by two thirds of the Senate and House of Representatives, according to the Rules and Limitations prescribed in the Case of a Bill.

Section 8. The Congress shall have Power To lay and collect Taxes, Duties, Imposts and Excises, to pay the Debts and provide for the common Defence and general Welfare of the United States; but all Duties, Imposts and Excises shall be uniform throughout the United States;

To borrow Money on the credit of the United States;

To regulate Commerce with foreign Nations, and among the several States, and with the Indian Tribes;

To establish an uniform Rule of Naturalization, and uniform Laws on the subject of Bankruptcies throughout the United States;

To coin Money, regulate the Value thereof, and of foreign Coin, and fix the Standard of Weights and Measures;

To provide for the Punishment of counterfeiting the Securities and current Coin of the United States;

To establish Post Offices and post Roads;

To promote the Progress of Science and useful Arts, by securing for limited Times to Authors and Inventors the exclusive Right to their respective Writings and Discoveries;

To constitute Tribunals inferior to the supreme Court;

To define and punish Piracies and Felonies committed on the high Seas, and Offences against the Law of Nations;

To declare War, grant Letters of Marque and Reprisal, and make Rules concerning Captures on Land and Water;

To raise and support Armies, but no Appropriation of Money to that Use shall be for a longer Term than two Years;

To provide and maintain a Navy;

To make Rules for the Government and Regulation of the land and naval Forces;

To provide for calling forth the Militia to execute the Laws of the Union, suppress Insurrections and repel Invasions;

To provide for organizing, arming, and disciplining the Militia, and for governing such Part of them as may be employed in the Service of the United States, reserving to the States respectively, the Appointment of the Officers, and the Authority of training the Militia according to the discipline prescribed by Congress;

To exercise exclusive Legislation in all Cases whatsoever, over such District (not exceeding ten Miles square) as may, by Cession of particular States, and the Acceptance of Congress, become the Seat of the Government of the United States, and to exercise like Authority over all Places purchased by the Consent of the Legislature of the State in which the Same shall be, for the Erection of Forts, Magazines, Arsenals, dock-Yards, and other needful Buildings;—And

To make all Laws which shall be necessary and proper for carrying into Execution the foregoing Powers, and all other Powers vested by this Constitution in the Government of the United States, or in any Department or Officer thereof.

Section 9. The Migration or Importation of such Persons as any of the States now existing shall think proper to admit, shall not be prohibited by the Congress prior to the Year one thousand eight hundred and eight, but a Tax or duty may be imposed on such Importation, not exceeding ten dollars for each Person.

The Privilege of the Writ of Habeas Corpus shall not be suspended, unless when in Cases of Rebellion or Invasion the public Safety may require it.

No Bill of Attainder or ex post facto Law shall be passed.

No Capitation, or other direct, tax shall be laid, unless in Proportion to the Census or Enumeration herein before directed to be taken.

No Tax or Duty shall be laid on Articles exported from any State.

No Preference shall be given by any Regulation of Commerce or Revenue to the Ports of one State over those of another: nor shall Vessels bound to, or from, one State, be obliged to enter, clear, or pay Duties in another.

No Money shall be drawn from the Treasury, but in Consequence of Appropriations made by Law; and a regular Statement and Account of the Receipts and

Expenditures of all public Money shall be published from time to time.

No Title of Nobility shall be granted by the United States: And no Person holding any Office of Profit or Trust under them, shall, without the Consent of the Congress, accept of any present, Emolument, Office, or Title, of any kind whatever, from any King, Prince, or foreign State.

Section 10. No State shall enter into any Treaty, Alliance, or Confederation; grant Letters of Marque and Reprisal; coin Money; emit Bills of Credit; make any Thing but gold and silver Coin a Tender in Payment of Debts; pass any Bill of Attainder, ex post facto Law, or Law impairing the Obligation of Contracts, or grant any Title of Nobility.

No State shall, without the Consent of the Congress, lay any Imposts or Duties on Imports or Exports, except what may be absolutely necessary for executing its inspection Laws: and the net Produce of all Duties and Imposts, laid by any State on Imports or Exports, shall be for the Use of the Treasury of the United States; and all such Laws shall be subject to the Revision and Controul of the Congress.

No State shall, without the Consent of Congress, lay any Duty of Tonnage, keep Troops, or Ships of War in time of Peace, enter into any Agreement or Compact with another State, or with a foreign Power, or engage in War, unless actually invaded, or in such imminent Danger as will not admit of delay.

ARTICLE II

Section 1. The Executive Power shall be vested in a President of the United States of America. He shall hold his Office during the Term of four Years, and, together with the Vice President, chosen for the same Term, be elected, as follows

Each State shall appoint, in such Manner as the legislature thereof may direct, a Number of Electors, equal to the whole Number of Senators and Representatives to which the State may be entitled in the Congress: but no Senator or Representative, or Person holding an Office of Trust or Profit under the United States, shall be appointed an Elector.

The electors shall meet in their respective States, and vote by ballot for two Persons, of whom one at least shall not be an Inhabitant of the same State with themselves. And they shall make a List of all the Persons voted for, and of the Number of Votes for each; which List they shall sign and certify, and transmit sealed to the Seat of the Government of the United States, directed to the President of the Senate. The President of the Senate shall, in the Presence of the Senate and House of Representatives, open all the Certificates, and the Votes shall then be counted. The Person having the greatest Number of Votes shall be the President, if such Number be a Majority of the whole Number of Electors appointed; and if there be more than one who have such Majority, and have an equal Number of Votes, then the House of Representatives shall immediately chuse by Ballot one of them for President; and if no Person have a Majority, then from the five highest on the List the said House shall in like Manner chuse the President. But in chusing the President, the Votes shall be taken by States, the Representation from each State having one Vote; A quorum for this Purpose shall consist of a Member or Members from two thirds of the States, and a Majority of all the States shall be necessary to a Choice. In every Case, after the Choice of the President, the Person having the greatest Number of Votes of the Electors shall be the Vice President. But if there should remain two or more who have equal Votes, the Senate shall chuse from them by Ballot the Vice President.

The Congress may determine the Time of chusing the Electors, and the Day on which they shall give their Votes; which Day shall be the same throughout the United States.

No Person except a natural born Citizen, or a Citizen of the United States, at the time of the Adoption of this Constitution, shall be eligible to the Office of President; neither shall any Person be eligible to that Office who shall not have attained to the Age of thirty five Years, and been fourteen Years a Resident within the United States.

In Case of the Removal of the President from Office, or of his Death, Resignation or Inability to discharge the Powers and Duties of the said Office, the same shall devolve on the Vice President, and the Congress may by Law provide for the Case of Removal, Death, Resignation or Inability, both of the President and Vice President, declaring what Officer shall then act as President, and such Officer shall act accordingly, until the Disability be removed, or a President shall be elected.

The President shall, at stated Times, receive for his Services, a Compensation, which shall neither be encreased nor diminished during the Period for which he shall have been elected, and he shall not receive within that Period any other Emolument from the United States, or any of them.

Before he enter on the Execution of his Office, he shall take the following Oath or Affirmation:—"I do solemnly swear (or affirm) that I will faithfully execute the Office of President of the United States, and will to the best of my Ability, preserve, protect and defend the Constitution of the United States."

Section 2. The President shall be Commander in Chief of the Army and Navy of the United States, and of the Militia of the several States, when called into the actual Service of the United States; he may require the Opinion, in writing, of the principal Officer in each of the executive Departments, upon any Subject relating to the Duties of their respective Offices, and he shall have Power to grant Reprieves and Pardons for Offences against the United States, except in Cases of Impeachment.

He shall have Power, by and with the Advice and Consent of the Senate to make Treaties, provided two thirds of the Senators present concur and he shall nominate, and by and with the Advice and Consent of the Senate, shall appoint Ambassadors, other public Ministers and Consuls, Judges of the supreme Court, and all other Officers of the United States, whose Appointments are not herein otherwise provided for, and which shall be established by Law: but the Congress may by Law vest the Appointment of such inferior Officers, as they think proper, in the President alone, in the Courts of Law, or in the Heads of Departments.

The President shall have Power to fill up all Vacancies that may happen during the Recess of the Senate, by granting Commissions which shall expire at the End of their next Session.

Section 3. He shall from time to time give to the Congress Information of the State of the Union, and recommend to their Consideration such Measures as he shall judge necessary and expedient; he may, on extraordinary Occasions, convene both Houses, or either of them, and, in Case of Disagreement between them, with Respect to the Time of Adjournment, he may adjourn them to such Time as he shall think proper; he shall receive Ambassadors and other public Ministers; he shall take Care that the Laws be faithfully executed, and shall Commission all the Officers of the United States.

Section 4. The President, Vice President and all civil Officers of the United States, shall be removed from Office on Impeachment for, and Conviction of, Treason, Bribery, or other high Crimes and Misdemeanors.

ARTICLE III

Section 1. The judicial Power of the United States, shall be vested in one supreme Court, and in such inferior Courts as the Congress may from time to time ordain and establish. The Judges, both of the supreme and inferior Courts, shall hold their Offices during good Behaviour, and shall, at stated Times, receive for their Services, a Compensation, which shall not be diminished during their Continuance in Office.

Section 2. The judicial Power shall extend to all Cases, in Law and Equity, arising under this Constitution, the Laws of the United States, and Treaties made, or which shall be made, under their Authority;—to all Cases affecting Ambassadors, other public Ministers and Consuls;—to all Cases of admiralty and maritime Jurisdiction;—to Controversies to which the United States shall be a Party;—to Controversies between two or more States;—between a State and Citizens of another State;—between Citizens of different States,—between Citizens of the same State claiming Lands under Grants of different States, and between a State, or the Citizens thereof, and foreign States, Citizens or Subjects.

In all Cases affecting Ambassadors, other public Ministers and Consuls, and those in which a State shall be Party, the supreme Court shall have original Jurisdiction. In all other Cases before mentioned, the supreme Court shall have appellate Jurisdiction, both as to Law and Fact, with such Exceptions, and under such Regulations as the Congress shall make.

The Trial of all Crimes, except in Cases of Impeachment, shall be by Jury; and such Trial shall be held in the State where the said Crimes shall have been committed; but when not committed within any State, the Trial shall be at such Place or Places as the Congress may by Law have directed.

Section 3. Treason against the United States, shall consist only in levying War against them, or in adhering to their Enemies, giving them Aid and Comfort. No Person shall be convicted of Treason unless on the Testimony of two Witnesses to the same overt Act, or on Confession in open Court.

The Congress shall have Power to declare the Punishment of Treason, but no Attainder of Treason shall work Corruption of Blood, or Forfeiture except during the Life of the Person attainted.

ARTICLE IV

Section 1. Full Faith and Credit shall be given in each State to the public Acts, Records, and judicial Proceedings of every other State. And the Congress may by general Laws prescribe the Manner in which such Acts, Records and Proceedings shall be proved, and the Effect thereof.

Section 2. The Citizens of each State shall be entitled to all Privileges and Immunities of Citizens in the several States.

A person charged in any State with Treason, Felony, or other Crime, who shall flee from Justice, and be found in another State, shall on Demand of the executive Authority of the State from which he fled, be delivered up, to be removed to the State having Jurisdiction of the Crime.

No Person held to Service or Labour in one State, under the Laws thereof, escaping into another, shall, in Consequence of any Law or Regulation therein, be discharged from such Service or Labour, but shall be delivered up on Claim of the Party to whom such Service or Labour may be due.

Section 3. New States may be admitted by the Congress into this Union; but no new State shall be formed or erected within the Jurisdiction of any other State; nor any State be formed by the Junction of two or more States, or Parts of States, without the Consent of the Legislatures of the States concerned as well as of the Congress.

The Congress shall have Power to dispose of and make all needful Rules and Regulations respecting the Territory or other Property belonging to the United States; and nothing in this Constitution shall be so construed as to Prejudice any Claims of the United States, or of any particular State.

Section 4. The United States shall guarantee to every State in this Union a Republican Form of Government, and shall protect each of them against Invasion; and on Application of the Legislature, or of the Executive (when the Legislature cannot be convened) against domestic Violence.

ARTICLE V

The Congress, whenever two thirds of both houses shall deem it necessary, shall propose Amendments to this Constitution, or, on the Application of the Legislatures of two thirds of the several States, shall call a Convention for proposing Amendments, which, in either Case, shall be valid to all Intents and Purposes, as Part of this Constitution, when ratified by the Legislatures of three fourths of the several States, or by Conventions in three fourths thereof, as the one or the other Mode of Ratification may be proposed by the Congress; Provided that no Amendment which may be made prior to the Year One thousand eight hundred and eight shall in any Manner affect the first and fourth Clauses in the Ninth Section of the first Article; and that no State, without its Consent, shall be deprived of its equal Suffrage in the Senate.

ARTICLE VI

All Debts contracted and Engagements entered into, before the Adoption of this Constitution, shall be as valid against the United States under this Constitution, as under the Confederation.

This Constitution, and the Laws of the United States which shall be made in Pursuance thereof; and all Treaties made, or which shall be made, under the Authority of the United States, shall be the supreme Law of the Land; and the Judges in every State shall be bound thereby, any Thing in the Constitution or Laws of any State to the Contrary notwithstanding.

The Senators and Representatives before mentioned, and the Members of the several State Legislatures, and all executive and judicial Officers, both of the United States and of the several States, shall be bound by Oath or Affirmation, to support this Constitution; but no religious Test shall ever be required as a Qualification to any Office or public Trust under the United States.

ARTICLE VII

The Ratification of the Conventions of nine States, shall be sufficient for the Establishment of this Constitution between the States so ratifying the Same.

DONE in Convention by the Unanimous Consent of the States present the Seventeenth Day of September in the Year of our Lord one thousand seven hundred and Eighty seven and of the Independence of the United States of America the Twelfth. IN WITNESS whereof We have hereunto subscribed our Names.

G⁰ Washington
Presidᵗ and deputy from Virginia

AMENDMENTS
ARTICLE I

[THE FIRST TEN ARTICLES PROPOSED 25 SEPTEMBER 1789; DECLARED IN FORCE 15 DECEMBER 1791]

Congress shall make no law respecting an establishment of religion, or prohibiting the free exercise thereof; or abridging the freedom of speech, or of the press; or the right of the people peaceably to assemble, and to petition the Government for a redress of grievances.

ARTICLE II

A well regulated Militia, being necessary to the security of a free State, the right of the people to keep and bear Arms, shall not be infringed.

ARTICLE III

No Soldier shall, in time of peace, be quartered in any house, without the consent of the Owner, nor in time of war, but in a manner to be prescribed by law.

ARTICLE IV

The right of the people to be secure in their persons, houses, papers, and effects, against unreasonable searches and seizures, shall not be violated, and no Warrants shall issue, but upon probable cause, supported by Oath or affirmation, and particularly describing the place to be searched, and the persons or things to be seized.

ARTICLE V

No person shall be held to answer for a capital, or otherwise infamous crime, unless on a presentment or indictment of a Grand Jury, except in cases arising in the land or naval forces, or in the Militia, when in actual service in time of War or public danger; nor shall any person be subject for the same offence to be twice put in jeopardy of life or limb; nor shall be compelled in any Criminal Case to be a witness against himself, nor be deprived of life, liberty, or property, without due process of law; nor shall private property be taken for public use, without just compensation.

ARTICLE VI

In all criminal prosecutions, the accused shall enjoy the right to a speedy and public trial, by an impartial jury of the State and district wherein the crime shall have been committed, which district shall have been previously ascertained by law, and to be informed of the nature and cause of the accusation; to be confronted with the witnesses against him; to have compulsory process for obtaining Witnesses in his favor, and to have the Assistance of Counsel for his defence.

ARTICLE VII

In suits at common law, where the value in controversy shall exceed twenty dollars, the right of trial by jury shall be preserved, and no fact tried by a jury shall be otherwise re-examined in any Court of the United States, than according to the rules of the common law.

ARTICLE VIII

Excessive bail shall not be required, nor excessive fines imposed, nor cruel and unusual punishments inflicted.

ARTICLE IX

The enumeration in the Constitution, of certain rights, shall not be construed to deny or disparage others retained by the people.

ARTICLE X

The powers not delegated to the United States by the Constitution, nor prohibited by it to the States, are reserved to the States respectively, or to the people.

ARTICLE XI

[PROPOSED 4 MARCH 1794; DECLARED RATIFIED 8 JANUARY 1798]

The Judicial power of the United States shall not be construed to extend to any suit in law or equity, commenced or prosecuted against one of the United States by Citizens of another State, or by Citizens or Subjects of any Foreign State.

ARTICLE XII

[PROPOSED 9 DECEMBER 1803; DECLARED RATIFIED 25 SEPTEMBER 1804]

The Electors shall meet in their respective states, and vote by ballot for President and Vice-President, one of whom, at least, shall not be an inhabitant of the same state with themselves; they shall name in their ballots the person voted for as President, and in distinct ballots the person voted for as Vice-President, and they shall make distinct lists of all persons voted for as President, and of all persons voted for as Vice-President, and of the number of votes for each, which lists they shall sign and certify, and transmit sealed to the seat of the Government of the United States, directed to the President of the Senate;—The President of the Senate shall, in the presence of the Senate and House of Representatives, open all the certificates and the votes shall then be counted;—The person having the greatest number of votes for President, shall be the President, if such number be a majority of the whole number of Electors appointed; and if no person have such majority, then from the persons having the highest numbers not exceeding three on the list of those voted for as President, the House of Representatives shall choose immediately, by ballot, the President. But in choosing the President, the votes shall be taken by states, the representation from each state having one vote; a quorum for this purpose shall consist of a member or members from two-thirds of the states, and a majority of all the states shall be necessary to a choice. And if the House of Representatives shall not choose a President whenever the right of choice shall devolve upon them, before the fourth day of March next following, then the Vice-President shall act as President, as in the case of the death or other constitutional disability of the President. The person having the greatest number of votes as Vice-President, shall be the Vice-President, if such number be a majority of the whole number of Electors appointed, and if no person have a majority, then from the two highest numbers on the list, the Senate shall choose the Vice-President; a quorum for the purpose shall consist of two-thirds of the whole number of Senators, and a majority of the whole number shall be necessary to a choice. But no person constitutionally ineligible to the office of President shall be eligible to that of Vice-President of the United States.

ARTICLE XIII

[PROPOSED 31 JANUARY 1865; DECLARED RATIFIED 18 DECEMBER 1865]

Section 1. Neither slavery nor involuntary servitude, except as a punishment for crime whereof the party shall have been duly convicted, shall exist within the United States, or any place subject to their jurisdiction.

Section 2. Congress shall have power to enforce this article by appropriate legislation.

ARTICLE XIV

[PROPOSED 13 JUNE 1866; DECLARED RATIFIED 28 JULY 1868]

Section 1. All persons born or naturalized in the United States, and subject to the jurisdiction thereof, are citizens of the United States and of the State wherein they reside. No State shall make or enforce any law which shall abridge the privileges or immunities of citizens of the United States; nor shall any State deprive any person of life, liberty, or property, without due process of law; nor deny to any person within its jurisdiction the equal protection of the laws.

Section 2. Representatives shall be apportioned among the several States according to their respective numbers, counting the whole number of persons in each State, excluding Indians not taxed. But when the right to vote at any election for the choice of electors for President and Vice President of the United States, Representatives in Congress, the Executive and Judicial officers of a State, or the members of the Legislature thereof, is denied to any of the male inhabitants of such State, being twenty-one years of age, and citizens of the United States, or in any way abridged, except for participation in rebellion, or other crime, the basis of representation therein shall be reduced in the proportion which the number of such male citizens shall bear to the whole number of male citizens twenty-one years of age in such State.

Section 3. No person shall be a Senator or Representative in Congress, or elector of President and Vice President, or hold any office, civil, or military, under the United States, or under any State, who, having previously taken an oath, as a member of Congress, or as an officer of the United States, or as a member of any State legislature, or as an executive or judicial officer of any State, to support the Constitution of the United States, shall have engaged in insurrection or rebellion against the same, or given aid or comfort to the enemies thereof. But Congress may by a vote of two-thirds of each House, remove such disability.

Section 4. The validity of the public debt of the United States, authorized by law, including debts incurred for payment of pensions and bounties for services in suppressing insurrection or rebellion, shall not be questioned. But neither the United States nor any State shall assume or pay any debt or obligation incurred in aid of insurrection or rebellion against the United States, or any claim for the loss or emancipation of any slave; but all such debts, obligations and claims shall be held illegal and void.

Section 5. The Congress shall have power to enforce, by appropriate legislation, the provisions of this article.

ARTICLE XV

[PROPOSED 26 FEBRUARY 1869; DECLARED RATIFIED 30 MARCH 1870]

Section 1. The right of citizens of the United States to vote shall not be denied or abridged by the United States or by any State on account of race, color, or previous condition of servitude.

Section 2. The Congress shall have power to enforce this article by appropriate legislation.

ARTICLE XVI

[PROPOSED 12 JULY 1909; DECLARED RATIFIED 25 FEBRUARY 1913]

The Congress shall have power to lay and collect taxes on incomes, from whatever source derived, without apportionment among the several States, and without regard to any census or enumeration.

ARTICLE XVII

[PROPOSED 13 MAY 1912; DECLARED RATIFIED 31 MAY 1913]

The Senate of the United States shall be composed of two senators from each State, elected by the people thereof, for six years; and each Senator shall have one vote. The electors in each State shall have the qualifications requisite for electors of the most numerous branch of the State legislature.

When vacancies happen in the representation of any State in the Senate, the executive authority of such State shall issue writs of election to fill such vacancies: PROVIDED, That the legislature of any State may empower the executive thereof to make temporary appointments until the people fill the vacancies by election as the legislature may direct.

This amendment shall not be so construed as to affect the election or term of any senator chosen before it becomes valid as part of the Constitution.

ARTICLE XVIII

[PROPOSED 18 DECEMBER 1917; DECLARED RATIFIED 29 JANUARY 1919]

After one year from the ratification of this article, the manufacture, sale, or transportation of intoxicating liquors within, the importation thereof into, or the exportation thereof from the United States and all territory subject to the jurisdiction thereof for beverage purposes is hereby prohibited.

The Congress and the several States shall have concurrent power to enforce this article by appropriate legislation.

This article shall be inoperative unless it shall have been ratified as an amendment to the Constitution by the legislatures of the several States, as provided in the Constitution, within seven years from the date of the submission hereof to the States by the Congress.

ARTICLE XIX

[PROPOSED 4 JUNE 1919; DECLARED RATIFIED 26 AUGUST 1920]

The right of citizens of the United States to vote shall not be denied or abridged by the United States or by any States on account of sex.

The Congress shall have power, by appropriate legislation, to enforce the provisions of this article.

ARTICLE XX

[PROPOSED 2 MARCH 1932; DECLARED RATIFIED 6 FEBRUARY 1933]

Section 1. The terms of the President and Vice-President shall end at noon on the twentieth day of

January, and the terms of Senators and Representatives at noon on the third day of January, of the years in which such terms would have ended if this article had not been ratified; and the terms of their successors shall then begin.

Section 2. The Congress shall assemble at least once in every year, and such meeting shall begin at noon on the third day of January, unless they shall by law appoint a different day.

Section 3. If, at the time fixed for the beginning of the term of the President, the President-elect shall have died, the Vice-President-elect shall become President. If a President shall not have been chosen before the time fixed for the beginning of his term, or if the President-elect shall have failed to qualify, then the Vice-President-elect shall act as President until a President shall have qualified; and the Congress may by law provide for the case wherein neither a President-elect nor a Vice-President-elect shall have qualified, declaring who shall then act as President, or the manner in which one who is to act shall be selected, and such person shall act accordingly until a President or Vice-President shall have qualified.

Section 4. The Congress may by law provide for the case of the death of any of the persons from whom the House of Representatives may choose a President whenever the right of choice shall have devolved upon them, and for the case of the death of any of the persons from whom the Senate may choose a Vice-President whenever the right of choice shall have devolved upon them.

Section 5. Sections 1 and 2 shall take effect on the 15th day of October following the ratification of this article.

Section 6. This article shall be inoperative unless it shall have been ratified as an amendment to the Constitution by the legislatures of three-fourths of the several States within seven years from the date of its submission.

ARTICLE XXI

[PROPOSED 20 FEBRUARY 1933; DECLARED RATIFIED 5 DECEMBER 1933]

Section 1. The eighteenth article of amendment to the Constitution of the United States is hereby repealed.

Section 2. The transportation or importation into any State, Territory or possession of the United States for delivery or use therein of intoxicating liquors, in violation of the laws thereof, is hereby prohibited.

Section 3. This article shall be inoperative unless it shall have been ratified as an amendment to the Constitution by convention in the several States, as provided in the Constitution, within seven years from the date of the submission hereof to the States by the Congress.

ARTICLE XXII

[PROPOSED 21 MARCH 1947; DECLARED RATIFIED 3 MARCH 1951]

Section 1. No person shall be elected to the office of the President more than twice, and no person who has held the office of President, or acted as President, for more than two years of a term to which some other person was elected President shall be elected to the office of the President more than once. But this Article shall not apply to any person holding the office of President when this Article was proposed by the Congress, and shall not prevent any person who may be holding the office of President, or acting as President, during the term within which this Article becomes operative from holding the office of President or acting as President during the remainder of such term.

ARTICLE XXIII

[PROPOSED 17 JUNE 1960; DECLARED RATIFIED 3 APRIL 1961]

Section 1. The District constituting the seat of Government of the United States shall appoint in such manner as the Congress may direct:
A number of electors of President and Vice President equal to the whole number of Senators and Representatives in Congress to which the District would be entitled if it were a State, but in no event more than the least populous State; they shall be in addition to those appointed by the States, but they shall be considered, for the purposes of the election of President and Vice President, to be electors appointed by a State; and they shall meet in the District and perform such duties as provided by the twelfth article of amendment.

Section 2. The Congress shall have power to enforce this article by appropriate legislation.

ARTICLE XXIV

[PROPOSED 27 AUGUST 1962; DECLARED RATIFIED 4 FEBRUARY 1964]

Section 1. The right of citizens of the United States to vote in any primary or other election for President or Vice President, for electors for President or Vice President, or for Senator or Representative in Congress, shall not be denied or abridged by the United States or any State by reason of failure to pay any poll tax or other tax.

Section 2. The Congress shall have power to enforce this article by appropriate legislation.

ARTICLE XXV

[PROPOSED 6 JULY 1965; DECLARED RATIFIED 23 FEBRUARY 1967]

Section 1. In case of the removal of the President from office or of his death or resignation, the Vice President shall become President.

Section 2. Whenever there is a vacancy in the office of the Vice President, the President shall nominate a Vice President who shall take office upon confirmation by a majority vote of both Houses of Congress.

Section 3. Whenever the President transmits to the President pro tempore of the Senate and the Speaker of the House of Representatives his written declaration that he is unable to discharge the powers and duties of his office, and until he transmits to them a written declaration to the contrary, such powers and duties shall be discharged by the Vice President as Acting President.

Section 4. Whenever the Vice President and a majority of either the principal officers of the executive department or of such other body as Congress may by law provide, transmit to the President pro tempore of the Senate and the Speaker of the House of Representatives their written declaration that the President is unable to discharge the powers and duties of his office; the Vice President shall immediately assume the powers and duties of the office as Acting President.

Thereafter, when the President transmits to the President pro tempore of the Senate and the Speaker of the House of Representatives his written declaration that no inability exists, he shall resume the powers and duties of his office unless the Vice President and a majority of either the principal officers of the executive department or of such other body as Congress may by law provide, transmit within four days to the President pro tempore of the Senate and the Speaker of the House of Representatives their written declaration that the President is unable to discharge the powers and duties of his office. Thereupon Congress shall decide the issue, assembling within forty-eight hours for that purpose if not in session. If the Congress, within twenty-one days after receipt of the latter written declaration, or, if Congress is not in session, within twenty-one days after Congress is required to assemble, determines by two-thirds vote of both Houses that the President is unable to discharge the powers and duties of his office, the Vice President shall continue to discharge the same as Acting President; otherwise, the President shall resume the powers and duties of his office.

ARTICLE XXVI

[PROPOSED 23 MARCH 1971; DECLARED RATIFIED 30 JUNE 1971]

Section 1. The right of citizens of the United States, who are 18 years of age or older, to vote shall not be denied or abridged by the United States or any state on account of age.

Secton 2. The Congress shall have the power to enforce this article by appropriate legislation.

Index

Aberdeen, Lord, 235
Ableman v. *Booth*, 265
Abnaki Indians, 5, 39
Abolitionists, 208, 226–28, 270
Acton, Lord, 296
Acts of Trade and Navigation, 32–33, 37, 39, 41, 45, 61, 62, 68, 70, 90
Adams, Charles Francis, 246, 347, 349
Adams, Henry, 171, 271, 296, 340, 348
Adams, John, 75, 80, 82, 89, 90, 97, 114, 115, 134, 197; portrait, 142; defense in Boston Massacre, 72; *Novanglus* letters, 76; and Declaration of Independence, 80; peace commissioner, 96; Massachusetts constitution, 98, 99; President, 140, 141, 143–45, 146, 153; in 1800 election, 145
Adams, John Quincy, 173, 174, 178, 186, 188, 194, 235, 237; portrait, 229; minister to Russia, 161; Secretary of State, 178, 180; and Monroe Doctrine, 180–81; President, 181–82, 185; character, 182; in *Amistad* affair, 228; and gag resolution, 230; Polk compared with, 241; death, 250
Adams, Samuel, 70, 72, 75, 115, 119; portrait, 71; Boston Tea-Party, 74; Constitution opposed, 119, 121
Adventists, 218, 220
Africa: Portuguese trade with, 9; slave trade in, 202; colonization plan for blacks, 226
Agassiz, Louis, 214
Agriculture: Indian, 2, 5; as occupation, population in, 123; machinery in, 257, 286; in prairie states, 257, 286; in South after Civil War, 323
Alabama, 175; Indian lands in, 169; statehood, 173, 177; cotton produc-

tion, 188, 201, 202; in 1860 Democratic convention, 267; secession, 269, 270; Reconstruction, 338, 341, 343
Alabama, C.S.S., 308, 347
Alamance, Battle of the, 73
Alamo, defense of, 239
Alaska: Russian trading posts in, 181, 232; purchase of, 345
Albany, 30
Albany Congress, 56
Albany Plan of Union, 56
Albert, Prince Consort, 297
Alcott, Bronson, 225
Alexander I of Russia, 181
Alexander VI, Pope, 7, 10
Alexandria, C.S.S., 308
Algeria, 147, 171
Algonquin Indians, 5
Alien Act (1798), 143
Allen, Ethan, 78, 105
Allen, Thomas, 101
Ambrister, Robert, 179–80, 188
America: Norsemen explore, 6; Spanish conquest and exploration, 6, 10, 11, 13–14; Columbus discovers, 7, 9–11; name, 11
American Academy of Arts and Sciences, 105
American Anti-Slavery Society, 226
American Board of Foreign Missions, 233
American colonies: foundation of: Raleigh's Roanoke Island attempts, 15, 17, Virginia, 18–19, 21–23, Maryland, 23, New England, 23–28, New Netherland, 28–30, Carolinas, 32, 33–34, New York, 30, 34, New Jersey, 34–35, Pennsylvania, 35–37, Georgia, 45, 47, 49; English trade with, 32–33; English government of, 41; colonial wars, 41,

43–45, 55–60; English settlements, 1607–1760, 42; immigration to, 45, 47; population, 45; charitable enterprises in, 47; trade routes, 48; industry and commerce, 49–50; social life, 50–51; government after 1763, 61–62; 1763–73, general survey, 63–66; moves toward independence, 79–80
American Colonization Society, 226
American party (Know-Nothings), 160
American Philosophical Society, 105, 214
American Society for Encouraging the Settlement of the Oregon Territory, 233
American System, 173, 174, 186, 267
Ames, Fisher, 135, 143, 146
Amherst, Jeffrey, 58, 59
Amherst College, 217
Amistad case, 228
Amnesty Act (1872), 356
Anderson, Richard H., 323
Anderson, Robert, 271–73
Andersonville prison, 333
Andros, Sir Edmund, 39
Anesthesia, discovery of, 217
Anglicans, *see* Church of England
Annapolis, 100
Annapolis Convention, 114
Annapolis Royal (Port Royal), 44
Ann Arbor, 217
Anthony, Susan B., 218
Antietam (Sharpsburg), Battle of, 306–7, 308
Antifederalists, 119, 121
Anti-Masonic party, 191–92, 218
Anti-slavery movement, 226–28, 230, 245, 246
Apache Indians, 3
Apalachee Indians, 5